CREATIVE
Experiences
for Young Children

Second Edition

Mimi Brodsky Chenfeld

Harcourt Brace College Publishers

Fort Worth   Philadelphia   San Diego   New York   Orlando   Austin   San Antonio
Toronto   Montreal   London   Sydney   Tokyo

Publisher	Ted Buchholz
Senior Acquisitions Editor	Jo-Anne Weaver
Developmental Editor	Tracy Napper
Project Editor	Angela Williams
Production Manager	Jane Tyndall Ponceti
Art Director	Jim Taylor
Cover Photography	Arthur Tilley

Address for Editorial Correspondence
Harcourt Brace College Publishers, 301 Commerce Street, Suite 3700, Fort Worth, TX 76102

Address for Orders
Harcourt Brace and Company, 6277 Sea Harbor Drive, Orlando, FL 32887
1-800-782-4479, or 1-800-433-0001 (in Florida)

ISBN: 0–15–501280-0

Library of Congress Catalogue Number: 93–80876

Printed in the United States of America

4 5 6 7 8 9 0 1 2 3   066   9 8 7 6 5 4 3 2 1

Preface

You will probably notice as you read this second edition of the newly named *Creative Experiences for Young Children* that this is more "rewritten" than "revised." That first edition, with the beautiful butterfly design on the cover, is like the recently shed skin of a brand new creature, a new being. This is essentially a new book.

So much has happened in this last decade. As this whirling, spinning planet of ours hurled us through space and time, our topsy-turvy lives accelerated—we zipped along in the fast lane. The fabric of our society tangled; in places, it shredded. Old patterns blurred. New threads interweave through worn stitches.

Since the publication of *Creative Activities for Young Children,* governments toppled, walls fell, old wars ceased, new wars began. More people found themselves homeless, poor, unemployed, and stranded. Families defined and redefined themselves in diverse ways. Boundaries changed, and countries were renamed. The earth under our feet quaked from geological shifts, and the ground under education shook from upheavals of ideas and demands—assessment, skills, integrated curriculum, multicultural education, vouchers, authentic learning, and restructuring.

Through it all, children did what children do: play, wonder, interact, respond, manipulate, question, observe, laugh, talk, sing, experiment, explore, discover, try to make sense out of their world, find connections, practice their language, and learn the ropes and the ways of their society.

As I studied the first edition, friends and colleagues were generous in their advice:

"Don't change anything except the photos!" some said.
"Leave everything alone. Just update references!" others said.

Thanking them all, I returned to the text. At the center of the first edition, I saw the children, living their lives and learning through play and active involvement with everything around them. The children must always be at the center of whatever we build around them—curriculum, theories, and materials. We want the children to live in the eye of that storm, in the calm peaceful place safe from the winds that blow around them.

As I studied the first edition, the expanding worlds of young children—from their immediate bodies and feelings ever outward—made more sense than ever. I wanted to keep those life themes beginning with the first world of "Our Fantastic Bodies/Our Amazing Senses" that expand to constantly widening spheres of awareness.

Because so many of our children are lonely, we need to give them even more support and reassurance. It seemed obvious to combine "Our Families/Our Friends" into one large chapter. Because our connections with nature have become so frayed, it seemed imperative to add a chapter highlighting our relationships with our environment, our natural world.

Because we have not made very much progress in becoming a more loving, empathetic, respectful and tolerant people, it was clear that the chapter "Others We Meet/Our Worlds Widen" had to be enriched. I still believe when we teach in the key of life (with inspiration, role-modeling, consistency of positive values demonstrated at all times), our children will lead the way to a better world.

Because many people said, "ho hum—borderline boring areas—necessary but unexciting," I *doubled* the food, shelter, clothing, shapes, and colors chapters.

Because language is at the core of it all, and because language is such a controversial topic, Chapter 12 offers numerous multidimensional suggestions for language enrichment.

Even though we are on the right track in teaching mathematical concepts and skills to young children, math is still accompanied by large doses of stress. Chapter 13 provides another example of the multiplication of ideas.

Because I can't hang out and spend time with you, talking, sharing, remembering, and planning together, I wrote this book. It's the closest I can get to being with you. Hundreds of teachers have shared ideas and experiences with me. Many are specifically highlighted in the book. Committed and loving teachers are hallowed cities of refuge for our children; they are magicians, caretakers, caregivers, guides, partners and lifeguards. They challenge, comfort, and inspire. I can't stop writing about the many items in the job descriptions of outstanding teachers. I thank them each and all for their always open hearts and minds.

Programs like the Leo Yassenoff Jewish Center's Early Childhood Program, Days of Creation Arts for Kids, and the Greater Columbus Arts Council's Artists-in-the-Schools Program continue to give me numerous opportunities to hang out with the children, learning with them and from them. Traveling the country, sharing ideas with parents, university students, inservice teachers, and children in conferences, conventions, staff development programs, and education organizations has enriched my life and work; I hope it contributed to the wealth of suggestions in these chapters. This book is a way of saying thank you to so many caring people who love the children.

Helping me, once again, make some order out of my chaos, Becky McAtee Moore gave shape to the knapsack books at the end of each chapter. Brenda Luco and Mary Campanelli at the Bexley Library and Lois Johnston at the Livingston Branch of the Columbus Metropolitan Library helped in the gathering of great books.

All communities have excellent resources. One of our community's resources is Michael Joel Rosen; his contributions to the field of children's literature are outstanding. Our friendship of many years has inspired my own work.

The consistent support and encouragement from the outstanding staff at Harcourt Brace College Publishers really made this second edition possible. They are wonderful people to work with. Thanks to Tracy Napper, Laura Lashley, Jo-Anne Weaver, Angela Williams, Jim Taylor, and Jane Ponceti. Thanks also to Leon Unruh, our copy editor, and Ann Burns Moyer, our proofreader.

Without friends and family, where would we be? All the friends who put up with me during this year of writing—the Berwick gang, the Hillel gang, all my "causes,"—thank you!

My parents, Iris and Joe Kaplan, who moved to Columbus, Ohio, in time to get caught in the making of this book—thanks for your patience! And to the family tribes: Walchers, Blooms, Kaplans, Cohens, Selingers, Rappoports, Chenfelds, Wilbats, Gandals, Frankels, Falveys, and Jacobsons, for unswerving love and support—thanks! And last and first, thanks to my anchor man, Howard.

Table of Contents

CREATIVE
Experiences
Second Edition
for Young Children

Hi my name is Anna Appelbaum, I live in Bexley, Ohio on Grandon.(Ave)
I'm special because I have red hair, and I am flexible. My best friends name is Claire Leblank, we both have red hair! I have I have 3 brothers, my little brothers name is Josh, My oldest brothers name is Moisha. Saul and me call him Moisha, Saul is my meidian brother (hes the nicest) Joshya's a pain! One time I was very
One time I was very special I got to go to my grandmas house in Flordia, on the way back to Columbus something funny happened! I was wearing a jean hat, there was a guy in back of me wearing jean pants. I lost my hat, and I started to look for it and I thought the guys new was my hat, so I took hold of his men, and he yell hat. So I apoligiesed and explained! That was the most embarrissing time of my life!
My favorite Singer is Micheal Jackson. My favorite author is Roald Deal. My favorite song is save the world, (by Micheal Jackson) My favorite movie is The Goonies. My 2 favorite books are The Witches, and the American girl collection, Felicia with red hair, Kristian with blond hair, Samantha with black hair, and Molly with brown hair. My 2 favorite shops are the Limited too, and the Gap. My favorite cartoon is Captian Planet.

Part 1

LETTERS OF INTRODUCTION

Dear Reader,

Welcome to the revised edition of *Creative Activities for Young Children*, now retitled *Creative Experiences for Young Children*.

Because of the warm and generous flow of letters from readers since the publication of the first edition, you will be introduced to this new book through responses to a sampling of questions raised in those letters. Readers target the most important concerns. As always, you, the reader, are the most important part of this exchange. If not for you, dear reader, this book would be just a number in a computer or a marking on a library card.

LETTER ONE

"Why did you rename your new book?"

Over the years, criss-crossing the country, talking with thousands of education majors and in-service teachers, I have come to realize that it's too easy to define "activities" in the most narrow, mechanical, isolated, product-centered interpretations. We are dealing with immeasurable opportunities for sharing and learning together in joyful, accessible, successful continuing time trips (moments-hours-days-weeks-months). "Activities" is too limited a concept.

"Experience" (both the verb and the noun) connotes total participation in the events, the happenings of our lives. Our minds, senses, feelings, attitudes, actions, and rhythms are involved in such times. Retitling the book "experiences" reminds us to invite ourselves and our students into sharing deeper, richer, more holistic ways of learning. "Experiences" help us to remember to "put our whole selves in" as we hokey-pokey along.

LETTER TWO

"Tell me about your new book. What's it about? How is it organized?"

This expanded edition continues the celebration of children and the excitement of the learning process—the creative process. Every suggestion comes from natural ways children best learn. And they all learn in their own unique ways, in their own peculiar combinations of styles. Howard Gardner's influential theory of multiple intelligences[1] encourages us to consider intelligence in more pluralistic ways. Instead of the notion of a singular intelligence, Gardner offers seven intelligences: linguistic, logical/mathematical, kinesthetic, visual/spatial, musical, and the two "personal intelligences"—interpersonal and intrapersonal. Such theories challenge us to add leaves to our smorgasbord tables of curriculum offerings, to add pigments to our palettes of "strategies," and to add instruments to our orchestras of ideas. Smug is out. No one approach, however meritorious, will be effective with every student. Last year's successful lesson may be this year's dud. The doors of possibilities and combinations are thrown open. Hello to the world of creative teaching!

Keeping in mind Gardner's seven areas as general guides, observe children learning at their own pace, following their own interests. They demonstrate the range of intelligences as they play with sounds, words, symbols, objects, drawing, writing, singing, building, acting, inventing, listening, and moving. . . . What are they doing? Trying to make sense of the world around them. Follow them as they search for meanings, discover relationships, build daily additions to knowledge and understanding, and achieve new levels of skills and comprehension.

Through direct, active, and interactive experiences, they learn about themselves and others; about how things work, about their own dazzling powers in this continually interesting world.

In language-rich environments of encouragement and acceptance, in safe and loving "communities of learners," children develop self-esteem, respect for themselves and others, and, we hope, a lifelong commitment to learning, a passion for living, and the desire to be good citizens making contributions to the betterment of the "world" (home/school/neighborhood/church/city/country/planet).

John Holt's provocative book, *What Do I Do Monday?*, and his theory of the "four worlds" still inspires. Holt's World One is the world of our bodies, the world under our skin. World Two is the world of our direct experiences, perceptions, and impressions. World Three is the world we have not directly experienced, but which we know something about (from books, TV, and stories). World Four is beyond our imagination, the unknown, the impossible-to-even-talk-about world. Holt believed that through learning, we expand Worlds Two and Three and reduce World Four.

I believe that the themes of this book flow along with the expanding worlds of the children from that primary world of the body to the more complicated world rich with symbols, shapes, colors, numbers, and letters. Just as the offerings in this book will coincide with Gardner's seven intelligences, you should also feel the spirit of John Holt's four worlds.

Important Note Even as you read each theme separately, know that each is intertwined with the others, inextricably connected. None exists in isolation. You cannot help but make combinations and new relationships. Each spills over to the others and enriches and is enriched. This is the magic of teaching, to help children make connections! And to help *you* continue to help your students see relationships, mix and match, arrange and rearrange, play with possibilities, integrate, we have created a logo/slogan to nudge you all along the way, so you never forget that ideas are linked together. Surprise and delight yourself with your own original fusions.

In response to so many of you who insisted that the subsections of each theme were practical and helpful, we have kept them virtually intact. Because there are still too many people who question the vital importance of the arts, of play, of talking, and of sharing in the lives of young children (of us old children, too), I have asked

a few outstanding educators to add their comments to the notes explaining the subsections. Add your own testimony. The subsections enrich every theme:

The Basics This subsection features a brief discussion of the theme. It's as important to know *why* as it is to know *where, when,* and *what.* If *you* don't consider a concept or an idea valuable or vital, you certainly can't teach it with enthusiasm.

Discovery Times/Wonder Times Wonder has been added, because wonder must be rooted at the core of every idea. Plato said that all learning begins with wonder. In our speeded-up, drive-in, media-manic world of dizzying machines and products, wonder, too often and too early, turns into a packaged bread; joy turns into a dishwashing liquid; bold into a detergent; and love into a cosmetic. The enchantment of wonder must be held in the forefront of our thinking, as must the joyful exploration of ideas, the boldness of discovery, and the love warming us as we journey together. Renaming the theme "Discovery and Wonder" helps you remember to leave room for discoveries the children make and share with you. Oh, the wonder of it all!

Suggested Vocabulary By the time children reach kindergarten, many of them have remarkable vocabularies. They know a lot! The words offered in each theme are samples of potential clusters of possibilities. A single word on your list can provide inspiration for countless activities and experiences. For example, the word *dog* can be illustrated by a drawing, a sculpture, a puppet show, a riddle, a game, a story, a poem, a chant, a game, a mask, a costume, a poster, a dream (shall we go on?). Think about the rich promise of words. Always invite the children to continually add to the thematic vocabulary. Each idea begets its own vocabulary list.

Some Starters These suggestions will help you get going. But any of the ideas can be used at any time, in any combination. You may decide to adapt a "starter" for a finale! Any of the offerings on any page of the book may serve as a "starter." Always look to your children for immediate resources. I have launched entire themes that lasted weeks from a design on a T-shirt or an object shared by a child. Be alert! Be open to the gifts the children bring each day. If you're excited about an idea, however small (however weird), it's almost guaranteed to help you begin. Remember, we can start but we can't *finish*. Ideas can't be finished. We can't *finish* our bodies, our feelings, colors, numbers, clothing, nature! Can we? If you think ideas can be finished, that's the way you'll teach. And your children will say (as kids said to me), "We finished the solar system!" "We finished Ohio history!" When a group of children told me they "finished the four seasons," I had to respond, "Hey, we might as well die!" *Your only limitation is time*. Ideas do nothing but beget.

Talk Times/Listening Times This newly combined theme celebrates probably the most important components of language. It is shocking to know that today many children learn in rooms of silence where talk is reduced to right/wrong answers and yes/no questions. Listening is limited to watching the teacher talk.

How can children of the human family learn their language without countless, daily experiences in talking and listening? Children want to, like to, need to talk. Think of your classroom as a *language immersion* environment where talking is the normal way people relate to each other as they work, play, plan, and problem-solve. From one-on-one conversations, to puppet dialogues, to small play groups, class sharing times, story telling, read-alouds, poetry breaks, brainstorming, direction giving, party planning—the list is endless—talk times are essential to the life of your class and to the lives of the children. When talking is valued, the importance of listening is elevated. Why should children learn to be active listeners if talking is discouraged?

Visual Arts Times Honoring one of the oldest and most basic means of expression and communication, the visual arts subsection offers shared experiences in practical and inspiring explorations using a variety of methods and materials. Remember, the arts should never be set apart from other subject areas, never viewed in isolation, but always as *part* of everything, as they have been throughout history and across geography.

Music Times A Zimbabwe saying reminds us, "If you can walk, you can dance. If you can talk, you can sing." Many people hum and sing *before* they talk! We humans sing our lives! Just think of all the songs you and your students know. What a resource! Our closets and basements are stocked with records, tapes, cassettes, instruments, and songbooks that cut across cultural and temporal boundaries. Music is a universal language. A keynote speaker at an educational conference said, "If you walk into a room where young children are learning and you don't hear music in fifteen minutes, leave!"

Don't think you have to be a specialist to share musical moments with your students. Just enjoy exercising and celebrating your birthright as a member of the human family.

Movement and Play Times When people ask me how long I have taught movement to children, I answer, "I have never taught one child how to move! Children are already movers and shakers. I only hang out with them and help them keep moving as long as possible."

Movement is a sign of life. We worry when something stops moving for a long time. Unless afflicted with physically or emotionally paralyzing conditions, all humans use movement to express feelings and concepts, to communicate messages. Movement, along with the other arts, is part of every culture on earth. Can we get more basic?

Education is a moving experience.

It's hard to believe, but some people may ask, "Why is *play* included in every theme?" Play is the way children learn. As Piaget said, it is their work. All the research supports the importance of play in the education of children. All the position papers of the major educational organizations regarding play[2] confirm the observations of my wandering son, Dan. He writes to us in a letter from the road, "I've driven through wealthy suburbs, Native American Reservations, farmlands, city streets, seaside towns all over the U.S., all over the world. The one constant I see is KIDS PLAYING. Everywhere, kids play. It's their subculture. It's their own 'kid' society. Kids have to play!"

Learning through play is developmentally appropriate for young children.

Don't downplay play! It's the way children learn![3]

I am happy that the first edition of this book has been included in courses teaching developmentally appropriate practices in educating young children because that edition was written before we had such a term, because the ideas in that book were in harmony with the newest and most hopeful thinking about early childhood education. Throughout both first edition and this new edition, active, interactive, hands-on, self-directed, arts-rich, open-ended, nonthreatening, cooperative, playful, and holistic ways of learning are encouraged. These old beliefs about the best ways children learn were written before such terms as "cooperative learning," "inclusion," "performance and portfolio assessment," "literature-based," and "whole language" became headlines. Yet, every page stresses cooperation over competition; making circles (as the poet Edward Markham writes, "We made a circle that let him in") in which every child is hallowed as an important, contributing member of the group; keeping good literature at the core of curriculum, inspiring myriad enriching activities and experiences; and valuing the works of the children and gathering them for the joy of it and for demonstrating their progress made in the process of learning. Portfolios tell more meaningful stories about children's levels of skill mastery and comprehension than statistical scores on impersonal tests. Yes, I am happy that our books are in harmony with the new (but old and good) philosophies.

Classroom Visitors and Field Trips In recent years, numerous books and articles have been devoted to the importance of school-community relationships. This subsection features excellent suggestions for strengthening those connections. Not only do positive experiences with classroom visitors and field trips increase our understanding of subjects, but they also provide valuable lessons in respect, appreciation, cooperation, listening, courtesy, communication, and wonder.

It All Comes Together Each theme will highlight an example of integrated experiences clustered and linked, interwoven and related, that demonstrate the wholeness of learning and learners. Michelangelo's motto was: "I am still learning." So, we are all learners walking along together in our shared time, learning from each other, helping each other.

Books From My Knapsack In the last decade, there has been a plethora of excellent materials for children and educators. Space permits the listing of just a few such offerings. It is hoped that these materials will inspire as well as inform.

note: underpinning every idea, interfacing all suggestions, is *language*. Asleep, awake, active or still, language is at the core of our lives. Language, that uniquely human gift, is the way we learn to think, perceive, comprehend, and manage. If you think in compartmental terms, you'll say things like this: "We're not having

Language Arts today because of the field trip" or "When the talking stops, we'll begin Oral Language."

As we believe, so we teach. If you believe that language is a separate subject, taught in isolation, confined to a time slot, then your teaching will be narrow and diminished. You and your children will be deprived of a rich, dynamic learning environment in which the magic of language is happening every second of the day. Language is all the time, a daily staple.

Nowadays we have a term for the interrelatedness, the integrating of curriculum and language. We call it "whole language," a new term for a very old, healthy, natural way human beings best learn.[4] In the first edition, I wrote, "It is important to understand that all sections of a guide are interrelated. In everyday life, words flow into songs and stories, games include movement and dance, talk spills into art and poems. The more you connect the various experiences, the more effective each one will be."

Please *make connections*. See possibilities for integrating, linking, changing, arranging, and rearranging. This is YOUR book, and you know your students and yourself. Make the ideas you like work for you. Make them your own.

LETTER THREE

"Can I use this book for my work with children with special needs? Exceptional children? Bilingual children? Gifted and talented? Children born in December?"

Over the years, teachers working with Gifted and Talented, with Learning Disabled children, with *all* of our alphabet children from A to Z, have been enthusiastic in their appreciation for the ideas we have shared. They have especially noted that we *don't* have separate sections for children with special needs. *All of our children have special needs.* Just as our children under law should be mainstreamed in our school programs as often as they are able, so ideas are mainstreamed throughout this book. These ideas are healthy and wholesome suggestions, good for everyone!

My friends, a good idea is a good idea if you like it. If YOU like it, you will shape it to fit your children, your situation. Many teachers take courses in Adaptive Physical Education. In creative teaching, everything we do is "adaptive" because each of our classes is a unique blend of individuals, not carbon copies of other groups.

In the first edition, Ronni Hochman Spratt[5] and Rhoda Gelles[6] contributed important philosophies to the introduction; Ronni, from the vantage point of working with children considered Learning Disabled, and Rhoda from working with children defined as Gifted and Talented. Both educators spoke in the same spirit, which applies now more than ever. Each articulated the need for all children to appreciate and respect one another, applaud one another's growth, differences, and achievement. They challenged teachers to create environments in which children across the spectrum can succeed. They reminded readers that in places where children care about each other, talk and work together, they are eager to praise, to applaud, to boast of their classmates' accomplishments. *All* of our children need attention, praise, and warmth.

Ronni said, "I want a clear conscience. I don't want to be on the list of teachers who make learning an unhappy experience for children." Rhoda said, "When all of our children are considered to be very important individuals, we help their self-concepts. All of our students bloom in classes where there is respect and appreciation for individuality."

Whether you are teaching in a Special Education setting, an English as a Second Language program, a Gifted and Talented enrichment class, the challenge is the same: Change and adapt any idea to your own situation to meet the needs of your unique group of children. With you, children will be safe at any speed! With you, they will be invited to succeed!

LETTER FOUR

"What about multiculturalism? Where does it fit?"

Dear reader, as you know, multicultural education is one of the top issues in the country. Hardly a day goes by without a news story about its importance, its controversy.[7] Everyone is for it, but the definitions and interpretations of what *it* is range across the board.

My feelings about multicultural education for young children are similar to my philosophy about language. Just as our young children need to learn in language-rich, language-immersed (I like to say language-drenched!) environments in which language in all its components is happening all the time, so young children need to learn to value diversity and respect and appreciate the cultural richness of others *at all times*. The curriculum should be saturated with the awareness of and knowledge of the gifts contributed to the human story by its peoples. The challenge is to celebrate diversity as we strengthen unity.

Yes, with you the children will learn songs, stories, customs, food, and clothing from cultures other than their own. They will also learn a deeper lesson: *that all the children of the human family make music, make stories, make art, make dances, celebrate, and share feelings and dreams.* Common threads tie people together even as they weave different patterns.

As you read this book, train yourself to blend multicultural awareness with all ideas. Photos, pictures, books, music, games, vocabulary, clothing, designs, and food are all obvious and delightful ways to enhance familiarity with and sensitivity to diverse cultures. But don't limit your multicultural curriculum to "things." A classroom community of respect and appreciation for others is the garden in which multicultural education takes root and flourishes. The poet Theodore Roethke said, "Teaching is one of the few professions that permits love." In classrooms of lovingness and acceptance, children learn every day about valuing and hallowing themselves and others. Isn't this where multicultural education begins and grows?

LETTER FIVE

"I don't think of myself as a very creative person. Is it possible to become more creative? I want to be a creative teacher."

Creativity has become one of those loaded buzzwords. Why is the idea of creativity so intimidating? Hasn't anyone told you that the human family is very creative? We constantly improvise, embellish, pretend, rearrange, play, imagine, and invent. Have you ever rearranged the furniture in your room? Twisted your scarf into a new design? Hummed a new tune? Mixed two ice cream flavors together?

I think that the most creative everyday activity in America is a salad bar! The spread of salad ingredients is the same for everyone. But does each diner's plate of salad wind up a carbon copy of the others? Heavens, no! Each plate is individually arranged. Watch how people select their ingredients. See the patterns they make. Some people heap everything into a huge pile. Some are neat and organized, color coordinated. What does your plate look like? How is it arranged?

Creativity is not a strategy or technique. It's not scheduled for Wednesdays after lunch if our dittos are finished! It's a *way* of being, thinking, and teaching. Teaching in the key of life means our teaching is brightened with enthusiasm, excitement, spontaneity, risk taking, open-mindedness, open-ended challenges, flexibility, divergent thinking, playfulness, imagination, and innovation.[8]

Before you can help your students develop their creative talents to maximum heights, you must believe in your own creative abilities. Practice helps. Here are four easy nudges to help you strengthen your own creativity. They can be arranged in any order.[9]

1. *What else?* Unless you are unconscious, the question "what else?" will trigger the response: more, more, more! What else can we find out about the early settlers? What else can we find out about Goldilocks? What else can we share about stars? What else can you share about gerbils? What else can we think of for our spring program?

"What else?" is not smug. It helps us expand our horizons and reminds us that we can never completely finish a subject or an idea. There is always more to discover, to learn, to ask, to wonder about.

2. *What if?* This question entices the imagination. What if the wolf in "Little Red Riding Hood" had been rehabilitated and reformed? What if we could understand the language of animals? What if it really did rain cats and dogs? What if we grew taller than trees?

3. *Show it!* This nudge invites us into the world of enriched, exciting, multilevel learning experiences. Here is an idea, a concept, a book, a poem, a fact, a lesson—show it! This nudge validates different ways of learning and comprehending. Think of how many ways we can show an idea! Here are but a few suggestions gathered by a group of second-graders: Say it. Sing it. Read it. Write it. Draw it. Make it. Play it. Act it. Touch it. Guess it. Find it. Map it. Sculpt it. Dance it. Wear it. Put it on a bulletin board, a T-shirt, a newspaper. Let a puppet tell it. Announce it on the PA system. Design it. Cut it out. Make a model of it.

4. *Fake it!* In the uptight, test-centered, anxiety-filled world of education, "fake it" gives permission to try something new or different. Try it! Take a stab at it. Make believe you can do it. Don't worry. Hang loose. Stay cool. If you can't do something perfectly, it's OK to try anyway. "Fake it" invites participation and encourages involvement. It draws a circle that encompasses everyone.

After watching *The Wizard of Oz,* I asked the preschoolers "What did the Tin Woodsman want from the Wizard?" "A heart!" they shouted. "What did the Scarecrow want from the Wizard?" I asked. "A brain!" they shouted. "And, what did the Cowardly Lion want from the Wizard?" "Porridge!"

We need hearts, brains, and yes, a lot of porridge in becoming creative teachers.

LETTER SIX

"I find it difficult to keep from being blown away by all the pressures in the field. I find myself on the defensive when we're having a good time *while* we're learning. Any advice?"

No doubt about it, this is a stormy time for educators—a time of changes and exchanges, reforms and upheavals. But, dear reader, remember that in the midst of these whirlwinds, children attend school each day with teachers who need to keep their calm in the eye of the storms. Because, no matter what is going on around us, we invite our students into classrooms where they are welcomed and regarded. Our time together is hallowed time. Harsh winds may be raging around us, even pounding the walls of our schools, but in *our* rooms, children are safe. With us, our students never feel humiliated, never alienated. We are "family." We are "community," working together, learning, sharing, helping, celebrating. Children are safe to ask questions, make mistakes, make discoveries, find ways to learn that give them the delicious taste of success. Our rooms must be Cities of Refuge; Eyes of the Storm; Home Plate, Charlotte's Web, where words are woven into webs that protect our children, that save their Wilbur lives.

To keep sane and strong, keep your eye on the first syllable of fundamentals—fun. Without it, we have a word that sounds like "demental," which I think is related to "demented"!

How do you keep sane and strong? This situation calls for more metaphors. Now, if your commitments and beliefs are as flimsy as the House Made out of Sticks or Straw, any wolf can blow you over. If your house of beliefs and commitments is as strong as the House Made of Bricks, nobody can blow you over. In your House Made of Bricks, you are bilingual. One language is for the spirit of the children, the joyous spirit of learning together in a loving environment. The other language is for the wolf, who usually is not interested in the spirit language.

Who is the wolf? The wolf can be a colleague ("Don't you think your children need more seat work? Want to borrow some dittos?"); an administrator ("There's too much laughter going on here. Where is the teacher?"); a parent ("How will my child ever get accepted into college without more of the basics and less of these frills?"); a child ("We already have this story on our video. You aren't telling it right!") or, the saddest wolf of all, *yourself* ("Oh dear, I just can't put on the storyteller's hat. I feel too silly!")

When you are bilingual, then you know what you are doing at all times. When the wolf asks, "What are you doing?" you spring into a thorough and valid response. For example, with first-graders, we worked out fourteen movement ideas for clowns. As we were putting the ideas together, a wolf asked, "What are you doing?" I did *not* say, "Clowning around!" I said, "Listening skills, following directions, paying attention, language acquisition, vocabulary recognition, cooperative learning, small and gross motor skills, physical fitness, learning things in a series, recognizing patterns, oral language, verbs, circus theme, reviewing information. . . ."

Before I could continue, the wolf changed into a lamb and apologized for interrupting the session.

Using your bilingual vocabularies in your House of Bricks, in the eye of the storm, winds will bluster around you but you and your students will be safe and warm.

Think of this book as another brick to add to your House of Bricks. Keep adding! Add strength to your commitments! Multiply ideas and delight!

LETTER SEVEN

"How do you keep up with all the resources available?"

It is virtually impossible to keep up with the avalanche of materials published almost daily. A complete bibliography would overflow the pages of this book and still be incomplete, as new pages are being printed as you read!

To answer your question in the most helpful, simple way, I'll share with you some of the materials now on my shelves and in my knapsack as I travel around the country being with children and teachers.

Music first! Children should never be without music. I share virtually every kind of music from the folk traditions of many cultures to classical to Broadway show tunes to disco to hip-hop. I share what I love. You must find the music, the songs that you love, and find room for them in the life of your class, in the lives of your students.

Following is a small sampling of some of my favorite music makers who make music especially for children. Each of these artists has numerous cassettes, CDs, and if you hunt for them, even good old albums! Personally, I am a phonograph and record person.

Ella Jenkins: Smithsonian/Folkways Records, Washington, DC 20560
Sylvia Wallach: Sylvionics, P.O. Box 60135, Chicago, IL 60661
Teddi and Fred Koch: Red Rover Records, Lake Bluff, IL 60044

Fran Avni: Lemonstone Records, 4841 Isabella, Montreal, Quebec
  H3W 1S6, Canada
Mr. Al: Melody House, 819 NW 92nd Street, Oklahoma City, OK 73114
Greg and Steve: Youngheart Music, 2413½ Hyperion Ave., Los Angeles,
  CA 90027
Rosenshontz: RS Records, Box 651, Brattleboro, VT 05301
Raffi: Kimbo Educational, P.O. Box 477, Long Branch, NJ 07740
Bing Bingham: Kimbo Educational (see above)
Pete Seeger: Smithsonian/Folkways Institution, Office of Folklife
  Programs, Washington, DC 20560
Woody Guthrie: Warner Brothers Records, 3300 Warner Boulevard,
  Burbank, CA 91505–4694
Gemini: 2000 Penucraft Ct., Ann Arbor, MI 48103
Thomas Moore: 4600 Park Rd., Suite 1000, Charlotte, NC 28209

What's in *your* knapsack? What's *your* music? What songs are humming in your mind? your memory? your heart?

Dear reader, my shelves are packed with so many wonderful books—old, new, borrowed, true. We are very lucky to live in a time of such challenging and inspiring ideas.

Here are examples of some books on my shelf:

Ashton-Warner, Sylvia. *Spearpoint*. New York: Random House, 1972.
———. *Teacher*. New York: Simon and Schuster, 1963.
Boyer, Ernest L. *Ready To Learn*. Princeton, NJ: Carnegie Foundation for
  Advancement of Learning, 1991.
Campbell, Joseph, with Bill Moyers. *The Power of Myth*. New York: Doubleday,
  1988.
Clay, Marie M. *The Early Detection of Reading Difficulties* 3/E. Portsmouth, NH:
  Heinemann, 1985.
Colgin, Mary Lou. *One Potato, Two Potato, Three Potato, Four! 165 Chants for
  Young Children*. Mount Rainier, MD: Gryphon House, 1992.
Czikszentimihalyi, Mihaly. *Flow: The Psychology of Optimal Experience*. New York:
  Harper & Row, 1990.
Goodman, Kenneth S. *Language and Thinking in School: A Whole Language
  Curriculum 3/E*. New York: Richard C. Owen, 1987.
Goodman, Kenneth S., Lois Bridges Bird, and Yetta M. Goodman. *The Whole
  Language Catalog*. American School Publishers, 1990.
Koch, Kenneth, and Kate Farrell (selected). *Talking to the Sun: An Illustrated
  Anthology of Poems for Young People*. New York: Metropolitan Museum of Art,
  Henry Holt, 1985.
Kohl, Herbert. *Growing Minds: On Becoming a Teacher*. New York: Harper &
  Row, 1984.
Kozol, Jonathon. *Savage Inequities*. New York: Crown, 1991.
Kreidler, William J. *Creative Conflict Resolution: More Than 200 Activities for
  Keeping Peace in Classrooms K–6*. Glenview, IL: Scott Foresman, 1984.
Moorman, Chick, and Nancy Moorman. *Teacher Talk: What It Really Means*. Bay
  City, MI: Institute of Personal Power, 1989.
Morrman, Chick, and Dee Dishon. *Our Classroom: We Can Learn Together*.
  Englewood, NJ: Prentice-Hall, 1983.
Neugebauer, Bonnie, ed. *Alike and Different: Exploring Our Humanity with
  Young Children* (revised ed.). Washington, DC: National Association for the
  Education of Young Children, 1993.
Prelutsky, Jack, and Arnold Lobel (illus.). *The Random House Book of Poetry for
  Children—A Treasury of 572 Poems for Today's Child*. New York: Random
  House, 1983.

Tegano, Deborah, James D. Moran III, and Janet K. Sawyers. *Creativity in Early Childhood Classrooms.* Washington, D.C.: National Association for the Education of Young Children, 1991.

Wood, George H. *Schools That Work: America's Most Innovative Public Education Programs.* New York: Dutton, 1992.

Yolen, Jane. *Touch Magic: Fantasy, Faerie and Folklore in the Literature of Childhood.* New York: Philomel Books, 1981.

What books are on *your* shelves? What are *you* reading now besides this wonderful book?

NOTES ❤

1. Howard Gardner. *Frames of Mind: The Theory of Multiple Intelligences.* New York: Basic Books, 1983.

2. Examples of major educational organizations with position papers on the importance of play are:
   National Association for the Education of Young Children (NAEYC), 1834 Connecticut Ave. NW, Washington, DC 20009–5786
   Association for Childhood Education International (ACEI) 11501 Georgia Ave. #315, Wheaton, MD 20902

3. Mimi B. Chenfeld. "Wanna Play?" *Young Children,* September 1991, pp. 4–6. Reprinted in *Teaching in the Key of Life.* Washington, DC: NAEYC, 1993. pp. 18–21.
   ———. " 'My Loose is Tooth!' Kidding Around with the Kids" *Young Children,* Nov. 1990, pp. 56–60. Reprinted in *Teaching in the Key of Life.* Washington, DC: NAEYC, 1993. pp. 31–35.
   Rosalie Blau, A. Zavitkovsky, D. Zavitkovsky. "Play Is . . ." *Young Children,* Nov. 1989, pp. 30–31.

4. Look for journals such as *Language Arts,* published by the National Council of Teachers of English; *Kappan,* published by Phi Delta Kappa; *Day Care and Early Education,* published by Human Sciences Press; *Educational Leadership,* published by the Association for Supervision and Curriculum Development; *Childhood Education,* published by the Association for Childhood Education International; and *The Reading Teacher,* published by the International Reading Association. They continuously feature essays and articles relating to whole language and integrated curriculum.
   To name a few books that will help you integrate ideas, see relationships and make connections:
   Boyer, Ernest L. *Read To Learn.* Princeton, NJ: Carnegie Foundation for Advancement of Learning, 1991.
   Goodman, Kenneth S. *What's Whole in Whole Language?* Portsmouth, NH: Heinemann, 1986.
   Hickman, Janet, and Bernice Cullinan. *Children's Literature in the Classroom: Weaving Charlotte's Web.* Norwood, MA: Christopher-Gordon, 1989.
   Katz, Lilian, and S. Chard. *Engaging Children's Minds: The Project Approach.* Norwood, NJ: Ablex Publishing Co., 1989.
   Kline, P. *The Everyday Genius: Restoring Children's Natural Joy of Learning—and Yours Too.* Arlington, VA: Great Ocean Publishing, 1988.
   Smith, Frank. *Understanding Reading* 4/E, Hillsdale, NJ: Lawrence Erlbaum, 1992.
   Strickland, Dorothy S., and Lesley M. Morrow. *Emerging Literacy: Young Children Learn to Read and Write.* Washington, DC: National Association for the Education of Young Children, 1989.

5. Ronni Hochman Spratt teaches special education at Hastings Middle School, Upper Arlington, Ohio, and consults with teachers around the country.

6. Rhoda Gelles is the coordinator of Extended Projects Programs for the Worthington, Ohio, schools. She is responsible for gifted and talented, outdoor education and the foreign language council.

7. The journals cited in footnote 4 are among those featuring numerous articles on multicultural education. Valuable materials in this area are growing daily, such as:

    Louise Derman-Sparks, and the A.B.C. Task Force. *Anti-Bias Curriculum—Tools For Empowering Young Children* 5/E. Washington, DC: National Association for the Education of Young Children, 1991.

    Multicultural Review, Greenwood Publishing Group, 88 Post Road West, P.O. Box 5007, Westport, CT: 06881–5007

    O. N. Saracho, B. Spodek. (ed) *Understanding the Multicultural Experience in Early Childhood Education.* Washington, DC: National Association for the Education of Young Children, 1986.

8. So many excellent resources are available to inspire your own creative process. To name a few:

    Baker, A., and E. Green. *Storytelling: Art and Technique* 2/E. New York: Bowker, 1987.

    Barlin, A. L. *Teaching Your Wings to Fly: The Nonspecialist's Guide to Movement Activities for Young Children.* Santa Monica, CA: Goodyear, 1979.

    Benzwie, Teresa. *A Moving Experience—Dance for Lovers of Children and the Child Within.* Tucson, AZ: Zephyr Press, 1987.

    Calkins, L. M. *Lessons From a Child—On the Teaching and Learning of Writing.* Portsmouth, NH: Heinemann, 1983.

    Chenfeld, Mimi B. *Teaching Language Arts Creatively* 2/E. San Diego, CA: Harcourt Brace Jovanovich, 1987.

    Cherry, Clare. *Creative Play for the Developing Child.* Belmont, CA: David S. Lake, 1976.

    Curtis, S. R. *The Joy of Movement in Early Childhood.* New York: Teacher's College Press, 1982.

    Fein, G., and M. Rivkin, eds. *The Young Child at Play,* vol. 4. Washington, DC: National Association for the Education of Young Children.

    McCracken, R. A., and J. McCracken. *Stories, Songs and Poetry to Teach Reading and Writing: Literacy Through Language.* New York: Teachers' College Press, 1986.

    Moustakas, C. *Teaching as Learning.* New York: Ballantine, 1972.

    O'Neill, C., and L. Johnson, eds. *Dorothy Heathcote—Collected Writings on Education and Drama.* London: Hutchinson, 1984.

    Paley, V. *Wally's Stories.* Cambridge, MA: Harvard University Press, 1981.

    Rosner, Stanley, and E. Lawrence, eds. *The Creative Experience,* New York: Grossman Publishing, 1972.

    Schirrmacher, R. *Art and Creative Development for Young Children.* Albany, NY: Delmar Books, 1988.

    Witkin, K., with R. Philp. *To Move, To Learn.* New York: Schoken Books, 1978.

    Yolen, Jane. *Touch Magic—Fantasy, Faerie and Folklore in the Literature of Childhood.* New York: Philomel Books, 1981.

Chapter

♥♥♥♥♥♥♥♥♥♥♥♥♥♥♥♥♥♥♥♥♥♥

1

Our Fantastic Bodies/
Our Amazing Senses

Four-year-old Kimani and 11-year-old Beth sat together watching the summer scene. Beth looked lovingly at Kimani and touched his curly black hair. "You have cute hair, Kimani," she said. "What about the rest of my body?" Kimani replied.

"Where are you going, children?" the visitor asked the preschoolers. "To Re-movement with Mim," they explained.

"I can't see," a VIP (Very Important Person) who is visually impaired, age 6, announced. "But," he continued before I could respond, "I can hear double!"

At four weeks old, Callie Rose performs daily demonstrations of amazing accomplishments. She now focuses; follows people, objects, light, mobiles, and shadows with her eyes; distinguishes familiar voices; turns her head toward sounds; holds onto her dad's finger for dear life; smiles (gas?); kicks and stretches; and makes weird and funny faces.

Callie's big cousin, Len, aka "the Muffin Man," at sixteen months old, is a role model of a dynamo in action: walking, jumping, dancing, clapping, throwing, running, singing, drumming, rolling, and falling.

Kimani, at four years old, comprehends and exhibits intricate movement patterns and sequences—making new combinations, multiplying ideas.

This always-fascinating first theme of Our Fantastic Bodies/Our Amazing Senses is not a curriculum area imposed by adults on children. *Children teach and remind adults about the importance of their bodies and senses.* We learn from them!

After a simple, ordinary (what *is* ordinary?) walk with the Muffin Man, I returned inspired to write notes on the experience. Enjoy these few excerpts from "Hangin Out With The Muffin Man."[1]

> . . . So many things to see when you hang out with the Muffin Man. Big things like buildings and cars. Little things like buzzing flies, eyes changing expressions, a leaf swaying in the wind. Far away things like clouds. Close up things like noses . . .
>
> Hanging out with the Muffin Man is a festival of sounds. He listens to sounds we hardly notice: the beginning of breezes, mobiles swinging, faucets dripping.
>
> Life is at our fingertips when we're with the Muffin Man because he reminds us about the fun of touching. Fingers want to hold other fingers, spoons, flower petals. If he can reach it, he wants to touch it. He grabs at dust particles shining in the bright noon window light and the flickering of passing shadows.
>
> The Muffin Man thinks the world is a big red apple waiting for him to sink his tiny teeth in and suck out its sweetness. Everything is on the menu of the Muffin Man: dirt, sand, paper, crayons, even food . . .
>
> Oh the patience, persistence and courage of the Muffin Man: sitting, crawling, standing, walking. Trying and failing. Pushing and falling. Up then down then up again and up, up, UP and down and up. Pouts and smiles. Whimpers and laughs.

Watch Callie grow and learn. Keep your eyes on Len and Kimani. At every stage, they will astonish you with their knowledge and skills. Just sit for a while at a neighborhood playground and observe the balance, coordination, and courage of young children sliding, swinging, climbing, playing.

Soon Kimani, Len, Callie, and all their friends will bounce, march, slouch, slide, glide, scurry into preschool, Head Start, kindergarten, first, second, third, and on and on through the grades. They will come into *your* room—eager to show you their muscles, how tall they are, how strong, how fast. They will urge you to give them opportunities to exercise and celebrate their senses. Pay attention to those worlds! Don't pass a flower without smelling it, hallowing it. Don't let a cloud float by without looking at it and wondering about it. Keep your doors and windows (mind and heart) open for spontaneous opportunities—serendipity. When the elephant walks into your room, do you say, "Sorry, we finished our E's!" or do you say, "Come on in—it's always the right time for an elephant!" and proceed to honor its presence with movement, sense poems, visual arts, songs, games, stories? It's up to *you*.

Because their accomplishments in mastering each physical challenge are so new, most children are proud and eager to demonstrate what they can do. They have not yet learned to inhibit their feelings, to repress their joy in accomplishment. Through movement, children express responses to their inner and outer worlds. Excitement and joy tingle the muscles and lift the limbs. Disappointment or sadness

lowers the head, slows the tempo. Infants move to the rhythm of human sounds. A mother's voice is the song of a baby's first dance. Your voice is the music of your classroom.

Young children never tire of "showing off" their bodies. They love repetition, familiar chants, games, and challenges. Some of their earliest words are body words. Their first accomplishments are skills of body coordination. One of their greatest delights is combining two or three movements, such as clap and turn; jump and clap; and jump, clap, and turn.

Through body movement, children express their understanding of ideas and language. Ask Len, "Where are your eyes?" and two tiny fingers point to two tiny eyes. Toddlers understand our words and their meaning. They learn about identification, location, comparison, and differentiation through activities that celebrate bodies.

When children are given opportunities to enjoy experiences involving their bodies and their senses, they feel good about themselves and others. Along with healthy bodies, they develop healthy self-concepts. They discover and rediscover the power of mind-body harmony. "My brain is the boss of all these muscles!" a five-year-old announced after a lively session of body movement and awareness.

The word "active" is highlighted in descriptions of Developmentally Appropriate practices for young children. It is shocking to me that, with all we know about how children best learn, it is still possible for Callie, Len, and Kimani to sit passively in silent, tightly structured, skill-centered, joyless rooms that make no time for celebrating that important *first* world—the world of the human body. So many opportunities are missed to teach valuable lessons across the curriculum.

Many years ago, before "mainstreaming," I was invited to participate in a movement session with all the children in what was then a public school for "handicapped" students. At the time, I was not prepared to see children who had no arms, who could not walk, and who had little muscular coordination. But there they were, eagerly awaiting the "creative movement" program in the gym. I had to toss out my usual directions, familiar vocabulary, and regular approaches that took for granted healthy bodies. We began with things everyone could do, with parts

everyone could move. We raised and lowered eyebrows, shrugged shoulders, wiggled noses, and turned our mouths into O's. We laughed and sang. I learned that it was possible to celebrate the body with children challenged by profound physical disabilities. I highlighted the *able* in disabled!

If you keep your activities flexible and open-ended, every child in your group will find meaningful and enjoyable ways to participate. In the case of children with special physical or emotional needs, concentrate on the things they *can* do. You will be surprised at the variety of ways human beings *can* express themselves through movement. Although some children have special challenges, they are whole persons who are both aware of their limitations and capable of enormous compensations. Most of these children can teach us about courage and humor.

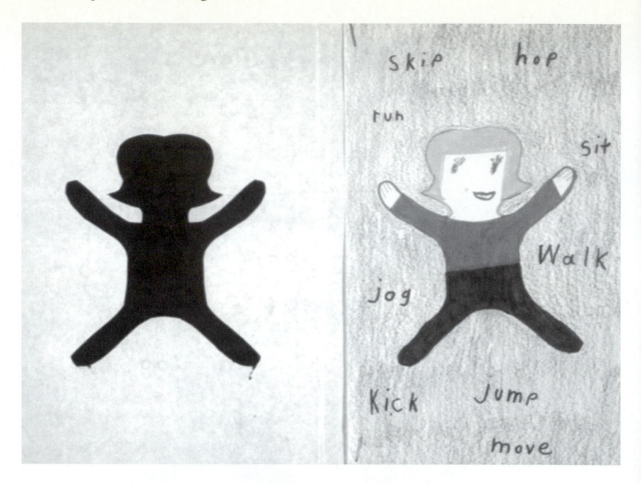

With all your students, celebrate these wonders throughout the year. Devote parts of every day to this always exciting, relevant focus. You will keep the attention of your students when they are involved in meaningful, enjoyable discussions or activities about their bodies, about their senses.

There's always a good reason and it's always the right season for enjoying moving learning experiences. You will be right on target with all the proclamations of every fitness report, of every president's commission, with every valid justification. When we offer our children numerous opportunities for movement activities and enrichment of the senses, we are encouraging language development, language acquisition, imagination, comprehension, small and gross motor skills, following directions, learning patterns, and listening skills. You will never be blown over if you *know* what you are doing and why!

DISCOVERY TIMES/WONDER TIMES

- Our bodies are made up of so many interesting, specific parts. They help us move in different ways. Aren't we lucky to be human beings and not jelly beans or baked beans?
- Each of our body parts has a name and more than one function (for example, fingers can do so many things, hands can move in so many ways).
- Most people have ten toes, ten fingers, two feet, two hands, and so on. But even though we all have thumbs, our thumbprints are unique.

- Some people, through accident or circumstances of birth or illness, do not have the usual number or function of body parts.
- People with physical disabilities can do extraordinary things with their bodies: blind people read through their fingers with Braille; deaf people use sign language and read lips; people with no hands learn to type, write, paint, and draw with their toes and even their mouths.[2]
- The human spirit is full of courage and determination!
- Our bodies can do so many amazing things—is there any end to the list? We can keep adding ideas every day of ordinary, marvelous body-works!
- Through practice, we teach our bodies to accomplish more complicated, challenging movement patterns.
- It is so important to take good care of our bodies by exercising, eating nutritious foods, and practicing safety and good health habits.
- Our brain is in charge. Our brain is the boss. Our brain is in our head—that's why we call it "headquarters"!
- Our amazing senses—seeing, hearing, tasting, touching, and smelling—help us to learn about everything around us. Every day, we should practice using our sensory powers.

Naming parts of the body leads to a variety of activities. Discover eye shapes, colors, and expressions. Count teeth; discover loose and missing teeth. Discuss numbers of body parts, such as two eyes, two lips, ten fingers, and two knees. Note that hands are big, small, chubby, skinny; that they clap, carve, weave, write.

SUGGESTED VOCABULARY

Body Parts

head	lips	fingers	ankles
hair	chin	fingernails	feet
eyebrows	face	wrists	toes
eyes	cheeks	heart	toenails
eyelashes	ears	chest	rear/bottom/tush/butt
nose	neck	stomach	bones
nostrils	shoulders	bellybutton	blood
mouth	back	hips	muscles
tongue	arms	legs	brain
teeth	hands	knees	skin

Bodies in Motion

big	loose	shake	skip
little	tight	wiggle	march
large	straight	flop	push
small	crooked	gallop	pull
tall	grow	leap	spin
short	shrink	hop	turn
heavy	curl	trot	lift
light	stretch	jump	forward
weak	fall	crawl	backward

(continued)

SUGGESTED VOCABULARY (continued)

strong	rise	walk	sideways
	reach	run	fast/slow

Bodies Coming to Their Senses

sight	sharp	dark	loud
feel	taste	spicy	shout
sweet	listen	sound	plain
rough	bitter	notice	crunchy
bumpy	soft	cold	see
decorated	colorful	whisper	watch
smell	dull	light	quiet
look	touch	gooey	lively
sour	hear	hear	peaceful
smooth	hot	observe	flowery
liquid	hard		

Some Exercises

sit-ups	jumping jacks	squats	stretches
push-ups	leg lifts	spin arounds	arm twirls
touch toes	twists	skips	rolls
jog	kicks	jumps	bends

SOME STARTERS

Start with a vocabulary word Words for body parts, bodies in motion, and exercises are excellent openers for talk, play, art, poems, and songs. There are worlds of possibilities in words.

Start with a warm-up exercise The exercise words turned into warm-up activities help children become aware of their bodies and of the variety of shapes and movements they can master.

Start with a challenge Children love challenges, especially if they can meet them. Be sure your challenge is accessible to everyone in the class. Here is an example: "My cousin says he can make five shapes with his body. He says that's very hard to do. Can you make five shapes with your bodies? I bet you can! That's not hard for you to do!"

Start with a photograph Show the children a photograph of the human body in some interesting and easily assumed position. "That position looks like fun. Let's try to do what the person in the picture is doing. I know you can do it even better. Let's hold the position for five seconds."

Start with a trick Children are proud of their physical accomplishments and are eager to show them off. "Isn't it amazing how many tricks we can do? My favorite trick is standing on one foot without falling down. Can you do that? What's your favorite trick? Show us. We'll all try it!"

Start with a loose tooth Never let a loose or lost tooth go unnoticed. That teeth fall out to make room for new ones is fascinating to young children and can prompt them to think about the wonders of the human body.

Start with a count of body parts Count the noses in your room. Count the fingers, hands, feet, toes, eyes. Children love to count and to look at each other. Here is a chance to talk about the universality and the uniqueness of our body parts.

Start with animal comparisons Discuss with the children some of the amazing things that animals can do. For example, snakes coil their bodies, crocodiles open their mouths very wide, and dolphins leap high out of the water. Compare and contrast such actions with those of humans. Ask, for example, if elephants do push-ups or if fish snap their fingers.

Start with an amazing observation Consider all the things the children did since they woke up in the morning. Here is a list that a group of kindergartners recalled in just a few minutes: woke up; stretched; sat up; got out of bed; went to the bathroom; washed; dressed; ate breakfast; played with the dog; played with toys; climbed into the school bus; and skipped into school. The list suggests ideas for pantomime, improvisation, art, story telling, and songs.

Start with a "What If . . . ?" What if you had to keep the shape you're holding now and never change it? (Demonstrate.) What if you could walk only one way or at only one speed? What if you could only crawl on your belly like a snake?

TALK TIMES/LISTENING TIMES

Children have important things to say about their bodies because they already have experiences and information to share. They are interested in all aspects of their bodies and show you every scratch and scraggly Band-Aid, their toenail and fingernail polish, bruises and splinters, new haircuts, and strong muscles. They make observations, ask questions, share their wonder. Leave time in your talks for appreciation and curiosity. You may not always have the answer; sometimes the answer is still unknown. But because you encourage questioning and wondering (the most important components of the learning process), your young students may grow up to find the answers.

Open-ended questions Such questions spur lively talk sessions. Examples of this kind of question are: "What do your eyes see right now?"; "What do you hear with your ears right now?"; and "What are your favorite ways to move?" One group of kindergartners responding to the question "How many ways can you move your eyes?" had some interesting observations: "Eyelashes are like little bugs' feet"; "When you sleep, your eyes are closed"; and "If I close one eye and open one other eye, it winks."

The question "What are some things *hands* can do?" triggered an outpouring of ideas from a lively group of prekindergartners. Here are some of the comments that were written on the chalkboard:

Hands can:

touch things	take pictures	tickle
scratch itches	shut doors	clap
pinch	pick up things	put socks on
write	paint	play with blocks
pick up the phone	pick apples	
pet animals	cut, comb, brush, and wash hair	

Adina added, "I know four *bad* things hands can do: Hit someone; pull somebody; push somebody; punch somebody."

The above discussion integrating sense awareness with body parts, provided resource material for activities in art, music, movement, pantomime, and games. The children turned the ideas into riddles, poems, and charts.

An example of how easily talking/listening evolves into other activities comes from a class of four-year-olds at the Jewish Center in Columbus, Ohio. For some reason, Jan Brown's students began movement sessions for about two weeks by chanting "feet, feet, feet" as they stamped into the room. Finally, I asked them, "What is so great about feet?" They sat down and told me all the fabulous things

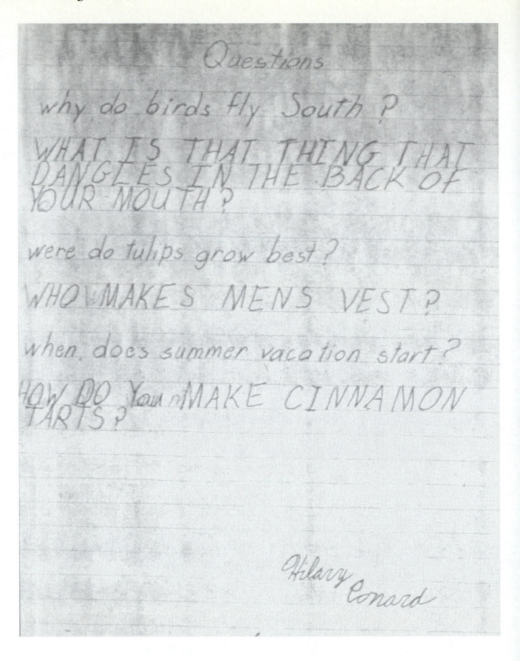

feet do. The participation and excitement was so intense that I told them I had to record their ideas. "Read them back to us," they bubbled. When their words were read aloud, we discovered that they had actually written a wonderful chant, which they then learned and turned into a dance. Each line was expressed in a specific movement. The chant became part of their lives that year and became even more enjoyable as they taught it to other children on the playground and in the gym.

feet	feet dance	feet take little steps
feet	feet kick	feet take big steps
feet	feet smell	feet jump high
feet	feet walk	feet jump like frogs
feet jump	feet run	feet jump like rabbits
feet hop	feet trip	feet scratch
feet hop backwards	feet slip	feet dig
feet stamp	feet fall	feet draw pictures

feet wiggle	feet slide	feet gallop
feet leap	feet turn	feet feet
feet tiptoe	feet jump and turn	feet feet
feet clap		

Observations Observations are excellent conversation topics. This simple observation stimulated a valuable session of experimentation and conversation in a kindergarten class: "You folks look so different when you sit up tall and straight. Your bodies seem to grow at least two inches in your seats!" We changed from slouched to straight backs and compared how our bodies felt. As we moved, we talked. Here are some excerpts from that activity: "Sometimes I stand straight and sometimes crooked"; "Sometimes I feel droopy, sometimes very tall"; "Do we *really* change size?"; "Once I felt all caved in, now I feel spread out"; and "It's fun to feel floppy-floppy." You can see how easily the verbal ideas translate into movement interpretations. Without doubt, "floppy-floppy" was the favorite experiment.

Shared experiences Armeda Starling's first graders in Indian Run School, Dublin, Ohio, were deeply involved in a fascinating discussion about their teeth. Loose teeth, lost teeth, new teeth—the children shared experiences about how they had lost their teeth. They listened attentively to this "storytelling" spurred by the question "Wouldn't it be fun to make up stories about missing teeth?" The children loved inventing tooth stories even more than they enjoyed telling "what really happened." The story telling led to story writing, and the result was a collection of tooth stories accompanied by original illustrations.

Leave time for humor After a lively discussion about losing teeth, I asked one of the first graders what he did with his loose tooth. "I put it under my pillow and in the morning, I found a quarter," he explained. "Who put the quarter under your pillow?" I asked. "The Truth Fairy!"

After the explosion of laughter subsided, we enjoyed a delightful brainstorming session about Tooth Fairies and Truth Fairies! Such "Talk Times/Listening Times" yield countless inspirational ideas for pictures, puppet shows, creative writing, improvisation, songs, and playful movement activities. (What do *you* think the Tooth Fairy looks like? Illustrate!)

Sense-full talks Delightful discussions center on favorite tastes, smells, sounds, textures, and sights. Center such conversations on seasons, weather, holidays, special events, and everyday ordinary (extraordinary?) days. Look out the window— what do we see? Smell this lovely flower—what kind of smell is it to you? What's your favorite sound? Chart the answers, illustrate them, turn them into poems, games, and surveys.

Add the dimension of sense-awareness to everything you do, every story, poem, or book you read, every idea you explore. Train yourself to challenge the children's imaginations with such questions as: "I wonder what the Three Bears saw out in the woods? Any suggestions?" or "That Winnie the Pooh sure likes honey. Let's taste some. How does honey taste to you?" or "Imagine the sounds the Wild Things are making! Anybody want to tell us about them or try out an idea about them?"

Including sensory images in your daily talks enriches vocabulary and expands appreciation for the power of language. Encourage all of the children to respond, but don't force them if they are shy or reluctant. Good teachers are like the Native American Trickster, Coyote, who tricks people into learning! Look up your sleeve for loving and playful ways to welcome children into participation. When they know you value their opinions, experiences, and questions, they develop good listening habits and respect for others as they practice language skills.

Let's look out the window. What do we see? Hear? Smell?

Let's look at this beautiful picture. What kinds of sounds can you imagine from the animals in the picture? Can you smell the field in the picture? What does it smell like to you?

Never let a day go by without practicing our powers of sensory enjoyment.

Stopping "Talk Times/Listening Times" is harder than starting them. My favorite way to end a discussion is by looking at the clock and remarking, "Time flies when you're having fun! We need to start moving!" You will never end a discussion because you run out of ideas, only because you run out of time.

VISUAL ARTS TIMES

Art projects devoted to our fantastic bodies/our amazing senses are so plentiful and enjoyable that I offer just a sampling. These projects will inspire you to develop your own ideas.

Handprints and footprints Children dip their hands or feet in finger paint or watercolor, then press them on a large piece of butcher paper. Write their names below their prints if they cannot write themselves. A variation of this idea is to outline each child's hand or foot on the paper and have the children color and decorate their own prints. Tape the paper to the wall to create an attractive mural.

Thumbprints, heel prints, etc. Think of the fun of discovering the variety of designs possible when thumbprints, heel prints, fingerprints, and toe prints are used. Eve Merriam's poem "Thumbprint" catches the wonder of our body parts. Surround her poem with thumbprint designs.

> **Thumbprint**
> In the heel of my thumb
> are whorls, whirls, wheels
> in a unique design:
> mine alone.
> What a treasure to own!
> My own flesh, my own feelings.
> No other, however grand or base,
> can ever contain the same.
> My signature,
> thumbing the pages of my time.
> My universe key,
> my singularity.
> Impress, implant,
> I am myself,
> of all my atom parts I am the sum.
> And out of my blood and my brain
> I make my own interior weather,
> my own sun and rain.
> Imprint my mark upon the world.
> Whatever I shall become.[3]

Helping hands Children trace their hands on separate papers, color them, and cut them out. Write their names on the hands. Hands can be used as indicators of daily chores or helpers of the day or just delightful decorations.

Ask the children what kinds of things hands and fingers can do. Write (or have the children write) some of those ideas *on* the hands.

Friendship hands Fold a piece of construction paper in half. On one half of the paper, handprint or outline a child's hand. On the other half, print the hand of a friend. Write the names below. This activity is an excellent way to introduce the concepts of likeness and difference.

Lei of hands I visited a kindergarten class and was welcomed with a lovely wreath of friendly hands. The children had outlined and cut their hands out of brightly colored construction paper. They decorated the hands and wrote their names on them. The hands were stapled together in a long chain. When a visitor came to the room, the children welcomed the visitor by putting the chain of hands around their shoulders.

Handouts Children trace their hands, cut them out and use them for the cover of a hand-shaped book that they will fill with original pictures and stories. This project works with feet as well.

Left and right hands An enjoyable way to learn right from left is to do something with the hand you want to focus attention on. Design a bracelet or ring, paint a design on that hand, or dot that hand with a chosen color to set it off. All day direct attention to the decorated hand and help the children learn that the hand is, for example, their right hand. After a few days, decorate the left hand and focus attention on it.

Finger and hand puppets These simple, popular little puppets can be made out of a variety of "scrounge" materials—paper, cotton, flannel, or even scrounge from nature. A group of five-year-olds had the best time taping little leaves and branches to their fingers to use as hats for finger puppets. An innovative teacher asked parents to send in old, torn gloves rather than throw them out. She and her students cut the fingers off the gloves and had enough fingers for each member of the class to decorate an original finger puppet. Be sure to go beyond the making of the puppets and give children plenty of time to play with their puppets. Improvisation is the most important element of the experience. De-emphasize formal performances and encourage informal interaction among the children.

Lollipop face puppets Use lollipop sticks or tongue depressors. Cut out cardboard circles and have the children draw eyes, noses, mouths, and hair to make faces. Tape or glue the puppet's face to the stick. When the face is added, a puppet is born, complete with name, voice, story, and song.

Paper-bag or sock puppets Of the easy-to-make puppets my favorites are paper-bag and sock puppets. Again, with plenty of scrounge material at hand, children can make puppets with distinctive features. Scraps of wool or material can be used for hair, buttons for eyes, cotton balls for beards and mustaches, and cardboard or felt for hats. With your children, make up names, stories, and songs for the puppets.

Eyes are probably the most distinguishing feature. Add eyes to anything and you have a creature or a character. Draw a circle, dot two eyes, and you have a face. Gather small stones, pinecones, and wood chunks. Paint eyes on them and you have little characters with their own names and personalities. Blow up balloons. Paint eyes on them and they become special characters. Add other parts, but start with eyes. What do these eyes see?

Shoe boxes of eyes, ears, noses, and mouths Children like to cut up magazines. From your plentiful supply of old magazines, children cut out eyes, ears, noses, and mouths and put each part in its own shoe box. After a while, you will have a shoe box full of eyes or noses. Create original faces on paper circles or paper plates using parts from each of the boxes. (Maybe this is how Picasso got his start!)

Collages and montages Body parts are the oldest, most popular artistic designs in human history. Here are two basic kinds of projects involving body parts. The children select one body part to cut out of magazines or draw. They compose an arrangement of, for example, eyes, and fill their papers with eyes of different colors, shapes, and sizes. Be sure to display all the children's work.

The other project involves a collage or montage of different body parts. The children cut out or draw body parts and arrange them in an interesting pattern on either their own paper or a large bulletin board to which all contribute.

Art appreciation Share great works of art with your students. Libraries often lend paintings. Art books usually have excellent reproductions of masterpieces. Use the names of the artists as you show the way individual artists painted or sculpted faces and bodies. Children enjoy looking at, for example, Modigliani's faces or Renoir's hair and faces. They marvel at how Michaelangelo carved such a perfect hand for *David* and find inspiration to model their own clay hands and feet.

Remember, many children are familiar with the Ninja Turtles: Leonardo, Michael-angelo, Raphael, and Donatello. I always describe the four great artists as Ninja Turtles' ancestors. Because the children are familiar with the names, they have a built-in interest in their arts.

Always include the dimension of sense-awareness to every activity focused on art. "How does red smell to you?" "We can almost feel those fluffy clouds." "How do they feel?" "What do you think the man in the picture is looking at? What does he hear?"

Body parts through the seasons This activity is a wonderful way to correlate understanding of changes in seasons with awareness of how the seasons affect what we do and what we wear. Here are excerpts from many classes' discoveries as they discussed the seasons in relation to body parts. Sense references are totally integrated into the explorations.

Winter Hands	Winter Feet	Winter Heads
wear mittens	wear boots	wear hats
make snowballs	make snow prints	wear ear muffs
build snowmen	slide on ice	wear scarves
throw snowballs	ice-skate	get snowflakes in eyes

Spring Hands	Spring Feet	Spring Heads
plant seeds	wear tennis shoes	wear baseball caps
fly kites	run on the grass	feel the sun and wind in hair
steer bikes	peddle bikes	

Summer Hands	Summer Feet	Summer Heads
splash in water	go barefoot	get sunburned
throw baseballs	wear sandals	wear sun hats
dig in sand and mud	squish mud and sand	get sweaty

Autumn Hands	Autumn Feet	Autumn Heads
rake leaves	wear school shoes	sometimes wear scarves
throw leaves	jump in crunchy leaves	or hats
pick apples	kick footballs	feel hair blowing in the wind
		get leaves in hair

One kindergarten class created a mural divided into four sections, one for each season. Each season had its own images—snowflakes and snowdrifts for winter, green grass and tulips for spring, inviting swimming pools and lush gardens for summer, and brightly colored leaves for fall. They drew, cut out, and pasted magazine pictures of boots, scarves, hats, caps, sandals, and mittens on the different seasons, and they added their own silhouettes of hands, feet, and heads to create a fascinating work of art. A variation of this activity is to feature bodies in movement through the seasons.

Remember—we can't go through the seasons without celebrating the senses. We see, hear, smell, taste, and touch so many different things during different times of the year (and day).

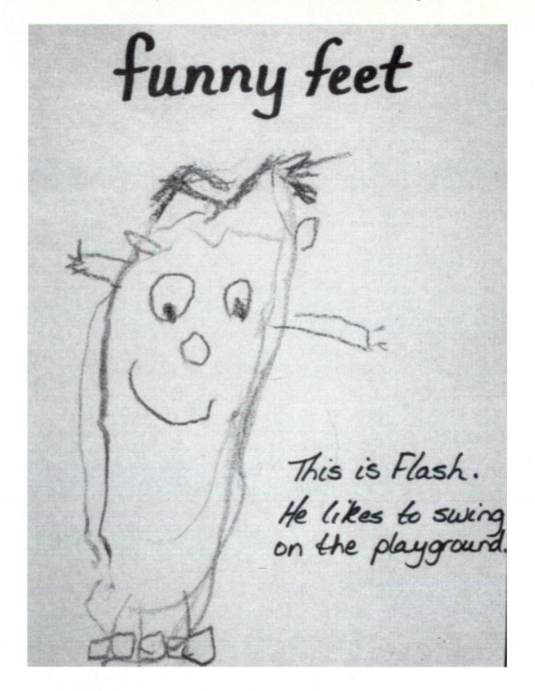

Body silhouettes Spread butcher paper, or any other inexpensive paper, across the floor. The children lie down on the paper in any position they choose. Outline their shapes with colored markers. Their body shapes are cut out and ready to be decorated with features, colors, clothes, and designs, or to be colored or painted with one color to make a silhouette.

I visited a first grade where the children's silhouettes were hung across the room on a clothesline. Another kindergarten class tacked their silhouettes on the four walls of the room.

Body works collage The children cut pictures out of magazines and newspapers that show bodies doing things such as playing, working, and resting. They create their own collages or together create a class collage. Both are exciting projects. Close in on dancers, athletes, or everyday activities of people in action.

Scrounge bodies Your supply of scrounge materials should always be ample. Give the children many opportunities to participate in the highest form of creative activity: making "something out of nothing." The children use whatever materials they find; they glue, paste, tape, or clip odds-and-ends together to make body shapes.

Favorite body-works books Here is a chance for children to gather pictures and designs of their favorite kind of body works and create their own books. (Staple the pages together; make it simple.) The first graders' body-works books featured joggers, mountain climbers, and construction workers.

Pipe cleaner bodies Pipe cleaners bend and twist and make wonderful bodies in motion. Give the children lots of time to experiment.

Stick figures Use Popsicle sticks, straws, toothpicks, or tongue depressors. Glue various lengths of material to shape a variety of figures.

Clay figures Roll, push, pull, twist, pat, clap, pinch—experiment with clay and encourage the children to find ways they most enjoy working with clay. "How many different body shapes can we sculpt today?" Display and celebrate all the works.

Body poses The children take turns modeling for their classmates. Encourage the children to sketch, paint, or color the model's position quickly, because it is a challenge for the model to hold a shape for more than a few minutes.

Exercise chart Devote a special place in the room—a board or portion of a wall—to pictures and diagrams of physical exercises. Children cut out pictures of exercises from magazines and newspapers. Label the exercises so that the name is prominently displayed next to the diagram or picture. Exercise "leaders" refer to the chart as different warm-up exercises are featured each day.

Exercise name tags Children write their names on a tag. Draw or cut out exercise shapes to add to their names. The tags will be used for some of the activities described later in this guide.

Exercise wheel Paint a large cardboard circle a bright color. Divide it into sections. Have children paste an illustration of a clearly defined exercise on each section. Be sure the exercises they choose for the wheel are familiar and easy to do. Cut a pointer out of cardboard, paint it a different color, and clip it to the center of the wheel. Spin the pointer and where it stops is the exercise the children will do. Assign different children to spin the wheel each day and lead the exercises.

Exercise cards Cut out or illustrate examples of exercises and paste one on each card. Design a special pocket or place for the exercise cards. Children choose a few cards each day to start their warm-ups.

Shape-up poster Divide the paper or portion of a wall into columns such as:

I CAN DO SIT-UPS   I CAN DO PUSH-UPS   I CAN JOG

The children write their names in each column and draw or paint a design next to their names to show "they can." Keep adding exercise sections. Children have lots of practice writing their names, creating designs, and feeling good about themselves.

Celebration of the senses As with all ideas, there are countless variations. Here are just a few suggestions for highlighting our amazing senses. Following walks, talks, shared classroom experiences, games, books, or holidays (every topic is relevant!), children love to illustrate their ideas with paints, markers, crayons, scissors, scrounge materials, creating murals, group pictures, posters, charts, and cards.

A group of first graders focused on one of the senses and created a beautifully illustrated poem called "The Sounds of Rain." It included excellent sound words like *patter, pitter, drip, shower,* and *sprinkle.*

Children love their own names. Here is LaToya's sense poem brightened with colorful pictures:

LaToya sees Woody, the spaniel.
LaToya hears Rachel singing.

LaToya tastes a strawberry ice cream cone.
LaToya touches her paint box.
LaToya smells her Mama's soup.
LaToya feels happy today.

Close in on those sense-related body parts for the text or captions accompanying sense-full pictures. Enjoy these few examples noted from the wall of a second-grade classroom decorated with delightful sense-posters:

"My fingers touch a shiny icicle." "My ears hear my brother's drumming." "My nose smells pizza. Yum." "My tongue tastes a green lollipop."

Be sure to celebrate the works of your students by sharing, appreciating, and displaying them in many imaginative ways.

MUSIC TIMES

Celebrate voices Children do not need to be taught to sing. They naturally sing, hum, and chant, echoing the words and rhythms they hear about them, inventing their own and combining musical ideas. Sing old, new, borrowed, blue, improvised, original songs. Sing about everything. Sing as you work, walk, play, and rest. Encourage the children to make up their own songs and celebrate them. Show them how by your own example.

Celebrate songs from around the world All people use their voices to sing. All people have songs, but their words, rhythms, and styles are often very different, reflecting the diversity of the human family. Borrow music from neighbors, family, the library, and children's families that highlight songs from different cultures. Play them (and sing along) as often as possible. Through these kinds of listening and learning opportunities, your children will learn something about the wonders of the human voice.

Songs of bodies at work Walt Whitman's poem "I Hear America Singing" introduces the theme of songs people sing while working and playing. In his poem Whitman describes the songs of carpenters, mechanics, masons, deckhands, shoemakers, woodcutters, and mothers. So many of our most popular folk songs are based on bodies at work—railroad workers, sailors, miners, ranchers, farmers, and migrant workers. Children love to sing such work songs as "I've Been Workin' on the Railroad"; "Erie Canal"; "Jump Down, Turn Around, Pick a Bale of Cotton"; and "John Henry." Share the idea with your students that as people work, songs flow. Make up your own songs.

Tune up body parts to make music Music is also the result of effort and practice. Musicians need nimble fingers, flexible wrists, powerful hands, and strong lungs to make music. As you listen to music and play your own, emphasize the importance of exercising special body parts and practicing for developing musical talents and skills. Invent such musical exercises as playing a piano, strumming a guitar, and blowing a wind instrument.

Body-parts rhythm band Our bodies are our first instruments. Hearts beat a special rhythm. Lungs exhale, inhale, their special breath rhythm. Feet jump, their special jumping rhythm. Hands clap—fast, faster, fastest; slow, slower, slowest; louder, softer—their special rhythms. Feet tap, their special tapping rhythms. Teeth click. Hands slap floor. Hands slap thighs. Hair swishes.

Experiment with body parts that make sounds and keep rhythms. Clap, tap, stamp, jump, whistle, sing, beat, and shake out rhythms. Listen to the sounds the body parts make. Work together and discover the joy of fusing energies and ideas. Play different kinds of music. Recite favorite poems and sing favorite songs accompanied by the body-parts rhythm band. Remember, musical instruments are extensions

of body rhythms and sounds. We blow our breath into wind instruments. We pluck and strum string instruments. We tap, pound, and shake percussion instruments.

Make rhythm instruments The earliest instruments came from nature, for example, dried gourds with loose seeds, animal skins pulled tightly over shells or wood, and stones and sticks with holes in them.

Here is Betsy Distelhorst's favorite way to make drums. Cut old inner tubes into circles that will fit over the open ends of coffee cans. Punch holes around the borders of the rubber circles. Carefully place one rubber circle on each end of the hollow coffee can. Connect the two rubber skins with string, from a hole on one side to a hole on the other. If you cannot find old inner tubes, use scraps of vinyl, suede cloth, or heavy canvas.

L'Eggs eggs or small milk containers are good for making rattles or maracas. Fill the egg or the container with seeds or pebbles. Close up the egg or glue the opening on the container. They can be held in hands and shaken or attached to wooden sticks, tongue depressors, or old rulers.

Before stapling two facing paper plates together, sprinkle some pebbles, beads, or seeds on them. Paint or color the outside of the plates in lively patterns. Attach string rings of bottle caps to the rims. Shake them up. Tambourines!

Experiment with objects that make sounds. Invent new instruments. Click two pencils together. Tap spoons on tabletops. Clap two wooden blocks together. Turn two pot covers into cymbals. Make songs, poems, and dances to accompany the rhythms.

Improvised "fantastic body" songs You have material in your knapsack of experiences to create delightful song sessions with your students that will enrich their appreciation and understanding of the fascinating ways our bodies work.

The popular song "This Is the Way We Go to School" can be adapted to verses such as "This is the way we clap our hands," "This is the way we blink our eyes." "This is the way we wiggle our nose," and "This is the way we shrug our shoulders."

I'm a terrific kid-arounder who loves playing with the children. They break into smiles of delight as I improvise to "Good Morning to You" with "Good morning, dear jumps" or "Good morning, dear elbows" or "Good morning, dear knees" (you get the idea). Or play with the old favorite, "If You're Happy and You Know It" by expanding the movement challenges:

Sing: "If you're happy and you know it, touch your toes."
"If you're happy and you know it, stretch stretch stretch."

I love surprising the children with "If you're *hoppy* and you know it, hop hop hop!" The point is to have fun!

Bodies respond to musical instruments "How do violins make you want to move?" "Bongo drums?" "Flutes or trumpets?" Experiment with the sounds of different instruments and the different ways children move to each of them. The children's bodies become the shape of the sound. Stretch this exploration of music and body responses through the school year. Highlight one instrument at a time. Start with your favorite instruments and musicians. With children of all ages I have shared my favorites, from Al Hirt on the trumpet to Carlos Montoya and Andrés Segovia on flamenco guitar. If you play an instrument, share it with your students.

Music for body relaxation In our often frenetic world, we need the feeling of inner peace and calm when the body relaxes with soothing, beautiful music. This is a time to help young children realize how much our bodies can do and still be able to rest comfortably and calmly. Encourage the children to let their minds daydream, wander, float. Later, you may want to discuss some of their imaginative sensory images; turn the images into pictures and poems.

Children need to find comfortable positions—sitting, leaning, or lying down. Pillows or mats on the floor are useful for those who want them.

As often as possible, tell your class the title of the music and its composer, not to test them but to give them the opportunity to hear and learn the names.

Choose lullabies, ballads, folk songs, and segments of longer pieces that are conducive to peaceful feelings and rich sensory experiences. The following are some old favorites you may want to hum or sing softly during this peaceful, easy time when the body works at relaxing: "Down in the Valley," "Clementine," "Red River Valley," "The Riddle Song," "Hush Little Baby," "Puff the Magic Dragon," "500 Miles," "The Water Is Wide," "On Top of Old Smokey," "Tell Me Why?" and "Day Is Done (Taps)."

If possible, sing your favorite lullabies or camp songs to the children. One of the best stories I ever heard came from a friend who substituted one day in a kindergarten class. The regular teacher always sang to the children after their snack. They asked my friend if she would sing to them. Reluctant because she felt she had a poor voice, my friend hesitated. The children urged her. Finally, she gave in, hoarsely whisper-humming a little song. When she finished, she shrugged apologetically. "That's OK," one child comforted her, "you did your best!" You are only being asked to do your best!

Music makes sense Create musical interpretations of sensory images. With rhythm instruments and voices, explore and enjoy ways to recreate such images as the sounds of the ocean, breezes in a forest, the excitement of people gathering for a festival, early morning on a farm, rush hour in a busy city, the sounds of a house filled with people. Accompany the sounds with movement, stories, poems, and visual arts. Which comes first? You decide.

Always be on the lookout for musical offerings from every cultural background and historical period to highlight your curriculum and enrich sensory awareness. For example, with children from kindergarten through the elementary grades, we honored Arnold Adoff's beautiful story, *Flamboyan*, about a little girl who lives on a tropical island surrounded by the soft blue sea.[4] I use my Harry Belafonte calypso records, my Ziggy Marlowe reggae, my old Hawaiian hula music, original children's songs, and rhythms of beach, waves, and birds to help create a total environment where our bodies feel the warm air, smell the brilliantly colored flowers, hear the songs of the gulls, see the flashing rainbow-colored fish, and imagine the feeling of waves of the sea and the sand under our feet. We move, dance, sing, talk, illustrate, and enjoy the story, adding our own feelings and ideas to Adoff's text.

Think of stories you and your students love and how they can grow more meaningful with music, movement, visual interpretations, and of course, lots of conversation.

MOVEMENT AND PLAY TIMES

Movement responses Raising hands seems to be the most accepted movement pattern in American schools. So many opportunities are missed when we limit choice of movement. Here are a few different ways children can answer questions. "Boys and girls, if you saw 'Sesame Street' last night, wiggle your nose." "Children, if you have ever heard of Alaska, tap your feet." "If you think you know the answer to two-and-two, clap it." "How many people here brought in their permission slips? Shake ten fingers if you did." Aren't these ways more interesting and fun than always raising hands?

Daily warm-ups What better way to limber minds and muscles than exercising for a few minutes every day? Correlate exercises with curriculum, and use a variety of musical selections to accompany the exercises. Include in these warm-up sessions exercises that you and your students create as well as familiar exercises such as sit-ups, push-ups, and jumping jacks. The following are some ways that exercises can become part of your daily schedule.

Follow the leader Children take turns leading a movement or exercise of their choice. If the leader does something difficult to follow, encourage the others to do their best. Leaders may choose from the exercise cards or spin the exercise wheel or put their name tags next to the exercise they want to lead on the exercise chart (see descriptions of these projects in "Visual Art Times" section above).

Exercises and numbers "It's January 6 today. Let's do six exercises in honor of the number 6." Write the exercises on the board and follow them in sequence. Or "Today we're celebrating the number 8. Let's do eight exercises. Which shall they be?"

Another aspect of numbers and exercises is to assign numbers to each warm-up. "How many jumping jacks shall we do?" Write the number on the board. "How many windmills?"

Another variation of numbers and exercises is for the birthday child to choose the exercises of the day to correspond to his or her new age. "Seven years old today? Jackie, choose seven birthday exercises!"

Animal exercises Consider the movements of animals that can be used in exercises: *hopping* (grasshoppers, frogs, rabbits, kangaroos); *running* (dogs, foxes, squirrels, wolves); *galloping* (horses, donkeys, zebras); and *crawling* (snakes, caterpillars, lizards, salamanders). Do them. Talk about them. Extend them into art projects and games.

Exercises for seasons and special occasions On a cold winter day, make up a few exercises based on seasonal activities such as snowball throwing, pulling on boots, and forming snow angels.

Turn the exercises into chants, into action stories. Illustrate.

Celebrate field trips by highlighting movement ideas. For example, following a trip to a local library to see a play based on *Jack and the Beanstalk*, some kindergartners returned to create their own "exercises" for Jack *walking*, the beanstalk *growing*, the giant *stamping*.

Exercise change game This is one of my favorite ways to enjoy exercises. Talk about all the exercises the children know. *Encourage them to make up their own for different parts of their bodies* (for example, shoulder exercise, knee exercise). Carefully explain. When the music goes on, each child may choose any exercise to do. Everyone will be different. When you give the signal (for example, shake tambourine, clap hands), everyone changes to another exercise. Minds and bodies work very fast. Children have the opportunity to choose their favorite movement and to enjoy a unique warm-up. Use any lively, rhythmical music you like. I have used everything from Arabic belly-dance music to Appalachian round dances. The only rule is that the children must stay in their own spaces. If they jog or kick, they must stay in their own "self space."

Taking inventory The most universally loved game of early childhood is "Show Me . . ." or "Where Is Your . . . ?" For example: "Where is your nose?" "Show me your belly button." Here is an opportunity for every child to feel success and delight. A silly variation of this game is to point to the wrong place. Pretend absentmindedness. Young children find great delight in these "mistakes" and will correct you with glee.

"Show me" can be extended from location to movement. For example: "What can your shoulders do? Show me." "How many things can your hands do? Show me." "What can you do with your eyebrows? Show me."

Many songs and poems take inventory. As the children sing or recite, they move and point to the appropriate parts. (Challenge the children to "show" you as the poem is read.)

Count the parts Here is an activity that combines counting body parts and moving them. Change the movement ideas. Once in a while, for fun and laughs, mix up the counting: "Three noses. Whoops! I mean *one* nose! Sorry!"

One head (shake it)	Two elbows (bend them)
Two eyes (blink them)	One mouth (make an O)
One nose (wiggle it)	Two shoulders (shrug them)
Two ears (twitch them)	One back (stretch it)
Two feet (stamp them)	One tummy (belly dance)
Ten toes (tiptoe)	

Movement machines Our bodies are like spectacular movement machines. When we are completely still, controlling all our muscles, we are on ZERO. While we are holding at ZERO, our minds are thinking about all the parts of our body that we can move. At the signal for ONE, everyone moves one part—no matter which one. The signal for TWO starts two parts moving—any two parts. Go on to five or six parts. Then "turn on" all the parts—move everything that can move. By then the "machines" will be ready for OFF or STOP. After the children are tired by an activity such as this one, take a few minutes to demonstrate the amazing versatility of our bodies. Some children, for example, will be lying on their stomachs, others on their sides or on their backs, and still others will be sitting.

Changing body shapes "Everyone keep your shape. As the tambourine shakes, find a *new shape* and hold it. Change again. Keep changing shapes and holding the new one for a few seconds." This activity is so successful and enjoyable that children often ask for it.

Dancing parts This activity begins with the following announcement: "Ladies and Gentlemen. For the first time in (your town and state), we are pleased to present a dance of the shoulders!" Play rhythmical music and experiment with shoulder dances. Follow this activity with dances featuring noses, fingers, heads, knees, and other parts.

"Which of our parts never gets its own turn?" "Elbows," six-year-old Dominique responded immediately. "Elbows never get a chance to dance!" The

children sympathized with the plight of the elbows and created an elbow dance to an old disco beat. Use music that you like, music that makes you want to move.

Hand dances to stories and poems There are dances thousands of years old that feature hand movements to tell stories. In keeping with that ancient tradition, children enjoy hand dances that they find in books or that they create themselves. Here is an example of an original story and accompanied by beautiful hand movements that the children agreed on.

> Once it was snowing. Everything was cold.
> Everything was asleep.
> Then the sun came out and warmed the ground.
> It started to rain.
> Seeds under the ground started to grow.
> Little caterpillars crawled around.
> They curled up and turned into butterflies.
> The sun got hotter.
> The seeds grew to flowers.
> Butterflies flew around.
> It was spring.

Each idea was expressed by different hand movements. The children loved the crawling caterpillars and flying butterflies so much that they insisted on doing that part over. John Denver's "Sunshine" provided the background as the story was read aloud. After two readings the children were able to recite the story; the movements helped them to remember the sequence. In so many cases, more reluctant children participate freely if movement is confined to a specific body part, such as hands. It seems safer to them. Always be ready to expand the movement.

Movement signals Nonverbal communication is very effective. "Wouldn't it be fun to make up some body movement signals for our class?" was the challenge to a group of first graders. With cooperation and enthusiasm, they created special body shapes and movements to convey the following messages: "Everyone please sit down"; "Attention, please"; "Time to clean up"; and "Time for a snack." The children responded to the signals immediately. They were part of the communication system for the year. Children love to learn sign language! Start a simple vocabulary. **"Turn yourself into . . ."** Here are a few examples guaranteed to succeed as long as they are shared with enjoyment, encouragement, acceptance, and enthusiasm.

> Animals (Combine with riddles and guessing games—"Which animal am I?")
> TV characters
> Weather (Challenge children with more abstract ideas such as interpreting wind, rain, thunder, snow, lightning, and sunshine with their bodies.)
> Something in the room (Give children the opportunity to use available shapes and designs as their inspiration.)
> Seasonal characters (snowman, snow shoveler, swimmer, ice skater)
> Letters of the alphabet
> Means of transportation
> Community helpers
> Story friends
> Athletes
> Fairy tale characters
> Nature ideas (mountain, rainbow, waterfall)

How many ways? Marlene Robbins challenges her students to demonstrate how many ways they can balance on one foot, twist, stretch, bend, wiggle, etc.[5] When the children are ready to move around the room (they are *always* ready!), she challenges them with such delightful offerings as, "How many ways can you walk? Run? Skip? Slide? Leap?"

Not only do the children develop strength and coordination, but they also begin to appreciate the incredible variations possible in human movement patterns. **Bodies around the clock, around the room, around the school, around the world** Consider *morning* exercises: Wake up! Stretch! Bend! Brush!

Consider *around the room* exercises: When you get to the back wall, do five hops. When you look out the window, do seven jumping jacks. . . .

Consider *around the school* exercises: Playground dance. Swing. Climb. Jump rope. Hopscotch. Choreograph these to any rhythmic music.

Consider movement from *around the world*. Use the music of the world. All children hop, skip, kick, twirl, slide, clap, jump, and bounce. Invite your students to "move to the music." You'll be amazed at how closely they come to the movement of ethnic and cultural dances! So often we drain the life out of "folk dances" by overemphasizing the *right* steps, the *right* position, that the children tense up. Teach in the key of life—be open to original interpretations to music and ideas. Incorporate them into group creations. Most important—have fun! **Bodies work together** If one human body is an amazing machine, imagine the possibilities when bodies work together. The challenge is: "Boys and girls, what can you make with all of your bodies working together?" Often, the teachers hide their eyes while the children meet the challenge. Joining bodies, children have created:

> A train (The children formed a line, one behind the other, and held onto each other's shoulders as they choo-chooed around the room.)
> A snake (The children sprawled on their stomachs, legs in a V shape, each child close to the one ahead and filling the space in the wide V. They all moved at once! Help!)

A rug (Bodies were spread out on the floor, arms and legs stretched, fingers and feet touching. "It's a rug with designs," the children explained.)

A fence (The children stood in a circle, arms joined at the elbows. Then one of the boys said, "Let's make a barbed-wire fence. A keepout fence!" It was astonishing to watch the children figure out how to convey this kind of fence with their jagged, pointy fingers, gnarled knuckles, and sharp elbows.)

A garden (Everyone in the group started as a seed and slowly grew into a special flower or tree.)

A fire (The children sat in a circle, put their feet into the center, and moved all their feet at once. It gave the feeling and look of a kindling fire. Finally, they leaned all the way back while their legs kicked higher and higher, like the flames of a bonfire.)

A house (The children arranged themselves in a square with their arms stretched at a pointed angle above them for the roof. Two children were the door and swung open and closed.)

A pizza (The children formed a circle, lying on the floor. Some were hunched and round like tomatoes; others were flat like cheese; still others were long and straight like sausage. "Put us in the oven," they instructed. The teachers pretended to push them into the oven. They made hissing sounds as they melted, oozed, and bubbled.)

Be more sense-full Children are natural mimes and mimics. They will *show* you faster than they will *tell* you. Using the magic words "show me," combined with sensory awareness, play such simple but enjoyable games as "Show me your expression tasting something delicious!" (After the improvisation, ask the children to tell you what the delicious food they were tasting was, or turn it into a guessing game.) "Show me how you look smelling a beautiful flower." "Show me a loud noise." After the movement interpretation, children can draw it, write it, or sing it. Or just go on to another challenge!

Stories, poems and songs are moving and playful experiences It's hard to imagine a children's story, poem or song that *doesn't* lend itself (even one line, refrain, or paragraph) to playful movement possibilities. From "Hokey Pokey" to poems like A. A. Milne's "Hoppity" to the chant from the Little Gingerbread Boy, "Run run run as fast as you can . . ." to Wee Willie Winkie "running" through the town—children can show you the action of the text. Be open to all their ideas. If you teach in the key of life, children will feel safe to offer their suggestions and interpretations. If you teach in the key of death, you'll permit only an official interpretation taught with rigidity and tension ("No, John, that's not how Hickory Dickory Dock ran up the clock.") Hang loose! When you hang loose, you invite your children to "shake out" stiff muscles, "take a wiggly break," "run to a story," "march to the rest room" and stretch their bodies and imaginations. Remember, children are movers and shakers.

CLASSROOM VISITORS AND FIELD TRIPS

Classroom Visitors

The families of your students and your own colleagues in school provide a treasure chest of excellent resources. As suggested in the Letters of Introduction, begin your school year with a letter inviting families to share their interests, hobbies, skills, and jobs with your children. Welcome their gifts as valued enriching experiences. You will be surprised and delighted at the willingness of family members to give of themselves. This is your most valuable resource. Keep strengthening the school/ family/community connections by inviting family and community members to contribute to the enrichment of your children's lives. Welcome all visitors to your class with a special song, symbol, poem, or gesture, maybe a lei of hands. One of my favorite mottos, an Arabic saying, reminds us that "every neighbor is a teacher." Look to your neighborhood!

Person who knows sign language This visitor will demonstrate and explain sign language and will teach the children basic words and expressions.

School custodian An important worker at the school is pleased to describe how he or she uses tools and hands to fix things and eyes to see what needs to be fixed.

Musician If you are unable to find a professional musician to invite, a parent, junior or senior high school student, or senior citizen is an excellent choice. Ask your guest to demonstrate and teach practice exercises.

Typist A school secretary, parent, or friend, armed with typewriter or word processor and willing to demonstrate the speed and facility of trained fingers at their best, is an effective visitor.

Seamstress or tailor This guest adds elements of delight when he or she demonstrates nimble art on dolls' clothes.

Senior citizen with magical hands A grandparent or other senior citizen is often expert in needle crafts such as knitting, crocheting, embroidering, creweling, or weaving. Invite such a person to be an "artist in residence" for a day and share his or her skills with your students.

Traffic cop A police officer who directs traffic with hand signals will entertain the children by demonstrating some of the signals.

Workers The kinds of workers you will be able to invite to visit your classroom will depend largely on where you live. Miners, lumberjacks, construction workers, steel workers, fishermen and fisherwomen, and stone cutters, all demonstrate their special skills. Do they lift? Dig? Chop? Climb?

Mime A mime is an outstanding classroom visitor. Children are fascinated by the makeup, humor, and body control. A mime demonstrates, probably more dramatically and effectively than any others, the incredible variety of body works.

Yoga teacher In many early childhood classes around the country, children are being introduced to yoga by teachers or by visitors. The children are challenged by yoga, the interesting names of the different positions, the philosophy of a harmony of mind and body that most yoga teachers communicate.

Magician Children who have trouble paying attention are cured instantly by a visit from a magician who dazzles the eyes with sleight-of-hand tricks.

Athlete No matter the sport, an athlete must stay in tip-top physical shape. Children have good questions about how an athlete takes care of the body, what exercises to do, what foods to eat.

Potter, sculptor, artist, craftsperson When human hands touch clay, stone, metal, or canvas, surprising shapes and designs appear. Be sure to encourage the artist to allow time for the children's participation.

Doctor, nurse A doctor and nurse make wonderful visitors, especially if they carry their little black bags filled with instruments and demonstrate on the children.

Dancer Whether a dancer performs jazz, ballet, folk, modern, or tap, discipline and practice are required. Ask your guest to demonstrate some of the warm-up techniques and to teach a few to your students.

Check your community resources and discover folk dancers from different backgrounds. Your children will enjoy learning how differently Scottish dancers move and look when compared to Turkish or Armenian dancers. Be sure your visitors teach you and your students some dances.

Make the most of the visits by following them with talks, art activities, games, songs and, of course, individual thank-you letters and pictures.

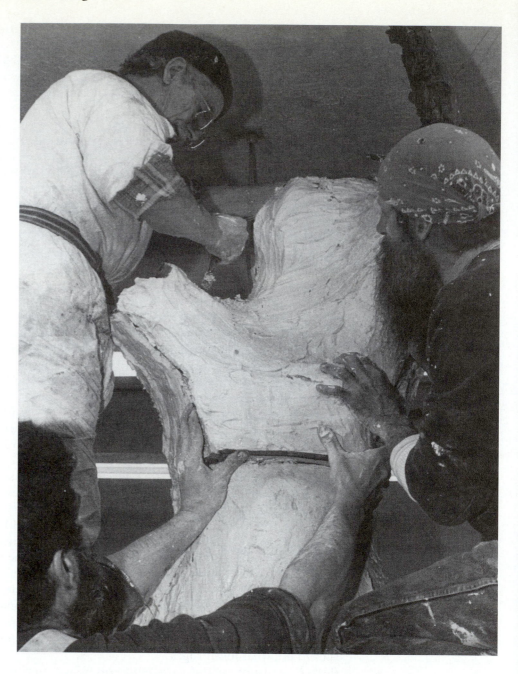

Field Trips

Gym Visit a high school, university, or community center. See and try the different pieces of body-building equipment. Watch teams or individuals practicing.

Dance school Ballet, modern dance, ethnic, jazz, tap—all are interesting and valuable experiences for the children as they see how people shape their bodies with determination and discipline.

Rehearsal of a marching band Find one at a high school or college. Enjoy the delightful patterns and shapes unfolding before you with rhythm and sound. Watch cheerleaders, twirlers, and drum majors.

Athletic field Watch a team practice or play. Football players move differently and do different things with their bodies than, for example, basketball players. Watch the fantastic feet of soccer players and the strong arms, hands, and legs of baseball players.

Ice-skating or roller-skating rink Add the magnificent balance and grace of the skaters to your growing list of body works.

Band or orchestra in concert or rehearsal Observe how disciplined and strong are the hands and fingers of musicians. Note how powerful and controlled breathing produces beautiful music.

Barber shop, beauty parlor, or animal grooming shop Focus on skilled hands curling, combing, brushing, setting, and cutting.

Secretarial office Speed and accuracy are the goals for skilled office workers. Fingers seem to fly on the keys.

Fast-food restaurant Workers' bodies are never still. Children watch as workers cook, wrap, count change, pour coffee, and write orders.

As you and your students enjoy field trips, correlate body awareness and movement patterns. Almost everything we do involves coordination, balance, skill, control, and practice.

Remember, survey your community, your children's families, and your own friends and neighbors for resources. When children visit carpenters, gardeners, computer programmers, artisans, construction workers, physical therapists, and auto mechanics, for example, their appreciation of the diversity of our fantastic bodies is enhanced. Field trips also inspire activities in music, story writing, drama, movement, art, and talk time.

Remember to send thank-you letters with original text and pictures.

IT ALL COMES TOGETHER

Any single idea on these pages can become the hub of a wheel of multidimensional activities and experiences. As you read through the suggestions, know that none of them happen in isolation. They are *part of,* not *apart from,* many other ideas, as connections happen all the time, naturally, easily, and with excitement. In these "It All Comes Together" sections, I am merely highlighting such integration. I hope as you read through the thirteen themes, you will constantly find ways in which "it all comes together." That's the magic!

Aliki's marvelous book, *My Five Senses*[6], inspired Marilyn Cohen and her kindergartners to launch an expanding, joyful web of interwoven learning strands.[7]

Each of the five senses was celebrated in numerous ways. Working as a class, in small groups, and as individuals, the children drew, discussed, painted, wrote, experimented, sang, demonstrated, and dramatized their findings. Every sense triggered its own interpretations. For example, here are a few of the components of the children's *sound* activities: They heard with their ears; drew pictures and cut out pictures of ears; chose images of "sound makers"; talked about and illustrated the sound makers (animals, machines, natural objects, instruments). They drew their own sound pictures, dictating and using their own inventive spelling to caption the pictures such as "tick-tock," or "clink" or "growl." They made rhythm instruments, listened to them, recorded them, and moved and played to them. They experimented with vibrations, from tuning forks to vibrations on their skin. They created a tape of sounds and turned it into a riddle game, turned it into a movement figure behind a screen, turned it into poems. They created books featuring each of the senses by using such challenging ideas to write and illustrate as "two smells I like," "two smells I dislike," and "I like to look at _____."

From books to riddles, from scientific experiments (comparing and contrasting textured materials, foods, and smells) to art projects, from charts to graphs to songs to more books and stories about the senses, Marilyn's kindergartners immersed themselves in learning. You can be sure that they will use their senses in everything they do. They will always appreciate their fantastic bodies and their amazing senses.

NOTES ♥♥♥♥♥♥♥♥♥♥♥♥♥♥♥♥♥♥♥♥♥♥♥♥♥

1. Mimi Brodsky Chenfeld. "Hangin Out With The Muffin Man." *Teaching in the Key of Life.* Washington, DC: National Association for the Education of Young Children (NAEYC), 1993, pp. 54–56.
2. See Association for Handicapped Artists, 5150 Broadway, Depew, NY 14043–4085.
3. Eve Merriam, "Thumbprint." *It Doesn't Always Have to Rhyme.* New York: Atheneum, 1964, p. 63.
4. Arnold Adoff and Karen Barbour (illus.). *Flamboyan.* San Diego, CA: Harcourt Brace Jovanovich, 1988.
5. Marlene Robbins is the movement specialist on the Arts Impact Team at Indianola Alternative Elementary and Reeb Avenue Elementary Schools of Columbus Public Schools in Columbus, Ohio.
6. Aliki, *My Five Senses.* New York: Crowell, 1989.
7. Marilyn Cohen, winner of the Kohl Award for Excellence in Teaching, teaches kindergarten at Bet Shraga Hebrew Academy of the Capital District in Albany, New York.

BOOKS FROM MY KNAPSACK FOR CHILDREN ♥ ♥

The following books are among the best available to use with young children. Some information may be somewhat advanced, but you can use your creativity in adapting the material to your children.

Baer, Edith. *The Wonder of Hands.* Photographs by Tana Hoban. New York: Macmillan, 1992.

Baylor, Byrd. *Sometimes I Dance Mountains.* New York: Scribners, 1973.

Bennett, David. *What Am I Made Of?* Illustrated by Steven Trotter. New York: Macmillan, 1990.

Berry, Joy. *Teach Me About Listening.* Illustrated by Bartholomew. Chicago: Children's Press, 1988.

Brown, Laurie Krasney, and Marc Brown. *Dinosaurs Alive and Well.* Illustrated by Marc Brown. Boston: Little, Brown, 1990.

Butterworth, Nick, and Mick Inkpen. *Field Day.* New York: Delacorte, 1988.

Buxbaum, Susan, and Rita Gelman. *Body Noises.* Illustrated by Angie Lloyd. New York: Knopf, 1983.

Cole, Joanna. *The Magic Bus: Inside the Human Body.* Illustrated by Bruce Degen. New York: Scholastic, 1989.

Dermuth, Patricia. *Inside Your Busy Body.* Illustrated by Paige Bitton Frye. New York: Grossett and Dunlap, 1993.

Evans, David, and Claudette Williams. *Me and My Body.* New York: Dorling Kindersley, 1992.

Grant, Sandy. *Hey, Look at Me!* Photographs by Larry Mulverhill. Scarsdale, NY: Bradbury, 1973.

Hall, Katy. *Skeletons! Skeletons! All About Bones.* Illustrated by Paige Bitten Frye. New York: Putnam/Grosset, 1991.

Hughes, Shirley. *Alfie's Feet.* Illustrated by Shirley Hughes. New York: Greenwillow, 1982.

Kent, Jack. *Hop, Skip and Jump Book.* New York: Random House, 1974.

Krementz, Jill. *A Very Young Dancer.* New York: Knopf, 1976.

———. *A Very Young Gymnast.* New York: Knopf, 1980.

Markle, Sandra. *Outside and Inside You.* New York: Bradbury, 1991.

Martin, Bill, Jr. *Here Are My Hands*. Illustrated by Ted Rand. New York: Henry Holt, 1987.

————. *Polar Bear, Polar Bear, What Do You Hear?* Illustrated by Eric Carle. New York: Henry Holt, 1991.

———— and John Archambault. *Listen to the Rain*. Illustrated by James Endicott. New York: Henry Holt, 1988.

Miller, Jonathan. *The Human Body*. Designed by David Pelham. New York: Viking, 1983.

Moncure, Jane Belk. *A Tasting Party*. Illustrated by Lois Axeman. Chicago: Children's Book Press, 1982.

————. *Sounds All Around You*. Illustrated by Lois Axeman. Chicago: Children's Book Press, 1982.

————. *The Look Book*. Illustrated by Lois Axeman. Chicago: Children's Book Press, 1982.

————. *The Touch Book*. Illustrated by Lois Axeman. Chicago: Children's Book Press, 1982.

————. *What Your Nose Knows*. Illustrated by Lois Axeman. Chicago: Children's Book Press, 1982.

Parker, Steve. *Skeleton—An Eyewitness Book*. New York: Knopf, 1988.

Rayston, Angela. *What's Inside My Body*. Illustrated by Richard Manning. New York: Dorling Kindersley, 1992.

Rocklin, Joanne. *Musical Chairs and Dancing Bears*. Illustrated by Laure de Matharel. New York: Henry Holt, 1993.

Shower, Paul. *How You Talk (revised edition)*. Illustrated by Megan Lloyd. New York: HarperCollins, 1992.

————. *What Happens to a Hamburg?* Illustrated by Anne Rockwell. New York: HarperCollins, 1985.

————. *The Listening Walk (revised edition)*. Illustrated by Aliki. New York: HarperCollins, 1991.

————. *How Many Teeth?* Illustrated by True Kelley. New York: HarperCollins, 1991.

Suhr, Mandy. *When I Eat*. Illustrated by Mike Gordon. Minneapolis: Carolrhoda, 1992.

Wright, Rachel. *Why Do I Eat?* Illustrated by Stuart Trotter. New York: Macmillan, 1992.

BOOKS FROM MY KNAPSACK FOR TEACHERS ♥ ♥

Borlin, Ann Lief. *Teaching Your Wings to Fly—The Non-Specialist's Guide to Movement Activities for Young Children*. Photographs by Hella Hammid. Santa Monica: Goodyear, 1979.

Cooper, Kenneth, M.D. *Kids' Fitness*. New York: Bantam, 1991.

Parker, Steve. *The Body and How It Works*. New York: Dorling Kindersly, 1992.

————. *The Body Atlas—A Pictoral Guide to the Human Body*. Illustrated by Guilanno Fornari. New York: Dorling Kindersly, 1993.

Rockwell, Robert E., et al. *Everybody Has a Body: Science from Head to Toe*. Mount Ranier, MD: Gryphon House, 1992.

Rojany, Lois. *Exploring the Human Body*. Illustrated by Linda Hill Griffith. New York: Barron's Educational Series, 1992.

Stein, Sara. *The Human Body: An Owner's Manual*. New York: Workman, 1992.

Walls, Bryn. *The Visual Dictionary of the Human Body*. New York: Dorling Kindersly, 1991.

————. *The Visual Dictionary of the Human Body*. New York: Dorling Kindersly, 1993.

Chapter 2

Our Feelings

Four-year-old Oren was teasing his baby sister by standing in front of the TV screen and blocking the picture. Of course, she cried. Oren's father told him not to do that, but Oren continued. Finally, his father took him by the shoulders and gently pulled him away from the TV set. Oren burst into tears. His father, shocked at such an extreme reaction, reasoned with him. "C'mon, Oren, you know I didn't hurt you. I just pulled you away from the TV set so your sister could watch it." Oren's crying intensified. "Oren," his Dad repeated, "you know I didn't hurt you. I barely tapped you!" Oren wailed through his sobs, "You're talking about the body and I'm talking about feelings!"

Dimitri was obviously down in the dumps. His teacher asked him what was the matter.

No answer.

"Do you feel sick?"

No.

"Do you feel sleepy?"

No.

"Well, Dimitri, what do you feel?"

Dimitri thought for a moment then answered, "I feel my feelings."

THE BASICS

Over the many years of our friendship, I have encouraged Michael Joel Rosen, artist/writer/educator, to devote some of his writing to concerns of teachers. One day, as we were visiting, Michael took a phone call in another room, and I, as always, skimmed through his manuscript in progress, which was spread out on the desk. Finally, he had taken my advice! I was thrilled to see pages of suggestions for educators. The section I read included such notes as:

- Be consistent. Help instill comprehension.
- Teach complicated lessons in stages so you build on success.
- If you notice more mistakes than usual, or the signs they are getting tired or bored, *stop*. Allow for a more playful period.
- Offer your biggest praises for their efforts.
- Remember, an excess of correction is discouraging.
- Always use their names. You are building trust and focusing positive attention.
- Offer praise immediately, warmly, sincerely, enthusiastically.

Michael returned. I was about to tell him that I planned to share his notes with teachers at a conference the following day when I noticed his last sentence: "If the session has been particularly successful, you might offer the occasional food treat: I've yet to meet a student who could resist a liver snap."

Huh? A liver snap? What's going on with this manuscript?

Dear reader, Michael's work in progress was the rough copy of *Kids' Best Dog Book*.[1]

Question: If consistency, praise, success, trust, reassurance, respect, understanding, and encouragement are good enough qualities for educating *dogs*, what are the implications for educating our *children*?

Let's talk about feelings and their importance in affecting every aspect of our lives, our behavior, of what and how we learn. Given our recognition of the prominent place emotions have in shaping and shading our life stories, isn't it distressing to know that many adults who should know better still believe that *real* emotions don't develop until sometime before puberty, perhaps in early adolescence, and so often dismiss and diminish the honest feelings of young children?

Infants as young as our seven-week-old Callie Rose exhibit clearly expressed feelings of comfort, distress, fright, well-being, and curiosity. Toddlers as young as our seventeen-month-old Len, the Muffin Man, demonstrate a wide range of deeply felt feelings such as disappointment, frustration, jealousy, grief, anger, joy, fear, possessiveness, and pride.

Although too many young children are learning at very early ages to begin to repress their feelings, most are still open in verbal and nonverbal expression. Pouty lips, quivering chins, and trusty blankets to stroke for comfort are some of the characteristics of hurt or sad feelings. In most instances, the body language of young children is still easy to understand. Do you need a postdoctorate degree to perceive a child sitting slumped in a corner of the room, eyes downcast, hands idle, tuned out of activity? You don't need advanced courses in communication to conclude that Jackie is happy today when she bounces into the room, flashes you a brilliant smile, hugs her playmates, and kisses the puppets! Of course, young children don't always express themselves so clearly. We who spend our time with young children must always be alert, sensitive, and responsive to all of our students, become familiar with their behavioral patterns, and understand their specific situations and relationships. The older the children, the more subtle their demonstrations of feelings. It's easier to fool adults who are not truly present and accounted for!

Anyone who works with young children knows how real and valid are their feelings. Anyone who knows young children appreciates the importance of teachers in the lives of those children.

From her thirty years of teaching in inner-city schools, Dawn Heyman speaks eloquently of the place of feelings in education. She generously shares some of her wisdom:

"You have to be aware of children's gut level feelings. Their feelings can either help them to learn or stand in the way. You can either be a hand reaching out to help them move forward or a hand holding them back. . . . Watch kids' faces. Watch yourself. Sometimes a smart alecky laugh hides a frightened child. Sometimes a show-off braggart covers an insecure, scared child. . . .

Children need to know we teachers have feelings, we're not always perfect. We're human beings. When I goof, I always apologize immediately. I say, "That wasn't very grown up of me" or "I'm sorry. That was thoughtless." I always try to be as honest as I can. When something wonderful happens, acknowledge it immediately. Oh, I have laughed and cried with the kids!

I try to understand them. Listen. Ask questions. So many of my students are angry children, lonely, alone. I try to talk to them. I say things like, "Nobody can tell you you can't be angry because you feel angry now. And you have a right to feel angry. Sometimes I feel angry, too. But, what do we do with that feeling? How do we handle it?" We talk about possible ways to work out our feelings. When I'm angry, I might tell the children, "I have to count to ten or I might lose my temper." Sometimes we count together. Then we might laugh. Humor is the most important saving gift. In tense situations, we can help the children learn the healing quality of humor. And, forgiveness. . . . I remember four girls who were furiously mad at each other. After we talked over the situation, I said, "Girls, I think we need a hug." So we held a group hug. A few days later, I had a serious incident that upset me. One of those four girls came to my desk and said, 'Miss Heyman, I think you need a hug!' "[2]

Dawn, an example of a gentle, consistent, understanding, very human teacher, was approached by one of her smallest, slowest students, who stuttered, "Mmm-misss Heyman, I-I-I have a r-r-riddle f-f-for you." "Oh, what is it?" "What-wha-what has two legs and l-l-l-loves you?" "I give up." "M-m-m-m-meeeee!"[3]

In this anxiety-ridden, often violent, and frightening world, teachers like Dawn create havens for children. As teachers, we have great, even awesome powers. We have the power of life and death over our students: life and death of the spirit, of curiosity, of imagination, of self-image and self-confidence, of courage and self-esteem. In the lives of young children, teachers are VIP (Very Important People). Great teachers have *ears* in the center of their *hearts!*

Recently, I found a kindergarten boy weeping inconsolably in the school office while the secretary dialed his mother to take him home. "Oh no, not the flu," I sympathized. "He doesn't have the flu," the secretary explained. "His teacher is absent today, and he's just sick over it." And he was—devastated.

Before we get carried away with our powers, which are formidable, let us acknowledge some other realities. Children have experiences outside of the classroom that are not in our immediate range of influence. Often they live in complicated family relationships and stressful homes. They come to us with emotional histories, carrying knapsacks of experiences and memories that have shaped their worldview, their images of themselves. Do they feel valued? Do they sulk? Do they pull hair? Withdraw? Do they hug? Share? Play happily? Is theirs a friendly or hostile world?

The focus on school/home communication is such an important development in American education. As parents and teachers open doors of communication, reaching toward each other with understanding and concern, helping and advocating, cooperating and brainstorming, the children's education and lives can only be enriched. Many times a child's home situation improves because of the greater understanding made possible by the mutual concern and communication between teacher and family. That new close relationship is a factor in the improvement of a child's learning abilities.

As you will be continually reminded, all the themes in this book are threads weaving through the daily fabric of our time with young children. None of these strands is more important than feelings. Even if you plan a special emphasis on feelings as a *theme* for a designated time period, know that feelings cannot be relegated to any specific curriculum schedule, because life doesn't permit airtight structures in the flowing, dynamic, challenging process of learning. Recognizing the importance of spontaneity, serendipity, and immediacy, Janet Stocker explained her approach: "We don't set aside special time to focus on feelings, because we deal with feelings every day. We are always ready with art, music, one-to-one talk, group discussion, stories, and games to respond to specific feelings as manifested by the group or by individual children. *Our teachers are always ready!*"[4]

Teachers like Jean Buker,[5] believe that they must not only provide support for children as they experience feelings, many of them *new* feelings, but also give children opportunities to express those feelings in healthy ways. She always has a table of pounding pegs, Playdough, and finger paints for children who need to pound, push, squeeze, and splash in order to work the anger out of their systems. She has a punching bag in the corner for children who need to actively express hostility. Jean introduced the children to these outlets by showing them that she herself felt better when she pounded a few pegs to vent her annoyance at an irritating situation. She "acted it out" by sharing her annoyance with her students, *sharing her feelings,* and then telling them that she was just going to pound some pegs very hard for a few minutes until she felt better. The children were fascinated. After she pounded in the pegs, she rolled some Playdough and slapped it against the table. "Now I feel better. Any time *you* need to pound some pegs or swish some Playdough to get rid of an angry feeling, come right over here." The children learned a few acceptable and satisfying ways to express their feelings.

Jean Buker's "pounding table" is an example of the ways teachers have designed environments that recognize the importance of feelings in the daily life of young children. Although most school budgets are limited, teachers design their space with originality and imagination. They are scroungers, scavengers, and thieves! They are geniuses!

Traveling around the country, I have seen wonderfully innovative rooms where young children live and learn and grow, rooms with room to express moods and feelings so children feel safe and accepted no matter what their mood may be. I have seen:

Cuddly corners These feature soft pillows and blankets and huggable teddy bears, for children who need an extra snuggle to make the day.

Alone house This is a large cardboard shipping box with a window cut out of it, for the one child sitting inside to be able to look out while retreating from the whirl of group activities.

Silly spot This is a box of wigs, mustaches, beards, and crazy hats, next to a mirror, where children can "mug" when they feel extra silly. A five-year-old girl explained the silly spot this way: "Sometimes you get up feeling like silly beans. Go right to our silly spot and put on a crazy face and make yourself laugh!"

Peaceful place In classrooms throughout the Penn-Harris-Madison School Corporation in Mishawaka, Indiana, the recommendation is: "Lamps, plants, and classical music." The glow of a lamp, the green beauty of plants and the soothing power of classical music help define peaceful places for children to enjoy. Variations abound around the country. Often, a bulletin board borders the peaceful place. On the board are photos and pictures of beautiful scenes and images. Children add to the display. On tables are sketchbooks and notebooks in which children draw lovely designs for others to see, and write poems or peaceful words. The music doesn't have to be classical. Melodies and songs from every culture reflect lyrical beauty, whether flute music from Native American tribes or soft strumming guitars from Spain. A student served as guide to his classroom. He explained, "Whenever you want to get beautiful inside, you can sit at our peaceful-place table and it always works."

Listening chair and talking chair Two chairs facing each other in a space apart from the main area of the room. One is labeled "listener"; the other, "talker." Whenever these first graders had an argument or disagreement, they sat in the special chairs and took turns talking and listening to each other until the dispute was settled. Some children nicknamed the chairs "argument chairs"; others called them "make up chairs."

Jane Johnson's Bears' Den Jane converted her space to a cozy Bears' Den, with bears abounding in pictures, dolls, and stories. The children wrote "Some Things I Like About the Bears' Den." Here are a few excerpts from their journals:

- "Sometimes we need Friday hugs on other days."
- "I love the Bears' Den. I like to read in the Bears' Den. I like to write, too. I like doing the calendar. It is fun to do things in the Bears' Den."
- "I like the magic. I like the fun."
- "We are smart in the Bears' Den."[6]

How will you design your environment so that it reflects your recognition of the importance of feelings?

I'm the Cowardly lion,
I'm scared at my own roar,
I'm Cowardly,
I don't want to be cowardly.

Suzanne Fraley

A word of warning While many of the activities you plan and the experiences you share with children will be addressed to specific feelings and will be successful in encouraging healthy expression and confidence in handling emotional situations, some children have serious problems that will not be easily soothed by a "comfort station" and will not be responsive to your efforts. Tragically, there are children like five-year-old Matty, who will not participate in school activities, not even snack time. She has never smiled or talked to anyone in class. Her teachers feel frustrated and often helpless in trying to break through the gloom that fills Matty. They have talked with her parents and a counselor, but to no avail. Yet they are stubborn and will not give up on Matty.

You are not a psychiatrist, a child psychologist, or a pediatrician. In many cases, a child has been treated by such persons for severe emotional problems but has finally responded to the continuous warmth and persistence of a classroom teacher who, after shooting hundreds of arrows of love, found one to touch the heart.

Theodore Roethke wrote: "Teaching is one of the few professions that permits love."[7] With all the methods and resources available for educational purposes, it is often love that is the best resource of all, and nowhere more needed and appreciated than with young children. When Steve Anderson began working with young children at the Leo Yassenoff Jewish Center in Columbus, Ohio, he said, "I've learned a lot about so many things—the creative process, curiosity, how language develops, imagination, and socialization. But, I've learned the most about the power of love."[8]

Love is probably the most important word for teachers of young children. Examine your own feelings and strengthen your reasons for working in early education, your feelings about yourself and about children. I want to say to students who are preparing for this career: *"If you don't love kids, go into another field!"* The best teachers love children and freely express that love. They are not inhibited about touching, holding, and hugging. They not only say they love but also *show* their love in everything they do.

Another necessary quality for teachers who work effectively with young children is *awareness*. You are alert and responsive. You don't miss a thing! You not only know but also act. Because of your influence, you have to take stands. Before modern education coined the term "values clarification," teachers clarified values. Your very presence, your words, gestures, and responses define values.

Connie Swain[9] clearly communicated to her first graders that putdowns would never be permitted. No child would ever be allowed to humiliate or insult another child. When Derrick said cruel words to tease Betsy, the whole class froze and looked at Connie with expectant expressions. Connie responded immediately by taking Derrick out of the group for a private conference. The children quietly comforted Betsy until Connie and Derrick returned.

What can children learn from their time with you? No matter what their home environment or family history may be, in your classroom children can learn safety, trust, respect, encouragement, acceptance, fairness, joy, and love. With you, children learn that they are unique individuals with many talents and strengths, with interesting thoughts and important ideas.

Because you provide success-oriented experiences and are supportive and responsive, your students develop positive and healthy self-images, confidence, and the freedom and courage to *try* without worry, to *risk* without anxiety, to *explore* and *experiment* without fear of failure or humiliation. Through your guidance and encouragement, children learn to deal with their feelings in healthy ways. They are offered many outlets for emotional expression and the safety to communicate. Because you are considerate of their feelings, sensitive to their moods, and aware of and responsive to their special needs, you will help them to become stronger individuals at peace with themselves and with others.

Anyone for a liver snap?

DISCOVERY TIMES/WONDER TIMES

- Isn't it amazing that no matter people's physical challenges, ages, languages, religions, cultures, countries, racial groups, customs, or regions, everyone has feelings? (Do animals have feelings?)
- Some feelings are positive and feel good, like happiness, friendliness, and love.
- Some feelings are negative and feel bad, like anger, jealousy, and fear.
- It is normal for people to have all kinds of feelings.
- It is important to be able to talk about our feelings with our families, friends, classmates, and teachers.
- We can express our feelings in many different ways.
- Our feelings are important, as are the feelings of others.
- Sometimes the way we express bad feelings hurts ourselves and others.
- We can learn healthy ways of expressing bad feelings.
- Everyone reacts differently to a situation. Each of us is unique.
- Even though we are different individuals, we share many feelings and can learn from each other.

SUGGESTED VOCABULARY

happy	eager	nice	kick
sad	impatient	stubborn	hit
glad	mischievous	ashamed	smile
mad	curious	divorced	hug
silly	brave	dead	died
serious	excited	sick	"feel good"
disappointed	nervous	hurt	"feel bad"
angry	calm	surprise	share
afraid	lonely	cry	give
shy	cuddly	laugh	love
scared	friendly	giggle	hate
jealous	unfriendly	tickle	comfort
proud	affectionate	break	forgive
pleased	mean	worried	care
listen	help		

You may be surprised at some of the words on the vocabulary list. Most children know many more words than we think they do. They are ardent TV viewers; they are part of many adult situations that children of earlier generations did not experience; they go to movies, fast-food restaurants, bowling alleys, and miniature golf courses; and they are readers of highway billboards, cereal boxes, magazine ads, and TV program schedules.

The astonished grandparents of a four-year-old boy related this incident to illustrate the rich vocabulary of young children. They were driving along, adults in the front of the car, the child in back, when an argument started over directions for their destination. Grandpa, the driver, grew exasperated with his wife's advice and became a little testy. From the back of the car, a child's voice asked, "Grandpa, why are you overreacting?"

Sometimes you can help your students change the way they feel by giving them a better word to describe their feelings. One of my young friends was worried about school. "I'm so depressed!" she moaned, "I'm so depressed!" I pointed out that "depressed" is a serious word describing a clinical mental state: "How about saying that you feel 'down in the dumps,' 'blue,' or 'yuk' instead of depressed?" When she came to school the next day, she cheerfully announced: "I think I feel better. Feeling down in the dumps is a lot better than feeling depressed!"

SOME STARTERS

Start with the word "sometimes" "Sometimes" is an excellent word and concept for young children. It helps them discover that feelings change, that when they are having a bad time, it usually passes. "Sometimes" is a very reassuring word. "Sometimes I get so mad at my dog for chewing my good shoes!" was the way one teacher introduced the feeling "mad." That was all she needed to say to encourage her students to join in with their own "Sometimes . . . ," which she wrote down for them and displayed on the bulletin board.

Start with an immediate situation (serendipity) The children planned a field trip to a pumpkin farm. On the day of the trip, it rained. Their teacher was the first to articulate disappointment. "I'm so sad that we're not going to the pumpkin farm today." This honest sharing opened the door for the children to express their own feelings of disappointment. After they planned the trip for another day, they decided to do something "very cheerful" to take their minds off the pumpkin farm. They made happy faces out of pumpkin-orange paper.

Every day you will have opportunities to respond to group or individual situations that can (if you wish) lead to a focus on feelings. Whether serendipity presents itself by Alan losing his new mittens or Keisha telling the class that her grandma had to go to the hospital, if you are alert and responsive, you will have many beginning ideas.

A gem of advice comes from the Talmud urging, "Before you begin a lesson, start with a story." Teachers like Debbie Charna have shelves, bags, and drawers that overflow with wonderfully effective stories for every reason, season, and occasion.[10]

Three of Debbie's favorite books that never fail to inspire lively shared experiences spinning off into myriad related activities are Judith Viorst's *Alexander and the Terrible, Horrible, No Good, Very Bad Day*, Bernard Waber's *Ira Sleeps Over*, and Sandra Boynton's *A Is for Angry*. Alexander's "bad day" helps children describe, recognize, and, through humor, accept and change their own "bad days." Sometimes Debbie and her students go the whole journey and end up talking, writing, and illustrating stories that describe their Most Wonderful Days! Ira gives the children permission to talk about times they were scared, afraid of ridicule, self-conscious, or reluctant to risk new experiences. Through the alphabet with feelings like B is for Bashful or K is for Kind, children learn that human beings experience a wide range of emotions. They are not alone in their feelings.

Collect your favorite books and poems. You will find that they are excellent starters as well as constant companions through the subsequent adventures in the celebration of feelings.

Start with a feeling word Share your feelings about the word first. "I feel so *happy* today because the sun is shining and we can go outside to play. How do *you* feel today?" This easily opens the way to an interesting, lively discussion of "What makes *you* happy?"

Start with a picture or photo From your own file, choose pictures or photos showing: a close-up of a person's face expressing a specific feeling; a scene that conveys a clearly defined mood (a nature scene, a traffic jam, a playground of children); or dramatic action (two children playing together, a grownup scolding a child, a broken toy and a tearful child, animal pictures). These types of pictures are excellent ways to stimulate discussion and focus on feelings. Children are very imaginative and empathetic and are brilliant interpreters. Such questions as: "What is happening in the picture?" "Why do you think the grownup is scolding the child?" "How do you think the child feels?" and "Let's tell a story about the picture. How shall we start?" encourage children to express their ideas and feelings. *It is often easier for them to talk about other people and someone else's toys and to interpret those feelings than it is to talk about their own.* Remember, every response a child gives is valid, to be accepted and respected.

Start with something weird Wendy Wohlstein and Rhoda Linder[11] began a discussion of "happy" and "sad" with their four-year-olds in an original and a dramatic way. Wendy made up her face as a happy face—turned-up lips; big, bouncy eyes; freckles; and apple-red cheeks. She wore lively overalls and a bright shirt. In contrast, Rhoda painted her lips downward; tears on cheeks; drab clothes. Wendy bounced; Rhoda slumped. Wendy wrote a poem that she read to the children first thing in the morning:

> I am so happy,
> I feel so good,
> I only wish that my friend could!
> She is sad. See that tear?
> She hates to look in the mirror.
> But me—I love it—yes siree!

A happy face is fun to see.
I look around from here to there
to see the kind of face *you* wear.
(Wendy stopped and looked at every child's face.)
Is it sad with a voice like a whine?
Or is it happy, I hope, like mine?
Happy or sad, which are you I say?
Please try to have a happy day!

The rest of the day was filled with activities and discussion about sad feelings and happy feelings.

Start with a T-shirt   I don't know about you, but my closets and dresser drawers are packed with T-shirts highlighting important messages and images, from "Love" to "Happiness" to "Friendship" to "Cooperation" to "Concerns for peace and the environment." My shirts can launch a blaze of activities and experiences in any curriculum area!

Observe your children. Notice their hearts on their sleeves! Pick up important messages such as the downcast eyes of a new older sibling wearing a bright and cheery shirt proclaiming, "I'm the New Big Brother!" Many of children's spirits at that traumatic time *don't* reflect the cheeriness of their shirts. Often, the birth of a baby evokes deep feelings of confusion, loss, and resentment. These are important areas for the group's attention and connection.

Start with a song   Songs, among our oldest ways of communicating, are often excellent poems. They also tell stories, express feelings, and reach out to catch you with their words, meanings, and melodies. Children's original songs (just *listen* to young children as they sing along their way) reflect their ideas, actions, and feelings. Old knapsack songs (camp? Scouts? youth groups?) connect us with feelings about love, comfort, safety, sharing, silliness, and reassurance. Leave no source of songs untouched. I use songs from camp like "You Are My Sunshine," songs like "Whistle a Happy Tune" from the musical *The King and I,* and old pop songs like "The Greatest Love of All." Songs of hopefulness are sustaining to young children. They love the optimism of "Tomorrow" from *Annie* or the Beatles' "Here Comes the Sun." Be a gatherer. What are *your* songs?[12]

Start with a puppet or stuffed animal   Young children clap their hands to keep Tinker Bell alive because they believe in fairies, puppet friends, and stuffed-animal classmates. Keep at least one character in the classroom to communicate with the children (through you), one that has a name and feelings and ideas.

With one timid class of very young children who hung back from participation and articulation at the beginning of the school year, the teacher told them that a special new friend had come to visit with them but that the friend was very shy. This friend was hiding behind the tambourine and was afraid to meet them. "Isn't that silly, to be afraid to meet *you?*" the teacher asked. The children were very concerned. "We won't hurt you," one of the children comforted the still unseen friend. "What can we do to make our new friend feel happier?" the teacher asked. "We can wave," another child offered. The group timidly lifted their hands in tiny friendly waves. The teacher peeked behind the tambourine. "Come on," she coaxed, "The children are waving to you. Don't be such a silly willy." She looked at the children, then continued talking to the shy, hidden friend: "They don't have *mean* faces. They have very happy faces." The children's faces brightened into smiles. Some were still waving. "Sometimes we're shy, too, aren't we?" the teacher asked. "Oh, yes!" Immediate agreement. By the time the little five-and-dime store toy appeared—a cuddly yellow bird which the children named "Chickie"—they had forgotten their own shyness in their eagerness to reassure Chickie. Thereafter Chickie was a regular member of the class.

TALK TIMES/LISTENING TIMES

Children should and must talk about their feelings. They talk about them through pictures, puppets, pantomime, songs, games, stories, and play times. They talk about them in large groups, small groups, and one-to-one conversations. Talking is valuable in itself. It gives children the chance not only to say how they feel, but also to find others who share those feelings. Children are reassured that they are members of the human family and have common experiences. It helps them reach out to each other and develop sensitivity.

When children are eager to talk about something, they are telling you that it is a subject relevant and interesting to them. As a responsive and active listener, you can take the hint and expand their interest into other activities. "Talk Times" lead to art, music, games, stories, dance, plays, improvisations, field trips, and visitors.

In Margie Goldach[13] and Carol Highfield's class of prekindergartners, talking about different feelings spilled over into creative writing and art. The children learned a lot about taking turns being good listeners, and being fair. No one person monopolized the conversation. Each child told about "things that scare me," "things that make me angry," "things that make me sad," and "things that make me happy." Their teachers wrote everything they said on large construction paper in a different color for each feeling. The children chose the colors for the four sections. Here are excerpts from the charts revealing children's feelings to parents who were not always aware of them.

Things That Scare Me
Dreams about monsters that eat me (Jason)
Being locked in my room (Michelle)
My mom yelling at me (Elissa)
Godzilla picking up my bed (Nicky)
Being spanked on my tushy (Jennifer)

Things That Make Me Angry
Someone breaking my toys (Nathan)
My brother hitting me (Nicky)
My mom throwing out my barber shop toy (Jamie)
My sister treating me like a baby (Elissa)
My mommy ripping my favorite papers on the way home from
    school (Joy)
My mom and dad sending me to my room (Jason)

Things That Make Me Sad
My mother not taking me to the store (Monica)
My sister not letting me in her room (Elissa)
My brother not playing with me (Jennifer)
My father not taking me to his office (Jamie)
My brother taking away my toys (Bret)

Things That Make Me Happy
Being tickled (Doug)
Mom and Dad reading to me (Jodi)
Ice cream (Nicky)
Playing with my friends (Yve)
Pretending I'm a kitty (Elissa)

The Magic of Humor One way of dealing with deeply felt negative feelings like anger is through humor. Children are gifted at name calling and put-downs, so when there are conflicts and hurt and angry feelings, don't be surprised at the display of epithets expressed by even the youngest students. The late Eve Merriam's poem "Mean Song" is a delightful example of changing insults and name calling to nonsense sounds and creative images. Even the most flush-faced, angry combatants often change grimaces to grins with such clever warnings as:

"Snickles and podes,
ribble and grodes:
that's what I wish you.

A nox in the groot,
a root in the stoot
and a gock in the forbeshaw, too.

Keep out of sight
for fear that I might
glom you a gravely snave.

Don't show your face
around anyplace
or you'll get one flack snack
in the bave."
(from *The Singing Green*, Eve Merriam. New York: Morrow, 1992).

Talking together about silly terms to express anger, gathering ideas, and changing discussions into class poems, vocabulary lists, and songs are healthier, more enjoyable ways to deal with the negatives. Try it or else I'll tackle your tickle toe!

Magic Circle Many teachers use this approach to talk about important topics.[14] Sitting in a circle on chairs or on the floor, children and teachers discuss thoughts and feelings. If children feel safe in your room, they feel safest in the Magic Circle, where they are encouraged to express their feelings and ideas. Some teachers set aside special times during the week for a Magic Circle session; others use it when the situation warrants.

A list of ways to make people feel happier resulted from a Magic Circle session with a group of kindergartners. Some of the suggestions that were recorded and displayed in a prominent place in the room were:

> **Ways to Make People Feel Happier**
> Share your snack (Eddie)
> Sing a song together (Eric)
> Look out the window together (Roosevelt)
> Play with Theodore (the class teddy bear) (Julie)
> Pat them (Michelle)

In this case the children not only talked about their own feelings and tried to understand the feelings of others, but also directed their thoughts and energies into compassionate responses. When you see children react this way, you can believe, with Anne Frank, that "people are really good at heart."

Children have so much to say about their experiences and feelings. Even shy children are reassured and encouraged through listening. Give your students many opportunities to talk—to you, to each other, to playthings and puppets. "There, I said it" is the kind of relief many children seem to feel after such sessions. The responses of teacher and classmates are also helpful in sorting out feelings. Through "Talk Times/Listening Times" you are teaching children that expression is healthy, that sharing is better than hoarding, that communicating about feelings is better than developing a sense of isolation and loneliness.

VISUAL ARTS TIMES

There is no theme that lends itself to a greater variety of enjoyable art activities and experiences than feelings. Feelings flow into colors, shapes, textures, and designs. Here are a few suggestions to start you thinking of your own ideas.

Paper plate faces Paper plates are just waiting for children to turn them into faces. Children draw features or arrange already-cut-out eyes, eyebrows, lips, and noses. The letters C and U are excellent models for drawing eyebrows and lips; the children discover that C's and U's facing up look happy and facing down look sad.

Add wool, carpet pieces, shredded paper, or cotton puffs for hair. Add ears and hats. Experiment with different facial expressions. Share ideas and observations. Add dialogue! Display all the faces on a bulletin board.

Feelings pictures If you are talking about a particular feeling, suggest that your students draw or paint a picture conveying that feeling. Another way to encourage this valuable expression is to ask the children to "Draw a picture about the way you feel right now." (Although you may not like the way some children feel, do not be critical or judgmental.) "Tell me about your picture" or "What is in your picture?" or "Why did you use these colors?" is the kind of response that invites children to interpret their artwork.

ABCs of happiness Draw or cut out images from A to Z that make you and your students happy. Border the room with your happiness alphabet; bill a board; cover a wall.

Happiness board I know I am highlighting feelings of happiness, but I'm concerned about so many young children being so out of touch with any moments of happiness. These projects are offered in the spirit of inviting children to be aware of, remember, recognize, and appreciate the positive people, places, times, and events of their lives.

With your students, brainstorm images that evoke happiness to them. Write all their suggestions. Create a bright and colorful display of their words. Mix the words with the children's original illustrations. On a first-grade corridor bulletin board called the Happiness Board, I was particularly delighted by a bright yellow balloon with these words: "Balloons are always happy because they are like round pieces of the sky."

Flowers and raindrops A kindergarten class had a long and intense discussion about good and bad feelings. They suggested things that made them feel good, and many children agreed that flowers fell into that category. The topic of rain came up, and one of the children said that when raindrops fell on her face, they looked like tears. The children liked the idea of teardrops and raindrops and decided that raindrops could make them feel sad.

The children then designed beautiful flowers out of colored construction paper and tissue paper, with green wool for stems. They taped their flowers to a strip of green paper on the bulletin board. The children named things that made them feel good, which they and their teacher wrote down. They taped their thoughts all over the beautiful garden. It looked as if the flowers were talking! Then they cut out raindrops of different colors and taped them to the blue-gray paper on the board. They wrote and dictated their sad thoughts to their teacher, and in a little while the sky was filled with teary raindrops and sad feelings.

Encourage children to design their own flowers and raindrops. Wouldn't it be dull if all flowers and raindrops were the same shape and size? Avoid dittos!

What "bugs" you? Lynn Thompson[15] and her third graders talk about the things that "bug" them, that annoy and anger them. The children design their own bugs (with help from Lynn, if necessary), color them, and cut them out. They make the bugs large enough to include written comments about what "bugs" them.

Feelings mobiles Each child has a hanger on which to hang pictures, shapes, and objects expressing different feelings. Not only do they add life and vitality to your room, but they also make great conversation pieces!

Feelings books With pictures and drawings, children create books dedicated to all feelings or to a specific feeling. Suggest that they add words to their images. If you have extra time, help children decide on a cover for their book and cut out the cover design as well as the pages that will form the contents. For example, Laura's book of feelings was in the shape of a house because, as she explained, "My house is my happiest thing." Brandy's book was in the shape of a baseball bat because "I'm getting a bat when I'm six and I can't wait! Ten more days!" Stephanie's book was in the shape of a circle. Every page had a circle: hula hoops, the sun, diamond rings, eyeglasses, and pizza. She smiled and said, "I love circles! See—pierced ears!" A variation is to have the children create their own ABC book of feelings.

Class book Using a large greeting card catalogue from which the cards have been removed, begin a class project. Ask the children to cut out pictures that make them feel happy, to paste them in the book, and to write their names next to the pictures or drawings they contribute. These catalogues are large enough to allow for many illustrations from each child. The book remains on display in a prominent place so that children feel happy when they look at the pictures.

A variation of this idea is to put faces expressing different emotions on the top of each page in the book. The children then paste pictures appropriate to the page.

Happy and sad tags This is a variation of name tags. On one side of a construction paper circle, children draw a happy face; on the other side, a sad face. They may want to glue on eyes and mouth with upward curves or downward curves, rather than drawing them. Attach a string so children can wear the circles as tags, on either side, depending on how they feel.

Happy greeting cards "You feel good when you make someone else feel good!" was one of the ideas a kindergarten teacher wanted to convey to her students. They decided to make "happiness cards," put them in a grab bag, and let everyone pick one. The children enjoyed making the cards. They drew or colored designs that made them feel good and that would also cheer someone else.

A variation of this activity is to have the children pick the name of one of their classmates out of a grab bag (keep it a secret) and then make a card for that child. In addition to the happy design or picture, the card includes the recipient's name. The cards are collected by the teacher, who then calls on one child at a time to deliver the card to the child whose name is featured. Every child has a chance to deliver "good news." Every child receives a special card with his or her name on it. Add another delightful suggestion: "You can deliver the card any way you want to—hopping, skipping, doing any happy movement!"

Make happy cards for parents and other family members and for friends outside the class.

Happy, sad, and mad faces on stones, etc. Children love to create expressive little creatures by painting and drawing happy, mad, sad, etc., faces on stones, buckeyes, shells, pom-poms, felt scraps, walnuts, buttons, wood chips, and pinecones. Add little hats, hair, and ears. Children enjoy naming and playing with their own special character. Encourage different expressions.

Paint or draw a shape "What kind of a shape is happiness? Draw it." "What kind of a shape is anger? Paint it." These questions stimulate good talk and expressive art. One first grader responded immediately: "Squiggly." She squiggled on her paper. "Happiness is squiggly." Another child chimed in, "My happiness is square like my room at home." Add movement!

Shape feelings in clay Danielle Leventhal, a young Arts Education student, described her feelings about working in the arts, clay in particular, and connections to feelings. She writes:

> Creativity is an expression from within of ideas, emotions, interpretations brought into form through a brush, fingers molding clay, muscles shaping metal, lungs blowing glass. . . . Creative art is a celebration of life. . . . Creative expression is also a way to release personal emotions. When I form clay, wedge it, pull it, stretch it, scratch it, pound it, smooth it, and crave details, I vent my feelings, a human need. I throw joy into my work as well as confusion, anger, love, awe and sadness. The clay retains what I release and I become balanced. Bringing emotions into a material form is a path to self-realization. . . ."[16]

Children need many opportunities to pour their feelings into clay. Sandy, a kindergartner, worked very hard on his shape. When he finished, he surveyed it with great seriousness. Then, pleased with himself, he explained to his tablemates, "My clay is very sad because my daddy is in Chicago."

One of the best stories I know about clay and feelings concerned a prekindergarten child who was angrily pounding away. He mashed, punched, and beat his clay. When it was "complete," he looked at it for a while, sighed as if relieved, and asked his teacher, "Can I press it and make a new shape?" "Of course," she said, "But why do you want to change it?" His answer was simple, " 'Cause I'm finished being angry."

"What colors do you feel today?" Young children and their teachers around the country are experimenting with colors and feelings. Talk about the different colors and the feelings they evoke. Again, *all* answers are correct. This is a time for original reactions and freedom of expression. After children interpret different colors, ask them to draw, poster-paint, or finger-paint a picture using one color that expresses their feelings at the moment. Terrence colored a completely brown picture. When his teacher asked him to tell her about the picture, Terrence grinned and replied, "Today is muddy, and mud is fun."

Insensitivity can kill anything. A kindergarten teacher invited her students to choose a color that matched their feeling at the moment and draw a picture with that color. One five-year-old chose black and, with thick and heavy strokes, created a grim design. The teacher's face tightened with displeasure. "Stephen, I don't think that's a very nice color. Why don't you pick a more cheerful crayon and do another picture?" Stephen tore up his paper and put his head on the table.

MUSIC TIMES

Music to paint feelings to Music inspires art. Feelings inspire music. Find music that expresses specific moods and feelings (lullabies evoke calm; shepherds' flute songs have a lonely sound; Spanish bullfight music flashes the red cape of excitement). Give the children paper and crayons, paints, or finger paints, and instruct them to listen carefully to the music, picture it, and discover how it makes them feel. "Listen and let the music go into your brushes and paint its feelings," one teacher instructed in a poetic way. *When there is no fear of failure, no worry about getting something right or wrong, children are absorbed by the musical challenge and often create wonderful works.*

Leave time to ask the children afterward, "Tell me about your pictures. Do they have a story? What were your feelings?" Encourage them to write titles for their works. One first grader filled a paper with a light blue color, hardly changing the shade or texture. He told his teacher, "The music made me feel like when I fall asleep and my room turns blue."

Vary the experience. Encourage the children to paint their responses to different kinds of music. None of their pictures will look the same. "Which did you like best? Did you have a favorite?" This question followed an art-music-feelings session in which the children interpreted three kinds of music: very noisy, dissonant, urban jazz; an instrumental rendition of a sad spiritual; and lively marching band music. "I liked the last one," Kent explained. "It made me happy to think I was in a parade. It was happy like a holiday." "I liked them all," Annie said. "Even the very sad one. I like my sad picture the best as a matter of fact."

Find a musical work that has a variety of mood changes and settle the children down for a longer listening-drawing-feeling session. One kindergarten teacher told her students that they could use larger-size paper and keep working on it for a while as the music and their feelings changed *or* use smaller sheets of paper and take new ones when different kinds of music were introduced. About half the children chose the large sheets and the result was an intriguing combination of design and color. One could really see how the moods and feelings changed. For this session the teacher used Grieg's *Peer Gynt* Suites no. 1, op. 46, and no. 2, op. 55—a dramatic and powerful work with interludes of peacefulness and sudden mystery and excitement. Let me add that this teacher considered *Peer Gynt* one of her favorite pieces of music. And so, I must repeat: *Choose the music that you enjoy, whether old favorites or newly discovered treasures.*

Familiar songs that evoke feelings Most young children love songs and singing, and they learn through rhyme, rhythm, and melody. You already know many songs that express feelings as well as provide springboards for further discussion and activities about feelings. Keep track of the songs you and your children enjoy. I visited a kindergarten class where a chart of songs and feelings was prominently displayed. Here are some of the items from that chart.

Silly Songs
"I Know an Old Lady that Swallowed a Fly"
"Pop Goes the Weasel"
"Boom Boom, Ain't It Great to Be Crazy?"
"John, Jangle Jingleheimer Schmidt"

Quiet, Sleepy Songs
"Kum Ba Yah"
"Michael, Row the Boat Ashore"
"Rain Rain Go Away"

Happy Songs
"Here Comes the Sun"
"He's Got the Whole World in His Hands"
"My Favorite Things"
"Puff the Magic Dragon"
"I Love You, You Love Me"

Original songs that express feelings Young children make up songs as naturally as they speak. They are very much like Winnie the Pooh, who is always making up hums and songs to match his moods. For example, one of the children's favorite Winnie the Pooh hums, "Sing Ho! for the life of a Bear!"[17] begged to be adapted into their own songs. They "sang" their hum with a little sing-song melody that followed the rhythm of the words. Here is the song that a group of prekindergartners created:

> Sing Ho! for the life of a girl!
> Sing Ho! for the life of a boy!
> I don't mind if I don't have toys.
> I don't mind if I don't make noise.
> We have lots of girls.
> We have lots of boys.
> Sing Ho! for the girls.
> Sing Ho! for the boys.

For weeks "Sing Ho" was the way those preschoolers expressed happiness.

Drumbeats and heartbeats Play a heartbeat rhythm on a tom-tom or a bongo drum, child-made or store-bought. If you do not have drums, cookie containers, coffee cans, or tabletops will do. Discuss the music of heartbeats with your students. Our hearts beat faster and louder when we are afraid, excited, angry, or full of energy. Our hearts beat slower and softer when we feel calm, safe, and loved. With your children, practice the different kinds of heartbeats.

Read or tell a story that expresses many different feelings. The children play the drums to accompany the feelings in the story—loud and fast for exciting and scary parts, soft and slow for peaceful, calm parts. Combine the drum rhythms of heartbeats with a round-robin story in which all of the children take turns adding to the action. Add other instruments to the basic drum rhythms. Encourage the children to tell or sing their own original stories and accompany them on the drums or other instruments.

Many Native American poems are drumbeat/heartbeat songs that evoke strong feelings. The repetition in such poems and chants helps children learn them easily. As you read them aloud, you cannot help chanting and feeling the pulse of the drumbeat/heartbeat.

Musical instruments play feelings   Either choose one instrument that children pass around and take turns playing, or give the children a chance to choose an instrument from the instruments box to express their feelings.

> **Teacher**: *I feel very bouncy and merry today. Like this. (She played a bouncy rhythm on the drum and passed the drum to a child.)*
>
> **First Child**: *I feel like marching. (He played a steady drumbeat.)*
>
> **Second Child**: *I feel like a silly rabbit. (She used both hands to create a hopping rhythm.)*
>
> **Third Child**: *I feel lazy and sleepy today. I want to go to bed. (She brushed the drum with her palms.)*

A group of first graders responded beautifully to a variation of this activity. The teacher introduced the idea by saying, "How do you feel today? I feel so cheery I could ring a bell." She took a bell from the instruments box and rang it. The children walked over to the box, most of them thinking about their choices, some immediately drawn to an instrument. Manuelo lifted the cymbals in the air and clapped them together five or six times. "How are you feeling, Manuelo?" his teacher asked. "Like a noisemaker. Pow! Pow!" And he added a few more cymbal claps for emphasis.

Music tells a feelings story   This is a challenging activity to accompany a puppet show, pictures, or a story (read or improvised). With the children, decide which instruments they want to use to express the different emotions that will be part of the story or play. "Which instrument shall we play for the sad character? How shall we play the instrument so that it sounds sad?" Work out musical ideas for each character, to be played when that character appears. One kindergarten class made up a story with these characters:

> Three bunnies: one shy, one happy, one glum
> One mean dog that chased bunnies
> Two nice children who chased the dog away

These were the instruments the class chose for each character:

> Shy bunny: triangle
> Happy bunny: jingle bells
> Glum bunny: kazoo
> Mean dog: all the percussion instruments
> Nice children: all the bells

As the story was told, the children listened with the sharpest ears, ready to express the feelings of the characters the instant they heard their names. Add movement.

Listen to music, tell a story   This activity involves listening, imaging, and sharing ideas. Choose music that conveys a specific feeling. Ask the children to listen to the music carefully and try to picture what is happening. Make up a story that goes with the music. Expand the idea into movement. Listen, make up a story, and turn it into a dance. Write it! Illustrate it!

Listen to music, make a wish or tell a dream Play mystical, dreamy music for the children as they relax and listen with imagination and feelings as well as ears. Many musical selections inspire a peaceful harmony that allows the mind to play with ideas and emotions that are rarely given time for expression. Unless you want the children to listen to words and respond to them, music without words is probably more effective for this experience.

With children of all ages, I share one of my favorite songs from *South Pacific,* "Bali Hai." We relax and stretch and let our minds go with the music. "This is dreamy music. It might make you have a beautiful little dream. This is music to make a wish to. Think of some wonderful wishes you want to make as you listen to this music." The children listen attentively, and when the piece is over, we talk about how they felt. "My dream was sunny, sunny. Nice and warm and toasty," one little girl sighed contentedly. Another child said, "My wish wanted a kite up in the sky." And yet another, "My dream was picking flowers all colors. . . ." The children listened to each other attentively and shared important feelings, not always easy to express. We followed the experience with art projects and asked the children to draw pictures of their dreams or wishes. Turn them into poems, songs, and dances.

MOVEMENT AND PLAY TIMES

Peek-a-boo faces Peek-a-boo is probably the most popular game of very young children. Hide your face in your hands. 1-2-3 peek-a-boo. Open your hands and show your face. Show your happy face. Show another happy face. Another! How about an angry face? Grrr! Another! Invite the children: "Hide your faces. Let's see some sad faces. Now some happy faces."

Mirror, mirror on the wall This activity is similar to the one above, but the children look in the mirror to see their own facial expressions. Then you can ask, "Which face do you like better, your happy face or your grouchy face? Why?"

Hands show feelings Happy hands look different from mean hands. Sad hands look different from angry hands. Let hands show feelings. Give children the opportunity to try at least five variations of an idea. *They should never feel that one try at something is the total experience.*

"Turn yourself into . . ." Probably no three words in the English language can spur children into movement faster than these three words. The possibilities are limitless. Here are just a few to start your mind buzzing.

Statues Angry statues, frightened statues, silly statues. (Remember, more than one version of each.)

Shapes The shape of happy, the shape of sad, the shape of angry, the shape of scared.

Present situations A child who just lost a puppy or who just found a puppy, a child whose friend is moving away, a child whose favorite toy just broke, a child whose grandma is very sick.

The Seven Dwarfs Bashful, Dopey, Grumpy, Sleepy, Sneezy, Doc, and Happy are excellent characters to help children express feelings. The children do shapes, walks, dances, pantomimes, and exercises for each dwarf. Bashful's dance, for example, contrasts greatly with Happy's dance. Expand the activity into art, music, and creative writing. Create seven new dwarfs. Name them, describe them.

Move your shape Ask questions to expand upon the exercise above. For example: "How does your angry shape (or statue) want to move? Want to walk? How does your angry shape run? How does your silly shape want to stand? Want to sit? How does your grouchy shape want to run? Can you do a grouchy dance? What's your grouchiest walk?" End each idea by asking the children to "shake out," "melt down," or "wiggle out" their sad, silly, or disappointed shapes. Shake a tambourine to give them transition rhythm as they prepare for the next feeling.

"What if" and other movement questions Think of real situations that involve special feelings. The best ones come from the children's own experiences. Ask such questions as:

"What if you were waiting for your friends and they didn't come? What would you do? Show me. How would you look?" (Encourage change of facial expressions as well as body responses.)

"What if your cat had kittens and they were so cute? What would you do? How would you look? Show me.

"What if you were scolded because you wouldn't let your baby sister play with your toys? How would you look? Show me.

"What if you could never change the expression on your face? What if it were always the same no matter what happened?!"

"When you're angry, jump!" and other advice to get things moving I visited a kindergarten class and saw a handmade poster showing a child having a temper tantrum and jumping in the air. The children had discussed their feelings and had decided on appropriate movements for the different emotions. "If you're angry, jump!" was one of the children's suggestions. The teacher explained that the day a visitor was scheduled but did not appear, the children were angry. They decided to follow their own advice and jumped very hard for about two minutes. They felt much better afterwards! Other suggestions the kindergartners made and followed were: "When you're silly, do a somersault"; "When you're sad, lie down on your tummy"; "When you're happy, skip"; and "When you're afraid, do jumping jacks and shout." I like to "play" with the kids and encourage them to have a "very jumpy or bouncy day!"

Feel your way around the room Divide the room into areas for different feelings, and use words and designs as labels. The front of the room can be labeled with a happy face and the word "happy"; the back of the room, a grouchy face and the word "grouchy." Practice by having the children go together to the happy part of the room, and experiment with happy shapes, designs, movements, and faces. Then change to the grouchy side of the room.

We tried this activity with a group of first graders and some of the phrases they used were interesting and surprising:

Grouchy Side	Happy Side
Go away	Hi
Stupid	Wanna play?
I'm not playing with *you*	Wanna dance?
I don't like you	Wanna be my friend?
Dopey	Let's go to the playground
I'm going home	Let's color
That's *mine*	Let's have our snack
	I like you
	Let's make a mobile

If the children understand the activity and show the changes for each feeling, expand the experience by letting them begin individually with the feeling place they choose or by making a grab bag of grouchy and happy faces and having the children grab a card to see which side they start on. Some children do happy things while others do grouchy things. The contrast is dramatic; it can stimulate discussion and increase awareness. After a few minutes, give a change signal. Everyone moves to another place and responds accordingly.

Add feelings Try a sad place, a silly place, an afraid place. Add art activities to further express the feelings of the place.

Puppet shows and other improvisations Puppets, stuffed animals, dolls, and toys all have an important place in the rooms and lives of young children. Children often express their feelings more readily through the lips of a puppet or toy animal.

If a situation that involves strong feelings occurs in your classroom, turn it into a puppet or toy animal scene. Initiate the improvisation by taking one of the puppets or toys and expressing its feelings: "Poor monkey is so sad today. What do you think is wrong with him?" The children may respond as themselves or involve other puppets and toys. "Wonder what we can do to cheer him up? Any ideas?" In one kindergarten, a downcast puppet was cheered only when the children made all the other puppets and toy animals sing a silly song to him. They applauded when the downcast puppet perked up and waved his arms gleefully.

Encourage children to play with puppets by themselves or in groups. All ways and approaches are valuable as long as the spirit is one of sharing and cooperating. *Remember: encourage, accept, enjoy, guide; do not criticize, humiliate, or reject a child's ideas or expressions.*

In one first grade, an ornery child who was having a bad day was encouraged to visit with one of the puppets. He handled the puppet roughly, called him names, and spanked him. "I'm gonna put you in the trash and the trashman will take you," he said. Smack. "You're naughty and you're going in the trash can." The children gathered around and watched, worried but fascinated. The teacher, thinking quickly, introduced another puppet. Her puppet had his head down and was crying. "Sniffle. Sniffle." She sniffled for the puppet until the ill-tempered puppeteer looked up from his drama. "Please don't put my friend in the trash can. I'll never see him again and I love him. Won't you change your mind, please?" The teacher's puppet begged, then whispered in the boy's ear. "If you don't put him in the trash can, we can play together." The boy thought about it. He visibly softened and said to his puppet, "OK. You don't have to go in the trash can." His puppet jumped up happily. The children clapped in relief as the two puppets danced together.

Masks and movement Using masks created in art activities, combine body movement with the feeling expressed by the mask.

Pictures, feelings, movement Have all the children respond in movement to a picture that expresses a specific feeling. "How does this picture make you feel?

Show me." Or give each child a picture depicting a particular feeling and have each child move in response. Turn it into a game by asking the child to do or show "the feeling of the picture" without revealing the picture to the other children. The rest of the children guess the feeling and only after the guessing is the picture shown.

Music and dance Play music with strong feeling. Ask the children to listen to the music, decide what feelings are in the music, and follow the feelings of the music with their bodies. Unless you are focusing on a specific body part, encourage the children to use the whole body.

After listening to a portion of *Scheherazade* by Rimsky-Korsakoff, a group of five-year-olds decided that the music was scary, and they did a marvelous dance showing all kinds of fright movement. After it was over, one little girl said, "I have lots of practice to dance about *frightened* now that my bedroom got moved upstairs."

Animals and movement Young children truly enjoy animals, and almost any activity with an animal is guaranteed to succeed. "Let's change into cats. Are you a big cat? Little cat? What color are you? Are you sleeping? Rolling a ball of yarn? Sunning by the window? Let's see. How are you cats feeling today? Very shy? Let's see those shy cats. Very mischievous? Full of tricks? Show me what you're doing. Very sad? Why are the cats so sad? What could have happened?"

A group of six-year-olds changed into turtles. They crawled slowly. They were curious. They were frightened and hid in their shells. They slowly stuck out their heads to see if it was safe outside. They walked happily because there was no danger. "How do you feel now? Show me. Tell me." One little boy-turtle lifted his head as he walked on all fours and expressed a feeling on his face that I had not seen before. "Very proud," he glowed. "My turtle isn't afraid of dogs anymore!"

Poems, stories, and movement Read, tell, and improvise stories and poems that express strong feelings. As the story is related, the children move and interpret it. To help this activity along, I ask the children to suppose that someone came in who did not speak our language. He or she could tell what was happening only by looking at what we were doing. So, even though the story is being told aloud, we also have to tell it with our bodies. Remember, the children do not have to move to every word or part of the story. Highlight the story with movement, unless it is that rare story with a different movement idea in every sentence.

Fairy tales like "The Ugly Duckling" by Hans Christian Andersen are full of feelings—loneliness, unhappiness, meanness, finally joy and surprise. Such classic stories as Maurice Sendak's *Where the Wild Things Are* invite children to play out feelings of fear and safety. The beloved *Babar*, as written by Laurent de Brunhoff, and all his friends and relations provide action-filled adventures with warmth, courage, disappointment, and happiness; Ezra Jack Keats' marvelous characters help children understand themselves and others.

A. A. Milne's wonderful poem "King John's Christmas" is an example of how easily poetry can inspire movement. King John is not a kind person and he has a very sad life. All he wants for Christmas is an India rubber ball, which he gets at the end through a happy accident. A poem like this gives the children a chance to express sadness, loneliness, meanness, hope, and finally a measure of happiness. Poems and stories help children to learn compassion and sympathy.

Crazy Circle makes you feel Draw a large circle on the floor with chalk or indicate it with your hands. Tell the children that some strange thing happened to the floor, to that circle, and gave it magical qualities. "Every time we walk into the circle, our feelings change. It's weird! Here we are just having a plain everyday day, and the minute we walk into the circle, pow!"

Most of the children will probably watch you the first time; some may follow you. Say something like, "Hope it doesn't fill with 'silly.'" Encourage the children to do the same: "It's making me do silly tricks"; "It's making me do a cartwheel"; "It's making me fall down. Plop!" The sillies have a wide range of expression! Guide by signaling, "Let's get out of this crazy circle. I'm going to jump out of it." And do so. When all the children are outside the circle, if they do not take up the game from that point, you can suggest something like, "One thing I know. I hope it doesn't turn me *grouchy*. I'm not in the mood to be grouchy today!" as you move toward the circle. Of course, the circle will make everyone act grouchy until you all get out safely.

We finished one Crazy Circle session by "abracadabraing" the circle out of existence. What was intended to be about a ten-minute activity took almost a half hour because the children had so many ideas: "It's turning us into show-offs!"; "That circle is making us into babies. Boo hoo!"; "That circle is changing us into bullies!" They never ran out of ideas, only time. Vary the activity by playing different kinds of music each time the children go into the circle.

Colors, feelings, dances Use brightly colored pieces of material, scarves, ribbons, yarn, or tissue paper to enrich this multifaceted activity. Colors evoke feelings. Colors can make us *do* things and *feel* things. *Red* makes us *stop* what we are doing. *Green* makes us *go,* keep moving. *Green* makes us *grow. Blue* makes us *blow* like the wind in the sky. "What else does *red* make you feel? How else does *green* make you feel?" Let the children explore one color at a time. After the children try many ways of moving to a particular color, ask them what kind of music that color wants to dance to. Fast? Slow? Loud? Soft? Choose music that fits their suggestions.

A group of first graders were working out their feelings about *orange.* "It makes me feel whirly"; "Cheerful like birthday parties and orange lollipops"; "Very bouncy"; "Sad because the leaves fall." The ideas expand into movement. Dance a rainbow of feelings!

Songs and movement Songs like "If You're Happy and You Know It Clap Your Hands" are popular with children and can be easily improvised. "If You're Happy and You Know It:

> stamp your feet
> blink your eyes
> tickle your nose
> touch your toes
> spin around
> run around
> hop around
> wave your arms
> tap your tummy
> wiggle your toes
> touch the sky
> point your elbows
> hug a friend

Jani Aranow[18] culminated a day of the "sillies" with an improvised song-movement game inspired by a slip of the tongue. The children were enacting a story about bears that kept climbing trees to find honey and the bees chasing them away. Of course, the bears got honey all over their bodies (make-believe) and at one point, instead of saying, "Get that honey off your face!" someone said, "Get that *funny* off your face!" which resulted in hysterics. Jani, her guitar always handy, improvised this song with the children:

> Get the funny off your face
> O my, how silly you look.
> Look in the mirror, go on, get nearer
> Your face is an awful sight.
> You say I'm wrong,
> Well so is this silly song
> So just get the funny off your face!

The children accompanied the song with crazy faces and silly movements.

Welcome a new day I saved this idea for the end of this section so you can see how beginnings and endings flow into one another and sometimes the beginning is really the ending and sometimes the ending is really the place to begin. We circular thinkers go with the flow!

Our students come to us with so many different home situations, so many knapsacks filled with often painful experiences and memories. Even at very young ages, some of our children are already labeled "difficult," "behavior problem," or "underachiever." Too often, yesterday's events hang around their necks like albatrosses.

I think it's important to begin each day in a fresh way. Even the youngest children understand the sacredness of that opportunity.

Hallow each day. Welcome the children to the new time together with special gestures, poems, songs, and ceremonies. Honor the new day and the new chance to do our best, to be our best selves.

With each class I teach, no matter the ages or grade levels, I begin with a special way to show appreciation and good wishes to everyone in the group, to the time we will share together. Maybe it's just a simple high-fives greeting. Maybe it's a song like Thomas Moore's "Good Morning To My Friends, Good Morning To My Teacher, Too . . ." Maybe it's a poem like Shel Silverstein's "Invitation," which begins, "If you are a dreamer, come in." Maybe it's a special book like Byrd Baylor's *The Way To Start A Day.* But, whatever the way, *your* way, the children begin with the magical feeling of being wanted and welcomed.

CLASSROOM VISITORS AND FIELD TRIPS

When planning programs that involve visitors and field trips, remember that you have an entire community as a resource. Draw on people and organizations in your community and you will be delightfully surprised at how many ideas you have to enhance your students' understanding of feelings. And keep in mind your first source—the gifts of your children's families.

Classroom Visitors

Folksinger This visitor can be a professional artist, grandparent, parent, or other member of the community who has a knowledge of music from a particular culture and the desire to share it. If the visitor wears a costume from the country represented, the session will be even more exciting. Ask your visitor to perform songs that express a variety of basic human feelings that are easy to understand in any language.

Storyteller Keep this ancient and vital art alive by inviting a storyteller from the community. Ask him or her to tell stories that evoke basic feelings, stories that encourage emotional involvement on the part of listeners, however young. Folk and fairy tales express strong feelings of disappointment, fear, love, hate, cowardice, and bravery. Our children need stories, poems, and songs to help them to *feel* that they are a part of the human family.

Mime Find a mime through your local arts council, theater departments of area schools, or the entertainment editor of a newspaper. Invite the mime to perform feelings for your children as well as to share exercises in mime that help children learn to articulate emotions with their bodies.

Musician Invite someone who enjoys playing a musical instrument to share his or her talent and feelings with your children. Explain to the musician that you have been paying attention to feelings and hope that he or she will be able to increase awareness of feelings through music. Violins can evoke great sadness as well as joy; trumpets are exciting and sometimes frightening.

Actor and actress Trained in expressing feelings clearly and articulately, an actor and actress are excellent visitors. They can demonstrate feelings with voice, facial expression, gestures, and movement. They can show the children that the same words can be said in many ways to express different feelings. Be sure to ask your guests to involve the children.

Dancer Dance is one of the oldest means of expression and has great emotional impact. Modern, ballet, and folk dancers all have important things to say about feelings with their bodies. Remember to ask your guest to involve the children in the experience.

Baby animal Baby animals evoke strong feelings of tenderness, protection, and love. Invite a person with a baby animal to visit your class, and be surprised at how much love even your most argumentative child will show.

Clown Clowns have cheered people for centuries and they can share their art with your children. Every community has at least one clown who enjoys performing for young children and passing on some secrets in the process.

Poet and writer Most writers and poets are very sensitive to their own feelings and those of others. It is a special challenge and privilege for writers to meet with young children and communicate what they feel and think as they write. Ask your local arts council or community resource program for the names of poets and writers.

Clergy, social worker, psychologist, counselor Helping people with problems, counseling people in difficult situations, and guiding people in handling their feelings are the main concern of these members of the "helping" professions. Invite them to share with your children the part of their work that is devoted to feelings. These visitors can also reassure the children that they are not alone in their feelings, that all people have good and bad feelings, and that sometimes people need help in expressing their feelings, in understanding their feelings.

Field Trips

Senior citizens center or home for the aged Here is an excellent way for children to learn the happiness of giving to and sharing with others. Children take gifts, perform songs, and visit with the senior citizens. This may become a regular field trip. Often elementary classes form an ongoing relationship with residents of such centers.

Art gallery Many paintings and sculpture express and evoke deep feelings. Talk with a guide about your special emphasis on feelings and he or she will be sure you find the works that fit your purpose. Celebrate the experience with your own artistic and creative writing responses.

Artist at work Many artists and craftsmen are glad to talk with young children about their feelings and their work. Again, be sure to tell the artist about your special interest in feelings so that he or she can focus on that subject during your visit. With your students, try some of the ideas.

Play, concert, or puppet show If you are lucky enough to have a special performance for children in your area, make every effort to have your class attend. Live performances are enriching experiences for children on many levels, especially in the way they help develop empathy.

Community center, recreation center, or "Y" This experience gives children a chance to see people of all ages doing things that make their lives happier. When we learn new skills, develop our talents, work with others, and strengthen our bodies, we are engaged in positive activities that enable us to have fuller lives. Learning, doing, and enjoying are excellent ways to ward off feelings of frustration, loneliness, and despair.

IT ALL COMES TOGETHER

By now I hope that you realize "It All Comes Together" sections are the magic stitches that connect ideas. This little section is highlighted only to remind you of that call for holistic, integrated learning in case (for just a minute) you forgot!

With all the excellent resources available at your fingertips, it is easier than ever before to find materials *you* love to share with your students.

One of Rose Stough's favorite books is *The Bears' House* by Marilyn Sachs.[19] It is a moving story told in the first person by the heroine, Fran Ellen, whose home life and school life combine to define her as an alienated and lonely girl. Even her teacher adds to her rejection by insensitivity and misunderstanding. As Rose's third graders listen attentively to the story, they easily empathize with Fran Ellen. The school and family situations and relationships are familiar to many of our children living through traumatic times. It's not hard for Rose's students to clearly imagine Fran Ellen's *only* comfort, happiness, and solace—playing with the Three Bears' dollhouse brought in by the teacher for the class's enjoyment. Fran Ellen has a beautiful imaginary life in the Bears' house. Playing with the dollhouse (when she's finished with her schoolwork assignments) is the only time Fran Ellen is happy. This strong and effective story ends on a note of hope as the teacher, who is going to retire at the end of the school year, decides to give the dollhouse to the child who has accomplished the most. That gift equals the other gift in the story—the gift of understanding and compassion on the part of the teacher who finally gains insight into Fran Ellen's painful situation.

Rose talks about the book and its influence on her own teaching about feelings. She says, "Every time I read this book it reminds me to evaluate myself on how I personally treat children. Over the years, I've had Fran Ellen in my room. The story really helps the children develop empathy and responsibility. It's a book that goes with them. . . ."

Discussions on every level (one to one, small group, whole class) happen throughout the reading of the story. Often, Rose will stop the reading and ask the children to "show" a scene, a reaction, or an expression of emotions.

"How would Fran Ellen sit?" "Imagine the big, strutty way the kids came into class. Let's show that feeling."

Role playing, dialogue exploration, and movement variations spin off from the reading of the story. Significant insights such as the difference between fantasy and reality and the importance of noticing the feelings of others are discovered. Because Rose's environment is a safe and loving place, her students make their own connections to Fran Ellen's experiences with the sharing of their own. The children turn themselves into counselors and brainstorm advice for Fran Ellen. They write Dear Abby letters from Fran Ellen to the newspapers and answer them.

As the Three Bears and their house provide Fran Ellen with her greatest feelings of warmth and joy, Rose shares the song "Waltzing with Bears" from the *Dr. Seuss Song Book*. The children waltz around the room with imaginary or real stuffed bears or bear substitutes to evoke the happiness Fran Ellen feels when she plays with the bears.

Each room in the Bears' house is described with such detail that the children easily picture the scenes, room by room. Their illustrations and posters reflect their thorough understanding of the people and places of the story. Langston Hughes' poem "Hope" conveys the promise of hope indicated at the end of *The Bears' House:*

> Sometimes when I'm lonely,
> don't know why,
> keep thinkin' I won't be lonely
> by and by.[20]

Rose's students love this poem. It inspires them to write their own poetry or illustrate the poem with their own visual images of hope.

When you encourage children to see relationships, make connections, and think in holistic ways, there is always hope for teaching and learning in the key of life. And it *feels* good!

NOTES ♥

1. Michael Joel Rosen's recent books include:
   All Eyes On The Pond. New York: Hyperion, 1994.
   Bonesy and Isabel. San Diego: Harcourt Brace, in press.
   Elijah's Angel. San Diego: Harcourt Brace, 1992.
   Kids' Best Dog Book. New York: Workman Press, 1993.
   Home. New York: HarperCollins, 1992.
   Speak! Children's Book Illustrators Brag About Their Dogs. San Diego: Harcourt Brace, 1993.
   Kids' Book of Fishing. New York: Workman Press, 1991.
   The Greatest Table. San Diego: Harcourt Brace, 1994.

2. Dawn recently retired from the Columbus Public Schools. She last taught in McGuffey School, where she still gives one day a week to be with the children.

3. Read about Dawn in Mimi Brodsky Chenfeld, " 'What Has Two Legs and Loves You?' Four Letter Words in the Classroom." *Language Arts,* Volume 66, number 4, April 1989, pp. 423–428. Reprinted in *Teaching in the Key of Life*. Washington, DC: NAEYC, 1993, pp. 64–69.

4. Janet Stocker was the director of the School for Young Children, Columbus, Ohio.

5. Jean Buker taught early childhood classes in central Ohio programs.

6. Jane Johnson is a Reading Recovery teacher at Deer Run School in Dublin, Ohio.

7. Theodore Roethke, *Straw for the Fire*. New York: Doubleday, Anchor, 1974, p. 205.

8. Steve Anderson taught at the Early Childhood Program of the Leo Yassenoff Columbus Jewish Center. He is now writing, producing, and directing plays for children in Columbus, Ohio.

9. Connie Swain cofounded the Community Learning Exchange in Columbus.

10. Debbie Charna teaches reading at the Evening Street Elementary School in Worthington, Ohio.

11. Rhoda Linder and Wendy Wohlstein taught in the Early Childhood Program of the Leo Yassenoff Columbus Jewish Center.

12. Listen to the music of those amazingly talented artists composing and singing for young children. Such outstanding musicians as Ella Jenkins; Thomas Moore; Greg and Steve; Pete Seeger; Tom Paxton; Peter, Paul, and Mary; Fran Avni; and Fred Koch are worthy of your attention. Keep your own list. Make your own discoveries.

13. Margie Goldach and Carol Highfield were co-teachers at the Early Childhood Program at the Leo Yassenoff Columbus Jewish Center.

14. Dr. William Glasser is credited with sharing the idea of Magic Circle. See *Schools Without Failure*. New York: Harper & Row, 1968.

15. Lynn Thompson taught at the Avalon Elementary School in Columbus.

16. Danielle Leventhal shared her paper, "Visual Art as Creative Experience."

17. A. A. Milne, "Expedition to the North Pole." *The World of Pooh*. New York: Dutton, 1957, p. 104.

18. Jani Aranow taught at the Leo Yassenoff Columbus Jewish Center.

19. Rose Stough teaches at Moler School in the Columbus, Ohio, Public School System. Read more about Rose's teaching in Mimi Brodsky Chenfeld's "The Ransom of the Rabbit in Room 15" (Educational Leadership, January 1991, p. 89) and Mimi Brodsky Chenfeld's "Stuff" (Educational Leadership,

November 1989, p. 97). Reprinted in *Teaching in the Key of Life*.
Washington, DC: NAEYC, 1993. pp. 11–13.

Sachs, Marilyn. *The Bears' House*. New York: Dell-Yearling, 1976.

20. "Hope" by Langston Hughes. *Selected Poems of Langston Hughes*. New York: Vintage, 1987.

BOOKS FROM MY KNAPSACK FOR CHILDREN ❤ ❤

Aliki. *Feelings*. New York: Morrow, 1984.

Asch, Frank. *Here Comes the Cat*. Illustrated by Vladimir Vagin. New York: Scholastic, 1989.

Avery, Charles E. *Everybody Has Feelings*. Seattle: Open Hand, 1992.

Baylor, Byrd. *I'm in Charge of Celebrations*. New York: Scribners, 1986.

Bayton, Martin. *Why Do You Love Me?* Illustrated by Martin Bayton. New York: Greenwillow, 1990.

Bunting, Eve. *Our Teacher's Having a Baby*. Illustrated by Diane de Groat. New York: Clarion, 1992.

Carlstrom, Nancy White. *Blow Me a Kiss, Miss Lilly*. Illustrated by Amy Schwartz. New York: HarperCollins, 1990.

Carlstrom, Nancy White. *Goody-bye Geese*. Illustrated by Ed Young. New York: Philomel, 1991.

Cohn, Janice. *I Had a Friend Named Peter*. New York: Morrow, 1987.

Conrad, Pam. *The Tub Grandfather*. Illustrated by Richard Egielski. New York: HarperCollins, 1993.

Denslow, Sharon. *Taylor's Place*. New York: Bradbury, 1990.

Girard, Linda Walvoord. *Adoption Is for Always*. Illustrated by Judith Friedman. Morton Grove, IL: Albert Whitman, 1986.

Grifalconi, Ann. *Kinda Blue*. Boston: Little, Brown, 1993.

Gross, Alan. *What If the Teacher Calls on Me?* Illustrated by Mike Venegia. Chicago: Children's Press, 1980.

Hiawyn, Oram. *Angry Arthur*. Illustrated by Satoshi Kitamura. New York: Dutton, 1992.

Honeycutt, Natalie. *Whistle Home*. Illustrated by Annie Cannon. New York: Orchard, 1993.

Hopkins, Lee Bennett. *It's About Time!* Illustrated by Matt Novak. New York: Simon and Schuster, 1992.

Johnson, Delores. *What Will Mommy Do When I'm at School?* Illustrated by Delores Johnson. New York: Macmillan, 1990.

Laskey, Kathryn. *The Tantrums*. Illustrated by Babette McCarthy. New York: Macmillan, 1993.

Martin, Bill, Jr. and John Archambault. *Knots on a Counting Rope*. Illustrated by Ted Rand. New York: Henry Holt, 1987.

Martin, Jane Read, and Patricia Marx. *Now Everybody Hates Me*. Illustrated by Roz Choat. New York: HarperCollins, 1993.

Marzollo, Jean. *Uproar in Holler Cat Hill*. Illustrated by Steven Kellog. New York: Dial, 1980.

Melmed, Laura. *The First Song Ever Sung*. Illustrated by Ed Young. New York: Morrow, 1993.

Modesitt, Jeanne. *Sometimes I Feel Like a Mouse*. Illustrated by Robin Spoward. New York: Scholastic, 1992.

Near, Holly. *The Grand Peace March*. Illustrated by Kiav Disimini. New York: Henry Holt, 1993.

Patron, Susan. *Bobbin Dustbobbin*. Illustrated by Mike Shenon. New York: Orchard, 1993.

Polacco, Patricia. *Thundercake*. Illustrated by Patricia Polacco. New York: Philomel, 1990.

Pringle, Laurence. *Octopus Hug*. Illustrated by Kate Sulley Palmer. New York: St.Martin, 1993.

Rogers, Jacqueline. *Best Friends Sleep Over*. Illustrated by Jacqueline Rogers. New York: Scholastic, 1993.

Ross, Dave. *A Book of Hugs*. Illustrated by Dave Ross. New York: Harper & Row, 1988.

Sachar, Louis. *Monkey Soup*. Illustrated by Cat Bowman. New York: Knopf, 1992.

Tews, Susan. *Nettie's Gift*. Illustrated by Elizabeth Sayles. New York: Clarion, 1993.

Tulloch, Richard. *Danny in the Toolbox*. Illustrated by Armin Greder. New York: Morrow/Tambourine, 1991.

Varley, Susan. *Badger's Parting Gifts*. Illustrated by Susan Varley. New York: Lothrop, Lee & Shephard, 1984.

Viorst, Judith. *Alexander and the Terrible, Horrible, No Good, Very Bad Day*. Illustrated by Ray Cruz. New York: Atheneum, 1972.

Waddell, Martin. *Can't You Sleep, Little Bear?* Illustrated by Barbara Firth. Cambridge, MA: Candlewich, 1992.

Zagwyn, Deborah Turner. *The Pumpkin Blanket*. Illustrated by Deborah Turner Zagwyn. Berkeley: Celestial Arts, 1990.

BOOKS FROM MY KNAPSACK FOR TEACHERS ♥ ♥

Conroy, Pat. *The Water Is Wide*. Boston: Houghton Mifflin, 1972.

Curry, N. and C. Johnson. *Beyond Self-Esteem: Developing a Genuine Sense of Human Value*. Washington, DC: NAEYC, 1993.

Kohl, Herbert. *Growing Minds—On Becoming a Teacher*. New York: Harper & Row, 1984.

Langone, John. *Spreading Poison—A Book about Racism and Prejudice*. New York: Little, Brown, 1993.

Lieberman, Alicia. *The Emotional Life of the Toddler*. New York: Macmillan/ The Free Press, 1993.

McCracken, J. B., ed. *Reducing Stress in Young Children's Lives*. Washington, DC: NAEYC, 1993.

Morrow, Gertrude. *The Compassionate School: A Practical Guide to Educating Abused and Traumatized Children*. Englewood Cliffs, NJ: Prentice-Hall, 1987.

Stuart, Jesse. *To Teach, To Love*. New York: World, 1970.

Terr, Lenore. *Too Scared to Cry*. New York: Harper & Row, 1990.

Chapter 3

Our Uniqueness

I am a nice nice boy
More than just nice,
Two million times more
The word is ADORABLE.[1]

See Me Beautiful

See me beautiful
Look for the best
in me.
It's what I really am
and all I want
to be.
It may take some time.
It may be hard to find
but
see me beautiful.
See me beautiful
each and every day.
Could you take a chance?
Could you find a way
to see me shining through
in everything I do
and see me beautiful?
  (chorus)

by Red Grammer
from *Teaching Peace*[2]

THE BASICS

Big sister Jackie, six years old,[3] is a great conversationalist. She breathlessly shares news updates about her schoolwork, "I'm writing a book about the rain forest. I love reading, spelling, math!" What about favorite colors? Without hesitation, she explains, "Now my favorite color is mostly red. I used to be yellow. Dad is blue like the sky, and I used to be yellow like the sun." Interrupt the colorful exchange to ask about her three-year-old identical twin sisters, Michelle and Annie, and Jackie's response is effusive:

"Well, Michelle is easier to be with. Annie sometimes is grumpier. Michelle doesn't wear earrings, you know. Annie loves earrings. . . . In the morning when she wakes up, Annie doesn't like me right away. But Michelle shouts, 'Jackie! Jackie!' . . . Annie mumbles when she's awake. Michelle screams! Annie's favorite thing is her cat and her Babar. Michelle's favorite things is my porcelain doll (but I won't let her). Annie's softer. She's not as wild. Michelle is wiggly. She's a bouncy wiggly girl. Oh, I love being the big sister!"

Even identical twins are unique individuals.

Think for a minute. *Who are you?* Do your features, feelings, intelligence quotient, imagination, body coordination, and personality add up? Does the sum of all your parts equal you? Despite social security number, zip code, and license plate, you are not so easy to identify. You are more than your fingerprints and dental structure. You are more elusive than your image in a photograph.

Though people may say you are "the image" of some near or distant relative, you are not that person. Sometimes you may share thought or behavior patterns with groups of people that fit a statistical study, but there are other aspects of you that will never fit a study. True, as we grow older, we give up much of our individuality to conform to society's expectations, but we still defy science to completely explain a single person.

Nowhere in human evolution has there been another person exactly like you, with your combination and arrangement of qualities, traits, and characteristics. Even identical twins, like Annie and Michelle, are not absolutely identical. Their thoughts, their special ways of looking at the world, their responses to people and situations, their dreams, fantasies, fears, and foibles are their own.

You are a special person. Because you have been born into the human family, you are gifted and talented. You have amazing strengths. You have seeds of interests waiting to be nurtured. You have abilities and skills waiting to be developed. You are bursting with potential! You have a knapsack of experiences, ideas, beliefs, and natural resources waiting to be opened, waiting to be used as a rich resource. When you feel good about yourself, you glow with a special light that brightens and warms others. When you feel down in the dumps, inadequate, incompetent, untalented, your light diminishes. The world around you droops and cools.

As you are, so you teach. It is vital that you reaffirm your belief in yourself: your own history, your own map of the journey of your life, your own ability to grow and learn, your own light that can warm you and others. It is important that you take time to remember the wonder of being human.

By the time most children come to preschool or nursery school, they have made astonishing strides in language usage and comprehension, physical coordination, and social awareness. They follow directions, initiate their own experiences, and are curious about the world around them and about the most fascinating world of all—themselves.

We are most unique and original when we are very young. In those early years, we have not yet learned what is "in," what is trite, what are the norms of our culture and the expectations of our society. When we were very young, we were honest and direct. We did not see the invisible clothes on the foolish emperor, even though the big people around us thought they did or should.

If we were lucky enough to be healthy and beloved children, our early years were years of enchantment, when we learned to love the sound of our own names and to bask in the warmth of a friendly universe. Celebrations were not limited to a few set calendar days; they were daily occurrences. When we said a new word, the people in our lives smiled and clapped. When we took a new step, we were cheered on. Our talk turned to song; our walk, to dance. We were delighted with our drawings, our toys, our make-believe games. We were proud of our accomplishments and discoveries. We were full of courage and mighty strength. We were giants. We could see through closed doors, cause rain, and play with imaginary friends.

Because healthy and cherished children learn that they are special and wonderful, they can see beyond themselves and appreciate the special qualities of others. Because they have been encouraged and praised for their works, they can praise others. The commandment "Love your neighbor as yourself" assumes that first you learn to love and cherish yourself.

We live in a difficult and complex world. National and international tensions are constant sources of anxiety. The security and order provided by traditional institutions are lost as mobility increases, families are disrupted, and communities grow. Individuals seek unhealthy remedies for feelings of alienation and rootlessness. Many of our young children come from single, multiple, and dysfunctional homes and carry their own knapsacks of disappointments and sorrows.

You could conclude that trying to teach the lessons of self-esteem, respect, and wonder in such difficult times is like trying to grow flowers in cement. But rather than becoming discouraged, let us pledge greater commitment to this challenge. It is probably more important now than ever before in history that people learn to love themselves and to love one another.

What is the "wonder of me" all about? It is about celebrating ourselves, enjoying our skills and powers, sharing our ideas and works proudly and joyfully, rejoicing in our unique talents, and translating this feeling about the immense importance of each child into concrete experiences.

When educators are deeply committed to the hallowing of their students every moment of the day, every day of the year (not relegated to a theme slot in a curriculum guide book), the very air the children breathe carries the message.

The motto of Indianola Informal Elementary School is "I'm an Original." Cindy Lalli, principal of Indianola, shares her passionately felt philosophy: "When children come to us, we start learning from them. We ask, what does this child bring to our school? Regardless of where they come from, transfers, new students, returning veterans, they have so much to contribute to our school. Even . . . no, especially the youngest children come to us from their special home environments, cultural backgrounds, environmental experiences. Each child is special. From day one and all the days, they know they are rich resources, They know they have their own contributions to share and we are waiting for them."[4]

Bill Dwyer, principal of Duxberry Park Arts Impact Elementary School,[5] is eloquent in his description of his school as one in constant process of renewal. "We are always shifting, adjusting, rearranging, looking for new and old ways to enrich the lives of the children and the life of the curriculum. Our teachers set the example— they are highly motivated, always learning themselves, always open to new ideas and experiences. We want to reach all of the children so we have to have many different ways, as we're all different individuals. Of course, we believe (and *know*) that the arts are the best vehicles for kids to express themselves, to learn about themselves and others. The arts are woven into everything we do. In this school, everything we do together recognizes the originality of every individual. All of our children come to us with so many combinations of qualities. We are always in the act of celebrating our good fortune to be learning from each other, with each other."

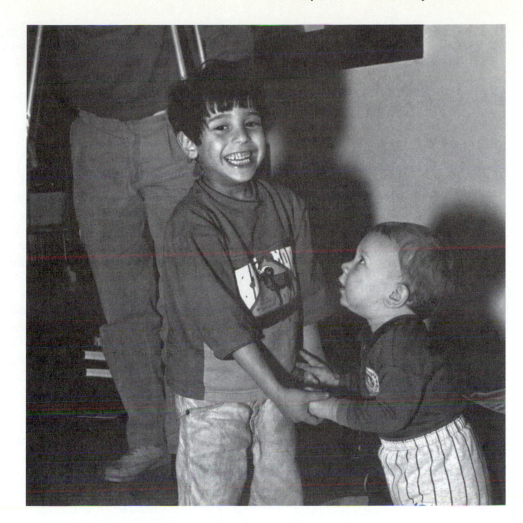

Mrs. A. Joseph Marsh wrote a letter to her daughter, who was about to begin a teaching career. These excerpts are excellent examples of philosophy translated into behavior:

Perfume the classroom with the sweet smell of success. Be kind to your kids. Show joy at even their small achievements. Sprinkle each day with praise—sincere praise that can withstand a child's windowpane vision of the adult heart. Accent the positive—the good try; the perhaps slow but steady progress—rather than poor work on a task. . . . Give your children . . . glittering souvenirs. Keep their senses awake. Take them on walks and encourage them to look . . . listen . . . touch . . . which brings up the specialness of each child. Not only does every child have unique gifts and attributes, but the same child sometimes seems to be several children—or at least several different ages in the same day. But, then, adults are like that, too. Don't you feel much more mature in some situations than others? I do. And, when I'm not feeling well, I just know I'm tiny and positively helpless. . . . I'm looking forward to hearing about your first weeks of teaching. Mine, I know, were full of frazzle. And, later, when I told my kids that, like them, I had been nervous and worried about the new situation, they couldn't believe it. Well, at least I let them know I'm human. Hope I let them know, too, that I cared about them. For caring, as I'm sure you've guessed, is what this letter is all about.[6]

Because you care so deeply about each of your children, everything you do will be stamped with that commitment. What will your students learn about themselves from you? How will you teach them?

A popular bumper sticker reads: "I Lost It." Another bumper sticker boasts: "I Found It." I have always wondered what it was that we lost, and I think it has something to do with this feeling of wonder and worth, of awareness and appreciation for ourselves and others. Let us help our children glue bumper stickers to themselves that shout: "We Never Lost It!"

DISCOVERY TIMES/WONDER TIMES

- Our human family is very inventive and creative. Just think of all the different kinds of objects, tools, machines, musical instruments, designs, and arts that came about from people's imaginations!
- We are part of that fascinating human family.
- Each of us is a very important person with unique personality, interests, habits, physical characteristics, talents, and wishes.
- Is there a limit to our learning and growing?
- Every day we learn something new about ourselves.
- We do things we have not done before; we learn new skills; we try different challenges. We keep practicing. (No one is perfect!)
- We are proud of our accomplishments and happy when our classmates share their interests and achievements with us.
- We are lucky to be able to enjoy our own imaginations, ideas, and questions. We have wonderful minds.
- We are capable of great learning and understanding.
- Every day we should celebrate our unique talents and appreciate and respect ourselves and others.
- We learn that through practice, difficult things become easier and obstacles can be overcome.
- It's exciting to exercise our special "powers." Sometimes we surprise ourselves.

SUGGESTED VOCABULARY

me	magic	different	share
myself	special	strong	celebrate
I	terrific	proud	surprise
you	interesting	original	congratulate
we	good	smart	thank you
us	wonderful	clever	please
names	funny	curious	discover
idea	beautiful	learn	I can
imagination	handsome	make	see
boy	pretty	understand	hear
girl	adorable	grow	touch (feel)
people	cute	question	smell
person	great	wonder	taste
human being	important	respect	know
practice	paint	laugh	think
draw	memory	appreciate	read
write	talent	like	talk
birthday	skill	build	sing

The above list includes many words of praise because the words that children hear and see contribute to the climate of their environment. Elizabeth Hunter reported children's responses to a questionnaire by the Association for Childhood Education International on their feelings about themselves, their teachers, and their parents. Here are some answers to the question "What are some things that people in your school (teachers, principals, etc.) do to help you feel good about yourself?"

> Don't yell a lot, love us, and say "Thank you!" when children do nice things
> I feel good when you say I'm a good person
> Compliment me on something I did
> Put my work on the bulletin board
> Treat me like I'm important
> Be kind
> Listen to us
> Have fun with us
> Respect us
> Care about us
> Treat us as individuals
> Tell children you love them[7]

Words are not just sounds. They represent things, events, experiences. They have power and influence. They can change our minds or our moods. Remember the special words that Charlotte spun in her web to save Wilbur's life. If you want children to learn to value themselves and others, surround them with words that convey those messages, words that say: You're safe; try again; don't worry; you're doing fine; share that with us; we're glad to have you in our class; you're important; aren't we all lucky to have each other and learn from each other?

Of course, there will be unpleasant times in your classroom. Children fight, insult, and hurt each other. Sometimes you may feel exasperated; your temper will be short. Your supply of kindness and patience may be at rock bottom. However, children survive those times if they are infrequent. With all of our faults, children always forgive us when we teach in the key of life.

Introduce words of praise regularly and you will find that the stormy times become rare. "The wonder of me" is a lesson learned only through a living vocabulary.

SOME STARTERS

Children learn from everything we do. Sometimes, what to us is insignificant may make all the difference in a child's day. Barbara Kienzle[8] put it beautifully when asked what activities she initiates with her students to convey "the wonder of me": "We get in the habit of sharing our appreciation all the time—for things the kids do, make, show, tell, fix, help. It's just part of everything that goes on."

As you become more conscious of how "the wonder of me" can be added, like sugar and spice and everything nice, to whatever you are doing, you will no longer need these starters.

Begin at the beginning At the beginning of your time together, greet each child in a special way; note something special about each of them.

> Come in, Jamil. I see you have a new haircut today.
> Good morning, Debby. I like your Donald Duck bracelet.
> Hi, José. You're standing up so straight. What wonderful posture!

Start with taking attendance in a special way Even the most mundane activity such as taking daily attendance has possibilities for joyful components. Taking attendance can be a wake-up call if you experiment with such offerings as: "Boys

and girls, when your name is called today, tell us your favorite color" (or number, season, food, book, exercise, place, etc.)

You immediately get important information for your treasure chest of resources, and your students will be always on the alert for creative responses that share something of themselves in a safe environment. Add the special perk of sharing a success experience with your students first thing in the morning!

Include possibilities for nonverbal responses such as: "When your name is called, show us your muscles" (or make a funny face or stand your tallest, etc).

Start with a book Two of my favorite examples of old, favorite books that start children thinking about their unique selves are Leo Lionni's *Frederick*[9] and Robert Kraus and José Aruego's *Leo the Late Bloomer*.[10] Combining outstanding illustrations and texts, these books help children develop awareness and appreciation of their abilities and their growing process. Frederick the mouse gathers bright words and warm images for cold winter days. He is a poet. Leo, who never does anything right, grows in his own time. As he blooms, he discovers that he can write, read, draw, and eat neatly.

All of our children are Frederick and enjoy the challenge of gathering words to brighten our days. And all of our children bloom in their own time. After one of our first graders wrote a delightful poem about a turtle, he said, "Just call me Frederick!"

Start with taking photographs Criss-crossing the country, in all kinds of schools, I am thrilled to see photographs of the children mounted on bulletin boards, on their own "mailboxes," on locker doors, over coat hangers, on classroom doors. When we launch a school year by taking time to highlight every child in front of the camera, we are saying in a dramatic way, "You are an important and special person. Our class is composed of a unique group of individuals." Perhaps that is the first time many of our children have been hallowed.

Start with a riddle This kind of game helps children recognize and pay attention to each other in positive ways. "I'm thinking of a person in our class who just loves

playing in the sandbox better than anything in the world!" Or "I'm thinking of a person in our class who just got beautiful new glasses." Or "I'm thinking of a person in our room who tells funny stories about his baby sister."

Start with a special name tag So often I see children wearing the traditional square white name tags (boring!). Invite children to choose materials from a collection of shapes, words, letters, and designs and let them decorate their own name tags expressing their own interests, moods, and ideas, their own individualism. During the course of the school year, encourage the children to design a number of name tags so they have a choice for whatever occasion.

Start with highlighting a different child each week This yearlong activity is an important component of such humanistic teaching systems as the Workshop Way, developed by Sister Grace Pilon, and of many teachers' best projects all around the country. Simply described, it is a way of giving every child special recognition and attention, over and above daily awareness and appreciation. Each week, a different child is the "Child of the Week." Many activities celebrate the special child. For example, here are some suggestions from classes around the country:

A bulletin board is devoted to the child, who may bring in pictures, photos, and souvenirs.

The child wears a hat, badge, name tag, shirt, or belt made especially for the occasion.

The class interviews the child and asks prepared as well as spontaneous questions. Sometimes the teacher pulls together the information from the interview and creates a pictograph about the child. Sometimes the class makes a collage about the child, based on the interview conducted earlier.

The child picks a game for the class to play, a song to sing, and a special recess activity.

The child starts as leader in a game of follow-the-leader.

The child picks the story to be read at story time.

Children make up a song, dance, game, story, or poem about or for the child.

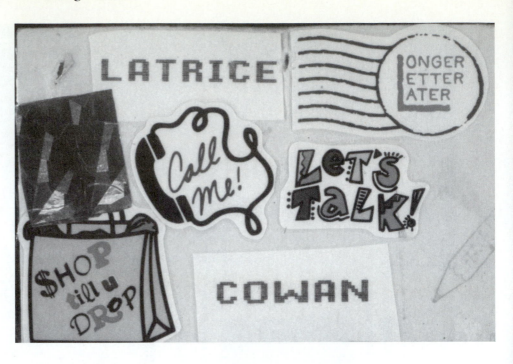

The child teaches a song, dance, or game. The child tells a story.

The child chooses a title to headline his or her name that week. An example comes from Linda Myer and Kathy Carter's[11] class, where one of the special children wanted to be known as *Patty Barker: Future Teacher.*

Classmates write special notes and letters and paint pictures for the child.

Sometimes, a party is given by the class to salute the child, and families and friends are invited. The child's bulletin board, collage, and crafts are featured. Songs, dances, and games are shared.

The special child can be selected in several ways. Few of the teachers I spoke with chose children in alphabetical order. As one teacher explained, "Kids with last names that start with T's and S's are always last for life when you use alphabetical order." She used a grab bag of blank papers, except for one paper that had a beautiful design on it. The child who picked the paper with the design was the next "Child of the Week."

Kathy Carter and Linda Myer explained that they selected the child, with an exciting ceremony, by drawing the name out of a hat or finding it magically written on the board. "This way," Kathy said, "we're not confined to a choosing system that doesn't give us flexibility. Sometimes a specific child will really *need* the extra attention the week gives. We want to be able to use the project to help those kinds through difficult times. Everyone gets a turn!" Kathy and Linda send home a list of the activities for the child's special week and invite families to cooperate and contribute stories, pictures, and photographs.

Note: Save a week for yourself and join the many teachers who enjoy being the VIP of the week.

Sign in From day one, teachers establish values and create positive learning environments in which children are taught that they are unique individuals whose ideas and experiences are highly regarded. I have seen many variations of what I call "sign in" charts and posters. The older children have no trouble immediately spotting a poster with colorfully printed instructions such as "Please sign your name," followed by informational categories such as "your lucky number," "your favorite animal," "your favorite holiday," or "ideas for field trips." The children sign their names and add their information or opinions under the indicated category space. By the end of the day, everyone has contributed. The chart is a resource for discussion, planning, art projects, creative writing, graphing, reporting, and decision making. Younger children need more explanation and directions for such responses, but they love to find their pictures on the chart, write the letters of their names next to their pictures (and printed names), and add samples of their favorite colors, shapes, designs, and animals.

TALK TIMES/LISTENING TIMES

Rebecca Kantor places the ideas, interests, and experiences of children at the very center of their learning. Her young students are constantly encouraged to develop their own observations and ideas through stimulating, challenging, enjoyable, open-ended discussions that evolve into diverse ways to expand those ideas.

In her lab program, Rebecca and her staff provide small collections of recyclable materials on open shelving throughout the room—materials and resources of every kind, fitting into every subject strand, are readily available. She explains:

> We are always talking and planning, exchanging ideas, finding ways to explore a topic. There's not a piece of the day that can't be opened up so that the children's ideas are at the center of what they're doing. Their interests are respected; their diversity is honored.

Talking in Rebecca's program is not limited to short answer responses in tightly scheduled time slots. Children have time to explore possibilities, elaborate on their ideas, and combine their own suggestions with others. Whether her students are brainstorming solutions for classroom problems or gathering options to celebrate a new season, they feel strengthened in their regard for their own opinions and those of others. They learn about their own uniqueness and the uniqueness of others in everything they say and do.[12]

When children feel secure and cared about, they become avid talkers and attentive listeners. "Our uniqueness" is an always fascinating topic for young children, as each day reveals changes and growth, new accomplishments, and new understandings. And don't just stop at talking and listening. Think across the curriculum; think of all the ways possible to enrich and develop ideas first articulated through talking!

I'm special because Your plan book must leave room for the surprise in store for you each day as the children walk (run?) into your room. Some days they are all bursting to tell some "news." Often, a few children have experiences or events to share. Creative teachers are always ready with conversation starters. Because they're observant, they notice a missing tooth, a new T-shirt, a shy smile, a mischievous twinkle, a defeated expression dimming the light in a child's eyes. Save time to talk about the ways we are special. Six-year-old Nick Wilbat thought about some of his unique qualities. He shared some of his findings:

> "I can run really fast. I still can't stop very good. I can jump high. I can even jump over my brother, Matt. I can roll like a ball and get dressed very fast. I can build really good stuff with Legos like my castle. . . . I give money to the poor people. I know a lot of stories. My birthday is on Valentine's Day. Know why July is my favorite? 'Cause of fireworks. Why is Matt special? 'Cause he's fun to be with. We're good dancers. We turn and jump and do tricks and we both pick up our toys."

When children are encouraged to honor their own special skills and interests, they are generous in turning their attention to others.

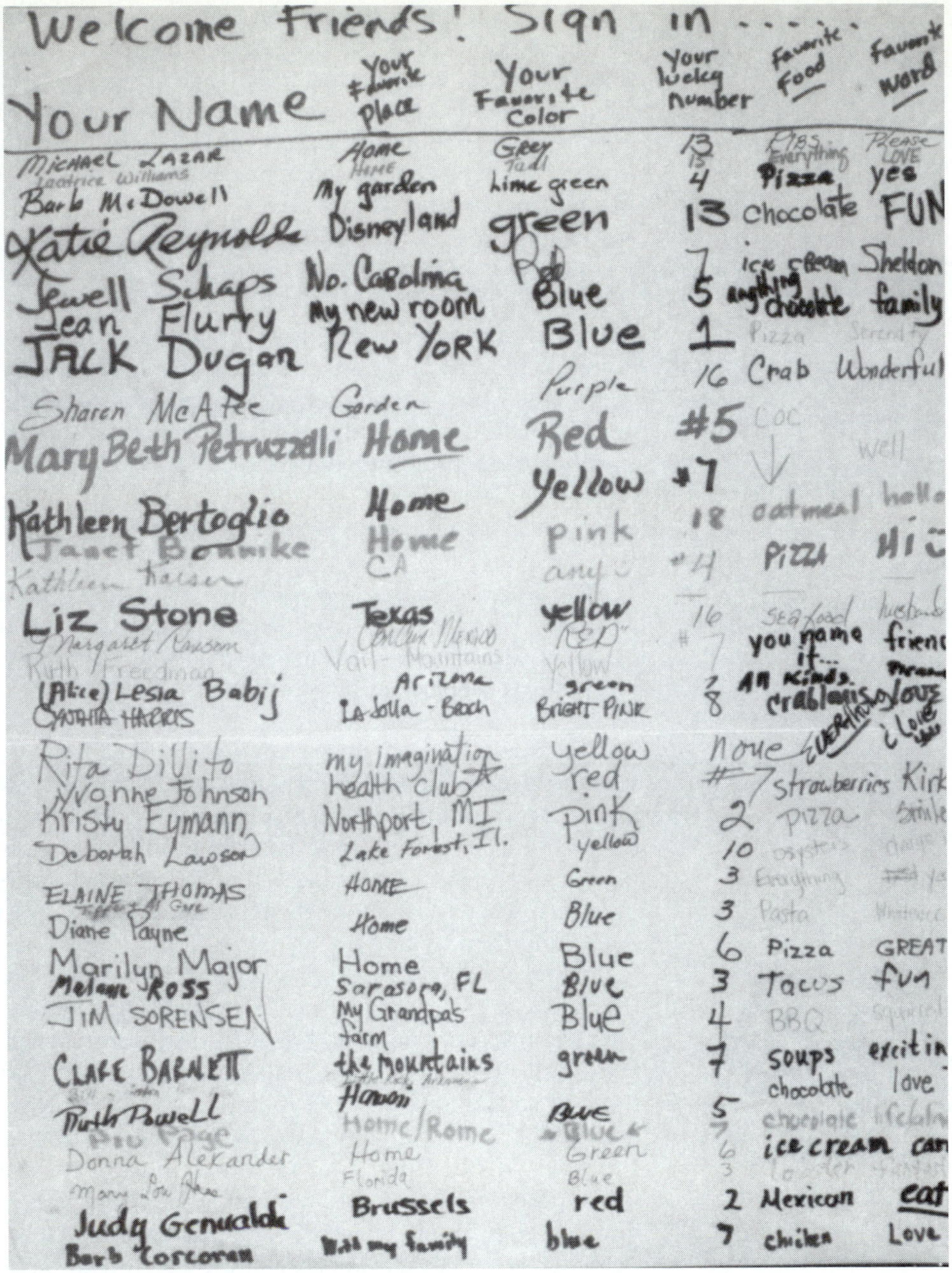

A handwritten sign-in sheet titled "Welcome Friends! Sign in..." with columns: Your Name, Your favorite place, Your Favorite Color, Your lucky number, Favorite food, Favorite word.

Imagine the delightful artworks following such talk times. Choreograph Nick's monologue! Use his words as lyrics to a new song! There is no end to possibilities.
Only me When Michael Joel Rosen talks with students of all ages, his conversation focuses on their special ways of seeing, of noticing, of remembering. As they talk of common experiences, Michael asks them to think about and share more surprising observations, more exceptional discoveries. "What did *you* see that we may have missed?" He encourages the students to think beyond their familiar experiences, to look more closely at their surroundings, to fill "their sensory banks." These discussions take shape in journal writing, sketch books, poems, and stories.
Imaginative questions Sometimes it's difficult for people to talk about themselves in factual terms. An enjoyable, challenging way of expanding self-expression and awareness is to invite the children to think of themselves in such unusual images as "What time of day are you—morning? night? What kinds of weather are

you? Which are you more like—an ocean or a mountain?" When Felicity Boxer-baum and Connie Swain[13] asked their students these kinds of questions, one of the boys answered, "I'm more like an ocean, 'cause an ocean changes a lot—sometimes calm, sometimes mad. That's me! Ocean!"

These comparisons, often turning into metaphors, are easily translated into creative writing, illustrations, collages, self-portraits, posters, dances, riddles, pantomimes, and musical compositions.

Keep asking, "what else?"

Memories Even the youngest children have collections of surprisingly rich memories. A popular topic of conversation is remembering "when we were little." Once the theme is established, it will be difficult to stop the flow of talk. "When I was a baby, I couldn't even turn over," reported Kyra. "But now I can do gymnastics!"

This topic inspires excellent movement possibilities that are shared later in this text.

All the things that I can do This is another source of delightful conversation. In one kindergarten the teacher added to a list that already covered two boards. Each day a few items were added as the children talked about them. This idea, as do all the others, spills over into art, music, movement, and drama. Each day provides opportunities to help children celebrate their abilities, differences, and unique qualities through talking/listening times—one to one, in small groups, and with the whole class.

Celebrate our marvelous imaginations Start talk sessions with observations such as these. Tad: "We can pretend we're a fish, but can a fish pretend he's us?"

Maria: "We can pretend to be a robot, but robots can't pretend anything." Kevin: "We can pretend we're monsters, but monsters can't pretend to be me."

Dreams I visited a kindergarten and found the children busy with an array of activities. Three children sat in a cardboard playhouse and talked softly. I listened for a few minutes as they told each other about dreams. Dreams are an important part of "the wonder of me." Adina told about a terrible nightmare she had the night before. "What was it about?" the others asked. "I dreamed that an elephant ate my sandwich!"

When your days are filled with talk times/listening times, you will find much to laugh about, care about, and share if you are alert and involved. You will have many opportunities each day to help children celebrate their countless "wonders." Talking about them is an excellent way to begin.

Encourage all of the children to participate. Sometimes a few children who are more verbal than the others may dominate the conversation. Taking turns is an excellent way to give each child a chance to talk. So is calling names: "Tasha, what was *your* dream about?" (Pause for a minute to give reluctant children a chance to respond). "If you can't think of a real one, make one up."

Made-up stories I will never forget Carmelita, who had nothing to contribute when she was called on to tell what she did on the weekend. Her teacher gave her the option of making something up. "I can't think of anything that really happened," Carmelita explained. Then her face lit up. "But here is a made-up story. . . ." She told a wonderful story about her dog (she doesn't have a dog) having three beautiful puppies. When she finished, one of the children said: "Carmelita, your made-up story was good." "What do we call that power to make up stories?" their teacher asked. "Imagination!" shouted an enthusiastic student, who tapped his forehead happily.

Word gatherings "Oh, my! We know so many words!" Think of it. Even your youngest children know (understand) words for things in the room and outside, things in their houses, people in their families, classmates, and animals. Talking about all the words we know leads to writing them, collecting them in "word boxes," and celebrating them in posters, collages, stories, poems, and songs. Part of our wonder is language, a dynamic process, the richest resource.

VISUAL ARTS TIMES

A room rich with materials and offerings We are all hunters and gatherers. Children are always hunting for unusual discoveries—pebbles, shells, twigs, leaves, Styrofoam packing chips, glittered greeting cards. . . . Gather materials. Sort them and make them available for many uses. Rebecca Kantor described her open-shelved, open-ended materials "everywhere." "If children want to write, pencils, pens, and markers are present and waiting all around the room. It's always the write time! Sometimes a particular material is the center of the children's attention. Perhaps they are fascinated by the possibilities of turning themselves into puppet characters. Today may be a day to decorate a forest scene with feathers, pebbles, and small pieces of colored cellophane. Today a child may feel 'blue' or want to paint the town red! Our uniqueness is expressed even in the choice of materials, even as we arrange commonly used materials. We are NOT carbon copies of each other." Flowers are *not* always red, nor is grass always green. A child in a class of a teacher who did not choose to teach in the key of life justified why he went out of the lines of his tree ditto: "My tree grew a branch."

Make something out of "nothing" From your ample collection of junk, children choose odds and ends to create works of art. These odds and ends may include toothpicks, stones, macaroni, shells, twigs, cloth scraps, pieces of wire, beans, pins,

beads, pieces of jewelry, and hanger wire. Use paste, glue, paper clips, tape, and wire to connect the parts.

Remember, all artists create something extraordinary out of the ordinary, and children, the best artists, need many opportunities throughout the year to exercise their imaginations and meet creative challenges.

Stars Every child is a star! Cut out stars of different shapes and colors and have each child choose one. In the center of the star, the children write their names, paste their photographs, and paint or color original designs. On each point of the star, help them to write a word that tells about their uniqueness. Spread the stars around the room so they brighten the walls and boards and give the children lots of places to look for words and pictures celebrating themselves.

Mind pictures An always delightful experience begins with having the children close their eyes. Sometimes simply inviting them to turn their minds into paintings or scenes is enough of a suggestion to launch satisfying visual arts activities, transferring their mind-pictures to paper! Or you might want to begin with a specific image: "Picture the sky. Is your sky clear or cloudy? Sunny or rainy? Under the sky is a field. What colors are your field? What textures? What season? Is there an animal in your field? A house? A fence?" As the children develop their ideas, their fingers will want to take brushes and crayons and depict their scenes.

One of my favorite series of suggestions is centered on trees, nests, and birds. First we stretch our bodies into strong tree shapes. Our arms, our limbs, our branches reach out and up. We imagine our colors, our leaves. Where would birds build a nest in our trees? And what if there were eggs in the nest, or hatched babies? Moving and imagining are magical ways to develop concepts, to express ideas, to demonstrate originality. The children's pictures or three-dimensional scenes of their trees, nests, birds, sky, and wind are souvenirs of an experience they will long remember.

Magic gardens Michael Rosen and a group of second graders in Columbus, Ohio, talked about seeds and gardens. They went from the real to the imaginary. "What if *everything* in the world grew from a seed? What would you plant in your garden?" The children bounced ideas around with enthusiasm. They would plant tennis-shoe seeds, bike seeds, swimming-pool seeds, ice-cream-cone seeds, even puppy seeds. The talk was followed by pictures of "my magic garden." Each child's garden was unique, reflecting individual interests and wishes.

What's in a name? Children love their names; anything that has to do with their names is a popular activity. Give each child a large piece of construction or drawing paper. Write or have the children write their names on the papers. Be sure the names stand out clearly. The children decorate their name posters by drawing pictures or designs and by cutting out and pasting pictures or words to the paper. Encourage them to draw or cut out pictures of things that mean something special to them, so the poster is a kind of personal collage. The children can also add photos of themselves to the poster. Join the activity and celebrate your name.

Silhouettes This popular project celebrates the faces of the children in your room. Tack white paper to the wall or board. Each child sits about six inches from the board. With a flashlight, slide projector, or opaque projector, throw light on the board and cast a shadow of the child's profile on the paper. Trace the outline. If the children are able, give them a turn to trace around the shadow and outline the profile on the paper. Cut out the silhouette.

The children enjoy choosing different colors for background mats for their silhouettes. Each child's immediately recognizable silhouette is a simple, enjoyable image. Variations include using the silhouette as the center of a collage of photos, illustrations, pictures, or words that tell about the child's favorite foods, places, hobbies, interests, and relationships. Joan Kalb[14] and her students feature their silhouettes with brief written statements about themselves in a display titled "We Are Special! Just Look at Us!"

Self-portraits Bring in an assortment of mirrors to be placed *carefully* on the ledge against the board or on shelves, or bring in a large dressing-room mirror. Invite the children to study themselves carefully and notice their own features.

Give out large pieces of paper and crayons or paint, and ask the children to color or paint pictures of themselves, self-portraits. Add names. Display all the self-portraits.

Children enjoy creating their own self-portraits as well as drawing or painting the portraits of their classmates. Give them many opportunities to celebrate themselves!

Dawn Heyman's third graders colored self-portraits but did not include skin color. This troubled Dawn, who cares deeply that children learn to love, respect, and accept themselves. She sat down with Audrea, with whom she had an especially close and loving relationship, and encouraged the child to find a color to match the "lovely, soft brown color of your skin." As they looked for the crayon that most closely matched Audrea's skin color, Nathan watched intently, then asked, "Miss Heyman, you wouldn't make fun of somebody's skin, would you?" Before she could answer, Nathan almost interrupted his own question by adding, "No, you would *never* make fun of us." Dawn did not need to reassure her students because they knew and loved her, but she reinforced her important message. "All of us are beautiful in our own shades, our own colors." By the time the session was over, every child had proudly added combinations of beiges, browns, and other flesh tones to depict his or her own skin color.

"Me" mobile Mobiles can be made many ways, but the easiest is the hanger mobile. The subject is "me" and the material is any picture, design, word, or image that reflects the uniqueness of that child. In one kindergarten class, a mischievous five-year-old, with great effort, tied a piece of chewed-up bubble gum to his mobile. When asked about it, he said "I chew so much bubble gum, my mom says I'm gonna turn into bubble gum!"

"Me" books Young children like to watch these books grow from a few blank pages to thick, colorful collections of feelings, ideas, favorite things, memories, and wishes. Many classes work on their books all year. These books run the gamut from randomly constructed, all-inclusive collections to well-organized presentations of selected topics, such as favorite foods and games, family, and plans.

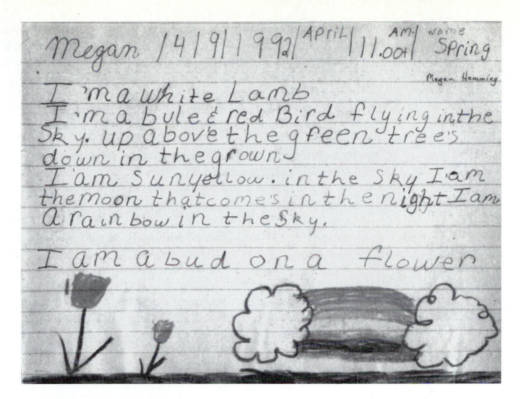

When children are free to choose what they want to include in their books, you will be in for some surprises. Kindergartner Eric glued in the first tooth that he lost. He asked his teacher to help him write the caption: "The tooth fairy gave me twenty-five cents for this tooth." Kimmy, almost five years old, taped a tiny pebble to a page in her book. "This is one of my treasures," she wrote, with a little help from a sixth-grade friend.

Aminah's amazing books Aminah Brenda Lynn Robinson is an artist of mud, buttons, ribbons, sticks, stones, shreds, clay, rags, glitter, and stitching. From found, collected, and scrounged materials, she creates extraordinary artworks.[15] She makes books out of everything, from the tiniest books hidden in pockets of pockets, in wheels, and in music boxes to books that unroll like scrolls. All her books are stories about her life, experiences, and interests. She inspires children of all ages to create their own books from scrounged and collected materials, to make books that reflect their uniqueness.

"I can . . ." mural Spread a large piece of paper across a chalk or bulletin board and encourage the children to think of all the things they can do. Share ideas *before* the pasting, writing, and drawing begin. Just talking about all the "I cans" gives such a boost to self-esteem that you may want to devote several sessions to this enthusiastic sharing of ideas.

Let four or five children at a time work on the mural (more, if it is larger). Each child writes his or her name and the word "can" after it. A word, drawing, or cutout picture follows the word "can."

Turn the mural into a follow-the-leader game with each child leading the others in performing or pantomiming the featured accomplishment.

A variation of this activity is to give the children large pieces of paper and invite them to make their own "I can" poster filled with as many of their accomplishments as there is room on the paper.

Pictures from our five sensational senses Devote shapes, images, and pictures to what we see, hear, feel, taste, touch, and smell. Encourage children to sharpen their senses and experience more of their world. Their painting, drawing, and sculpture reflect their sharpened awareness, their original ways of experiencing the world.

Clay play   Ancient traditional materials like clay that children can really "get into" are excellent vehicles for carrying the spirit of originality. In their research following 1600 children from Columbus, Ohio, as they explored ways of using clay to give shape to information, observations, feelings, and beliefs, Helen Lewis, Sara Smilansky, and Judith Hagan[16] painstakingly recorded their findings. The children clearly demonstrated development in perceptual, motor, emotional, cognitive, and artistic/creative areas. Giving children many opportunities to work and play in clay is really getting back to the basics.

"If they are to have the inner resources to make sense of the vast amount of knowledge that surrounds them, children must have time to experiment, to explore, to dream, to imagine: to simply 'fool around' and delight in living. . . . By engaging in the arts, children experience, interact, contemplate, integrate, discriminate, create—in other words, find ways to give meaning to those daily patterns of living which so easily can become monotonous and frustrating," the researchers wrote.[17]

Let clay be a symbol of our need to give our ideas shapes—to totally participate in the creative process. With heads, hearts and hands, we plunge in!

Potpourri   Our four nudges ("What else?" "What if?" "Show it!" and "Fake it!") will help you continue opening yourself to new materials, methods, and ideas in the interconnectedness of curriculum, in the often mysterious, magical, amazing, and surprising ways humans make sense out of it all. Whenever children are offered choices, are welcomed to open-ended challenges, are invited to be part of decision making and to express their ideas, they will delight you with their unique spirits. Join them!

MUSIC TIMES

The incredible creativity of the human family is demonstrated clearly through music. Every culture that ever lived on the planet Earth made/makes music! Chants, songs, lullabies, play songs, love songs, war marches, mourning dirges— the songs of every aspect of life are sung and played by the nations and tribes of the world. The human voice is astonishing in the variety of tones and sounds it can express. *Your* voice trained in another culture would adapt the qualities of singing familiar to that tradition. Listen to the high-pitched Japanese women's voices or the throbbing, exaggerated, strange-sounding (to American ears) dramatic voices of Chinese opera. Many men's voices from Middle Eastern cultures convey songs in low registers. Listen to mountain yodeling from Swiss villages; Macedonian women's voices loudly calling the community together; the mesmerizing blend of drumbeats and Native American chants made of vocables and phrases; pulsating, exciting rhythms of African tribal songs; hoarse, scratchy, whiny power-words of Bob Dylan; voices of the human family! Rap, madrigals, ditties, arias, spirituals, reggae, symphonic choirs—our planet throbs with musical rhythms, with songs. *The children will make music. The children will make songs.* They will sing in happier tones and melodies, however, if they are given numerous opportunities to express themselves through the language of music.

The following suggestions are only a few reminders of how easy it is to keep the music going. Add your own ideas!

Songs of sound   Children enjoy experimenting with different sounds and are quick to imitate new sounds that they hear. Part of the wonder of human beings is that we can make so many sounds. Discuss this idea with the children before you begin this activity.

Encourage each child to make up a sound and practice it for a few minutes in order to remember it. Sit in a circle and ask the children to begin making their sounds. Start with one child and continue until all the children are making their sounds at the same time. Then, one by one, each child stops until the last single sound is made.

Children may also use instruments or body claps to accompany their voices. They can hear the dramatic development from silence to crescendo and back to silence.

Another variation is to talk about animal sounds. "We can imitate most animal sounds, but most animals can't imitate human sounds!" Someone may mention parrots, which are an exception. "Let's make a song of animal sounds," one teacher suggested to her class after talk time. Each child contributed an animal sound as they built the rhythms in the manner described above. The result was fantastic! The children were so excited that they asked the teacher to tape it and play it for their parents at open house.

Our names are songs All of our names have rhythm. We can chant them, clap them, and turn them into wonderful music. Sit in a circle and invite the children to make rhythms out of their names. *Charley Anderson*—slow/slow/fast-fast-fast (clap it, snap it, stamp it, chant it). Try it another way. Stress different syllables. The group, of course, joins in. Shyer children need encouragement. Watch their expressions change when they hear their names turned into music! In one class the children enjoyed their name rhythms so much that the teacher called attendance by clapping their names.

Add rhythm instruments to enrich the experience—create a symphony of names. Add words to the name-songs (they do not have to rhyme). Here is an example composed by a group of first graders.

Elizabeth Ann Washington
(E LI za beth ANN WASH ing ton)
(slow/fast-fast-fast slow slow/fast-fast)
(soft/loud/soft-soft loud loud/soft-soft)
Elizabeth Ann Washington,
Elizabeth Ann Washington.
Plays the drum. Rum. Tum. Tum.
It's such fun. Drum. Drum. Drum.
Elizabeth Ann Washington.

Name-calling songs Once you realize how much children enjoy hearing their own names called, you will get into the habit of using their names in almost every song you sing. A well-known song such as "Michael, Row the Boat Ashore" can be used to celebrate each child in your class: "Denzil, row the boat ashore, hallelujah"; "Stacey, help to stem the tide. . . ."

There is an old chant that goes like this:

Hello everybody and clap your hands.
Clap your hands. Clay your hands.
Hello everybody and clap your hands.
And clap your hands today.

There are many variations of its "melody," so feel free to improvise. A class of four- and five-year-olds had fun with the song when they and their teacher changed it to:

Hello, Tim O'Brien, turn around.
Turn around, turn around.
Hello, Kira Kaplan, turn around.
Turn around today.

One kindergarten teacher reported that after a workshop in which this idea was discussed, her entire morning had been changed by using the children's names in

"Rockabye Baby." "Just before our rest time," she said, "I thought I'd try the idea with one of our lullabies. We always sing a lullaby before we rest—so I thought it would take only a few minutes, but the children were so entranced and waited for their turn before they *fell* and rested that it practically became our major morning activity! And today, as I came into the room, the children asked if we could do it again!"

> Rock-a-bye Nicole, on the tree top.
> When the wind blows, the cradle will rock.
> When the bough breaks, the cradle will fall.
> Down will come Nicole, cradle and all.

> The children sang with her, of course.

Songs like "He's Got the Whole World in His Hands" can be easily modified to celebrate each child:

> He's got Brett and Neal in His hands,
> He's got Gabriella and Misha in His hands . . .

A group of four-year-olds squealed with delight when we sang a special version of "The Bear Went Over the Mountain":

> The bear went over the mountain
> Who do you think he saw?
> He saw Rachel, Seth, and Billy
> He saw Laura, Bob, and Anthony
> He saw Billy Ray and Iris
> And who else did he see?
> He saw . . .

The wonder of me and my magical musical note One day Jani Aranow talked with her young students about how numbers are a special language for counting and letters are a special language for reading and writing. "There is a special language for writing music," she explained, and she showed them a music book filled with notes. They talked about whole notes and quarter notes, what notes look like on paper, and how people follow the notes when they play instruments and sing melodies.

Jani drew five long lines for a staff on large white paper taped to the wall. She gave each child a round "note" cut out of construction paper. The children colored and decorated their notes and wrote their names on them. One by one she called the children to put their notes somewhere in the four measures she drew on the paper. "Wherever you put your note will be a special sound. On the lines or between the lines." The children's notes filled the four measures.

Jani looked at the melody created by the children's notes and played it for them on the guitar. They were amazed at the sound. "Play it again!" She did. They realized that she was "reading" their notes and making the music from their special language. They added words to their song: "We love music. We sing all day. When the sun shines."

Gather songs. I saw a poster that read: *A bird doesn't sing because he has an answer, he sings because he has a song.* Sometimes we have more songs than answers. The number of songs we remember is often astonishing. Two-and-a-half-year-old Jessie received a double album of popular songs from her aunt. Three weeks later, when Jessie's aunt visited her again, Jessie knew every one of the *fifty-five* songs on the records!

In appreciation of the human mind, talk with your children about all the songs they know and remember. Begin a class list of songs and add to it daily. Sing as many of the songs as often as possible.

One kindergarten teacher encouraged the children to draw pictures and designs next to the song titles on the large song chart that was titled: "We Know All These Songs." Each day, a different child was appointed song leader and tacked his or her "helping-hand" name tag (see Chapter 1) beside the chosen songs. The teacher was surprised to see how quickly the children not only remembered the songs but also recognized the words and pictures describing the songs.

During my visit to this kindergarten, I admired the chart and praised the children. "You people know so *many* songs. How do you remember them all?" One small spokesman pointed to his head and said, "They all fit right in here!"

Pass the instruments around Once again, sit in a circle. Ask the children to shut their eyes and not to peek as you place rhythm instruments in their hands. Then they can open their eyes and explore their instruments. Ask a child to play a rhythm or melody on his or her instrument and have the others join in, one at a time, to accompany or play a variation until all the instruments are playing. Then signal each child to stop, one at a time, so that the music diminishes. Exchange instruments and begin again.

Part of the "our uniqueness" is the discovery that we have such a range of choices and abilities. "I played a hundred instruments today," a young musician puffed proudly.

Our own original songs Most ancient poetry was originally sung. Songs and poems are terms often used interchangeably by traditional cultures who honored all aspects of life with songs passed down through the ages.

Young children hum, sing, and chant their lives. They sing-song their experiences, they compose their own symphonies of daily life. In my gatherings, I have collected the "songs" of thousands of children who have given them titles, taught them to others, and added them to their own treasure chests of musical resources.

Shawn's proud song "I'm Big, I'm Big," Rosa's exciting song of anticipation about "Going to Grandma's for Easter," and Harry's funny ditty about "feeling silly silly silly" are all examples of the imaginative human spirit expressed in musical forms. Native American tribal chants have Songs for New Babies, Morning Songs, Songs for Winds, Songs for Rain, Songs for Recovery. Part of living each day is honoring that time with songs that mark events, feelings, and hopes.

Encourage your children to make songs about many relevant topics. There is *no* boring topic! I even heard a first grader softly singing a song about using an eraser!

Is it too obvious to remind you to share *your* songs, *your* music with your students? Bring the instruments you play into the classroom and enrich learning across the curriculum as the spirit of learning is hallowed. Tom Griffin's guitar is part of the life of his class. He plays songs the children sing together as well as songs he sings to them. He makes up songs about favorite stories and poems. Tom and his music are an important part of the *way* his students learn every day.[18]

MOVEMENT AND PLAY TIMES

As mentioned earlier, young children are movers and shakers. Marlene Robbins helps children move and shake in imaginative and often startling ways.[19] Trying to describe how Marlene moves with children is virtually impossible. It would be like trying to catch the magic of David Copperfield and conveying the "information" on the back of a cereal box! Ask Marlene about her work in movement with children, and she explains in poetic terms. Her eyes glow as she describes her students leaping around the gym higher, wider, more joyfully, lighter.

"When we were working on the Japanese folk tale, the Stone Cutter, we were playing with the idea of the kids doing a dance about the power of the sun—a sun dance. Each child, inside, would hold a spark of the sun and when we leaped into the scene, it would be as if the sparks of the sun were shining and shimmering. Even though we were all practicing basically the same movement—leaps—every child was different. They made their sun-sparked leaps their own. They flew through the space—each child original, each unique. . . ."

One of Marlene's favorite movement challenges is to work with all of the children using three basic movement ideas such as run, jump, and freeze, or timid, silly, and bold or forward, backward, and sideways. Even though everyone is centering on the common themes, "these same moves are different for each child. They stamp the movement with their own expressions, intensity, courage, sense of risk. They interpret it in their own ways—revealing their special qualities. Some kids are gentle, some humorous. Maybe Stuart feels rambunctious today. Pietro is thoughtful."

The movement will shape mood, feelings, and qualities of character.

"Remember," Marlene says with a grin, "even in a field of daisies, every petal is different! As a teacher, that's the joy—to see the look on the children's faces when they realize the ownership of what they do. You see the thinking and doing—the live child in front of you!"

No matter what the idea or theme, Marlene encourages the children to use their own interpretations, to assimilate suggestions in their own ways. She doesn't do dittos. She doesn't do formulas. As the students and teachers develop ideas together, comprehension deepens and imaginative ways of expressing those ideas evolve. Be open to the many possibilities inherent in any suggestion. Take a risk!

The wonder of growing Nothing celebrates "our uniqueness" as delightfully and effectively as discovering how we grow and what we can accomplish now that we could not accomplish before. This activity can be presented in a variety of ways. As you read the two general approaches described here, think about the many ways you would enjoy sharing the ideas and experiences with your students.

"Talk Time" introduces this activity. Talking about babies and when we were babies is probably one of the most popular topics of discussion for young children, who glow with pride as they realize their newly achieved powers.

The story of growing has been improvised and shared by thousands of young children. Every idea is expression in movement and drama as well as speech. Here is an example of part of the story told by teacher and children together as they interpret it through gestures, sounds, expressions, and movement.

> When we were very new babies, we were very tiny and small. How tiny and small can we make our bodies?
> We could hardly do anything except sleep (soft snore), make funny noises (googly goo sounds), and cry (Waaaaaaa!).
> We couldn't even turn over from our tummies to our backs or our backs to our tummies. We were stuck.
> We tried and tried to turn over. Lots of times. Finally, we did it! Turned over by ourselves. Yaaaaay.
> But, we couldn't turn back over and we kept trying and trying, until we finally did it! Yaaay.
> When we were babies, we didn't know that our hands and feet belonged to us, belonged to our bodies. We thought they were toys or mobiles.
> We couldn't even sit up by ourselves. Every time we sat up, we flopped right back over.
> But, we kept trying and trying to sit up and finally, one day, we did it! We sat up all by ourselves without falling over.

The story continues with crawling, reaching, standing, and walking. Each accomplishment is the result of great effort, patience, and determination. The development of the story is exciting and dramatic. After reenacting all the steps along the way, children burst into enthusiastic demonstration:

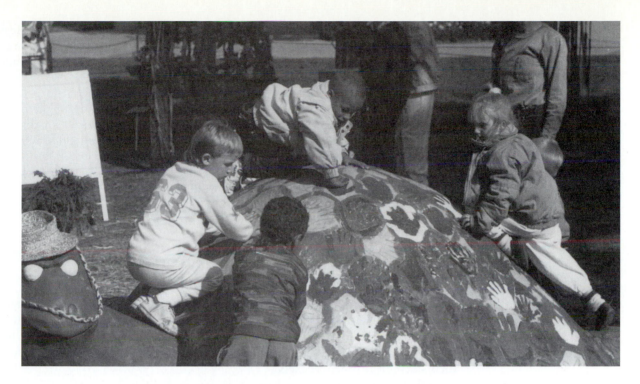

Now we can walk, lots of ways—quietly, noisily, tip-toe, sideways,
    backwards, bouncy, stiff, high, low.
We can hop, skip, jump, turn, leap, slide.
We can march, run, dance, race, prance, gallop.
We can . . .
There is no end to what we can do now that we are growing more
    every day. (Show us!)

This activity may take one twenty-minute session or it may be continued for
days. Add illustrations and creative writing.

Another approach to this activity takes one item at a time rather than developing the whole idea:

When we were babies, we couldn't even turn over.
Now we can turn over.
When we were babies, we could only crawl.
Now we can walk (explore).
When we were babies, we couldn't stand up without falling down.
Now we walk, run, hop, skip, and jump.

Try it another way Children are the true explorers. Through free-spirited experimentation, they make great discoveries and learn in satisfying ways. To avoid getting into ruts ("This is the way I do this, and don't show me any other way!") try
this fun challenge as often as possible. If you're walking, try to walk a different way.
How many ways can we sit? Let's experiment with thirty-six varieties of jumps! We
can change heights, stretch and bend, show angles, show curves, express qualities
such as bouncy, heavy, straight, crooked . . . we keep amazing ourselves!

Musical moves Welcome into your minds and hearts the rhythms and melodies
of diverse musical offerings and instruments. Shake out all preset choreography! Let
the music fill you. Let the music decide how you want to move! It is astonishing
how close to traditional movement patterns children dance in response to totally

unfamiliar music. Our bodies will move differently to Scotch bagpipes, to Mexican mariachi bands, to Appalachian dulcimers, to Russian balalaikas, to Arabic ouds, to percussive/brassy circus music, and to Peruvian flutes. Add creative writing; add illustrations. Create designs for the music and movement.

Magic Only human beings create magic tricks with imagination and a sense of fun. As one kindergartner observed, "Changing to a butterfly wasn't the caterpillar's idea!" Children are fascinated by magic and their earliest "trick" is hiding their faces and playing peek-a-boo. The following magic "tricks" celebrate what only human beings can do.

Magic show Talk with the children about magicians. Here are some ideas about magicians and magic from a group of kindergartners.

> Magicians do tricks.
> Magicians have special wands.
> Magicians make bunnies come out of hats.
> Magicians make things disappear.
> Magicians have tricky hands.

Scrounge around for colorful nylon squares to use as scarves. Find enough for all the children. Ask the children to close their eyes. Tell them you are going to put something magical in their hands. As soon as they feel it, they are to hide it somewhere in their clothing. You may have to help a few children hide their scarves up their sleeves or in their pockets.

When all of the children have their scarves hidden, the magic story begins. Here is an example of the kind of magic show we have shared with many early childhood classes.

> We have some magic scarves. But where are they? Are they in our hands? (Show fingers, front and back.) No. Are they in our mouths? (Open mouths). No. Are they in our ears? (Show ears.) No. Are they in our elbows? (Point elbows.) No. Are they in our noses? (Wiggle noses.) No. Where could they be? Are they under our arms? (Lift arms.) No. Are they under our feet? (Jump.) No. My goodness, where could the magic scarves be? (Children add ideas.)
>
> We need some magic words. (Work them out with your class.) Let's say the magic words. (The following incantation was created by a group of first graders.)
> *Abracadabra peanut butter and jelly*
> *Watch my magic tricks or I'll tickle you in the belly.*
> (Pull out the scarves and hold them up.) Here are the magic scarves. (Twirl them, wave them.) They can go anywhere they want to. They can make any designs in the air. They can make circles. They can make up and down lines. They can fly into the air and come down. (Throw the scarves into the air.) They can fly by themselves. (Throw the scarves up and blow them up higher.) They can fly in the air and land wherever they want to. (Throw the scarves up or blow them up and try to catch them on heads, arms, legs.)

"My scarf can land on the floor if it wants to!" said Mohammad. Rather than getting frustrated because his scarf kept missing his head and falling to the floor, Mohammad turned the situation into a trick.

Here are some more ideas for the magic scarves: Bunch them up in hands so they practically disappear and fling them suddenly into the air; turn them into butterflies and birds; turn them into flowers; spread them on the floor, turn them into horses' tails and gallop around; lay them down and blow them across the floor; put them together and turn them into a rainbow; drape them over chests or backs and turn them into queens' and kings' robes; and hold them up in front of faces, say the magic words, drop the scarves, and reveal the faces. Add your own.

This activity may be accompanied by music or an improvised story or poems.
Razzle dazzle   I like to kid around with teachers in workshops. I say, "When God gives you lemons, don't make lemonade! Make a lemon meringue pie! Or a lemon chiffon!" Years ago, my group of middle school folk dancers sang (with relentless repetition) a cheer from the high school that had a variation of the chant "Razzle Dazzle" and a few snappy handclaps. They sang it so many times on this particular long bus ride that when I tried to sleep that night, all I could hear was "Razzle Dazzle" and the clapping rhythms. The next morning, I made up a "cheer" for my classes at an early childhood program. By now, it has been enjoyed by thousands of all ages of kids throughout the country. It's a group celebration. It's a follow-the-leader activity. It feels good; try it (or something like it)!

Razzle dazzle (claps)
Razzle dazzle (claps)
Her name is Atina, she's like the sun
Her Razzle dazzle has just begun!

(Atina does something—anything. Everyone follows the clapping hands as the chant continues.)

Razzle dazzle (claps)
Razzle dazzle (claps).

We all have our own "razzle dazzles"! Make room to celebrate everyone and their own special contributions. Turn one of the sessions into a chart, marking the dazzling varieties shared. For example:

Our Razzle Dazzles
Kristen snaps her fingers.
Phuong does jumping jacks.
Shamika moon walks.
Juanita waves her arms.
    Keep adding!

Kids love cheers and gladly add movement and enthusiasm to the contagious playful spirit of cheers. The simplest:

Give me a T (T)
Give me an O (O)
Give me an M (M).
What does it spell? TOM! Yaaay!
(This will often turn grimaces to grins.)

DYOT and/or playing favorites   Even the youngest children understand something of their own uniqueness. We give information, directions, and suggestions to children. We demonstrate patterns and ideas. We offer them components of concepts. It's spread before them. The next step is to invite the children to *Do Your Own Thing*. For example, we practiced clapping and jumping and turning around. This gave us three ideas. After the children are familiar with the three ideas, suggest that they DYOT. Encourage them to arrange the material as they want to. Play with it! Or, I like to say, "Do your favorite part!" After a minute, I'll challenge them to "Change—show another favorite part!"

The children are constantly asked to come up with their own arrangements, with their own combinations. From day one, they realize that they are learning in the key of life and their handling of common materials is very individual and special.
What else?   At work, at play, moving or still, children learn to expand their thinking and their expressing when invited to show "what else" they can add to any idea.

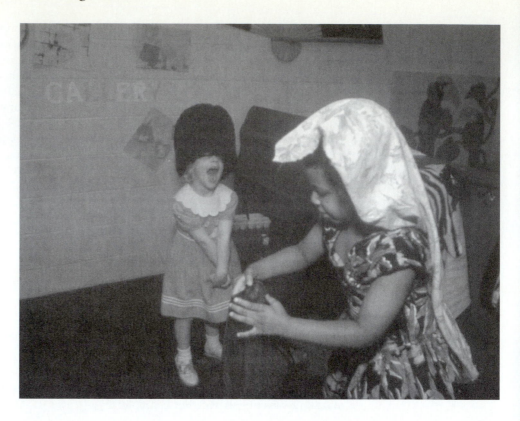

"What else were the Three Bears doing on their walk in the woods? Show us!" "What else can you add to the Wild Things Dance?" "What else can your leprechaun do to trick everyone?" "What else could Cinderella say to her fairy godmother?"

Birthdays Of all the holidays on the calendar, the most important holiday to each young child is his or her birthday. On that special day, the world revolves around the "birthday" child. "Six years old! Jon is six! Let's clap a six! Let's count to six. One. Two. Three. Four. Five. Six. What can we do *six times* for Jon's birthday?"

Here are just a few of the ideas suggested by young children: clap; snap fingers; stamp feet; turn around; hop; sit up; take bites of cake (imaginary); blow out candles; touch toes; wave; wiggle fingers; and do jumping jacks. Each action is performed six times in honor of the birthday.

We like to end our birthday celebration with six tricks. We play rhythmical music, from disco to dervish, and the children practice "tricks" such as balancing on one leg, waving their arms, and shrugging their shoulders.

Jokes and laughs One of the best wonders of being human is to make jokes, to make people laugh. Children have a marvelous wild and wacky sense of humor. They seem to be tickled by certain things at particular ages. For years and years I have experimented with early childhood children from ages two to five with variations of similar kinds of humorous ideas. Often what sends three-year-olds into explosions of laughter triggers cool and sophisticated (over the hill) four-and-a-half-year-olds to shake their heads and say, "Mim, you're so silly!" with hardly a smile. Play around. Find the kinds of situations that your students really enjoy. Discover how many ways you can celebrate times of laughter. Children don't need to be told to "play" or to "act out" a story or to "show you" with their bodies. They already know those languages. Our job is to see that they are strengthened in their confidence and joy in continuing creative and healthy means of expression!

Masks, wigs, costumes, and props help children play out real life situations, fantasy scenes, storybook themes, schemes, and dreams. One idea can continue indefinitely. First graders loved Diane Paterson's *Smile for Auntie*[20] as they demonstrated eager little people trying to make a grouchy huge person smile. Their ideas to get the grouchy person smiling took every possible form from body shapes to body tricks to dialogue to joke-telling.

Humans laugh! Laughter in your room (not put-down, ridiculing laughter, but healthy, positive, sharing humor laughter) is like music!

Shadows On a sunny day, go outside with your children and study their shadows. Depending on which way they face, they will discover that: their shadows are behind them; their shadows are in front of them; no matter how fast they run, they will always be ahead of, or behind, their shadows; and no matter what shape they make with their bodies, their shadows will do the same. Talk about shadows. Experiment with shadows. Read poems about shadows. Robert Louis Stevenson's "My Shadow" is a classic.

Take "sense walks" On clear days, take the children for walks to celebrate the five senses. Take a *sound* walk and listen to everything you see. Take a *smell* walk and focus on the smells along the way. Take a *touch* walk. Experience the different textures of tree bark, leaves, pebbles, dirt, grass, and flowers. Follow up this activity with art, music, poems and stories, talk, and creative dramatics when you return to the classroom.

Children who use only one speed My favorite metaphor to remind children to use all their powers goes like this: "Kids, if you have ever heard of a ten-speed bike, clap your hands (or stamp feet or wiggle noses). Kids, if you have ever seen anyone ride a ten-speed bike, hold up ten fingers" (or blink ten times). After establishing that the children are familiar with a ten-speed bike, I tell this story.

> Once there were kids who had ten-speed bikes (show me ten fingers). But, they used only one speed (show me one finger). When they went up hills, they could hardly pedal (pantomime effort and strain). When they went down hills, they practically fell off (wobble). We met these kids and said, "You have ten speeds; why are you using only one?" Those kids looked surprised. "We forgot about our other speeds. Thanks for reminding us!" Now they use all ten speeds, all their powers. They go up and down hills. Easy!

Then we talk about how we have even more than ten speeds. We have so many powers, but sometimes we use only one.

For the rest of the year, the children use the metaphor to remind themselves and each other to do more, not less; to expand, not shrink.

Ten-Speed Jumps, Ten-Speed Runs

We can jump only a short distance off the floor (speed one).
We can jump a little higher (speed two).
All the way to *ten* and we're flying off the floor with high, high jumps!
(Do the ten-speed runs outdoors or in an indoor area with lots of space.)
Everyone runs in a large circle, in the same direction.
We start with a slow-motion run (speed one).
We run a little faster (speed two).
All the way up to our fastest ten speed.

Remember—Education is a moving, playful experience!

CLASSROOM VISITORS AND FIELD TRIPS

As with all suggestions, *how* you envision an idea and *what* you do with that idea shapes its effectiveness and determines its life. Classroom visitors and field trips are *events* in the lives of young children. Maximize their potential for inspiring enriching experiences. Before visitors arrive, the children are ready with interesting questions, curiosity, and active listening. Visitors will present ideas possible for adaptation by you and your students. Try them! Children follow visitors and field trips with letters, pictures, and projects inspired by those programs. It's up to you to either celebrate creatively all that is possible within an experience or minimize it, limiting the experience to its allocated hour in your schedule.

Classroom Visitors

Baby This visitor will definitely enrich the activities about growing described in this guide. If one of your students has a baby sister or brother, invite the parent and baby to your classroom. The children will see how little, helpless, and uncoordinated the baby is. Watch your students stretch with newly emerging self-image as you wonder aloud, "I bet this baby wishes he could do all the wonderful things these big kids can do! Don't worry. He'll be able to do them when he grows up some more."

Artist This visitor can help children discover the creative process by starting with a blank paper or board and filling it with people, animals, shapes, and colorful designs. Cartoonists are especially delightful classroom visitors.

Magician Invite a magician to talk about how he or she learned magic as well as to demonstrate magic tricks. Ask your guest to teach the children a simple trick.

Poet On a blank piece of paper, the poet scribbles lines and curves that magically become letters and words and eventually poems.

Weaver This person's work is intriguing to watch. Encourage the visitor to share a skill with the children, such as making pot-holders or lacing cardboard with material.

Inventor Ask the inventor to tell the children the story of his or her invention in order to illustrate originality and innovation. Children should be encouraged to try inventing something themselves.

Storyteller Storytellers are excellent examples of creativity in action. They may tell a familiar story in their own way. They encourage children to think about the universality of storytelling and the individuality of every storyteller. Often the children's discovery of common themes or common story types is exciting and guaranteed to enrich their learning and appreciation.

Musician I hope your room is always open to music makers from every culture and background. When children practice enjoying the music of many instruments, voices, and peoples, they become advocates of the uniqueness of the human spirit.

Interior designer/Decorator Here is an empty room. What colors, furniture, draperies, and designs change it into a special room? After a decorator visited a first-grade class, Nikki announced, "Now I know what to be when I grow up!"

Cake decorator Children need to learn that creativity and imagination play important roles in more surprising areas, such as cake decorating.

Any person involved in an activity that features improvisation, arrangements, rearrangements, combining patterns, making something out of "nothing," or filling blank spaces and time is an excellent resource for demonstrating originality.

Field Trips

Sculpture or pottery class Children discover how responsive human beings are to natural materials like clay, stone, and wood. Out of the materials nature provides, people make original shapes and designs that are both useful and beautiful.

Community or high school theater The children will have an outstanding experience whether the set is being constructed or the stage is set for a play. Ask the manager if the children can walk carefully on the stage. Talk about the play that will be performed. What kinds of things are on the stage? What kind of scene is it? Discuss the power of imagination and the need for people to "make believe," whether they are children or adults.

Gymnastics class in a school or community center After experimenting with so many "tricks" themselves, the children appreciate the mind-body coordination that results in spectacular gymnastic combinations. Stress practice, good health habits, and confidence as essential qualities of a gymnast. Ask the instructor to show the children an easy gymnastic exercise.

Jazz group Improvisation should be stressed on this field trip. Children discover that jazz musicians play what they feel as they respond to the other instruments. They "make up" the music as they play it. They create new musical arrangements— the process becomes the product.

Arts festival What an experience in imaginative possibilities! Aren't human beings fascinating?

IT ALL COMES TOGETHER

Take a group of children. Mix them with an interesting, relevant idea. Blend in high-quality materials and resources and there's no end to exciting possibilities.

Debbie Charna's students enjoy such books as *I'd Like to Be*[21] and *I'm Terrific*.[22] Both books inspire the children to recognize their uniqueness, to accept their own strengths and weaknesses, and to recognize their own special gifts. Debbie and her students read and talk, talk and read. They discuss "things they're really good at and things they want to improve in." Debbie reassures them with the revelation that "no one is perfect at everything!" The children draw pictures of those areas they're "really good at." They chart the areas in which they want to show improvement. They turn their interests, skills, and qualities into pantomime, games, and riddles. "Guess what hobby I really love!" (show it). They have a parade of "Terrific People." They become experts at specific skills, crafts, and techniques. Debbie tells how a reluctant, not very confident boy found that he could sculpt beautiful shapes out of clay. Many of the ideas discussed and read were shaped into clay objects by Jim. Soon, the children referred to Jim as our "clay expert." Jim's increase in self-confidence was visible. The "We're Terrific" board displays illustrations, portraits, posters, creative writing descriptions, charts, and stars (all the children have stars with descriptive words written on each point). "Practice helps us improve," Debbie says. The children discover daily through myriad activities and exchanges that they are each unique individuals and, as one child summarized, "being *me* is the best of all!"[23]

Remember the four little nudges for creativity:

1. What else? (more more more)
2. What if? (wonder, imagination)
3. Show the idea! (so many ways)
4. Fake it! (Porridge!)

NOTES ❤

1. Martin O'Connor, *Miracles*, edited by Richard Lewis. New York: Bantam, 1977, p. 146.
2. Red Grammer, "See Me Beautiful," from *Teaching Peace*. Children's Group c/o B.M.G. Distribution, 1133 Avenue of the Americas, New York, NY 10036–6758; (212) 930–4000.

3. I wrote about Jackie Cohen in an article, "On the Trail with Jackie." Mimi Brodsky Chenfeld, *Day Care and Early Education*. Summer, 1990, pp. 35–37. Reprinted in *Teaching in the Key of Life*. Washington, DC: NAEYC, 1993. pp. 50–54.

4. Cindy Lalli is the principal of Indianola Informal Elementary School in the Columbus, Ohio, Public Schools. Indianola's Arts Team has been highly acclaimed.

5. Dr William Dwyer is the principal of Duxberry Park Arts Impact Elementary School in the Columbus Public Schools. Duxberry Park was the recipient of *Redbook* magazine's Certificate of Recognition as one of the 177 best schools in the country in 1993.

6. Mrs. A. Joseph Marsh, "Letters to a Fledgling Teacher." *Early Years,* September 1975, pp. 36–37.

7. Elizabeth Hunter, "Tuning into Children." *Childhood Education*. October 1975, pp. 13–19.

8. Barbara Kienzle is a teacher at Hamilton Alternative Elementary School, Columbus Public Schools, Columbus, Ohio.

9. Leo Lionni, *Frederick*. Pinwheel, 1973.

10. Jose Aruego, *Leo the Late Bloomer*. Simon & Schuster, Windmill, 1971.

11. At the time, Linda Myer and Kathy Carter taught at Worthington Hills Elementary School in Worthington, Ohio.

12. Rebecca Kantor is associate professor of Early Childhood at Ohio State University. She directs the A. Sophie Rogers Lab for Children and Family Studies.

13. At the time, Felicity Boxerbaum and Connie Swain team-taught at Worthington Hills School, Worthington, Ohio.

14. Joan Kalb teaches in Woodward School, Delaware Public Schools, Delaware, Ohio.

15. Aminah Brenda Lynn Robinson illustrated *Elijah's Angel* (story by Michael Joel Rosen; San Diego: Harcourt Brace Jovanovich, 1992), and *The Teachings* (drawn from African-American spirituals; San Diego: Harcourt Brace Jovanovich, 1992).

16. See Sara Smilansky, Judith Hagan, and Helen Lewis, *Clay in the Classroom*. New York: Teachers College Press, 1988.

17. Ibid. P. 173.

18. Tom Griffin teaches at Cassingham Elementary School in the Bexley, Ohio, public schools.

19. Marlene Robbins is the dance specialist on the Arts Team at Indianola Informal Elementary School and Reeb Elementary School, Columbus, Ohio.

20. Diane Paterson, *Smile for Auntie*. Dial, 1976.

21. Steven Kroll, *I'd Like to Be*. Illustrated by Ellen Appleby. New York: Parents Magazine Press, 1987.

22. Marjorie Weinman Sharmat, *I'm Terrific*. Illustrated by Kay Choroao. New York: Holiday House, 1977.

23. Debbie Charna teaches in the Evening Street School, Worthington, Ohio.

BOOKS FROM MY KNAPSACK FOR CHILDREN ♥ ♥

Akass, Susan. *Number Nine Duckling*. Illustrated by Alex Ayliffe. New York: St. Martin's, 1993.

Bradbury, Ray. *Switch on the Night*. Illustrated by Leo and Diane Dillon. New York: Knopf, 1975.

Bruchac, Joseph. *The First Strawberry*. Illustrated by Ann Vajtech. New York: Dial Books for Young People, 1993.

Burningham, John. *Aldo*. New York: Crown, 1992.

Cazet, Denys. *Born in the Gravy*. New York: Orchard, 1993.

Cole, Babette. *The Silly Book*. New York: Doubleday, 1990.

Cole, Sheila. *The Hen That Crowed*. New York: Lothrop, Lee & Shephard, 1993.

Collins, Annabel. *You Can't Catch Me*. Boston: Little, Brown, 1993.

Denslow, Sharon Phillips. *Bus Riders*. Illustrated by Nancy Carpenter. New York: Four Winds, 1993.

Diaz, Jorge. *The Rebellious Alphabet*. Illustrated by Oivind S. Jorfald. New York: Henry Holt, 1993.

Exley, Helen, ed. *What It's Like to Be Me*. New York: Friendship, 1984.

Fleming, Virginia. *Be Good to Eddie Lee*. Illustrated by Floyd Cooper. New York: Philomel, 1993.

Frasier, Debra. *On the Day You Were Born*. Illustrated by Debra Frasier. San Diego: Harcourt Brace Jovanovich, 1991.

Greenfield, Eloise. *Daydreamers*. Illustrated by Tom Feelings. New York: Dial, 1981.

Haldane, Suzanne. *Helping Hands: How Monkeys Assist People Who Are Disabled*. New York: Dutton, 1991.

Hartmann, Wendy. *All the Magic in the World*. New York: Dutton, 1993.

Henkes, Kevin. *Chrysanthemum*. Illustrated by Kevin Henkes. New York: Greenwillow, 1991.

———. *Sheila Rae, the Brave*. Illustrated by Kevin Henkes. New York: Greenwillow, 1987.

Hoffman, Mary. *Amazing Grace*. Illustrated by Caroline Binch. New York: Dial, 1981.

Hopkins, Lee Bennett, ed. *Happy Birthday*. Illustrated by Hilary Knight. New York: Simon and Schuster, 1991.

Horton, Barbara Savadge. *What Comes in the Spring?* Illustrated by Ed Young. New York: Knopf, 1992.

Howard, Jane R. *When I'm Sleepy*. Illustrated by Lynn Cherry. New York: Dutton's Children's Books, 1985.

Howe, James. *I Wish I Were a Butterfly*. Illustrated by Ed Young. San Diego: Harcourt Brace Jovanovich, 1987.

———. *Rabbit-Cadabra*. Illustrated by Alan Daniel. New York: Morrow Junior Books, 1993.

Huck, Charlotte, ed. *Secret Places*. Illustrated by Lindsay Barrett George. New York: Greenwillow, 1993.

Hudson, Wade. *Pass it On—African American Poetry for Children*. Illustrated by Floyd Cooper. New York: Scholastic, 1993.

Huston, Gloria. *My Great Aunt Arizona*. Illustrated by Susan Condie Lamb. New York: HarperCollins, 1992.

Johnson, Angela. *Do Like Kyla*. Illustrated by James E. Ransome. New York: Orchard, 1989.

———. *The Girl Who Wore Snakes*. Illustrated by James E. Ransome. New York: Orchard, 1993.

Johnson, Delores. *The Best Bug to Be*. Illustrated by Delores Johnson. New York: Macmillan, 1992.

Karas, Jacqueline. *The Doll House*. Illustrated by Judith Riches. New York: Morrow, 1993.

Kherdian, David. *By Myself*. Illustrated by Nonny Hogrogian. New York: Henry Holt, 1993.

King-Smith, Dick. *Ace, the Very Important Pig*. Illustrated by Lynette Hemmant. New York: Crown, 1990.

Kirby, David, and Woodman, Allen. *The Cows Are Going to Paris*. Illustrated by Chris Demarest. Ottowa, IL: Caroline House, 1991.

Kiser, SuAnn. *The Catspring Somersault Flying One-handed Flip-Flop*. Illustrated by Peter Catalanotto. New York: Orchard, 1993.

Krementz, Jill. *How It Feels to Fight for Your Life*. New York: Knopf, 1990.

Kroll, Virginia. *Masai and I*. Illustrated by Nancy Carpenter. New York: Four Winds, 1992.

Lear, Munro. *Ferdinand*. Illustrated by Robert Lawson. New York: Viking, 1936.

Macauley, David. *Black and White*. Illustrated by David Macauley. Boston: Houghton Mifflin, 1990.

Mandelbaum, Pili. *You Be Me, I'll Be You*. Illustrated by Pili Mandelbaum. Brooklyn: Kane/Miller, 1990.

Markum, Patricia Maloney. *The Little Painter of Sabana Grande*. Illustrated by Robert Casilla. New York: Bradbury, 1993.

Marshall, Rita. *I Hate to Read*. Illustrated by Etienne Delessert. Mankato, MN: Creative Editions, 1992.

Marzollo, Jean. *Close Your Eyes*. Illustrated by Susan Jeffers. New York: Dial, 1978.

Mathers, Petra. *Maria Theresa*. New York: HarperCollins/Harper Trophy, 1992.

McCully, Emily Arnold. *Mirette on the High Wire*. Illustrated by Emily McCully. New York: Putnam, 1992.

McLerran, Alice. *Roxaboxen*. Illustrated by Barbara Cooney. New York: Lothrop, Lee & Shephard, 1991.

Mendez, Phil. *The Black Snowman*. Illustrated by Carole Byard. New York: Scholastic, 1989.

Merriman, Eve. *The Singing Green—New and Selected Poems for all Seasons*. Illustrated by Kathleen Collins. New York: Morrow, 1992.

Moss, Thylias. *I Want to Be*. Illustrated by Jerry Pinkney. New York: Dial, 1993.

Pfister, Marcus. *The Rainbow Fish*. Illustrated by Marcus Pfister. New York: North-South Books, 1992.

Robinson, Nancy. *Ten Tall Soldiers*. Illustrated by Hilary Knight. New York: Henry Holt, 1991.

Roy, Ron. *Move Over, Wheelchairs Coming Through!* Photographs by Rosemarie Hauserr. New York: Clarion, 1985.

Scarry, Richard. *Things to Love*. Illustrated by Richard Scarry. Racine, WI: Golden, 1987.

Scieszka, Jon. *The Frog Prince Continued*. Illustrated by Steve Johnson. New York: Viking, 1991.

Shields, Carol Diggory. *I Am Really a Princess*. Illustrated by Paul Meisel. New York: Dutton Children's Books, 1993.

Trivizas, Eugene. *The Three Little Wolves and the Big Bad Pig*. Illustrated by Helen Oxenbury. New York: Macmillan, 1993.

Van Laan, Nancy. *The Tiny, Tiny Boy and the Big, Big Cow*. Illustrated by Marjorie Pressman. New York: Knopf, 1993.

———. *People, People Everywhere*. Illustrated by Nadine Bernard Westcott. New York: Knopf, 1992.

Vertreace, Martha M. *Kelly in the Mirror*. Illustrated by Sandra Speidel. Morton Grove, IL: Albert Whitman, 1993.

Weisner, David. *Tuesday*. Illustrated by David Weisner. New York: Clarion, 1991.

Weiss, Nicki. *An Egg Is an Egg*. Illustrated by Nicki Weiss. New York: Putnam, 1990.

Wild, Margaret. *All the Better to See You With*. Illustrated by Pat Reynolds. Morton Grove, IL: Albert Whitman, 1992.

Wilson, Beth P. *Jenny*. Illustrated by Delores Johnson. New York: Macmillan, 1990.

Young, Ruth. *Golden Bear*. Illustrated by Rachel Isadora. New York: Viking, 1993.

BOOKS FROM MY KNAPSACK FOR TEACHERS 💜 💜

Armstrong, Thomas. *In Their Own Way*. Los Angeles, Jeremy Tarcher, 1987.

Bredekamp, Sue. *Developmentally Appropriate Practice*. Washington: NAEYC, 1987.

Carlson, Laurie. *Kids Create: Arts and Crafts Experiences for 3–9 Year Olds*. Charlotte, VT: Williamson, 1990.

Coleman, D., Kaufman, P., and Ray, M. *The Creative Spirit*. New York: Dutton, 1992.

Duckworth, Eleanor. *The Having of Wonderful Ideas and Other Essays on Teaching and Learning*. New York: Teachers College Press, 1987.

Hamilton, Martha, and Weiss, Mitch. *Children Tell Stories*. Katonah, NY: Richard Owen, 1990.

Isenberg, Joan P., and Jalongo, Mary R. *Creative Expression and Play in the Early Childhood Curriculums*. New York: Merrill/Macmillan, 1993.

Johnson, James, Christie, James, and Yawkey, Thomas. *Play and Early Childhood Development*. Glenview, IL: Scott Foresman, 1987.

Koral, April. *A Great Wave of Immigration*. New York: Franklin Watts, 1992.

Lazear, D. *Seven Ways of Knowing*. Pallatine, IL: Skylight, 1992.

LeShan, Eda. *What Makes You So Special*. New York: Dial, 1992.

Piaget, Jean. *Play, Dreams and Imagination*. New York: Norton, 1951.

Polloway, Edward; Patton, James; and Payne, R. *Strategies for Teaching Learners with Special Needs*. Columbus, OH: Merrill, 1989.

Samples, Bob. *The Metamorphic Mind: A Celebration of Creative Consciousness*, 2d edition. Rolling Hills Estates, CA: Jalmar, 1992.

Part 2

Our Families/Our Friends

Others We Meet/Our Worlds Widen

Our Natural World/Our Environment

Chapter

4 Our Families, Our Friends

". . . A family is like a building. . . . If you take a part of it out, it all collapses. So—you have to keep them together. . . . Make sure that even if your parents are divorced, you don't get into the problems they're in.

Friends are kind and nice. They share with you. . . . They understand each other. All the things friends are, families should be to each other. . . ."
Natalie, age 8

THE BASICS

All human endeavors are performed as we move through time, even the writing of a book such as this one!

As I begin this chapter, which combines the themes of Our Families and Our Friends chapters from the first edition, Callie Rose is three months old. Oh, how intently she looks at everyone and everything. Listen to her cooing, chirpy infant language. Smiling, she snuggles to the comforting conversation of her soft-voiced, gentle mother. So familiar and reassuring is the loud, deep, excitable voice of her cheering, jeering dad, who is watching his beloved Chicago Bulls on TV, that she swings serenely in the midst of the Bulls' fans shouting around her!

Remember Callie's big cousin, Len, "the Muffin Man"? He's a year and a half and has a new nickname: "Jelly." He's a ballplayer, puzzle doer, book "reader," and phone "talker." He's hooked on that popular TV dinosaur character, Barney. Clapping and dancing, he recites his numbers and letters. He loves all kinds of music, but most of all, he adores the two most important people in his world—those two words on the list of his "key vocabulary"[1]—Mama and Dada.

Almost four and a half, Kimani is a sharp, funny, smart, kind boy. He knows his phone number, his address, and his numbers. He recognizes and names everything around him but especially his favorite people: his parents, his baby brother Jared, his Grandma Matty and his baby-sitter, Keneisha. Ask Kimani about his family, and he'll name those people as well as his turtle, Shelley, his aunts, his cousins, his neighbors "across the street," and his "next door's dog, Pharaoh."

The young of the human species are not like sea turtles left to hatch themselves then run for their lives to the water. They are not like insects, curled in cocoons until they must wing it on their own. The most helpless of all infants, human babies are totally dependent on the care of others. Why? Maybe a first grader had the best answer of all when he explained, "That's so we have to help each other."

Callie Rose, Len, and Kimani are lucky children. They live in warm, secure, loving homes where they are encouraged, reassured, and cherished. Each of them receives many more than their minimum daily requirement of twelve hugs.

Tragically, many of our children are not so lucky. They are born into families that *don't* hold them, talk to them, sing to them, or reassure them with sheltering arms. While Len, Callie, and Kimani are learning lovingness, too many of our country's babies are learning loneliness. While Callie holds our fingers as tenaciously as a hand grips a lifeline, how many of our babies reach for hands that aren't there, cry for food that never satisfies, or lie in wet beds waiting for diapers to be changed, waiting for their lives to be changed?[2]

Bob Dylan's always relevant song, "The Times They Are a Changin'" wails and strums to the cacophony of alarming statistics and discordant dialogues about families and family values.

Who decides the composition of *family* anyway? And what definitions of *family* will meet with majority approval? Our traditional definitions are out of synch with the realities of these changing times. While our leaders agonize over terminology, definitions, and statistics, our children *live* the statistics and the definitions.

Here are some of our children's family situations. These are just a few simple facts, not explanations of the quality of life provided to the children. (As you know, a single-parent family may be one of security and joy, while a seemingly intact two-parent, more traditional family may be overly strict and harsh. Look past statistics. Look past labels. *Look to the children.*)

- Molly lives with her grandmother.
- Jose lives with his father, stepmother, three siblings, and one niece. On weekends he lives with his mother, her boyfriend, and a new baby.

- Justin and Daryl live with their mother. They rarely see their dad.
- Senta's father has custody of Senta and her two brothers. One weekend a month she visits her mother and her mother's "friend," Aunt Vicki.
- Han Su lives with the third foster family since he started school two years ago. He hardly ever sees his brother, who lives with another foster family.

We could go on. And on and on.

Who decides the definition of family anyway?

Fifteen-year-old Tony, abused and neglected by his parents, wanted only one thing. On all his wish lists, he printed in block letters, "Get hugs and kisses like everyone else." He endured indescribable hardships before he "escaped" and was taken from his parents and adopted by new parents. How did he survive with his spirit so miraculously strong?

"... A patchwork of characters had provided a soul-saving counterpoint to the soul-killing world he knew at home. ... There were teachers who instilled in him a sense of self-respect; the Muppets and the make-believe neighborhood of Mister Rogers. ... There was PG, a stray cat, ... most of all, there was a best friend named David, who escaped his own unhappy home by taking care of his schoolmate. ..."[3]

Thousands and thousands of teachers across the country have heard Don Bartlett's own story about an unbearable childhood of physical disabilities, total rejection, abuse, and alienation from family as well as teachers and classmates. One woman in his town befriended him, believed in him, and helped him. Don is now a Ph.D., a professor, an educator, and a national lecturer. To me, the most moving words of his emotionally hitting lectures are these: "I just wanted what every child wants—someone to walk along with me."

In her role as Director of Publications for the National Association for the Education of Young Children, Polly Greenberg is eminently qualified to share her ideas, feelings, and observations. I wish you, dear reader, could not only read Polly's very important words but also hear the dedication and compassion in her voice as she spoke to me:

"I'm glad you're combining Families and Friends. They go together.

As most of us know, the world can be a harsh, unkind, and even cruel place. And harsher are the facts that the homes of so many of our children—no matter the economic levels or cultural or racial backgrounds—are often harsh, unkind, and cruel. Large numbers of our children come from homes saturated with severe problems such as drugs, alcohol or substance abuse, domestic violence, or destructive relationships. Even our children whose homes appear "normal" may be very hurried children whose parent or parents are preoccupied with earning a living and the other innumerable duties involved in running a household. There may be no one at home who meets this child's emotional needs for leisurely friendship and fun.

The less time a child gets for family conversations, activities and projects, the more time the child needs that in school.

The less a child's life permits play with siblings, neighbors, relatives, or interested adults, the more urgently the child needs an abundance of such opportunities for spontaneous discussions, activities and play in the classroom.

You and I know that each of us is better able to focus on learning and is more open to learning when we feel secure, when we're not emotionally or socially desperate, and when our basic human needs for acceptance, appreciation, and friendship are met: Then our minds are freed for learning.

Our children come from such a diversity of family relationships—single parents; grandparents as caretakers; foster homes; multiple families; and interfaith and

interracial, multigenerational, same-sex parents, to name just a few! This is such a difficult time for teachers. We may find what we know about some of our children's families to be appalling, but *it is not our job to judge*. We must accept and welcome each child.

In every classroom, there is a lonely child, and in many classrooms, there are quite a few. Aren't all of us lonely sometimes?

One thing we can offer to all of our children—regardless of academic deficiencies or emotional and social difficulties, is a comforting, kind, and encouraging classroom rich with colorful and attractive materials, manipulatives, games, and books; an abundance of art supplies; and teachers who mix and mingle, assist, challenge, reassure, and encourage. In such classrooms, children are able to work and play with others in partnerships and small groups. Generally, children seek out others from whom they will learn as they play and work together. They need many opportunities to get emotional fulfillment from such friendships. Providing time for spontaneous play—language games, math games, make-believe—helps children strengthen their sense of self and appreciation of others. We are always trying to pull in the left-out child!

Yes, I'm glad Families and Friends are now combined! Especially for children whose families are *not* their friends. Many children can count among their best friends members of their family, but, unfortunately, many can't. That's why committed and loving teachers must create family-style classroom communities for all of our children. . . ."[4]

The central place school occupies as a "family-style community" in the life of a child from a troubled family was most eloquently described by Lynda Barry as she shared a memory of a lonely and neglected child who one morning, before the sun rose, left a house tense with parental fighting and made her way to her school. Lynda writes:

"The high levels of frustration, depression and anger in my house made my brother and me invisible. We were children with the sound turned off. And for us, as for the steadily increasing number of neglected children in this country, the only place where we could count on being noticed was at school. . . ."

Soon the janitor arrived, let her into the building, and invited her to help him open the school. The school secretary waved to her as she arrived. When her own teacher walked toward her, calling her name in a very happy and surprised way, she remembers,

"Suddenly my throat got tight and my eyes stung and I ran toward her crying. . . . It's only thinking about it now, 28 years later, that I realize I was crying from relief. I was with my teacher, and in a while I was going to sit at my desk, with my crayons and pencils and books and classmates all around me, and for the next six hours I was going to enjoy a thoroughly secure, warm and stable world. It was a world I absolutely relied on. Without it, I don't know where I would have gone that morning. . . ."

Lynda's teacher asked her to carry her purse in and then asked if she wanted to paint.

"She believed in the natural healing power of painting and drawing. . . . In the back of her room there was always a drawing table and an easel with plenty of supplies and sometimes during the day she would come up to you for what seemed like no good reason and quietly ask if you wanted to go to the back table and make some pictures. . . . By the time the bell rang that morning I had finished my drawing and Mrs. LeSane pinned it on the special bulletin board she reserved for drawings. . . . It was the same picture I always drew—a sun in the corner of a blue sky over a nice house with flowers all around it."[5]

Families and friends . . . friends and families The news isn't always so grim. The good news is that families, neighbors, and communities are demonstrating new, vigorous commitment and involvement in schools. *Call us,* they say. *Let us help you. Use us. Invite us in. We are partners. We'll be there for you with projects, parties, field trips, celebrations, story-times. Keep us in mind and in sight!* In so many classrooms and schools, the active presence of family members and friends is a very hopeful development. You won't get a hundred percent involvement from all your families but you will be surprised at the readiness and eagerness of many of your families to be participants in enriching the education of their children. Of *our* children!

A child asked Bertha Campbell, "Have you been a teacher for a long time?"
Bertha, a master teacher, answered, "Oh, for many many years."
"I guess you can do it by heart," the child said.
This whole book is written by heart, but this chapter, especially, is written in the deepest heart language. I truly believe that if you are *not* moved by the importance of your role in creating, as Polly Greenberg described, "a family-style classroom community" where every child is hallowed and welcomed, where trust and friendships develop, where, no matter the season outside, the weather inside your space is warm, then you should consider entering a profession other than teaching. For the children, you must be strong and dedicated. They need you so much.
What are the implications if you, despite the difficult challenges of today's times that are a-changin', heed the calling to teach? I offer you four blended ideas: awareness, acceptance, respect, and communication.
Without awareness, we are handicapped. When children talk, we must listen wisely, with all of our senses. When children don't talk, we must observe with the *ear* inside our hearts. (Isn't there an "ear" inside of "heart"?) Awareness implies

sensitivity and caring. Because you are aware, your behavior changes, your communication changes. Because you know that seven children in your room do not live with their mothers, you change your celebration of Mother's Day. You respect and accept their dignity and the variety of their home situations. You no longer automatically say "Mommy or Daddy" as your major reference to family without watching the pain of sudden loss sadden the face of a young child. Aware, respecting, accepting teachers learn new ways to refer to the adults at home. They say things like, "Ask a grownup at home to please sign this note." "Everyone in your family is invited to our party." "Maybe a baby-sitter or friend or someone bigger than you at home will help you cut out pictures of flowers for our project."

Our language is the language of inclusion. Our vocabulary features words of reassurance, caring, understanding, respect, and acceptance.

Don't be surprised if the children call you Mommy or Daddy.

Don't be surprised if your classroom is a home away from home, a City of Refuge, a haven, and a hearth.

Look on your roster. You may see names like Callie Rose, Len the Muffin Man, Kimani, Molly, Jose, Justin, Daryl, Senta, Han Su, Tony, Don, and Lynda. They are ready to fall in love with learning, with sharing, with playing together, with you.

Are you ready for them?

DISCOVERY TIMES/WONDER TIMES

- Family is basic to all people. Just think: no matter where people live in the world, most belong to some kind of family.
- Families have many members, including mothers, fathers, stepmothers, stepfathers, sisters, brothers, grandmothers, grandfathers, aunts, uncles, nieces, nephews—so many interesting relationships!
- Sometimes we have such good friends and neighbors that we think of them as members of our own family.
- Friends come in all ages, shapes, colors, nationalities, and religions.
- It's fun and easy to make new friends.

- Friends and family members are usually people who care about us.
- People are very individualistic (unique). They have many ways of showing feelings and approval. Aren't we lucky we're not all exactly the same? We're not robots!
- There are many kinds of family arrangements. Children are intelligent; they usually understand even the most complicated family relationships!
- It's sad when parents divorce or when a family member or friend is sick or dies. It's good that children have teachers and friendly classmates to talk to and share feelings with.
- Sometimes family members and friends may disagree or argue, but it's often possible to settle differences in healthy ways.
- When people respect the feelings and ideas of others, a climate of trust and safety grows. It's always amazing to know that we can learn to cooperate and be with others in friendly ways.
- When a baby is born in the family, it's fun to be a big sister or brother—sometimes! But sometimes new babies can be a "pain in the neck." Remember, everyone was a new baby once! We have a lot of experiences to share with friends and family.
- Aren't we all members of different kinds of family? Our school family? Our church, mosque, or synagogue family of friends? Our scouts or after-school program family of friends? *The human family?* (Many children who come from negative family situations find very great comfort in their membership in other kinds of family-type groups.)
- Whether at home or at school, life is more pleasant when people help each other, care about each other, and share.

SUGGESTED VOCABULARY

mother	neighbor	trips	shop	let's plan
father	partner	outings	hug	together
mommy	classmate	picnics	kiss	stories
daddy	teacher	visits	smooch	songs
mom	meals	parties	listen	poems
dad	breakfast	birthdays	share	riddles
parents	lunch	holidays	friendly	laugh
stepmother	supper	care	happy	cry
stepfather	bed	praise	sad	jokes
sister	bath	invite	glad	church
brother	clothes	celebrate	scared	synagogue
stepbrother	medicine	company	lonely	gifts
stepsister	games	come in	disappointed	puzzles
baby	toys	house	excited	blocks
grandmother	books	apartment	please	greeting cards
grandfather	bikes	laundry	you're welcome	hold hands
uncle	pets	clean	thank you	company
aunt	dolls	take turns	may I?	forgive
niece	trucks	cooperate	I'm sorry.	babysitter
nephew	chores	agree	excuse me.	school
cousin	helpers	disagree	I love you.	help
friend	car	argue	you're nice	apologize
buddy	van	make up	you're funny	
pal	give	talk	let's play	

Note: Your vocabulary "list" will be unique and represent your particular group of children. "Buenos dias," "amigo," "jambo," "shalom," "salaam," "aloha," and "yo" may be words your children use to communicate friendliness, greetings, or welcome. They may have different terms for family members and friends—especially grandparents! Continue gathering all their words, remembering that the qualities of friendliness are manifested in many ways. No matter our particular list of words, I hope that we are teaching our children the vocabulary of friendliness in everything we do!

SOME STARTERS

Start with a special welcome message What is the daily, constant, never-ending "theme" of your room, of you? *welcome!* (I knew you'd guess!) Words, signs, visual images, mobiles, posters, bumper stickers, and poems expressing the idea of *welcome* are welcome sights to children of all ages (especially when they are validated in action). Special songs, gestures, and rituals that take just a few short moments but have long-lasting effects are excellent daily starters for expressing warmth and an invitation to "come in—I'm so glad you're here today! We all need each other!"

Start with naming names As I have mentioned throughout this book, the children's own names are high-priority words on their "key vocabulary" lists. Even very young children recognize their letters or the designs and configurations of their names. Seeing their names proudly displayed on boxes, boards, posters, pictures, and charts is an immediate message of reassurance. Very quickly they learn the names of their classmates. Expand that knowledge and information to an invitation to share "the names of some of the people in your family or who live at home with you or are people you care very much about." Imagine a whole wall devoted to the names of your own children and the important names in their lives. I like to call this "the gathering of the tribes." Each name is a word that defines a relationship. Think of how many ways you can enrich this initial gathering with art, drama, music, and movement. It helps children remember that they are not alone.

Start a year of friendliness and cooperation with a room full of helpers Even the youngest children love to "help" even if their "job" is "Len, please give the keys to Mommy." When everyone participates in the upkeep and well-being of the group, cooperation is strengthened and a feeling of cohesion brings everyone together. Here's a challenge. Figure out enough real jobs for every child in your class every day. If you have twenty-nine children, you can think of twenty-nine classroom helpers! Look everywhere: plants (number them), pets (number them), weather reporter, exercise leaders, "poem for the day" reader, messages, Pledge, welcome leader, calendar helper, song leaders, announcer, art center helpers . . . the list goes on! Everyone is needed and important. Here is a true story:

> Four-year-old Tara told her father, "When I grow up, I'm going to marry Josh." "Josh?" her father joked. "How are you going to live? Where does he work? How can you get married? He doesn't even have a job!"
>
> Tara's spirits sagged until, suddenly, she brightened and ran to her father with the good news, "Wait a minute, Daddy, he *does* have a job! He's the *line leader!*"

These vitally important lessons in responsibility, thoughtfulness, and cooperation are so relevant that we will focus further on family and friendship themes.

Start with humor Psychologist/joyologist Steve Wilson[6] crosses the country spreading life-affirming, lifesaving information about the high-priority place of humor and laughter in almost every aspect of human existence. Steve reminds us that laughter is the natural sound of childhood and that when we grin or giggle our immune systems are activated! Not only do humor and laughter open pathways in the brain that help us retain information, but humor also helps get kids' attention and relaxes, energizes, and refreshes them. Steve likes to quote Victor Borge, who said that laughter is the shortest distance between two people. Which brings us to the idea of starting your day with humor—a joke, an experience, a playful situation, a silly song, a riddle, or a cartoon. Healthy laughter (never at anyone's expense, never to ridicule or put down) provides shared positive experiences to your ever-growing mutual history. When people share joyful times, they feel closer to each other. The chances that friendship and family-style classes of children will develop are great. Try it. You'll like it!

Start with a personal snapshot Sharing goes both ways! Because you are happy to share photos of members of your family or friends, the children must discover, if they don't already know, that we are all part of family groups, friendships, and neighborhoods and these relationships are very important in our lives.

Start with buddies Even very young children often fall into cliques, and without loving "management" by a caring teacher, lonely children too many times remain outsiders. Encourage children to work and play with others in spontaneous relationships of their own choosing. But be ready, if needed, to offer the children opportunities to "buddy up" with others so that by the end of the school year, most of your children will have worked and played together, if only for a day.

Organize "buddy" systems in playful ways. For example, give each child a card with a special color, number, letter, word, design, picture, or animal. Tell them that someone in the room has a matching card, and when they find the people with the matching cards, they will find their buddies for the day. The buddies may walk together, sit together for snacks, play together, draw or build together, do puzzles together, or work on projects together. These partnerships are valuable even if they are only for one day.

Start with a puppet, stuffed animal, or doll In many early childhood classrooms, special beloved puppets, stuffed animals, and dolls are VIP and enjoy high-priority positions in the lives of the children. My own little dog puppet, Snowball, now about thirteen years old and hugged and kissed by thousands of children, communicates ideas better than most "experts." Snowball has inspired children to be more caring and thoughtful of others when he shares painful experiences with unfriendly behavior. Because he doesn't always "get it," the children are patient in their explanations to him. When he visits his Grandma over school break, he invites the children to talk about their families. If you've never tried it, I urge you to find a puppet, stuffed animal, or doll that you love. With your children, name it and make it your own important classroom "character."

Start with a poem or a story Unless the effectiveness of the material is squeezed dry by a stiff, expressionless delivery, children are usually happily caught in the magical power of poems and stories. The poems of Eloise Greenfield, especially her collection *Honey, I Love*,[7] inspire Joan Kalb's students to talk about their own feelings about family relationships and write their own poems. Joan and her students enjoy starting lively talk times about the many dimensions of friendships by reading together Byrd Baylor's *Guess Who My Favorite Person Is*.[8] A good story or poem shared in a safe, loving environment generates important and meaningful ideas and activities. Find the materials you and your children love!

Start with pets and plants Caring for classroom pets and plants is a wonderful way for children to work together, learn responsibility, and contribute to the welfare of other living things. When pets and plants are important inhabitants of your room, children learn gentleness and sharing. Numerous observations, language activities, art, music, and movements experiences grow from seeds, tanks, and habitats.

Reminder: Any idea that's interesting and exciting to you is a potentially excellent starter. Be open to exploration! Songs, stories, poems, games, and celebrations are examples of effective ways of launching important concepts.

TALK TIMES/LISTENING TIMES

Some time ago I read a powerful saying on a bulletin board of a teachers' lounge: "The Best Way to Send an Idea Is to Wrap It Up in a Person."

This book is full of people who embody ideas in everything they do. They *are* the ideas! For example, there's Alice Aron.[9] Listen to Alice as she talks about her New York City kindergartners and talk times/listening times.

"We talk all the time! We talk, sing, discuss, share, exchange. We sit together, help each other, ask questions, solve problems. There's always room for sharing. The more the children listen to each other, the more they learn about each other. Our kids have real conversations. I encourage them to help each other, to listen to each other. Cooperation develops. We have a close group feeling that just keeps growing!"

An Arab proverb reminds us: "Talking together is loving one another."

Open-ended questions At all times, remember to emphasize open-ended questions rather than conversation-killing yes-no, wrong-right prompters. Talk times turn into boring cut-and-dried times if you ask only short-answer questions.

Be open to how open-ended questions keep begetting more interesting responses. First graders were discussing "What does a family do?" and one of the responses was "a family teaches us stuff." Alert teachers will pick up on another language and thought-provoking question, "What are some things that a family teaches us?" Children's thoughts on that topic ranged from "telling time" to "how to be nice to animals." Note that this example featured "family" as a topic, but don't be surprised if children refer to family members and events as part of every topic!

As often as possible, write the children's ideas, suggestions, and responses on the board so they see the relationship between oral and written language. Let their own words inspire pictures, games, songs, and crafts activities.

Involve children in planning Schedules, field trips, walks, arts activities, open house programs, holidays, and celebrations are all excellent subjects that need the input of the children to truly succeed. Even the youngest children discover that their opinions and the opinions of others are valuable when they are full participants in planning their own learning activities. Exchanging ideas, listening to others, making choices, and cooperating to carry out class decisions are valuable experiences through which children learn cooperation, friendliness, respect, and responsibility. Use large chart paper to gather the names of children and their suggestions. Not only are such charts excellent souvenirs from stimulating talk times/listening times, but they are also conversation "pieces" in themselves.

Talking chair/listening chair In case you didn't know, life isn't perfect! Even the most cooperative, cohesive family-feeling classrooms have moments of conflict and tension. If two children are fighting or arguing, encourage them to take turns telling the other what the problems are. The person in the "talking chair" talks while the other listens. Then they change places. This kind of exchange of views usually results in reconciliation.

Rose Stough sat two of her fighting third graders in chairs facing each other. She told them that they couldn't go out for recess until they found three positive, interesting things about each other. They asked each other questions, talking and listening, taking turns. Rose heard them share information and feelings about their families, pets, hobbies, TV shows, and friends. When they came to Rose with their "assignment" completed, they found that they both liked the same color, TV show, and clothing style. They played together that recess, and, Rose reports, "They've been friendly ever since, with never a negative word."

Family circles/magic circles/friendship circles Sometimes these kinds of "gatherings" are scheduled in daily or weekly programs. Sometimes they respond to the situation of the moment. Often, especially with young children, you'll find that almost everyone has something important to say. This is the time to gather in your special place, sit quietly together, and give each child a chance to share feelings, questions, or concerns. This is a time for solving problems, for planning, or for simple human sharing and fellowship.

Talking sticks It's ancient but relevant and exciting! Decorate a cane, wand, branch, or baton. Pass it around. The person holding the "talking stick" is the speaker. Everyone else listens. When the talking stick is passed to you, it's your turn.

Snuggle talk Teachers who spend time with very young children have special equipment that need not be budgeted or allocated—laps! Small children fit perfectly into their teachers' laps and usually consider laps their favorite places for hugging, talking, and being soothed and comforted. When a child misbehaves, a few minutes of snuggle talk resolving the "problem" can be more effective than a reprimand or punishment.

Happy talk This kind of talk includes daily, numerous, small doses of positive reinforcement for cooperation, helpfulness, and thoughtfulness demonstrated by the children. So often, even with all we know about the importance of positive reinforcement, we respond so much more to the negative, defining negative behavior as more important than positive. Train yourself to respond to friendly, caring behavior. Take the time to comment, "Isn't it nice to be all together sharing this story? Everyone is listening so attentively!" or "Cody, I noticed how quickly you helped Max pick up all the things that spilled from his desk. You're a good friend and a good citizen!"

Season your sessions with generous sprinklings of happy talk! Keep it relevant.

Book talks Nothing ignites more interesting and relevant conversations and discussions than sharing the rich experience of good literature. Aren't we lucky to have so many excellent resources waiting at our fingertips? Eavesdrop on any group of interested children gathered around a book, and you will hear them talk about: "My favorite part was . . . ," "I liked it when . . . ," "Once that happened to me and I . . . ," "I know how (the character) felt . . . ," "If I was in the story I would. . . ."

Two of Linda Goldsmith and Jo Ann Bell's[10] favorite books are older stories that never fail to evoke lively talk among prekindergartners. The children empathize with *Katy No Pocket*.[11] How can she carry her baby kangaroo without a pocket? The delightful story helps children share feelings about how friends care about each other and reach out toward one another. A Caldecott winner, *Sylvester and the Magic Pebbles*,[12] can never be read enough times. Linda and Jo Ann's children talk intently about Sylvester and the little donkey's sad disappearance from his family and friends after he accidentally touches a magic pebble and turns into a rock. Friends and families miss him so! At the happy ending, embraces, kisses, questions, and answers launch sensitive talks about the interdependence of relationships. We all need each other!

When children come in to the Cover to Cover Bookstore, Terri Li finds they gather around and easily relate to a little boy named Ling Sung, who is trying to make new friends in his class in the book *Cleversticks*.[13] Ling Sung's special contribution to his class reminds the children that every person has unique gifts to share with others.

Even though many of the children in the bookstore are not from Hispanic backgrounds, they feel very close to Rosalba and her abuela (grandmother) in *Abuela*.[14] Rosalba and her abuela find their experiences in the big village of Manhattan warmed by family and friends.

Across the country, children are learning that friends come in many different ages, races, cultures, and religions. These are exciting discoveries to talk about. Michael Joel Rosen's *Elijah's Angel*[15] and Patricia Polacco's *Mrs. Katz and Tush*[16] invite boys and girls to explore the rich fabric of family and friendship relationships as they fall in love with marvelous characters from African-American and Jewish American backgrounds.

Kids have a lot to say about *The Hundred Penny Box*.[17] An African-American child helps a grandmother keep her memories, a penny a memory! How can we keep our memories, and how do we find imaginative ways to help friends and family members when they need us? You can easily find a hundred excellent books to stimulate talk times/listening times and adventures to follow.

Hearts to hearts When trust, safety, and respect are key elements in the air you breathe, children will share their deepest concerns. These special talk times/listening times are there when needed to help children understand the most difficult of personal experiences and feelings—divorce, separation, sickness, death, relocation, or

rejection. You may not be able to come up with solutions, but the fact that you and the children are "there" for each other, to talk and express empathy and support makes *all* the difference!

Remember, feelings, wishes, dreams, fears, fantasies, jokes, memories, experiences, and relationships are as important for children to talk about as is factual information. Talks turn into myriad language, music, art, or drama field trip celebrations. Keep making connections!

VISUAL ARTS TIMES

Visual arts times are excellent times to encourage cooperative, friendly classroom relationships. Through success-oriented, enjoyable arts activities, children learn to rejoice in their own works and in the works of others. Because you respect and appreciate their works and continually encourage their originality and creativity, they learn to respect and appreciate those of their classmates. Once again, key phrases to remember in sharing art projects with young children are "open-ended" and "safe at any speed." Rigid rights and wrongs have no place in the encouraging, supportive, and safe environment you want to create for our children. As shocking as it is, I still hear some teachers of young children chastise their students for not "staying in the lines" on their flower dittos! And children (sadly) still hear, "This color is wrong. Leaves are green!"[18]

Because family and friends hold positions of high priority in the children's lives, arts times devoted to creating works about, for, or inspired by family and friends have far-reaching impact. Mix and match. Combine and change. Connect and add.

Family and friendship trees After talking about families—who do *you* live with?—the children enjoy cutting out different tree shapes from cardboard or construction paper. Of course, our trees need leaves, and cutting leaf shapes is so much fun. On each leaf, the children draw, color, paint, or paste a picture or name of someone in their family or someone special to them. The leaves are pasted to the branches of their trees. Find a wall big enough to display your forest of family and friendship trees. A variation of this popular idea is to bring a small bare-branched tree into the classroom and paste or tape the leaves to the wooden branches.

Collage of shared family/friends activities After talking about such happy times together, gather the ideas and suggestions on a chart or a section of the chalkboard to keep as reminders. The children cut pictures, draw, or paint as many of the activities suggested as they enjoy with friends and family. They paste their drawings or cutouts on large sheets of paper arranged and designed as they choose. These collages are not only interesting and lively, but they also tell a lot about the children's lives. In five-year-old Lynette's collage, I noted a cutout picture of a car, a TV set, an outdoor grill, a garden, and cat food. Included was an original drawing of two happy faces: "That's me and Mom at the Ice Capades."

I always make room for even the one child who may feel "left out" because of home situations that are marked more by deprivation than by enrichment. Add to your suggestions, "If there are some activities you haven't enjoyed yet but think you would love to experience someday, draw about them or cut them out."

Family/friendship scrolls The children are fascinated by stories of long ago. Talk with them about how long ago, before people learned how to make books, they used scrolls to tell stories. Cut butcher paper into long sheets that roll easily. Give all the children a sheet. Encourage them to write names of family members or special friends and to put next to each name drawings as well as descriptive words to highlight their characteristics. Stories about the family and/or the friendships can be added with words and colorful illustrations. When the scrolls are finished, the children choose a strand of colored wool to tie them. Be sure to share and celebrate all of the scrolls before they are given to families and friends as gifts.

She likes me and buys me clothes and books.   Shanna Harris

KIM

Grandmother Ruth Williams

my cousin, Jackie

Scrounged material sculptures Artists like Aminah Brenda Lynn Robinson inspire children to use an amazing array of found, scrounged, tossed away, and overlooked common materials for sculptures and constructions. In your always-available, always-packed-with-materials "scrounge box" are bits of cloth, leather, buttons, wool, shells, sticks, pebbles—you name it—for children to use to create sculptures of family members and/or friends. You will be surprised to see the energy and originality of such three-dimensional structures.

Family symbols/classroom symbols Scottish clans have tartans, Cub Scouts have animals names for their dens, Native American nations have totems honoring animals or natural forces. Talk with the children about choosing a symbol for their family—perhaps it's a star or a fish. Tyrone said that his family went to church "almost all the time," so he chose a church steeple for his family's symbol. After the children chose their symbols, they used them as often as they wanted. One first-grade teacher wrote all the children's names on a large sheet of paper. The children signed their names after the printed list; next to their own signatures, they drew their family symbols. Soon the children knew the symbols for everyone in the class! How many ways can you think of for these designs to be used?

Family and friends place mats I personally have learned more from some place mats than I have from lectures! On plain sheets of paper, the children design place mats for their family members or the people they live with. Encourage them to create a special place mat for each person, including the person's name and any designs or pictures that person would enjoy. Somewhere on the place mats, include the family symbol. Louie's place mat for his baby brother, Harry, featured a collage of pictures of baby-food jars. "That's his main thing," Louie explained. "Eating!" Laminate them if possible. Clear contact paper can be stretched over them if no laminating machine is available. They make wonderful gifts.

Gifts for friends and families Doesn't "gifted education" mean giving gifts to others? Children enjoy making special gifts for special people. With scrounged materials, bits and pieces, hunks and chunks, chips and scraps, children create charm

bracelets, earrings, pins, "treasure boxes," posters, picture albums, and T-shirts with original designs using tie-dyeing, markers, or paint (to name just a few popular ideas from around the country). Of course, an original greeting card should accompany each gift!

As we have said throughout the book, the lovely challenge for teachers is to create a family feeling within the classroom. I am inspired by the numerous examples of such cohesive, loving groups of children learning in environments rich with caring and warmth. Enjoy these few samplings from schools across the country.

Group projects Along with individual or small group activities, as often as possible (preferably all the time!) plan projects with your children that invite them all to participate. Everyone's contribution is needed! I like the idea of beginning with a blank space and watching what happens as the children fill that space with words, colors, shapes, and pictures. For example:

Wallpaper As a group, the children decide the pattern for their wallpaper. Cover a portion of a wall with paper and ask the children to contribute their portion to the whole. I have seen walls of footprints, handprints, circles, stars, and animal designs. One class worked in small groups on specific sections of the wallpaper and celebrated the colors blue and green to create an ocean wallpaper. Of course, their fish filled the waters!

More trees On your constructed or real tree, leaves can come in many shapes. I have seen Happy Face Trees, with each child's self-portrait and name on a happy-face leaf. The tree is a cheery greeting as one enters the room. A group of second graders turned themselves into originally named ice cream flavors and added their cones to an ice cream tree! My favorite flavor was Jenny Fudge Berry.

Zoos, gardens, circuses, villages, rain forests When everyone contributes to a large theme, the plot thickens! A blank wall that begins with just a sign—Zoo— soon evolves into pathways, animals grazing, baby animals in a "petting" section, giraffes munching on the leaves of tall trees, flamingoes balancing on their skinny pink legs. Every child in the class added visual ideas to the evolving wall. Whether you're working in three-dimensional materials or your basic murals and walls, people create a more marvelous piece of art *because* they have worked together.

Quilts In the last few years, quilts using many materials, from paper to cloth, have become very popular. Family quilts or "Our Class Friends" quilts are excellent projects for cooperative learning and group enjoyment. A quilt can't be complete unless it has a section from everyone!

Turn your whole room into . . . Nothing brings children together more quickly and effectively than deciding on a story or theme that is especially exciting to the group and turning your whole room into the idea. For example, one kindergarten class so enjoyed *Charlotte's Web* that they decided to turn their room into a web. They connected string from corner to corner and place to place by taping it. The project emphasized cooperation because the process of deciding where and how to connect the string was complicated. The children wrote their favorite words on colored construction paper, cut out and taped to the string of the web. They made a marvelous mobile of baby spiders, shiny and twinkling.

I have seen whole classrooms turned into rain forests, oceans, Iroquois longhouses, and gardens. These ideas go on, sometimes for weeks. Stories, poems, songs, games, play activities, and art projects related to the theme continue throughout the duration. The only limitation is time!

Panels and pages Beloved poems, read-aloud tales, and just plain favorite books, as well as original class stories, are celebrated in extraordinary ways by asking the class to divide up into small groups, partners, or individuals and creating a page or panel of that story. Each child's or group's contribution to the story—in words and pictures—is essential. Together, the children create a work that evokes great pride and pleasure.

Two by two buddies Combining children's free choices of buddies as well as matching-up games that help children work and play with as many of their classmates as possible during the year, activities for twos inspire cooperation and classroom friendships. Buddies can enjoy many activities, such as: *draw a buddy*—Sit together, look at each other, be observant, and paint or draw your friend's portrait; *buddy prints*—Dip hands into pans of paint, a different color for each buddy. Each has a large sheet of paper. Both children with their different colored handprints design each paper. Messages or favorite words are written. The children keep their papers to remind them of their fun together. All the pictures displayed make a lively, colorful exhibit. Try this with thumbs, feet, and fingers.

A classroom of friends Shirley Duncan described an art project that demonstrates awareness, appreciation, and friendliness. It begins on the first day of school and continues through the school year.

> On the first day, I ask the children to draw a picture of themselves. We put all the pictures on the board. "This is Me. My Name. My Picture."

The next day, I ask them to draw a picture of a classroom friend. We put them all up, with the children's names and the name of the artist.

A few weeks later, I ask them to draw a picture of our classroom *friends* and not to forget their names on the picture. They draw more children. We put them all up, of course.

After just a few months, when I ask them again to draw pictures of classroom friends, invariably they draw pictures of *every kid in the class!* Names and features! We display them, admire them and talk about them. I remind them that only a few months before, they didn't know anyone in the class and we started with a picture of just ourselves. Now they know and can draw every person in the class! Look how many new friends we have made![19]

MUSIC TIMES

Throughout this book, music times are highlighted as times to celebrate ourselves, each other, and the creativity that stamps us as part of the human family. Any musical suggestion in this book fosters feelings of friendliness if it is shared with warmth and fun. Throughout history and around the world, all people have made music, do make music. Many babies sing before they ever talk. Songs bring people together; singing together is a delightful human experience. Families, friendship groups, interest groups, communities, and organizations (groups and subgroups of every kind) have their favorite kinds of music and songs both learned and improvised. Many families have songs they sing when going places, lullabies, work and play songs, and songs for holidays and special events. When we honor family songs, we honor the cultural heritage of the families. We share the richness of their musical gifts. In your knapsack of memories and experiences, you have collected songs that you can trace back to family times, camps, schools, friendships, and games. This is a treasure box of resources for you to use and share with your children. You will be surprised at the diversity of songs young children easily learn and enjoy.

Don't limit yourself to packaged songs for children. Be eclectic in your selections. Music is a universal language. It helps us continue to make those life-affirming connections that bring us closer to one another.

In an interview, Joseph Shabalala, leader of the South African nine-member acapella group, Ladysmith Black Mambazo, spoke movingly about his love of songs and making music. He said,

> In our culture, we believe that music is something to make people know each other. Once you have a chance to stand and dance, the people are going to know who you are, where you're from, who's your mother, who's your father. You're not just dancing for yourself. When I sing, I know that I'm standing for my people, for my family. Now I must try to do a good thing, so my people will be known.[20]

In the classes you would want *your* children to attend, singing and music happen throughout the day, part of everything they do. They sing their lives and their time shared together.

At three months old, Callie Rose responds to music. Her expressions change, and her movement patterns are energized. She even has favorite music box songs that lull her to sleep.

At one and half, toddler Len, the Muffin Man now sings: "Old Macdonald," "Baby Beluga," "No More Monkeys Jumpin on the Bed," "Baa Baa Black Sheep," "Row Row Row Your Boat," "I Love You—You Love Me," "Twinkle Twinkle Little Star," "Open Them—Shut Them," "Eensy Weensy Spider," "The Noble Duke of York," "Ring Around the Rosy," and "The More We Get Together."

At four and a half, Kimani and his friends know so many songs that their titles alone would fill this page!

Sing with them, sing to them, ask them to sing for you and they will be your friends forever!

Welcome and greeting songs Start your days with songs. Instead of saying, "Good morning," sing it! Instead of saying, "Hello everybody," sing it! Make up your own melody:

> Where is Florindo?
> Where is Florindo?
> Here I am.
> Here I am.
> How are you this morning?
> Very well I thank you.
> Give me five! Give me five!

With children, I sing the gamut of selections from original, improvised songs to Raffi's "One Light, One Sun" to Thomas Moore's "Good Morning to My Friends" to Woody Guthrie's "How Doo Do" to Steve and Greg's "Good Morning," and from "The World Is a Rainbow" to Rosenschontz's "Hey, We'll Fill the World With Love" to Ella Jenkins' "Jambo"—I could fill this book with favorite songs. Add to your own knapsack. Because you have shared so many wonderful songs with your children, they become leaders of daily greeting songs. Include those high positions in your collection of helpers. The children love to select the songs that are sung. Give them many offerings.

Songs that celebrate the human family Our children must know that in addition to the family they live with and their extended families, their family of friends at school, they belong to the great Human Family. Especially in these difficult times for so many children who feel alienated and abandoned, their relationship to greater family structures is important and appreciated. Older songs like "He's Got the Whole World in His Hands," "Give Peace a Chance," "If I Had a Hammer," James

Taylor's "You've Got a Friend," "Kum Ba Ya," and "We Are the World" are just starters for a gathering of songs that link us to each other.

Lullabies Peaceful, soothing, and loving songs that lull babies to sleep, lullabies are probably the most basic kinds of musical messages. Lullabies come in every language, representing every culture on the planet. During quiet times or after snacks or strenuous activities, share lullabies from around the world with your children. Make room for their own lullabies, original or learned. Listen as they sing to their "babies," to each other, to themselves.

Family songs When children feel safe and cared about, they are eager to share songs they sing with their families. Many of these are hums or chants sung while doing something or going somewhere or "clean up your room" songs.

Patty, age six, laughed as she taught her mommy's "silly song." Her mother sang this song when the children forgot to wash their faces. "You forgot to wash your face. It's a disgrace! A dirty face!" Anaciato's aunt (he lived with his aunt) had a "scolding song" that he shared with his kindergarten classmates: "No! No! A thousand times no!" The children sang it often throughout the year.

The old song "Over the River and Through the Woods to Grandmother's House We Go" was cheerily rearranged by a group of kindergartners to include their own family visits. They sang, "Over the river and through the woods to Cousin Desiree's house we go." Theresa objected, "We don't go over a river to Desiree's house! We go on the freeway and on a bridge!" The song became, "Over a freeway and over the bridge to Desiree's house we go. . . ."

Most children compose songs almost daily. They are usually about family members, special friends, and pets. Write down their words. Ask them to teach their songs to classmates. Gather the songs children create into a songbook that they illustrate. All the songs the children know and hear should be printed and prominently displayed so they see the connections between the songs in their minds, in their mouths, in their ears, and in words they see with their eyes.[21]

Remember that your children will represent some of the rich diversity of our country. Your learning community will be enriched with "gifts" from homes including songs, music, instruments, rhythms, chants, and dances reflecting the cultural backgrounds of your students and their families. Because yours is a safe and accepting environment, children will want to share their songs. *We begin with the world in our room!* Sing out its praises.

Choruses, bands, orchestras—cooperation at work! Whether we get voices together or instruments together, the underlying value is the same—we must work together to create the musical piece, whether a rap song or a symphony. Sing and play familiar songs together. Go beyond those experiences to improvise music. Play with rhythms. Begin with a heartbeat rhythm. Ask each instrument to pick up the rhythm and join in. Invite the children to experiment with sounds, words, and melodies to accompany the instruments. As often as possible, ask the children to pass their instruments along so they experience different sounds. Experiment with melody, tone, pitch, and tempo so children appreciate the range of possibilities for their voices. Together, create some new music.

Songs as gifts Because, as Thoreau noted, children begin the world anew, they understand the ancient tradition of giving one's own songs, dances, poems, or artwork to others.

> I have a song that I love
> I want to share it with you.
> I want to give it to you as my gift to you.

My Shinnecock princess friend, Bess Chee Chee Haile, told me long ago about a Native American tradition of giving songs as gifts.

Write the words to the children's songs. Illustrate them and keep them prominently displayed and enjoyed.

Rounds, call-and-response chants When children sing rounds, such as "Row, Row, Row Your Boat," they must listen attentively, sing closely with their group, and learn their place in the whole scheme. They also hear how much richer a song sounds when different parts are sung at the same time. Harmony is a musical term, but it is a fitting word for a chapter on families and friends!

Call-and-response chants are rooted in tradition. They are almost extensions of conversations.

> Come out and play.
> OK.
> Come out and play.
> OK.

This is an example of a simple call-and-response song improvised by two children as they climbed a jungle gym.

A group of five-year-olds sang a call-and-response song as they hiked along. They made up the words as they walked.

> If you come with us
> You'll have fun.
> If you walk with us
> You'll have fun.
> If you swim with us
> You'll have fun.

Dante told his classmates about his baby sister, Jewel. The class made up a song about her.

> Jewel keeps crying.
> Waah waah.
> Jewel keeps crying.
> Waah waah.
> Jewel stopped crying.
> Yaaaay. Yaaaay.

Ella Jenkins was one of the most popular and earliest of the nation's singers to introduce children to the fun of call-and-response songs. She sings call-and-response songs and chants from Hebrew, Arabic, Spanish, French, African, and American traditions.

When children sing together, friendliness and goodwill prevail. Because music is the most universal language, we feel close to those with whom we share musical experiences.

Accompany singing and musical moments with visual arts, movement, drama, poetry, and stories . . . keep connecting!

Special instruments bring people together Throughout history, musical instruments and rhythms have communicated important messages to groups. Families sometimes ring dinner bells. Drums call people to gather for a special event. Bagpipes begin the excitement. Blowing a whistle for order or for instructions and directions is probably a relative of this old tradition. I use my tambourine for numerous signals and messages. Marlene Robbin's conga drum, Lester, is listened to attentively by her students. Tom Griffin's guitar strums have ideas to share with his students.

If possible, bring your instrument into class. Give it a language. Let it become an important part of your day.

Let it truly gather your children together.

Sing your days Fans of the comedy show *Saturday Night Live* remember the fabulous character Opera Man, who sings the news events in an operatic style. Imaginative and free-spirited teachers turn many spoken moments into improvised songs.

Instead of saying, "Let's all clean up so we can go outside," try singing it! Trust me, the children will listen more attentively than ever before and express more delight with an invitation to clean up than you can imagine. Turn reading and speaking into singing.

Mrs. Smith's second graders were encouraged to write letters to the incoming second graders telling them what to expect from their new teacher and grade. When the incoming second graders received the sealed letters, one of the letters warned: "Beware! Mrs. Smith sings and dances the spelling words!"

The bottom line is this: I can't imagine celebrating families and friends *without* music. If you can talk, you can sing! Sing out!

MOVEMENT AND PLAY TIMES

"Family" is the first game children play. With or without props, children become mommies, daddies, babies, grandparents, and siblings. With accessible props and costumes (hats, handbags, ties, belts, shoes, furniture, and kitchen utensils), children plunge into the game of family. Tune into their role playing. Who takes which parts? Be a good listener and observer. You may need to introduce a new character so that a child who is always relegated to a minor role in the family gets to play a more important part.

"Left out" children who "want in" can always be included by your suggestion that cousins or aunts and uncles are about to visit. Encourage the drawing of circles that "take people in."

Children naturally blend movement, improvisation, singing, music, dialogue, and costumes into total activity. They live whole language. They already make connections. Creative teachers often encourage further avenues of expression with such challenges as: "Well, how does that mommy walk?" or "That's a great way to show Baby trying to stand up by herself."

Three-and-a-half-year-old Ophelia, tiny feet in high heels, a droopy flowered bonnet on her head, stood at the entrance to her "house" waiting for her family to join her. Shifting her weight to one side, hands on hips, she shouted, "Come now! I'm giving you three. One. Two. Three. Time's up!" No one had to teach her that dialogue!

Young children need time and space to play. As they play, you will be astonished at how much they express themselves, how well they communicate and how quickly skills, language acquisition, and comprehension develop. In their play, the children will demonstrate meaningful, authentic learning as they explore their roles in relationships and events.

Sometimes, teachers take on a more direct role in children's play. Jay Brand, working with his elementary students in creative dramatics, talks about more active roles for teachers:[22]

> When we create stories together, we have to work together. We brainstorm. We share ideas. Let the process happen. Even impractical ideas are freely given. A lot of communication is going on and trust. . . . My role? Roles? I have to be a good listener. Ask good questions. Questions that help the direction of the story, of the idea to play. It's hard to do—to give children responsibility for their ideas, to let them take charge, to make decisions. They have 25 ideas for every one I have. We can't use all the ideas—I help them pick, choose, select, combine. . . . It's a matter of faith. We must believe in the kids' knowledge and abilities. They always know more than we think they know!

Jay and his students make plays from favorite books, folk tales, poems, songs, familiar situations, events, and holidays. Any idea is valid if the children are excited about it. They work as a large group, in smaller groups, and as partners. Sometimes the whole class is turned into experts helping to solve problems. Sometimes they become tour leaders leading tours of their houses. Many times the stories have to do with relationships and friendships.

"Kids need opportunities to devour ideas!" Jay sets a good example by joining the excitement and contributing his own suggestions to the shaping of the ideas.

When school becomes, as Polly Greenberg described, a family-style community, children have numerous opportunities to play with each other in enjoyable, cooperative ways. Be aware of the ways in which furniture arrangements, design, and materials encourage friendliness and cooperation. Blocks, puzzles, cars, trucks, dolls, stuffed animals, sandbox, scrounge corner, puppet stage, hat rack, arts supplies, and interest centers are examples of materials that invite interaction, experimentation, and the discovery that individual contributions help create joyful, whole-group experiences.

When you walk into a room where young children learn, notice the places and objects that need more than one child at a time to play with or in them. Watch how children play together. Many children, as we sadly noted, have little experience in playing happily with others. They must learn how to enjoy free play time. Innovative teachers have devised ways to organize free play so that children work and play cooperatively. Taking turns, sharing, listening to others, planning and building together, being open to unfamiliar materials and activities, and encouraging and celebrating the work of classmates—all of these contribute to a friendly environment where family-style communities are strengthened.

Ideas for organizing free play time It's important that children be introduced to materials, centers, and play areas and clearly understand them. Often, symbols, drawings, and photographs are prominently displayed to represent toys, games, and activities. Material and interest centers often are color coded. Let's say yellow represents the water table. Today the children who picked yellow cards from the Free Play Time Grab Bag will have a chance to play at the water table. You'll find that there will be times that children need to be directed to play in different areas. Turn that kind of organization itself into an enjoyable game!

I visited a kindergarten class that was bubbling over with supplies, projects, conversations, laughter, activities, songs, and games. Children played, painted, read, and acted out stories alone, in twos, and in small groups. Occasionally, they came together for a read-aloud book or puppet show. Many of their artworks and stories with invented spelling were on the walls, hanging from the ceiling, and draped across the windows. A chart of the class rules caught my eye.

"The rules," the teacher explained, "came out of a long class discussion that followed a noisy, unpleasant argument. We tried to figure out a few rules that would improve our classroom life. These are the ones that everyone voted for:"

Our Rules

1. Please try to take turns.
2. Please try to talk in friendly voices.
3. Please try not to fight.
4. Please try not to break toys.
5. Please try to be friends with everyone in the class.

Remember, play is the work of young children. Keep them moving! Education is a moving experience!

Playful movement songs that feature friends and families Popular songs such as "The Wheels on the Bus" that already name family members ("The mommies on the bus go sshh sshh sshh . . .") can be easily expanded to cousins, uncles, sisters, and brothers. Change the basic song into an active game by giving every friend in the class a chance to be on the bus doing something that is demonstrated by movement.

"Pierre on the bus does jumping jacks . . ."
"Crystal on the bus can touch her toes . . ."

"Farmer in the Dell" turned into a family affair when all kinds of relatives were "taken":

"The baby takes a brother . . ."
"The brother takes a sister . . ."

or a friendly gathering when the teacher turns into the farmer and takes each child in the class.

"Mrs. Reedy takes a Yael . . ."
"Mrs. Reedy takes a Yael . . ."

Exercise families This is a variation of the game, "Mother, May I?" or "Giant Steps," in which children differentiate between giant steps and baby steps. Children enjoy doing "baby jumps" then increasing the height of their jumps to "big sister (brother) jumps" to "baby-sitter jumps" and finally to "mother (father, stepmother, stepfather, grandmother, grandfather) jumps."

Choose any exercise that the children enjoy. Give them a steady beat on tambourine or drum or play music with a steady lively rhythm. Increase the volume as you increase in exercise. Always begin with the "baby" category because even the most reluctant movers will show they can do "baby jumping jacks" or "baby hops."

Animal families exercises Children love animals and animal movement. Adapt the above activity to the theme of animals. Kanga, a mom kangaroo, is a big jumper. Baby Roo takes little jumps. Grandfather horses have high prances and strong gallops. Baby horses have little prancing feet. The children enjoy the fun of demonstrating animal families in action, with specific movements for different family members. This is a great way to learn differentiation. Make up stories to go with the exercises.

Guess what members of my family and my friends do In this improvisation/pantomime guessing game, the children act out something done by a family member or friend. The rest of the children try to guess. Juan curled up on the floor and sucked his thumb. The class had no trouble guessing what Juan's baby brother did! Melissa's classmates loved her imitation of her big sister's favorite thing to do—Melissa looked in a pretend mirror and put on pretend lipstick and eye makeup.

Turn all the ideas into charts with names and actions. Illustrate!

Classmate riddles Children cannot become friends until they begin to know each other. Every day should be a time of celebrating classmates through songs, poems, stories, greetings, and games.

Children love guessing games. Ask the children to turn on their Power Lights, lift their antennas, charge up their batteries, and get into gear for this challenge. Here are a few examples:

"I'm thinking about a boy who is wearing a blue T-shirt with the number 3 on it. If you know who he is, say his name." Or "I'm thinking about a girl with lots of extensions, beautiful beads in her hair, and a big smile. If you know who it is, say her name, hop over to her, and touch her hand."

Use physical characteristics, clothes, jewelry, possessions, hobbies, personal qualities, and skills as clues. Here is a lovely way to emphasize positive attributes and feelings toward others and to ensure success for all who participate.

Twenty ways to love a circle A circle is a perfect shape for encouraging friendship. It has no beginning and no end, no front and no back of the line. Everyone faces one another and no one is left out. A circle provides a feeling of belonging and safety. (I am not an advocate of games played in circles where people are tagged out or cast out!)

Arnold Adoff's lovely poem strengthens the powerful message that circles can convey:

I Am Making a Circle For My Self
I am making a circle for my self
            and
I am placing into that
            circle: all who are for me,
            and
            all that is inside.[23]

Of the thousands of circle activities, twenty are offered to start you thinking about your own family circle of friends.

1. Sit in a circle and shake hands with one another.
2. Wave to everyone in the circle.
3. Sing songs, clap hands, slap thighs, and stamp feet while keeping the circle.
4. Blink your eyes, wiggle your nose, and make a funny face for everyone around you in the circle.
5. Tell round-robin stories while sitting in a circle. Everyone has a turn to continue the story.
6. Roll the ball to each child in the circle and ask a question like, "What's your favorite color?" or "What's your favorite food?" The child responds and rolls the ball back to you.
7. Sit in a circle and pass around an imaginary shape that changes as each person receives it.
8. Sit in a circle and listen to a story, poem, or song. Improvise hand and body movements to accompany the action.

9. Pass an expression like "hello" around the circle. Everyone gets a chance to say it in a different language or different way. The children discover that even a wonderful phrase such as "I love you" can be said with anger or meanness. They are astonished that a playful phrase like "You cucumber!" can be hurtful when spoken in a negative way.

10. In your circle, talk about sign language and the language of gesture. Learn signs for phrases like "I like you" or "friend." Make up gestures for familiar ideas.

11. Sit in an unfriendly/friendly circle. Take turns making mean, unfriendly faces and body shapes. How does that feel? Change the circle into a friendly circle with friendly expressions, words, and body shapes. How does *that* feel?

12. Hold hands. How many ways can the circle move? Experiment. Walk into the center. Walk back. Hop, jump, kick, slide. Move the circle clockwise, then counterclockwise. Work out a sequence. Accompany it with music.

13. Play follow-the-leader. Choose your favorite music and give everyone a turn to lead some kind of movement in the center of the circle. (Don't force a shy child to be leader. Skip to the next person. Minimize tension!)

14. Turn your circle into a balloon. Stand very close together, bunched up and holding hands. Take deep, exaggerated breaths and expand into a large circle. Then breathe out and walk into a small circle again. Children enjoy pretending that the air went out of the balloon and pulled everyone into the middle.

15. Form a noisy circle, quiet circle, musical circle, clapping circle, tiptoeing circle, marching circle.

16. Turn your circle into a circle of giants, trees, robots, animals, elves, or characters from stories.

17. Turn your circle into a tribal dance circle. Play African, Native American, or Caribbean music (for example). Let the children dance freely to the music inside the sacred dance circle.

18. Make a circle of slow-moving, fast-moving, sideways-moving people.

19. Make a ten-speed circle. Everyone holds hands and walks very slowly. Begin walking a little faster, then faster and faster. Speed it up ten times until the children are moving in their fastest gear. Accompany with drum or tambourine or handclaps.

20. Brainstorm circle ideas with your children and turn your circle into a wheel, a pizza, a merry-go-round, a melting ice cream cone, the moon, or a puddle.

I know you can easily think of twenty more ways to love a circle!

Sticking together Continuing with a variation of the above suggestion, remember that togetherness is a way to foster friendship. If children improvise movement to The Three Pigs, they will find that the wolf will have no trouble blowing down their loosely arranged bodies, representing sticks and straw, but that wolf will never blow down their closely arranged bodies representing a solid house of bricks!

Migrating birds rarely fly awry. They fly in formation and follow a leader. Take the children outside. Turn yourselves into a flock of migrating birds. The children love to take turns being the leader bird as their classmates swoop with them across the grassy sky.

Ducklings usually stay together, near or behind their mother. Invite the children to waddle behind you, exploring the room, school, halls, and playground. Swimmy swimming alone was in danger. But swimming together surrounded by friends and family, Swimmy was safe![24] The children love to be turned into a school of fish swimming together.

Create dances for the group to do together. The children have excellent ideas. Use as many of them as possible. Combine ideas. Make simple but delightful patterns. **Stories, poems, and songs are moving experiences** Think of how easily you and your children can enrich poems, stories, and songs with movement interpretation and accompaniment. Keep the spirit of playfulness and adapt the materials to fit your children. Everyone is *in* when Bill Martin Jr.'s beloved book, *Brown Bear, Brown Bear, What Do You See?*[25] is changed into an active "game" using everyone's name—"Nina, Nina, what do you see?" "I see Duane jumping to me!" A. A. Milne's "Us Two" is a perfect poem for pairs of buddies to interpret. The rhythm of the poem is music to link arms, sway together, play patty-cake, and skippity-do walk together.

After listening to *Together,*[26] pairs of buddies enjoy the demonstrating/miming/acting out/dancing activities that friends can do together—different activities performed simultaneously or one activity performed by both children.

Don't feel you must move to every word in a story, song, or poem. Select phrases, paragraphs, or ideas in it to celebrate in movement. How can we not move to vivid and exciting ideas?

Walking together An ordinary walk can be transformed into an extraordinary experience that strengthens camaraderie, friendliness, and cohesion while encouraging authentic learning.

On clear days in any season, take your children outside. Find old and new places to explore. A simple walk around the school or around the block when mixed with imagination and fun can become a peak experience. "That was more fun than a field trip!" exclaimed a bright six-year-old. With a group of kindergartners, we walked through a silent school (third-grade standardized tests were going on) to a school bus waiting to take them on a field trip. To keep the children quiet so they didn't disturb the test-takers, we walked as if we were invisible, as if we were snowflakes falling, as if we walked on magical tiptoes. The children waved goodbye to me and rolled off to their trip. Later in the day, I stopped back to see the kindergartners who had just returned. They were gathered in front of a language experience flip chart writing responses to their afternoon. When the teacher asked the children what was their favorite part of the field trip, one of the children said, "Walking to the bus!"

Here are a few suggestions. Add your own!

Buddy walk Buddies walk holding hands.

Singing walk Hold hands, swing hands, sing, and "bouncy walk."

Animal walk The children walk like animals. Monkeys walk differently from giraffes.

Noah's ark walk A variation of the above is a procession of animals walking two by two. Buddies choose which pair of animals they want to be.

Hello walk Greet everyone and everything you pass with a friendly word or movement.

Stop-look-listen walk Walk with your senses in high gear. Stop and look behind you, around you, above you. What do you see? Listen; what do you hear? Share observations.

Walk tall Heads high, shoulders straight, muscles strong—make big footsteps.

Discover-the-world walk Wear your imaginary magical glasses, which help us see everything more clearly. Close in on a specific spot. One group of kindergartners

spent almost a half hour on a patch of grass noticing ants, ladybugs, caterpillars, birds, seeds, worms, roots, weeds, blades of grass, and holes in the dirt.

Storybook characters walk Walk softly like Hiawatha. Walk rigidly like the Tin Woodsman, loosely like Scarecrow. Walk *big* like a giant, *big* like Paul Bunyan. Walk like a monster from *Where the Wild Things Are*. Skippity-walk like Dorothy on the Yellow Brick Road. Walk like best friends, Frog and Toad.[27]

When you return from your walk, invite the children to talk about, sing about, draw, paint, construct, or dance about the experience of walking together.

CLASSROOM VISITORS AND FIELD TRIPS

Family members Family members are a source of creative and important learning experiences. Parents, stepparents, uncles, aunts, grandparents, cousins, and siblings have much to contribute to children's lives. When family members are invited, encourage them to share something with the children such as a skill, hobby, story, song, tradition, game, food, or object. Of course, letters of appreciation not only enrich the time together but teach children about courtesy as they develop language competency.

Your own family members Young children are excited to meet their teacher's spouse, children, parents, or cousins. Encourage older family visitors to reminisce with the children about earlier times.

Foster Grandparents This is a marvelous program sponsored by the federal government to bring young children together with older adults in a grandparent-grandchild relationship. If you do not want to become involved in official programs, invite older members of your community to establish such relationships with your children. Americans are so mobile that grandparents are often hundreds of miles away. All of the generations need each other.

Friends and neighbors If yours is an open, welcoming door, people will want to become part of your classroom family. Whenever Mrs. Gresham walks her dog, she stops in to visit the kindergartners. Friendly custodians develop close friendships with children and see them daily.

Storytellers and folksingers They are relevant to every theme!

Family businesses Often you will find businesses operated by your children's families. These family businesses are usually flattered and eager to have their children's classmates visit them. Many trades are passed down from one generation to another, and children need to see this kind of traditional relationship at work. The walls of restaurants, offices, and laboratories are bright with pictures sent to them by appreciative children after enjoyable visits.

Places where families and friends work You'll be surprised at how responsive friends and family members are to visits by the children. Children visited Tina's cousin who worked at McDonald's, Deidre's aunt who was a dental hygienist, and Stephanie's neighbor who sold at a bakery.

Athletic teams, marching bands, drill teams, symphony orchestras, construction workers When children watch these kinds of activities in action, they see teamwork, cooperation, and friendliness clearly demonstrated.

IT ALL COMES TOGETHER

"It" can all come together at any and every moment of every idea. See the immeasurable possibilities for integrating learning. To inspire you, meet Janis Pechenik.[28]

The children in Janis's integrated kindergarten define the idea of "inclusion." Children with special needs are members of a "regular" full-day kindergarten. Janis's "physically challenged" children receive services in speech, language, physical, and occupational therapy within the day's program. *All* of Janis's children almost immediately grow into a loving family-style community. How does she do it?

Before school even begins, she sends each child a picture postcard welcoming them with a personal message. From the very first day of school, they find individual welcome messages in their cubbies.

One of Janis's favorite ways to help the children learn about each other and the school is to tell the story of the Little Gingerbread Man with puppets or flannel board. Together, they bake a big Gingerbread Man. The children soon discover that their Gingerbread Man is missing. From the next day on, they travel as a class, searching together. They find clues in different places in the school—the nurse's office, the custodian's room, the cafeteria. Their search ends in the principal's office with the last clue. As you can see, Janis involves everyone in the story. Of course, when the Gingerbread Man is found, there's a celebration. By then, the children know each other—they've worked together, traveled around the school together, and succeeded in their journey together.

We always have playmates—to watch over and watch out for each other. Especially on the playground. When I blow my whistle, the children must find their playmates.

There are always lots of choices about where they're playing, what they play and with whom. With more introverted children who choose not to have play partners, I take out something very exciting like puppets or snapblocks and play with that child. Invariably, the others drift over and join in.

I love to play songs for the children like Thomas Moore's "I Am Special" or "At the Easel" or "I Like You." We sing together then tell each other what we like about each other. We draw each other and draw pictures for each other. . . . Oh, we make up lots of circle games. We sing and dance to Thomas Moore's "Hokey Pokey Dokey." Then we make up our own verses and take turns being leader. . . . There's always singing and moving going on in our room. Through movement, singing and playing, the children are always developing higher level skills. . . . Talking goes on all the time. Lots of cooperative learning. Children more skilled in one area may not be skilled in other areas. We help each other and learn to respect each other. One of my kindergartners reads on an eighth-grade level but can't skip. The other kids try very hard teaching him how to skip. His best friend in the classroom is a child with Down's syndrome. . . . Throughout the day we work and play together as a whole group. The first hour of every day we are all together. It takes us an hour to go through the calendar, days of the week, counting. We sing and dance the days of the week and our numbers. We like Hap Palmer's "Days of the Week Rap" and the "Alphabet Rap." . . . Unless they're listening to a story, five-year-olds won't sit still more than a few minutes! As long as I keep the kids moving, they're happy. . . . We learn a new poem every single week. We write them in our classroom poetry book. Most of our children are doing inventive spelling with lots of pictures. My children who scribble think they're writing in cursive! My child reading on an eighth-grade level prints in all capital letters. . . . In our room there's room for everybody in every stage of development. . . . We respect and acknowledge each other's specific gifts and talents. . . . Learning is an ongoing process in our class, among all members of our classroom family!

NOTES ♥

1. See the work of Sylvia Ashton-Warner and her concept of the "key vocabulary," especially *Spearpoint,* New York: Random House, Vintage, 1974.

2. I wrote about this situation in the article, "Only One Child In the World: Notes from a Doting Grandma." *Day Care and Early Education.* Summer 1992, p. 35.

3. Tony's story was described in an Associated Press article that appeared in the Columbus, Ohio, *Dispatch,* April 11, 1993. The headline was: "Extraordinary Boy Survives Terrible Pain to Find Love." The book about Tony is *A Rock and a Hard Place* by Anthony Godby Johnson. New York: Crown, 1993.

4. Polly Greenberg, publications editor of the National Association for the Education of Young Children, is the author of numerous articles, essays, and books. These two books are widely known and highly regarded: *Character Development: Encouraging Self-Esteem and Self-Discipline in Infants, Toddlers and Two Year Olds* (Washington, DC: NAEYC, 1991) and *The Devil Has Slippery Shoes: A Biased Biography of the Child Development Group of Mississippi (CDGM): A Story of Maximum Feasible Poor Parent Participation* (originally published by Macmillan in 1969; reissued by Youth Policy Institute, Washington, DC: 1990).

5. Lynda Barry's essay, "The Sanctuary of School," appeared in *The New York Times,* January 5, 1992, p. 58.

6. Steve Wilson, joyologist and psychologist, has three delightful books in print: *Eat Dessert First* (1990), *SuperHumor Power* (1992), and *The Art of Mixing*

Work and Play (1992). Especially note the section "Fifty Practical Ideas Teachers Can Do in a Classroom" from the last book. All are available by calling 1–800–669–5233.

7. Eloise Greenfield, *Honey, I Love*. Illustrated by Diane and Leo Dillon. New York: Harper & Row, 1978.
8. Byrd Baylor, *Guess Who My Favorite Person Is*. Illustrated by Robert Andrew Parker. New York: Charles Scribner, 1977.
9. Alice Aron teaches kindergarten in Public School 153, in the Bronx.
10. Linda Goldsmith and Jo Ann Bell teach at Leo Yassenoff Jewish Center, Early Childhood Program, Columbus, Ohio.
11. Emmy Payne, *Katy No Pocket*. Illustrated by H. A. Rey. Boston: Houghton Mifflin, 1944, 1972.
12. William Steig, *Sylvester and the Magic Pebbles*. New York: Simon & Schuster, 1969.
13. Bernard Ashley, *Cleversticks*. Illustrated by Derek Brazell. New York: Crown, 1991.
14. Arthur Dorrow, *Abuela*. Illustrated by Elisa Kleven. New York: Dutton, 1991.
15. Michael Joel Rosen, *Elijah's Angel*. Illustrated by Aminah Brenda Lynn Robinson. San Diego: Harcourt Brace Jovanovich, 1992.
16. Patricia Polacco, *Mrs. Katz and Tush*. New York: Bantam, 1992.
17. Sharon Bell Mathis, *The Hundred Penny Box*. New York: Puffin Books, 1986.
18. Harry Chapin's moving song, "Flowers Are Red" (published by Five J's Songs, ASCAP, 1978, Elektra Records) powerfully states how creativity can be squelched by rigidity and authoritarianism.
19. Shirley Duncan teaches kindergarten at Lindbergh Elementary School in the Columbus school system.
20. From "The Forest and the Trees" by John Lahr. *New Yorker* magazine, April 12, 1993, pp. 105–107.
21. Many beloved children's songs have been adapted for picture books. For example:
    Raffi, *One Light, One Sun*. New York: David McKay, 1990.
    ———. *Five Little Ducks*. New York: Crown, 1988.
    Mary Ann Kovalski. *The Wheels on the Bus*. Boston: Little Brown, 1987.
    ———. *Take Me Out to the Ballgame*. New York: Scholastic, 1992.
    Nadine Bernard Westcott. *There's a Hole in the Bucket*. New York: HarperCollins, 1990.
22. Jay Brand teaches drama on the Arts Impact Team at Indianola Alternative Elementary School and Reeb Elementary School, Columbus.
    I recommend that you learn something of the work of Dorothy Heathcote, who has inspired so many teachers and programs in the use of drama in education. See Liz Johnson and Cecily O'Neill (editors), *Dorothy Heathcote: Collected Writings on Education and Drama*. London: Hutchinson, 1984.
23. This poem appears in Arnold Adoff, *All The Colors of the Race*. New York: Lothrop Lee Shepard, 1982, p. 13.
24. Leo Lionni, *Swimmy*. New York: Pantheon, 1963.
25. Bill Martin Jr., *Brown Bear, Brown Bear, What Do You See?* New York: Holt Rinehart and Winston, 1983.
26. Ella George Lyon, *Together*. Illustrated by Vera Rosenberry. New York: Orchard Books, 1989.
27. Arnold Lobell's delightful series about Frog and Toad help the children understand many aspects of friendship.
28. Janis Pechenik teaches kindergarten at the Green Meadow School, East Greenbush, N.Y., Central School System. She has received many honors, including Teacher of the Year, for her school district.

BOOKS FROM MY KNAPSACK FOR CHILDREN ♥ ♥

Ackerman, Karen. *Song and Dance Man*. Illustrated by Stephen Gammell. New York: Knopf, 1988.

Aliki. *We are Best of Friends*. New York: Mulberry, 1982.

Aylette, Jenness. *Families—A Celebration of Diversity, Commitment, and Love*. Boston: Houghton Mifflin, 1990.

Banish, Roslyn, and Jordan-Wong, Jennifer. *A Forever Family*. Photographs by Roslyn Banish. New York: HarperCollins, 1992.

Barrett, J. *Willie's Not the Hugging Kind*. Illustrated by Pat Cummings. New York: Harper & Row, 1989.

Belton, Sandra. *From Miss Ida's Porch*. Illustrated by Floyd Cooper. New York: Four Winds, 1993.

Booth, Barbara. *Mandy*. Illustrated by Jim Lamarch. New York: Lothrop, 1992.

Bornstein, Ruth L. *A Beautiful Seashell*. New York: Harper & Row, 1990.

Bremmer, Larry Dann. *The Migrant Family*. Minneapolis: Lerner, 1992.

Browne, Anthony. *Willie and Hugh*. New York: Knopf, 1991.

Bunnett, Rochelle. *Friends in the Park*. Photographs by Carl Sahelhoff. New York: Checkerboard, 1992.

Bunting, Eve. *A Turkey for Thanksgiving*. Illustrated by Diane deGroat. New York: Clarion, 1991.

———. *The Wednesday Surprise*. Illustrated by Donald Carrick. New York: Clarion, 1989.

Butterworth, Nick. *My Grandpa is Amazing*. Cambridge, MA: Candlewick, 1991.

———. *My Grandpa is Wonderful*. Cambridge, MA: Candlewick, 1991.

Butterworth, Oliver. *A Visit to the Big House*. Illustrated by Susan Avishai. Boston: Houghton Mifflin, 1993.

Byars, Betsey. *The Seven Treasure Hunts*. New York: HarperCollins, 1991.

Carlstrom, Nancy White. *Baby-O*. Illustrated by Sucie Stevenson. Boston: Little, Brown, 1992.

Cazet, Denys. *Great-Uncle Felix*. New York: Orchard, 1988.

Choi, Sook Nyul. *Halmoni and the Picnic*. Illustrated by Karen M. Dugan. Boston: Houghton Mifflin, 1993.

Cole, Brock. *Nothing But a Pig*. New York: Farrar, Straus & Giroux, 1990.

Crews, Donald. *Bigmama's*. New York: Greenwillow, 1991.

Crews, Donald. *Shortcut*. New York: Greenwillow, 1993.

Cuyler, Margery. *Shadow's Baby*. New York: Clarion Books, 1989.

Daly, Niki. *Not So Fast, Songololo*. New York: Macmillan, 1986.

Davol, Marguerite. *Black, White, Just Right*. Illustrated by Irene Trevas. Morton Grove, IL: Albert Whitman, 1993.

dePaola, Tomie. *Tom*. New York: Putnam, 1993.

DePaolo, Paula. *Rosie & the Yellow Ribbon*. Illustrated by Janet Wolf. Boston: Little, Brown, 1992.

Dionetti, Michelle. *Coal Mine Peaches*. Illustrated by Anita Riggiio. New York: Orchard, 1991.

Dowling, Paul. *Meg and Jack are Moving*. Boston: Houghton Mifflin, 1990.

Dragonwagon, Crescent. *Home Place*. Illustrated by Jerry Pinkney. New York: Macmillan, 1990.

Drescher, Joan. *Birth Order Blues*. New York: Viking, 1993.

———. *My Mother's Getting Married*. New York: Dial, 1986.

Duffy, Betty. *The Math Wiz*. New York: Viking, 1991.

Ehrlich, Amy. *Parents in the Pigpen, Pigs in the Tub*. Illustrated by Steven Kellogg. New York: Dial, 1993.

Fowler, Susan Gregg. *When Joel Comes Home.* Illustrated by Jim Fowler. New York: Greenwillow, 1993.

Garza, Carmen Lomas. *Family Pictures: Cuadros de Familia.* Emeryville, CA: Children's, 1990.

Girard, Linda. *Alex, the Kid with AIDS.* Illustrated by Blanche Sims. Morton Grove, IL: Whitman, 1993.

———. *Who Is a Stranger and What Should I Do?* Illustrated by Helen Cogancherry. Morton Grove, IL: Whitman, 1993.

Gomi, Taro. *My Friends.* Illustrated by Taro Gomi. San Francisco: Chronicle, 1990.

Greta, Susanna. *Frog, Duck, and Rabbit.* Illustrated by Susanna Gretz. New York: Four Winds, 1992.

Heine, Helme. *Friends.* Illustrated by Helme Heine. New York: Macmillan, 1986.

Hendershot, Judith. *Up the Tracks to Grandma's.* Illustrated by Thomas B. Allen. New York: Knopf, 1993.

Henkes, Kevin. *Julius, the Baby of the World.* New York: Greenwillow, 1990.

Horowitz, Ruth. *Mommy's Lap.* Illustrated by Henri Sorensen. New York: Lothrop, Lee & Shephard, 1993.

Hort, Lenny. *How Many Stars in the Sky?* Illustrated by James Ransome. New York: Tambourine, 1991.

Hudson, Wade. *I Love My Family.* Illustrated by Cal Massey. New York: Scholastic, 1993.

Hughes, Shirley. *The Snow Lady.* New York: Lothrop, Lee & Shephard, 1991.

Hunt, Nan. *Families Are Funny.* Illustrated by Deborah Niland. New York: Orchard, 1990.

Johnson, Angela. *The Leaving Morning.* Illustrated by David Soman. New York: Orchard, 1991.

———. *When I Am Old with You.* Illustrated by David Soman. New York: Orchard, 1990.

Johnston, Tony. *Grandpa's Song.* New York: Dial, 1990.

———. *Yonder.* Illustrated by Lloyd Bloom. New York: Dial, 1988.

Joose, Barbara. *Mama, Do You Love Me?* Illustrated by Barbara Lavallee. San Francisco: Chronicle, 1992.

Jordon, Mary Kate. *Losing Uncle Tim.* Illustrated by Ron Wennekes. Morton Grove, IL: Whitman, 1989.

Koehler, Phoebe. *Making Room.* Illustrated by Phoebe Koehler. New York: Bradbury, 1993.

Komaiko, Leah. *Earl's Too Cool for Me.* Illustrated by Laura Cornell. New York: HarperCollins, 1988.

Lager, Claude. *A Tale of Two Rats.* Illustrated by Nicole Rutten. New York: Stewart. Tabori & Chang, 1991.

Lash, Michele, et al. *My Kind of Family—A Book for Kids in Single Parent Homes.* Burlington, VT: Waterfront, 1990.

Lillie, Patricia. *When This Box Is Full.* Illustrated by Donald Crews. New York: Greenwillow, 1993.

Lyon, George Ella. *Together.* Illustrated by Vera Rosenberry. New York: Orchard, 1989.

Martin, Bill, Jr. *Barn Dance.* Illustrated by Bill Martin, Jr. New York: Henry Holt, 1988.

Mitchell, Margaret King. *The Barber Shop.* Illustrated by John Ransome. New York: Simon and Schuster, 1993.

Passen, Lisa. *Fat, Fat Rose Marie.* Illustrated by Lisa Passen. New York: Henry Holt, 1991.

Pearson, Susan. *Well, I Never!* Illustrated by James Warhola. New York: Simon and Schuster, 1990.

Peters, Lisa Westburg. *Good Morning, River!* Illustrated by Deborah K. Ray. New York: Arcade, 1990.

Pinkwater, Daniel. *Doodle Flute.* Illustrated by Daniel Pinkwater. New York: Macmillan, 1991.

Polacco, Patricia. *The Keeping Quilt.* Illustrated by Patricia Polacco. New York: Simon and Schuster, 1988.

Pomerantz, Charlotte. *Halfway to Your House.* Illustrated by Gabrielle Vinient. New York: Greenwillow, 1993.

Potok, Chaim. *The Tree of Here.* Illustrated by Tony Auth. New York: Knopf, 1993.

Ringgold, Faith. *Tar Beach.* Illustrated by Faith Ringgold. New York: Crown, 1991.

Rosenberg, Maxine B. *Brothers and Sisters.* Photographs by George Ancona. New York: Clarion, 1991.

Rubenstein, Gillian. *Dog In, Cat Out.* Illustrated by Ann James. New York: Ticknor & Fields, 1993.

Russo, Marisabina. *A Visit to Oma.* New York: Greenwillow, 1990.

Rylant, Cynthia. *The Relatives Came.* Illustrated by Stephen Gammell. New York: Bradbury, 1985.

Sadler, Marilyn. *Elizabeth and Larry.* Illustrated by Marilyn Sadler. New York: Simon and Schuster, 1990.

Say, Allen. *Grandfather's Journey.* Illustrated by Allen Say. Boston: Houghton Mifflin, 1993.

Schreffrin-Falk, Gladys. *Another Celebrated Dancing Bear.* New York: Scribners, 1991.

Senisi, Ellen B. *Brother & Sister.* Photographs by Ellen B. Senisi. New York: Scholastic, 1993.

Sharp, N. L. *Today I'm Going Fishing with My Dad.* Illustrated by Chris L. Demarest. New York: St. Martin's, 1993.

Simon, Norma. *All Kinds of Families.* Illustrated by Joe Lasker. Morton Grove, IL: Albert Whitman, 1976.

Smalls-Hector, Irene. *Jonathan and His Mommy.* Illustrated by Michael Hays. Boston: Little, Brown, 1992.

Smith, Lane. *The Happy Hocky Family.* Illustrated by Lane Smith. New York: Viking, 1993.

Smothers, Ethel Footman. *Down in the Piney Woods.* Illustrated by Ethel Footman Smothers. New York: Knopf, 1992.

Spohn, David. *Winter Wood.* New York: Lothrop, Lee & Shephard, 1991.

Tyler, Anne. *Tumbel Tower.* New York: Orchard Books, 1993.

Vigna, Judith. *Black Like Kyra, White Like Me.* Illustrated by Judith Vigna. Morton Grove, IL: Albert Whitman, 1992.

———. *I Wish Daddy Didn't Drink So Much.* Illustrated by Judith Vigna. New York: Morrow, 1993.

Waber, Bernard. *Ira Says Goodbye.* Boston: Houghton Mifflin, 1988.

Waddell, Martin. *Owl Babies.* Illustrated by Martin Waddell. Cambridge, MA: Candlewick, 1992.

Wahl, Jan. *Mr. Owl and Mr. Pig.* New York: Lodestar, 1991.

Walter, Mildred Pitts. *My Mama Needs Me.* New York: Morrow, 1983.

Wassonm, Valentina. *The Chosen Baby.* Illustrated by Glo Coalson. New York: HarperCollins, 1977.

Watson, Jane Werner. *Sometimes a Family Has to Move.* Illustrated by Irene Travis. New York: Crown, 1988.

Williams, Vera B. *More, More, More, Said the Baby.* Illustrated by Vera B. Williams. New York: Greenwillow, 1990.

Winthrop, Elizabeth. *Asleep in a Heap.* Illustrated by Mary Morgan. New York: Holiday House, 1993.

Wynot, Jillian. *The Mother's Day Sandwich.* New York: Orchard, 1990.

BOOKS FROM MY KNAPSACK FOR TEACHERS ♥ ♥

Baldwin, Paul. *The 125 Most Asked Questions about Adoption.* New York: Morrow, 1993.

Bernard, B. *Fostering Resiliency in Kids: Protective Factors in the Family, School and Community.* Portland, OR: Western Center for Drug-Free Schools, 1991.

Cohen, D. *Families.* Minneapolis: Simon and Schuster, 1990.

Dishon, Dee, and O'Leary, Pat. *A Guidebook for Cooperative Learning.* Holmes Beach, FL: Leary, 1984.

Kidder, Tracy. *Among School Children.* New York: Avon, 1990.

Perske, Robert. *Circle of Friends.* Nashville: Abingdon, 1988.

Polakow, Valerie. *Lives on the Edge—Single Mothers and Their Children in the Other America.* Chicago: University of Chicago, 1993.

Ramsey, Patricia. *Making Friends in School.* New York: Teachers College, 1991.

Thomas, Marlo, and Friends. *Free to Be—A Family.* New York: Bantam, 1987.

Chapter 5

Others We Meet/
Our Worlds Widen

If I am not for myself, who am I?
If I am only for myself, what am I?
Separate yourself not from the community.
Rabbi Hillel

It takes a whole village to educate a child. African proverb

Every neighbor is a teacher. Arab proverb

Mitakuye oyasin. (We are all related.) Lakota nation

THE BASICS

Just as the themes in this book have blurry boundaries, overlapping and continuously interconnecting, so the many worlds of human beings flow one into another. As we journey from wombs to rooms, to, as John Holt describes in his concept of World Three, "the world on the other side of the door,"[1] our awareness, knowledge, and experiences expand. Beyond our closest circles of family and friends, other people and other ideas wait for our recognition. Beyond that door (or those doors) is a greater community. Creating caring communities that welcome all who enter, especially the children, is a challenge debated throughout the country. Preparing young children to move into those worlds of unfamiliar faces and places, ideas and events, can be exhilarating as well as frightening.

In a country as vast, heterogeneous, and complicated as ours, the idea of building or rebuilding communities may seem too impossible to envision, but we Americans are known as creative problem solvers. We are doers! From California to the New York islands, schools, families, agencies, and institutions work together to enrich the education of children by strengthening the interwoven strands of the fabric of community. Read any issue of any educational journal or magazine and you will read terminology that tells the story. Phrases like "coordinated network," "multiple resources," "foreign alliances," and "building through collaboration" provide vocabulary for this dynamic period of cooperation bringing diverse interests together with common goals.

Even in some of our most distressed communities, individuals, groups, and institutions are embarked on enterprises of healing. Read all about it—businesses are adopting schools; volunteers tutor across the grades; families are becoming more responsibly involved in the education of their children. Articles with titles like "Cooperation Between the School Board and the Corporate Board Creates a Kindergarten"[2] share good news from Fargo, North Dakota. Find out what's happening in Baltimore by reading "Linking a City's Culture to Students' Learning."[3] Check out the Brookstown School in Baton Rouge, Louisiana, through "Growing Up with Options."[4] In their excellent article, "Beyond Parents: Family, Community and School Involvement,"[5] Patricia A. Edwards and Lauren S. Jones Young write: "These proposals call for greater inclusion of adults who are important in children's lives and in vastly different ways from our traditional conception. . . . The time has come to reframe home/school relations diligently and seriously in light of the old African saying: 'The whole village educates the child.' "

It is reassuring to know that examples abound of how schools, families, and communities converge in full support of children.[6] I think it's valuable to close in on one group.

Project Reach[7] is a model of cooperation between institutions and individuals to smooth the transition from a smaller, more secure environment to a larger, often more dismaying scene. In this outstanding venture (adventure!) in Columbus, Ohio, Head Start teachers and assistants and public school staff, family counselors, and families create a welcoming community for young children as they leave Head Start and begin the big world of public school.

At the lunch break of an all-day Project Reach seminar, participants talked thoughtfully about preparing young children to learn about "others we meet."

In the excerpts that follow, you'll note that, as always, caring educators begin with the children. (It's in the blood!)

"I tell my children: Be proud of who you are. Do your best. Keep strong self-concepts. Share your knowledge with others, people unfamiliar to you, different from you, and they will share their gifts and knowledge with you. Don't be afraid to explore. Be open to new people and new experiences."—Donna Robinson

"When we have confidence in ourselves, in our skills and abilities, we learn to respect others. We learn we're all individuals in a world community."—Dan Cunningham

"The world is getting smaller. Our children have a place in the world. They have to see themselves as part of *we*. Aren't we all in the process of reaching toward each other?"—Joyce Calamese

"We talk a lot about the things people have in common. Even though people do things differently, our needs are the same. We share the basic things! This year my kids had to learn to understand and accept a classmate who had a speech handicap. We all learned patience and to wait and listen so we could understand her. We all benefited. She became a happy, playful child. We became better people."—Jerlyn Saunders

"In everything we do, we keep discovering that different is not bad; it's just different! The important lesson is to see the worth of every individual."—Carole Moyer

"It's exciting—learning about new people, new ideas. We can help make it positive, make it wonderful, if we don't view those wider worlds with dread. So many adults lock themselves out. Even our youngest children sometimes lock themselves out. Those earliest habits carry through a lifetime. I'm always interested in different cultures, different professions, people of different ages. I'm always asking them to 'tell me.' I like to pass that curiosity, interest on to my children. Get them ready for the world."—Celestine Shipp

Before our workshop resumed, Steve Schack, Anne Sylvan, Becky Bible, and Julie Watt presented their Project Reach song still in progress. Here is their chorus:

Reaching out to make a connection
Reaching out to help children grow.
Reaching out to one another—that's our goal.
Reach for the dream that all children hold in their hearts.
Search for the ties that bind us all.
We can soar high if we but try—it's possible
To build a foundation to last our whole life long.[8]

Because you are such a significant influence on the lives of young children, your attitudes toward reaching out to others we meet, your feelings about the expanding worlds beyond the door, will be as much *caught* as taught. If you share the excitement of the challenge with the Project Reach participants, the experiences your students will have as they explore the wider community will be positive and life-affirming. But if you approach this inevitable expansion with dread, that negative energy will permeate the very air your children breathe. We may teach facts or information. What else are we teaching? As you read through this book, remember that you have the keys to open all the locks, especially the locks that close our hearts to ourselves and others.

All themes evoke a range of responses from the most narrow to the widest possible. How open is your mind? When Liz Harzoff[9] learned that this section would be titled "Others We Meet/Our Worlds Widen," she went into automatic, enthusiastic brainstorm! Numerous ideas flowed through her imagination. She jumped far beyond the familiar, traditional categories of community helpers such as firefighters and police officers. As with any idea, enough material can be generated to last a year long (a lifetime long!). These are just a few samples of Liz's notes for "Others We Meet."

All kinds of "otherness": language, age, gender, ethnic, rural-suburban-urban, racial, cultural, family grouping, diverse abilities. . . .

What about the world of work? Who are the people around us who help us? Around school? Around the neighborhood?

How can we approach people of different ages? Older adults? Teenagers? Babies? What about people from other ethnic groups who live in our community? Who speak other languages? What can we learn from people who participate in service projects?

How do we approach people who may have physical challenges? People from environments different than ours?

Start close to the students and yourself. Move outward to the rest of your school or center, the neighborhood, the area, the nearest population center, other parts of the U.S.A. and finally to other countries.

As young children grow in curiosity and comprehension, they are reassured to learn that the greater communities around them (their widening worlds) are functioning. They need to see people working together, contributing to the success of the whole structure. They are strengthened by the discovery of the interdependence of people. They must learn that they are part of the pattern, connected to all that they see. They are valuable members of the community!

Empowerment is another popular word today. Even the youngest children must know that their contributions are important. They are people of worth who can make things happen! As they reach out to others in positive, loving ways, they see that they can make a difference. Very young children form relationships with residents of nursing homes, rehabilitation centers, and shelters. Very young children launch pen-pal projects with children in a school across the city, across the corridor! Discover the many important ways friendships form among older and younger children.

Children are fascinated with the idea of work, of what people do. They have dozens of questions for the bus driver, the trash collector, and the auto mechanic. They are curious without labeling or judging, without looking up or down at occupations. Young children too soon will learn some of the prejudices and stereotypes that accompany various job descriptions and workers. Most young children still have a horizontal view rather than vertical. In this competitive, success-oriented, high-tech society, it's our challenge to preserve an open, respectful, appreciative attitude of children to the world of work.

We are living through a social revolution in the way we look at and aspire to that world. Today men are nurses, dancers, and homemakers. Women are surgeons, governors, and plumbers. Our children must be enlightened and strengthened with imagination, motivation, and self-confidence as they confront the opportunities now open to them.

Beware! Even when our purpose is noble, our language often reflects stereotyped thinking. Become aware of gender-specific words, especially pronouns. An easy way to avoid such language is to use the plural form. For example, instead of saying "a doctor" and then referring to the doctor as "he," say "doctors" and "they." Try to change traditional titles like mailman, policeman, and fireman to letter carrier, police officer, and firefighter.

As children play, they explore possibilities and experiment with concepts. Encourage them to respect and cooperate with each other, to do whatever they are pretending to do with a sense of pride (if they are baking pretend pies, encourage them to bake their very best; if they are washing cars, to wash their very best), and to have confidence in themselves that their play will be infused with regard for their own work and that of others.

Aren't we really talking about extending the philosophy and practices of family and friends toward that widening circle of neighbors, of others who, in their own special ways, help us in our everyday lives?

Take the wide road when you think about "others we meet." Any suggestion from the Project Reach conversation collage or from Liz's notes can be the grain of sand through which you discover the world! Be inclusive in your definition of "others." In the expanding worlds of young children, TV characters, storybook characters, animals, and puppets are often as real and believable as the neighbors across the street.

In this ever-changing, dynamic society, new experiences knock at both sides of the children's doors! The classmate who is difficult to understand because of a speech impediment or because she speaks a different language is waiting to be welcomed, accepted, and respected by your children. Yours may be a homogeneous group of children who share the same race, religion, and cultural background, but their ever-widening worlds will encompass people and ideas from around the globe and across the city.

DISCOVERY TIMES/WONDER TIMES

- The success of a community depends on everyone doing a good job, taking responsibility, and caring about and cooperating with others.
- Everyone's work is important and should be appreciated. Isn't it astonishing to think about all the kinds of work possible for people to do? Explore the yellow pages!
- People, in their work and in their lives, contribute to the well-being of others.
- People depend on one another and have responsibilities toward one another. (I bet you can think of a hundred ways people help one another!)
- We all have different talents, skills, and interests that are important and should be valued.
- If people work hard, learn special skills, practice a lot, and achieve certain levels of accomplishment, they should be able to do any job to which they aspire.
- No matter what kind of work people do, they should do their very best and be proud of their accomplishments.
- Sometimes the work people do is easily recognized and understood, but there are many kinds of jobs that are not as immediately obvious (doesn't someone shape the holes in doughnuts?). Obvious or subtle, all contribute to the working of the whole community.
- So many kinds of people, languages, and cultures appear different from our own; we can find ways to learn about, get to know, and understand them. People always have ways of connecting with one another. It's fascinating to realize that with all the diversity, we are still members of the human family and have so many things in common. (Can you think of ten?)
- Sometimes personalities we read about in the newspapers and see on TV are real to us. We feel as if we know them personally. Even characters in stories soon became part of our lives. Our imaginations are magical. They help us see the world in such interesting ways.
- We have so many strengths, talents, skills, questions, and ideas about how our world works and the many wonders of our world. We have important contributions to make to others.

SUGGESTED VOCABULARY

neighbor	work	delivery	telephone	Asian-American
school	job	mail carrier	typewriter	Hispanic
teacher	chore	police officer	computer	Native American
classmate	assignment	mechanic	word processor	Christian
partner	responsible	doctor	equipment	Jewish
principal	cook	dentist	tools	Hindu
nurse	clean	social worker	ladders	Moslem
bus	store	clinic	art supplies	church
bus driver	gas station	volunteer	artist	synagogue
custodian	post office	Scout leader	studio	mosque
helper	fire house	ambulance	theater	world
community	laundry	subway	sculptor	senior citizen
neighborhood	factory	taxi	symphony	nursing home
street people	office	airplane	instruments	college
different	hospital	fire engine	TV	university
same	market	library	movies	welfare worker
share	supermarket	museum	videos	radio
repair	shopping center	zoo	cassettes	news
fix	beauty parlor	farm	tape recorder	newspaper
collect	barber	city	magazines	president
sort	shoe repair	country	books	governor
clean	garage	machinery	cameras	
customs	uniform	skills	languages	
accent	food pantry	mayor	understand	
worker	truck	librarian	African-American	

Note: Continuously add to these vocabulary suggestions with your students. Each word is a universe of possibilities!

SOME STARTERS

Start with serendipity and spontaneity Be open to the wonderful, unexpected gifts offered to you every day—the new child, a visiting relative, a telephone repair truck, or something shared by one of your students that ignites imagination and exploration. When the three exchange teachers from Kenya walk down the halls of your school, do you say, "We're not ready for Kenya yet!" or do you say, "Come on in!"?

Start with a classroom visitor Be spontaneous and invite the mail carrier to say hello to your class and share a few minutes with your children. Or plan ahead and ask a community helper or a member of a different background to visit your room. Prepare the children for the exciting event. Encourage them to ask the guest questions and to share ideas. Continue with activities that are related to the visit.

Start with a walk around the neighborhood This delightful activity is an excellent way to stimulate response on all levels, especially if children are encouraged not just to walk but to stop, look, listen, and learn.

A class of kindergartners filled a chalkboard with their observations and discoveries, which included:

On Our Walk Around Our Neighborhood, We Found

two mailboxes	one newspaper store
one traffic light	our school
twelve houses	street signs
one doctor's office (M.D.)	"block parent" house
streetlights	one carry-out store
sewers	fire hydrants
telephone poles and wires	

The walk provided them with more than enough material to begin their study of community and community helpers.

Start with pictures Show children pictures of community helpers and people from different backgrounds and ask them to guess who they are and what they are doing. Their answers will stimulate ideas for further activities.

Start with the Yellow Pages Show children the local Yellow Pages and explain that it lists most of the people in the community who provide services. Read some of the types of services offered.

Start with a riddle "I'm thinking of someone who helps us. That person wears a special uniform and sometimes directs traffic. That person will help you find your way if you are lost. That person tries to keep you safe from harm. Who is it? Can you guess?"

Start with a question Spark discussion with questions such as "What do you want to be when you grow up?" "What kinds of work do you like to do?" and "What are important kinds of work needed by us all?"

Start with a poem Poems are a wonderful way to help children think about the possibilities that await them. Examples include A. A. Milne's "Busy" and "Cherry Stones"[13] and Walt Whitman's "I Hear America Singing."

I wrote a poem that has been enjoyed and added to by children of all ages. It is printed so that you can use it. Better still, write your own!

When We Grow Up

I

I'm going to be a football player
when I grow up.
I'm going to kick that football
when I grow up.
You'll watch me at the game.
You'll see my speed and strength.
I'm tackling right now
so I can be a football player
when I grow up.

I'm going to be an artist
when I grow up.
I'm going to paint pictures
when I grow up.
You'll see my flower prints.
You'll love my bright designs.
I'm doodling all the time
so I can be an artist
when I grow up.

I'm going to be a scientist
when I grow up.
I'm going to discover things

when I grow up.
I'll find a cure for ills.
I'll search those mysteries.
I ask questions every day
so I can be a scientist
when I grow up.

II
When we grow up, when we grow up,
we want the world to be
a place of friendly people
with room for you and me.
    doctor, lawyer, ice-cream scooper, cook, tailor, trash collector, governor,
    gardener, shoemaker, teacher, dancer, baker, builder, plumber, taxi driver,
    artist, scientist, football player
The world needs us all
to carry it along,
to build its bridges,
sing its song,
to feed its children,
to cheer its sad,
to paint its pictures,
to make it glad.

The world needs us each
and every one,
whatever our ages, whatever our shapes,
whatever our colors, whatever our lands,
to open our hearts
and reach out our hands,
to use our minds wisely
to live days of joy,
to help build a better life
for each girl and boy.

When we grow up, when we grow up,
we want the world to be
a place of friendly people
with room for you and me.

Start with pantomime Pantomime different kinds of work for the children, and ask them to guess each one. For example, pantomime a police officer blowing a whistle and directing traffic; a doctor examining a patient (use the children, puppets, or dolls as patients); and a mechanic repairing a truck or car (use one of the classroom vehicles). If you want to emphasize one helper, pantomime several activities of that occupation. If you want to introduce the idea of community helpers, pantomime several occupations. Invite the children to pantomime their own ideas.
Start with clothing Wear a police officer's cap or a fire fighter's helmet to introduce the idea of community helpers. Hold up a shovel or a paintbrush. Ask the children: "Boys and girls, do you notice I'm wearing something unusual?" They will have no trouble meeting the challenge of your question, and you can easily start them off on a monthlong or yearlong study of others who help us.
Start with a song There are so many excellent songs to help enrich every idea! Share songs you love with your children. A few of my favorite songs that help children

connect to others in our ever-widening worlds are Raffi's "To Everyone in All the World," and "Like Me and You"; Ella Jenkins' "The World Is Big—The World Is Small"; Woody Guthrie's "How Doo Do"; and "Everybody Loves Saturday Night" (in many languages). Make up your own songs! Sing the children's songs!

Start with a story Stories are the oldest ways to teach! No matter the lesson, start with a story. Make up your own story about meeting a person from a different background who may speak a strange language and have an unfamiliar-sounding name. Make up a story with your children about people who help us. Share some of the excellent children's literature waiting to be celebrated. Some of my favorite children's books that cannot help but stimulate talk and thought are Peter Spier's *People,*[10] a beloved book that opens the minds and hearts of all readers to the amazing diversity of human beings on this little planet of ours; and Michael Joel Rosen's *50 Odd Jobs,*[11] a delightful introduction to thinking about less obvious jobs people do, such as, who decides new shapes for noodles? There is a lot of fun and laughter thinking about odd jobs people do in this world! Tana Hoban's marvelous photographs and Edith Baer's simple text introduce the world of healing, helping, building, creating, and loving through *The Wonder of Hands.*[12] Begin, continue, and never end with stories and songs.

TALK TIMES/LISTENING TIMES

Even our very young children have many experiences, questions, and observations to share. Encouraged in safe and loving learning environments, knowing their contributions are important and respected, most of them will be eager to participate in talk times as speakers and as active listeners. Creative teachers use the children's suggestions to generate activities and further explorations. The process is exhilarating. Learning from the inside out is the most meaningful kind of learning. As often as possible, write (or with older children, assign a scribe as a classroom helper) the children's ideas so they continually see the relationship between the spoken and written word. Remember, talk times/listening times cannot be relegated to a time slot. Talk times/listening times are happening in loving, lively classrooms throughout the day.

When Pat Stumhauzer and Cliffy Withers asked their three- and four-year-old students about their ideas of "people who help us," they had enough topics to last a lifetime! Here is their list:[14]

doctor	person who mows lawns	clothes cleaner
nurse	person who shovels snow	house builder
minister	veterinarian	truck driver
salesman (-person)	street cleaner	zookeeper
mailman (letter carrier)	trash collector	candy shop lady (clerk)
policeman (officer)	telephone man	diaper man (service)
fireman (-fighter)	wireman	TV newsman (reporter)
ambulance man (driver)	toy maker	tape recorder man
soldier	car mechanic	newspaper boy
teacher	circus man (performer)	(deliverer)
dentist	highway fixer	rug cleaner
barber	car washer	guy who fixes broken
taxi driver	librarian	stuff in house
bus driver	furniture repairman	Girl Scout leader
gas station man	Salvation Army man	Boy Scout leader
(attendant)	(collector)	airplane pilot

It should be noted that young children still identify most occupations by gender. Teachers have the opportunity to teach new vocabulary and a new way of thinking.

Following a storytelling session in a local bookstore, I sat with Emily and Travis Irvine[15] talking about their idea of "others we meet." Many of their ideas corresponded to those on the list above. I won't repeat those words in the following response by Emily and Travis. Add these suggestions:

the president	comedians
baby-sitters	cooks
counselors	news reporters ("help us know what's going on")
social workers	

"People who are trying to save the world. People who know the world's in trouble and are trying to help like planting trees and stopping smoking."

sailors	naturalists
the principal	lawyers
deejays on the radio	scientists
actors	Native Americans
basketball, soccer, softball coaches	characters like Johnny Appleseed
artists	plumbers
writers	people who speak different languages
mayor	governor

So many ideas poured out immediately that we had to stop and catch our breath. In that pause, Emily's eyes widened. She exclaimed, "I never knew there could be so many!"

Observations Fascinating discussions develop from shared observations. When I was a child, I was amazed that whatever needed to be done, someone did it! I shared with the children my feeling about the ingenuity and industriousness of human beings and their ability to meet whatever needs arise. "Isn't it amazing, boys and girls, that someone is always able to do a job that needs to be done? For example, if you need your car fixed, someone knows how to fix it!" The children could hardly contain their ideas.

> If your lights go out, you can call and get someone to get them on again.
> If you fall down and hurt yourself, you can go to the doctor.
> If your tree gets sick, a tree doctor can make it get better.
> If your bike breaks, you go to the bike store and get it fixed.

Later we improvised plays based on the children's comments. "My dog is sick. Who can make him better?" asked a child who held a stuffed dog close to her. "I can. I'm a 'vesternarian'!" a future vet responded immediately.

Questions, based on observations, that also spur lively discussions are: "What kinds of workers come to your house?" "What kinds of people do you see in your neighborhood?" "What skills and qualities are needed for certain jobs?" and "I wonder how people get to be doctors, mechanics, teachers, and cooks?"

We are lucky to spend time with young children, most of whom still have hearts and minds open to people and ideas different from themselves, who have not yet been "carefully taught" stereotyping and prejudice. Children are famous for their honesty, their sharp awareness of even the most minute details in faces and places. Their often matter-of-fact comments expressing their observations and experiences are often refreshing, sometimes embarrassing. "That man has a big nose!" "Why is that lady in a wheelchair?" I'll never forget when our oldest son, Cliff, was three years old and answered the front door to find three nuns in full habit. He looked at them without critical or judgmental eyes. His eyes brightened with curiosity. He asked them, "Who are you guys?"

When we teach in the key of life, we help children learn how to meet new situations with courtesy and respect. Sometimes that's a challenge! Our own attitudes toward others spread easily. We need to take care with our own words and expressions so our fears, suspicions, and prejudices are continually reduced. *We have to teach ourselves.* We need to be wise talkers and fair and compassionate listeners.

When Indira's mother visited school wearing her bright red and yellow sari, Jason commented that she looked "weird." A special talk time/listening time immediately followed the comment. A few minutes of honest discussion among the kindergartners gave them the opportunity to express opinions freely, such as:

"Saying 'weird' can hurt someone's feelings" (Kim said).
"I don't think Jason meant to hurt my feelings" (Indira's mom said).
"I never saw a sari before. It's pretty" (Nikki said).
"Do all the ladies in India wear saris?" (Rebekka asked).
"My mom wears jeans" (Shawn said).

By the time the little discussion stopped, the children, including Jason, agreed that Indira's mom's sari was, indeed, beautiful.

Be ready to talk about any kind of narrow, prejudiced, stereotyped comments at the time. Don't wait a week, checking your plan book to see if there's an open slot in your schedule! *Nothing in your schedule is more important than talking together about the way we look at ourselves and others.*

Let's continually say, with Celestine Shipp, "Tell me," and keep interest and curiosity on our way to understanding.

And remember, with Carole Moyer, "Different is not bad, it's just different!"

Unemployment Because unemployment is a fact of life for millions of people in our country, it is likely to be a topic of discussion, especially if you have an open, trusting relationship with the children in your class.

"My Daddy doesn't have a job," shy, five-year-old Cindy said in the middle of a class talk about work. Her teacher replied: "Your Daddy may not have a job where he goes out to work every day right now. He may get one sometime. But doesn't he still do things for you and your family?" Cindy quickly responded: "He takes me to school. He takes my brother to Scouts. He brings in groceries for my mom. He helps me with puzzles. . . ." The teacher noted, "He does a lot of important things that help you. It's hard work being a daddy." The teacher's comments changed Cindy's expression from dull to bright. "Yes, he does," she smiled.

Be as open as possible to find ways to express respect and compassion for all of the situations that may be introduced during talk times/listening times. You may not be able to do anything about unemployment or welfare programs, but you can do something about attitudes and feelings—your own and those of your students. You can help them to see that people must not be defined by their jobs alone. Even though Cindy's father is unemployed, he is a good daddy, a good neighbor, a good citizen, a person who makes a contribution to society. Try not to be judgmental; look within yourself for ways to understand and accept situations and relationships that may be unfamiliar to you. Your commitment is to help strengthen your young students with feelings of confidence, courage, and self-worth, however diverse their situations, talking and listening helps!

Appreciation for volunteers The children in Jan Hammock's class[16] discussed their feelings about volunteers who come from the community and help in so many ways. Bethany Higginbotham translated her thoughts and conversation about those special people into a poem.

> **Volunteers**
> Someone knocking on our classroom door.
> Who is it?
> Who is it?
> He walks in.
> It is field day.
> He cheers us on
> like an untrained cheerleader.
> She drives us to our field trip,
> singing happily with us
> like a little, sweet bird.
> He tutors us,
> encouraging like a
> mother duck
> pushing her babies into the water.
> Now the volunteer leaves us.
> A tear streams down our faces.
> Thank you![17]

Questions, observations, appreciation, comparisons, memories, information, and clarification are all components of talking and listening times.

I am in shock when I observe classrooms of silence. What can we learn about ourselves and others without communication?

VISUAL ARTS TIMES

I hope that by now you can't help but think of your room as a dynamic space/environment that is always in process—full of action, exploration, and participation. Your space is more than a room, more than, say, "Kindergarten Room 4." It's a gallery. It's a museum. It's an archeological dig. It's a convention center. It's an exhibit hall. Walls are for pictures, paintings, murals, collages, posters, and portraits. Hooks are for hanging mobiles, balloons, and sculptures. Windows are for painted colors. Your room tells a story. Is it product-centered or process-centered? Does it reflect the excitement, the energy of what's happening with your children, or is it perfectly framed in static, packaged images mail-ordered from manufacturing companies?

Be eclectic in your gathering of visual materials, especially if your group of children is more homogeneous; the need for them to be surrounded by faces and images that reflect diversity grows urgent. In many classrooms around the country, the only faces different from themselves seen by the children are pictures on their walls. Always make room for the faces of people, for people at work, for the rich complexity and fascinating heterogeneity of the human family. Keep the images flowing throughout the year.

Because your "scrounge" materials will always be plentiful, you will never be short of magazines, cards, scraps, snips, ribbons, and buttons, or treasures that most people toss, like Styrofoam packing chips and fast-food containers. You and your children will be able to enjoy hands-on visual arts experiences daily.

Classroom helpers Remember that a feeling of community begins in the classroom, where children take specific responsibilities and contribute to the welfare of others. Your challenge is to think of enough classroom helper jobs so that every child has a job every day.

If you travel across the country, you will see as many visual variations of helpers as there are teachers. Basically, there are two ways to organize: the children's names/symbols/photographs are on a permanent chart and the symbols/words/images of the jobs are changed around, or vice-versa.

This project is probably one of your first visual arts activities. The children's input into gathering the jobs themselves is important. Be open to adding jobs as you and your students think of them. Encourage the children to illustrate each idea. Laminate the designs/symbols/words for each job and devise a way to display them next to the children's names or pictures.

In my travels, I have seen job wheels, space journeys (each child's rocket lands on a different job in the shape of a planet), circus trains (each car represents a job and the children's name cards are in the shape of circus animals and characters). In one kindergarten I saw a board of kangaroos representing every child. Classroom jobs were printed on baby kangaroos that slipped into the big kangaroos' pouches. The board's headline was: "Let's do our jobs! Hop to it!"

Portrait galleries Beginning with portraits of class members (be sure to title and name each one), expanding to portraits of families and friends (including pets), discuss with the children the importance of people in the school—clerks, other teachers, secretaries, custodians, school nurses or counselors, tutors, volunteers, cooks, cafeteria staff, and so on. After visiting and observing, the children enjoy honoring those people with portraits. Now your walls are covered with images reflecting our widening worlds.

Turn yourself into a community helper Many community helpers have easily identifiable uniforms and equipment. Here are some suggestions for making these articles for the children to play with.

Nurses and doctors' surgical lights Rhoda Linder and Wendy Wohlstein and their four-year-olds played doctor for days with their official-looking headbands. They gave each child a strip of paper for a headband and small circles to color yellow or orange (for light). The children pasted their circles in the middle of their headbands and fastened the headbands around their heads.

Stethoscopes Rhoda and Wendy and their students also made stethoscopes. They cut the little sections out of egg cartons, punched holes on each side, and attached pipe cleaners.

Stethoscopes can also be made from spools. Wrap the spool in aluminum foil, thread a strong piece of string or wool through the spool, and fasten the two ends of the string or wool together.

Furniture Collect small twigs and sticks, tongue depressors, and toothpicks for making furniture. Glue them together to make chairs, beds, tables, and couches for dollhouses. Other materials for young furniture makers are assorted boxes and flaps and sheets of cardboard of all sizes.

Telescopes Ask parents to send in the cardboard cores from rolls of paper towels. The children paint them black or another dark color. When dry, they make perfect telescopes. How about a canopy of stars and moons to view?

Barbershop clients Blow up balloons. With Markers, the children paint faces on the balloons. When dry, they are ready to be sprayed with shaving cream and shaved with dull knives or tongue depressors. "Who's next?"

Instrument panels Give each child a sheet of shirt cardboard or a medium-sized cardboard box. Encourage the children to create their own panel by gluing on materials from the scrounge collection, such as buttons, pins, spools, paper clips, scraps of material, jewelry, and pebbles, or drawing different shapes on the panels with Magic Markers. Old lamp frames, hanger wire, and long pipe cleaners make fine steering wheels.

TV announcers' microphones Clothespins or cardboard toilet paper rolls make excellent microphones. Paint them an appropriate color. Give each child a chance to report the news.

TV sets TV announcers feel better when they are surrounded by a TV set. Turn a medium-sized box into a TV set by cutting off the bottom of the box, gluing or taping the rest of the box tightly, and cutting out a screen in the front. The children paint the box and take turns slipping up into the box so their heads fill the screen area.

Zookeepers' animals Draw or sculpt animals that live in the zoo. Or shape zoo animals with pipe cleaners, clay, Playdough, rocks, electronic wire, driftwood, yarn, cotton, and scrounge materials. Or glue or paste animals to the bottom of a shoe box. Each child makes a small zoo and pretends to be the keeper. Or create a class zoo.

Interior designers' windows Interior designers, painters, and artists help make a community more beautiful through their creative works. Paint original designs and pictures on your windows with poster paint. Give all the children an opportunity to add their own contributions to the pattern. Poster paint looks terrific on windows and is easy to wash off when you need a change of color or mood.

Police officers' badges Cut badge shapes out of cardboard and give one to each child, or have them cut out their own.

Wrap each badge in a piece of aluminum foil. Using double-sided masking tape, attach the badges to the children's chests.

Police officers' hats Motorcycle police officers wear helmets; traffic police wear white hats; and patrol officers wear blue hats. Give the children strips of paper for headbands. Outline the different hats on paper. Cut hat shapes out of construction paper. The children color or paint the hats according to the shapes. Tape the hats to the headbands.

Police officers' walkie-talkies Paint small cereal boxes any walkie-talkie color. Punch a hole in each box. Connect two boxes with a long piece of string. Now police officer buddies can communicate emergencies and other information to each other.

Firefighters' hats You can create a simple firefighters' hat by following the basic directions for police officer's hats.

Draw or shape yourself as a community helper Following your own discussion with your children about people who help us, gather the ideas, write them, and display them. Your gathering will be as rich as those included in the Talk Times/ Listening Times section. Using their own materials, invite the children to imagine

which jobs they would enjoy doing the most. Pictures and sculptures (clay, wire, paper mache, pipe cleaners, and so forth) of themselves *at work* are delightful activities for the children. Don't forget to exhibit them and celebrate them.

Collage of community helpers Based on their ideas and observations, the children cut out pictures of community helpers or people who help us from magazines, catalogues, and newspapers.

They draw or paint their own illustrations. All the children contribute cut-out or original pictures of community helpers to a large collage. With markers, print the names of different helpers over the pictures and in the spaces (if there are any spaces).

Make gifts for a community helper Paint or draw cards, pictures, or posters, and present them to a favorite community helper. I had the good fortune to be in a school office when a kindergarten class knocked on the door, came in beaming with smiles, and gave the school secretary love letters, greeting cards, and pictures. She was moved to tears! (So was I!)

A more personalized look at the world of work and people who help us Taking the widest view but closing in on the collective knowledge and experience of your class, horizons immediately expand when you talk together about people they know who do things that contribute to the betterment of others. We talked with preschoolers about their ideas; here are a few excerpts from that session:

> "Grandpa Bob makes chairs." "Susan and Igor deliver papers." "Bobo knits cute baby clothes." "Kanika beads earrings and sells them at festivals." "Annie's mom stamps your library books." "Greg's band is 'Shades of Grey'—they play good." "Pietro talks on the phone a lot—he writes down what they say."

Here are opportunities, once again, to move beyond traditional ways of looking at how people work and help each other.

The children can honor these people with pictures and projects. Add them to your ever-growing gallery! A delightful variation is to invite the children to create images representing the works like: Grandpa's chairs, Bobo's baby clothes, Annie's

mom's library books, Kanika's beaded earrings, Pietro's telephone, and Greg's musical band. Remember to title all the pieces.

What's in a snack? This is the story of how a simple snack of milk, cookies, and bananas led Louise Johnson and her first graders into new understandings of the interrelationship and interdependence of people as the children enjoyed a series of stimulating activities.[18]

One day, as the children were sitting down for snack, Louise thought of all the people and processes that made that taken-for-granted snack possible. She asked questions like: "Where does the milk come from?" "How did it get to us?" "Where do bananas come from?" and "What goes into an oatmeal cookie?" The questions elicited answers that produced more questions. "We get bananas from the supermarket." "Yes, but where did the supermarket get them?"

Before she realized what was happening, Louise and her children were having fascinating discussions, heads bent over globes and maps, looking for banana-producing

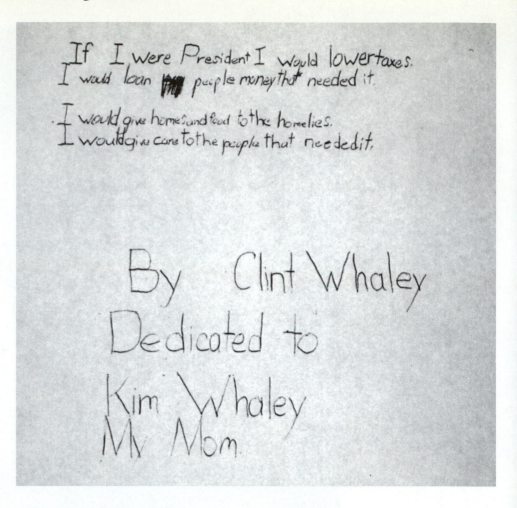

If I were President I would lower taxes.
I would loan ███ people money that needed it.

. I would give homes and food to the homelies.
I would give care to the people that needed it.

By   Clint Whaley
Dedicated to
Kim Whaley
My Mom.

countries and tracing railroad lines and truck routes. These are just a few of the persons who were identified as having helped to produce the snack of the day.

dairy farmers	cookie factory workers
cows	grain elevator operators
banana pickers	delivery people
sailors of banana boats	people who load milk cans
truck drivers	store clerks
freight train conductors	paper workers who make the package for
store owners	the cookies
grain farmers	workers in the milk container factory
sugar cane plantation workers	

Pictures of containers of milk, a banana, and an oatmeal cookie were pasted to a large bulletin board. "Then the fun began," Louise said. "The children drew any aspect of any of the people or processes that had a part in their snack. We drew lines going out in all directions from our center snack design. The children pasted up their pictures of farmers, banana pickers, sailors, truck drivers, all of the 'helpers.' It was really an amazingly enlightening as well as thoroughly enjoyable project!"

Not only did Louise's children understand and appreciate their simple snack of milk, bananas, and oatmeal cookies, but they also learned that hands of many colors, from different cultures, crossing lands and seas, all contributed in important

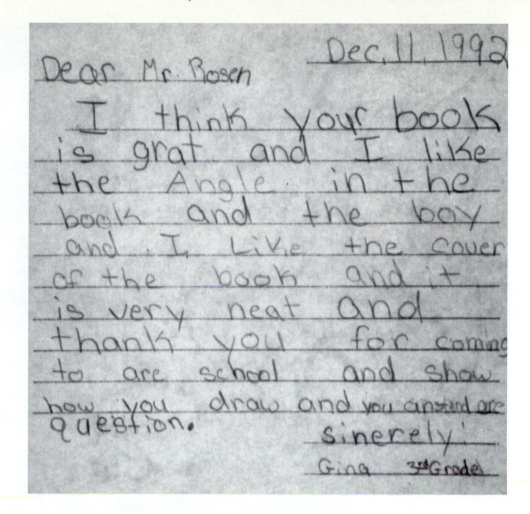

ways to that ordinary snack! From the coffee-colored hands of Caribbean banana pickers to the diversity of truck drivers, factory workers, clerks, and packagers to the hands of the children, the journey was fantastic!

Community helpers booklets Encourage the children to make booklets celebrating community helpers. When children make a booklet about one kind of helper, each page is a picture, story, or symbol associated with that helper. When children make a booklet celebrating many helpers, each page is labeled; stories or words are added to the pictures to enrich the project. Staple the pages together. Ask the children to make wonderful covers. Share them. Celebrate them!

A people procession As the children talk about, read about, visit with, and observe people coming into your room and your lives, honor those experiences with symbols, cards, pictures, posters, collages, sculptures, and mobiles—works of every style and dimension.

For years I have worked in the Greater Columbus Arts' Council's Artists in the Schools program, which has given me the opportunity to be with children in hundreds of schools in central Ohio. Throughout the country, variations of our Artists in the Schools programs abound, and American children are widening their worlds by sharing time with people from diverse backgrounds who work in interesting and colorful fields. A typical program for a school reads: Scottish dancers—September. Japanese paper artist—October. African drummers and dancers—November. Storytelling from Mexico—December. And on through the year. Now, more than ever

before in our history, American children are learning about people unfamiliar to them. Add to this procession characters in books who are as beloved as flesh-and-blood humans and TV personalities and characters who become "my Barney" and "my Mr. Rogers."

As we design our appreciation for the experience of meeting new people, as we demonstrate our new knowledge and awareness in colors, shapes, forms, and textures, we carry on an ancient tradition of expressing feelings and experiences in art forms. Whether you make masks, cartoon drawings, stick figures, scrounged-material portraits, or crayon drawings, you help the children connect their daily lives with art forms that hallow our time.

Picture books inspire picture books   This is a glorious time for children's literature! There are so many excellent picture books for children. When children read such treasures as Arnold Adoff's *Flamboyan*,[19] how can they *not* rush to their paints and crayons to catch flaming colors of people and nature on a tropical island? Imag-

ine children learning of *Flamboyan* as they sit in a Vermont classroom surrounded by winter. Children who may never have seen a Native American read *Dancing Tepees*[20] and see the connection between Native Americans, their love of nature, and their designs and symbols. Our children can't wait to create their own.

MUSIC TIMES

Work songs Throughout history people sang as they worked—on canals, railroads, ships, ranches, and farms. Work songs popular with children of all ages include "Sixteen Tons," "Pick a Bale of Cotton," "Erie Canal," "Banana Boat Song," "Rock Island Railroad," and "John Henry." When you enjoy work songs with your children, be sure to include songs from other cultures.

Fill your room with the sound of singing and music!

Rearranged golden oldies "I've Been Workin' on the Railroad" already celebrates a community helper—the railroad worker. This song was easily turned into a community helpers song when a group of first graders and their teacher added these stanzas:

We've been working as firefighters.
All the live-long day.
We've been working as firefighters
Just to keep the fires away.
Can't you hear the fire bell ringing?

Hurry and slide down the pole.
Can't you hear the fire bell ringing?
Hurry and put out the fire.
Firefighters go! Fire fighters go!
Hurry and put out that f-i-r-e!
Firefighters go! Firefighters go!
Hurry and put out that fire!

A group of five-year-olds adapted "The Bears Went Over the Mountain" into a fine community helpers song.

The bears went over the mountain.
The bears went over the mountain.
The bears went over the mountain.
And what do you think they saw?
They saw a bus driver.
They saw a bus driver.
They saw a bus driver.
Stopping at a bus stop.

Later in the year the class visited the local library and talked to the librarian. They remembered their song and improvised the lyrics:

And what do you think they saw?
They saw a librarian.
They saw a librarian.
They saw a librarian.
Stamping all the books.

Of course, the songs are accompanied by improvised movement.

Community helpers bands What kind of music would traffic officers play? Anything with whistles and horns, of course! That was the answer kindergartners gave their teacher. They distributed homemade and rhythm instruments that made whistling or honking sounds. After experimenting for a while with fast, slow, loud, soft, high, and low sounds, the children composed a police officer's fugue with two distinctive melodies.

These are the kinds of discoveries children make through discussion and translate into music.

Librarians' music would be very quiet. . . .
Firefighters' music would be first real quiet when they're sleeping in the firehouse, then very loud and noisy when the siren blows, then fast as anything when the fire engine races to the fire!
Letter carriers' music is real steady, like walking!
Secretaries' music is like tapping sounds on a word processor—rat rat rat rat rat—very fast.
Police officers' music is like sirens—stop and go.

Songs and music for community helper puppets When children create community helper puppets, invite them to think of songs for their puppets to sing to the rest of the class about their work. Also encourage the children to play music appropriate to their puppet's work.

Singing telegrams and other musical mail Discuss the kinds of mail that letter carriers deliver: happy mail, which includes invitations to parties and news of visitors coming; sad mail to say that someone is sick or that someone cannot come to visit; angry mail, such as a notice about an overdue payment; emergency mail to be answered immediately; and beautiful mail that brings greeting cards and picture postcards.

The children take turns picking a piece of mail from a mail pouch (sack or shopping bag). They decide what kind of mail it is and think of or make up a song that describes the mail. The other children guess the inspiration. Five-year-old Felicia chose a letter and, without hesitation, burst into the song "Happy birthday to you!" The children guessed immediately—happy mail!

What are possibilities for air mail letters from different parts of the world? Beginning with the families and friends of your children as resources (include yourself), think about a postcard from Germany (German songs), a letter from Ghana (West African songs), a greeting card from Brazil (Mardi Gras music).

Accompany the activities with art challenges of designing stamps for all these pieces of mail.

Community helpers singing games After discussing community helpers, ask the children to put on signs (you may have to write them) or special clothing or equipment turning themselves into specific community helpers. When they are ready, form a circle and enjoy a community helpers "Farmer in the Dell."

"Have You Ever Seen a Lassie?" is another popular singing game that lends itself to celebrating community helpers. Here is how one group of children sang it, as each community helper was called into the center of the circle, improvised a movement, and was imitated by the other children.

> Have you ever seen a house builder go this way and that way (hammering)?
> Have you ever seen a house builder go this way and that?
> Have you ever seen a house painter go this way and that way?
> Have you ever seen a house painter go this way and that?

Musical gifts to community helpers Extend the gifts of song to helpers in school and the surrounding neighborhood whom the children have come to know. Whenever possible, find out the names of people you see and meet regularly, such as letter carriers, secretaries, custodians, delivery people, bus drivers, librarians, other teachers, and clerks.

Singing special songs for people expresses appreciation. Here is an example of such an offering.

A group of Detroit kindergartners made up and practiced a song and walked to the office to present it to their school secretary, Mrs. Goldenberger.

> (To the tune "Skip to My Lou")
> Run run run to our friend,
> Clap clap clap for our friend.
> Mrs. Goldenberger is our very good friend.
> Sing sing sing to our friend.
> Make a circle around our friend.
> Mrs. Goldenberger is our very good friend.

Songs for classroom helpers What a challenge! With your students, compose a song for every classroom job. Why not songs for emptying wastebaskets, songs for feeding fish, and songs for leading the salute to the flag? Write, illustrate (with the children), and display the words prominently so they can be shared throughout the year.

Music for books and stories People and places introduced to children through literature, as we said, often become important parts of the children's lives. Enrich the experiences of discovering the worth of new and unfamiliar people by sharing music from the cultures of those people. When you read a story like Angela Johnson's *The Leaving Morning*,[21] your students will empathize with a family on moving day—the African-American children bid goodbye to friends and neighbors and businesspeople. Here is a chance to share moving-on, goodbye, blues, soul, and journey songs to enhance the story with music. The children can even create their own rap song to catch the feelings of the story. Patricia McKissack's *A Million*

Fish . . . More or Less,[22] set in the bayou swamps in Louisiana, introduces children to lovable characters who fish together and tell tall tales. Find Cajun and zydeco music to highlight the story. Add movement to everything!

The rhythms of the world Basic instruments like drums come in every size and shape, design and style, from drums that fit in the palm of your hand to the nine hundred pound drums pounded by the Japanese Kodo drummers. Children are fascinated by the similarities within the diversity of instruments as they explore their widening worlds. How many ways cultures have designed and shaped strings, wind instruments, and percussion instruments. Shake, rattle, and strum your way through the cultures of the world as new people are introduced to your children, whether on paper or coming through that open door.

An opera of people who help us All around the country, teachers and children delight in creating operas. The theme of people who help us naturally lends itself to an original opera. Each kind of helper/worker the children honor can have a specific song describing a specific contribution. All the children can sing the chorus, connecting the ideas. Gilbert and Sullivan brightened the lives of people as they created operatic songs to introduce marvelous characters through arias. Your songs can introduce the kinds of workers. Add movement, props, and masks. Enjoy! (Note: When you embark on any big, ambitious project, don't squeeze the fun out of it by overrehearsing or prolonged preparation. Keep these kinds of experiences spontaneous and playful.)

MOVEMENT AND PLAY TIMES

The good news is that young children play and move! The best news is that your room invites imaginative, free play and your schedule provides time for the children to do what they do best and learn in ways they learn best—through play. Simple materials and props should be available at all times. Set aside spaces and places for blocks, sand boxes, water tables, clothing racks, house furniture, tool chests— whatever themes are closest to the children's lives. Classroom visitors, field trips, songs, stories, pictures, and books may inspire the setting up of a specific idea like a dentist's office, a hairdresser's shop, or a supermarket. As the worlds of your children grow wider, those worlds become part of the lives of the children and the life of your room. The Emerald City, a rain forest, an airport, or a fast-food restaurant take shape before your very eyes.

What is your role? Often a participant, occasionally a director, you are always a loving, aware, sensitive, supportive, responsive, responsible adult. In your observations of the children's play, watch for children who are more inhibited, who sit on the outside and long to be included. Often a simple prop like a badge or a hat transforms them into participants. If you prod, they may pull back. Many times, a puppet will evoke a positive response. Never stop trying to help children freely enjoy their gift of imagination. Keep drawing circles that take them in!

As you enjoy these smatterings of ideas, remember: keep things moving! Young children are already moving. Adults are the ones who tell them to stop. Minimize those stop signs!

Hat rack In addition to the hats children make as art projects, keep a good collection of helpers' hats hanging in easily accessible places for children to play with. In one class, I saw these hats hanging on a hat tree: railroad worker's striped cap; police hat; construction worker's hard hat; nurse's cap; cowboy hat; sailor's cap; fire helmet; mommy's hat; and gentleman's hat. "I'm a hat snatcher," the teacher explained. "Wherever I go, and whomever I meet, I ask if they have a hat to give me for my kids."

Shoe rack While you are scrounging, collect shoes of different types: cowboy boots, fisher's boots; lady's high heels; fire fighter's boots; men's shoes; moccasins.

Four-year-old Emily was looking through Grandma Anita's closet. She found a foldable pair of gold-threaded discount store slippers and gasped with excitement. "Grandma," she called, holding them up. "Are these the slippers you wore when you were a prince?"

Costume box Old shirts make excellent uniforms for doctors, nurses, and hairdressers. Bags of every size and shape, from knapsacks to mommy's pocketbooks to medicine bags, are very popular. Overalls, vests, shirts, ties, jackets, dresses, scarves, veils, and shawls are constantly used by children in their play. Be sure to include wigs, mustaches, beards, and makeup; and to have at least one mirror safely propped in an accessible place. (Children are not vain; they are curious.) They love facepaint!

Community helpers puppet shows Informal, spontaneous puppet shows are often a daily feature of students' lives when puppets and formal or makeshift puppet stages are always available. Occasionally, you may want to encourage specific puppet situations. Here are a few suggestions.

Interview community helper puppets. The children ask the puppets questions about their work.

Invite community helper puppets to be guests of the class and tell the children what they do.

Introduce one community helper puppet to another and start a dialogue in which they compare jobs.

Ask the puppets to sing a song about their work.

Ask the puppets to show the rest of the children what they do and have the children guess which helper they are.

Invite the community helper puppets to do their work in the classroom. For example: "Boys and girls, this is our new mail carrier, Mrs. Envelope. She will be giving out your letters today." Or "Children, our friend Dr. Sandy Sniffles wants to check your ears and chins to see if you're all in good health!"

In all of these situations, the children are manipulating the puppets. If you think children need extra encouragement, try something like this: "Metria, will you bring over Freddy Fire Fighter and ask him to tell us about fire safety. Thank you!"

Parades of community helpers A parade of scientists would certainly look different from a parade of house builders. Put on some sprightly marching music and

experiment with different parades. Encourage the children to think of specific actions that describe each helper so that the parades look different. Their body shapes and movement change with each idea.

Helping hands Think of some things helpers' hands do: cut, sew, stamp, write, type, dial, fix, hammer, paint, draw, repair, comb, press, build, polish, sort, steer, tap, mix, shake, lift, push, and pull. Talk about this first so that the children's minds are full of ideas for helping hands. Play follow-the-leader and give each child a turn to demonstrate a hand movement that the others follow.

Community helper movement collage Focus on one community helper and discuss the various activities of that helper. Write the ideas on the board as reminders of how many wonderful suggestions young children can offer in only a few minutes.

Here are some ideas about a school custodian's actions suggested by a group of first graders.

Our School Custodian—Mr. Esposito

walks around school	stops the school bus
sweeps	answers the phone
shovels snow	checks the furnace
turns on electricity	connects broken pipes
fixes wires	helps us with moving our projects
carries stuff	helped us look for our rabbit
tells kids things	moves very fast in emergencies

After the children talked and gathered ideas, they brainstormed about each as they read them on the chart. Then they practiced "showing" them. They moved through the list changing at each idea. The list of ideas was the choreography—walking, sweeping, shoveling, electricity going on. We told the children, "When the music starts, choose any one of the custodian's movements. When the music stops, freeze. Shake out. When the music goes on, choose another idea to move to." Because they talked, shared, and practiced, the children had no trouble expanding familiar ideas to new experiences involving changes and music. Find any music that you like with a steady rhythm. Don't feel that you must have a specific piece of music to do any improvised creative movement activity. Children and music are flexible. There are resources at your fingertips that you never thought of using.

What other kinds of helpers lend themselves to these types of movement celebrations? Make your own list! Illustrate and write about the movement.

Movement games of the world's people   Even when they meet a person who initially appears to be different, the children soon learn that people of unfamiliar backgrounds and situations offer much to share and enjoy and have many things in common.

Every culture features circle games/dances in which people take turns going into the center, performing some movement that the others follow, and choosing another person to be the leader in the center of the circle. These variations of "follow-the-leader" are universal. Find chants that you know and love, use music easy to circle to, and dance to any and every culture. Discover the ways your children enjoy this kind of game. Books like Mary Lankford's *Hopscotch Around the World*[23] or

Jane Yolen's *Street Rhymes Around the World*[24] are examples of excellent resources that inspire you to play with your children in old and simple ways.

Every culture has variations of hand-clapping games like patty-cake. Nowadays, our city kids have lifted those patterns to new heights of complexity and creativity. Watch children sit together on stoops or playground benches and perform dazzling feats of eye/hand coordination, small gross motor skills, high-level language development, sequential learning, listening skills, comprehension, rhythm, and timing as they show you their hand-clapping routines.

When children learn to love the songs, dances, games, and stories of cultures and people unfamiliar or strange to them, they break down barriers and turn keys in locks that open new doors.

Dances of the world's people   Very often dances from different cultures express various kinds of work—numerous dances from around the world show aspects of farming, transportation, healing, and dressing. Not only can we honor the work people do in dances, but we can also honor their cultures. All people have processions for special occasions. You can't go wrong if you honor a visitor from another culture by finding music from that culture and presenting a welcome parade or procession. If you can learn simple dances from other cultures, that's wonderful. If not, use music from the different cultures. People the world over dance in circles. Listen to the music. Let the rhythms move you. Circles can walk, march, stamp, and skip. They can change directions: clockwise and counterclockwise. They can face the center and clap and jump. Your children will have excellent movement ideas that will fit perfectly to the music no matter how unfamiliar.

In my sessions with children of Dances from Around the World, held at the Columbus Cultural Arts Center, the children (ranging in age from toddlers to intermediate graders) accompany all the music with rhythm instruments. The children follow the rhythms, from West African to calypso, as if they were born into those cultures! Our dances are simple, often children-choreographed, and loyal to the music and the traditions.

Remember, it was a pianist who broke through some of the barriers of fear and distrust between peoples involved in the Cold War. Van Cliburn's brilliant playing of Tchaikovsky's *Piano Concerto* thawed the icy feelings between the two peoples, just as dancer Nureyev leaped across the ocean and into the hearts of Americans who found, through the beauty of the gifts he shared, the humanity that lies in all peoples.

Music, dance, poetry, literature, and the visual arts are strands of the universal language of our human tribe. In our widening worlds, these are good languages to know!

CLASSROOM VISITORS AND FIELD TRIPS
Classroom Visitors

An open-door policy   Because you and your children are interested in learning about others and because hospitality is the atmosphere of the air you breathe, family members, neighbors, school staff, and volunteers will be happy to share their experiences with you. Always leave time for serendipity—the unexpected resource. Often the person who spontaneously looks in at your group has valuable material to bring you. One day a kindergarten class invited a man who walked his dog around the school every day. He turned out to be a veterinarian and fascinated the children with stories from his life and work.

In addition to police officers, fire fighters, and letter carriers, children enjoy meeting mayors and other government officers, and workers from community ser-

vice organizations such as the Red Cross, the Society for Prevention of Cruelty to Animals, the Kiwanis Club, the Society for Prevention of Blindness, and the YW or YMCA. It is important for children to know that people work at many different kinds of jobs and that people who do volunteer work are often as dedicated as professional staff. Iris Kaplan, the most honored community leader in Yonkers, New York, spent a great deal of time arranging for visitors to share with schoolchildren the many ways in which social service agencies improve the lives of people. A first-grade class had a memorable visit from a spokesperson for the city's United Way. The children were astonished at the number of agencies devoted to helping people.

Unless a visitor pops in unexpectedly, the preparation time with the children is as important as the visit. What do we want to know about, say, Mr. Puchovich's training to be a physical therapist? What are questions we want to ask him? As often as possible, encourage the visitor to bring something tangible for the children to see—a tool, an instrument, or a uniform. Encourage the visitor to share something concrete with the children—a song, a story, or a skill. Of course, thank-you letters and pictures should follow the session, along with projects and activities inspired by the session. A visit from an antique dealer inspired a group of prekindergartners to collect old "treasures" and stock their own "antique store" in a corner of the room.

Field Trips

Walk around and throughout the school   That often-formidable greater world of school has many interesting facets for children to learn. Those halls, corners, fields, other rooms, offices, and all the people who staff them, as well as other children who work and play in them, are major adventures for our newest students.

Your community as a resource   Len, our Muffin Man, is growing up in New York City, so the possibilities for numerous field-trip destinations will be very different from his cousin Rachel, who lives in a small, suburban community outside of Cleveland, and totally different from his friend Vincent, who lives with his grandparents on a farm in West Virginia.

What resources are provided by your community? Check them out. Museums? Galleries? Factories? Libraries? Post offices? Clinics? Service stations? Firehouses? Police stations? Orchards? Farms? Food pantries? Homeless shelters? Recreation centers? Packaging plants? Colleges or universities? Hospitals? Parks? Theaters? Government offices? Shopping malls? Pizzerias?

Your list of possible field trips will be unique, as are the ways you celebrate the experiences. Connect them to rich learning moments, encourage a continual unfolding as the children keep "playing" it. It's up to you. Wide or narrow? Open or closed?

Community events   Include in your gathering of community resources special events and commemorations. If at all possible, organize field trips to such ethnic celebrations as Native American powwows, Cinco de Mayo festivals, Kwanzaa, arts fairs, and international festivals and celebrations. It is important for your children to witness people from diverse backgrounds coming together in positive ways.

IT ALL COMES TOGETHER

I hope you are making it all come together as you read every page of ideas and imagine how they combine with others, fusing into multifaceted, meaningful experiences for the children.

Carol Highfield and Debbie Lamden's four-year-olds enjoyed a fantastic year of joyful, richly textured experiences.[25]

One of their students was an Asian-American child. To celebrate his cultural background, Carol and Debbie immediately embarked on what turned out to be a yearlong journey on the open road. Let Carol tell the story:

> We invited Lee's dad to come in and show us his abacus. Oh, the children loved it. We made abacuses by connecting strings across meat trays and putting beads on the strings. . . . I found a book with Chinese lettering and we wrote "Happy New Year" in Chinese to Lee's dad. One of the other parents who practiced calligraphy came in and showed us how to do calligraphy. She brought calligraphy pens and the children tried lettering with them. We read *Liang and the Magic Paintbrush*[26] and the children pretended they were the Chinese boy who painted magical pictures with his magical paint brush. We painted our own magic pictures! That led us to *The Eye of the Dragon*,[27] a wonderful book about a real Chinese artist, T'ang Yin, who painted dragons.
>
> The children were so excited when T'ang Yin in the story used an abacus for counting! Lee's dad told us about the seven standard puzzle pieces of different shapes called "tangrams" and we found the book *Grandfather Tan's Story: A Tale with Tangrams*.[28] We recreated the tangram shapes, made our own and gave the children the chance to arrange them and rearrange them into their own puzzle pic-

tures. . . . Oh my—our Chinese New Year's Celebration was terrific! We read *The Lion Dancer*[29] about a little boy who does his first Lion Dance in the New Year's parade. *Gung Hay Fat Choy*[30] is the Chinese New Year's greeting. It helped the children imagine the celebration. We painted a huge dragon on our wallpaper. We had a procession to Chinese music. We wrote fortunes for our own fortune cookies which we made out of small paper plates, folded over and stapled. We "smooshed" our strips of fortunes inside of them. . . . Don't worry, we did eat *real* fortune cookies (kosher). . . . On a huge chart, we wrote every kid's name and the fortune they made. We made red and orange scrolls that said, "Good health/long life/ happiness" and hung them around the room. The children were reminded about the same kinds of blessings they learned in Hebrew. . . . The kids loved the little red envelopes for good luck called laisees. I scrounged enough from a stationery store so every child had one. We filled them with play money. . . ."

As Carol enthusiastically shared some of these experiences that, as you can imagine, lasted weeks, I grew breathless with her. She paused for a moment, thought, then brightened with new energy. "Wait, don't I have time to tell you all the wonderful ways we celebrated Dr. Martin Luther King Jr.'s birthday?" Before I could answer, she continued, "The children's dreams and wishes for the world were amazing. After we talked about them and wrote them, we drew them inside of dream "bubbles" and mounted them around Dr. King's "I Have a Dream" speech near our beautiful friendship wreath of hands of all colors. Our rainbow people banner was one of the highlights. . . . Our two favorite songs were "Go Down Moses" (we talked a lot about the experiences of the African-American people and the Jewish-American people) and "If I Had a Hammer." David A. Alder's *Picture Book of Martin Luther King, Jr.*[31] is outstanding and we. . . ." Carol interrupted her story. "Gosh, which theme will you include in your book?"

This chapter, as all chapters, doesn't end. It just stops because we're caught in the limitations of time and space. What can be more important in our "work" than walking along with children as they enter ever-widening worlds, meeting many other people new to them? We can only pray that the experiences we share will be positive and have a lasting effect on their attitudes and philosophies. We want our children to become healthy, competent, respectful, caring people—citizens of the world, children of the earth!

NOTES ♥

1. John Holt, *What Do I Do Monday?* New York: Dutton, 1970. See chapters 3 and 4.
2. Liz Severn, "Cooperation Between the School Board and the Corporate Board Creates a Kindergarten." *Young Children.* Vol. 47 number 4, May 1992, pp. 62–64.
3. Richard Allen Chase and William G. Durden, "Linking a City's Culture to Students' Learning." *Educational Leadership.* September 1992, pp. 66–68.
4. Dana McDaniel Docherty and Beverly Irby Davis, "Growing Up with Options." *Educational Leadership.* March 1992, pp. 58–59.
5. Patricia A. Edwards and Lauren S. James Young, "Beyond Parents: Family, Community and School Involvement." *Kappan.* September 1992, pp. 72–80.
6. Ibid.
7. Project Reach is a National Head Start Public School Transition Demonstration Project. Under the umbrella of the Child Development Council of Franklin County, Ohio, a partnership project was created between

the CDC and Columbus Public Schools. Ann Bardwell is the director. For information on Project Reach, write to 398 S. Grant Ave., #205, Columbus, OH 43214.

8. Donna Robinson teaches at Southside Head Start in Columbus. Dan Cunningham and Joyce Calamese are family service counselors at Weinland Park School, Columbus. Jerlyn Saunders teaches at Koebel School, Columbus. Carole Moyer teaches at Salem School, Columbus. Celestine Shipp is family service coordinator for Project Reach. Steve Schack teaches at Windsor Alternative Elementary School, Columbus. Julie Watt teaches at Reeb Elementary School, Columbus. Anne Sylvan and Becky Bible are with the Early Childhood Department of the Columbus Public Schools coordinating programs with Project Reach.

9. Liz Harzoff is a folklorist working with children, teachers, and families in central Ohio. Her special commitment is to multicultural education.

10. Peter Spier, *People*. New York: Doubleday, 1980.

11. Michael Joel Rosen, *50 Odd Jobs*. Worthington, OH: Willowisp Press, 1987.

12. Edith Baer, *The Wonder of Hands*. Illustrated by Tana Hoban. New York: Macmillan, 1992.

13. A. A. Milne, *The World of Christopher Robin*. New York: Dutton, 1958. pp. 132–136, 137–139.

14. Pat Stumphauzer and Cliffy Withers taught in the Learning Unlimited School, Columbus.

15. Emily and Travis are students at Montrose Elementary School, Bexley, Ohio. This discussion took place in Chene's Books, Bexley.

16. Jan Hammock teaches at the Duxberry Park Arts Impact Alternative School, Columbus, Ohio.

17. Bethany Higginbotham teaches third grade.

18. Louise Johnson taught at Avery Elementary School, Hilliard, Ohio.

19. Arnold Adoff, *Flamboyan*. Illustrated by Karen Barbour. San Diego: Harcourt Brace Jovanovich, 1988.

20. Stephen Gammell, *Dancing Teepees*. Selected by Virginia Driving Hawk Sneve. New York: Holiday House, 1989.

21. Angela Johnson, *The Leaving Morning*. Illustrated by David Soman. New York: Orchard Books, 1992.

22. Patricia McKissack, *A Million Fish . . . More or Less*. Illustrated by Dena Schutzer. New York: Knopf, 1991.

23. Mary Lankford, *Hopscotch Around the World*. Illustrated by Karen Milone. New York: Morrow, 1992.

24. Jane Yolen, *Street Rhymes Around the World*. New York: Boyds Mill, 1992.

25. Carol Highfield and Debbie Lamden teach at the Leo Yassenoff Jewish Center, Early Childhood Program, Columbus.

26. Demi, *Liang and the Magic Paintbrush*. New York: Henry Holt, 1980.

27. Margaret Leaf, *The Eye of the Dragon*. Illustrated by Ed Young. New York: Lothrop Lee Shepard, 1987.

28. Ann Tompert, *Grandfather Tan's Story: A Tale with Tangrams*. Illustrated by Robert Anders Parker. New York: Crown, 1990.

29. Kate Walters and Madeline Slovenz-Low, *The Lion Dancer*. Photos by Martha Cooper. New York: Scholastic, 1990.

30. June Behrens, *Gung Hay Fat Choy*. Photos by Terry Behrens. Chicago: Childrens' Press, 1982.

31. David A. Alder, *Picture Book of Martin Luther King, Jr.* Illustrated by Robert Casilla. New York: Holiday House, 1989.

BOOKS FROM MY KNAPSACK FOR CHILDREN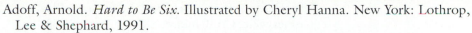

Adoff, Arnold. *Hard to Be Six*. Illustrated by Cheryl Hanna. New York: Lothrop, Lee & Shephard, 1991.

Begay, Shonto. *M'aii and Cousin Horned Toad*. New York: Scholastic, 1992.

Clifton, Louise. *Three Wishes*. Illustrated by Michael Hays. New York: Doubleday, 1992.

Cross, Verda. *Great-Grandma Tells of Threshing Day*. Morton Grove, IL: Albert Whitman, 1992.

Dugan, Barbara. *Loop the Loop*. Illustrated by James Stevenson. New York: Greenwillow, 1992.

Everett, Gwen. *Li'l Sis and Uncle Willie*. Illustrated by William H. Johnson. New York: Rizzoli International Publishers, 1991.

Faber, Doris. *The Amish*. Illustrated by Michael E. Erkel. New York: Doubleday, 1991.

Florian, Douglas. *A Painter*. New York: Greenwillow, 1993.

————. *An Auto Mechanic*. New York: Greenwillow, 1991.

Fox, Mem. *Wilfred Gordon McDonald Partridge*. Illustrated by Julie Vivas. Brooklyn: Kane Miller, 1985.

Goble, Paul. *The Lost Children*. Illustrated by Paul Goble. New York: Bradbury, 1993.

Gordon, Ginger. *My Two Worlds*. Photographs by Martha Cooper. New York: Clarion, 1993.

Grifalconi, Ann. *Osa's Pride*. Boston: Little, Brown, 1990.

Gunning, Monica. *Not a Copper Penny in Me House*. Illustrated by Frane Lessac. Homesdale, PA: Boyd Mills, 1993.

Hirschi, Ron. *Seya's Song*. Illustrated by Constance R. Bergum. Seattle: Sasquatch, 1992.

Hopkinson, Deborah. *Sweet Clara and the Freedom Quilt*. Illustrated by James Ransome. New York: Knopf, 1993.

Howlett, Bud. *I'm New Here*. Photographs by Bud Howlett. Boston: Houghton Mifflin, 1993.

Hoyt-Goldsmith, Diane. *Hoang Anh, A Vietnamese-American Boy*. Photographs by Lawrence Migdale. New York: Holiday House, 1992.

————. *Pueblo Storyteller*. Photographs by Lawrence Migdale. New York: Holiday House, 1992.

Johnson, Delores. *Now Let Me Fly*. Illustrated by Delores Parker. New York: Macmillan, 1993.

Kahlman, Maeria. *Sayonara, Mrs. Karkleman*. Illustrated by Maeria Kahlman. New York: Viking Kestral, 1993.

Keats, Ezra Jack. *Louie's Search*. New York: Four Winds, 1980.

Kendall, Russ. *Eskimo Boy—Life in an Inupiaq Eskimo Village*. Photographs by Russ Kendall. New York: Scholastic, 1992.

Knight, Margy Burns. *Talking Walls*. Illustrated by Anne Sibley O'Brien. Gardiner, ME: Tilbury, 1993.

————. *Who Belongs Here—An American Story*. Illustrated by Anne Sibley O'Brien. Gardiner, ME: Tilbury, 1993.

Kroll, Virginia. *Africa Brothers and Sisters*. Illustrated by Vanessa French. New York: Four Winds, 1993.

Kuklin, Susan. *Fighting Fires*. Photographs by Susan Kuklin. New York: Bradbury, 1993.

Lankford, Mary. *Hopscotch Around the World*. Illustrated by Karen Milone. New York: Morrow, 1992.

Leigh, Nila. *Learning to Live in Swaziland*. Illustrated by Nila Leigh. New York: Scholastic, 1993.

Littlechild, George. *This Land Is My Land*. Illustrated by George Littlechild. Emeryville, CA: Children's Book Press, 1993.

MacGill-Callahan, Sheila. *And Still the Turtle Watched*. Illustrated by Barry Moser. New York: Dial, 1991.

Martin, Rafe. *The Rough-Faced Girl*. Illustrated by David Shannon. New York: Putnam, 1992.

Mathis, Sharon. *Red Dog Blue Fly*. Illustrated by Jan Spivey Gilchrist. New York: Viking, 1991.

McKissack, Patricia. *A Million Fish . . . More or Less*. Illustrated by Dena Schutzer. New York: Knopf, 1992.

McPhail, David. *Farm Boy's Year*. Illustrated by David McPhail. New York: Atheneum, 1992.

———. *Pigs Aplenty, Pigs Galore!* Illustrated by David McPhail. New York: Dutton Children's Books, 1993.

Meredith, Susan. *Why Are People Different?* Illustrated by Annabel Spenceley. Tulsa: EDC, 1993.

Pinkwater, Daniel. *Author's Day*. Illustrated by Daniel Pinkwater. New York: Macmillan, 1993.

Pitre, Felix. *Juan Bobo and the Pig*. Illustrated by Christy Hale. New York: Dutton, 1993.

Polacco, Patricia. *Babushka Baba Yaga*. Illustrated by Patricia Polacco. New York: Philomel, 1993.

Powers, Mary Ellen. *Our Teacher's in a Wheelchair*. Photographs by Mary Ellen Powers. Niles, IL: Albert Whitman, 1986.

Rohmer, Harriet. *Uncle Nacho's Hat*. Illustrated by Mira Reisberg. Emeryville, CA: Children's Book Press, 1989.

Rohmer, Harriet; Chow, Octavio; and Vidaure, M. *The Invisible Hunters*. Emeryville, CA: Children's Book Press, 1987.

Rosen, Michael J., ed. *Speak! Children's Book Illustrators Brag about Their Dogs*. Illustrated. San Diego: Harcourt Brace, 1993.

Rylant, Cynthia. *Appalachia: The Voices of Sleepy Birds*. Illustrated by Barry Moser. San Diego: Harcourt Brace Jovanovich, 1991.

San Souci, Robert. *The Snow Wife*. Illustrated by Stephen T. Johnson. New York: Dial, 1993.

Schroeder, Alan. *Ragtime Tupie*. New York: Little, Brown, 1989.

Shemie, Bonnie. *Houses of Bark—The Woodland Indians*. Illustrated by Bonnie Shemie. Pittsburgh: Tundra, 1993.

———. *Houses of Snow, Skin and Bones—The Far North*. Illustrated by Bonnie Shemie. Pittsburgh: Tundra, Press, 1993.

Sis, Peter. *A Small Tall Tale from the Far Far North*. Illustrated by Peter Sis. New York: Knopf, 1993.

Soto, Gary. *Neighborhood Odes*. Illustrated by David Diaz. San Diego: Harcourt Brace Jovanovich, 1992.

Spier, Peter. *Circus*. Illustrated by Peter Spier. New York: Doubleday, 1992.

———. *People*. Illustrated by Peter Spier. New York: Delacorte, 1980.

Steptoe, John. *The Story of Jumping Mouse*. Illustrated by John Steptoe. New York: Morrow, 1984.

Tompert, Ann. *Bamboo Hats and a Rice Cake*. Illustrated by Demi. New York: Crown, 1993.

Turner, Robyn Montana. *Frida Kahlo*. Boston: Little, Brown, 1993.

Valens, Amy. *Danilo the Fruit Man*. Illustrated by Amy Valens. New York: Dial, 1993.

Walker, Barbara K. *Laughing Together—Giggles and Grins from Around the Globe*. Illustrated by Simms Tab. Minneapolis: Free Spirit, 1993.

Waters, Kate. *Samuel Easton's Day—A Day in the Life of a Pilgrim Boy*. Photographs by Russ Kendall. New York: Scholastic, 1993.

———. *Sarah Morton's Day—A Day in the Life of a Pilgrim Girl*. Photographs by Russ Kendall. New York: Scholastic, 1989.

Williams, David. *Grandma Essie's Covered Wagon*. Illustrated by Wiktor Sadowski. New York: Knopf, 1992.

Williams, Karen Lynn. *When Africa Was Home*. New York: Orchard, 1991.

Williams, Shirley Anne. *Working Cotton*. Illustrated by Carole Byard. San Diego: Harcourt Brace Jovanovich, 1992.

Wilson, Sarah. *Garage Song*. Illustrated by Sarah Wilson. New York: Simon and Schuster, 1991.

Yagelski, Robert. *The Day the Lifting Bridge Stuck*. New York: Bradbury, 1992.

Yolen, Jane, ed. *Street Rhymes Around the World*. Illustrated by seventeen artists. Homesdale, PA: Boyds Mill, 1992.

Zak, Monica. *Save My Rainforest*. Illustrated by Bengt-Arne Runnerstrom. Volcano, CA: Volcano Press, 1992.

Zubizarreta, Rosalma. *The Woman Who Outshone the Sun*. San Francisco: Children's Book Press, 1991.

BOOKS FROM MY KNAPSACK FOR TEACHERS ❤ ❤

Bierhorst, John. *The Mythology of North America*. New York: Morrow, 1986.

Bierhorst, John, ed. *Lightning Inside You and Other Native American Riddles*. Illustrated by Louis Brierl. New York: Morrow, 1992.

Chalofsky, Margie, et al. *Changing Places: A Kid's View of Shelter Living*. Mount Ranier, MD: Gryphon House, 1992.

Dawson, Mildred Leinweber. *Over Here It's Different—Carolina's Story*. Photos by George Ancona. New York: Macmillan, 1993.

Derman-Sparks, L., and The A.B.C. Task Force. *Anti-Bias Curriculum: Tools for Empowering Young Children*. Washington: National Association Ed. Young Children.

Hamanaka, Sheila. *The Journey: Japanese Americans, Racism and Renewal*. New York: Orchard, 1990.

Harris, Violet, ed. *Teaching Multicultural Literature in Grades K–8*. Norwood, MA: Christopher-Gordon, 1992.

Hirschfelder, Arlene, and Singer, Beverly R. *Rising Voices: Writings of Young Native Americans*. Selected by Arlene Hirschfelder. New York: Scribner's/Macmillan, 1992.

Milord, Susan. *Hands Around the World*. Mount Ranier, MD: Gryphon House, 1993.

Myers, Walter Dean. *Now Is Your Time! The African-American Struggle for Freedom*. New York: HarperCollins, 1991.

San Souci, Robert D. *Cut From the Same Cloth*. Illustrated by Brian Pinkney. New York: Philomel, 1993.

SANKOFA/Anderson, David A. *The Origin of Life on Earth—An African Creation Myth*. Illustrated by Kat. Mount Airy, MD: Sights Production, 1991.

Smith, Charles A. *Peaceful Classroom/162 Easy Activities to Teach Pre-School*. Illustrated by Nancy L. Dow. Mount Ranier, MD: Gryphon House, 1993.

York, Stacey. *Roots and Wings: Affirming Culture in Early Childhood Programs*. Mount Ranier, MD: Redleaf, 1992.

Chapter  6

Our Natural World/
Our Environment

May green be the grass you walk on.

May blue be the skies above you.

May pure be the joys that surround you.

May true be the hearts that love you.

Old Irish Blessing

THE BASICS

After they cooled down from morning exercises, the children listened intently to Sekou as he told them about the treasures they have inside of themselves and the treasure hunt outside.

"But, we must be very, very quiet," Sekou told the live-wire kids. In his story-telling voice, he said: "We're searching for the spirit of Nature, the spirit of the Arts. Use your special powers, your senses, your imaginations, as we walk. Sssshhh. Pay attention and you'll find signs of the spirit of Nature!"

The motley group of children walked two by two in a hushed journey through the thick woods behind the Recreation Center. Not a sound came from the kids except their footsteps. They listened for the chirp and twitter of birds, for the wind rustling leaves. They smelled the sweetness of damp grass and the richness of pine. They caught the red flash of a cardinal high in the thick branches.

"We're finding lots of treasures, Sekou," Christina whispered as she took his hand.[1]

Three-year-old Jackie and her dad, Seth, made mountains out of small hills in their backyard. They called the tiny pathway zig-zagging around the "mountains" a "trail."

"Don't run on the trail," Jackie warned. "Be careful!"

She led me up her "mountains." We hiked her "trail," discovering rust-colored berries gleaming in the cold, bright autumn afternoon; billowy clouds changing shapes as they floated above us.

From her lookout on her "mountain," Jackie announced, "This is a beautiful day!"[2]

In the middle of Manhattan, the day-care children sat quietly on the pebbly shore of the lake in Central Park observing ducks. As they watched the ducks play, swim, and fish, they noticed many things, like the ducks' beautifully colored feathers; the cute way ducklings follow the mother; the waddling walk of the ducks as they step to shore. . . .

Whether they live in high-rise tenement houses in urban neighborhoods or on farms miles from their nearest neighbors, it seems that most of our young children have a built-in readiness to revere nature. One look around at the play of lights, shadows, colors, movement, shapes, and designs—the swirl of the natural world—and young children immediately understand Liese Millikin's delightful description, "The world is flipped and damzled about!"[3]

Our young children are like Ptolemy. Not only is the earth the center of it all, but they are also at the center of the earth! Most young children think that the world is a big, red, juicy apple waiting for them to sink in their new teeth and suck out its sweetness. Nothing is ordinary. Noticing everything, they catch the beginnings of breezes, dust particles shining in the noon window light, a stray ant carrying a crumb.[4] A young child looks at the moon and the moon looks at the young child. The child doesn't say "The moon!" The child says, "*My* moon!" Stars twinkle and shine so children can wish upon them. Those early years are rich with ownership!

All cultures have ceremonies for welcoming newborn children into the world. From the Great Plains, the Omaha Nation chants the birth of a child by summoning sun, moon, stars, wind, clouds, rain, mist, hills, valleys, rivers, lakes, trees, grasses, birds, animals, and insects, all to welcome the new child, to "make its path smooth."[5] At birth, Omaha children are immediately connected to everything in

the natural world. All the tribal peoples of the world teach the relationships, the interdependence, the connectedness among living things on this planet Earth that we share as home.

How relevant, vibrant, and engaging is this curriculum of Our Natural World/Our Environment—indeed, our very survival may depend on it. It's a treasure chest and a treasure hunt. Long before children come to us, they have already begun this theme. They are children of the earth and already communicate with animals, plants, trees, sun, moon, and stars.

In her excellent article, "Nature Education and Science," Ruth A. Wilson suggests some goals for nature education:

1. The development of a sense of wonder
2. An appreciation of the beauty and mystery of the natural world
3. Opportunities to experience the joy of closeness to nature
4. Respect for other creatures.[6]

The simplicity of these goals reminds us that children learn through interaction; through hands-on experiences with accessible, concrete materials; and through ample time to explore, experiment, observe, and reflect. This is a curriculum, as are all our life-affirming themes, that goes beyond information, beyond the gathering of facts. Wilson writes, "Nature Education offers a way of knowing that includes, but is not limited to, rational knowledge. Its focus is on a way of knowing that moves the heart and soul and imagination of the one involved. . . . While it is, indeed, good to have factual information about the natural world, it is also important to have a sense of connectedness, love, and caring for the world of nature."[7]

Observe Sekou and his group of treasure seekers. Walk with Jackie on her "mountain." Sit with the children watching ducks. You will witness children actively involved in encounters with the world of nature. So many important skills are strengthened and developed. Trying to make meaning out of experience, they observe, compare, question, hypothesize, count, predict, manipulate, analyze, initiate, construct, and arrange. Whole language happens all the time, integrated learning crisscrosses curricula strands when children are given opportunities to put "their whole selves in," as the Hokey Pokey song says.

We shouldn't even need a chapter in a textbook about the vital importance of such a topic as Our Natural World/Our Environment. Its limitless wealth of offerings should require no explanations, no persuasion. Yet, our journals highlight sincerely felt questions and concerns facing teachers: What to teach? How to teach? What materials? What if I don't like animals? What if I'm not an outdoors person? How can I teach Nature in the city? What if my children are scared of bugs? We already "did" dinosaurs![8]

No one person has all the answers; we certainly know that. But the experiences and examples of others are valuable additions to our own cache of wisdom. With that motivation in place, I called on Mary Rivkin, an articulate advocate who inspires and prods people to reconnect their lives to the world of nature. Her deeply held beliefs are always challenging.[9]

When Mary walks into a classroom, shades fly up and windows open. When she visited a class of second graders sitting in a darkened room watching a film about air pollution, her response was immediate.

"Outside," she reported, "it was the most beautiful day in America! I wanted to say, 'Why are you not outside looking at trees, at the sky, at wildflowers?' What are we doing to our young children by emphasizing the destruction of our environment? How can young kids take on the whole world's problems? Yes, encourage children to help take care of, take responsibility for *what's around them*. All over America, children are waiting and ready to help, to care for, to nurture nature! They clean up, recycle, lobby for clear rivers, replant. Isn't that part of the kinds of values inherent in this curriculum? But, at the same time, let's not be so desperate about nature!"

To the many teachers who express insecurity in the teaching of environment, of nature, Mary's approach is reassuring and simple. Here is what she says: "Appreciate where you are. Develop a sense of place. Start anywhere, anytime! Thoreau said, 'The earth is more to be admired than used.' Learn to become attuned, not controlling. Notice and respond. Keep your sense of wonder and your curiosity. We're natural creatures and we need to be connected with the 'unbuilt environment.' Don't worry about memorizing the names of things. That's the least important part. What's important? Take the kids out. Sit together. Close your eyes. Listen. Tune in. Walk to a park. If you don't have a park, look at a puddle! See the reflections in it? Sit and watch. Let yourselves experience the fullness of things. I like to tell the kids, 'I don't want to take it home. I don't want it. I just want to look at it!' But the children *do* love to collect things like pebbles, stones, rocks, shells, leaves, and twigs. We have to guide, inspire, model. We have to help our children look for beauty, patterns, predictability, cycles, seasonality. This is not a passive study. We have to respond creatively, poetically, figuratively to nature's gifts. We help our children experience both interaction and transformation. What can we do? What can we make? How can these experiences, this knowledge be transformed into poems, maps, songs, exhibits, games, paintings?"

Mary is always inspired by the work of others. She interrupts her conversation by reminding me of the excellent writing available in the country.

"I like my students to read such books as Joseph Cornell's *Sharing Nature With Children*, Rachel Carson's *The Sense of Wonder*, James Greenman's *Caring Spaces, Learning Places,* and Molly Cone's *Come Back, Salmon.*[10]

I ask Mary about her deepest concerns in regard to the teaching of nature. Children of poverty, children living broken lives in depressed neighborhoods are children who hold a special place in Mary's heart. She sees nature providing unique lessons for all of our children, for all people, but especially for children who feel hopeless.

"Nature can be an antidote to despair," she says. "It's important for a sense of hope for children to see the incredible abundance of nature. They need to see the

spaciousness of sky and the beauty of clouds. That's available to everyone. Even weeds in sidewalk cracks and insects in asphalt remind us of the enduring and adaptable qualities of nature, that ongoing intensity to *live*. And our children living in these confused and chaotic times are comforted by the reassurance of orderliness, night and day, cycles and seasons. It's tragic that so many of our children say, '*If* I grow up.' Nature says to them, 'I want you to grow up. Everything young is supposed to grow, to get older. You are part of the natural order of life.' "

As Mary so passionately states, the study of nature, the love of nature in the lives of children is one of hopefulness, of *life*, and of continuation. We are part of nature, children of the natural world. We are caretakers as well as residents!

This is the curriculum beyond information. This is the curriculum of wonder and appreciation, of connectedness and caring, of ownership and of empowerment.

There is enough material in the rich offerings of nature to select areas of study you love, are fascinated by, and feel comfortable with. If you're not an animal person, look at rocks and plants. If you are allergic to plants, keep your eyes on the sun, moon, and stars. Millions of animals, plants, and rocks are waiting to find their way into your classroom. All across America, children and teachers are going outside to discover nature's treasures, and all across America, children and teachers are inviting nature in.

Mary Rivkin advised, "Start anywhere, anytime." Whether you and your children are blowing the fuzz from dandelions, watching chicks hatch from eggs, sunning your plants, or filling an entire school with birds, fish, reptiles, mammals, plants, and recycling centers, you are participating in a life-rich curriculum, totally engaging the children, demanding interaction, inviting "hands on," connecting minds and hearts.

There are many lessons in this study. One is humility. Throughout history, humans have tried to fathom the mysterious workings of nature. Even today, with our incredible technoscientific instruments, many of nature's secrets have not been revealed. Theodore Roethke wrote, "Our ignorance is so colossal that it gives me a positive pleasure to contemplate it."[11] Coming to this study with a sense of wonder, an open mind, lively curiosity, and questions (even questions that may take centuries before answers are in sight!) is an antidote to smugness. Closed-in, right/wrong, short-answer questions and answers learned by rote and recited for grades are not the stuff of inquisitive, adventurous, and courageous minds. Plato said that there is no other beginning of learning than wonder. Einstein believed that imagination is more powerful than knowledge! Wonder, imagination, curiosity, courage, patience, caring, responsibility, and enthusiasm are some of the qualities necessary for this journey.

Are *you* ready for this journey? Are you prepared to soar beyond information? Are you ready to turn Earth Day into a continuum of Earth Days rather than a single event determined by a calendar date?

The children are always ready and waiting. Hurry! Jackie is holding a place for you on her "mountain." She'll guide you along the "trail."

Come on! Sekou and his treasure hunters have so much to share with you. Oh, the discoveries they made!

Sit for a moment. The day-care kids exploring in Central Park want to tell you everything they know about ducks.

Are you ready?

DISCOVERY TIMES/WONDER TIMES

- Our planet is called Earth.
- Even though people speak different languages and live in different places, we all live on the planet Earth.
- Our planet has air for us to breathe, water and land, a sky above us, and countless plants and animals of every size, type, design, and color.
- Not even the smartest scientists know all the answers to how our planet works, how plants and animals grow and change. Questions and curiosity are the best ways to begin learning about things.
- There are many beautiful parts of Earth: oceans, rivers, mountains, fields, valleys, deserts, and forests. Each part has special features: special animals, birds, kinds of weather, plants, and so on.
- Even though it seems impossible to count all the trees and fish and plants, they can be used up or wasted. It's very sad when people don't appreciate the gifts nature gives us and wastes them or destroys them (like forests and rivers)
- We need to take care of our home, our Earth. There are many ways we can help keep it clean and clear.
- All living things are connected. We are all a part of life, of nature.
- Nature is very orderly: morning and night, dark and light, season, tides, birth and death, growing and changing.
- We have fantastic "instruments and machinery" for study and for caring for nature: our senses, our language, our memory, our curiosity, our understanding, our imagination, and our creativity.

SUGGESTED VOCABULARY

Every word included in this starter vocabulary is a universe of possibilities for joyful learning experiences. The words themselves are motivating and inspiring! "Start anywhere, anytime."

sun	earth	roots	mammals	weather
moon	dirt	hibernate	endangered	parks
stars	stone	feathers	pollution	animal shelters
wind	air	paws	clean	veterinarians
clouds	fly	shells	clear	park rangers
mist	dark	claws	recycle	greenhouses
hills	light	wings	protect	naturalists
valleys	twinkle	beaks	swamp	scientists
rivers	sky	hop	fossils	herbs
lakes	rain	crawl	shore	gourds
trees	sprinkle	fins	pebbles	patterns
grasses	thunder	grass	webs	designs
birds	lightning	crops	cocoons	rainbows
animals	snow	grow	gallop	hurricanes
insects	ice	harvest	scurry	tornadoes
mountains	breeze	preserve	morning	flowers
oceans	sand	fruit	night	plants
sea	water	vegetables	afternoon	gardens
lakes	waves	eggs	winter	swim
puddles	fish	hatch	summer	climb
forests	branches	bugs	spring	environment
sky	leaves	insects	autumn	environmentalists
mud	seeds	reptiles	seasons	astronomers

Obviously, if we included all the specific words under "animals" or "plants," every page in this book would be covered with names. You and your children will continually add to this very small group of suggestions. Your vocabulary will reflect *your* geography and *your* experiences.

SOME STARTERS

By now you should have no trouble starting any idea, subject, or theme! But, in case this is a time when you just need an extra push, here are a few suggestions to get you going.

Start with wonder Whether your inspiration is a single raindrop, the strange shape of a saguaro cactus, or a spider swinging on an almost invisible thread, the natural world constantly supplies you with subjects of wonder. Someone sent me a card featuring a quotation from John Muir: "When we try to pick something by it-self, we find it hitched to everything else in the universe." A single raindrop can start an outpouring of ideas!

Start by looking out of the window What do you see when you look out your window? Think of your window frame as a picture frame. One tree can branch out ideas for the rest of the year. The story is told that Albert Einstein, when he was a child, kept looking out of the window in his classroom at the sky and wondering, "Why is the sky blue?" From this question grew a lifetime of scientific inquiry. What questions do you and your students have about sky, trees, streams, and hills? Keep looking and sharing your observations. Is the view from your window the same every day? Will the view in a desert school in Tucson, Arizona, be the same as the scene seen through a kindergarten window along the Gulf of Mexico in Pensacola, Florida? What do you and your children experience every day?

Start with a pocket garden Children love to close their eyes and hold out their hands and feel something in their palms. All you need is a bean seed, a wet square of paper towel and a clear plastic sandwich bag. The seed nestles in the paper towel, closed into the sandwich bag. Be sure the seed faces the side of the bag so the children can see the miracle. The bags go in their pockets. Keep the paper damp and warm to help the seed sprout. When the seeds sprout, replant them in soil. A variation is to give each child a plastic drinking cup to plant the seed in. Watch the seed sprout!

Start with a class pet Animals are important members of classrooms. Gerbils, fish, turtles, hamsters, rabbits, and guinea pigs are among the most popular classroom animals in the country. As children learn about, care for, observe, and share the responsibility of keeping their pets healthy and happy, they are immediately launched into a study of nature.

Start with pictures or photos We are lucky to live in a time of excellent visual images. Children are very responsive to ideas conveyed by pictures. Single paintings or photographs of landscapes, seascapes, or animals are excellent for inspiring discussions, observations, and inquiry. Books of photographs or paintings multiply opportunities. Keep seed and flower catalogs well used. Always ask for open-ended responses, rather than closed-in, yes-no answers. Questions such as "What do you think this owl is looking at?" or "Imagine how it feels to cuddle up in a nest" start the kids wondering.

Start with a song Old favorites like "Old MacDonald Had a Farm" that feature so many animals and their sounds are excellent, playful ways to begin thinking about nature's wonders. Classical music like Ferde Grofe's "Grand Canyon Suite," which conveys the rhythm of donkeys clip-clopping along the winding trail, evoke images of canyons, hills, sand, and animals. Listen to any selection from Fran Avni's *Daisies and Ducklings*[12] and you and your children will bounce into a yearlong celebration of nature. Don't forget to create your own songs to honor your pets, plants, window scenes, and pocket seeds!

Start with (surprise!) serendipity In rooms of trust and sharing, children are always bringing in little gifts such as fossils, rocks, crystals, feathers, souvenirs they've purchased in state and national parks, or stories about trips and discoveries. Be aware of the designs on T-shirts, socks, notebooks, and tennis shoes! Often children wear marvelous T-shirts commemorating animals, rain forests, and natural wonders. Any of these gifts are marvelous starting-off points.

Start with your own experience One sentence coming from you that invites children to add their own is an excellent way to begin: "Last night I saw the most fascinating program about elephants. Did anyone see it? What do we know about elephants?"

Start with a walk, a look, a listen, a smell, a taste, a touch . . . in other words, come to your senses! The simplest activity yields a rich variety of responses and inspires more . . . more . . . more. Take a walk. What do we see? Listen. What do we hear? Smell? Pine? Mint? Roses? Gently touch this stone. How smooth. There's hardly a wrinkle or a line on it. What's its story? Leave the doors wide open to make room for imaginative, creative discussions.

Start with a story, start with a poem Children's literature abounds with materials about nature. Animals are children's favorite characters and subjects! Whether presented in fact or fiction, animal books draw children to their pages like no other topic. Any component of nature is attractive to children when presented in a nontechnical way. From Edna St. Vincent Millay's "Afternoon on a Hill" to Christina Rossetti's "Who Has Seen the Wind?" to David McCord's "Every Time I

Climb a Tree," the range of poetry honoring nature is practically limitless. Share poems you love with your children. Not only will they be inspired to write and illustrate their own poems, but they also will be caught in the magical web of learning and exploration. I have so many favorite books that inspire a loving focus on our natural world that the titles would run off these pages. Old, old favorites like *Where Does the Butterfly Go When It Rains?, Make Way for Ducklings, The Cloud Book,* and *Charlotte's Web*[13] always start minds spinning their own webs. The next-to-last paragraph of *Charlotte's Web* is probably one of the most beautiful odes to stepping into our natural world you could ever share with children: "Life in the barn was very good—night and day, winter and summer, spring and fall, dull days and bright days. It was the best place to be, thought Wilbur, this warm delicious cellar, with the garrulous geese, the changing seasons, the heat of the sun, the passage of swallows, the nearness of rats, the sameness of sheep, the love of spiders, the smell of manure, and the glory of everything."

Old and new, borrowed and true, there are many books, poems, and stories that you will love to share with your children.

TALK TIMES/LISTENING TIMES

As we have repeatedly pointed out, talk times may occur throughout the day and are never confined to a limited schedule. We must exchange ideas about what we see, how we see our experiences, and how we feel. Language happens all the time. With that in mind here are a few suggestions.

Questions and more questions Young children's challenging questions help us see life in fresh ways. They come to experiences with few preconceptions or prejudices. We have a lot to learn from the children! Gary Rosen and Bill Shontz's wonderful song "These Are the Questions"[14] invites the kids to sing along and add their own questions about everything. Designate a special space in your room to feature children's questions. Value the questions themselves even if you don't know

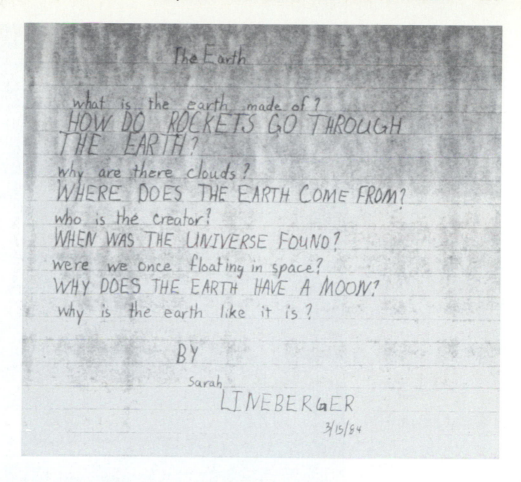

the answers. Each question is a seed. Questions beget questions, and before you know it, your children may give you the direction and guidelines for an enriched curriculum on the natural world. Be sure to feature the name of the questioner as you write children's ideas on poster board or any large chart paper.

Work and talk As children dig, plant, water, feed, and clean animals and plants, they talk. They observe, compare, and share. They learn to take turns, to take responsibility, and to respect others. This incidental talking and listening is so important, perhaps the most valuable kind of language enrichment. Caring for classroom pets generates important conversations about responsibility and caretaking. Even very young children clearly discover that the actual lives of the pets depend on being cared for by people. "Before we eat our snacks," kindergartners decided, "we should be sure our rabbits and turtles are fed." We learn by doing. Caring for pets and plants means *doing*. It's important work, and talking together about such life-affirming work is essential. Write and illustrate the ideas generated and discussed.

Play and talk Hands in mud, clay, dirt, water, or sand are busy hands. Children "mess around" with natural materials—free-flowing materials—and have much to say about what they feel, what they are doing, their plans for the work, and ideas that come to them as they work and play.

Book talk—a room of talk times Whenever I am in a school, if possible, I wander around in between my own scheduled sessions, investigating and eavesdropping. At a break in a tight schedule, I strolled into a first-grade room. The children were at recess on the playground, so I had a chance to look around. No question about the focus of these children: Earth! Earth! Earth! There were so many books and children's magazines, not just displayed, but open, lying on tables and cushions, left with the warmth of hands still on them. Some of the books I noted: *Lily*

Pad Pond, Tree of Life (*The World of the African Baobab*), *Tiger with Wings* (*The Great Horned Owl*), *Earth Songs, The Life Cycle of a Grasshopper, A Crack in the Pavement, Rain Forest Stories, The Tiger,* and *Volcano and Earthquake*.[15] It was clear that the children were following their own interests, Earth at the center, but branching toward their specific curiosities. The way the books were opened and scattered, one could easily see that they were in use, inspiring many children's projects about grasshoppers, volcanoes, and lily pads. Pictures, diagrams, stories, journal writing, posters, and drawings packed the room. And, in the silence of the child-empty room, I could *hear* conversations rich in information, ideas, and discoveries. After all, the child reading about the great horned owl sat next to the child reading about nature and city children and cracks in sidewalks. Collections of pictures, postcards, and other objects were displayed everywhere. The room was like a museum; every shelf featured exhibits. Names, titles, labels, and information highlighted the displays. I wanted to wait for these children to return so I could see them in action. I think from my brief visit to their room, I could tape record the sounds of learning!

Share your knowledge As children delve into a topic they choose, initiated by their own questions and their own interests, they need time to share some of their discoveries with their classmates. Keep this kind of talk time/listening time loose. Young children don't need the anxiety of scheduled oral reports! Whenever they are

ready and excited about telling their friends about their findings, make time for that event. Encourage respectful listening, active questioning, and appreciation.

Problem stating/problem solving A story, news report, direct experience, or class-sharing item are examples of ways problems can be introduced to your children. Perhaps the playground is littered. Maybe the gerbils' habitat is neglected. What about the smog-clogged sky? Why are fish dying in a nearby stream?

These are important opportunities for encouraging problem-solving discussions. Be sure that everyone understands the situation being discussed. Write on the board or a chart as the children talk. They must always see the connections between oral and written language. Listen with respect to all ideas and suggestions. Brainstorming means all contributions are welcomed; put judgment on hold. Once all the ideas are gathered, the group can begin selecting, arranging, and combining. Remember, a silly idea may trigger a really significant idea! That's the way the creative process works.

The children may decide to write rules for Habitat Cleaners. They may form a Litter-Busters Club. They may send letters and pictures to government officials about regulating pollutants.

Problem-solving discussions usually result in some kind of agreed-upon action. It's very important for young children (and all people) to know that their concerns are valid, that their ideas have value, and that their solutions are practical and can be effective. This is empowering. The children learn about communication as they strengthen their connections to each other and the world about them.

Very often, the children themselves generate important discussions about nature and ecology. At the Richmond Elementary School in Richmond, Rhode Island, Alex Sovet-Pett created his own questionnaire about ecology and shared his concerns with his schoolmates.[16] Alex asked such questions as "What are you doing now to make our planet Earth a cleaner and better place to live?" and "How do you think we can help our parents and teachers to make our planet Earth a better and cleaner place to live?" The children's responses, from the youngest students to the oldest, demonstrated great awareness and deep concern for the environment. Danielle, a six-year-old, talked about recycling garbage. Samantha, a first grader, related how she helped "clean up trash on the beaches with my Dad and sisters." Andrea, a third grader, recommended that we "plant more trees for oxygen."

Talk times/listening times generate thought and action.

Shared observations Perhaps it's a bird's nest found abandoned under a tree or a crystal Cody's aunt sent from New Mexico. As you and your children pay attention to the special object, many observations and questions are exchanged. We all may look at the same object but we look with our own eyes. It's important for children to know that even in sharing common experiences, we maintain our uniqueness.

Changes and cycles Nothing is more fascinating to young children (and old children like us!) than the seemingly magical changing of life forms—tadpoles to frogs, caterpillars to butterflies, seeds to flowers, winter to spring, infants to toddlers to kids. Nature is constantly in motion (even mountains erode or erupt). Talks generated by the ideas of changes, metamorphosis, and cycles are dynamic talk times. Extend discussions into written language, poetry, literature, music, visual arts, movement, and drama. Remember, talking and thinking inspire a multitude of enrichment possibilities.

VISUAL ARTS TIMES

As you begin this section, I want you to meet Kaye Boiarski, who has wisdom, practicality, and delightful ideas to share with you.[17] In her work with Days of Creation Arts for Kids as well as numerous school and recreation programs, Kaye is well known in central Ohio for her energetic creativity. At the moment, she is most excited about a project she is doing with an integrated group of preschoolers (medically fragile children with special needs mainstreamed with "typically developing" children) for the Nisonger Center at Ohio State University. They are designing and building an outside playground featuring an undersea theme. On a tall post, they wound soft, cloth-stuffed sculptures of sea plants and sea creatures. Out of the tips of the sculptures were tree branches with tufts of heavy monofilament strings in bright colors. Kaye related how she was most moved by two visually impaired young children who sat for over two hours in their wheelchairs touching, playing with, and enjoying the pole of sculptured sea creatures and plants. Patricia Wynn Brown had this to say about the playground: ". . . a very special playground for children (with special needs) was constructed this past fall. With the theme, 'Under the Sea' it is both aesthetically pleasing and accessible to kids who rarely get to play outside. Art plays an important part in its design. . . . A blue canopy covers a structure that shelters children from weather and sunlight. Behind it is a bright interactive

mural in a sea motif. . . . Soft sculpture coral, starfish and lobsters to be created by Kaye Boiarski will offer tactile experiences. A gently sloping hill allows even the least agile child a chance to climb and roll. And the best way to develop gross motor skills is, of course, to crawl through the play area's giant whale."[18]

When Kaye talks about sharing visual arts experiences with children, she throws out a delightful metaphor. "It's like a baseball that you toss out and the game is on! Once you make the first suggestion and provide the materials, it's out of your hands. The kids take over! What do *you* do? Run around, watch, see what they need, respond, help if asked, applaud. . . ."

Natural materials, kids, and Kaye are the mix that make for joyful times together. With the exception of dandelions, Mary Rivkin[19] instructs children to pick only what they plant. Kaye would go along with this philosophy, urging the children to gather such materials as pebbles, stones, fallen leaves, twigs, sticks, gourds, pinecones, grasses, nuts, fallen ferns, seashells, dropped birds' feathers, and so on. Nature leaves so much in our paths, on the ground, for us to recycle into artistic offerings.

Some of Kaye's favorite adventures in the visual arts using natural materials and nature as the focus follow. As you read, imagine them, add on to them, change them to fit your spirit, your children, your ideas, your unique situation.

From Kaye's treasure chest of arts adventures

- Tree jewelry. We decorate and dress trees, circling them with tree jewelry made from sticks, string, paint, glitter, and sequins. After we decorate them, we circle them, singing and saying poems to them.
- Branched stick-people dancers. We look for branched sticks on the ground in interesting shapes and bring them back to our table covered with lots of scrounged materials. We decorate the sticks to look like dancing people, dancing for joy to honor nature.
- Wind chimes. It's so easy to make wind chimes. Gather seashells or small stones, drill holes in them (if they don't already have holes), pull strings through them, and hang them.
- Dream catchers. From the Native American tradition, we share the idea of the dream catchers. We shape grapevines into a circle, take thin string and design it into a spider web pattern inside the circle,

add tiny stones, little feathers, and beads to it, and hang it in our room or over our beds. Only the good dreams are caught; the bad dreams float away. In old traditions, we talk about making gifts for others, always sharing our gifts.

- Nature prints on T-shirts and materials. We gather dropped flowers, leaves, pebbles, ferns, grass, and stones and arrange them on T-shirts. Then we fill plant-misting bottles with diluted acrylic paint and mist the shirt with the paint. We remove the materials when the paint dries, and we have marvelously designed shirts featuring patterns from nature. Use sheets and mural paper to create larger designs.

- More nature prints. This kind of print is the reverse. Coat leaves, stones, and pebbles with acrylic paint and press them on paper and materials. They make excellent gifts as well as lively wall hangings and colorful prints.

- Outdoor nature sculptures. We mix peat moss, sand, and a little Portland cement. This mixture makes weatherproof sculptural material that kids shape into animals and place outside. We always like to give back to the outside. A variation is to press into the mixture things from the environment like rocks, sticks, leaves, and our own handprints and footprints. After the shapes dry, add them onto and arrange them into three-dimensional bas-reliefs. We think of these as records of what we want to keep, remember, and honor. The children love to create models of their own hands and feet in this soft material.

- Rubbings. We press sheets of paper against the trunks of trees. As the papers are pressed, we rub them with the sides of crayons to pick up the texture of the bark. The variety of patterns and designs is amazing, especially when they are all displayed together.

- Pinecone necklaces. The kids love jewelry. Pick small pinecones, string them together, and wear them.

- Three-dimensional books. We write our own stories and poems, illustrating them with natural materials so you open pages to three-dimensional scenes.
- Assemblages. On matboard, tagboard, or cardboard, assemble twigs, leaves, stems, and stones. Create original nature scenes.
- Making paper. We always talk about how trees give us so many materials, so many gifts. We talk about all the products and ideas we get from trees. Making paper is one way of honoring trees and teaching the kids not to waste anything. We gather materials for texture like leaves, flower petals, carrot scrapings, recycled newspapers, and lint from laundry. We slur it all in the blender, then pour the mix on a framed screen. We strain the mixture through the screen, draining the water. Only the pulp remains and dries into a large sheet of paper.
- Bird nests. When we find abandoned bird nests, we paint little stones and pebbles and put them in the nests. Then we glue together paper strips, party streamers, and dried grass, making our own nests. The kids love nests!

As Kaye goes back to the children, she stops to remind us that in sharing these ideas, she's not talking about teaching skills in a formal way or teaching a highly structured "art class." She's talking about being with the children, exploring with them, sharing a freedom of spirit together in that important time to play with materials and ideas in the excitement of the creative process.

There's no end to suggestions in any celebration of ideas. These are just a few samples for you to enjoy and play with. From my travels around the country, I have seen many outstanding works of art created by young children in learning environments that protect and care for the earth. Here are a few more items from my notebooks.

Waste nothing Americans toss out so many materials of value! In classrooms around the land, children discuss ways to use such throwaways as fast-food containers, egg crates, paper towel tubes, boxes, Styrofoam food boxes and packing chips, plastic bags, and plastic utensils. After lively talk times, a group of first graders gathered many uses for these materials. For example, they mixed paints on Styrofoam trays, spread paints with plastic knives, and stored glitter, small beads, and silver stars in the compartments of egg crates. They also used the egg crates to create insect creatures.

Constant reminders to the children about the source of materials are of great value. Trees provide many of our favorite materials like paper, wood, pencils, furniture, floors, and boxes. I ask the children to remember that "A tree was cut down so you could write and draw and paint on the paper made from it. Honor the life of that tree and always do your best work! Don't waste the precious materials. Don't just scribble-scrabble and be deliberately sloppy and messy. Think about your designs, your words, your patterns. Be proud of all your works!"

Scrounged sculptures Pablo Picasso's amazing use of found, scrounged, and broken materials to create marvelous animal sculptures is inspirational. Note how he transformed old automobile parts into a baboon sculpture. Did he throw out old bicycle parts? No. He shaped them into an unforgettable goat! What can your children create, honoring ideas from nature, with materials that normally would be tossed away? Waste nothing!

An inspiring example of a unique and gifted artist who creates scenes, people, animals, and memories with scrounged natural and environmental materials is Aminah Brenda Lynn Robinson. At any given moment you see branches, tree roots, gourds, nuts, glitter, buttons, beads, and bits and pieces of throw-away materials in the process of transformation (magic!) into powerful art works.

Greeting cards for all seasons Why should we limit greeting cards to those occasions prescribed on calendars? Children enjoy sending seasonal cards—"Happy Spring!"—with their own original messages, poems, designs, and images, as well as weather cards, animal cards, flower cards, and sky cards. Display, enjoy, share, and most importantly, *use* the cards for thank yous to classroom visitors, helpers, field trip guides, classmates, and families.

Mobiles, wall hangings, clotheslines, hanging sculptures Walls are for decorating with beloved images using a variety of materials from laminated cutouts to three-dimensional abstract forms to representational images (flowers, stars, rainbows, trees) to illustrated words. Ceilings are for hanging mobiles or sculptures; clotheslines are for stringing from one part of the room to another, adding another dimension to displaying artistic creations. I have looked up in classrooms to see cotton clouds, glittering stars, and moon-and-planet mobiles. I have looked across rooms to see paper birds nesting in cardboard trees. I have felt the spray of aluminum foil/crepe paper strips flowing as fluidly as a waterfall. Bring the wonders of our natural world *into* your classroom!

Collages, montages, assemblages Nature is so inspirational a subject for children that practically any aspect of it is immediately responded to with creativity. Children decide whether they want to celebrate one idea like "fish" or "deer" or take a broader view and focus on "jungle" or "river," with all the components possible to interpret. Glue, paste, tape, nails, staples, and tacks hold images to paper, cloth, bulletin boards, shirt cardboard, boxes, and poster board. Sky, water, and land provide myriad choices for the children to select. Weather assemblages are especially enjoyable—raindrops, snowflakes, clouds, and sky variations challenge imaginations. Any aspect of nature under discussion provides inspiration for such collected, arranged designs. Be sure to keep normally discarded materials. Cut pieces of construction paper into confetti to dot landscapes and seascapes. Gather magazine pictures and add them to painted and colored images. Choose materials from scrounged nature materials to include in assemblages. Encourage experimentation and willingness to risk in the exploring of new ideas.

Think small William Blake urged us to "see a world in a grain of sand." Begin with one leaf, one stone, one twig, or one grain of sand and see what happens. What can we do with our gift from nature? How can we combine it with others? Rearrange and arrange it? Change it? Add to it? As children work and play with the limited materials, they soon realize that no two pieces look exactly alike.

Even when all the children start their projects from a single leaf, every piece evolves differently. Some children highlight their leaves as centerpieces. Others make their own original leaves to add to the real one given to them. Some children create a whole scene from nature around their original leaves.

Illustrate everything Calendars, songs, poems, stories, words, and ideas need illustrations! Encourage your children to add design, color, and images to all their resources and materials. If you're talking about the four seasons, create pictures for each season. Divide papers into four sections, bulletin boards into fourths. If you read a poem like Emily Dickinson's "Bring Me the Sunset in a Cup" or "A Bird Came Down the Walk" or if you share a poem like Langston Hughes's "April Rain Song," print it in beautiful letters. Fasten it to the center of a mural and invite the children to add their own pictures inspired by the poem.

Quilts Throughout the country, children are designing and decorating their "squares" on numerous themes, many from nature. Whether of paper or cloth material, the children's offerings may be sewn or pasted together to create a beautiful quilt.

The designs of nature Nature provides multitudes of ideas for patterns, designs, and colors. With your children, *always* notice and appreciate the stripes, spots, swirls, blends, blotches, and dots found on animals, fish, birds, and plants. Children enjoy choosing their favorite nature designs and painting, coloring, or drawing them on paper or cloth swatches.

Nature symbols Animals, plants, and flowers as well as stars, sun, and moon have throughout history symbolized qualities such as strength, peace, harmony, and nationhood. Flags, totems, banners, and coats of arms feature symbols drawn from nature. A challenge to the children is to design their own symbols from their favorite nature ideas to express their feelings. What natural objects or life images would you choose for *your* own flag, banner, or totem? In the midst of such creative efforts, six-year-old Latrice explained the two animals she was painting on her banner: "The kitten is for cuteness and the squirrel is for cuteness, too."

It's impossible to "finish" ideas. We stop because time and space limit us. I'd like to be able to suggest such delightful offerings as Windowpane Pictures, Our Changing Tree Through the Season, Collecting Nature Words (asking the children to choose their favorite words from nature, illustrate them, and create posters); Artworks That Demonstrate Changes in Nature (from weather to animals, from acorns to trees, from seeds to gardens, the children enjoy expressing these ideas on one large paper, in three-dimensional shoe box scenes, or on unfolding accordion pages or original books)—I'd love to include writing poems on the shapes of the poetic theme (write animal poems on the cut-out shapes of the animals, cloud poems on cloud shapes, rainbow poems on rainbow shapes), but time's up! We move on.

MUSIC TIMES

How can we even think about our natural world without a special focus on music?

Sylvia Wallach took time from her work with inner-city Chicago children to share some of her philosophy about the importance of music in the realm of nature.

> All the instruments we ever knew came from nature—for example, drumming on tree trunks, shaking seeds in pods from trees, blowing into seashells. . . . Nature has always been the stimulus for all of our music, dance, poetry, visual arts. . . . In ancient days when we experienced storms, lightning, thunder, phenomena we didn't understand, we tried to make it more accessible, more understandable by replicating it. . . . The big word is *imitation*. Maybe by imitating the sounds and rhythms of natural events, we lessened our own fears. We said to Nature, "Listen. We're a part of you. We're honoring your powers." We became the composers, performers and listeners. . . . All properties of nature became more human through music, for example—high/low, long/short, loud/soft, fast/slow, uneven/even.[20]

Often Sylvia will accompany city children on an "outdoor education" field trip or a visit to a city park. Together they gather materials to form a Mother Nature Rhythm Band. They pick nothing but find everything: tree bark, pebbles, rocks, sticks, and seed pods. They bring their "instruments" together and create and score their sounds, experimenting freely with wide ranges of possibilities. Together, they compose a Mother Nature Rhythm Band piece.

Many of the children Sylvia knows are city children who see cement and steel and very little grass, trees, squirrels, rabbits, or crickets. Often there are few if any opportunities for "outdoor education" trips. All children, but especially city children, love making Mother Nature Soundscapes with Sylvia. You can't miss the excitement in her voice as she describes such experiences:

> It all happens in the classroom. We determine where we "go." We may go to the ocean or to Lake Michigan before a storm, maybe a rain forest or to a farm in the country. Wherever we "go," we create our Mother Nature Soundscape of that place using only our imagination, voices and body percussion. For instance, we decided to "go" to a pond just before a rainstorm. We talked about the kinds of sounds we would find there and wrote them down. Crickets, birds, frogs, raindrops, wind rustling the trees are some suggestions from the list. We take each

idea and experiment with our interpretation of its sounds. Sometimes I invite the children to choose one idea to express. In this class, I divided the children into insects, birds, wind and rain. We played with different ways to organize our symphony. One group at a time? Three groups simultaneously? It's exciting to hear the variations. When we finally agree, we tape the Soundscape. Now that new and original music can be the background for the singing of a very familiar song like "Rain Rain Go Away." Our Soundscape can illustrate a story or poem. We always leave time for visual images of our special place and the sounds we created. For our Pond Before A Rainstorm, we created a large mural which everyone worked on. We wrote haiku-style poems about our experiences then placed the poems in the middle of the mural with the visual images all around. Of course, we included movement for each of our sound sections.

As you continue reading the following ideas for enjoyable musical experiences featuring themes from Our Natural World/Our Environment, apply them to your situation. Your students may represent a very heterogeneous group. Be sure to highlight songs and music from the cultures shared daily by your own students. If yours is a more homogeneous class of kids coming to you from one basic cultural background, they need to know (and enjoy knowing) that the peoples of the world honor the world of nature in music and song. Every child on the planet learns songs about animals, rain, sun, stars, seasons, and plants. Nature is a universal theme. Be open to the widest and richest array of musical celebrations!

Sing a song about the world of nature You already know that young children sing about everything in their lives, accompanying virtually all of their activities with little improvised hums, songs, and tunes. Building on this built-in resource, encourage the children to create songs about the gifts of nature and their environment. Songs about any aspect of nature—flowers, weather, animals, or mountains— are beloved favorites and will be sung repeatedly by the children.

Note: These are ancient ideas. All the tribal peoples sang poems, called their poems "songs," and honored every aspect of nature. Just thumbing through an old book, *American Indian Poetry,*[21] I see titles of short chants/songs/poems such as "Song of the Earth," "Rain Song," "Summer Song," "Mouse Song," "Bear Song," "Beaver Song," "Dog Song," "Butterfly Song," "Coyote Song," "Lightning Song," and "Thunder Song." Think how many "songs" you and your children can create. Accompany them with visual images, stories and movement.

Music inspired by stories and poems Nature is a major theme in many of our favorite works of literature. As you read, note those aspects of the material that most easily inspire musical interpretations. When we read the Slovenian folk tale, *How the Sun Was Brought Back to the Sky,* the children created music, songs, and movements for each of the animals who climbed to the sky to find the sun and bring it back to the cold and dark world. You can imagine that the chick's song and rhythms were very different from the rabbit's song. In *How the Sun Was Brought Back to the Sky,* the children especially loved: "Sun, sun, world's delight. Come out, give us warmth and light." That became their chorus.[22]

There are many examples of literature-related musical experiences, but because of space, we'll include only a few samples. From *The Snowy Day,* the children composed a playful chant to, "Down fell the snow—plop! On top of Peter's head. . . ."[23] Many imaginative responses were evoked during our celebration of *The Emperor's Nightingale* when the children were challenged to create their own song of the nightingale and their own music of the mechanical bird. And what about composing lyrics for the song of the nightingale? The children's own voices and body percussion accompanied the reading of Aileen Fisher's poem, "Weather Is Full of the Nicest Sounds," featuring such music words as "rustles," "strums," "sprinkles," "bangs," "splishes," "flashes," and "crashes."

Instruments of scrounged, discarded human-made materials In keeping with the deeply felt goal of cleaning our environment and not wasting any useful materials, children enjoy collecting such objects as buttons, rods, beads, cardboard containers, nuts, bolts, small pipes, and tubes—junk! After talking about and exploring the varieties of musical instruments familiar to the children, ask them to experiment with the junk material and invent original instruments. They can even name them! Remember, most musical instruments are based on blowing through them, pounding and tapping them, or shaking, strumming and vibrating them. You'll be amazed at the variety of imaginative sounds the children produce.[24]

Tone poems With Sylvia's Mother Nature Rhythm Band instruments, instruments invented from human-made scrounged materials, or classroom orchestra instruments, invite the children to paint musical pictures of times of day, seasons, weather, part of the Earth, animals and plants, stars, sun, and moon. How many ways can a rainstorm be expressed in musical variations? Sunset? A clap of thunder? A jab of lightning? A beautiful rainbow? Falling snow? Buzzing bees? As you experiment together, close your eyes and try to imagine the pictures the music paints. Extend the experience by adding paintbrushes and crayons and creating pictures and poems in response to the music.

Tape your musical compositions. Use them by themselves or to enrich poems, stories, and songs. Play them to inspire visual arts experiences. Choreograph movement to accompany the music.

Note: Nature already provides us with aesthetically pleasing melodies, harmonies, and rhythms. When we pay attention, we listen to and record in our imaginations and memories the sound around us, whether the jangle of birds, the splash of streams, the rush of winds, or the patter of rain. Let us hope that our children will be able to hear the sweet music of the ancient Anasazi legendary character, Kokopelli the flute player, who with his beautiful flute songs makes the wind talk and calls the clouds. Better yet, turn the children into Kokopelli and listen to their magical music that helps the sun shine and paints the sunset!

Gather your own collection of songs and music celebrating nature Draw on your own memories and experiences to collect the songs and music you know and love featuring any aspect of the world of nature/our environment. You know many more songs about nature than you think you do! As this is being written, three telephone calls interrupt. I ask three callers to name "nature" songs they know and I will jot them down in one minute. Here are their lists:

Becky Moore[25]

"On Top of Old Smoky"
"Red River Valley"
"The River is Wide"
"Baa Baa Black Sheep"
"Oh, What a Beautiful Morning"
"There's a Hole in the Bottom of the Sea"
"This Land Is Your Land"
"Frog Went a'Courtin'"

Anna Grace[26]

"Summertime"
"Nature Boy"
"On A Clear Day You Can See Forever"
"The River"
"Blue Skies"
"Sunrise, Sunset"
"Somewhere Over the Rainbow"

Leslie Zak sings in fifteen languages.[27] She knows hundreds and hundreds of songs. She verifies that every language features songs that honor nature: animals, weather, and seasons. I asked her to list some songs in English for our list. Here they are:

"Whose Garden Is This?"
"Inch by Inch, Row by Row"
"I Love the Mountains"
"Down by the Bay"
"Little Arabella Miller Found a Fuzzy Caterpillar"
"All God's Children Got a Place in the Choir"
"Ten Little Monkeys"

She paused in her suggestions to sing a little song composed by a five-year-old Russian child:

"May there always be sunshine
May there always be blue skies
May there always be Mama
May there always be me."

Continually add to your treasure chest of songs and music centered on nature. Most important of all, include the songs your children bring to you. (Remember, one of their first songs is "Twinkle Twinkle Little Star." You can go far with that twinkly little star to brighten themes of sky, earth, and sea.) Be sure to gather some of the excellent music available for young children.[28]

May you and your children always make music and share it to celebrate the wonders of nature and to document the caring, planning, and wishing for a clean, healthy environment.

MOVEMENT AND PLAY TIMES

Chances are that your students are already playing and moving in response to themes from Our Natural World/Our Environment as those ideas are central to the imagery of young children. Bess-Gene Holt believed that personal ecology is "the individual child interrelating, interweaving and interacting with the phenomena that make up his own environment."[29] And how do children interrelate, interweave, and interact as they make meaning out of their lives? They do it through thinking, talking, singing, creating visual arts, reading, writing, moving, and playing. Our happy challenges are to enrich and expand opportunities for such important experiences.

Show me! Choose any of the suggested vocabulary words or the words on your list. Talk about it, sing about it, illustrate it, and ask the children to demonstrate it. "Show me" always evolves into the expression of more ideas. As you talk together, comprehension is strengthened and choreography clarified. "Show me a bird!" easily leads to "How about a bird flying?" "What about birds pecking for worms and seeds?" "What about birds snuggling in their cozy nests?"

Every aspect of nature can be shown through movement and body designs. When children "show you" on a daily basis, movement becomes a stronger integral component of their vocabularies. Because they are moving purposefully all the time, they are able to develop more complicated movement ideas. Working individually, in small groups, or as one large group, we have demonstrated and celebrated "ocean" (complete with water, tides, fish, and sea plants) and "solar system" (including the revolution of the earth around the sun as well as the rotation of the earth on its axis). Do it slowly, with dreamlike music, so no one gets dizzy (especially you). From the crawling of the smallest snail to the buzzing/blowing/swinging/climbing/hiding/blooming/pulsating life of a forest, children delight in expressing ideas through movement. You'll find that after they actively interpret themes and suggestions through movement and play, their visual arts creations as well as their original writings are extraordinarily enriched. Move and play first! Settle down to the visual arts and creative writing *after* the movement session.

Metamorphosis/changes/cycles From seeds to trees, plants, and flowers; from caterpillars to butterflies; from tadpoles to frogs; from winter to spring; the possibilities for movement celebrations abound. Wrap the thematic material in a story and the experiences are enhanced. After a kindergarten group's movement story about chicks hatching (we began curled up on the floor oh so tightly, feeling our shells around us as we grew, we felt closed in, crowded—we had to get out—*crack*—we jabbed our shells but were too exhausted to push out—*crack* again—we

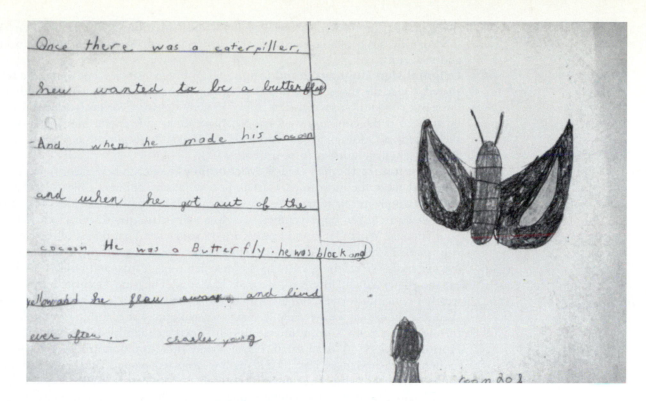

Once there was a caterpiller, he wanted to be a butterfly. And when he made his cocoon and when he got out of the cocoon He was a Butterfly. he was block and yellow and he flew away and lived ever after. ___ charles young

room 201

kicked, we pecked—finally, we hatched—and our new lives began), a few children came back to the multipurpose room. "Tasha can't find her earring." We looked for it on the floor. One of the children asked, "Tasha, where were you when you hatched?" We found the earring!

After we talked about and "practiced" ideas for a movement story highlighting a storm (the children enjoyed demonstrating clouds thickening, wind blowing, trees swaying, rain pattering—they used finger taps, snaps, and claps to accompany their rain movement), I suggested that during a storm, many of these components happen at once. "Decide which part of the storm you want to express. If there's anything we left out, just do it!" Marvelous, dramatic movement followed, with each child clearly expressing a relevant storm idea through body language. In the midst of the swirl, one little girl lay still in a curled position. I leaned down and whispered to her, "What are you?" She whispered back from inside her shape, "A puddle!"

Think about the children interpreting the melting of snow, the forming of ice, the frozen shapes, the melting again, the changing of frozen shapes, puddles, and evaporation—there are so many movement possibilities in the dance of nature!

Snowy footprints With delicate, snowy music, add fingers and hands to fill your room with the movement of snow. Sssshhh. Snow is very quiet. Now your room is a field of snow, a forest of snow. Imagine the prints of animals in the snow. Deer? Ducks? Little birds? Show it. Do it! Move it! Snowy pictures of animal prints and human prints are lovely images that enrich studies of animals and winter.

What if? Turn yourself into . . . (More words to get kids moving.) "What if you were a deer? How would you leap?" "What if you were a sunflower? How tall would you grow?" "What if you were a monkey? What tricks could you do?" "Turn yourself into a river—how would you flow?" "Turn yourself into a star. How would you shine?" "Turn yourself into a horse. How would you gallop?" These are examples of the most simple and delightful of invitations to moving. The children are always ready. Within each challenge are many possibilities. Encourage the playfulness of experimentation. This is not a right/wrong situation. Make circles that take everyone in. Keep asking questions that invite and encourage children to explore and take risks.

Original sign language/hand language As poems, stories, and songs are being shared, especially those with themes from our natural world, invite the children to "pretend you know a special sign language with a gesture for every idea." You will be amazed at the common ways people share similar movement interpretations for such words as "mountain" or "darkness" or "forest." It's almost as if we have pre-existing language waiting to be articulated!

Favorite nature themes (magic vocabulary) We each have favorite words and ideas that mean the most to us. Certain people, places, animals, objects, and events are held deeply in our hearts. We are very ready to celebrate these ideas in as many ways as we are given opportunities. Our lists will be unique to ourselves. Who are your animals? What plants and flowers are on your list? What places of the earth are your places? Children have their lists, too. When we surround them with stimulating materials—magazines, posters, pictures, paintings, cards, and books—their lists expand. They fall in love with certain creatures. They are fascinated by specific weather conditions, trees, or land forms. From their "magic vocabulary" list, invite them to choose an idea—draw it, paint it, make it, write about it, and show it through movement. Turn it into riddles and guess its identity. Choreograph it.

Honor dances Just as all tribal peoples create literature honoring every aspect of nature, so their dances imitate and hallow animals, plants, land, sky, and water forms. I reach to three well-used albums in my collection. With children of all ages, I have improvised movement sequences and dances to the offerings on these records. Note the nature titles of the selections: From the album *China: Shantung Folk Music and Traditional Instrumental Pieces:* "Beautiful Spring," "A Happy Evening," "Moonlit Night," "Silent Evening," and "Chirping of a Hundred Birds." From *Songs of Earth, Water, Fire and Sky (Music of the American Indian):* "Rabbit Dance" (Northern Plains), "Butterfly Dance" (San Juan Pueblo), "Eagle Dance" (Northern Arapaho), and "Alligator Dance" (Seneca). From *Music from the Kabuki (Geza Music of Japan),* intricate explanations are included to indicate that the mizuoto is a drum theme that signifies water; another drum theme signifies waves; the yamaoroshi drum symbolizes mountains, the kazaoto is the sound of wind and the shinobisanju is the motif for darkness. Nature is honored in instruments, movement, rituals, dramas, and dances.[30]

Working as a group, in small groups, or individually, children enjoy creating and choreographing their own dances to animals and natural themes they especially love. Add masks, colors, costumes, rhythms, stories, and poems. Or, just "do" them by themselves! Wrap them in stories.

Sacred directions Go back to ancient traditions from the tribal peoples. Many Native American nations precede every ceremony, celebration, powwow, gathering, and story with gestures or offerings to the directions "above," "below," "before," "behind," and "all around." Numerous ancient peoples honored the north, south, east, and west every day and before special programs. The Aztec peoples honor seven directions—north, south, east, west, above, below, and the space inside of themselves. Try showing the ideas of these directions with movement. Play any steady rhythmic music from any culture. Create your own heartbeat rhythms. Reach toward the sky. Bend toward the earth. Stretch your arms before you. Pull them back to indicate the space behind you. Circle around slowly to mark a curve all around you. Or, with the group, clap, snap, and wave to each of the four directions. As you turn to each direction, jump, hop, bounce, or tap so the rhythms are enriched. Ask the children to explore ways to designate and honor the directions.

Many of our children feel disconnected, alienated from others and from life-affirming forces. These kinds of old ritual movements connect us to the great natural forces around us (we are part of the miraculous story) and are very reassuring.

Watch demonstrations of African dance from any region and you will see the dancers honor the sky above, the earth below, and the drum that keeps the music going.

This Navajo chant is repeated over and over in many variations:

With beauty above me, I walk.
With beauty below me, I walk.
With beauty before me, I walk.
With beauty behind me, I walk.
With beauty all around me, I walk.

Turn this chant into a simple, beautiful dance. The good wishes inherent in the words will be clear with only the movement, once the children know it, love it, and do it. Adapt the directions/prepositions for original chants and poems. Mix in the senses. And, as we care for our environment, look in all the directions. Miss nothing!

Above us we see the sky.
Below us we feel the grass.
Before us we see birds in the trees.
Behind us we hear a dog barking.
All around us it's sunny.
May we walk with friends.
(Kindergarten class poem)

The following is an example of choosing horses as our favorite animals, improvising rhythms of horses galloping, choreographing horse dances, talking about the colors of horses, and combining senses and directions in a third-grade class poem:

We honor horses
O horses.
We sing of horses.
From the North, we hear the hooves of horses galloping.
From the South, we see the black, brown, grey, white manes of horses flying in the cold wind that blows from the North.
All around us we hear the wind rushing and the water flowing gently.
May we always honor horses.

(Ms. Wolf's third graders, J. W. Reason Elementary School, Hilliard, Ohio)

Animal movements Chart them, graph them, turn them into games and riddles, and choreograph them. Start with the specific animals, kinds of animals, or the movement itself. For example, "slithering"—what kinds of animals slither? Let's write them down. Let's demonstrate how slithering makes us move. What about "galloping"? So many animals have a galloping movement. Name them. Illustrate them. Let's do a galloping dance! Within each movement or animal idea is a universe of extended ideas. Are we talking about baby animals? Fast or slow? Heavy or light? Scared or happy? Tired or energetic? Remember, our only limitation is time! Keep it loose and give the children many choices. Combine animal movements with animal sounds. Mix and match!

Dance a landscape, skyscape, or seascape When your children move every day, amazing possibilities emerge. (If you rarely move with your students, their creative energies will be shriveled. They'll be as tight as the Tin Woodsman before Dorothy loosened him with a drop of oil.) Children shape their bodies into mountains, forests, rivers, oceans, and beaches. Children's bodies convey sunrise, sunset, sun hiding behind clouds, sun emerging, and sun shining! Young children *love* to hide, then emerge. Accompany the movements with carefully selected or originally created music, stories, and poems.

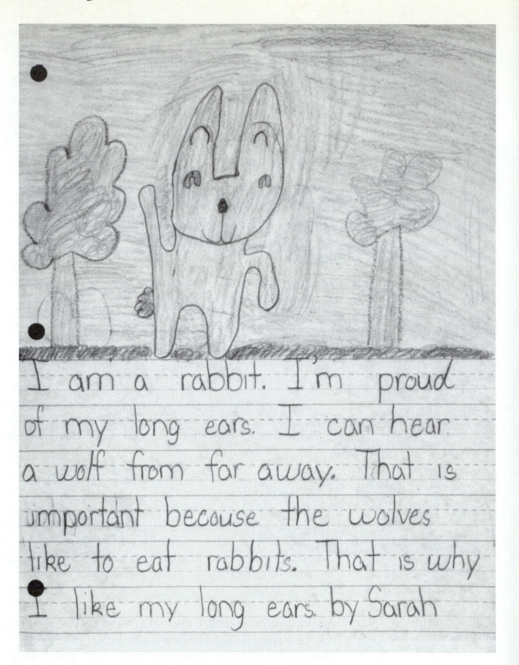

I am a rabbit. I'm proud of my long ears. I can hear a wolf from far away. That is umportant becouse the wolves like to eat rabbits. That is why I like my long ears. by Sarah

Moving museums Turn yourselves into animal exhibits, planetariums, or botanical displays. Keep your shapes. When the music signal goes on, the shapes are animated. When the music stops, the children return to original shapes. Add the dimensions of movement and music to collections of objects and to exhibits and displays.

Literature is a moving experience I can't think of a children's story or poem without thinking movement, even if the inspiration for movement is only one sentence or paragraph in the story.

Two examples come to mind. Marie Hall Etts' *Play With Me*[31] is about a child who goes out to play. As each animal (grasshopper, frog, or turtle) comes near her, she tries to catch it and it runs away. Finally, she sits quietly, listening and watching. One by one, all the animals join her. "Oh, now I was happy, as happy could be! For

ALL of them—ALL OF THEM—were playing with me." The children move and play all the parts. (I never choose parts; we all dance everything!) They experience frog hopping away, snake crawling into a hole, fawn leaping away as they shout, "Play with me!" It's a simple, lovely story with numerous movements and an important lesson.

A First Little Golden Book, *Good Morning, Muffin Mouse*[32] provides simple, inspirational series of greeting to different gifts of nature. As the little mouse character wanders through a day, it hails "friends" with greetings such as "Hi, tall grass." "Hello, cool water!" and "Greetings to all you little bugs that crawl and fly." Young children have such a wonderful time greeting their day and its wonders with salutations, imitations, gestures, and movements. As you read, encourage the children to express a greeting, then turn themselves into the object of the greeting.

Legends, myths, and folklore Our earliest legends were explanations for natural phenomena. Human imagination, over millennia, has created stories about animals, earth, stars, and sea; every single aspect of the natural world has been celebrated in stories such as the idea of Mother Nature, Father Time, Father Sky, Sister Moon, the myriad ways humans played with the awesome world around them. Children love stories from around the world: how did the stars get up to the sky? Why does the moon seem to disappear? Is lightning the thunderbolt of Zeus? Why does the earth freeze during winter? Byrd Baylor's beautiful Caldecott Honor book, *The Way to Start a Day,*[33] catches the poetry and magic of human endeavors to live in harmony with natural forces.

Children enjoy reading legends, myths, and folktales, improvising on the stories, making up dances about them as well as making up their own legends and folktales. They will be fascinated by the similarity of legends explaining natural phenomena; for example, "turtle" is honored by both Native Americans and Chinese people as the animal who dove to the bottom of the sea and brought up land on its shell. The best resource material for original legends about nature comes from the questions and wonderings of your own group of children. The seeds of stories grow from thinking times and talk times. Make time!

Celebrations and special occasions Our calendars are a rich resource of events and holidays commemorating themes from nature. Across the planet and through centuries, the human family has celebrated the change of seasons, harvests, new moons, and trees with religious, cultural, and social holidays. Most of these have prescribed activities, songs, games, colors, food, and symbols. In Holland, people celebrate their most popular flower, the tulip. Egyptian families celebrate Sham al-Nessim in mid-March to enjoy the spring. Italian children love St. Joseph's Day on March 19. Flowers and food are in abundance as the new season begins. Even swallows return to San Juan Capistrano in California! All around the world, people celebrate the first of May with cheerful festivals and customs. African-American children celebrate the harvest and family unity with candles and special colors and customs for the holiday of Kwanzaa. Jewish children have special songs, prayers, and symbols for the harvest festival of Sukkot (Feast of Booths). Earth Day is a relatively new holiday for children around the world.

Learn about the special celebrations enjoyed by the children in your class. Share the songs, games, colors, and stories. Go beyond designated holidays. With your children, choose a theme from nature (animals? plants? trees? flowers? fish? stars?) and create your own holiday, with your own colors, songs, games, signs, symbols, and dances. Posters, cards, banners, poems, chants, processions, paintings, and sculptures are delightful ways for you and your children to introduce celebrations to families, friends, and the school community.

The wonder lab When Penni Rubin comes into a classroom, she "brings the magic" with her.[34] In this instance, the children were deeply fascinated by creepy, crawling creatures. From her collection of STUFF (Stimulating Tools Useful for

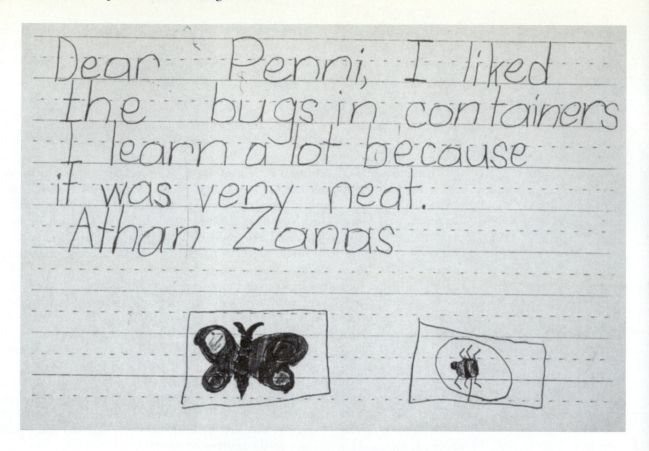

Fun and Fundamentals), Penni fills her suitcase with rubber snakes, alligators, ants, spiders, cloth creatures, plastic, and string. She's dressed as a "bug collector." Under one arm is her guitar. "Bug-collecting nets" are packed in her bulging suitcase. It's time to play Wonder Lab.

The children dive into the suitcase of insects, lizards, and turtles. Out come empty boxes ready for itemizing and categorizing. The children are "hired" as staff bug collectors, museum curators, and exhibit designers. Together, they decide how to categorize the creatures. They name, count, list, compare, and collect. Labeling and designing, they create excellent exhibits. Penni asks them, "Two legs? No legs? Four legs? Six legs? Thousands of legs?" They invent shadow plays of insects with a sheet and a light and expressive bodies. They fold paper in half, cut it into bug shapes, drop paint in the middle, press the cut paper together, and string up original bug mobiles to enhance their museum. They act to the Shel Silverstein poem, "I'm Being Swallowed by a Boa Constrictor"[35] and "The Eensy Beensy Spider." They celebrate Eric Carle's *The Very Hungry Caterpillar*[36] with a puppet show featuring striped knee socks. Penni describes her approach:

> We attach a set of pipe cleaners and pompoms as antennas to both socks, and add two button eyes on both. One of the socks we stuff and make into a butterfly with net wings attached. The other we leave wiggly. As the story goes along, we feed the wiggly caterpillar sock puppet clay and plastic fruit. We let that caterpillar crawl into a dark, cozy bag. As the story unfolds, we push out the other sock puppet, the butterfly one with net wings and wow—is it magic!"

The children love to play scientist, archeologist, and meteorologist. Without you, they sort, collect, and categorize. With your encouragement and guidance, they extend those natural, Curious George-like qualities to higher levels of thinking and learning.

Children collect, arrange, improvise, sort, exchange, experiment, infer, and communicate as they "mess with" and "play with" materials that invite interaction.[37]

Give them time and space, the "real" stuff of playful learning.

Penni Rubin wanders the country with her Wonder Lab of playful ideas. What's happening with the wonder in your room? I wonder. . . .

Improvised stories The stories we have made up could fill library shelves! Over the years, with children of all ages, we have made up stories (played and moved them) about such plots as: The Absentminded Caterpillars Who Forgot What They Were Supposed to Turn Into; The Baby Birds Who Learned How to Fly; The Hibernating Bears Who Kept Sleeping Even When Spring Had Arrived; The Baby Horses Who Wanted to Run and Gallop with the Big Horses; The Thunderstorm That Chased All the Animals and People Back to Their Warm, Dry Shelters[38]; The Polluted Stream That Got Cleaned Up; the Happy Fish; and Pele—Angry Goddess of Volcanoes! Oh, how much fun it is to make up stories with our children! Add movement, drama, dialogue, music, illustrations, and words.

CLASSROOM VISITORS AND FIELD TRIPS
Classroom Visitors

Animals Animals are wonderful classroom visitors, especially when accompanied by articulate human companions willing to share information and feelings. Children enjoy having the animals of families, neighbors, school staff, community friends, or institutions be at the center of attention. Encourage intelligent questions and discussion and always do follow-up letters, pictures, and projects.

Authors Many prominent authors of children's literature travel the country and visit classrooms and schools. Three influential writers whose works reflect their deep commitment to themes from our natural world and our environment are Ron Hirschi,[39] Michael Joel Rosen,[40] and Lois Ehlert.[41] Before the actual visits from such artists, the children immerse themselves in their books. Slowly, the school halls and walls will fill with art works, poems, writings, displays, collections, posters, and stories inspired by the literature. When writers such as Hirschi, Rosen, and Ehlert spend time with the children, they don't just read to them, talk to them, or lecture. They share ideas and activities. They walk together, gather materials, plant gardens, collect ideas for caring for animals and plants, observe natural phenomena, and explore ways to create a healthier environment and preserve the treasures of nature.

Gardeners Devoted gardeners can be found on any class list of families, friends, and neighbors. You'll find gardening people eager to share their enthusiasm and knowledge with your students. Highlight the visit with the planting of seeds outside your room or inside in pots, pockets, or plastic cups. I enjoyed visiting a classroom that featured a plastic children's swimming pool filled with soil and 23 bean plants, one for each child. It was a classroom garden planted with the help of a visitor who loved gardening.

Environmentalists Representatives of community organizations concerned with environmental issues are very willing to visit with your children and share information and materials. Always encourage such visitors to devote a large amount of time discussing solutions so the visit is not one of despair, but one of hope that leads to effective action—recycling, picking up litter, writing letters to newspapers, and so on.

Artists, photographers, and craftspeople who specialize in themes from nature Most communities are rich in resources. Be aware of opportunities for valuable and enjoyable visitors who will share experiences as well as examples of

their works. What do artists who paint landscapes and seascapes look for? What do they notice? How do they work? What about photographers who take excellent pictures of animals, of landforms, of skies? How do woodcarvers carve the feeling of life into wooden animals? These visits always inspire children to create their own pictures, sculptures, or collages.

Veterinarians Children are fascinated by and compassionate toward hurt or sick animals. Encourage your veterinarian visitor to highlight incidents or personal experiences of success in healing wounded or ill animals. Children need to discover, over and over, that nature (that life) has often (not always) the ability to rebuild, renew, and rehabilitate.

Astronomers/stargazers When astronomers or stargazers visit children, they bring not only information on skies and space, on solar systems and galaxies, but also stories of how constellations were named, how ancient peoples viewed the passage of the sun across the sky and the journey of falling stars. After the visit and the star-filled thank yous, the children will play astronomer and create beautiful art works that honor "the space above."

Botanists/florists Botanists carry colorful materials about seeds, plants, flowers, and trees. They also carry a message of awe that inspires children to appreciate the astonishing variety of plants and flowers growing on our fertile planet. Your children will become "flower children" for a long time after your visitor departs!

Geologists/rock collectors Rocks tell stories. Fossils stamp stones with the record of their lives. Professional or amateur geologists in classrooms motivate collections of stones, pebbles, rocks, petrified wood, painted sand, and mud. Mountains, volcanoes, and earthquakes are themes that mesmerize young children. Caves, deserts, canyons, mountains, and valleys are places that invite imagination and curiosity.

Oceanographers/scuba divers Scientists of the seas and waterways, and specialists studying fish and creatures of the waters, are especially welcome in classrooms of young children. The oceans provide mysterious and amazing arrays of animal and plant life. Creating artworks honoring sea life is a favorite endeavor of young artists. Challenge them to design original fish or to create their own ocean exhibit.

Ornithologists/bird watchers   Our winged friends are a vast and varied curriculum that never fails to fascinate. Most of us know so little about the lives of birds that information shared is like a gem to be savored. Be sure to ask your bird-watching visitor to bring many photographs and examples of different types of birds, eggs, and nests. Often bird-watchers tape the songs of birds. Children will want to make their own charts, recording the names and pictures of birds they observe in their own environment. There are no boring birds! Even the common city pigeon is astounding.

Meteorologists   Weather people have interesting stories of how they predict the weather. Ask the visitor to mix in legends and superstitions about weather predictions. *Farmers' Almanacs* are full of folk beliefs about cold winters, short winters, heavy rainfall, drought, and so on. Just think of our basic groundhog and the presence or absence of a shadow! The children enjoy playing weather reporter in daily scheduling. They enjoy making up new superstitions.

Member of a tribal culture   When Emma Bailey visits a classroom, she shares the deep-felt respect and love for all the works of nature as expressed by the designs, dances, and music of her Blackfoot background.[42] Be aware of organizations or individuals in your community who represent older, less technically sophisticated traditions and who will help the children find their connections to nature. When I visited Taiwan, I was happy to see that every class had a garden on school land. Every school cared for animals. We, in modern America, are relearning those old relationships.

Field Trips

Visit a field   Bring paper and crayons, markers, or pencils. Sit quietly in one spot. Look closely at that one spot and draw what you see. Pay attention to the lines of grass, the curl of stems, and the texture of earth and pebbles. Are there insects crawling through the blades of grass? Do you see the ladybug on the petal of clover? Catch the beauty of the dandelions.

Visit a farm/ranch   Barns, animals, crops, and sense-rich impressions wait for young children. What better place to learn about the harmony of nature than in the interwoven relationships obvious in farms and ranches?

Visit a park, preserve, or conservatory   In such places, children learn that adults do take responsibility for the care of nature and of our environment. Be ready with intelligent questions and concerns. How can the adventure be celebrated back at school? What lessons and experiences seem most vivid in the children's minds, and how can those facts and impressions be expressed most joyfully?

Visit an aquarium, planetarium, arboretum, or zoo   Look at your community. It will feature sights unique to itself. Take advantage of all it offers. Design posters, cards, commercials, slogans, songs, and dances to honor the adventure.

Visit a recycling center   When children see aluminum cans, plastics, newspapers, and other materials considered "trash" gathered in specific places, placed in storage areas and ready for machinery that recycles them for useful purposes, they are reassured that adults are taking responsibility for the upkeep of the environment. And

Field trip capped fourth-graders' in-depth study of rain forest

In response to David W. Thiel's recent letter to the editor regarding my fourth-grade class's rain-forest project, I offer more information about this special learning experience to clarify its objectives and outcomes.

Our class trip to Arhaus Furniture was the culmination activity of a five-week, in-depth study of tropical rain forests. During this time students read, discussed, wrote and gathered information from a variety of sources.

The student used math, science, social studies, reading and writing skills to construct a three-dimensional simulated rain forest in the classroom. They gave tours to more than 350 other students, parents and community members, sharing their knowledge and concerns for this worldwide endangered habitat.

The students wrote a book, compiled a scrapbook, made a video and constructed rain-forest terrariums from recycled bottles. They also were interviewed by newspaper, radio and television staff members. They were immersed in their learning.

The culminating activity at Arhaus took place during related arts, recess and lunch times. The activity, including T-shirts, was entirely paid for by John Reed of Arhaus.

The money earned by the students through working at the store was used to purchase 16 acres of rain forest, with the legal land title going to indigenous people in the Equadorian Amazon. The land was purchased through the Central Ohio Rain Forest Action Network, 1519 Aberdeen Ave.

During this motivating, meaningful study, the students became informed and involved. They applied basic skills, bolstered their self-esteem, interacted and cooperated with others and developed a better understanding and appreciation of their environment.

I am truly proud of my students and excited to be part of the Worthington City School system, which allows students and teachers to be creative and to collaborate with parents, with community members and with businesses to make a difference not only locally, but also in a global way.

Judith F. Tabor, teacher
Bluffview Elementary School
Worthington

when they are encouraged to do their part, they are very enthusiastic about participating. Never underestimate children's willingness to help, to work, and to make important contributions.

Visit a museum Museums remind children that we keep and learn about things we care about. Exhibits about the earth, space, and time, themes from our natural world, evoke great interest and concentration. Children remember so much. When you return to the classroom, of course, recollect and share experiences and observations. You will probably be inspired to set up your own classroom museum, creating your own materials and information.

The opportunities available to us based on our unique group of children, their families, the extended community of school and neighborhood, as well as organizations and individuals from nearby towns and cities, afford excellent ideas for field trips and visitors. Sometimes a simple ordinary, spontaneous visit by a passing neighbor may be the most meaningful and memorable. When one volunteer tutor finished his lesson, he stopped on the way out to greet his friends in the kindergarten room. They remarked on his safari-design T-shirt. He spent the next forty minutes keeping the children spellbound with his adventures on an African safari. Be open to serendipity!

A garden a street away from your school may be one of your best field trips (and you don't even need to order a bus).

A large squirrels' nest in the highest branches of an old maple tree around the corner from the school was the destination of a group of first graders who sat under the tree and filled their journal pages with illustrations of the tree and the nest. They wrote descriptions of the tree and their thoughts and questions about trees, squirrels, and nests. Every child had interesting observations to share.

IT ALL COMES TOGETHER

Thousands of examples of integrated, holistic connections could be offered in this small space to remind you of the interwoven strands of authentic learning experiences. For your enjoyment, I have chosen the story of the "galupe" bird as related by Kaye Boiarski.

Before we took the children outside for a silent walk, we told them that we were interested in finding the "galupe" bird, a bird many people heard of but no one ever saw. Maybe, in our explorations, we would actually see this very rare bird! We walked in total silence for about twenty minutes, listening to nature sounds, noticing nests, birds, animals, designs. As we walked, we imagined what the "galupe" bird looked like, sounded like. When we returned to the classroom, we talked about our ideas. With construction paper and paper plates, we made bird masks, adding folder paper for beaks, adding feathers and colors. How do you think the "galupe" bird sounds? What kind of song does it sing? We shared our sounds. We wrote everyone's name on a chart and the phonetically spelled sounds suggested. How do you think the "galupe" bird moves? Is it big, small? Bright, dull? Wide wings or tiny fluttery wings? Every child had original movement interpretations. We chanted the sounds as the children demonstrated their bird dances, wearing their "galupe" masks.

Kaye reports that the children's interest in giving beaks, wings, lives, and legends to their "galupe" birds continued for days. Kaye was most affected by the reaction of the children who had rarely been outside except to play soccer, baseball, or basketball. It is shocking that so many of our "couch potato" children have so

few experiences playing and enjoying nonstructured outdoor activities like walking, seeing, listening, touching, smelling, or following our noses or imaginations. Believe it or not, Kaye reported, "Those children with the fewest outdoor experiences were the *most* excited. They'll never forget our adventures in search of the 'galupe' bird!"

They may not have found the bird, but they did find that they loved entering the world of nature.

Sekou's students are gathering the "treasures" they found on their walk and deciding how to show and share them.

Jackie is climbing down from her "mountain" to draw a picture of fluffy clouds and rust-colored berries.

The day-care children are waddling single-file behind their teacher like ducklings behind the mother duck. They're singing a quacking song.

Where do we go from here?

NOTES ❤

1. Phillip Sekou Glass is a storyteller and teacher well known in the Midwest. The "treasure hunt" was shared with children participating in Days of Creation Arts programs.
2. I wrote about Jackie Cohen in "On the Trail with Jackie," Mimi Brodsky Chenfeld, *Day Care and Early Education,* summer 1990, pp. 35–37. My article is reprinted in *Teaching in the Key of Life.* Washington, DC: NAEYC, 1993. pp. 50–54.
3. Liese Millikin wrote a poem called "Arruning Raway," which was included in a twenty-year retrospective of *Writers in School* and *An Anthology 1982–1985,* published by the Ohio Arts Council. The line from her poem became the title of the anthology. Liese was in fifth grade when she wrote it.
4. I wrote about this theme in "Hangin Out with the Muffin Man," *Young Children,* September 1992. Reprinted in *Teaching in the Key of Life.* Washington, DC: NAEYC, 1993. pp. 50–54.
5. This chant comes from "The Child Is Introduced to the Cosmos at Birth" from the Omaha people. *American Indian Poetry—Anthology of Authentic Songs and Chants,* edited by George W. Cronyn (renewed 1962); Liveright, Ballantine Edition, pp. 53–54.
6. Shel Silverstein. "Forgotten Language" from *Where the Sidewalk Ends;* New York: Harper & Row, 1974. p. 149.
7. Ruth A. Wilson. "Nature Education and Science." *Day Care and Early Education.* Summer 1993, pp. 15–17. Wilson is director of Environmental Education for Pre-Schoolers, Bowling Green State University, Bowling Green, Ohio.
8. Ibid.
9. For example, see *Young Children,* May 1992. "Science Is a Way of Life" edited by Mary Rivkin, pp. 4–8.
   See also the 1992 annual theme issue of *Childhood Education* (Association of Childhood Education International), titled "Promoting Ecological Awareness." Stewart Cohen, guest editor.
   Also, see the *Phi Delta Kappan* special report, May 1993. "Environmental Education: Bringing Children and Nature Together," edited by Yvonne Baron Estes, pp. K1–K12.
10. Mary Rivkin coordinates Early Childhood Education at the University of Maryland-Baltimore County. Through her numerous articles, reviews, and presentations, her work as a consultant in science education is well known around the country. This interview is based on a conversation with Mary.

11. The books Mary recommends are: Cornell, Joseph. *Sharing Nature with Children*. Nevada City, CA: Dawn, 1979.
    Carson, Rachel. *The Sense of Wonder*. Photos by Charles Pratt and others. New York: Harper & Row, 1965.
    Greenman, James. *Caring Spaces, Learning Places*. Redman, WA: Exchange Press, 1988.
    Cone, Molly. *Come Back, Salmon*. San Francisco: Sierra Club, 1992.
12. Theodore Roethke. *Straw for the Fire*. Garden City, New York: Doubleday Anchor Press, 1974, p. 163.
13. For information on Fran's music and programs, write to Lemonstone Records, P.O. Box 607, Cote St. Luc, Quebec, H4V2Z2, Canada.
14. Mary Garelick, illustrated by Leonard Weisgard, *Where Does the Butterfly Go When It Rains?* New York: Scholastic, 1961.
    Robert McCloskey. *Make Way for Ducklings*. New York: Scholastic, 1972.
    Tomie DePaola. *The Cloud Book*. New York: Scholastic, 1975.
    E. B. White, illustrated by Garth Williams, *Charlotte's Web*. New York: Harper & Row, 1952, p. 183.
15. "These Are the Questions." Words by Michael Thaler, from *Rosenshontz Tickles You*. RS Records, Box 651, Brattleboro, VT, 05301.
16. Bianca Lavies. *Lily Pad Pond*. New York: Dutton, 1989.
    Barbara Juster Esbensen, illustrated by Mary Barrett Brown, *Tiger with Wings (The Great Horned Owl)*. New York: Orchard, 1991.
    Myra Cohn Livingston, illustrated by Leonard Everett Fisher, *Earth Songs*. New York: Holiday House, 1986.
    Jill Bailey, illustrated by Carolyn Scrace, *Life Cycle of a Grasshopper*. New York: Bookwright, 1990.
    Ruth Howell, photos by Arline Strong, *A Crack in the Pavement*. New York: Atheneum, 1970.
    Arthur Dorros. *Rain Forest Secrets*. New York: Scholastic, 1990.
    Lynn M. Stone. *The Tiger*. Vero Beach, FL: Rourke, 1989.
    Susanna Van Rose. *Volcano and Earthquake*. (Eyewitness Book.) New York: Knopf, 1992.
17. Alex Sovet-Pett, "Kids on Ecology." Annual theme issue. *Childhood Education*, 1992, p. 261.
18. Kaye Boiarski is the assistant director of Days of Creation Arts for Kids as well as a popular costumer and teacher of arts for children. This section features excerpts from a long conversation with Kaye.
19. Patricia Wynn Brown. "Playing for Dreams," an article about the Nisonger Center and the playground. *Ohio State University Alumni Magazine*. January/February 1993, pp. 11–14.
20. From Mary Rivkin and Gail Perry. "Becoming Teachers of Science." *Young Children*, May 1992, p. 16.
21. Sylvia Wallach is a national consultant in music education. For information on her programs, write Sylvionics, Box 61035, Chicago, IL 60660. (312) 465–4583. This section is based on a conversation with Sylvia.
22. See note 5.
23. Mirra Ginsburg, illustrated by Jose Aruego and Ariane Dewey, *How The Sun Was Brought Back to the Sky*. New York: Macmillan, 1975.
24. Ezra Jack Keats. *The Snowy Day*. New York: Viking Press, 1962.
25. Always encourage the children to catch the rhythms of nature with their exciting new instruments.
26. Becky Moore retired from a teaching career with the Columbus Public Schools to help bring good literature to children. She is a major help in organizing the bibliographies in this book.

27. Anna Grace is a well-known singer performing in central Ohio. She presents musical programs with Artists in the Schools.

28. Leslie Zak, the director of Days of Creation Arts For Kids, is a multilingual singer presenting programs to schools under Artists in the Schools. Leslie also shares creative dramatics programs with children. She can be reached at 65 W. Como, Columbus, OH, 43202.

29. My own collection of music to share with children is eclectic. We love the songs of Woody Guthrie; Pete Seeger; Tom Paxton; Ella Jenkins; Mr. Al; Steve and Greg; Fran Avni; Harry Belafonte; Peter, Paul, and Mary; and Red Grammer. Music from cultures around the country and around the world is our favorite kind. What music do you share with the children?

30. Bess-Gene Holt. See note 24, p. 118.

31. Most of these are old albums, probably out of print. Libraries, used record, and old cassette shops have useful materials. Keep looking and gathering.

32. Marie Hall Etts. *Play with Me*. New York: Viking/Seafarer, 1968.

33. Lawrence Di Fiori. *Good Morning, Muffin Mouse*. Racine: Western, 1989.

34. Byrd Baylor. *The Way to Start a Day*. Illustrated by Peter Parnell. New York: Macmillan, 1978.

35. Penni Rubin is an educational resource specialist, educational consultant, teacher, musician, performer, and author. With her sister, Dr. Eleanora Iberall Robbins, Penni wrote *What's Under Your Feet?* (Earth Science For Everyone) published by the U.S. Department of the Interior/U.S. Geological Survey, 1992. Penni can be reached at 3538 Ingleside Road, Shaker Heights, OH 44122.

36. Shel Silverstein. "I'm Being Swallowed by a Boa Constrictor" from *Where The Sidewalk Ends*, p. 45.

37. Eric Carle. *The Very Hungry Caterpillar*. New York: Philomel, 1987.

38. An excellent article on the subject of the importance of interactive experiences is "Science Activities for Young Children" by Jean Shaw, Sally Blake, and Mary Jo Cliatt. *Day Care and Early Education*. Autumn 1992, pp. 15–17.

39. This improvised, original story was described in my article, "From Catatonic to Hyperactive: Randy Snapped Today" in *Young Children*, May 1989, pp. 25–27. Reprinted in *Teaching in the Key of Life*, NAEYC, 1993.

40. Ron Hirschi's commitment to protecting the environment, to sharing his deep appreciation and understanding of nature is carried in the messages of his well-loved books and his direct experiences with children and teachers across the country. A sampling of Ron's books honoring themes from nature are:
    What Is a Bird? Photos by Galen Burrell. New York: Walker, 1987.
    What Is a Horse? Photos by Linda Quartam Younker. New York: Walker, 1987.
    Where Do Birds Live? Photos by Galen Burrell. New York: Walker, 1987.
    Who Lives In . . . Alligator Swamp? Photos by Galen Burrell. New York: Dodd, Mead, 1987.
    Who Lives In . . . The Forest? Photos by Galen Burrell. New York: Dodd, Mead, 1987.
    Who Lives On . . . The Prairie? Photos by Galen Burrell. New York: Putnam, 1989.
    Note Ron Hirschi's *One Earth* project, published by the National Audubon Society.

41. Michael Joel Rosen's books, as well as his visits to schools, encourage children to become appreciative and responsible caretakers of animals. He challenges children with ideas that evoke imaginative artistic and poetic responses. Some of Michael's books enriching themes from our natural world are:

> *All Eyes on the Pond.* Illustrated by Tom Leonard. New York: Hyperion, 1994.
> *Kids' Best Dog Book.* New York: Workman Press, 1993.
> *Kids' Book of Fishing.* New York: Workman Press, 1991.
> *Speak! Children's Book Illustrators Brag about Their Dogs.* San Diego: Harcourt Brace, 1993.

42. I visited a school that had transformed itself into a Lois Ehlert celebration! Brilliant images and colors inspired by Ehlert's beloved nature books filled every space. Some of the books highlighted were:
    > *Nuts to You.* San Diego: Harcourt Brace Jovanovich, 1993.
    > *Feathers for Lunch.* San Diego: Harcourt Brace Jovanovich, 1990.
    > *Fish Eyes: A Book You Can Count On.* San Diego: Harcourt Brace Jovanovich, 1990.
    > *Planting a Rainbow.* San Diego: Harcourt Brace Jovanovich, 1988.
    > *Red Leaf/Yellow Leaf.* San Diego: Harcourt Brace Jovanovich, 1991.

43. Emma Bailey is an example of an excellent community resource. She is on the staff of Days of Creation Arts for Kids and Artists in the Schools. In addition, she teaches workshops and performs for programs in greater Columbus, Ohio.

BOOKS FROM MY KNAPSACK FOR CHILDREN ♥ ♥

Anholt, Laurence. *The Forgotten Forest.* San Francisco: Sierra Club, 1992.

Baker, Jennie. *Where the Forest Meets the Sea.* New York: Greenwillow, 1988.

Banks, Merve. *Animals of the Night.* Illustrated by Ronald Himler. New York: Scribner, 1990.

Baur, Laura. *First Discovery Books—The River.* New York: Scholastic, 1992.

Behm, Harry. *Trees.* Illustrated by James Endicott. New York: Henry Holt, 1992.

Bond, Ruskin. *Cherry Tree.* Illustrated by Allan Eitzen. New York: Boyds Mill, 1991.

Brenner, Barbara, and Garelick, Mary. *The Tremendous Tree Book.* Illustrated by Fred Brenner. Homesdale, PA: Boyds Mills, 1979.

Cherry, Lynne. *The Great Kapok Tree.* San Diego: Harcourt Brace Jovanovich, 1990.

Chinery, Michael. *All Kinds of Animals—A Child's First Encyclopedia #1.* New York: Random House, 1993.

Cole, Joanna. *The Magic School Bus at the Waterworks.* Illustrated by Bruce Degen. New York: Scholastic, 1986.

———. *The Magic School Bus Inside the Earth.* Illustrated by Bruce Degen. New York: Scholastic, 1987.

Cotler, Joanna. *Sky Above Earth Below.* Illustrated by Joanna Cotler. New York: Harper & Row, 1990.

Cowcher, Helen. *Rain Forest.* New York: Farrar, Straus and Giroux, 1988.

Davol, Marguerite. *The Heart of the Wood.* Illustrated by Sheila Hamanaka. New York: Simon and Schuster, 1992.

Dawe, Neil and Karen. *The Bird Book and the Bird Feeder.* New York: Workman, 1988.

Dorros, Arthur. *Follow the Water from Brook to Ocean.* New York: HarperCollins, 1991.

Elkington, John, et al. *Going Green: A Kid's Handbook to Saving the Planet.* Illustrated by Tony Ross. New York: Viking, 1990.

Fleming, Denise. *In the Small, Small Pond.* New York: Henry Holt, 1993.

———. *In the Tall, Tall Grass.* New York: Henry Holt, 1991.

Gackenbach, Dick. *Mighty Tree.* Illustrated by Dick Gackenbach. San Diego: Harcourt Brace Jovanovich, 1981.

George, Jean Craighead. *The Moon of the Bears*. Illustrated by Ron Parket. New York: HarperCollins, 1993.

————. *The Moon of the Monarch Butterflies*. Illustrated by Kam Mak. New York: HarperCollins, 1993.

————. *The Moon of the Owls*. Illustrated by Wendell Minor. New York: HarperCollins, 1993.

Gibbons, Gail. *Stargazers*. Illustrated by Gail Gibbons. New York: Holiday House, 1992.

————. *Surrounded by Sea: Life on a New England Fishing Island*. Illustrated by Gail Gibbons. Boston: Little, Brown, 1991.

————. *The Seasons of Arnold's Apple Tree*. Illustrated by Gail Gibbons. San Diego: Harcourt Brace Jovanovich, 1984.

Guiberson, Brenda Z. *Cactus Hotel*. Illustrated by Megan Lloyd. New York: Henry Holt, 1991.

Halpern, Shari. *My River*. Illustrated by Shari Halpern. New York: Macmillan, 1992.

Havill, Juanita. *Sato and the Elephants*. Illustrated by Jean and Mou-Sien Tseng. New York: Lothrop, Lee and Shephard, 1993.

Heard, Georgia. *Creatures of Earth, Sea, and Sky*. Illustrated by Jennifer Owings Dewey. Homesdale, PA: Boyds Mills-Wordsong, 1992.

Hughes, Shirley. *The Big Alfie Out of Doors Story Book*. Illustrated by Shirley Hughes. New York: Lothrop, Lee & Shephard, 1992.

Iverson, Diane. *I Celebrate Nature*. Dawn, CA: 1993.

Javna, John. *50 Simple Things Kids Can Do to Save the Earth*. New York: Andrews and McMeel, 1990.

Jones, Brian. *Space: A Three Dimensional Journey*. Illustrated by Richard Clifton-Day. New York: Dial, 1991.

Jones, Hettie. *The Trees Stand Shining—Poetry of North American Indians*. Illustrated by Robert Andrew Parker. New York: Dial, 1971.

Kerrod, Robin. *The Children's Space Atlas*. Illustrated by Janos Marffy. Brookfield, CT: Millbrook, 1992.

Ketterman, Helen. *The Year of No More Corn*. New York: Orchard, 1993.

King, Elizabeth. *Backyard Sunflower*. Photographs by Elizabeth King. New York: Dutton's Children's Books, 1993.

Kovacs, Deborah. *Moonlight on the River*. Illustrated by William Shattuck. New York: Viking, 1993.

Kurjurian, Judi. *In My Own Backyard*. Watertown, MA: Charlesbridge, 1993.

Lamb, Marjorie. *2 Minutes a Day for a Greener Planet*. New York: HarperCollins, 1991.

Leslie, Clare Walker. *Nature All Year Long*. Illustrated by Clare Walker Leslie. New York: Greenwillow, 1991.

Lionni, Leo. *A Busy Year*. Illustrated by Leo Lionni. New York: Knopf, 1992.

Lotz, Karen F. *Snowsong Whistling*. New York: Dutton, 1993.

Madgwick, Wendy. *Animaze! A Collection of Amazing Nature Mazes*. Illustrated by Lorna Hussey. New York: Knopf, 1992.

Newton-John, Olivia, and Hurst, Brian Seth. *A Pig Tale*. Illustrated by Sal Murdocces. New York: Simon and Schuster, 1993.

Orr, Katherine. *My Grandpa and the Sea*. Illustrated by Katherine Orr. Minneapolis: Carolrhoda, 1990.

Pearce, Fred. *The Big Green Book*. Illustrated by Fred Pearce. New York: Putnam, 1991.

Rockwell, Anne. *Our Yard is Full of Birds*. Illustrated by Anne Rockwell. New York: Macmillan, 1992.

Ryder, Joanne. *Hello, Tree!* Illustrated by Michael Hays. New York: Lodestar, 1991.

Schlein, Miriam. *Let's Go Dinosaur Tracking*. Illustrated by Kate Duke. New York: HarperCollins, 1991.

Schwartz, Linda. *Earth Book for Kids: Activities to Help Heal the Environment*. Santa Barbara: Learning Works, 1990.

Shaw, Kiki and Kathryn. *Maya and the Town that Loved a Tree*. New York: Rizzoli International, 1993.

Stephen, Oliver. *My First Look at Seasons*. New York: Random House, 1990.

Stevenson, James. *Grandpa's Too-Good Garden*. Illustrated by James Stevenson. New York: Greenwillow, 1989.

Stock, Catherine. *Where Are You Going, Manyoni*. New York: Morrow Junior Books, 1993.

Tresselt, Alvin. *The Gift of the Tree*. Illustrated by Henri Sorensen. New York: Lothrop, Lee and Shephard, 1992.

Udry, Janice May. *A Tree Is Nice*. Illustrated by Marc Simont. New York: Harper, 1956.

VanAllsburg, Chris. *Just A Dream*. Illustrated by Chris VanAllsburg. Boston: Houghton Mifflin, 1990.

Yolen, Jane. *Welcome to the Green House*. Illustrated by Laura Regan. New York: Putnam, 1993.

Zolotow, Charlotte. *The Seashore Book*. Illustrated by Wendell Manor. New York: HarperCollins, 1992.

BOOKS FROM MY KNAPSACK FOR TEACHERS ❤ ❤

Caduto, Michael, and Bruchac, Joseph. *Keepers of the Earth*. Illustrated by John Kahionhes Fadden. Golden, Colorado: Fulcrum, 1989.

Chaillé, C., and Britain, L. *The Young Child as Scientist: A Constructivist Approach to Early Childhood Education*. New York: Harper College, 1991.

Collis, M. *Early Explorations*. Great Britain: Macdonald Educational Teachers' Laboratory, 1989.

Earthworks Group. *50 Simple Things You Can Do to Save the Earth*. Berkeley: Earthworks Press, 1990.

Gore, Al. *Earth in the Balance: Ecology and the Human Spirit*. Boston: Houghton Mifflin, 1992.

Hollander, Jeffrey. *How to Make a Better Place*. New York: Morrow, 1990.

Hopkins, Susan, and Winters, Jeffrey, eds. *Discovering the World*. Philadelphia: New Society, 1990.

Jobb, Jamie. *The Night Sky Book—An Everyday Guide to Every Night*. Illustrated by Linda Bennett. Boston: Little, Brown, 1977.

Lewis, Scott. *The Rainforest Book*. Los Angeles: Living Planet Press, 1990.

Peppin, Anthea. *Nature in Art—Millbrook Arts Library*. Designed by Paul Fielder. Brookfield, CT: Millbrook, 1991.

Petrach, Carol. *Earthways: Simple Environmental Activities for Young Children*. Mount Ranier, MD: Gryphon House, 1992.

Delicious Work

PIZZA

Pizza
by Paul Tyson

Our class made pizza in October in our classroom. We rolled the dough, we spread the sauce, then put pepperonis on.

Pizza
by Justin Gerwe

Our class made pizza in October in our classroom. Then we rolled The dough and spread the sauce and put pepperonis on. Then we baked it. Then we ate it.

Pretzels
by Justin Gerwe

Our class made pretzels in our classroom in April. We put the flour on the table, then we spread the dough, then we baked it.

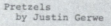

Pretzels
by Paul Tyson

Our class made pretzels in April in our classroom. We made the dough, we shaped it and baked it. Then we ate them.

Peanut Butter
by Karen Larson

Our class, Mr. Hohwald and Miss Susi made peanut butter. We peeled the nuts and then we crushed the nuts and then we put salt on them. Mrs. Lehman got some crackers out and we put peanut butter on the crackers.

Part 3

The Food We Eat

Where We Live

The Clothes We Wear

Chapter 7

The Food We Eat

Let us sit down soon to eat
with all those who haven't eaten;
let us spread great tablecloths,
put salt in the lakes of the world,
set up planetary bakeries,
tables with strawberries in snow,
and a plate like the moon itself
from which we all can eat.[1]

Pablo Neruda

THE BASICS

Of all our basic themes, none is more basic than food. Food means life. Can we get more fundamental than that?

From weddings to funerals, from baptisms to bar mitzvahs, food is a central component of every celebration. In every religion, blessings of thanksgiving for food are rituals of vital importance. Food is a symbol of life, of love: a parent's first responsibility to a baby, a nation's first responsibility to its people. In the last decade, we have witnessed the devastated faces of starvation in lands where crops have died and water supplies have dried. On such a fertile planet as Earth, it is incongruous and unacceptable for millions of people to know only hunger. In our own country, the statistics on hunger are shocking. These terrible realities add another dimension to our theme of Food. Collecting food for those in need is an event happening in schools and communities throughout the land. As you read this chapter, you will note the many ways teachers, children, and families share with others less fortunate.

Every mouthful of food we taste is laced with ingredients from all curriculum strands! For example, cereal is named for Ceres, the Roman goddess of grains and fruits. Spaghetti dates from the thirteenth century, when the Venetian explorer Marco Polo brought back from the Orient his "discovery" of noodles, which the Italians turned into pasta. We know that Christopher Columbus was not searching for America but for a short route to India to collect spices. The Old Testament's description (Numbers 13:27) of a land that "does indeed flow with milk and honey" is a factual report citing the abundance of goats and wild bees in ancient Israel. When you devour your next pizza, find out something of its fascinating history from books such as Louise Love's *The Complete Book of Pizza*.[2] How many cultures feature meats, cheeses, and vegetables wrapped in some kind of dough? Include on your list crepes from Sweden, tacos from Mexico, ravioli from Italy, blintzes from Germany, and egg rolls from many lands of the Far East. Wouldn't the Earl of Sandwich be astonished at the variety of sandwiches available throughout the world since the seventeenth century, when he instructed a servant to put a slice of roast meat between two pieces of bread so he could have his dinner without interrupting a card game?

In thinking about food, human creativity must be appreciated. Consider the varieties of bread throughout the world! Ann Morris's *Bread Bread Bread* in simple text and photographs will give you an around-the-planet whirlwind tour of bread from pita to pizza, from toasted to roasted to baked.[3] Better yet, roll bread dough into a story like *Tony's Bread,* full of fancy and delicious ingredients![4] If bread isn't your dish, read about rice, another staple of the world's peoples. Books like *Rice* by Lynne Merrison[5] have information about the many ways this basic crop is eaten. Call it jambalaya or paella. Drink it in soups, mix it into puddings, crunch it in cereals, or press it with raw fish, seaweed, and vegetables and name it sushi.

We can learn so much about the dynamics of our own society through our study of food. Even infants like Callie, now six months old, are already developing their own particular tastes. In addition to milk, Callie enjoys butternut squash, bananas, sweet potatoes, applesauce, and rice and barley cereals. Len, the Muffin Man, almost two years old, has definite predilections. He says *yes* to pizza, hot dogs, apple juice, scrambled eggs, and toast. Kimani and his prekindergarten buddies could be hired by Madison Avenue to advertise every fast-food product in America. When asked about their favorite foods, these almost-five-year-olds don't hesitate for a second: tacos, pasta, pizza, french fries, hamburgers, cheeseburgers, hot dogs, and egg rolls.

Just how did such dishes as pizza, pasta, tacos, and egg rolls become favorite foods of American children? As educators around the country debate goals and

definitions for multicultural programs, children are eating daily dosages of multicultural materials! Regional, ethnic, and cultural foods are familiar items on the menus of American children, who sip New England clam chowder and Creole gumbo, munch gyros, and chew Tex-Mex burritos and hot chili while adults around them drink espresso and cappucino. I am always surprised when I visit teachers in rural areas with few or no Jewish residents to find bagels and cream cheese for brunch! There's a tie between Thai food and Mexican food for the unofficial title of the fastest-growing food in America. An idea whose time has come is Glory Foods,[6] the first widely distributed line of African-American specialties like okra, black-eyed peas, collard greens, corn muffins, hot sauce, sweet potatoes: soul food. Maybe the way to our hearts really is through our stomachs!

What *is* American food anyway? If we go back to beginnings, we must include some of the foods grown by Native peoples before the coming of Europeans. Corn, beans, and squash—sometimes called "the three sisters"—were mainstay crops. Peanuts, cacao beans, pumpkins, peppers, and vanilla were native to the people of the Americas.

Food is a cluster of sensory experiences! The sight, smell, taste, or texture of a particular food often evokes images of people, places, and events from earlier times. For the great French novelist Marcel Proust, the sweet smell of a particular pastry he enjoyed in his childhood triggered memories that inspired the classic *Remembrance of Things Past*. The brain's memory center is located near the brain's center for smell and taste. What foods do you remember from your childhood?

Food is often enmeshed with emotions. We make up after an argument by going out to dinner. Guests hear, "I'm so happy you're visiting us, I'll prepare your favorite dish!" A fourth grader wrote: "Anger is the smell of supper burning."

Food is a theme that must be directly experienced! How many skills are involved in folding napkins, setting places, piling, selecting, cleaning, washing, preparing, and counting portions? ("Be sure we have a snack for everyone!") Snack time, usually the most popular time of a young child's school day, is a time for interactive activities, cooperative learning, language development, and multicultural understandings ("What kind of delicious snack did Maria's aunt bring in today to celebrate Maria's birthday? Oh, my, a piñata, too!"). We could list every curriculum component, every theme from fantastic bodies to letters and numbers, all revolving around food!

Michael Joel Rosen talks poetically about food:

> The preparation of any food is an ordeal, a ritual, a procedure, a narrative event—something to do with plot, with drama! One thing happens after another. Things marinate, rise, heat—all while you are somewhere else. The plot thickens, literally! Finally, we find out what happens, we wait and see. We are as much the observer, the reader, the watcher as we are the actor, the observed, the reading. The meal, the menu, the dish all depend on a kind of mystery: Will it turn out? What will it taste like? God made this fruit; someone else made the recipe, and I followed it. There is something of discovery, of imagination.
>
> Children are awed—I am—by the fact that dough rises and that water, sugar, butter, yeast, and flour make almost all the different cakes, cookies, noodles, and breads in the world! Bacon shrinks, concentrated orange juice expands, a drop of food coloring turns a whole cake pink, egg whites foam and become stiff. Who dreamed of beating egg whites and why? That question, that mystery, is part of cooking.
>
> There is the whole idea of hands, the ritual of hands on—manipulation, stirring, kneading, straining, twisting, peeling, slicing. Sacred gestures, spellbinding movements . . . passing the hands over the mixing bowl three times.
>
> There is the whole curative, healing, growing part of cooking, the whole aspect of doing a good deed, gracing the table with tastes, offering your best to those you love.

Did you know that the word *company* means "with bread"? *Companionship* means people who eat bread together. Until a few decades ago, meals were occasions for families to eat and talk together. The most important family times were mealtimes, when parents and children shared events of the day, concerns, and plans. The warm, rich smells of home-cooked meals blended with conversation in what for many people were the best times of their childhood.

Those days seem to be gone forever. More and more people skip breakfast or eat it on the run. Most families do not have lunch together. Although for some families dinner time is still a time of companionship, for many it is accompanied by loud music or television. Individual TV trays have replaced the family table. Often, children eat by themselves.

Laurel Robertson expresses her feelings about this contemporary scene in her book *Laurel's Kitchen*.

> If breakfast is the most important meal to the body, dinner may be to the spirit; not the food so much as the simple precious fact of coming together with those you love. The world we live in now is so rushed and hectic that by the end of a day, people very often find themselves feeling depleted, confused, and fragmented. This is the time of day when the warmth and conviviality of a family meal can make all the difference in the world.

She urges parents to "Be fierce as a mother lion to protect the sanctity of this hour. Fight football coaches, drama teachers, and scout leaders if you must, but keep the dinner hour intact."[7]

Despite the fact that good health habits and nutrition are widely taught in our schools, many young children still develop poor eating habits. Mary T. Goodwin, who with Gerry Pollen wrote the widely used book, *Creative Food Experiences for Children*,[8] is eloquent in her concern. She says the four F's—formulated, fabricated, fake foods—are displacing wholesome foods in the diet. She notes that many children eat food that comes in boxes, packages, bags, bottles, and vending

machines—food designed to be eaten on the run. She reminds us that the foods children eat affect their growth, development, ability to learn, and general behavior. We have all read newspaper reports linking diet with emotional problems, antisocial behavior, and hyperactivity.

How children eat is as important as what they eat. Mary writes, "The presentation of food in a comfortable, relaxed atmosphere, together with love, care and eye appeal, can greatly affect the way the child feels about himself and those around him. Early experiences with food may lay the foundation for lifelong eating habits . . . *Children have to be educated to make good food selections.* Food habits which build good health are not acquired naturally; they must be learned."[9]

Mary told me a delightful story about her own children. When they were very young, they formed their own concept of her work as a nutritionist, which was revealed when Mary stayed home with the flu. Her son, then five years old, was upset that Mary was home sick: "Mom, you can't stay home!" "Why not?" Mary asked hoarsely. "Because all the junk-food pushers will get ahead of you!"

Because many homes are not places of warmth, safety, and security centered around traditional mealtimes, because the mass media bombard children with commercials about junk food, and because many foods lack nutritional value, it is important that teachers help children develop good eating habits and provide opportunities for children to share and enjoy meals with other persons (your classroom may be the only place where they learn the meaning of *company*).

If, as a teacher, you link food activities with everything you do, this guide will add to your knapsack of ideas. If you are a teacher who has not really thought about making "your daily bread" a part of the curriculum, be ready to be moved as you read. Those who believe in the importance of food as a central activity in early childhood education speak in one voice. They are powerful advocates of enlightened, nourishing, and loving education.

In the schools that feature cooking in their classrooms, you can smell the sweet aromas of friendly atmospheres. Food always connects with good conversation and warmth.

You can feel everyone relaxing. . . . Food provides success experiences for all children. It brings teachers and children closer together, minimizes the gap. Everyone participates in the project—food experiences break down sexist roles. This is one avenue where children can learn to be more grown up, responsible, to take charge. Cooking and food-related activities touch every subject, every area of the curriculum, from table manners to science and math. I see cooperation, thoughtfulness, appreciation, and courtesy developing through cooking activities. Oral language is enhanced; talk naturally comes with a process that involves children.[10]

America's favorite cook, Julia Child, in her book *Julia Child and Company,* encourages the participation of children in the cooking process:

> I am all for encouraging children to work productively with their hands. They learn to handle and care for equipment with respect. . . . A knife is a tool, not a toy. . . . Talk to children as you plan menus. Let their small, sensitive noses sniff the fish. . . . Work together at the counter. Let your children arrange platters. The small rituals, like the clean hands and clean apron before setting to work; the precision of gesture, like leveling off a cupful of flour; the charm of improvisation and making something new; the pride of mastery; and the gratification of offering something one has made—these have such value to a child."[11]

Perhaps you are shaking your head and saying, "How can I encourage cooking activities when I don't have the equipment for it? I don't have appliances and supplies. I'll just have to forget it!" Wrong. You do not need large appliances and the latest gadgets to share cooking experiences with children. Schools with sinks, stoves, refrigerators, and ovens are in the minority. Think "scrounge." Teachers around the country call on families to send in toasters, crock pots, electric frying pans, mixing bowls, hot plates, blenders, corn poppers, whatever is needed. Don't get complicated. Keep it simple!

Diane Biswas describes how three-year-olds preparing bread and butter:

> . . . [they] smiled and were genuinely tickled at having put butter on bread and then . . . eating it! The pat on the head, the encouragement from the teacher, the words "good for you" help children feel good inside. And the teacher feels good, too. It's contagious! Cooking with children does wonders for their self-concepts. The most important thing we stress to our children is that they are loved by their teachers and we care what goes into them. We care about their health. We want them to be healthy because we love them![12]

Not all children want to participate immediately. Some may have a "wait and see" attitude. Some may be starting careers as excellent "guests" at early ages. Five-year-old Ariela was asked to help set the table, fold the napkins, and fill the glasses with water. Ariela replied politely, "I'll be the person who says 'Thank you.'" It is to be hoped that all children will say "Thank you." Courtesy, good manners, and thoughtfulness are integral parts of this learning-by-doing process. It is amazing how children learn to cooperate through cooking experiences.

Even when learning social skills, we learn more successfully in joyful, playful ways. *Pass the Fritters, Critters!* is a delightful book that encourages children to learn the magic power of "please," a word necessary for pleasant mealtimes and all other times.[13]

There are as many ways to arrange food preparation and cooking activities as there are teachers. Small groups are the most popular. Many teachers give small groups of children the chance to make something or prepare something while the rest of the class works on a different activity.

"Sometimes one child at a time is involved in the process," explains Sue Coomer.[14] When her kindergartners make butter or ice cream, one child at a time stirs. Usually Sue combines the stirring with numbers and counting. "Everyone stirs six times when we're talking about the number six!"

The many benefits of cooking with children are clearly described in the following evaluation received by Marilyn Cohen and her kindergartners who were visited in the middle of an exciting gastronomic experience.

Evaluation of Marilyn Cohen by Jeanne Jacobson

The kindergartners had made vegetable soup with alphabet noodles, and during this period they ate the soup, cleaned up, and got ready for play. Such a lot of learning in cognitive and affective domains occurred during this happy period. In their conversation, children talked about fruits and vegetables, giving specific examples and telling or finding out how they should be classified. (Previously, children had visited an apple orchard and had made a fruit salad.) They identified the cooked pieces of vegetables and talked about which children had brought each one.

They found seeds and talked about what made the seeds grow and whether they would grow inside the person who ate them! They named alphabet letters and found those in the soup that were part of their names. Although Ms. Cohen was not, of course, present at each of the tables, she had established an atmosphere of learning and inquiry such that the children talked about intellectual concerns appropriate for their age level. The children enjoyed eating, talking, and sharing ideas. Bruno Bettelheim holds the view that we must literally feed those whom we hope to teach. Ms. Cohen feeds her children and gives them a gentle, caring environment full of exciting things to do and concepts to learn. . . . She teaches them that school is a happy and safe place to learn and live. She is an exceptionally gifted teacher. . . .[16]

This guide is packed with ideas, recipes, and experiences generously shared by many teachers who never heard of the phrase "burn out" because they are too busy simmering, boiling, toasting, frying, and melting! Every activity in this guide can be used in other guides in this book. Activities involving food easily relate to numbers, letters, shapes, colors, community helpers, our fantastic bodies, family, and friends. Fit them into your scheme, your scene.

Let us end this section with a reminder that the fruits of the earth are gifts that we often take for granted, squander, and waste. There is no age young enough to begin learning compassion for those less fortunate, appreciation for the miracle of the earth, respect for the environment, and a commitment to help "spread great tablecloths,/put salt in the lakes of the world,/set up planetary bakeries,/tables with strawberries in snow,/and a plate like the moon itself/from which we all can eat." Perhaps in the lifetimes of our young children, the people of the earth will truly break bread together and no one will go hungry.

DISCOVERY TIMES/WONDER TIMES

- Everything that is alive must eat to live.
- Healthy bodies require nourishing food.
- We need to eat something every day from each of the four basic food groups. They are: dairy products; fruits and vegetables; poultry, meat, fish, and eggs; and grains and cereals.
- Preparing food together and eating together is an enjoyable experience.
- We can learn about cultures, customs, and traditions through food.
- We are always amazed at the many ways people prepare the same basic ingredients. It demonstrates the imaginative powers of the human family. The variety of cooking methods, combinations, and presentations is infinite!
- Our earth is abundant with food for people. People have to learn how to farm and grow crops and take care of the earth. Aren't we lucky to live on a planet that has fertile soil, waters, and forests?
- Because we are thankful for our food, we should not waste it.
- We should share our food with others.

SUGGESTED VOCABULARY

food	hunger	share	follow
vegetables	menu	dry	measure
meat	teaspoon	creamy	rinse
eggs	tablespoon	eat	slice
milk	sugar	drink	digest
cereal	flour	chew	stir
bread	salt	swallow	peel
fruit	pepper	sip	bake
food groups	sauce	taste	knead
junk food	batter	boil	roll
restaurant	liquid	steam	pit
table	delicious	simmer	seed
plates	hot	scramble	grow
soups	cold	fry	leaf
stews	warm	toast	stem
cups	sweet	dip	root
bowls	sour	add	farm
knives	spicy	melt	orchard
forks	cool	pour	dairy
spoons	frozen	shape	recipe
pots	lumpy	cut	set the table
pans	smooth	taste	clean up
mixing bowl	sticky	smell	sweep
glass	crisp	squeeze	clean
napkin	soft	mix	

Each word on the list is a seed-word that yields many more. The word "fruit," for example, leads to apple, orange, pear, cherry, berry, banana, peach, and melon.

You'll notice that the list does not include the hundreds of specific foods like cornflakes, pepperoni pizza, egg-drop soup, etc. This is a vocabulary that is immeasurable in yielding rich language, social studies, and multicultural learning experiences. This vocabulary list will be created by you with your unique group of children sharing their particular knowledge based on families, communities, and regions. Don't be surprised if the youngest children make daily contributions to your ever-growing vocabulary list with such words as "goulash" or "knockwurst."

Children are amazed at how much they know. Food is a category guaranteed to astonish them. Through talking with your children, discover their favorite foods and you will have an excellent topic for class discussion and projects. Among a child's earliest words are those relating to food. A child sitting in a supermarket basket is picking up vocabulary words in every aisle.

SOME STARTERS

Start with a taste Nothing launches a food activity with more excitement than a taste of something wonderful. An old Yiddish joke ends with the line, "Eat first. You'll talk later!"

Start with smell Pass around an orange, a lemon, or a grapefruit. Encourage the children to smell the citrus flavor with their eyes closed. Then, with eyes open, talk about the experience. Compare and share!

Start with texture Feel the fuzziness of a peach, the smooth, hard shell of an egg, the ridges on a stalk of celery, the creaminess of peanut butter. These activities are excellent ways to begin discussions about healthful foods.

Start with a work of art For centuries food has been a popular subject for artists. With art books or prints from the library, introduce children to paintings such as Manet's *Still Life with Melon and Peaches,* Picasso's *Le Gourmet,* and Cezanne's *Still Life with Apples and Peaches* or his *Still Life* (bowl of oranges). Most children are amazed at how brilliantly artists capture the color, shape, and texture of the food.

Start with an announcement A kindergarten teacher launched a unit on nutritious food this way: "Boys and girls, starting tomorrow, we are going to have healthful and delicious snacks. Do we have any suggestions on the kinds of snacks to make?" Presto: a chalkboard full of ideas and activities.

Start with a color Nature painted foods such beautiful colors! As you admire purple and green grapes, yellow bananas, and red apples, take time to appreciate the variety of hues in the most ordinary foods.

Start with a special way to take attendance A simple direction such as this will launch conversation and activities: "Boys and girls, when I call your name today, please tell us a good food to have for breakfast (or snack)."

Start with a wonder Children are the best wonderers, and unless they have already learned to fear being wrong, they usually have excellent responses to such questions as "I wonder where apples come from," "I wonder how bread is made," and "I wonder how peanuts turn into peanut butter."

Start with Popeye Everyone knows that Popeye the Sailor Man has super muscles because he eats spinach! "What else can we eat if we want to grow as big and strong as Popeye?"

Start with feeding an animal Young children are usually concerned about the welfare of animals. If you even suggest to them that you can feed gerbils fish food or fish birdseed or birds dog food, they will be horrified. This is a wonderful way to begin helping children develop an appreciation for the correct foods for animals . . . and for people!

I was kidding around with a group of five-year-olds and deliberately mixed up all the animals and food in my house. "Boys and girls, I was in such a rush today. I think I goofed everything up! I gave our bird a dog biscuit (the children laughed and screamed), I poured fish food into our dog's dish ("Fish food into the dog's dish! Oh no!"), and then—the worst thing—I poured birdseed into the fish tank!" The children showed a mixture of shock, dismay, and skeptical laughter ("Is she kidding?"). Gretchen couldn't contain herself: "Mimi! You're gonna make those animals very sick!" That was the perfect response for introducing the topic of nutritious food for healthy children.

Start with sharing an experience Children want to know everything about their teachers. Telling them about something delicious and healthful that you enjoyed will prompt questions and activities.

Start with an intriguing story Rose Stough challenges her children to find out what George Washington's breakfast consisted of! After she shares the book *George Washington's Breakfast*[17] and everyone knows the "menu," Rose and the children make the breakfast and eat it. This leads to a yearlong celebration of nutrition and foods. In the delightful book, *Eat Up, Gemma,*[18] Gemma, the toddler of the family, just won't eat. She throws her food down, plays with it, and refuses to eat it. Her big brother solves the problem in an imaginative way. Children love the chance to suggest ways they could encourage Gemma to eat and not to waste food. Their solutions are just as clever as Gemma's brother's plan. Important ideas about the value of food and teaching people not to waste food are launched with stories such as these.

Start with a song Old folk songs made popular in the children's field like "Oats and Beans and Barley Grow," "Goober Peas," or "The Banana Boat Song" are songs the children love to sing and talk about. Musical theater songs like "Food" from the show *Oliver!* can provide the overture for a multidimensional food theme.

Start with a silly Nothing is more attention-getting in positive ways than a session of imaginative, playful humor. Books like *Cloudy with a Chance of Meatballs*[19] invite children to share silly ideas of their favorite foods falling from the sky. The children will respond with their own adaptation of the book and will provide a terrific gathering of food items. Another silly old favorite is Maurice Sendak's *Chicken Soup with Rice.*[20] As the children smile through the months, they love reciting the refrain, "Sipping once, sipping twice, chicken soup with rice!" The kids have many original ideas about what they would enjoy every month of the year. Maybe they will offer a refrain like this: "Sip for one. Sip for two. Have a hot dog in your stew!" As you read through these pages, read for two, read for one, gather ideas and have some fun!

Start anywhere! Just start!

TALK TIMES/LISTENING TIMES

Children, who like to talk about almost everything, especially enjoy talking about food, because everyone has something to say. I received a call from a teacher who needed advice on helping her unusually shy group of five-year-olds to begin expressing themselves more openly. I gave her about ten ideas. The next day she called back, thrilled with her morning.

"This is the first day all year that every child wanted to say something. We spent a good twenty minutes at high-speed talking!" And she used only one of the suggestions! "What's your favorite food?"

Some talk starters that always work (unless the children have learned to be afraid) are

TALK TOGETHER ABOUT

What do you like for breakfast?
What do you like for lunch?
What do you like for a snack?
What do you like for supper?
Why do we eat?
Do animals need to eat?
What kinds of foods do animals eat?
What are some healthy foods?
What foods are not good for us?
Did you ever help make food?
Where do vegetables and fruits come from?
What are some things we use when we eat?

One on one/Two by two Even very young children often have surprisingly deep feelings about food and its place in their lives. When Lisa, age seven, announced that she was going to be a vegetarian, her family was amazed at such a decision at such a young age. I had a long talk with Lisa, whose explanation was thoughtful and clearly articulated.

> "I really love animals and I really don't want to eat them because I love them. . . . I was really thinking about this for a long time . . . like when I was growing up and my dad told me that meat was animals. . . . It was a hard decision to become a

vegetarian, 'cause I really like the taste and I knew I was giving it up. . . . But, I feel better in my heart that I'm not eating animals anymore."

Aaron, Lisa's older brother, age twelve, shared his feelings about his sister's decision.

"When she told us, I asked her why? I wanted to see if she really meant it and if she thought about it. . . . I was concerned about the protein—we need protein—but she had answers so I knew she would take care of that with soy and eggs and cheese. . . . I like animals very much, but I think it's part of nature that humans need animals for food. . . . I'm not becoming a vegetarian but I respect Lisa's decision."[21]

As you can see, once you close in on a topic, especially one close to children such as food, they openly express opinions and feelings. In environments of warmth and trust, children will want to talk about everything. As they think and talk, language develops, comprehension develops, and healthy human beings develop!

Problem-solving discussions Hunger hurts! Children are aware of current events; TV, radio, and newspapers bring images immediately to the awareness of children and plunge the children into the events.

Most young children feel compassion for others less fortunate. Unless they have been toughened by their own traumatic histories, young children will want to share their food and feed animals, dolls, puppets, and other people.

When the kindergartners looked at the photograph in the newspaper of people in a community shelter waiting for Thanksgiving dinner, they talked about hunger, poverty, and homelessness. Their eyes widened with surprise and caring. They were disturbed to know that children like themselves went to bed hungry. They talked and worried about such tragic situations and collected suggestions for how to help such as:

"We can write them letters to make them feel better."
"We can draw them pictures."
"We can share our snacks."
"Our church has a box for cans. We can save cans of food."

And they did all of the above. As children make suggestions, write them on the chalkboard or on a chart so they always see the shape of their spoken words. Include their names. For example: Cavin: "We can pick apples and bring them to the hungry people." Shawn, Melissa, and Maddy agree with that idea.

Very often, even our young children are involved in helping to prepare and serve food (through churches, synagogues, and service organizations) at community kitchens. An example of a young child accompanying his uncle to his volunteer job helping in a soup kitchen is found in *Uncle Willie and the Soup Kitchen*.[22] As the story is shared, children are encouraged to contribute their ideas of how people can help in such settings. It's so vitally important for our children to not only recognize the reality of our poverty problems but to know that we are all responsible for helping to solve them.

Snack times/Talk times I am still shocked when I visit schools that do not permit talking during snack or meal times. Food should be mixed with the idea of company (with bread), and to forbid children to talk together while they eat is depriving them of a very human, very important activity. How else can language develop but through using it, and using it in many ways for a multitude of purposes?

Feeding pets/Talking together When children care for classroom pets, interesting and valuable talk is generated. What kind of food? How much? How do you encourage a reluctant pet to eat? We must provide an environment of safety and reassurance for an animal—are your hands gentle? Is your voice soft and friendly? Is their eating space clean?

Planning talks What shall we have for snacks? How can we celebrate the March birthdays, with what kinds of food? What ideas do we have for cooking up something special to welcome winter? What refreshments shall we offer our guests for Open House? How shall we prepare them?

Children have so many wonderful and weird ideas! Encourage active listening and taking turns talking. Combine/adopt/adapt as many suggestions as possible and turn them into realities!

VISUAL ARTS TIMES

By now you need no reminders (so why is this paragraph being written?) to appreciate the theme of food as a cluster of visual arts experiences. Celebrating all of our senses, food provides a plethora of visual arts possibilities. Enjoy the following smorgasbord of suggestions. Think of how even the most ordinary salad bar or buffet reflects the remarkable creativity of the human mind to mix, match, arrange, combine, select, and rearrange.

Note: We never use food as materials for art activities and projects. That contradicts our asking children *not* to waste food!

Colorful charts Let your talk times/listening times expand to visual records of opinions and feelings. "What Is Your Favorite Food?" easily provides material for a large, colorful chart featuring the children's names, photos or self-portraits, names of foods they like, and illustrations of those foods. Children love to give their opinions on things familiar to them. Success is built in. Everyone is included. These kinds of colorful charts can wallpaper your room! Try such ideas as: "Food that Helps Me Grow"; "Super Snacks"; "Four Food Groups"; or "Fruits and Vegetables for Fabulous Kids."

Books good enough to eat All over the country, children are "making" individual as well as class books. I have seen hundreds of variations of simple themes. Your students will enjoy creating books based on their favorite foods, such as *Juan's Favorite Foods,"* in which each page features one of Juan's selections with words and pictures. Sometimes children love choosing their very very favorite food and creating a book about that food alone, such as *Gabriella's Book of Strawberries.* Every page was highlighted by a strawberry design or picture. Class books are delightful to compile, as all the children contribute their own pages to the whole. Laminate the pages, connect them in loose-leaf style, and you have a resource that is guaranteed to be well-used and enjoyed.

Michael Joel Rosen's *The Greatest Table*[23] inspires children to create scenes of eating and sharing on pages that connect and unfold in accordion style. Books of poems like Arnold Adoff's *Chocolate Dreams* and *Eats*[24] encourage children to make up their own poems and illustrations about their favorite foods. Eric Carle's beautiful picture book *Today Is Monday* is based on an old folk tune that lists different foods for each day of the week, for example, "Tuesday—spaghetti; Monday—string beams. . . ." Use the lyrics of the old song and ask the children to illustrate their own page or pages based on the days of the week. Better yet, make up your own lyrics of food for each day of the week. As the week progresses, the list grows longer. By Sunday you may have:

Sunday, ice cream
Saturday, fresh fish
Thursday, roast beef
Wednesday, ZOOOP
Tuesday, spaghetti
Monday, string beans[25]

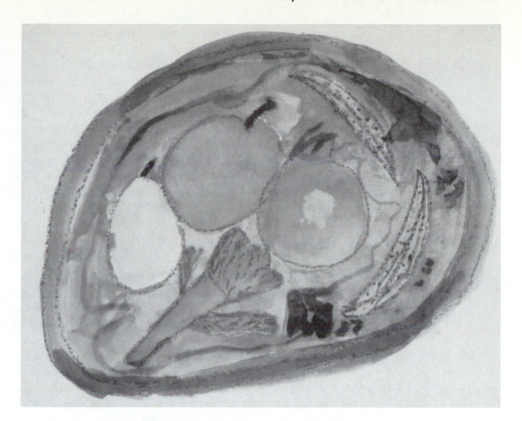

Recipe books and how-to books Joan Kalb[26] and her students enjoy creating their own recipe books and how-to books complete with descriptions, illustrations, and explanations in a celebration of sequential thinking. After all, you can't stir the eggs until you have broken them! Joan always reminds the children to be clear in their instructions. The books are excellent for sharing as well as eating the products described! Enjoy experimenting with different ideas with your students.

Fill your plates Paper plates are excellent materials for visual arts ideas. Following talks about favorite foods, healthy foods, or colorful foods, invite the children to paste on their plates magazine pictures of nutritious food or pictures that they drew, painted, or colored. Each plate can represent a meal. It may feature the children's favorite foods, be divided into four food groups, or demonstrate beautiful designs of food as art objects or collages. Prominently display all the plates.

Still-life studies Using postcards, inexpensive posters, and art books for inspiration, talk with your students about the beauty, colors, textures, and shapes of food and how famous artists throughout history have been drawn to food as subjects for paintings. Arrange your own patterns of still-life food designs and invite the children to create their own beautiful pictures as they study the unique qualities of such items as oranges, grapes, apples, bananas, and peaches. After the arts session, share the fruit in a fruit salad or as individual pieces. Be sure the children title and sign their works and, of course, feel the pride and excitement of seeing their works as a class exhibit.

Be clear in your explanations and instructions.

The first graders were working on still lifes. After a while, the session broke into free play. Katie was bored and complained to her teacher that she had nothing to do. Her teacher suggested that she "paint the fruit." About ten minutes later, the teacher walked around to see what people were doing and there sat Katie, completely engrossed in painting designs on the bananas and oranges!

Clay food Even if you do not suggest it, children often roll clay into food shapes. Expand on this interest by talking about and looking at the shapes and contours of different foods—the flatness of a slice of bread, the roundness of pumpkins, the squiggliness of noodles or spaghetti, and the smooth, oval shape of eggs. Label and display the children's work. Encourage them to play with their "clay food."

Clay pots and bowls Archeologists discover cups, plates, pots, bowls, and pitchers made and decorated by ancient peoples. Modern young potters find pleasure in creating these objects to play with, use, give as gifts, or display.

Fruit salad "This fruit salad is as pretty as a rainbow!" observed five-year-old Douglas as he and his kindergarten colleagues marveled at the brightly colored fruit in a large glass bowl. Encourage the children to paint fruit designs on notepaper and wall paper.

Holiday and seasonal foods When you and your students create a mural for a holiday or season, leave space for the foods associated with that event. Leave a circle shape, plate, basket, or rectangle for a table to celebrate the foods that symbolize the special times. Cook, bake, mold, and decorate your own holiday or seasonal treats such as heart-shaped cookies for Valentine's Day, orange pumpkin cookies for autumn or Halloween, and eggs for spring. Paper plates can be illustrated to highlight events, seasons, or holidays. Cover the plates with plastic wrap or spray them to preserve the colors.

Please sit under the apple tree Teachers like Sue Coomer cannot resist "planting" fruit trees in their rooms. Sue twists a large hunk of brown wrapping paper to make the trunk, and staples on branches. The tree is ready for the apples, which come in assorted colors of red, yellow, and green. The children choose circle shapes for apples, triangles for leaves, and long rectangles for stems. They color them and add them to the tree. Sue pastes the children's pictures on their apples and tells them, "You're the apple of my eye!"

A variation of this activity is to encourage children to add any fruit that grows on a tree. They make shapes of apples, peaches, cherries, bananas, and so on, color them, and tape them to the branches.

Mary Goodwin described yet another variation of the tree idea.[27] Take a walk with your children and collect unusually shaped fallen branches. Back in the room, sink the branches in clay in a shoe box. Cover and decorate the box with green paper "grass." Hang paper, clay, Playdough, or papier-mâché fruit from the tree.

Food groups mobile Give children a different hanger for each food group, or give them one hanger from which to hang four kinds of food, one from each group. Children cut out pictures of food, paste the pictures on construction paper and, with help if needed, cut out the shape. Now their food pictures are sturdier and better balanced, as they are stapled or taped to colored yarn that is tied to the hanger. Many teachers use smooth sticks and twigs, gathered by the children, instead of hangers. Children enjoy creating mobiles based on their favorite foods.

Contrast collage Build upon talk time sessions contrasting the value of nutritious food and the dangers of junk food. Divide a large sheet of paper in half. On one side draw a happy face at the top; on the other side, an unhappy face. Invite the children to add pictures of healthful food to the happy-face side, junk food to the other.

Food posters Ask the children to create messages they would like to write on posters about healthful food habits. Ask them where on the paper they want the message—top, bottom, or center. Help them write the message, if needed. Write the message in pencil so they can outline the letters themselves. Add illustrations. Older children, obviously, write their own ideas. Exhibit the posters and invite other classes as guests. Serve nutritious snacks as refreshments.

Four-year-old Patti's poster was a surrealist design of a large carrot and an eye. Her message was "Eat a Carrot for Your Eyes."

Pretzel sculpture Annetta Dellinger's four-year-olds enjoy a variety of food activities, but one of their favorites is to shape bread dough into original designs, such as the letters of their names, numbers, and animals. Annetta uses the simplest of dough recipes:

2 loaves (16 ounces each) frozen bread dough, thawed
1 egg white, slightly beaten
1 teaspoon water
Coarse salt (optional)

Arrange the pretzels 1 inch apart on a well-greased baking sheet. Let them stand for 20 minutes. Brush them with a mixture of egg white and water. Sprinkle them with coarse salt, if desired. Place a shallow pan containing 1 inch of boiling water on the lower rack of the oven. Bake pretzels at 350 degrees for 20 minutes or until golden brown on a rack above the pan of water.[28]

The children enjoy shaping their pretzels, comparing designs, smelling the pretzels as they bake, and eating them.

Alphabet good enough to eat Here is a good way to combine ABCs with nutritious foods. Print a letter of the alphabet on a sheet of white paper. With your students, decide on delicious, nutritious foods that begin with that letter. Print the names of the foods. Children draw or cut out pictures to go with the letter. Use the alphabet to make a border around the room.

A variation of this activity is to invite the children to make their own alphabet books.

Tablecloths, bread covers, napkins Use paper or scrounged white sheets for these functional yet beautiful objects. With paint, crayon, or markers, the children create designs on the material. Use their creations in the classroom during snack time or present them as gifts to families.

Place mats Children enjoy designing and illustrating their own place mats. Laminate them and use them!

Spice braids Betsy Distelhorst [29] enriches a talk and smell session about the spices of life with this excellent project. Each child chooses strands of yarn to braid or weave together. Tie the strands at the top and the bottom. Children choose tiny squares of scrounge material. From an offering of such spices as nutmeg, cloves, cinnamon, vanilla beans, mace, and allspice, the children pick samples and put them carefully in the middle of their squares of material. Pinch the four corners together and tie with a rubber band or string. Tie each pouch of spices to the braid. Put a stick or loop through the top of the braid. Hang the braids in your room for marvelously rich and spicy smells. They make wonderful family gifts.

Kitchen witches The Scandinavians have a delightful tradition of hanging witches in their kitchens to keep pots from boiling over and food from spoiling, and generally to protect culinary activities. Children, who love folklore, respond enthusiastically to the idea of the kitchen witch.

You can make kitchen witches in a variety of ways (just as puppets are made). One of the simplest kitchen witches I saw hung in a kindergarten class in Michigan. The children cut out their witches from construction paper and used buttons for eyes, wool or cotton for hair, and scraps of material for clothes. They glued their witches to tongue depressors and taped them (with masking tape) to the wood panel around the "cooking corner." "Since we put up our kitchen witches," one of the children explained, "all our food comes out perfect!"

Five senses sampler Sue Coomer collects Styrofoam meat trays, washes them, and uses them for projects like this one.

It is better to smell, taste, touch, see, and hear food than simply to talk about doing so. After discussing such words as bitter, sweet, sour, salty, crunchy, smooth, soft, and hard, Sue gives children Styrofoam plates of food to sample, such as potato chips, pretzels, lemon, banana, peanuts, grapes, celery, apples, salt, sugar, honey, and onion. Illustrate the samplers after the sensory session.

Peanut shell art Julia Crabbs believes in wasting nothing. First the children make peanut butter using the following recipe, which requires no cooking.[30]

> 1 pound roasted peanuts
> 2 tablespoons salad oil
> Crackers

> The children shell the nuts and put them through a grinder or in a blender. Add oil until the mixture is spreadable. Spread peanut butter on crackers.

The children use the peanut shells for projects such as pasting the shells on cardboard or on boxes for mosaic designs, and combining the shells with scrounge materials such as felt, wood scraps, Popsicle sticks, and glitter to create sculptures, puppets, or "peanut people."

Eggshell mosaic Teachers like Sherri Bishop[31] share the wonders of eggs with their students. One of Sherri's most popular projects is to color hard-boiled eggs and display them in different color combinations for a few days. Then she and the children peel them and eat them with celery or carrots, or mash them together with mayonnaise and scoop the deviled eggs onto crackers. The children salvage the colored eggshells and arrange the pieces of shells in mosaic designs by pasting or gluing them to cardboard, wood, or boxes.

Vegetable prints This popular activity is a by-product of making salad or vegetable soup. After talking about the different vegetables the earth yields and preparing salads and soups for the class to enjoy, instead of throwing out the inedible ends of the vegetables, give each child a small piece. Children paint the bottom of the vegetable pieces with watered-down tempera and stamp the design on paper. Encourage them to make their own patterns, using different vegetables or just one. When the pictures are displayed, play a game of guessing which vegetables made which prints.

Picture stories of seeds Young children are fascinated by the magic of seeds. After discussing the amazing changes from seeds to vegetables, fruits, and flowers, ask each child to draw a seed on a sheet of drawing or construction paper. Suggest that the children color, draw, or paint as many ideas about the seed's changes as they can think of.

Centerpieces from the earth With hand-designed tablecloths and centerpieces, an ordinary snack becomes an event. Take a walk with the children and gather pebbles, small branches, leaves, ferns, twigs, buckeyes, acorns, pinecones, and so on. Give each child a paper plate or a small aluminum pie plate on which to arrange their "treasures" into lovely designs. Use glue or paste if necessary.

Wild carrots or Queen Anne's lace A friend of Betsy Distelhorst told her, "There's no such thing as a useless weed. A weed is simply a plant growing in the wrong place!" Betsy takes her children for a spring walk to gather one of the most common weeds, Queen Anne's lace. The children are encouraged to pull up the plant by the roots and smell them ("They smell like carrots!"). Back at school, the children cut and wash the roots, which can be eaten raw or cooked.

After the feast, the children tie the stems together, hang them upside down, and wait for them to dry out. The design of Queen Anne's lace is beautiful. The children use it alone, mounting it on construction paper or colored cardboard and covering it with wax paper, or add it to other dry flowers for long-lasting arrangements to enjoy in class or present to family or friends as gifts.

The earth's garden Planting a *real* garden is the best activity! Second best is creating a beautiful garden by using torn or cut pieces of colored construction paper, tissue paper, or painted newspaper. Encourage the children to tear long, skinny pieces for stems and short, oblong pieces for leaves. Tack a large sheet of paper to a bulletin board or wall. Children paste up stems, roots, leaves, fruits, vegetables, grains, trees, and so on.

A preschooler evaluated their garden by saying, "I think it needs to be mowed!"

Magazine pictures, and seed, flower, and vegetable catalogues offer marvelous images for the children to enjoy. Books like the beautiful *Vegetable Garden*[32] with simple and brilliantly colored illustrations inspire the children to paint or color their own interpretations of vegetable gardens.

Salad bar designs Children love making/drawing/cutting/constructing ingredients for a class art salad bar. Choosing from the group offerings, the children create their own combinations on their own paper plates. The variations will be amazing!

Walnut zoos, boats, and Thumbelina beds Nuts are an excellent source of protein. Walnuts are especially delicious, and their shells make delightful animals. After the children enjoy eating the meat of the walnut, ask them to turn the shells into zoo animals by gluing on bits of felt and straw, tiny buttons, and so on. Markers can be used to draw on the shell. If you put a tiny ball or marble under the shell, the walnut animal will scoot down a slanted board or book.

Walnut shells also make excellent little boats. Glue, paste, or tape a toothpick or tiny stick to the bottom of the shell to make a mast. Give each child a paper sail to color or design before attaching it to the mast. Now you have a fleet of walnut ships! Turn them into "wishing boats" by standing around a tub of water and giving the children time to make a wish before gently pushing or blowing them on their journey.

Children love Thumbelina, who is no bigger than their thumbs. Make a Thumbelina out of tiny scraps of material and cotton balls. Remember, the Thumbelina must fit into the walnut-shell beds. A four-year-old kept his Thumbelina for the year. His mother said it was one of his most precious possessions.

Peanut butter play dough [33] Sandy Morgan's students enjoyed the following treat.

½ to 1 cup dry milk
1 cup peanut butter
4 tablespoons honey

Mix ingredients by hand and shape the dough into animals, letters, numbers, people, and designs. Look at everyone's wonderful works and eat them!

Be sure all hands are washed before you begin. You will probably want to wash hands after the sculpting and eating as well.

Poems good enough to eat Many poets write about food. Share delightful poems with the children. Print them on large poster paper and invite the children to illustrate them. Poems like Jack Prelutsky's "I'm Hungry," Leland B. Jacobs's "Taste of Purple," and Shel Silverstein's "Pie Problem" offer the children lively images for visual arts extensions. Nikki Giovani's "Knoxville, Tennessee" describes lovely summers eating foods like greens, barbecue, and buttermilk and starts children on their own poetic list of memories, seasons, and food. Create your own class food poems and poetry posters to be displayed and illustrated.

Food and dreams Older children find books such as *An Angel for Solomon Singer* by Cynthia Rylant[34] inspiring of thought, talk, compassion, imagination, and creativity. A lonely man lives alone in a shabby room in New York City. He wanders around and finds a restaurant, The Westway Cafe, "Where All Your Dreams Come True." The smiling-eyed waiter welcomes him. Solomon reads the simple menu of such ordinary items as tomato soup, biscuits, and grapefruit juice, and as he eats, he enjoys dreamy memories of his happy childhood in the midwest. The friendly waiter, the simple menu, and the chance for remembering as he ate made Solomon happy. Children paint imaginative pictures, memory pictures, for Solomon as he enjoys the eating of simple foods. A good story for developing empathy as well as imagery.

Although space and time limit us (our only limits!), I don't want to stop this section without reminding you of how much children enjoy creating jewelry, quilts, wrapping paper, notepaper, T-shirts, sculptures, bookmarks, greeting cards, and invitations based on food themes and designs. Always keep adding to your cache of treasured ideas.

Are you ready to sing for your supper? Do you hum as you prepare lunch? Do you turn on the background music as you clear the table? If you do, then you already know about food and music times!

MUSIC TIMES

Songs that celebrate food Many songs from folklore, musical shows, and TV programs have food as their main themes. Play them. Sing them. Teach them to the children. Invite the children to share songs they know about food. You'll be surprised at their repertoire! As I write this, I am thinking about corn as high as an elephant's eye from "Oh, What A Beautiful Morning" in the show *Oklahoma!* What about "Plant a Radish" from the longest-running show in American history, *The Fantastiks*? I reach down to my pile of well-used records and cassettes and with no searching, I find: Fran Avni's "Artichokes and Brussel Sprouts," Pete Seeger's "All Around the Kitchen," Ella Jenkins's "Way Down Yonder by the Apple Tree" and "Annie My Cooking Friend," Thomas Moore's "Corn on the Cob," and Malvina Reynolds's "Artichokes, Griddle Cakes, and Other Good Things." Be eclectic! Be a gatherer and a hunter!

Improvised songs to munch on Any song you and your children enjoy becomes the perfect food song when mixed with imagination and fun. Gwen Marston[35] and her students changed the old folk song "Old John Rabbit" into a nourishing experience.

> Old John Rabbit—Yes Ma'am.
> Jumping in my garden—Yes Ma'am.
> Eating all my vegetables—Yes Ma'am.

"What kind of vegetables?" Gwen whispered between lines of the song. The children had no trouble supplying excellent lines.

> Eating all my carrots—Yes Ma'am.
> Eating all my potatoes—Yes Ma'am.
> Eating all my lettuce—Yes Ma'am.

They continued through the vegetables to the fruits.

The familiar children's song "Found a Peanut" was transformed to a complete eating experience when a group of kindergartners made peanut butter and sang about it.

Found a peanut, found a peanut, found a peanut last night.
Last night we found a peanut, found a peanut last night.
Found another one, found another one, found another one last night.
Last night we found another one, found another one last night.
Broke them open, broke them open, broke them open last night.
Last night we broke them open, broke them open last night.
Put them in the blender, put them in the blender, put them in the blender
last night.
Last night we put them in the blender, put them in the blender last night.
Mushed them up, mushed them up, mushed them up last night.
Added oil, added salt, made peanut butter last night.
It was delicious, it was delicious, it was delicious last night.

The beloved song "If I Had a Hammer" became a food-celebrating event by the year-long musical improvisations of a group of kindergartners.

If I had an apple
I'd eat it in the morning.
I'd eat it in the evening
All over this land.
I'd eat it for breakfast.
I'd eat it for supper.
I'd eat it with all my friends and sisters and brothers
All, all over this land.

Children never tire of the things they enjoy. Use a favorite song over and over, adding new words and ideas as they are discovered and discussed.

Recipe songs Children learn everything better by singing it. Use the steps and ingredients of easy recipes as the words for original songs, or fit the recipe words into familiar melodies. A first-grade class making applesauce with a recipe adapted from *Kids Are Natural Cooks*[36] followed brightly lettered instructions written on a large chart.

1. Cut apples into pieces
2. Add a little water
3. Cook and stir the apples
4. Mash the apples
5. Add a little honey
6. Add a little lemon juice
7. Add a bit of cinnamon
8. Stir and eat

The recipe perfectly fit the melody "Bow Bow Bow Belinda," a favorite game-dance. The children turned the recipe into a song.

Cut the apples into pieces.
Cut the apples into pieces.
Cut the apples into pieces.
Won't you make some applesauce?
Add a little water to the apples.
Add a little water to the apples.

As you write recipes for the children to follow (add illustrations or pictures to each step), hum the rhythm of the words. There is your recipe for a new song!

Nutritious singing games Change "Farmer in the Dell" to vegetable soup. Change "Hokey Pokey" to a salad bar. Steve Anderson and his four-year-olds made

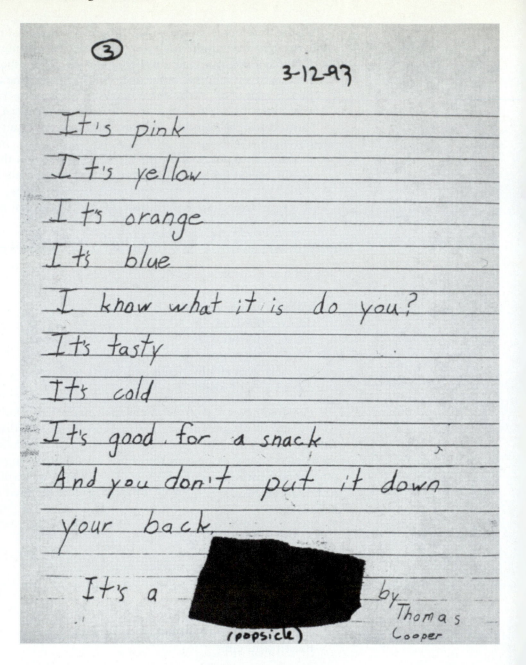

3-12-93

It's pink
It's yellow
It's orange
It's blue
I know what it is do you?
It's tasty
It's cold
It's good for a snack
And you don't put it down
your back.
It's a ████████   by
                                  Thomas
(popsicle)   Cooper

sandwich boards of vegetables. On large sheets of tagboard, the children drew or pasted pictures of specific vegetables—one vegetable for each child, the name of the vegetable on the board. Steve punched two holes at the top of each board and tied pairs of boards together with string. The children put them on and were ready for "Farmer in the Dell" vegetable soup. "The farmer needed peppers./The farmer needed peppers. Hi Ho the derry-o, the farmer needed peppers." As each vegetable was needed for the soup, a child entered the circle.

A group of five-year-olds made bib pictures that they hung around their necks. Each picture featured a different fruit and its name. They sang and danced a "Hokey Pokey" fruit salad.

You put a banana in. (banana enters circle)
You put a banana out. (banana jumps out)
You put a banana in (banana jumps in again)

and shake it all about. (banana shakes it up)
(Everyone) You do the hokey pokey and you turn around.
(Clap and jump) That's what it's all about.

Continue until all of the children have entered the circle. Then sing:

You put all the fruit in.
You put all the fruit out.
You put all the fruit in
and shake it all about.
You do the hokey pokey and you turn around.
That's what it's all about.

Music for every taste When you dine at a fine restaurant, you usually enjoy soothing music. Sometimes one person entertains, sometimes a group of musicians plays, and sometimes the music is recorded. Discuss this with your students so they learn that music is part of many eating experiences.

When you have food in the classroom, try to match the music with the kind of food you are eating. For example, if you are having pizza or pasta, play Italian folk music; pita bread sandwiches, Arabic, Greek, or Israeli music; corn bread or corn pudding, Native American music. As you eat tacos, enjoy flamenco or mariachi music. Explain the relationship between the food and the music.

A delightful variation of this idea is to give the children, one at a time or in partners, the opportunity to play music as people eat. You may want to designate one day a week for "live entertainment." The child or children who will perform eat their snacks before the others so that they do not feel deprived. Emphasize the need for soft, pleasant, soothing rhythms. You will be surprised when even your champion noise-maker plays mellow tones.

Eat first, sing later Snacks or meals become favorite times when they are followed by a few favorite songs. As soon as the children are finished with their food and before they clear the table, invite them to sing some of their favorite songs together. Choose the songs spontaneously; have the children take turns choosing songs (song leaders); or write all the songs they know on small colorful index cards or song charts, or put them in a box or bag, and have the children draw a song card grab-bag style and sing it.

Cheers and chants for favorite foods Young children are excellent cheerleaders. Improvise cheers that your children know, and celebrate nutritious foods.

A group of first graders had a marvelous session celebrating whole-grain cereals and breads with cheers such as this one.

Don't eat Twinkies.
No. No. No.
Eat whole wheat!
Yes. Yes. Yes.

The children worked out percussive rhythms and movements to accompany their cheer. On the yes, yes, yes part, they took three giant jumps, arms flung in the air.

Songs of thanks for food Songs of thanksgiving are daily events in many schools, camps, and community centers where people break bread together. You do not have to be involved in religious dialogue to convey to children an appreciation for the gifts of the earth and for our good fortune in having enough food to eat and share with others. Many graces and songs run the gamut from "Rub a dub dub, thanks for the grub" to a jazzy, hand-clapping number such as:

God is great.
God is good.
Let us thank Him for our food.

We're gonna thank Him in the morning,
noon and night.
We're gonna thank our Lord
'cause He's out of sight.
Amen (clap clap clap clap)
Amen (same)
Amen (same)

To an original song composed and sung by four-year-olds to the tune of "Good Morning to You":

We're thankful for food.
We're thankful for food.
We're thankful for this food.
We're thankful for food.

Special sounds for food and cooking "Snap, crackle and pop" are not the only sounds celebrating special foods. There are sizzling, boiling, simmering, crunching, munching, pouring, sipping, melting, seasoning, cracking, sifting, scraping, and a few dozen other sound effects of the cooking process. Challenge the children to use their bodies, voices, or instruments to express these actions. From simmering to boiling is an exciting musical idea. After one such experience, five-year-old Nathan remarked: "That boiling hurts your hands!" He had been playing a drum and when the boiling started, the drum beats came fast and furiously.

Special events, holidays, seasons—music to eat to What do people eat at the circus? The children will tell you: hot dogs, peanuts, cotton candy, and popcorn. Include a component of food celebrating in your circus theme. Percussive marching band music helps the real or play food go down!

What kinds of food will people eat on a cold winter day? The children will tell you: hot chocolate, hot soup, and hot cereal. Here is a chance to mix your wintery music and your winter songs in a blender with real or play foods.

A kindergarten class had a "slumber party." The children came to school in pajamas with their stuffed animals and favorite nighttime books. They decided that their favorite last snack of the day (their bedtime snack) would be crackers and milk. They sang a medley of goodnight songs. When they snuggled into sleeping bags and mats, their teacher played soft, soothing classical music.

As you celebrate such well-known and beloved holidays as Thanksgiving, Christmas, Hannukah, Kwanzaa, Chinese New Year, Japanese New Year, Halloween, Valentine's Day, birthdays, Earth Day, and Arbor Day in addition to the special events and occasions unique to your group of children and families, think creatively about the food shared and prepared. Can human beings celebrate festivals without food? See the bibliography at the end of this chapter for holiday ideas.

Whistle while you work (clean-up songs) An essential part of any cooking activity is the inevitable clean-up time. Working together, singing as you work, will practically guarantee cheerful clean-up times. Begin with the Seven Dwarfs's favorite song from *Snow White*—"Whistle While You Work."

MOVEMENT AND PLAY TIMES

I walked through a room of young children and as I passed each cluster of children at play, I heard: "Want a cup of coffee?" (in a tiny toy cup); "We're making 'begetable' soup. You can have some" (play kitchen corner); "This cake is coming out good. Do you like carrot cake?" (sandbox cake); and "What do you want on your hamburger?" (cardboard play food).

Food and eating is one of the most popular themes of children's games. A popular center of many classrooms is the play kitchen, where one usually finds table and chairs; dishes and silverware; pots and pans; toy stove, sink, and refrigerator; and a closet or shelf with boxes and cans of food (homemade or scrounged). The area is usually occupied by at least one "family," eating, cooking, and talking together.

Playing store or restaurant When children study foods, they explore the wonders of the grocery store, fruit stand, and supermarket where most of their foods are bought. Talking about food and visiting food stores introduces the delightful game of playing "store." Likewise, a trip to a restaurant or a lively discussion about restaurants leads to playing "restaurant."

These two popular games were developed to extraordinary lengths by Helen Speyer and Lori Salczer and their four-year-olds.[37] Joe's Supermarket was created when the children drew, painted, and cut out pictures of food from the four food groups and pasted them on the walls. The children found a large cardboard carton in which a refrigerator had been packed. They cut out a window and door and decorated the box with pictures of food and the name Joe's Supermarket. They collected empty cereal boxes and rinsed out empty cans and jars of food that still had labels. They also made their own food out of clay, cardboard, Playdough, and miscellaneous materials. They made money out of cardboard and paper. A table and shelves were pulled to the refrigerator box. The children stocked the bottom of the refrigerator box and lined the table and shelves with "food." Toy telephones and a toy cash register were added for authenticity. Paper bags were collected for packing groceries. The children took turns buying, selling, checking out, and packing food. Joe's Supermarket was in business for well over a month.

Helen and Lori and their four-year-olds had such a good time learning about healthful food habits that the children talked about creating a restaurant where only nutritious foods would be served. They decided to name their restaurant Lamb's Restaurant.

A field trip to a local health food restaurant followed. The children were full of questions on their grand tour and offered practical ideas for their own restaurant, including a poster of restaurant workers.

When the children returned, they set up Lamb's Restaurant. They made place mats, menus, food posters, and table decorations. Using the same play money from Joe's Supermarket, they played waitresses, waiters, cooks, and customers. One day, they invited another class to be the customers and served them real banana pudding. Lamb's Restaurant was a favorite game for many weeks.

The children are already playing kitchen, restaurant, market, and cooking. Foods, utensils, pots, dishes, and bowls are natural manipulative materials. Mixing, stirring, scooping, cutting, and kneading are the kinds of direct-involvement activities children need and enjoy. These kinds of experiences are as nourishing to the mind and spirit as a good diet is to a healthy body. Give the children places to play and time to develop these important kinds of play times. You'll hear language enriched, imagination expanded, and cooperation strengthened as children play in such positive ways.

Food stories/poems are moving experiences So many of the children's favorite works from literature highlight foods, such as Pooh's love of honey, Peter Cottontail's attraction to Mr. McGregor's delicious vegetables, and Johnny Appleseed's habit of planting apple seeds throughout the land. These kinds of stories become even more special when movement, pantomime, dialogue, props, costumes, and music are integrated. Consider the following examples:

Little Red Hen In this story, Little Red Hen asks everyone to help her till the soil, plant the seeds, water the ground, reap the grain, grind the flour—all the way to baking the bread. No one helps. But when the bread is baked and smells delicious, everyone wants to eat it. This story is helpful in teaching cooperation as well as the process from seed to bread.

We have played and danced this story many ways with children of all ages. Be creative! Improvise! Encourage the children to decide who they want to be (we have had everything from horses to clowns to Superman). When the Little Red Hen approaches each character, that character does something special—horse gallops, clown does tricks, kangaroo hops—and the Little Red Hen interrupts to ask for help.

When one kindergarten class reached the end of the story, where everyone wanted to taste the bread and the Little Red Hen said, "No, you didn't help!", the children, as if rehearsed, sincerely said, "We're sorry! Can we have another chance?" The children played the story again, and this time everyone helped.

Stone Soup This old tale has been told and retold through the ages. Marcia Brown's *Stone Soup*[38] tops the list of children's favorite versions. The story involves one or two strangers (probably related to the tricky tailors who convinced the Emperor to strut down Main Street with new clothes no one could see) who come to a village. They tell the villagers that they can make stone soup. No one believes them. "We can prove it," they say. They boil a stone in a pot of water. They taste it. "Hmmmm. Very good. It might need a little carrot." Each time they taste the plain hot water, they think of another vegetable to add. The silly villagers bring the vegetables, never realizing that they are making vegetable soup. The trick works. Everyone loves the stone soup.

This is a story children truly enjoy listening to as well as improvising. We have played variations, using pictures, play food, or pantomime food to add to the pot. Each child has a turn to run home and "get a vegetable" for the soup. At the end, everyone dips an imaginary cup into the pot and murmurs how delicious stone soup tastes. The mischievous tricksters wink and giggle.

This story provides practical suggestions for vegetable soup, which many classes of young children cook and eat with gusto. They combine the story with the making of real vegetable soup.

Every story has so many interpretation possibilities. I especially love to be the person coming into town and asking the children to help make the stone soup. They all contribute as the story goes along using body movement, sounds, rhythms, and dialogue. After each ingredient is added, we all stir the "pot," sometimes singing a little improvised tune to words like "Stone soup . . . Stone soup . . . Stir, stir the stone soup." Sometimes we add a circle dance, dancing around the "pot" after each item is "stirred" in. Sometimes the children *are* the food, jumping into the middle of the room (the pot) and plopping down together.

The children will delight in the book *Group Soup,*[39] a variation of the Stone Soup story. Keep it loose and enjoy the imaginative contributions of the children as the soup simmers!

No formulas! No recipes! You can't go wrong if you sprinkle your soup with fun, safety, trust, and success.

You and your children can have so many enjoyable sessions incorporating food into well-loved stories and poems. A few more suggestions to get you started: The Three Bear's Porridge (how did it taste? Shall we make some?). What shall we include in Little Red Riding Hood's basket of goodies for her grandmother? How tall did Jack's beanstalk grow? If we tasted one of the beans, would we grow? What were those magic words for Strega Nona's amazing pot of pasta? How did they go? The children chant and sing,

> Bubble, bubble, pasta pot.
> Boil me up some pasta, nice and hot.
> I'm hungry and it's time to sup.
> Boil enough pasta to fill me up.[40]

as they play and move to the folktale about a town overflowing with pasta!

Anita and Arnold Lobel's *On Market Street*[41] inspires children to create their own markets with their own favorite items to sell and trade. Enrich this story with pictures and props.

An old, old favorite story is Ruth Krauss's *The Carrot Seed*.[42] A little boy plants a carrot seed, and everyone says it won't grow. Every day the little boy takes care of it, sprinkling water and pulling weeds away. One day, *it came up!* Our favorite way to "play" the story is to plant ourselves as the curled up seeds. From our curled up positions, we call out, "It won't come up!" Finally, we start growing! Here come the carrots! Sometimes we divide the group in half—one group of children are the seeds, the other group of children play all the people who say "it won't come up!" Of course, you may want to celebrate in songs and dances the exciting growth of the carrot seeds!

One of the most beloved stories children play and act out is *If You Give a Mouse a Cookie*.[43] Oh, so much happens if you give a mouse a cookie! You just can't imagine, but the children will be happy to show you, complete with voices, movement, gestures, pictures, and props. Try creating variations of the original story. We laughed throughout the whole improvisation of "If You Give a Baby a Pizza," composed and performed by a very silly group of first graders.

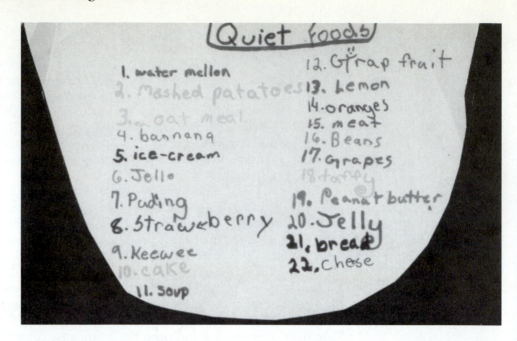

Poems like "Food and Drink" by David McCord inspire imaginative movement interpretation. There are ten parts to this poem, each dedicated to a different aspect of food and drink. Children enjoy listening to each section and using their bodies to express the ideas.

A group of kindergartners listened to section 9, entitled "Salt and Pepper," and began jumping and bouncing. "We're salt and pepper shakers," they explained.

My young students love bouncing and dancing to Dennis Lee's "Bouncing Song":

Hambone, jawbone, mulligatawney stew,
Pork chop, lamb chop, cold homebrew.
Licorice sticks and popsicles, ice cream pie:
Strawberry, chocolate, vanilla![44]

They create their own rap food songs with steady percussive rhythms. Naming foods is a delightful language exercise as well as an effective way to gather material for chants, stories, songs, raps, and rhythms.

Be open and flexible in your celebration of a story or poem the children especially like. If only one part of the piece lends itself to movement and interpretation, play with that one part. The bibliography at the end of this guide contains other stories and poems to be improvised.

Cooking words are moving words Children respond immediately to this challenge. "I'll say a word and you show me with your body that you know what this word means." Use words from recipes, cooking stories, and discussions—words such as mix, rise, chew, melt, sprinkle, taste, smell, measure, and bubble.

"Turn yourself into . . ." During discussions about various foods and their qualities, challenge the children to:

Turn yourself into a sunflower. How tall can you grow?
Turn yourself into a banana. How do you peel? (Small groups of children may work together.)
Turn yourself into an alfalfa seed. How do you sprout?
Turn yourself into a milkshake. How do you shake?

Turn yourself into peas in a pod. How does that look?
   (Small groups again.)
Turn yourself into a piece of toast in a toaster. How do you pop up?
Turn yourself into a whistling, steaming tea kettle.

Healthy kids, blobby kids In the past few years, this kind of movement story has been thoroughly enjoyed by young children throughout the country. Here are excerpts that can be changed or rearranged to fit your children.

"Once upon a time, there were these terrific kids who were so healthy and strong. Let's see how these kids looked." Stop so the children can demonstrate their strengths. "These children ate healthy food like milk, eggs, cheese . . ." (pantomime drinking and eating). After a few starter words, ask what other kinds of good food the healthy children ate. You will be amazed at the long list suggested by your students as they gulp and chew imaginary food.

After you have mentioned all the foods, continue the story. "Because those kids had such strong bones and muscles, great energy and coordination, they were fabulous joggers. Here's how they jogged!" (Play music with steady beat as the children jog.) "Because they had such straight backs, good eyes, and strong legs, they were terrific skippers. Here's how they skipped!" (Have the children demonstrate their best skips.) Continue in this way; for example, "Here's how they did jumping jacks . . . touched their toes . . . hopped . . . danced."

After a while, ask the children to freeze and hold their last position. Then shake out that position and turn into a group of blobby kids. How do those kids look? "Those kids ate the worst junk. They ate things like candy bars for breakfast (boo) and whipped cream and chocolate syrup for lunch (boo). What else do you think they ate?" The children come up with the most creative junk-food combinations, such as: "Baby Ruth sandwiches with potato chips on top!"; "Bubble gum soup!"; and "Chocolate kisses in their oatmeal!" Five-year-old Mark made an awful face and declared, "That's disgusting!"

After a list of "disgusting" junk-food combinations are suggested, the real fun begins. "Well, these junk-food kids were so blobby and rusty and uncoordinated they could hardly jog. This is the way they jogged." (Students love to show this heavy-footed, fatigued-looking semijog.) "Here's how they touched their toes!" (Accompany the attempt with moans and groans.) Repeat the sequence used earlier for the healthy children.

Sometimes the story ends here, with the moral so obvious the children can recite it in their sleep: Junk food messes up your body; nutritious food gives you energy, muscles, strength to do lots of fun things. Other times, the children want a finale that gives the junk-food group a chance to change their bad habits and become physically fit.

Animals and food A variation of the above idea focuses on animals. Tell and demonstrate a story about horses eating delicious oats. Watch how fast they gallop! Other horses eat dog and cat food and can hardly run. One group of rabbits are such good hoppers because they eat yummy vegetables, while another group eats birdseed and peanut butter and practically fall down when they hop. After a while, through the laughter and motion, the children understand that animals also have to eat food that is nourishing and appropriate for them.

Junky and Strongy and other puppets Creating puppets dedicated to their favorite foods was a popular experience for a group of first graders. Such puppet characters as Carrie Carrot, Robert Egg, Appie Apple, and Timmy Tuna Sandwich played happily for weeks.

Junky and Strongy were two puppet characters in a kindergarten class. Junky ate the worst food and was always complaining about his health. Strongy ate nutritious food and was always trying to persuade Junky to change his evil ways. Children took turns throughout the year creating dialogue for the puppets.

Dances and ceremonies Native peoples perform rituals involving movement, music, masks, and chants to honor the powers of nature. They perform Corn Dances to help the corn grow tall and healthy. They perform Rain Dances in hopes that enough rain falls to nourish their crops. Legends such as the Native American stories about Young Corn Man, Pumpkin Maiden, and Bean Maiden are dramatically enacted. Symbols of fruits, vegetables, soups, and stews are common designs in the artistic language of Native peoples.

Make up your own stories about corn growing, rain falling, Pumpkin Maidens, Bean Maidens, and Young Corn Men. Create your own legends about rain and sun and fertile earth. Beat steady, heartbeat pulses with your children and their real and improvised instruments as well as body rhythms. Find (in libraries, basements, families, and museums) music from Native cultures.

Explore the process of planting with the children: hands on the floor, softening the earth, making furrows for the seeds, placing the seeds, and smoothing the earth over them. Ask the children to interpret rain falling, sun shining, and seeds growing, then round pumpkins, tall corn, and tiny berries.

Always use songs and dances of thanksgiving, of celebration when crops are harvested, when food is shared. Those ideas should be adapted to all themes.

Recipe dances Clearly print familiar recipes on large poster board. Accompany them with illustrations. Use the steps in the process as choreography. Such directions as "peel bananas," "beat eggs," "shake drink," "chop walnuts," and "stir ingredients" are excellent movement suggestions for a cooking dance. (And there's no mess to clean up!)

Aprons, chef's hats, oven mitts, pots, pans, shelves, tables, stoves, real and imaginary foods, stories, legends, poems, recipes, and songs—how can we go wrong when we stir play and movement into our bubbling curriculum cauldron?

CLASSROOM VISITORS AND FIELD TRIPS
Classroom Visitors

Remember that company means "with bread." Every visitor is company and should therefore be greeted by you and your students with warm hospitality, which, of course, includes refreshments. Serving refreshments to your guests provides opportunities for planning and preparing nutritious, delicious food.

There are also many wonderful classroom visitors whose lives and work are directly related to food.

Family and community members who love to cook and bake This is a marvelous way for young children to discover the wealth of cultural, religious, ethnic, and regional customs and food specialties that contribute to the rich diversity of our country. Encourage family members and community members who enjoy cooking and baking to share their feelings, customs, and expertise with your children. Stress the importance of specific holidays and the food associated with them.

Even though there is only one Chinese child in a class of second graders, the children enjoyed an exciting Chinese New Year's celebration complete with egg rolls and almond cakes. On Martin Luther King's birthday, the grandmother of one of the African-American children in a kindergarten class came to school and helped the children cook a traditional meal of greens, sweet potato pudding, and fried chicken. On Hannukah, an aunt and two mothers visited a class of four-and-a-half-year-olds and spent the morning cutting up potatoes, blending them with onions, and frying them into the favorite treat of the holiday, potato "latkes." The children ate them with applesauce and sour cream.

Materials and resources abound for enriching such familiar holidays as Thanksgiving, Halloween, Valentine's Day, and birthdays. Don't limit yourself to commemorating only those events printed on your wall calendars. Create your own harvest festivals, seasonal celebrations, and special events. Because eating—breaking bread together—is part of the tradition of all cultures, be sure that you and your children mix food into your blender of delicious and creative curriculum ingredients.

Find out who your families are, what holidays and occasions they celebrate, what family specialties they are willing to share, what variations on commonly observed events (birthdays, first day of spring, and so on) they will introduce, and roll out the welcome mat. Emphasize to all classroom visitors the importance of direct involvement with the children as activities are enjoyed. When children experience the deep satisfaction and comraderie of breaking bread with others, they are likely to become more understanding, appreciative, and respectful adults.

Naturalists and other "wild food nuts" If you live in a smaller community, with splashes of green between roads of concrete, you will most likely be able to discover a person who knows about folk foods and edible herbs, weeds, and roots. Doris Berry calls herself a "wild food nut" and enjoys sharing her knowledge and appreciation with young children. Her three favorite edible wild plants that she helps children recognize and gather are dandelions, curly dock, and wild onions. The children take them back to the classroom, wash them thoroughly, and cook them or use them in salads.

If you are lucky, someone like Doris Berry lives in your community and will be delighted to visit your children. You can also obtain information from the Park Service and local museums.

Junk Food Junky and other zany visitors Jay Jacobs turned himself into Junk Food Junky. His approach really hit the target and helped strengthen the children's resistance to junk food.

If you have an uninhibited colleague, parent, relative, friend, or neighbor who enjoys kidding around with young children, create a guest character based on a food idea. I saw a wonderful Mr. Carrot, dressed in orange with a pointy carrot hat, who told the children: "Look into my eyes. Let me look into your eyes. You need to eat more carrots!" In another school, the study of the letter P turned into a group of area teenagers dressed as Protein People. They helped children learn a lot more than that letter of the alphabet.

Athletes, cheerleaders, dancers, joggers, bikers, and physical fitness advocates Area athletes, cheerleaders, and dancers are held in awe by young children. Invite some of these community friends to talk to your children, demonstrate some of their exercises and drills, and, most important, emphasize the importance of good nutrition and diet in the making of strong bodies.

Representatives from 4-H, dairy council, health department If you invite people with expertise in food and nutrition to speak with your children, be sure to ask them to bring colorful pictures, posters, and props and to dramatize their messages rather than presenting straight lectures.

Chef/cook You may find a family member or neighbor who is a chef or cook by profession. By all means, invite that person to meet your children and share some experiences and techniques. Involve the children in the "active" session.

Volunteer for community kitchen The mass media and many direct experiences have already educated our young children in the realities of poverty and hunger. Once again, we need to work with our children on situations they can understand and affect. In schools and programs around the country, children respond to visits and explanations from community representatives with great compassion. Food drives, penny collections, and making and giving food to shelters, as well as discussions, letters, pictures, and visitors are part of the lives of young children as they attempt to make a difference in their small world. Always accompany a visit or

discussion about a "problem" such as hunger with suggestions for solutions. Our children must know that the adult world is responsible and caring.

Storytellers When storytellers come to visit, encourage them to include or feature stories good enough to eat. Many of our folktales, myths, legends, and stories highlight food: magic foods that make us grow, shrink, or sleep, enchanted foods that are always in abundance even when the pot or pan or cupboard looks empty. Nursery rhymes simmer with food items: Miss Muffet's curds and whey; this little pig's roast beef; Jack Horner's plum; Tommy Tucker sings for his supper, Georgie Porgie's pudding and pie; Hickety pickety, my black hen's eggs. With the storyteller (or with just yourselves!) enjoy a lively, moving, and chanting nursery-rhyme time, then continue with the story that might just be about the City Mouse and the Country Mouse and their distinct meals. You might want to follow up the visit, after the thank-you pictures and letters, with a pot of curds and whey and a dish of plums.

Artists and craftspeople Working with food motifs, potters form useful objects for eating: trays, dishes, bowls, and cups. Glassblowers shape bottles, pitchers, and platters. The presentation of food is often more important than its taste! Ask your guests to share with the children their talents as well as their interest in creating beauty in useful objects. The children will be inspired to create their own!

Animal caretakers Look to the community for a person taking responsibility for animals, whether in a zoo, park, farm, forest preserve, veterinarian's office, or household. Talking together with your children about the importance of good diet and proper foods for animals is an excellent way to bring home the importance of a good diet and proper foods for people.

Community resource people representing different cultures and food styles As noted, our country is blessed with a diversity of peoples, customs, and traditions. Our lives can only be enriched by continually learning about others and incorporating our new knowledge into our own lives.

Look to your community for those willing to share skills, knowledge, and experiences with young children. For example, Alycia Diggs spent two years in the Peace Corps working in Mali (formerly French Sudan). There she met and married Issa Kone. The couple now lives in Columbus, Ohio, where they are very happy to spend time with young children, giving them a taste of Mali and foods from that part of Africa. Children are fascinated by stories about villagers, who—even though they can purchase staples at the markets—prefer to pick the crops, pound them with wood, mortars, and pestles, and cook the food themselves. In the villages of Mali, people eat hot porridge called "moni" for breakfast. Lunch is always a hot meal. Children enjoy hearing how Issa finds American fast food a strange experience.[45]

Check your own community resources for outstanding classroom visitors like Issa and Alycia.

Field Trips

Each geographic area has its own resources for children and teachers to discover. The following list includes places young children around the country have visited.

> School cafeteria
> Bakeries
> Supermarkets
> Fruit and vegetable markets
> Fruit orchards
> Pumpkin patches
> Egg farms
> Dairy farms
> Cooperative food stores
> Bagel factories
> Ice cream factories
> Canning factories
> Restaurants
> Cafeterias
> Health food stores
> Fast-food restaurants
> Community food pantries
> Grain elevators
> Dairies
> Food processing plants
> Zoo (especially at feeding time)

Festivals   Most communities celebrate the cultural diversity of their residents. The most popular feature of these festivities, whether they are United Nations festivals, Greek festivals, or St. Patrick's Day parties, is food. If possible, take your children to the party. Have your own!

Historical restorations and museums   Many area museums feature historical exhibits. Food and food preparation are fascinating features of these exhibits. If you live near a restored village or house, your children will find the trip an amazing adventure into a time before fast-food drive-ins and refrigeration.

Reminder: Classroom visitors and field trips provide motivation for arts projects, writing, reading, puppetry, vocabulary building, language development, social skills, story telling, play, and movement. For example, the extended activities preceding and following Marilyn Cohen's kindergartners' visit to an apple orchard could fill this book. Apples became not only the sauce, but also the source of myriad delightful learning experiences that crisscrossed curriculum. A few apple-centered, core experiences the children enjoyed were counting apples, discovering the five-seed star shapes when cutting apples, adding apples to fruit salad, baking apple pies, singing songs about apples, drawing apple pictures, and creating apple puppets!

Your only limitation is time!

IT ALL COMES TOGETHER

All suggestions in this book (and in all books) are ideas packed with potential for integrated, multifaceted, multicultural enrichment possibilities. The following is just a small sample of how, in the hands of imaginative teachers, it all comes together.

A spring festival The winter was so long and dreary! It seemed to go on forever. The children felt as if they were really hibernating! Like Frederick, they gathered colorful words and images to warm them through the cold months. When the first signs of spring were spotted by the watchful children, their excitement was boundless! Spring pictures, murals, and posters covered their walls. When the last puddles dried up and the first crocuses showed their yellow and purple colors, the children planned a spring festival. How should they celebrate? Food headed the list. What kinds of food? Cheerful food, colorful food. Planning and flurries of activities kept the children busy and directed: Who to invite? How to decorate? Entertainment? A parade? Songs? Costumes? Stories? Games? Sharing? Greetings?

Invitations were designed, printed, and delivered. Families, neighbors, school-mates, school staff, and friends were invited with:

Come to Our Spring Festival
Pot Luck (Please bring a favorite food to share)
Bring a Can of Food for the Community Kitchen
Wear Bright Spring Colors
Singing** Stories** Dances** Fun**
Happy Spring!

On the day of the festival, the children had their specially decorated cloths and place mats covering the tables. Spring-bright flower arrangements and centerpieces were on every table. It wasn't meant to be an international or multicultural festival, but, of course, it was, as it always will be when community and family members are invited to share their gifts. For example, on the tables—in addition to bowls of fruit, cookies in the shapes of flowers and animals, vegetable plates, and homemade bread and rolls—were such treats as: Keneisha's aunt's sweet potato pie, Ken Lee's mom's fortune cookies with special fortunes tucked inside, Angie Taldone's grand-mother's little paper cups of fruit salad, and Musaf Assad's dad's bowl of hummos (paste made from chick peas) and small pieces of pita bread.

Festive meals are always accompanied by entertainment. The children sang "Miss Mary Mack" and did their Popcorn Dance. Everyone joined in a maypole dance with colorful ribbons and bouncy rhythms. Their procession included movement celebrating spring animals.

Clean-up time was a continuation of the festival as the children nibbled on left-overs, sang, talked, and, yes, some even whistled while they worked.

NOTES ❤ ❤ ❤ ❤ ❤ ❤ ❤ ❤ ❤ ❤ ❤ ❤ ❤ ❤ ❤ ❤ ❤ ❤ ❤

1. Pablo Neruda, "The Great Tablecloth." *Extravagaria,* translated by Alastair Reid. New York: Farrar, Straus and Giroux, 1976, p. 47.
2. Louise Love, *The Complete Book of Pizza*. Evanston, IL: Sassafras Press, 1980.
3. Ann Morris, photos by Ken Heyman, *Bread, Bread, Bread*. New York: Lothrop Lee and Shepard, 1989.
4. Tomie de Paola, *Tony's Bread*. New York: G.P. Putnam's Sons, 1989.
5. Lynne Merrison, illustrated by John Yates, *Rice*. Minneapolis: Carolrhoda, 1990.
6. For information on Glory Foods, write to Box 328949, Columbus, OH 43232.
7. Laurel Robertson, Carol Flinder, and Bronen Godfrey, *Laurel's Kitchen*. Petaluma, CA: Nilgiri Press, 1976, p. 144.
8. Mary T. Goodwin and Gerry Pollen, *Creative Food Experiences for Children*, revised ed. Washington, DC: Center for Science in the Public Interest, 1980.
9. Ibid, pp. 13–14.
10. When Jeannette Lauritsen was principal of Edison Elementary School in Grandview Heights, Ohio, cooking was a highlighted activity. Jeannette described some of the benefits of cooking with children.
11. Julia Child, *Julia Child and Company*. New York: Knopf, 1979, p. 147.
12. At the time of this interview, Diane Biswas was director of the Summit United Methodist Preschool in Columbus, Ohio.
13. Cheryl Chapman, illustrated by Susan L. Roth, *Pass The Fritters, Critters*. New York: Four Winds Press, 1993.
14. Sue Coomer shared these activities with her kindergartners at the Easthaven School, in Columbus.
15. Verna Willis was on staff of the Summit United Methodist Preschool, Columbus.
16. Jeanne Jacobson was principal of Bet Shraga Hebrew Academy of the Capital District in Guilderland, New York. Marilyn Cohen teaches kindergarten at the academy.
17. Jean Fritz, *George Washington's Breakfast*. Boston: Houghton Mifflin, 1989.
18. Sarah Hayes, illustrated by Jan Ormerod, *Eat Up, Gemma*. New York: Lothrop Lee and Shepard, 1988.
19. Judi Barrett, illustrated by Ron Barrett, *Cloudy with a Chance of Meatballs*. New York: Atheneum, 1978.
20. Maurice Sendak, *Chicken Soup with Rice*. New York: Harper & Row, 1962.
21. Lisa and Aaron Huber attend Granby School in Worthington, Ohio.
22. DyAnne Disalvo-Ryan, *Uncle Willie and the Soup Kitchen*. New York: Morrow, 1991.
23. Michael Joel Rosen, illustrated by a collaboration of the best artists in children's literature, *The Greatest Table*. San Diego: Harcourt Brace, 1994. Proceeds from this book will be contributed to Share Our Strength, 1511 K Street NW, Suite 600, Washington, DC 20005, (202) 393–2925.
24. Arnold Adoff, illustrated by Turi MacCombrie, *Chocolate Dreams*. New York: Lothrop Lee and Shepard, 1989.
    Arnold Adoff, illustrated by Susan Rousso, *Eats*. New York: Morrow, 1992.
25. Eric Carle, *Today Is Monday*. New York: Philomel, 1993.
26. Joan Kalb teaches at Woodward School, Delaware, Ohio.
27. Goodwin and Pollen, p. 150.
28. Annetta Dellinger taught at Trinity Lutheran School in Marysville, Ohio.
29. Betsy Distelhorst worked with children throughout central Ohio in folk crafts and foods.

30. Julia Crabbs taught at the Edison School in Grandview Heights, Ohio.
31. Sherri Bishop taught at Summit United Methodist Preschool in Columbus, Ohio.
32. Douglas Florian, *Vegetable Garden*. San Diego: Harcourt Brace Jovanovich, 1991.
33. Sandy Morgan taught at the food-loving Edison School in Grandview Heights, Ohio.
34. Cynthia Rylant, illustrated by Peter Catalanotto, *An Angel For Solomon Singer*. New York: Orchard, 1992.
35. Gwen Marston's fun-filled music sessions were well-known by Michigan children.
36. Roz Ault, *Kids Are Natural Cooks*. Boston: Houghton Mifflin, 1974, p. 147.
37. Helen Speyer and Lori Salczer shared this delightful activity at the Leo Yassenoff Jewish Center Preschool in Columbus, Ohio.
38. Marcia Brown, *Stone Soup*. New York: Scribners, 1977.
39. Barbara Brenner, illustrated by Lynn Munsinger, *Group Soup*. New York: Viking Penguin—A Bank Street Book, 1992.
40. Tomie de Paola, *Strega Nona*. Englewood Cliffs, NJ: Prentice-Hall, 1975.
41. Arnold Lobel, illustrated by Anita Lobel, *On Market Street*. New York: Greenwillow, 1981.
42. Ruth Krauss, illustrated by Crockett Johnson, *The Carrot Seed*. New York: Harper & Row, 1971.
43. Laura Joffe Numeroff, illustrated by Felicia Bond, *If You Give a Mouse a Cookie*. New York: Harper & Row, 1985.
44. Dennis Lee, illustrated by Frank Newfeld, *Alligator Pie*. Boston: Houghton Mifflin, 1975, p. 10.
45. Alycia Diggs and Issa Kone were featured in the Food section of the *Columbus Dispatch* in a story written by Karin A. Weiszel and titled "Out of Africa: Couple Adapt Native Dishes to Columbus Kitchen," August 4, 1993.

BOOKS FROM MY KNAPSACK FOR CHILDREN ♥ ♥

Adoff, Arnold. *Eats.* Illustrated by Susan Russo. New York: Lothrop, Lee & Shephard, 1979.

Anderson, Gretchen. *The Louisa May Alcott Cookbook.* Illustrated by Karen Milone. Boston: Little, Brown, 1985.

Anderson, Joan. *The First Thanksgiving Feast.* Photos by George Ancona. New York: Clarion, 1984.

Bourgeois, Paulette. *Too Many Chickens!* Illustrated by Bill Slaven. New York: Little, Brown, 1990.

Brown, Marc. *Your First Garden Book.* Boston: Little, Brown, 1981.

Burns, Marilyn. *Good for Me! All About Food in 32 Bites.* Boston: Little, Brown, 1978.

Carle, Eric. *Today Is Monday.* New York: Philomel, 1993.

Cobb, Vicki. *Science Experiments You Can Eat.* Illustrated by Peter Lippman. New York: Lippincott, 1972.

Coplans, Peta. *Spaghetti for Suzy.* Boston: Houghton Mifflin, 1993.

Demarest, Chris. *No Peas for Nellie.* New York: Macmillan, 1988.

dePaola, Tomie. *Pancakes for Breakfast.* San Diego: Harcourt Brace Jovanovich, 1978.

————. *The Popcorn Book.* New York: Holiday House, 1978.

Dobrin, Arnold. *Peter Rabbit's Natural Foods Cookbook.* New York: Warne, 1977.

Dooley, Norah. *Everybody Cooks Rice.* Illustrated by Peter J. Thornton. Minneapolis: Carolrhoda, 1991.

Drucker, Malka. *Grandma's Latkes.* Illustrated by Eve Chwast. San Diego: Harcourt Brace Jovanovich, 1992.

Ehlert, Lois. *Eating the Alphabet—Fruits and Vegetables from A to Z.* San Diego: Harcourt Brace Jovanovich, 1989.

————. *Growing Vegetable Soup.* San Diego: Harcourt Brace Jovanovich, 1987.

Evans, Kate. *Hunky Dory Ate It.* Illustrated by Janet Morgan Stoeke. New York: Dutton, 1992.

Falwell, Cathryn. *Feast for 10.* New York: Clarion, 1993.

Fleming, Denise. *Lunch.* New York: Henry Holt, 1992.

Gallimard, Jeunesse, and deBourgoing, P. *First Discovery Books—Fruit.* Illustrated by P. M. Valet. New York: Scholastic, 1989.

Gibbons, Gail. *From Seed to Plant.* New York: Holiday House, 1991.

————. *The Milk Makers.* New York: Macmillan, 1985.

Giblin, James Cross. *From Hand to Mouth: Or How We Invented Knives, Forks, Spoons and Chopsticks & the Table Manners to Go with Them.* New York: Crowell, 1987.

Hayes, Sarah. *Eat Up, Gemma.* Illustrated by Jan Ormerod. New York: Lothrop, Lee & Shephard, 1988.

Hines, Anna Grossnickle. *Daddy Makes the Best Spaghetti.* Illustrated by Anna Grossnickle Hines. New York: Ticknor, 1986.

Houston, Gloria. *But No Candy.* Illustrated by Lloyd Bloom. New York: Philomel, 1992.

Howard, Jane R. *When I Am Hungry.* New York: Dutton's Children's Books, 1992.

Kasza, Keiko. *The Wolf's Chicken Stew.* Illustrated by Keiko Kasza. New York: Putnam, 1987.

Khalsa, Dayal Kaur. *How Pizza Came to Our Town.* Illustrated by Dayal Kaur Khalsa. Pittsburgh: Tundra, 1989.

Kimmelman, Leslie. *Frannie's Fruit.* Illustrated by Petra Mathers. New York: HarperCollins, 1989.

Klutz Press Editors. *Kids Cooking: A Very Slightly Messy Manual.* Illustrated by Jim M'Guinness. Palo Alto, CA: Klutz Press, 1987.

Koscielniak, Bruce. *Bear and Bunny Grow Tomatoes.* Illustrated by Bruc Koscielniak. New York: Knopf, 1993.

Kovalski, Mary Ann. *Pizza for Breakfast.* Illustrated by Mary Ann Kovalski. New York: Morrow, 1991.

Krementz, Jill. *The Fun of Cooking.* New York: Knopf, 1985.

Lasky, Kathryn. *Sugaring Time.* Photographs by Christopher G. Knight. New York: Macmillan, 1983.

MacGregor, Carol. *The Fairy Tale Cookbook.* Illustrated by Debby L. Carter. New York: Macmillan, 1982.

McFarland, Cynthia. *Cows in the Parlor: A Visit to a Dairy Farm.* New York: Atheneum, 1990.

Micucci, Charles. *Life and Times of the Apple.* Illustrated by Charles Micucci. New York: Orchard, 1992.

Morris, Ann. *Bread, Bread, Bread.* Photographs by Ken Heyman. New York: Lothrop, Lee & Shephard, 1989.

Needham, Kate. *Why Do People Eat?* Illustrated by Annabel Spenceley. Tulsa: EDC, 1992.

Numeroff, Laura Jaffe. *If You Give a Mouse a Cookie.* Illustrated by Felicia Bond. New York: Harper & Row, 1985.

Penner, Lucille Recht. *Eating the Plates—A Pilgrim Book of Food and Manners.* New York: Macmillan, 1991.

———. *The Tea Party Book.* Illustrated by Jody Wheeler. New York: Random House, 1993.

Perl, Lila. *Hunter's Stew and Hangtown Fry: What Pioneer America Ate and Why.* Boston: Houghton Mifflin, 1979.

Pillar, Marjorie. *Pizza Man.* New York: Harper & Row, 1990.

Pinkwater, Daniel. *The Phantom of the Lunch Wagon.* Illustrated by Daniel Pinkwater. New York: Macmillan, 1992.

Polacco, Patricia. *Chicken Sunday.* Illustrated by Patricia Polacco. New York: Philomel, 1992.

Radlauer, Ruth. *Breakfast by Molly.* Illustrated by Emily Arnold McCully. New York: Simon and Schuster, 1988.

Rattigan, Jama Kim. *Dumpling Soup.* Illustrated by Lillian Hsa–Flanders. Boston: Little Brown, 1993.

Rice, Eve. *Benny Bakes a Cake.* Illustrated by Eve Rice. New York: Greenwillow, 1981.

Snow, Pegeen. *Eat Your Peas, Louise.* Chicago: Children's Press, 1987.

Steig, Jeanne. *Alpha Beta Chowder.* Illustrated by William Steig. New York: HarperCollins, 1992.

Stock, Catherine. *Thanksgiving Treat.* Illustrated by Catherine Stock. New York: Macmillan, 1990.

Thomas, Elizabeth. *Green Beans.* Illustrated by Vicki Jo Redenbaugh. Minneapolis: Carolrhoda, 1992.

VanAllsburg, Chris. *The Sweetest Fig.* Illustrated by Chris VanAllsburg. Boston: Houghton Mifflin, 1993.

Watanbe, Shigeo, and Yasuo. *What a Good Lunch!* New York: Philomel, 1991.

Watson, Susan. *Sugar-free Toddlers.* Mount Ranier, MD: Gryphon House, 1992.

Wilson, Sarah. *Muskrat, Muskrat, Eat Your Peas!* Illustrated by Sarah Wilson. New York: Simon and Schuster, 1989.

Wittstock, Laura. *Ininatig's Gift of Sugar—Traditional Native Sugarmaking.* Photographs by Dale Kakkak. Minneapolis: Lerner, 1993.

BOOKS FROM MY KNAPSACK FOR TEACHERS ❤ ❤

Carey, Diana, and Large, Judy. *Festivals, Family and Food*. Mount Ranier, MD: Gryphon House, 1993.

Hess, Mary Abbott, et al. *A Healthy Head Start*. New York: Henry Holt, 1990.

Van Leuven, N. *Food to Grow On: A Parent's Guide to Nutrition*. Penanal, VT: Storey Publishers, 1988.

Chapter 8

Where We Live

The walls come close around me
In a good way.
I can see them;
I can feel them;
I live with them.
This house is good to me.
It keeps me . . .[1]

Ann Nolan Clark

THE BASICS

"Let's play house!" Chances are, you and billions of children throughout history played in or constructed some kind of shelter, even if the walls were imaginary and the roof invisible. You probably built homes for toys, pets, dolls, stuffed animals, puppets, and yourself as you moved through those early childhood years.

I can clearly see my sister, Laura, my brother, Mike, and myself playing in one of our favorite settings: an open umbrella spread over the living-room floor, a sheet spread over the umbrella to make a draped shelter, and we three kids cozy inside our wonderful "house," making up stories.

Felicity Steele[2] remembered when her son, Alexander, was barely two years old. She recalls that he worked hard at playing with blocks, Legos, and cardboard boxes. He turned a large cardboard box into a house. Felicity helped him cut out doors and windows. Alexander loved keys and locks, and they installed one end of an old chain lock on the box and the other on the door. Alexander brought in his animals, dolls, toys, and friends. He dragged in his blanket and pillow and pretended to sleep in his house.

Pam Slater[3] reminisced about her Head Start children transforming a large packing box into a house. It was their most exciting game. They, too, cut out doors and windows and decorated the walls with designs and pictures. One little girl taped up a towel for a curtain. The children carried in their favorite dolls and toys.

When Lisa Stevens was five years old, she told about her favorite game, house. She and her friends used any kind of boxes and made houses for their toys and dolls and themselves. They had picnics in their houses and built little furniture out of sticks and blocks.

Pam's Head Start students and Lisa shared a common rule: "We all have to take good care of our house. We take turns, we share."

All children want the protection of a shelter. Houses make them feel good and safe. They want to bring in their favorite playthings and friends to share in the game. Playing house gives them opportunities to try their wings at adult roles as they dress their dolls and stuff animals into "jammies," sing lullabies to them, and arrange and rearrange the contents of their shelter.

In A. A. Milne's wonderful story, "In Which a House Is Built at Pooh Corner for Eeyore," Eeyore's friends are concerned because poor Eeyore has nowhere to live.[4] Pooh says, "You have a house, Piglet, and I have a house, and they are very good houses . . . but poor Eeyore has nothing. So, what I've been thinking is: Let's build him a house!"

So Pooh and Piglet agree to the grand idea and fetch sticks to build Eeyore a house at Pooh Corner. When the usually grumpy Eeyore discovers his beautiful house, he manages a rare show of gladness.

"It just shows what can be done by taking a little trouble," said Eeyore. "Do you see, Pooh? Do you see, Piglet? Brains first and then Hard Work. Look at it! That's the way to build a house."

Feelings of pride and possession play a large part in our need for shelter. No matter how humble a house, it is someone's home.

Pause here for a wonder break. Shelter is one of those universal themes that demonstrate human creativity and ingenuity.

If we were robins, we would not build eagles' nests. If we were beavers, we would not need a course in dam building to construct our shelters of mud and sticks. And if we were ants, we would not call on architects to design the intricate structures of our colonies. Animals have strong instincts for survival and amazing capacities for learning to hunt food and find or build shelter. Perhaps more amazing is the ability of human beings to learn, invent, innovate, and improvise.

Our human instincts tell us to get out of the cold, rain, wind, snow, and heat. When we see wild, scary animals, our instincts tell us to run and hide. But where? Where to hide? How? How to find ways to protect ourselves from the elements?

Our earliest ancestors lived in trees, protected by leaves and branches from the heat, rain, and wind. The height of trees kept the people safe from unfriendly animals and from floods. When our ancestors found hollows in rocks, hills, and mountains, they came down from the trees and took shelter in the caves. Over the centuries, humans learned to make a variety of shelters, including tents, tepees, huts, adobes, stilt houses, houseboats, stone cottages, skyscrapers, igloos, castles, tenements, farmhouses, longhouses, yurts, mansions, trailers, log cabins, Quonset huts, and glass houses.

Wherever in the world people settled, they had to respond to three major questions as they decided how to build their houses: What is the climate? What materials can we use? How do we want to live? (Unfortunately, many people must substitute "have to live" for "want to live.") People who lived in cold places found ways to use ice, snow, and animal skins. Those in dry, desert lands built homes of clay, mud, sand, dung, straw, and animal hair. People who settled in jungles and forests had an ample supply of lumber, bark, leaves, twigs, mud, straw, and grass.

Other questions about housing arrangements include: How big shall our houses be? How many people shall live in a house? One family? One generation? Many families? Several generations? How close shall we build our houses to each other? Shall we have one large room or a house divided into smaller rooms? The solutions to these questions result in homes running the gamut from isolated farmhouses to high-rise apartment houses sheltering hundreds of families.

You no doubt have your own favorite kinds of houses and daydreams about them. Here are some of my favorite fantasies. I want to spend some time with a Bedouin family on the Sinai Desert and see what is inside their sprawling tents. I would give anything to be adopted by a Rumanian gypsy family and live with them in their caravans. Let me spend a year with a Chinese family on their sampan, floating down the Yangtze River. Take me into your hogan, Navajo friend. What is inside? What kinds of houses fascinate you?

We educators can't live on fantasy alone! We need to ground this house-hunting spree and come back to reality.

Reality: The children who come to your room each day probably leave many different kinds of homes. Some live in more than one home, with more than one family.

Some leave mansions with closets of clothes and luxurious toys; others leave small, tattered rooms crowded with people, secondhand playthings, and hand-me-down clothing. Some leave painfully the security and safety of their homes; others

leave gladly, eager to begin a new experience in a new place. Some do not want to go home at the end of the day, because their homes fail to provide safety, protection, and warmth.

Avoid stereotyped thinking. Children find security and love in humble, shabby homes as well as neglect and rejection in wealthy homes. And the reverse.

I once heard a saying. It went something like this:

If a child comes from a warm home to a cold school—there is a chance.
If a child comes from a cold home to a warm school—there is a chance.
If a child comes from a warm home to a warm school—many chances!
But if a child comes from a cold home to a cold school—no chance!

Tragically, in this decade of homelessness and increasing poverty, our children are coming from cold "homes," shelterless shelters. For too many of our children, school is the only safe, loving, responsible shelter in their lives. That responsibility is awesome.

Where children live is a deep representation of themselves. These themes cut closest to the hearts and souls of people, along with their languages, clothing, families, and food. When we want to hurt others, we stab them with words insulting to their most basic situations. "Your mother dresses you weird." "You look funny." "You eat gross food." "You talk crazy." "You live in a dump."

I remind you: you are not a judge or a critic. Here is where our own stereotyped attitudes and prejudices must be defeated, because our acceptance of and respect for our children's homes, no matter how different from our own, is vital in the building of trust and love in our rooms, our shelters. These can be heartbreaking times. I am reminded of an incident with a kindergarten class I visited the day after the classic movie *The Wizard of Oz* was shown for the umpteenth time on TV. Through my whole session with the group, one child stood apart, unresponsive. Even though he was continually invited to participate and was included in everything we did, he hung back. Only at the end of the session, as we were getting ready to go, did he respond when I asked the children if they had seen *The Wizard of Oz*. He jumped into action, waving his hand enthusiastically.

"And what did you think was the best part of the movie?" I asked him. Without hesitating, he said, "I saw it on TV in Room 14 of the Bluebird Motel."

I stammered a show of comprehension as the children waved and left. Later, the kindergarten teacher explained that this little boy and his mother and brother were found living in an abandoned automobile for days before a police officer helped them to a community kitchen and arranged with a local agency to put them up in a motel. They stayed in Room 14 at the Bluebird Motel, a temporary shelter.

From her many years of experience with Head Start, Mattie James[5] is fervent in her belief that school is an extension of home and a primary shelter for young children. Schools now, she explains, bring families, teachers, and community representatives together to create positive support systems for the children. She remembers in the early years of Head Start when many of the programs were located in meager, dark facilities. "But we were always able to brighten them with teachers sensitive to children's needs. We brightened the drab spaces with love! And, with all our power, we tried to 'dress up' the dull walls." Mattie is happy to report that today Head Start programs have evolved from "basements and holes in the walls to our shinier places in the sun!" She points out that children who come from homes reflecting great economic deprivation *need* surroundings of beauty and aesthetics. They need to see bright colors, designs, flowers, and paintings. Mattie's priorities, however, are clear and emphatic. "Just colors, equipment, and materials aren't enough if the place isn't filled with love and warmth! Teachers are the architects of the buildings. After a few days, school becomes like home. Teachers become almost like family."

As teachers of young children, as "architects" of our space, how shall we design our shelter? Mattie James and Pam Slater have a lot to say about turning school into a warm place.

> We don't need the best equipment in the world. We need to be ingenious enough to use our imaginations and create special places and activities out of our beautiful junk! Our rooms have special places for the children's things: shoe boxes, cardboard liquor boxes, plastic trays, shelves with hooks. Their names are on everything! This is *their* room!
>
> The housekeeping areas are the most popular. We have tables and chairs, dress-up clothes, stoves, refrigerators, sinks, and, believe it or not, mirrors! Most mirrors in homes are usually too high up; they're only good for "big people." We put mirrors on our walls low enough for children to clearly see themselves.
>
> We spend a lot of time taking care of our "home." A lot of people think "poor" means "dirty." This is a tragic stereotype! We see our children learning to care for their things, keep them clean, put them away, pick up.
>
> Because parents are involved in all aspects of the Head Start Program, family life is enriched, enhanced.

Probably no educator wrote more eloquently about the effect of environment on the development of young children than Maria Montessori. She believed that children should learn in an environment that conforms to their size, energy, and intellectual and psychic faculties. In her excellent book *The Child in the Family* many recommendations about a school environment were offered:

> A school, a place built for children, must have furniture and equipment scaled to the proper size and adapted to their physical strength, so that they can move it with the same ease with which we move the furniture in our homes. . . . The child must be able to use everything he comes across in the house and he must be able to do the ordinary tasks of everyday life—sweep, vacuum the rugs, wash and dress himself. The objects surrounding the child should look solid and attractive to him, and the "house of the child" should be lovely and pleasant in all its particulars; for beauty in the school invites activity and work.[6]

Maria Montessori constantly encouraged teachers to give children freedom of opportunity to choose their own activities and objects as well as the time to concentrate on whatever fascinates them. How else is discovery possible? She believed that

> The environment itself will teach the child. . . . Little by little, it will seem to the child that he hears the silent language of objects advising his actions: "Pay attention, look! I am a newly varnished end table; don't scratch me or make me dirty!"
>
> Through constant active involvement with the environment, children learn responsibility and appreciation in addition to the countless intellectual, motor skills that are part of the simplest activity.
>
> "The house of the child," our school rooms, must be places where the children can touch, move, manipulate, change, build, invent and rearrange![7]

Judy Tough[8] emphasized another aspect of shelter that must be remembered as teachers design their space.

> Young children are very territorial. We have to allow them to stake their claims. Remember, many children don't have their own rooms or space of their own at home. At school, they need a special group of chairs, rugs, or mats—special

places—respected as quiet spaces within areas of activity to rest, think, wonder, and observe. If it's not built into equipment, then you have to set it aside, designate it. Those places are best if they're behind some low barrier (a form of protection), a corner, a place against a wall, a special little circle.

Scrounging, that familiar activity, is the most popular way creative teachers find materials and items for their classrooms. They send notes to community and families, rummage through basements, visit garage and lawn sales, and nudge neighbors to find such excellent shelter items as umbrellas (open them, throw a sheet or blanket over them); folding wooden clothes dryers (the top is like a roof; they make excellent little houses); floor pillows; mats and rugs; cardboard boxes of all sizes (safety is the first item of business with any box or compartment in which children enjoy playing or hiding; always be sure there are openings, and discuss safety); coffee tables and end tables; odd sheets; clotheslines (hang two clotheslines near each other and turn a corner of the room into a tent by draping a sheet over the lines); blocks, Legos, Tinkertoys, any building materials; old Monopoly games (save the houses and hotels); miniature cars, farms, animals, and trees of cardboard and plastic; tongue depressors and toothpicks; and scraps (carpet, wool, rugs, contact paper). Children have fantastic imaginations and do not need exact replicas to be able to play.

Simplicity and accessibility are important criteria in the classroom. And, as Maria Montessori affirmed, "The aesthetics, too, both of things and of the environment itself, encourage attentiveness in the active child; for this reason, everything ought to be multi-colored, brushed brightly colored. . . . Attractive objects invite the child to touch them and then to learn to use them."[9]

It is no accident that Maria Montessori, Mattie James, Lisa, and the Head Start children talk about aesthetics. Nearly two thousand years ago, the Roman architect Vitruvius described three goals of architecture that have been adopted by architects throughout the world: use, strength, and beauty. Shelter has been discussed above as useful for protection and safety. Obviously, such a practical structure must be strong. Whether built of sod, sand, stone, straw, or stained glass, our houses must withstand wolves and winds. Beauty, unfortunately, is often considered an extravagance rather than a basic goal. Yet, every civilization has decorated its structures, within and without.

Children need not read Vitruvius or study architecture to embrace beauty as one of their primary interests in exploring shelter. Recall that the very first thing Pam Slater's Head Start children did with their "house" was paint it, decorate it. I had an interesting talk with my friend Ruthie, who is three years old. She told me why she likes to visit people in their houses: "All houses are different. Some are blue, some are white. . . . I like to see people's pretty fish tanks, plants, and books with nice pictures. . . . I paint pretty pictures for Mommy and Daddy to hang up in our house."

When Ruthie comes to your class, your room, your sheltering walls of safety and welcome, she will learn about other people who may live in houses that don't have blue and white walls or pretty plants. She may find new friends who live in trailer parks, public housing projects, apartment houses, community shelters, migrant worker camps, condominiums, castles, houseboats, or bungalows. A greater challenge is to introduce children of homogeneous environments to the idea of diversity. Here is where excellent materials and activities provide direct experiences so even our children from more insulated communities expand their awareness, knowledge, and understanding.

Read the following sections of this guide and keep making connections as you find ways to make room in your room (and in your heart) for every child who shares your space and time in a school or program where the climate is warm. The children already know:

"We are the people/Living together/All of us together."[10]

DISCOVERY TIMES/WONDER TIMES

- All people and animals live in some kind of shelter.
- Animals build their shelters through instinct. Wouldn't it be fascinating to watch birds build their nests from the first twig to the finished shelter? Have you noticed that even nests resting on the ends of limbs or branches stay put even through storms and winds?
- People build houses out of the materials they have around them.
- Houses protect people from cold, heat, snow, and rain.
- There are many kinds of houses! It really shows how imaginative human beings can be when they try to solve basic problems like the need for shelter.
- Sometimes people share one house or apartment. Sometimes only one person lives in a house. Some apartment houses have hundreds of people living in them. People are very versatile.
- No matter what kind of shelter people live in, it is home to them and very important.
- Sometimes people find themselves in tragic circumstances and have no place to live. Communities and cities, along with organizations,

churches, synagogues, and mosques, try to help provide temporary shelter for them. It's everyone's responsibility to try to help others less fortunate.

- A neighborhood or community or city is made up of houses near each other, with stores, shops, services, and streets that help people live better lives.
- School is like a house. Everyone in a house, in school, should be responsible for taking care of the things and people in it.
- We should always respect people, even if they come from homes very different from our own.
- Each of us can help make our homes and schools happier places to be. When people cooperate with each other in keeping their houses in order, family life and community life are enriched. Everyone benefits.
- We share the planet Earth, a home to us all.

SUGGESTED VOCABULARY

house	floors	shower	fireplace
home	rooms	garden	clothes washer
apartment	windows	lawn	clothesline
tent	doors	steps	clothespins
hut	pipes	stairs	magazines
cabin	wires	stoop	mailbox
mobile home	closets	elevator	mail
farmhouse	key	fire escape	outside
tenement	lock	shades	inside
shelter	bedroom	curtains	warm
igloo	kitchen	table	games
tepee	living room	chair	parties
nest	paint	bed	visitors
hutch	make	couch	share
den	build	pictures	decorate
ant colony	wood	fish tank	village
beehive	stone	community	city
doghouse	brick	neighborhood	farm
Habitrail	glass	refrigerator	street
watch TV	straw	freezer	block
sleep	cement	stove	neighbor
eat	mud, clay	oven	friend
play	painter	TV	vacuum
read	carpenter	stereo	fix
study	electrician	lights	clean
homework	plumber	lamps	dust
food	porch	books	sweep
family	yard	toys	pick up
room	basement	dishwasher	put away
ceiling	attic	sink	telephone
roof	laundry	toilet	address
walls	bath	shelves	colors
rent	landlord	chimney	work

Young children's knowledge of words associated with their homes and neighborhoods is extensive and cannot be contained in a short vocabulary list. In addition, children have special vocabularies based on their housing arrangements. If they live in trailer parks or on houseboats, they will probably have different vocabularies from children who live on farms. Likewise, city children will have their own set of words that contrast with those of children who live in rural areas.

All words are little universes of their own. They beget and beget!

When your children look around them, they will be able to create their own vocabulary books based on the contents and natures of their homes. *In a People House*[11] by Theodore Geisel (aka Dr. Seuss) is full of words and illustrations showing readers all the items that might be found in a People House, like stairs, chairs, toothbrushes, and clocks. See how your vocabulary list immediately expands?

City children just need to look around to see clusters of vocabulary words that might be unfamiliar to children living in rural neighborhoods. *Taxi: A Book of City Words*[12] is an example of that more specialized list that includes "skyscraper," "museum," "hotel," and "tunnel" accompanied by lively illustrations and descriptions.

Many children live in more than one household and travel between homes and neighborhoods, dividing their time (and their lives) between divorced parents who share custody. Although they divide their time, these children multiply their vocabularies and experiences. This situation common to so many of our children is sensitively caught in such books as *My Mother's House, My Father's House.*[13] As you can see, words are not just configurations on paper—they have their own little universes of expanding experiences.

You will learn from your children as they introduce you to words and ideas from their own lives that describe and clarify their concepts of shelter. Your word list will evolve each day as you and your students share, learn, and grow together.

SOME STARTERS

The following section is probably unnecessary because most of your young children already know how to think about and play "shelter." But, in the event that your students are the rare exception, enjoy the following suggestions or mix and match and make your own.

Start with a bird's nest Here come my young friends, Louie and Ben with their Grandpa Marvin. They found a fallen bird's nest and are running to show me. These fascinating demonstrations of animal ingenuity and instinct compel the attention of children and adults alike. Entwined in the materials of the nest are curiosity and wonder. How are birds' nests made? How many birds help make the nest? Imagine: they have no hands and fingers, just beaks! How many birds live in a nest? Do different kinds of birds make different kinds of nests? What kinds? Imagine how it would feel to have a nest as a home.

Start with classroom pets The value of classroom pets as resources for learning on all levels, across all subjects, is immeasurable. Add to your list of important experiences for children the observation of gerbils, turtles, hamsters, rabbits, guinea pigs, frogs, even fish, and the idea of shelter. As children watch their classroom pets at work, play, and rest, they see how nests are made as animals nibble shredded papers to build cozy shelters. There are lots of ideas for the children to nibble on as they pay attention to the habits of their pets, care for them, keep notes and illustrations, read books like *Animals That Build Their Homes,*[14] and compare questions and explanations.

Start with photos or pictures of animals and their houses On your walls and borders of colorful and interesting images, be sure to include animals and their "homes." These subjects are among those most interesting to young children. One photograph or painting can evoke enough response to launch your theme for the rest of the year.

Start with a large box If you have not already discovered firsthand how eagerly children turn boxes into houses or have not been inspired by Alexander and the Head Start children, bring in a box and see for yourself.

Start with a challenge Raggedy Ann and Raggedy Andy dolls started a group of first graders on a study of shelter. The teacher asked the children: "Where can Raggedy Ann and Raggedy Andy live?" The children built them a small house out of blocks, in a protected part of the room, and even gave the house an address. The project was an excellent way to stimulate the children's thinking about shelter and what it means in our lives.

Start with a song You need not be a musician or singer or even know the melody or all the words to enjoy singing with your children. I love Graham Nash's lovely song "Our House," and even though I do not know all the lyrics or even the tune, that did not stop me from sharing parts of the song with a group of kindergartners as a way of introducing the topic of shelter!

When the song was over, I asked the children: "Do you have two cats in your yard? Do you have flowers in a vase? What do you have in your house, your very very very fine house?" Here are just a few of the answers that were written on the board as the children spoke. Note how many important points were introduced by the children's responses:

> We have no cats and two babies.
> We have gerbils in the basement.
> No pets. My dad's allergic. Just rooms and people.
> Just make-believe pets like my teddy and new TV.
> My own room with my brother to share. All our toys.

Start with a walk around the neighborhood Look, listen, talk, and compare as you walk. A group of second graders saw an apartment house with lots of windows, an "old pointy house" with a drugstore below and an apartment above, two men painting a house white, and a wooden house with a hex sign on the outside door. A simple walk around the school neighborhood yields many rewards, specific impressions rooted in specific places. The children at Indianola Alternative and Duxberry Park Alternative schools in the middle of Columbus—surrounded by crowded streets, shops, shoppers, a mix of houses, lively traffic, and pedestrian hubbub—will find different scenes than the children taking a walk around their school neighborhood in Granby, Connecticut, or Albuquerque, New Mexico.

Ezra Jack Keats' Sam, in *Apt. 3*, and Peter, in *A Letter to Amy*,[15] introduce children in any region in the country to a city neighborhood. *Irene and the Big, Fine Nickel*[16] takes readers to the streets of Harlem. Contrast Sam, Irene, and Peter's city houses to the rural family's in the wordless book of self-explanatory illustrations going through the months of the year in *Our House on the Hill*.[17] It's a very different walk around the neighborhood!

Be sure to leave time for discussion, illustration, and creative writing, celebrating the initial experience.

Start with pictures of different kinds of houses/books about different kinds of houses Igloos, tepees, grass huts, sod cabins, castles, skyscrapers, and houseboats—all are captivating images to young children (and old children like us). Shelter is a theme that demonstrates human creativity. Books like *Anno's USA*[18] intrigue children with the unfolding drama of a country beginning with untamed nature, a few canoes, and a few simple houses growing into a complex nation of cities. Josephine Karavasil's *Houses and Homes Around the World*[19] gives the children a glimpse of the variety of houses built by people around the world from a floating town in Hong Kong to houses made of rushes in Peru. The photographs are crystal clear and feature children in most of the scenes. Such materials spark high interest and encourage imaginative responses to "How would you like to live in a house

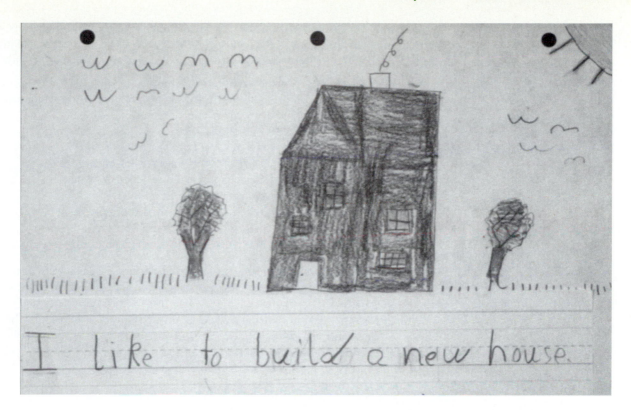

on stilts?" and "What do you think it would be like to live in this house of palm leaves and mud?"

Start with a sign You will be amazed at what happens with the appearance of a sign on your door saying, "Welcome to the Houses of the Children in This Room" or "Follow the Arrow to the Houses of the Children." Given time to read and interpret the sign, the children will plunge into their collections of scrounged and play materials to construct original houses.

Start with a wonderful story Teachers over the years have been enthusiastic about *A House Is a House for Me,*[20] that old book taking young readers through many ideas about shelter from animals such as "A hive is a house for a bee" to castles for duchesses, oceans for whales, and garages for cars, to more imaginative concepts of houses such as: "a pod is a house for a pea" or "a cooky jar's home to the cookies." The reassuring refrain throughout the book is, of course, "a house is a house for me." Children love the story and are truly engaged in its provocative expansion of the idea. They come up with excellent variations such as: "My pocket is a house for my marble" and "My closet is a house for my clothes." I especially like the last two lines of Hoberman's text: "Each creature that's known has a house of its own. And the earth is a house for us all."

TALK TIMES/LISTENING TIMES

If you eavesdrop on young children, you will find that much of their conversation concerns their homes: what happens there, who lives there, games and toys played with, and chores performed. Unless their shelter is not a safe and secure place, children will always have a lot to say about where they live. Often, children growing up in hostile homes don't/won't share their wishes and fantasies. These are even greater reasons for assuring *all* children that where we live together in school is a safe, loving, welcoming home.

At a staff development program for Head Start teachers and assistants, Pam Slater encouraged the group to be a curriculum of welcome to children walking toward them. She read a poem she had written, and I am happy to share it with you:

Act as if you see magic in the twinkling of those rainbow eyes.
Act as if you could jump out of your skin when they give you a BIG surprise.
Act as if your smile is true even when you're feeling blue.
Act as if you don't mind 20 questions or 2.
Act as if they're warm blessings in a winter's storm.
Act as if your hugs are blankets to keep them ever-so-warm.
Act as if they are Kings and Queens just waiting to be crowned.
Act as if you are their pillows, never letting them hit the ground.
Act as if they were rainbows, each with their own golden treasure.
Act as if the love they give turns gloom to instant pleasure.
Act as if their dreams will come true. Martin Luther King did—so can you!

When children are lucky enough to live and learn in such caring environments, they will have much to say and they will be responsive listeners. Talk times will be most of the times!

Wonder questions We humans are curious about shelters. Encourage the children to wonder aloud, to ask their questions to contribute to the group's collection of ideas and thematic directions. Here are just a few samples to spark your own list (display the children's questions and add to them).

Some Wonder Questions

Why do we need houses?
How did people learn to build houses?
Do all people live in the same kinds of houses? Can we think of different kinds of houses?
What is your house made of?
What's in your house? Do all people have the same things in their houses?
If you were a bird, where would you live?
Who lives in your house?
Do you like to visit people in their houses? Why?
How do people help take care of your house/apartment?

Enjoy these few excerpts from a long discussion among prekindergartners inspired by some of the above questions:

"Houses are to keep us warm."
"We need houses to watch TV in."
"We need houses for our beds to stay so we can go to sleep."
"If I'm in my house, I don't get wet when it rains."
"My house gets messy when my brother comes home."
"Doors are my favorite parts. I like to turn the doorknob and ring the bell."

We were talking about a severe thunderstorm that hit our city the night before. I asked the children if anything unusual happened last night. One of the boys jumped up and announced dramatically, "I had a thunderstorm in my house last night!"

Animal houses This is a strand of the shelter theme, which is a source of constant fascination for the children to ask about, discuss, investigate, inform, compare, conclude, and wonder about. And, it's an emotionally safe (relatively) area. Often, children living in dysfunctional homes find talks about houses in general very uncomfortable. But when attention is focused on animals and their habits and habitats, those children have a green light into the conversation and activities.

City kids/country kids Imaginations are fed with that wonderful "what if" question. "What if we lived in a tall apartment house?" to children living in a farm community evokes lively responses. And, of course, the reverse is also true. Books like *Farm Morning*[21] or *When I Was Young In The Mountains*[22] add vivid images to nourish imaginative possibilities. "Country" children enjoy such "city" children books as *Mrs. Katz and Tush*[23] for a taste of life in apartments with neighbors of diverse backgrounds living closely together. Kids love to pretend to live in houses other than their own!

Problem-solving discussions The tragedy of homelessness in our country is not lost on even our youngest children who listen to adults, TV announcers, radio commentators, and each other. Very often, children from a community shelter will attend school and bring the experience directly to the awareness of their more fortunate classmates. It's important to remember that even in shelters, many families live together and attempt to keep family life viable. Children do homework. Parents come in for conferences. Children have birthdays. When they know safety and reassurance in the environment you create, your children will share information and feelings from their situations. Always make it possible for every child to participate. Try to find ways to help children see as much as they can of anything positive in whatever their circumstances. They will always have positive relationships and activities in the shelter you provide.

Young children are direct and honest. Their solutions to even the most complex problems are often the most logical and compassionate!

Here are a few suggestions from first graders to help solve the homelessness:

"They could stay in our living room."
"We could make our garage a house."
"When no one's in school, people could live here."
"We could call the President."

Again, children as well as adults need to follow discussions with some kind of action, whether it's a letter-writing project, planning an activity with a group at the shelter, or inviting people who live in a shelter to share a holiday or commemoration.

Shelter is a moving experience In our society, people move frequently. No matter how often families may move (and some families move many times in the childhood years of their offspring), moving is a traumatic experience. It's an emotional time for the child who is leaving as well as for the "new child" entering your room as a stranger. Books like *I'm Not Moving, Mama!* and *Anna's Secret Friend*[24] catch the anxiety of that event and help the children talk about not only the characters in the stories but themselves through vicarious involvement and people in their direct experiences. Empathy and hospitality are qualities that need tending to all the time. Through the free-spirited sharing of concerns and feelings, children are strengthened and feel more confident as such events occur around them and within their own lives. In both these stories, the children find positive ways to handle that difficult journey. These are important lessons for American children living in a transient society.

Encourage the children to collect ideas for welcoming new students to the class, new neighbors to their streets. How would we want to be received if we were new children coming to a new house and school for the first time? The kids will surprise you with their enlightened thinking and suggestions.

Remember, talking leads to doing!

VISUAL ARTS TIMES

Our shelters, our houses hold much fascination for us. Photographs, paintings, and models of houses are among our favorite subjects. At two recent art exhibits, this theme's centrality was reemphasized. Thousands of people visited the Columbus Museum of Art to see an exhibit by Elijah Pierce, woodcarver.[25] Animals, athletes, action-packed stories, people, and Biblical events carved in wood and painted in bright colors drew appreciative crowds. The crowds were so thick in front of Pierce's "Doll House" that people waited in line to view it. The large house was filled with furniture, dishes, little paintings on the wall, cooking utensils, and people. Children in one program, DepARTures,[26] sketched and wrote poems in their notebooks. Many chose the Doll House to write about. For example:

> **The House**
> Far in the East, Far below,
> There was a house built.
> A house for me.
> A delightful house made of sticks and stones.
> In the delightful house,
> I built another house.
> A house of love.
> The delightful house.
> The delightful house made of love, was not a house.
> It was a home.
>
> Jenny Kocher, fifth grade, Cedarwood School, Columbus, Ohio

Something about the rooms—the warmth, the coziness, the liveliness—drew these people near. There's something about houses!

Across the city, at Capital University, the ceramics of Marjorie Bender were on exhibit.[27] Marjorie's work, colorful, original, and imaginative, never fails to evoke delightful responses. Marjorie's house is a story-house, a house of imagination and fantasy. Marjorie's house began with stories she told her son, Matt, about a boy named Jonathon Level and his family and characters she invented, such as the Kickle-Kackle Chicken and a displaced witch. When a friend found a junk table in an alley in Greenwich Village and gave it to Marjorie, the visualization of Jonathon Level's house took form! Marjorie built a house around that scrounged table.

Marjorie's house of clay, wood, fiber, paper, paint, and fantastic stories and Elijah Pierce's Doll House of wood, paint, fiber, and memories are both examples of visual arts celebrations of where we live.

In your room rich with inviting and easy-to-use materials, young children will create images and designs from their own experiences. Enliven your building centers and construction areas with books about houses and construction. Young children especially enjoy such selections as *I Can Build a House, The Little Red House,* and *Up Goes the Skyscraper* for colorful ideas and inspiration.[28]

Chances are your children will already be embarked on many projects that express their feelings and understandings about shelter. While you are reading the following section, the children will, most likely, already be busy constructing and creating!

Construction sites Set aside a building area in your room and stock it with blocks, boxes, Tinkertoys, Legos, and Erector Sets. Children who like to constuct houses, cities, and worlds will work with great concentration and energy. If there is a lull in the activities, suggest that some children build a house for puppets, dolls, and stuffed animals, and that those who want to sit quietly by themselves for a little while also make important contributions to the class. They may be gathering ideas!

Sandbox structures It is hoped that your room or playground has a sandbox available, because children truly enjoy building castles, tunnels, bridges, walls, cities, and houses of sand. Wet sand holds shapes. Powdered tempera dusted on the sand adds life and color. Enhance the sand community with clay sculptures, shells, pebbles, leaves, toy cars, plastic people, and pinecones.

Milk carton houses Save small houseshaped milk cartons. The children rinse them out and cover them with markers, colorful construction paper, and paste-on designs. Use a tabletop or set aside floor space to arrange the houses into neighborhoods, with streets and toy cars, animals, and people.

Shoe box housing projects Shoe boxes are the right size for a variety of housing projects. Alexandra Stoddard, in her lively book *A Child's Place*,[29] shares experiences with a group of six- to eight-year-old children who were given boxes and challenged to create an environment inside the box. The children asked such questions as "Am I allowed to make mine a garden?" "Does mine have to be my own bedroom?" "Am I allowed to divide it into more than one room?" Stoddard reassured them: "You may do anything you wish."

The children used materials such as wallpaper, rugs, paints, markers, fabric swatches, scissors, glue, tape, and excellent scrounge materials. Empty spools of thread were made into end tables. Wooden coffee stirrers became posts on a canopy bed. The top of a can of shaving cream was used as a lamp shade. A lace doily was colored and decorated to be used as a hook rug on a kitchen floor. Paper cups were cut in such a way that they became modern chairs. The children were asked to bring in treasures from home that could be adapted to the project and to cut out pictures from magazines of things they liked.

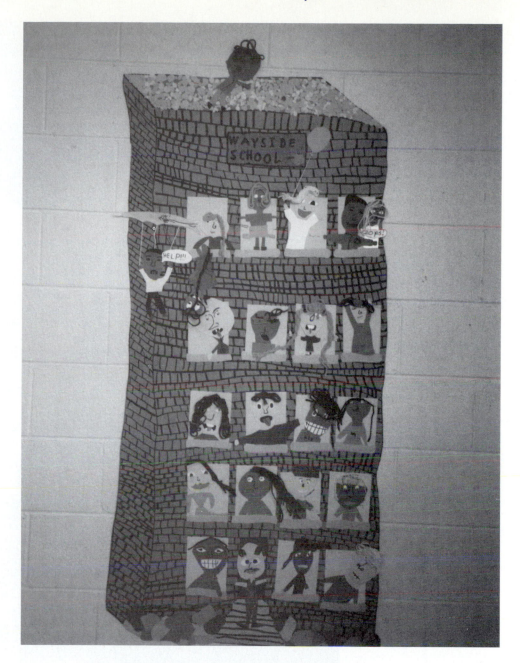

As Stoddard explained, "The imagination and creative input was inspirational. . . . I realized that these children didn't want it to end with an eighteen inch cardboard box, they wanted to create their own rooms. . . ."[30]

Cardboard cities   Large milk cartons (rinsed, painted, and decorated) and paper towel rolls make excellent high-rise buildings. The children design their own buildings, paint or draw windows and wall designs, and put the rolls and cartons together for a fine cityscape.

Lean-tos   The lean-to is a very old form of housing that is still used in many parts of the world. Children enjoy building small lean-tos for their toy animals and people, and larger lean-tos for themselves.

Small lean-tos   Gather twigs, lollipop and Popsicle sticks, strong leaf stems, cutoff match sticks, and similar materials. The children lean a group of the sticks against the side of a box, shelf, or wall to create miniature lean-to communities.

Large lean-tos Scrounge long wooden sticks or poles. Place the bottoms in pots of clay or plaster of Paris; lean the tops against a wall. Drape a sheet or blanket over the sticks, and you have a perfect lean-to for children to play in. Paint or color pictures and designs on the material.

Tents Here are just a few examples of easy and successful tents.

Tiny tents Use lean-to materials of sticks and twigs. The children create their tents in boxes or on sheets of cardboard. They tape, glue, or paste the tops of the sticks together. Some teachers use rubber bands or tie them with wool or thread. The children cut scraps of colorful material or paper to paste or tape to the outside of the sticks. Surround the tents with animals and articles to complete their Native American village.

Annelyn's tepee Annelyn Baron[31] and her kindergartners created a marvelous tepee to enrich their study of Native Americans. They tied the tops of a few broomsticks together and steadied the other ends on the floor with cement blocks (the kind many people use to support shelves for bookcases). They spread a large sheet on the floor and painted it with Nature symbols for moon, snake, tree, and water. They draped the sheet over the poles and pinned back a front flap. Four children could fit in the tepee at a time. They surrounded their tepee with a village, large cardboard pictures of trees, a make-believe red-crepe-paper fire, and a picture of a river.

The tepee and the meeting circle around the "fire" became the center of the children's play for many days. Stories, songs, original plays, and other art projects developed.

Quiet-time tent At a conference in Michigan, a first-grade teacher told about her students who noticed that there was no place in their room where someone could be alone and quietly relax for a little while. So they created one. They decorated a sheet in lovely, relaxing colors and images—"quiet ideas," one shy boy explained. They draped their sheet over a bridge table (donated by one of the parents) in a special corner of the room. Over their tent was the sign "Quiet-Time Tent."

Class tent A parachute was hung from the ceiling and walls of a classroom by hooks, tacks, masking tape, and clothespins to create an all-encompassing tent. Everything in the room was inside the tent. This excited the children and stimulated stories, drama, and games. "Let's pretend we're in a forest. . . ." "Let's be long ago. . . ."

Cornstarch igloos Hilary Talis and her young students are excellent builders of challenging structures.[32] They crushed newspapers into balls and formed a large round shape. Then they made a paste of cornstarch, salt, and water (see cornstarch box for recipe) and smeared and patted the mixture over the round structure. When it dried they had a marvelous white igloo. With colored flow pens, they drew lines for ice blocks. The igloo was large enough for one child at a time.

Egg-cup igloos Egg cartons are among the best scrounge materials. Save white egg cartons, many of which are Styrofoam, and cut out each cup. The children can make individual scenes of an Eskimo village using a box or a sheet or shirt cardboard as a base, or contribute to a large class project based on a table or a special area of the floor. Cotton puffs surrounding the egg-cup igloos make wonderful snow. Cut colored construction paper for water, trees, and animals.

Scrounge village Nancy Rosen[33] likes to take her young students for a walk to gather materials to create villages. Leaves, pebbles, twigs, bark, Popsicle sticks, pinecones, and wood scraps are among the most popular resources. These are added to the scrounge collection, which usually includes small boxes of all varieties and sizes, Styrofoam packing materials, fabric scraps, bits of jewelry, Christmas tree ornaments, discarded parts of model railroad villages, and charms from cereal boxes. The children create buildings out of tongue depressors, Popsicle sticks, twigs and bark, glued and pasted together. Some children make houses in the oldest way by piling up little stones and pebbles to build structures. Toilet-paper rolls painted the colors of tree trunks and covered with real or paper leaves make excellent trees.

Clay furniture and housewares Like a sandbox, an ample supply of clay is essential in the classroom. Young children enjoy working with clay and creating furniture for shoe box, sandbox or large box houses and rooms; jugs, mugs, pots, pans, plates, and bowls for play box kitchens; and people and animals to live in newly furnished homes. Clay is excellent material for holding down trees, street lamps, bridge supports, and other vertical structures.

What's-inside-a-house collage chart/book Use a bulletin board, a chart, or a large sheet of poster paper in the shape of a house. Follow a talk time about the things found inside houses with naming, cutting pictures out of magazines and shopping catalogues, drawing original pictures, and filling the board or paper with the images. Label as many of the items as possible.

Books like *In Our House*,[34] rich with household objects and activities, or the bilingual *My House—Mi Casa*,[35] featuring colorful and clearly defined rooms and objects printed in Spanish and English, provide ideas for words and illustrations yielding amazing visual suggestions. Note that Emberly also has two other excellent bilingual picture books, *Taking a Walk, Seeing the Park*.

Language is enriched when children have many opportunities to illustrate, label, and celebrate familiar objects and activities in English and any other languages spoken in your class.

House portraits The children enjoy drawing or painting pictures of their houses. Themes include:

The Outside of My House (apartment, mobile home, and so on)
The Inside of My House
The Shape of My House
My Room (or Where I Sleep)
The People in My House
The Colors of My House
The Feelings of My House
The Sounds of My House
What I Like Best in My House
My Favorite Places in My House
Things I Do in My House
My House in the Morning
Holidays in My House

Encourage the children to tell you about the pictures. Their real or imagined stories and experiences are valuable. Be a good, sensitive listener, not a critic. As often as possible, write and tape the stories to the pictures. Display them all.

Housing arrangements Cut out pictures of different kinds of houses or the shapes of different kinds of houses. Cut out pictures and construction paper shapes of other buildings, trees, cars, and children. Children arrange their own housing scenes by choosing pictures to paste on a sheet of white or colored paper. Be sure there is an ample supply of interesting house shapes from which to choose.

Our sheltering tree Pam Slater tells of another memorable Head Start project that started as a talk and walk time. The children discussed shelter and decided that trees provided shade, protection and safety for birds and animals, and enjoyment for people.

On a walk, the children found a tree that had been cut down. They took one of the large limbs, carried it back to their room, set it in a bucket of plaster of Paris and called it "Mr. Tree." Mr. Tree was part of the room for the whole school year. The children celebrated holidays by decorating Mr. Tree with colorful designs. They put signs on Mr. Tree to welcome people to their room. They sat under Mr. Tree and read, sang, and told stories. They changed the colors of Mr. Tree's leaves for different seasons.

What is a house without a tree?

Who's looking out the window? One of Annelyn Baron's favorite projects follows a discussion of windows, which are, as one child described, "The eyes of a house." All the children receive construction paper cut in the shapes of houses with large window areas. The children color and design them in original patterns. Now the question "Who's looking out the window?" is discussed and is turned into pictures of: "Daddy"; "My cat"; "My fish in their tank"; and "Me." The pictures are pasted to the windows of the house. It is amazing how much life one little face looking out a window adds to a scene.

Picture these unusual houses Children are intrigued by such challenging questions as

Can you draw, paint, or build:

a clown's house?	a good witch's house?
an elf's house?	a zoo keeper's house?
a giant's house?	Cinderella's house?
a space-person's house?	the Three Bears' house?
a king or queen's house?	the President's house?
a wicked witch's house?	a snail's house?

What color is it?
What's in it?
What kind of rooms, furniture, and paintings does it have?
Is there a yard?
What's in the closets?

Encourage the children to talk about their drawings. Write or have them write their comments and titles on or near their pictures.

Develop your own community On a large bulletin board or sheet of paper tacked to the wall, encourage the children to draw, paint, or paste on images describing the season and the landscape. Enjoy looking at it and talking about it for a few days. When it becomes part of the room, introduce the idea of adding animals to the picture. Enjoy that enrichment for a while as children look at and talk about squirrels, deer, rabbits, dogs, and birds scattered throughout their seasonal scene. Now it is time to develop the area by adding houses. The children draw and cut out their own houses and place them in the scene.

Before your eyes, this pastoral scene is dotted with communities. Houses mean people and people add a special dimension. Make house and street signs. Title the houses with the children's names.

An old but very loved book is *The Little House*,[36] which begins with one little house that, through the seasons, grows surrounded with other houses, fields, farms, factories, and city tumult until finally, the little house is almost lost to sight. The great-great-granddaughter of the person who built the little house hires a truck to pull it to a grassy field to begin a new life. Children enjoy creating their own picture book stories beginning with one house.

Names, addresses, and phone numbers When you think of houses, you think of addresses and telephone numbers. Young children usually learn their addresses and phone numbers quickly because they are drilled on that information by cautious family members who have vivid images of lost children.

A large, illustrated, colorful chart with the children's names, addresses, and telephone numbers is an excellent focal point of discussion and comparison, as well as a popular room decoration. Write in the addresses and telephone numbers for children who do not know their own.

Decorative house symbols If you drive through Pennsylvania Dutch Country, you will see hex signs on the barns and houses. Many people believe that hex signs are intended to ward off evil spirits, but students of the Pennsylvania Dutch culture believe that the signs celebrate those things that play important roles in the life of the people and are "chust for nice."

Show and talk about the diverse and colorful Pennsylvania Dutch signs with your children. They will notice symbols that include birds, hearts, flowers, stars, petals, and geometric shapes in bold colors. Discuss the things that are important in the children's lives and encourage them to create their own symbols and designs on construction paper circles. Display all the signs before sending them home as family gifts to be taped or tacked to doors or windows—not for superstition, "chust for nice."

Your children and their families may share customs and traditions of house decorations that inspire visual arts activities as well as contribute to appreciation and awareness of others. Always make room for the unique contributions of your classroom community.

Because your room is a safe and loving shelter, you and your children may decide on a special symbol or design that represents your class/room. They may want to design a banner, a flag, a totem, or a logo. What if you named your room and group and decided on its design? I passed a first-grade room with a huge welcome sign on its door that announced: "Come In! Welcome to the Rainbow Village of Smart Kids!" Of course, they had chosen a rainbow for their symbol.

Going home These extended experiences follow stimulating talk times/listening times as well as stories and poems highlighting different kinds of shelters. Beautifully illustrated books like Brian Wildsmith's *Animal Homes* or Jan Pienkowski's *Homes*[37] add to children's knowledge and spark ideas about creating many kinds of shelters, such as bird nests, fish tanks, squirrel holes, beehives, turtle shells, and spider webs. Arrays of painted, sculpted, constructed, or improvised shelters make excellent displays, exhibits, and backgrounds for stories and games. I saw excellent bird nests made by kindergartners from straw, string, grass, and glue, as well as spider webs woven out of thread. With pictures, toys, or clay-modeled animals and people, play a mix and match game, helping the different characters "go home."

Poems like John Ciardi's " 'I Am Home,' Said the Turtle," which begins:

"I am home," said the turtle, as it pulled in its head
And its feet, and its tail. "I am home, and in bed."[38]

encourage the children to compose their own poems about nests, dens, webs, lairs, holes, and homes.

Home! Michael Joel Rosen's *Home: Collaboration of Thirty Distinguished Authors and Illustrators of Children's Books To Aid the Homeless*[39] celebrates ordinary and extraordinary features of "home" such as closets, attics, hiding places under the back porch, elevators, even comfortable old chairs. I was excited to contribute a page remembering my favorite part of our New York City houses: stoops! Karla Kuskin's page, "Comfortable Old Chair," illustrated by Karen Barbour, begins like this:

A bird has a nest
A fox has a lair
A den is home
If you're a bear.
I have a comfortable old chair.

With your children, gather ideas for your own original book inspired by Michael's *Home*. Invite the kids to choose their own topic to write about and illustrate. Talk about how the proceeds from Michael's *Home* will help children in need, children who are homeless. Perhaps your artists and writers will find a way to contribute to an organization such as Share Our Strength or to a local shelter.

MUSIC TIMES

Songs of welcome and hospitality What is a house without guests? What better way to say "Come in, make yourself at home!" than with a song? Even the grumpiest people cannot resist being cheered by children singing them a welcome.

The old, familiar camp song "We Welcome You to _____" can easily be turned into a welcome song for your class.

We welcome you to our room
We're mighty glad you're here.
We'll set the air reverberating
With a mighty cheer.
We'll sing you in.
We'll sing you out.
For you we'll raise a mighty shout!
Hail! Hail! The gang's all here and
You're welcome to our room!

The melody of "Happy Birthday to You" was adapted for a welcome song sung by first graders to all their visitors.

Come into our room.
Come into our room.
Come into our room.
We're glad you're here.

Any familiar melody can be changed to a welcome song. Better yet, with your children, make up an original song of hospitality.

If you have named your room and chosen symbols to represent the spirit of your classroom home, songs and chants naturally celebrate those ideas. The Rainbow children had rainbow songs to welcome guests. I remember a preschool room called "The House of Happy Children" and the little song they had composed to welcome people:

If you're happy and you know it, come on in!
If you're happy and you know it, come on in!
If you're happy and you know it, come on in and play with us . . .
If you're happy and you know it, come on in!

Looking out the window "Windows are the neatest part of houses!" a first grader concluded after looking out the window. Stand at the window and see what you see. You can draw it, talk about it, pantomime it, or sing about it. Songs like "I See the Moon and the Moon Sees Me" are perfect for musical observations: "I see a car and the car sees me," or "I see the school bus and the school bus sees me." The children take turns making up a lyric about what they see out the window. Songs turn into drawings, stories, poems, games, and dances.

Taking inventory: counting songs Children enjoy counting and singing about it. After you and your children have built a community of houses, take inventory with some counting songs. The popular children's song "My Hat It Has Three Corners" was delightfully changed to an inventory song about a kindergarten room. Here are two of the verses.

> Our room it has four windows.
> Four windows has our room.
> And if it didn't have four windows.
> It wouldn't be our room!
>
> Our room it has six closets.
> Six closets has our room.
> And if it didn't have six closets.
> It wouldn't be our room!

Chairs are fun to count. A group of first graders formed a line behind their teacher and sang a kind of chug-a-lug cheer as they counted chairs. Later she told me, "It was the simplest thing and so much fun! The children didn't want to stop!"

Sounds of houses Houses are full of sounds. Each sound is a challenging musical idea for exploration and experimentation. Talk with the children about sounds heard in houses, and write their ideas on a board or chart as a guide for many activities.

The following are some house sounds suggested by young children around the country. See how easily they turn into exciting musical experiences.

People knocking on doors Some people knock once. Some have a special knock, a signal. The children enjoy using percussion instruments; tables, desks, and floors; and their bodies and voices to create knocks.

Wind chimes I have heard young children imitate the delicate sounds of wind chimes with their voices as well as with tiny bells, pipes, and flutes. Encourage a variety of musical expressions.

Telephone ringing Suggest that the children practice different voice pitches and rhythms to catch the steady, predictable "song" of the telephone. They enjoy finding instruments that express the urgency of the ringing as they work on creating sound patterns.

Teakettle whistling The telephone rings, stops, rings. The teakettle keeps whistling till someone removes it from or turns off the heat. "The teakettle doesn't stop calling you till you get it," a first grader commented. Children enjoy practicing "teakettle songs" of long, steady notes with voices and instruments.

Clocks ticking The tick-tock of clocks is so much a part of the music of houses that we hardly notice it. The song of the clock is like a pulse. Children try it many ways—tapping, snapping, clapping, clicking, and "tch-tch-tching" voice sounds. One little girl even clicked her teeth! What about a cuckoo clock?

Now that you have the idea of using body sounds, voices, musical instruments, and furniture, imagine how much fun you and your students will have turning the following house sounds into songs.

water splashing	door bells ringing	birds chirping
alarm clocks ringing	people talking, laughing,	dogs barking
music boxes playing	whispering, yelling,	cats meowing
doors banging	snoring, singing	people practicing piano,
feet walking	TV, stereo, and radio	guitar, violin, drums
dishes scraping	playing	rain hitting the window

There is no formula for developing any of the above suggestions. Here are only a few possibilities for you to consider.

Explore one idea at a time with the whole class   After experimenting and practicing, the group as a whole demonstrates a house sound set to music.

Small groups concentrate on different ideas   One group of children may want to focus on door knocking while another works on teakettle sounds. The process may be cacophonic, but the results will amaze you.

Each child chooses a sound to practice and share   Some young children are independent and self-initiating. If your children like to work on their own, encourage them to pick their own house sound and improvise musical representations to share with the class.

Sequence of house sounds   After the children have practiced individually or in small groups, decide on a sequence of sounds. Add a dynamic dimension by agreeing on one sound to repeat throughout the composition.

Symphony of house sounds   What a fabulous experience it is for children to discover the interesting combinations of sounds. Experiment with different groups of house sounds and create your own symphony. Encourage the children to take turns as conductor.

Tape the house sounds   Children enjoy hearing recordings of their voices and music. They really listen!

Make up a story featuring the sounds of a house   Your musicians will be eager to supply the sound effects and music.

City sounds, country sounds   City children like Len, the Muffin Man, know the cacophony of horns, brakes, sirens, traffic, crowds, airplanes, and subways. Country children like Vincent living on a farm in West Virginia know the good morning song of roosters, the comforting clucking of hens, the funny quack quack of ducks, and the gentlest beginning of rain tapping on the roof. With your children, talk about the sounds they hear in their homes, neighborhood, and school. Use voices, bodies, instruments, and lyrics to capture the flavor of natural and environmental sounds. Encourage city children to imagine the sounds of the country and vice versa. Stimulate imagery with brightly illustrated books, pictures, and photographs. Don't limit yourself to city and country. Mountain, desert, and coastal children have sounds and music unique to those regions. Keep your ears, doors, and windows open!

Ethnic and cultural sounds   Walk into the Alibertis's house and you'll hear the glorious voice of Pavarotti filling all the rooms. Visit the Sanchez family and you'll hear rhythmic salsa, reggae, and jazz. Spend time in Arye and Miriam's house, and you'll hear Klezmer music, hora medleys, and Middle Eastern melodies. But, wait! *There are no simple formulas.* An Irish family could love Italian opera, and an Italian family could blast Irish jigs from CDs and cassettes. Every household has its own combination of musical tastes. When children feel safe in the shelter of your classroom, they are willing to bring in the music of their families, of their homes, to share with classmates and you. We must always encourage children to develop appreciation of and respect for the rich diversity of our country. We are a nation of immigrants, a people of peoples, and the music in our households reflects the combination of cultures and subcultures that comprise our country.

My aunts have lived in the same apartment house in Manhattan for over forty-five years. When I walk up Broadway to visit them, I hear music playing from open windows, doors, stores, cars, and boom boxes along the way. On my last trip home, I noted reggae, zydeco, rap, Vietnamese, salsa, and Cambodian rhythms unfamiliar to my ears. I walked through streets of soul, jazz, New World, African, and South American melodies and percussive patterns.

Who lives in your neighborhood? What songs do they sing? What music do they play? What sounds are familiar to you and your children? What sounds are new to them?

Whistle while you work: clean-up songs   Children are never too young to begin learning responsibility for the quality of their environment. When children learn to care about their immediate surroundings, it is only a short step away from caring about their larger environment. Because of the daily practice of straightening and cleaning their room, they become aware of litter in the streets and begin to assume responsibility for their behavior.

Clean-up time can be a special time when music enlivens the process. Songs like Woody Guthrie's song "Pretty and Shiny-O" (Folkways Music), for example, help children smile and sing as they clean the room.

It is easy to improvise simple little clean-up songs to old, familiar tunes. A group of first graders conscientiously completed their jobs as they sang (to the tune of "Pickin' Up Paws Paws, Put 'Em in Your Pocket"):

> Pickin' up papers, put 'em in the basket.
> Pickin' up papers, put 'em in the basket.
> Pickin' up papers, put 'em in the basket.
> Cleanin' up our room.

A delightful singing game was improvised to the tune of "A Tisket, a Tasket." After projects that left a mess all over the floor, the children picked up and disposed of the materials while they sang the following song.

> A tisket, a tasket,
> Throw litter in the basket.
> If you miss, you don't get a kiss
> Till you throw it in the basket!

Encourage the children to compose songs for other chores, such as dusting, putting away toys, sweeping, folding clothes, and storing art supplies.

Good morning/Good night Many homes ring with songs to greet each day. In fact, some parents sing the day through from sunup to sundown. Nancy Rosen greets each day with songs like "Mr. Sun, Sun, Please Shine Down On Me" or "Good morning, good morning, good morning to you." She sings so much that one day, Benjamin, age four, sat at the table, looked at her seriously and suggested, "Mommy. Stop singing. Just drink your coffee!"

You and your children will enjoy (except possibly for Benjamin!) greeting each day together in the warm safety of your classroom home. Always write the words to the songs you sing (whether learned or improvised or composed) so they become familiar reading materials known and loved by your group. Illustrate the songs; add to them.

Lullabies are part of every known culture. At rest time or nap time, you and your children will feel the beauty and comfort of lullaby–good night songs. Add songs to stories, to games, to poetry. When children are playing house, suggest that when they put their dolls and animals to bed, they sing lullabies to lull them to sleep.

Poems and stories need music Just imagine how many ways you and your children could chant/sing/play the first four lines of the poem "Squares and Angles":

> Houses in a row, houses in a row,
> Houses in a row.
> Squares, squares, squares,
> Houses in a row.[40]

Robert Louis Stevenson's "Block City" demands that you sing it as you recite it. Read the first stanza out loud. Do you hear yourself humming along with the words? (Remember, many early poems were sung!)

> What are you able to build with your blocks?
> Castles and palaces, temples and docks.
> Rain may keep raining, and others go roam,
> But I can be happy and building at home.[41]

Aunt Nina, Goodnight[42] joins the nieces and the nephews who sleep over at Aunt Nina's house and miss their families and pets in their own homes. They finally settle down in bed with a story read to them by Aunt Nina. The only thing missing from the book is a lullaby! You and your children can easily compose a lullaby for Aunt Nina to sing to her nieces and nephews.

Music for animal shelters What about animal lullabies for baby animals sleeping in their special homes? Children eagerly compose songs and hums for birds cuddled in nests and prairie dogs dry and safe in their burrows. The children will be abuzz with songs for bees in hives and very soft and whispery for snails in their shells. Illustrate the lyrics! Display them prominently.

MOVEMENT AND PLAY TIMES

Young children's homes and schools are their primary shelters. Throughout this book, suggestions have been made to ensure that school is a shelter for children—keeping them safe, protecting them from dangers, providing feelings of warmth and companionship. For too many young children, school is the only such shelter.

Home and school are places where children learn and grow through play. In the schoolroom, they create dynamic mini-environments: stores, gas stations, spaceships, boats, and—the most popular and basic—houses or shelters. Give them a room of blocks, boxes, sand, clay, and scrounge toys and materials, and they will build as instinctively and eagerly as beavers. They build homes for puppets, pets, dolls, stuffed animals, and themselves.

Children want to be involved in the arrangement and architecture of their classroom. Encourage their participation in solving such familiar problems as how to arrange furniture, where to put toys, and how to display artwork. When young children feel they have contributed to the structure and activities of their school day, they feel important and responsible for the success of the program.

A small group of five-year-olds had created a neighborhood in an area of their room. One of the structures they were using for a house was a small stepladder. Its location was clumsy and two children not in the neighborhood game had already tripped on it. Joshua watched for a while from his racing cars across the room. He walked over quietly and in the most diplomatic voice suggested, "Can you guys move this building? Someone's gonna get hurt. I'll help you." Without a note of tension, the group rearranged their buildings. This kind of responsibility in play is not rare. Watch children in a room where their input is welcomed by responsive, encouraging teachers, and you will see them caring about each other and their environment.

Rearrange everything Tune into your group of children. If they are flexible and open about new experiences, they will enjoy occasional challenges to rearrange their room. Talk about it. Decide what should and should not be changed. Enlist the cooperation and effort of all the children as they see that out of disorganization can come a new order, one that they design, one evolving from their interests.

Name the places in your room Children enjoy giving special names to different areas of their room. After the names are chosen, you or the children (depending on their ability to print or write) make lively signs to tape or tack throughout the room. Here are a few examples from various rooms where young children live.

Book Nook	Circus Village	Picture Wall
Storytown	Costume Closet	Sticky Shelf
Block City	Paint Place	(glue and paste)
Sand Land	Art Gallery	Paper Drawer
Animal House	Artists at Work	Seed Center

"Turn yourself into . . ." walk Using the places in the room as stops along the way, encourage the children to extend the idea of a special place. For example, at the Book Nook, turn yourself into a person reading a funny book, a sad book, a scary book, and so on; at the Paint Place, turn yourself into a great artist and pantomime the way you paint or sculpt; and at the Paper Drawer, turn yourself into a large, flat sheet of paper, a crumbled paper, a blank piece of paper, a paper filled with colorful pictures, and so on.

Transportation trip around the room Instead of walking, tour the room by different modes of transportation. Between the Book Nook and the Paint Place, turn the children into a train; from the Paint Place to the Paper Drawer, airplanes.

Hands and arms tell it all After gathering ideas about houses, sit comfortably in a circle and suggest that the children use just their hands and arms to show such interesting actions as knocking on a door, ringing a doorbell, turning a doorknob, putting a key in a lock and turning it, opening and closing a door, sliding a door open and shut, picking up a telephone, turning water faucets on and off, flushing the toilet, and going upstairs and downstairs. Hands also make wonderful shapes for roofs, windows, peepholes, doors, window shades, and rooms.

Encourage children to experiment. Remember, there is no one way, or right way, to demonstrate these concepts. Let the children find their own ways. Make up songs, poems, or finger and hand plays.

What goes on in our homes and school: pantomime riddles Discuss the children's responses to the question "What are some things people do in their homes?" Then invite the children to choose an answer to pantomime. The rest of the group guesses.

Animal shelters: "What if . . . ?" The following ideas related to animal shelters provide opportunities for children to explore imaginative movement experiences. "What if you were a turtle? Let's crawl. Feel your shell. Uh-oh, something scary! Quick! Hide in your shell! OK. Safe to peek out."

"What if you were a bird? How would you build your nest? Let's fly around and pick up straw and tiny twigs with our beaks!" After this activity, you will be amazed at the awe you and the children feel about this bird behavior.

"What if you were a bear? Bears hibernate in caves or hollows. Let's lumber around, fill our tummies, and find a nice, warm cave to sleep in all winter. How's this? (Try several places.) Too small! How's this? Too low! How's this? Just right! Goodnight. See you in the spring."

Now that you have the idea of how simple these activities are, encourage the children to respond to the following. "What if you were a fish? Some fish make bubble nests! What if you were an ant? How would you build an ant colony? What if you were a bee? What would it be like to live in your hive? Buzz around and show us!"

All of these ideas correlate with songs, stories, art projects, creative writing.

People shelters: "Let's pretend . . ." After talking, reading, and looking at pictures of various kinds of human shelter, children usually play "pretend" games by themselves. If they do not, encourage them by suggesting: "Let's pretend we're Native Americans and this is our village"; "Let's pretend we're Eskimos and these are our igloos"; and "Let's pretend we're Bedouins and these are our tents." Such follow-up challenges as "What are we doing? Where do we sleep? What shall we eat? Where shall we cook? What are we saying to each other?" help develop the game if the children have not caught the momentum themselves.

Use all the crafts projects and props possible to enhance the game. Always try to expand art activities into drama, play, and creative writing experiences. Imagination needs nourishment.

Walls, rooms, floors: group shapes When children discover that shelters usually have common elements like walls, floors, windows, doors, rooms, and roofs, they are delighted to show that they understand these concepts in ways that go beyond pictures and building models. How? Through body movement.

Ask a group of children to use their fantastic bodies to show the idea of a floor. Without hesitation, most children will lie flat, arms and legs extended.

When they lie near each other, they really convey the feeling of a floor. Many children will extend the simple initial shape to demonstrate designs on the floor. "Hey, if we all touch hands and feet, we can make tiles!" "Let's make squares like my aunt's linoleum!"

Walls are excellent movement challenges. Children line up side by side, touching, and, in a matter of minutes, show a solid wall of bodies.

Their wall can easily turn into a room if they form themselves into a square pattern. Now they have an inside and an outside.

Puppets are marvelous helpers in developing ideas with children.

Puppets can say something like: "Look at this room. Wonder who lives inside. What kind of a room is it? We can't see through the walls. Let's look around and maybe we'll find a window or a door." This stimulates the children to create a door and windows in their room. Then puppets can look inside.

Create a story, a plot, an adventure, a character, and so on for the room children build with their bodies. After the game, write the story and illustrate it.

Different houses for different folks   Kings and queens live in castles; Peter Pan and the Lost Boys live in an underground hiding place; giants live in gigantic houses; and munchkins live in tiny dwellings. Turn your room into a castle, a giant's house, an underground hiding place, a munchkin village. Turn your room into a gingerbread house, a house for each of the Seven Dwarfs (Grumpy's house certainly looks different from Happy's house).

Questions celebrating the five senses are relevant to this theme. "What do we see? Hear? Smell? Taste? Touch? What do we do? How do we feel? What's in this house? How do we sleep? Eat? Relax? Work? Care for this house?" Within each of these improvised environments, encourage the children to explore, through movement, drama, dialogue, art, and music, their specific features and qualities.

Strange and mysterious shelters   Hans Christian Andersen's Thumbelina lived on a water lily floating on a pond before a friendly mole took her to his dark, cold, underground home. She finally married a tiny prince who lived in a flower. The Old Woman Who Lived in a Shoe had so many children, she didn't know what to do. For a little while, Jonah lived in the belly of a whale. Antoine de Saint Exupéry's Little Prince lived on his own little planet, scarcely larger than a mouse.

What if we lived on a leaf?
What if we lived in a house in a flower?
What if we lived in a shoe?
What if we lived in a pumpkin shell?
What if we lived in a whale?
What if we lived in a house on a star?

What if we lived in a house in the rainbow?
What if we lived in a house deep inside a birthday cake?
What if we lived in a house inside a carrot?

Draw or tape a door or window shape to a picture of any object, animal, plant, or place. This suggests that inside the original image is a house. Suppose you drew a little door on a picture of an apple. It is easy to imagine someone living inside the apple. "Let's pretend it's us! What do we see, hear, smell, taste, touch, say, do, feel? Where do we sleep, eat, work, play?" Pretend it. Play it. Move to it. Draw pictures of it. Make up poems about it. Create stories about it.

Stories and poems and playful and moving experiences The illustrations in a book or a scene from a story may be the focus of movement-drama improvisations. Perhaps only one part of a longer piece lends itself to the theme you are discussing. Do not hesitate to enrich that segment with movement and play. Enjoy the following examples of stories and poems that children have enthusiastically explored.

With young children of all ages, we have acted out parts of Ann Nolan Clark's book *In My Mother's House* as it is read.[43]

The delicately illustrated, poetic story *Where Does the Butterfly Go When It Rains?* suggests excellent ideas for movement interpretation.

And the mole
and the bee
and the bird in the tree—
Where do they go when it rains?
A mole can stay in his hole.
A bee can fly back to her hive.
I've heard
that a bird
tucks its head under its wing.
But, where does the butterfly go
when it rains?[44]

Children easily dramatize moles, bees, and butterflies, as well as birds, cats, snakes, and grasshoppers. They definitely comprehend shelter as protection from the elements.

"Skyscrapers," by Rachel Field, is a good example of how poetry can provide ideas for movement and drama. The first stanza of the poem clearly points the way for bodies, hands, and arms reaching to the sky.

Do skyscrapers ever grow tired
Of holding themselves up high?
Do they ever shiver on frosty nights
With their tops against the sky?[45]

"Oh, Joyous House" by Richard Janzen is an example of a child's poem that celebrates the warm recognition of our own house.

When I walk home from school,
I see many houses
Many houses down many streets.
They are warm, comfortable houses
But, other people's houses
I pass without much notice.
Then as I walk farther, farther
I see a house, the house.
It springs up with a jerk

That speeds my pace; I lurch forward.
Longing makes me happy, I bubble inside.
It's my house.[46]

We have "danced" this poem many ways. One of the simplest and most satisfying is to talk about how we feel about our own houses; read the poem to the children; then take a walk together, keeping a steady, casual rhythm, arms swinging, holding hands. "I see a house, the house" is the line that changes everything. We stop. We focus on an agreed-upon image or place in the room for "the house." We walk faster, faster, break into a run, and run all the way home.

Old, beloved books like *Mushroom in the Rain*[47] turns a mushroom into a shelter, with animal after animal hiding beneath it to keep dry. As it rains, the mushroom grows larger, providing protection to butterfly, mouse, sparrow, ant, and rabbit. Each character has its own choreography—let the story direct the movement and dialogue!

Children adore rabbits and are happy to hop along loyal to the dance and spirit of one of their favorite animals. *Home for a Bunny*[48] weaves a simple, lovely story of a bunny trying to find a home of his own. He asks different animals about their homes but rejects them all, continuing his search "under a rock or a log or a stone. Where would a bunny find a home?" Finally, he meets another bunny and finds his home! We play the story with all of the children moving and improvising to all of the parts and characters. They change from one to another with no trouble. Keep it loose!

Eric Carle's *A House for Hermit Crab* and Leo Leonni's *The Biggest House in the World*[49] invite children to explore the feeling and movement of snails, crabs, shells, land, and sea. After these stories, which so vividly catch the wonder of shells as shelters, children will illustrate their own shell designs with clarity and beauty.

The Rains Are Coming,[50] set in the African land of Zaire, gives the children the chance to create rain movement: run run run (around the room, in the same direction) to their village of huts, which will keep them dry.

A Yiddish folktale retold by Marilyn Hirsh titled *Could Anything Be Worse?*[51] provides the children with a lot of room for imaginative movement/music/dialogue/sound effects in a story about a frustrated man who finds his house too small, with no room for all the people and activities. The Rabbi instructs him to add animal after animal to his household, which is getting more and more crowded. Just as the man is about to really go crazy, the Rabbi instructs him to remove each animal, one at a time. By the end of the story, the man is back to the original inhabitants of the house and feels peaceful. He says to his happy family, "Our home is a paradise now!" With children around the country, I have experimented with this story, asking them to create movements for each of the characters. As the story develops, the characters multiply and the movement patterns are added, lengthening the story and movement sequence. Children have created their own sound interpretations to illustrate each character as they move. We have danced this to Herbie Hancock's jazzy rhythms and to Middle Eastern belly dance music! We always start out saying, "Once upon a time, there was a house," and demonstrating the idea of a house with our arms overhead as the roof (a natural movement for the idea of shelter).

Houses mean company and visiting Group discussions, visual arts projects, and music activities ("My cousins bring their banjos. They play in a bluegrass band.") are enriched with such excellent books as *The Doorbell Rang,*[52] in which many cousins visit a family for cookies. But no one makes cookies like Grandma! Finally, the doorbell rings, and it's Grandma with enough cookies for everyone. Children love to play the story, ringing the bell and entering the "house" in their unique styles, until everyone in the class is in and here comes Grandma (you? a parent? a colleague?) to pass out a tray of cookies.

Bigmama's[53] is the story of a family's trip by train and car to Cottondale and a visit to Bigmama and Bigpapa in their wonderful farmhouse. It has descriptive words and pictures the children easily interpret in movement. Washing (pantomiming) their hands, faces, and feet; looking for nests; sitting together around the big round table; and looking at stars are actions easy to "show." After playing the story one afternoon, a kindergartner told me, "I felt as if I really went to Cottondale!"

I Go with My Family to Grandma's[54] is a memory book about all the grandchildren in a family and how they visit their grandmother. Set in New York City at an earlier time, this simple story gives the children a chance to "go with my family on a red and yellow bicycle" or "on a golden yellow trolley" to finally meet at Grandma's. Transportation connects shelters!

Cynthia Rylant's *The Relatives Came*[55] is a bouncy story about the relatives' annual trip from Virginia. After their journey (children love moving to journeys!), they arrive for hugging, laughing, talking, eating, playing, singing, and just being together. It is a glowing story in which every child feels the warmth of hugs and fun. This is an example of enchanted education providing experiences for children on many levels. How reassuring for children, whose own homes may be cold and empty, to have times of sharing and lovingness in the warm home of school!

Folk tales and nursery rhymes to improvise   Shelter is an important theme in many folk tales and nursery rhymes. Children often know them already and are imaginative in interpreting and expanding upon them.

"The Three Little Pigs" is an excellent story for movement-drama interpretation. The children form three small groups or one large group and demonstrate the three houses with their bodies. A house made of straw falls down fairly easily; a house made of sticks is a little harder to blow down; a house made of bricks withstands the strongest gusts.

The different kinds of houses challenge the children to differentiate body shapes and movements. A house of straw does not require nearly as much muscle and body control as does a house of bricks. After a movement session, a first grader explained why he liked the house of bricks best: "I used all my muscles!" One of his classmates preferred the house of straw: "Because I like feeling floppy!" Don't forget Goldilocks and the Bears' House, with furniture and dishes of different sizes for baby, mother, and father bear!

Many nursery rhymes lend themselves to challenging movement activities. After reciting what I remembered of "There Was a Crooked Man," a class of second graders and I "played" this rhyme many ways. One of my favorites was to ask the children who wanted to be the crooked house to form their "crooked house" shape together, and to ask the children who wanted to be the man, wife, cat, and mouse to walk their crooked mile to the crooked house. After our movement session, the children drew pictures of and wrote stories about the crooked house and its crooked inhabitants.

Original hand and finger plays are so easy to invent to accompany cumulative folk poems like "This Is the House That Jack Built." How many ways can you and your students interpret this poem? With one group of children, we encouraged individual interpretation, and the variety of finger and hand plays was astonishing. With another class, we decided as a group how we would show the many ideas.

Chants, games, movement songs   Ella Jenkins revived enthusiasm and interest in the street games and chants she learned as a child in her urban neighborhood.[56] Now children around the country are singing, dancing, and prancing to "Miss Mary Mack," patty-cake songs, and jump-rope chants.

The chants, games, and movement songs children learn at home and in their neighborhoods are resources of value: language, counting, rhythms, poetry, drama, coordination, cooperation, and imagination are but a few of the skills and talents developed through such activities.

Always make it possible for children to teach classmates (and you) the words, rhythms, and movements to the material they have learned at home and in their families and friendship groups.

Time and space are our only limitations in celebrating any idea. Movement and play possibilities enhancing a theme like Where We Live are immeasurable. Be open to the interrelationships of every song, game, story, shape, image, poem, or word you enjoy.

Continue finding ways for your children to strengthen their connections to ideas and to each other in the safety of your House of Happy Kids.

CLASSROOM VISITORS AND FIELD TRIPS
Classroom Visitors

Maintenance person, plumber, carpenter, repair person, electrician People who take care of your school building are honored to be invited to visit with your children and talk about their work. The children learn to appreciate the effort and competence needed to keep shelters clean, efficient, and safe.

Turn the experience around and create a "mini-field trip" by visiting these people in their work areas as they work.

The children's thank-you notes and pictures are always appreciated by the people who "keep a building going," as one school janitor explained.

Interior decorator, architect, designer Ask these visitors to bring some of the materials and tools they use in their work of making shelters beautiful. Children like to look at illustrations and sketches.

If these people cannot come to the classroom, try to arrange for a trip to their studios or shops.

Gardener, groundskeeper, landscape architect The land around houses is almost as important as the houses themselves. People mow, plant, cut, prune, and spend a lot of time caring for their lawns and gardens. Invite to your classroom people involved in beautifying and caring for the land. Many urban areas have mini-parks (pocket parks). They will welcome the opportunity to share their work and feelings about land with young children. Correlate these visits with challenging art and writing projects.

Locksmith, quiltmaker, and others Each community has its own special resources, but chances are yours has more people and places than you realize to enhance children's understanding of "where they live." Invite some of the following people to talk with your students (or visit them to watch work in progress): locksmith, quiltmaker, cabinet maker, furniture maker, furniture salesperson, furniture repair person, lumberyard worker, window washer, house cleaner, carpet cleaner, and antique dealer. You will not only help expand awareness of important aspects of shelter, but also introduce the children to different kinds of work and careers.

Pets in the classroom Pets are very important long-term visitors because children can observe their habits, express feelings about and toward them, and learn to take responsibility for their well-being. The most popular classroom pets are turtles, fish, gerbils, birds, hamsters, guinea pigs, chicks, and rabbits. Whether your pets live in commercially manufactured Habitrails or improvised environments, each will have a special dwelling place and a special kind of care to go with that shelter. Be a collector of nests, hives, cocoons!

Family members, neighbors, and community resource people share Every household, every house is unique. Even in an urban housing project with every apartment identically designed, no two apartments look exactly alike. Children (and adults) are very interested in how and where people live. My mother, Iris Kaplan, who was born in a small village in Rumania and came to America in her teens, shares her experiences and memories with schoolchildren. They want to know everything about her house and village: "Did you sleep in beds? Did you have your own room? What kind of furniture did you have? Did you have toys?" Asking people from different cultural backgrounds to share their memories of childhood will invariably center on where they lived. Encourage your visitors to teach the children a song or game associated with their homes. Juan and Carmella tell children about the beautiful birthday parties they remember with candy-filled piñatas and funny games and songs about burros. In the Wu house, one month after the birth of their baby, the family excitedly prepares for the Chinese Red Egg party. The house is buzzing with activity, food smells, red dye, talking, and singing. Children listen in fascination to classroom visitors with homespun stories like these.

We live in our houses, our shelters, but *how* we live is as fascinating as the physical construction.

Safety first and last It is very important to give young children information about safety precautions, because many serious accidents occur at home. In many communities, police officers or fire fighters visit classes and explain home safety to the children. In other communities, the Red Cross, Safety Council, and PTAs provide volunteers to visit with children and speak about safety in the home. Encourage these speakers to keep it simple (too many rules and warnings are confusing) and interesting, to demonstrate as well as talk, and to ask the children to participate.

Perhaps you have a well-informed, articulate, fun-loving parent or friend who will come to your classroom dressed as a favorite TV, fairy tale, animal, or original character and present the information in an entertaining way. Or turn yourself into a mysterious classroom visitor! Puppets, mimes, and clowns are also outstanding in presenting important points to young children.

After the visit, bring on your own classroom puppets, stuffed animals, and dolls for a repeat home safety lesson by the children. Repetition is a must, but make it fun.

Field Trips

House being built, painted, repaired, or renovated City children have the advantage of nearby construction sites and are able to watch high-rise buildings emerge from the debris. If you live in a suburban or rural area, be alert to the housing activity in your vicinity. If a house is being built, painted, repaired, or renovated, take a field trip to the site. When children see how things happen, comprehension and appreciation are increased.

Homes of children in your class During the school year, a group of prekindergartners in Michigan visited eight classmates' homes. At each home they had a guided tour and lunch or a snack. Of course, this kind of program is not possible with all groups of children (geography, economics, and parent cooperation are factors), but if you have families who are unusually involved in the school and are willing to host a field trip, try it. Honor your hosts and hostesses with creative thank yous!

Unusual homes or housing areas in your neighborhood Do you live near a Native American reservation? Ask someone in that community if you and your children may visit and learn about the interesting kinds of shelters there. (Turn the experience around and invite someone from the community to visit your class and tell about their homes, as well as other interesting aspects of their lives.) Do you live near a historically restored area like Old Town in San Diego; Old Town in Alexandria, Virginia; German Village in Columbus, Ohio; or Market Area in Philadelphia?

Do you live near a trailer court, a harbor with houseboats, a street of old brownstones, a proud Southern mansion, rambling farmhouses and red barns, wooden shacks near a swamp, or glass and steel condominiums? Look at them. Think about them. What stories do they tell? Talk to people who live there. What would it be like to live there? Talk, ask, wonder, share ideas and feelings. The secret ingredient is respect.

Climb a hill; look down and around Florence, Italy, is known as much for its red clay rooftops as for its magnificent cathedrals. The white stone houses in Jerusalem blaze in the noonday sun. People call Jerusalem "The City of Gold" because of the way light shines on the white stone.

If there is a hill near your school, take the children for a ride and look down on your community. Children enjoy discovering the shapes, colors, patterns, and designs of buildings, rooftops, trees, bridges, streets, and parks. Take paper and crayons and sketch the scene. Use all your senses. Encourage the children to write their ideas and observations. Share the pictures and stories.

Animal preserves, parks, and museums If there is a state or national park nearby, the rangers will show the children bird nests, beaver dams, and squirrel holes. Many museums and wildlife centers have exhibits featuring animal shelters. The variety of bird nests is always intriguing. If you live near a zoo, visit the bird house to see tiny hummingbird nests and huge eagle nests. The insect house, with ant colonies and varieties of webs and cocoons, is amazing.

You may have a beekeeper in your community and not even know it. Check the Yellow Pages. A visit to a beehive is a real event. Ask the beekeeper to explain some of the remarkable rituals of the bees.

Walk around the street Walk around the neighborhood and look at different houses and buildings. As you walk, talk. What are the shapes? Do they all have the same kind of roofs? Do they have stairs? Are they on one level or more? Are the houses attached to each other? Is there cement or grass between them? What are they made of? Are the buildings old or new? Notice the doors and windows. Count the houses. When you return to the classroom, the children have a lot to write, draw, sing, move, and play about.

Other homes Children throughout the country are visiting retirement homes, rehabilitation centers, group homes, and shelters for the homeless. It's important for our kids to know that people of all ages, of every background, live in diverse arrangements. Our young children bring honesty, innocence, and openness to new situations. They immediately befriend residents of a home for the aged and share holidays and special times with them. With your children, reach out to less traditional, less familiar shelters that are home to millions of people. Exchange cards, letters, pictures, and projects. Sharing means mutuality. Sharing means caring. If enough people care, we hope and pray, someday shelters for the homeless will be part of our history and not a field trip suggestion in an early childhood text.

IT ALL COMES TOGETHER

With teachers participating in a course sponsored by National College of Education at the Kohl Center for Learning in Wilmette, Illinois, we took a few minutes to pool ideas and experiences about the theme of shelter. Playfully, we began with a take-off from *If You Give a Mouse a Cookie*. We called it: "If You Give Children Boxes." Here are excerpts from the three pages of language experience chart paper filled with immediate suggestions:

If You Give Children Boxes

They will build them into houses.
They'll decorate them inside and out with markers, fabrics, pictures, posters, mobiles, banners, curtains, shades, sculptures, and objects.
They'll use glue, scissors, chalk, tape, hammers, clips, and paints.

They'll climb through them, sit inside them, and take stuffed animals, toys, books, games, instruments, and pencils into them.

They'll make a family, work together, eat snacks, play and sleep, sing and hum, plan and hug, have birthday parties, have company, create rooms, make furniture, and write signs and letters (mail to be delivered).

They will drape them with sheets and turn them into tepees.

Add them to one another and make apartments.

Roll cars and trucks in front of them and build a street.

Turn them upside down and make houseboats.

Cut out windows and doors.

Build fireplaces to tell stories around and sing near.

Carry in clothing to try on make-believe characters like family members, neighbors, storybook friends, or personalities like those seen on *Mr. Rogers' Neighborhood* or *Sesame Street* or the street of your school.

The important thing is to give the kids some boxes and time to play . . . and time to play.[57]

NOTES ♥♥♥♥♥♥♥♥♥♥♥♥♥♥♥♥♥♥♥♥♥♥♥♥♥♥♥♥♥

1. Ann Nolan Clark, "Home," *In My Mother's House*. New York: Viking, 1972, p. 10.
2. Felicity Steele teaches at Columbus School for Girls in Columbus, Ohio.
3. Pam Slater coordinates programs for the Child Development Council of Franklin County, Inc. (Ohio).
4. A. A. Milne, "In Which a House Is Built at Pooh Corner for Eeyore," *The World of Pooh*. New York: Dutton, 1957, pp. 157–172.
5. Mattie James is Executive Director of the Child Development Council of Franklin County, Inc. (Head Start).
6. Maria Montessori, *The Child in the Family*. New York: Avon, 1970, p. 96.
7. Ibid. pp. 66–67.
8. At the time of this discussion, Judy Tough was director of the North Broadway Children's Center, Columbus.
9. Maria Montessori, *The Child in the Family*, p. 67.
10. Ann Nolan Clark, "The People," *In My Mother's House*. New York: Viking, 1972, p. 12.
11. Theodore Geisel, illustrated by Roy Mckie, *In a People House*. New York: Random House, 1972.
12. Betsy and Giulo Maestro, *Taxi*. New York: Clarion, 1989.
13. L. B. Christiansen, illustrated by Irene Trivis, *My Mother's House, My Father's House*. New York: Atheneum, 1989.
14. Robert McClung, *Animals That Build Their Houses*. Washington, DC: National Geographic Society, 1976.
15. Ezra Jack Keats, *Apt. 3*. New York: Aladdin, 1971.
   ———. *A Letter to Amy*. New York: HarperCollins, 1968.
16. Irene Smalls-Hector, illustrated by Tyrone Gester, *Irene and the Big, Fine Nickel*. Boston: Little Brown, 1991.
17. Phillipe Dupasquier, *Our House On The Hill*. New York: Viking Kestrel, 1988.
18. Mitsumasa Anno, *Anno's USA*. New York: Philomel, 1983.
19. Josephine Karavasil, *Houses and Homes Around the World*. Minneapolis: Minnesota Dillon Press, 1986.
20. Mary Ann Hoberman, illustrated by Betty Fraser, *A House Is a House for Me*. New York: Viking, 1978.

21. David McPhail, *Farm Morning*. San Diego: Harcourt Brace Jovanovich, 1985.

22. Cynthia Rylant, illustrated by Diane Goode, *When I Was Young in the Mountains*. New York: Dutton, 1982.

23. Patricia Polacco, *Mrs. Katz and Tush*. New York: Bantam, 1992.

24. Nancy White Calstrom, illustrated by Thor Wickstrom. *I'm Not Moving, Mama!* New York: Macmillan, 1990.
Yoriko Tsutsui, illustrated by Akiko Hayashi, *Anna's Secret Friend*. New York: Viking, 1987.

25. The woodcarvings of Elijah Pierce are in exhibits around the country.

26. The DepARTures program is a unique venture (adventure) bringing together docents and education staff of the Columbus Museum of Art, a poet, visual arts teachers/coordinators from the Columbus Public Schools, and classroom and art teachers with funding from foundations and corporations and highlighting children in the Columbus Public Schools. Coordinating the entire program is Carole Genshaft, educator for School Programs and Resources, Columbus Museum of Art. Jenny's poem was included in the 1993 DepARTures art and literary journal, *Splashed with Inspiration*.

27. Marjorie Bender's original sculptures of mixed media have delighted folk art lovers in exhibits throughout the country. For information on her work, she can be reached at 3062 Dale Ave., Columbus, OH 43209.

28. Shigeo Watanabe, illustrated by Yasuo Ohtomo, *I Can Build A House*. New York: Philomel, 1983.
Norma Jean Sawicki, illustrated by Toni Goffe, *The Little Red House*. New York: Lothrop, Lee, Shepard, 1989.
Gail Biggons, *Up Goes the Skyscraper*. New York: Four Winds Press, 1986.

29. Alexandra Stoddard, *A Child's Place*. New York: Doubleday, 1978, p. 67.

30. Ibid. p. 68.

31. Annelyn Baron teaches at the Leo Yassenoff Jewish Center's Early Childhood Program in Columbus, Ohio.

32. Hilary Talis directs the early childhood program for Children's Hospital in Columbus.

33. Nancy Rosen's creative work with children is well known around Columbus.

34. Anne Rockwell, *In Our House*. New York: Crowell, 1985.

35. Rebecca Emberly, *My House—Mi Casa*. Boston: Little, Brown, 1990.

36. Virginia Lee Burton, *The Little House*. Boston: Houghton Mifflin, 1969.

37. Brian Wildsmith, *Animal Homes*. Oxford University, 1980.
Jan Pienkowski, *Homes*. New York: Julian Messner, 1979.

38. John Ciardi, illustrated by Merle Nacht, " 'I Am Home,' Said the Turtle" from *Doodlesoup*. Boston: Houghton Mifflin, 1985, p. 15.

39. Michael Joel Rosen, *Home: A Collaboration of Thirty Distinguished Authors and Illustrators of Children's Books to Aid the Homeless*. New York: Charlotte Zolotow Books, HarperCollins, 1992. The proceeds from this book are contributed to Share Our Strength, 1511 K Street NW, Suite 600, Washington, DC 20005. (202) 393–2925.

40. Alfonsina Storni (translated from Spanish by Seymour Resnick), "Squares and Angles" from *On City Streets—An Anthology of Poetry*, edited by Nancy Larrick, photos by David Sagarin. New York: Bantam-Pathfinder, 1969, p. 100.

41. Robert Louis Stevenson, "Block City," *A Child's Garden of Verses*. La Jolla, CA: Green Tiger Press, 1975, p. 67.

42. Franz Brandenberg, illustrated by Aliki, *Aunt Nina, Goodnight*. New York: Greenwillow, 1989.

43. Ann Nolan Clark, *In My Mother's House*. New York: Viking, 1972.

44. May Garelick, *Where Does the Butterfly Go When It Rains?* New York: Scholastic, 1972.

45. Rachel Field, "Skyscrapers," *Arrow Book of Poetry*. Edited by Ann McGovern. New York: Scholastic, 1965, p. 65.

46. Richard Janzen, "Oh, Joyous House," *Miracles*. Edited by Richard Lewis. New York: Bantam, 1977, p. 144.

47. Mirra Ginsburg, illustrated by Jose Aruego and Ariane Dewey, *Mushroom in the Rain*. New York: Macmillan, 1974.

48. Margaret Wise Brown, illustrated by Garth William, *Home for a Bunny*. New York: Golden, renewed 1984.

49. Eric Carle, *A House for Hermit Crab*. Saxonville, MA: Picture Books Studio, 1987.
Leo Lionni, *The Biggest House in the World*. New York: Pantheon, 1989.

50. Sanna Stanley, *The Rains Are Coming*. New York: Greenwillow, 1993.

51. Marilyn Hirsh, *Could Anything Be Worse?* New York: Holiday House, 1974.

52. Pat Hutchins, *The Doorbell Rang*. New York: Greenwillow, 1986.

53. Donald Crews, *Bigmama's*. New York: Greenwillow, 1991.

54. Riki Levinson, illustrated by Diane Goode, *I Go with My Family to Grandma's*. New York: Dutton, 1986.

55. Cynthia Rylant, illustrated by Steven Gammell, *The Relatives Came*. New York: Bradbury, 1985.

56. Ella Jenkins is one of America's most beloved music makers for early childhood education. Her work is known around the world.

57. The teachers who participated in this brainstorming session at the Kohl Center for Learning teach in schools throughout the Chicago area: Virginia Sharwell, Rosalie Kaufman, Joan Spears, Karen Sullivan, Cheryl Gopenberg, Mary Ann Egan, Eleanor (Lou) Hoover, Lisa Feltman, Faresa Hussain, Shpresa Jusufi, Tamara Walsh, Mary Rosic, Diane Sharp, and Jim Parker.

BOOKS FROM MY KNAPSACK FOR CHILDREN ♥ ♥

Bial, Raymond. *Frontier Home*. Photographs by Raymond Bial. Boston: Houghton Mifflin, 1993.

Buchanan, Ken. *This House Is Made of Mud*. Illustrated by Libba Tracy. Flagstaff, AZ: Northland, 1991.

Burton, Virginia Lee. *The Little House*. Boston: Houghton Mifflin, 1942.

Cumeo, Mary Louise. *How to Grow a Picket Fence*. Illustrated by Nadine Burnard. Westcott, NY: HarperCollins, 1993.

Dorros, Arthur. *This is My House*. New York: Scholastic, 1992.

Dtagonwagon, Crescent. *Home Place*. Illustrated by Jerry Pinkney. New York: Macmillan, 1990.

Emberley, Rebecca. *My House/Mi Casa*. New York: Little, Brown, 1991.

Goodall, John. *Great Days of a Country House*. Illustrated by John Goodall. New York: McElderry Books, 1992.

Grifalconi, Ann. *The Village of Round and Square Houses*. Illustrated by Ann Grifalconi. Boston: Little, Brown, 1986.

Hoberman, Mary. *A House Is a House for Me*. Illustrated by Betty Fraser. New York: Viking, 1978.

Kahlman, Bobbie. *A Colonial Town—Williamsburg*. New York: Crabtree, 1992.

———. *The Kitchen*. New York: Crabtree, 1992.

———. *Visiting a Village*. New York: Crabtree, 1992.

Komaiko, Leah. *My Perfect Neighborhood*. Illustrated by Barbara Westman. New York: HarperCollins, 1990.

Maynard, Joyce. *New House*. Illustrated by Steve Bethel. San Diego: Harcourt Brace Jovanovich, 1987.

McDonald, Megan. *Is This a House for Hermit Crab?* Illustrated by S. D. Schindler. New York: Orchard, 1990.

Peet, Bill. *Farewell to Shady Glade*. Illustrated by Bill Peet. Boston: Houghton Mifflin, 1969.

Rudstrom, Lennart. *A Home*. Illustrated by Carl Larsson. New York: Putnam, 1974.

Sendak, Maurice. *We Are All in the Dumps with Jack and Guy*. Illustrated by Maurice Sendak. New York: HarperCollins, 1993.

Shemie, Bonnie. *Houses of Hide and Earth—The Plains Indians*. Illustrated by Bonnie Shemie. Pittsburgh: Tundra, 1993.

———. *Houses of Wood—Native Dwellings, the Northwest Coast*. Illustrated by Bonnie Shemie. Pittsburgh: Tundra, 1993.

Stow, Jenny. *The House That Jack Built*. Illustrated by Jenny Stow. New York: Dial, 1992.

Van Rynbach, Iris. *Everything from a Nail to a Coffin*. Illustrated by Iris Van Rynbach. New York: Watts, 1991.

Yue, Charlotte and David. *The Igloo*. Illustrated by Charlotte and David Yue. Boston: Houghton Mifflin, 1988.

BOOKS FROM MY KNAPSACK FOR TEACHERS ❤ ❤

Berck, Judith. *No Place to Be—Voices of the Homeless Children*. Boston: Houghton Mifflin, 1992.

Rosen, Michael Joel, ed. *Home: A Collaboration of Thirty Distinguished Author and Illustrators*. New York: HarperCollins, 1992.

Chapter

9

The Clothes We Wear

We dress
to keep dry
to stay warm
to keep cool
to be cool
for work
for school
for sleep
for dinner
for sport
just to have pockets
to please our mothers

to imitate
to disguise
to fantasize
for support
for protection
to attract attention
for self-expression
as a sign of class
to be one of the guys
to mask our identity
for formal occasions

in style
up
down
to kill
to look thinner
to celebrate mass
to undress
for battle
for partying
for comfort
for kicks[1]

THE BASICS

Hanging out with the kids is always an education. On this hot, end-of-August day, Aleah Allen (four), Tamara Billups (six), Nick Wilbat (six and a half), Josh Appelbaum (six), and Anna Appelbaum (nine) talked about one of their favorite topics—clothing. Eavesdrop on the conversations for a moment:

> *"What kinds of clothes are your favorites?"*
>
> **Aleah**: *"Black and green and yellow and blue clothes."*
>
> **Tamara**: *"Dresses—long-sleeve purple dresses."*
>
> **Nick**: *"Jurassic Park."*
>
> **Josh**: *"Wayne's World and Terminator T-shirts."*
>
> **Anna**: *"Blouses with ruffles in plain, you know, solid colors."*
>
> *"What other kinds of clothes do you especially like?"*
>
> **Josh**: *"Tie-dye stuff, boxer shorts, long denim jeans. White."*
>
> **Aleah**: *"African clothes. White dress-up clothes for church."*
>
> **Anna**: *"I like stripes and colorful solid colors."*
>
> **Tamara**: *"Black pants and stuff with stars and moons."*
>
> **Nick**: *"Dinosaur designs on everything."*

Take a picture of these five American children in this last decade of the twentieth century. Note Aleah's beaded, braided African-inspired hairstyle that is so popular nowadays. Even people with blond hair are wearing their hair in cornrows, extensions, and finger curls. Note Nick's sandals and loose cotton shorts, Josh's white denim jeans and Disney World T-shirt. Catch Anna's colorful sneakers, fluffy bow in her hair, and friendship bracelets. Tamara's sleeveless pinafore matches her little necklace. Ask the children who chooses their clothes on most days, and they'll answer in one voice, "We do!"

Any one of the items mentioned above—clothing, jewelry, and accessories—is a key that opens you to a journey, a fascinating journey through time and place, to the beginning of human history.

Ever since the snake dangled that apple in front of Eve, people have been devoted to thinking up clever variations of the fig leaf. The challenge of clothing has stimulated human inventiveness in countless ways. Throughout history, people have covered themselves with skins, furs, feathers, shells, grasses, eaves, wood, jewels, and metals. They have hidden their heads behind veils, scarves, hoods, and helmets; draped themselves in capes; strapped themselves into girdles, belts, and corsets; and stuffed their feet into pointy-toed, spike-heeled, platformed shoes, or thigh-high boots.

Clothes reflect geography, history, religion, socioeconomic background, cultural heritage, and individual personality. They identify and describe us; they express our beliefs, allegiances, occupations, and status. The Amish, for example, wear no buttons because buttons are associated with the uniforms of Prussian soldiers, who oppressed them. Muslim women wear veils and robes as a sign of modesty. Orthodox Jews always cover their heads in deference to God. In ancient Rome, togas were worn by free male citizens. The higher the status, wealth, and position, the bulkier, longer, and larger the toga. The colors and designs on togas indicated the rank of the wearers. Purple was the color of royalty. In China, the color of royalty was yellow. Only members of the royal family were permitted to wear yellow. Ancient African hunters wore the skins of their prized hunted animals to demonstrate their courage and skills and to honor the spirits of the animals. In many Native American tribes, eagle feathers are sacred objects, worn proudly in headdresses. Mussolini's Fascist soldiers were called Brownshirts. A group of tough American soldiers are known worldwide as the Green Berets. We all know one of the warning shouts of the American Revolution, "The Redcoats are coming!"

Every society has its fashion and customs, sometimes set by tradition, other times influenced by a famous person or by other cultures. Because Charles II of England liked elaborate clothes trimmed with laces, ribbons, and ruffles, seventeenth-century English aristocrats followed in his red high-heeled footsteps. Even Anna Appelbaum, an American nine-year-old, loves ruffled blouses! Amelia Bloomer, a women's rights champion at the turn of the century, wore baggy pants. It took fifty years to catch on, but her "bloomers" revolutionized the world of clothing. In her fascinating book, *From Top Hats to Baseball Caps, from Bustles to Blue Jeans: Why We Dress the Way We Do,* Lila Pearl's delightful chapter, "Who Wears the Pants?"[2] will take you on a scenic route through clothing history, beginning with the rejection of pants by ancient Greeks as they snubbed their noses at the Scythians, who galloped out of Asia wearing boots, hoods, and tight leather riding pants, to Bloomer and her comfortable, practical trousers. Pearl writes:

> Today women dress with more variety in trousers alone than Amelia Bloomer could have imagined in her wildest dreams. They wear long pants in forms that range from athletic warm-up suits to the dressiest of evening outfits, and short pants in versions as brief as short shorts and bikini-style bathing suits.
>
> As for the ancient Romans, they would certainly be shocked if they could see the men and women of today. It was unthinkable to them that the loosely draped robes worn by both sexes in their day would ever be discarded in favor of fitted garments, and especially "barbarian" trousers![3]

We can imagine our earliest ancestors of fifty thousand years ago in the warm climates of Africa. In those places people didn't need to wear clothing for protection against the cold. But they did wear clothing for status, for demonstrating bravery, or for magical reasons. Archeologists have found numerous amulets, ornaments, bits of jewels, and other decorative body adornments in the museum of the earth. If you think our African ancestors were "primitive" in the wearing of necklaces made of bone, ivory, claws, feathers, or shells to honor sacred powers or to ward off evil powers, check yourself right now. Are *you* wearing a good-luck charm, amulet, or religious symbol? Has it brought you luck or protection?

Thousands of years of tying, knotting, and "pinning" materials together went by before an ingenious ancestor invented sewing needles made out of ivory, bone, or antler. Archeologists date that amazing device about 40,000 years. Skip millenniums to the mid-1700s, when James Hargreaves invented the spinning machine and Edmund Cartwright invented the power loom. Along came Singer's wonderful sewing machine, revolutionizing the making of clothes. Today, clothing is one of the major industries of the world, and the United States is one of the leading manufacturers and style-setters.

Probably no individual has had more influence on clothing than San Francisco tailor Levi Strauss, who, in the 1850s, used canvas tent cloth to make work pants for farmers, miners, and cowhands. He soon softened the canvas with less stiff denim and dyed the material blue. Now, at the end of the twentieth century, blue jeans of every style, from overalls to dress-up, are probably the most universally worn and loved article of clothing around the world.

I began teaching in the Albany, New York, area in 1956. If I had eyes to see into the future, I would have been reassured to know that in the '90s, teachers, parents, kids—everyone would wear slacks and jeans to school, as well as denim skirts, headbands, bandanas, and wraparounds. Male teachers and administrators wear T-shirts, jeans, and earrings. My friend Marvinia Bosley, the principal of Johnson Park Middle School in Columbus, Ohio, wears lively, colorful African dashikis, robes, and tunics to school. I wear my jeans and T-shirts. My T-shirts blaze messages about peace, the environment, and education. They are reading experiences in themselves!

Many of our articles of clothing are image- and language-rich. They promote causes, events, places, and personalities. Just as our earliest ancestors crossing the African and Middle Eastern plains and deserts painted images of their deities, sacred forces, animals, and natural phenomena on their walls, animal skins, belts, capes, and tunics, so Nick and Josh want dinosaurs, Mickey Mouse, and Terminator designs on their clothes. Anna wants stripes. Tamara wants stars and moons on solid black. We found Ohio State University T-shirts in the markets of Florence, Venice, and Rome, in the Shuk in Jerusalem, and in the markets of Taipei. Under their traditional embroidered robes, Bedouin men and women wore American tennis shoes in the markets of Beersheba. When our friends visited the Soviet Union fifteen years ago, the universal request by Russian families was, "Bring blue jeans!" America's spirit of informality, comfort, irreverence, individuality, and playfulness has stamped clothing fashion around the globe.

And now, surrounded by books and materials on clothing, I look through reference materials like a National Costume book, *Japan,* and the Children of the World series edition of *Cuba.*[4] Here we see "typical" children of Japan and Cuba, their activities, and their clothing. I think to myself: Could American children be represented by a few images of fashion? Which child would represent America? Would it be the newborn baby in Wyoming who already has two pairs of Western boots in infant sizes to go with his Western outfits? The teenager in front of me on the movie line wearing a dashiki shirt, harem pants, a kente kufi cap, and an African medallion of red, black, and green? Malia in her flowing, flowered muumuu and thongs? Carlos in a bright red ruffled shirt and jet black pants, dancing in the Cinco de Mayo celebration in San Diego? Holly, wearing a fringed leather skirt with beaded designs sewn by her grandmother to match her leather moccasins as she walks the Shinnecock reservation in South Hampton, New York? I don't think one book in a series could represent American children in their clothing. We need a series of our own! Perhaps the cover children should be Nick in his dinosaur T-shirt, Josh in boxer shorts with tie-dyed "stuff," Anna in her ruffled blouse, Tamara wearing black pants and "stuff with stars and moons," and Aleah in her "white dress-up clothes for church."

And what about you? Lila Pearl talks about clothing as a "sign language." She challenges us to think about such questions as: "Is your personality upbeat or subdued? Are your tastes adventurous or rather quiet? Are you neat or sloppy? Do you dress to please yourself, to impress others, or to attract the opposite sex? Even the mood that you are in on a particular day can express itself in the clothes you are wearing. What, in fact, do you think that the clothes you are wearing at this very moment may be signalling to others about you?"[5]

Your students will notice every thread of every garment you wear. What is the story you are telling?

I was met at the airport by the teacher responsible for driving me to the conference. There was something unusual about this delightful person. After a few minutes (it takes me a while!) I figured it out. She was wearing barrettes with cows on them, a cow necklace, a blouse with cow designs, a cow belt, a skirt with cow shapes, and ankle socks with cow images.

I asked her, "What's with the cows?"

She sweetly answered, "I'm a theme dresser!"

What's your theme?

Recall your own childhood and try to remember the clothes you loved, what they looked like, and why they meant something to you. Our clothes put us in touch with special people, places, events, and times of our lives. They are part of our memories and experiences. We need clothes for protection against the elements, but we seem to have a universal need to decorate ourselves, to express our

individuality, and to link ourselves with others through the mysterious power of clothing. As you enjoy sharing the ideas in this guide, see how naturally the theme of clothing connects to every thread of the curriculum. Keep stitching!

DISCOVERY TIMES/WONDER TIMES

- Clothes protect us from cold, heat, rain, snow, wind, and hail.
- We wear different clothes in different seasons and for different reasons.
- People like to decorate their clothing with bright colors, designs, jewels, feathers, and other interesting materials.
- Clothes are made by people—sometimes by hand, other times by machines.
- Most raw material for clothing (cotton, flax, silk, wool, fur) comes from plants and animals.
- We take care of our clothing by cleaning and laundering it, hanging, and folding it.
- Putting on clothes often involves buttoning, zipping, tying, and snapping. If we practice these actions, we will learn how to do them. It is fun to practice.
- People from different countries, regions, cultures, occupations, religions, and hobbies often wear special types of clothing.
- Learning about clothing of all kinds helps us increase our understanding of our inventive human family.
- Even if someone's clothing seems strange to us, it is important to that person. We should be respectful toward that person and toward all people who look and dress differently from us.

SUGGESTED VOCABULARY

clothing	tennis shoes	unbutton	sandals
clothes	earrings	snap	clogs
dress	cap	wash	galoshes
outfit	denim	Velcro	rubbers
shirt	clean	used	gloves
blouse	laundry	new	mittens
jacket	scarf	sweater	hat
coat	socks	slacks	sewing machine
pants	stockings	jeans	tight
shorts	tights	dungarees	wool
sleeves	leotard	overalls	price
money	costume	snowpants	department store
shoe store	mask	gym shorts	shoelaces
necklace	western hat	dressmaker	play clothes
bracelet	zipper	long	party clothes
jogging shorts	pocket	short	factory
T-shirt	belt	kimono	big
skirt	dress-up clothes	daishiki	small
pajamas	plaid	skullcap	unsnap
pj's	cotton	shawl	tie
bathrobe	sweatshirt	sombrero	untie
flannel	dry cleaner	embroidery	fold
dirty	put on	stripes	put away
store	take off	solid	dry
shoes	iron	prints	shop
slippers	zip	loose	needle
boots	button	sneakers	thread

Young children will amaze you with their extensive vocabulary of clothing. They know not only the generic names of items, such as pants, dungarees, and socks, but also the brand names (thanks to television commercials). Their ability to add descriptive words, such as colors, types, and sizes, is impressive. In addition to the physical description and definition of their clothing, young children often tell the circumstances as well. "This shirt my Aunt Barbara brought when we saw her at the Columbus International Airport from New Jersey," five-year-old Billy explained as he showed off his new shirt. "My Nana Rosa sent my blue pants with this Mickey Mouse belt and look at how many pockets for my birthday present," Pietro told his fellow kindergartners.

Display words identifying pictures and parts of clothing all around your room. The children soon associate the written words with their meanings. Their sight vocabulary increases daily, painlessly and joyfully.

I visited a kindergarten room one stormy winter day and over each clothing hook was a card bearing the child's name and the clothes worn. For example:

Anthony's	Jean's	Keneisha's	Kristi's	Neal's
coat	jacket	snowsuit	jacket	coat

The teacher laughingly told me that one of the children had two winter outfits and when he wore his jacket, he asked the teacher if he could change the label from "coat" to "jacket." What better way to enrich language development than the magic of creative teaching?

SOME STARTERS

Start with weather Rainy days mean raincoats, rubbers, and umbrellas. Snowy days mean boots, mittens, hats, scarves, snowpants, and jackets. Take advantage of special weather to introduce the main reason for clothing—protection against the elements.

Start with a class poll Most children respond immediately and with enthusiasm to questions such as: "What is your favorite thing to wear?" or "Why do we need clothes?" Brighten large chart paper with the names of the children, their answers, and, if space permits, illustrations. For example, next to Tony's name is his answer to what are his favorite kinds of clothing—"tennis shoes and baseball caps." In the column next to the answers is room for Tony to color in or paste cut-out illustrations of tennis shoes and baseball caps. You'll gather enough material to continue connecting ideas for weeks and weeks!

Start with a room full of resource books about clothing Children love to look at colorful photos or illustrations of clothing. When I was sitting in the library looking through many books about clothing, I was not surprised to be joined by a few children who wanted to look at the pictures of clothes with me. Books like the Eyewitness Books series on *Costume* or the Timelines book, *Clothes For Work, Play and Display*[6] practically mesmerized the kids. As we turned the colorful, illustration-packed pages, the children had many comments. As we looked at pictures of people in clothing in medieval times, one of the children remarked, "Oh, look, fairy-tale clothes!"

One child looking at one page in one of those excellent resource books could launch your whole celebration!

Even a coloring book like *Everyday Dress of the American Revolution*[7] borrowed from an older sibling had the kindergartners poring over the illustrations of characters from Revolutionary times and their clothing. The hands-down favorites of the children were the Quaker couple and the Cherokee chief.

The children can't help but notice the colorful clothing in *People, People Everywhere.*[8] Even the cover is draped with swinging clotheslines that brighten the city buildings.

Start with a doll from a specific background Dolls come in every shape, size, style, sex, race, and age. They represent all occupations, hobbies, and cultures. What is even better than having a doll? Why, dressing a doll, of course, and discussing what the clothes mean, what they express. Flore is a beautiful doll who wears a black lace mantilla, high-heeled dancing shoes, and a wide flamenco skirt of floral colors. Flore intrigues the children. They want to know all about the flamenco dances she does and where she comes from. Stopping in the nurse's room to make a phone call during a break from my Artist-in-the-School residency, I noticed two "medical" dolls, one with a Red Cross insignia, that probably were used to demonstrate safety and health rules to the children. What a great opportunity to launch a study of clothing as well! The clothes on these dolls tell us the kind of work they do. What other jobs require special kinds of clothes? The air in your room will buzz with answers and the chalkboard will fill with suggestions.

Start with a storybook or poem There are many storybooks with clothing as a central subject that are practically guaranteed to start you off. A delightful old favorite like *No Roses For Harry!*[9] introduces a silly woolen sweater with roses on it, a present for Harry, the dog, from Grandma. Harry hates the sweater and for the rest of the story tries to lose it. Finally, a bird unravels the wool in the sweater and flies away. The children clap in surprise when they discover that Harry's sweater has been transformed into a bird's nest! Grandma then sends Harry a sweater that he likes. I'm sure you'll have no trouble imagining the children's discussions and art projects designing their own sweaters for Harry. Pick up the threads!

A richly illustrated newer book like *Red Dancing Shoes*[10] is about another Grandma who brings a present. This time she brings everyone presents like a tie for Daddy and a yellow blouse for Mama. Best of all, she brings a pair of red dancing shoes to the little girl of this African-American family. Children love the story. They are ready to talk, move, sing, draw, and write about magical shoes—shoes that make them run fast, shoes that help them jump high, dancing shoes. Put those shoes on and fly!

You don't need to find a book *about* clothing as the subject to start you off on a clothing theme! Unless a story takes place in a nudist colony, the characters in any story will wear clothing! Be aware of all the possibilities waiting in any given word, on any page, in any corner of a picture. For example, in Ann Grifalconi's books like *Darkness and the Butterfly* and *Osa's Pride,*[11] young readers cannot help but notice the soft, simple, beautifully colored tunics and robes worn by Osa and her family and friends in her African village. There's no need for snowsuits and boots in warm, African climates. In Steven Kellogg's exciting retelling of *Pecos Bill,*[12] every page pulses with characters dressed in rough-and-tumble rugged western clothing. Arnold Adoff's *Flamboyan*[13] invites you to a Caribbean island and surrounds you with the sun, sea, birds, and clouds. Oh, you definitely will notice the bright, lively, easy-to-move-in clothes of Flamboyan's family and neighbors. The children will want to fill their own sketchbooks and canvases with original designs for Caribbean clothes.

Note the exquisite illustrations of Native American people dressed in modern traditional clothing in the haunting story, *Knots on a Counting Rope*[14] or the delicately illustrated characters in thong sandals and kimonos on every page of Japan's most beloved folktale, *The Crane Maiden.*[15]

Poems like "The Mitten Song"[16] that you say and sing and demonstrate are examples of poems *about* articles of clothing. Any weather poem, like "Snow,"[17] about "playing and straying and staying" in the snow will generate creative energy about clothes to wear in the snow as compared to clothes to wear in summer. And you're on your way!

Start with a pantomime of dressing Challenge the children to guess what you are doing. Give them clues such as: "We do it every day, right after we get up in the morning. You did it this morning!" When they have guessed, ask them to join you in a group pantomime. Elaborate with, "What are you putting on? How is the weather outside? Do you need help with your zipper?"

Start with a puppet who does not know what to wear Any classroom puppet will do to involve the children in a delightful advice-giving session on clothing. If you want to evoke terrific responses, make your puppet the absent-minded type who does not realize shoes go on feet, gloves on hands, hats on heads. The children will eagerly correct their puppet friend and feel proud of their knowledge.

Start with an item of clothing The spotlight is on sweaters or mittens or whichever item you find the most fun to discuss. Use a real article of clothing or a photograph or cutout. Tape it or tack it to a bulletin board in a central place so the children can gather round and focus their attention on it.

Start with a clothing hook Play a game: "What is on the clothing hook?" Hang different articles of clothing on a hook and ask the children to guess each one. When the game has run its course, talk about the kinds of clothing we wear and why. This will hook the children on the topic.

Start with a celebration Everyone enjoys celebrations, and what better idea to celebrate than everyone's clothing? Here is how one kindergarten teacher started a monthlong series of experiences centered around clothing: "Let's have a cheer for Michael's Yankees T-shirt!" "Let's hear it for Joey's long sleeves!" "Everyone clap hands for Brett's brown belt!"

No one is left out. Everyone is wearing something that becomes special because a fun-loving teacher makes it so. Follow the celebration with a discussion highlighting questions, answers, and observations that will provide material for the weeks to come.

Remember: Stories, poems, pictures, songs, chants, riddles, cheers, classroom visitors—even one word—are all excellent starting activities. Most beginning activities from other guides in this book can be adapted to clothing. Better still, make up a starting activity of your own.

TALK TIMES/LISTENING TIMES

Unless they feel threatened or anxious, young children are eager to talk about things they know about. Clothing is one of their favorite topics. In safe, loving environments with no put-downs or teasing, boys and girls will enrich your curriculum with their suggestions and ideas. I have read that toddlers and young children laugh as often as fifteen times an hour. With that item in mind, let's begin with laughter.

Kidding around What if animals wore clothes? What kinds of clothing would fish wear? Birds? Alligators? Books like *Animals Should Definitely Not Wear Clothing*[18] add a spark to an imaginative, fun-filled session. The children will want to illustrate and demonstrate their ideas. What if the grown-ups were trying to get dressed to go out and the children were so full of mischief that the adults could barely get their clothes on all in one piece? Putting on clothes takes a lot of coordination and comprehension. Anyone could get mixed up putting on clothes! Did that ever happen to you? *All in One Piece*[19] is an example of another silly story good for loosening up talk times and good for playful creativity.

I love to kid around with kids! Even though today's popular style is wearing baseball caps backwards, mixing up clothing is funny to the children. The simple, silly sentence like, "Now, let's see, where do these gloves go, on my feet?" will have the children laughing and clarifying!

Wonder questions In addition to short-answer, right-wrong kinds of questions like "What part of our bodies wear shoes?" (these are important, necessary kinds of questions, but don't limit them to close-ended inquiries) children love to play with ideas responding to such questions as:

> What *are* clothes, anyway?
> Where do clothes come from?
> How do we get clothes?
> Why do we wear so many clothes?
> Did people always wear clothes?
> Can we tell what some people do by their special clothes?
> Can babies put on their own clothes?
> How do clothes make us know we grow?

Here are a few children's comments and explanations collected through the years. Many of their follow-up questions and ideas formed the basis for activities and further discussions in the weeks following the initial group talk time.

> Clothes come from moms. (Amy, age 5)
> We get clothes from our closets and house. (Randy, age 7)
> Grandmas and grandpas give us clothes. (Petie, age 4)
> We need clothes or all our skin will show. (Terry, age 5)
> Clothes are the stuff we put on after breakfast. (Nancy, age 4)
> My socks grow. They stretch bigger. (Neal, age 4)
> Babies can't put on their diapers. They'll stick theirselves. (Judy, age 4)
> Spacemen need special flying clothes. (Todd, age 5)
> I know I growed 'cause my shoes don't fit my big boy feet!
>   (Timmy, age 4)
> I think clothes got started by the underwear. (Heather, age 8)
> Clothes are if you have to get dressed up when you don't want to.
>   (Mikey, age 5)
> Clothes are to keep you warm when it's cold; otherwise, they're for fun!
>   (Howie, age 6)

As often as possible, gather the children's ideas and write them (or have the children write them) on large charts featuring their names, the questions, and their answers. Be sure every child's name is included on every chart!

What will you take on a trip? You can use a real or imaginary suitcase. With the children and yourself in a circle, talk together about a wonderful trip—"We'll need lots of clothes!" Go around the circle, giving every child a turn to add an item of clothing to your suitcase. Encourage the children to be very good listeners so they remember everyone's contribution! Review as you go along. "Darren's taking

his Chicago Bears sweatshirt. Vanessa's taking her ballet shoes. Pedro's taking his jeans with the zipper pockets." By the time the game is "over," your suitcase will be bulging with clothing and ideas for illustrations, songs, pantomimes, and charts. Change the idea with the season and weather. If you go to Hawaii your suitcase will certainly be filled with different clothing than for a trip to Alaska. You'll be surprised at how many articles of clothing the children remember!

Riddle talk Children love guessing games. Success is built in when clothing is the topic of the guesses. With real articles, pictures, or pantomime, ask the children to guess the kinds of clothing described. Encourage full participation. I remember a grinning first grader who asked the kids to guess: "You can wear me on anything, even your face, even your knees. I'm plain and designs and big and small." His classmates finally gave up after tossing around many ideas. The class exploded in laughter when he told them, "A Band-Aid!"

Among the best books I've seen highlighting clothing and guessing/talking/discussing/identifying are Margaret Miller's *Whose Shoe?* and *Whose Hat?*[20] and Ron

Roy's *Whose Hat Is That?* and *Whose Shoes Are These?*[21] The excellent photographs and relevant styles and text in all four of these books will encourage conversation and help children connect clothing to occupations, seasons, occasions, and hobbies. These kinds of books help reinforce nonsexist attitudes: boys and girls wear, for example, construction workers' hard hats. *Encourage children to think in non-stereotyped ways.* Clothing items help!

Sharing significant clothing In rooms where children want to share because the air they breathe is sweetened with trust, acceptance, and respect, they will often bring in "gifts" that have deeper meanings. The locket Tamicka wears came to her from Aunt Quinetta. It's special! The warm sweater Kendra wears in the winter is the sweater her mom wore when she was a little girl. It's Kendra's "best" sweater. A tiny piece of lace passed through the generations in the book *From Me to You*[22] generates lively talk times/listening times as children share their own experiences. Patricia Polacco's touching story, *The Keeping Quilt*,[23] tells the story of how her Great-gramma Anna came to America "wearing the same thick overcoat and big boots" she had worn for farm work. With worn items of clothing from Russia woven together, Anna's mother weaves a quilt that takes on meanings as it is passed along. Your children will have many stories to tell of items passed along in their families.

Problem-solving discussions Even our very young children are painfully aware of the tragedies of poverty. Your own children may be children of poverty, and the strengthening that comes from loving environments of respect and acceptance is even more essential in such situations. Children *want* to help solve problems, *want* to care for others. As they collect cans and packaged food to contribute to shelters, as they sell their pictures and projects to raise funds for community kitchens, so they collect clothing for those in need. A teacher told me that during a discussion about how the kindergartners could help people who didn't have much clothing prepare for winter, one of the children immediately volunteered, "I can give one of my mittens." When the teacher asked what about the other hand, he answered, "I'll put it in my pocket."

Be open to all suggestions. Don't forget: write them down!

Caring for clothes Children have many fine ideas for how to keep their own clothes and their "dress-up" center in order. Add "clothing straighteners" and "clothing hanger-uppers" to your list of classroom helpers. Organize the way boots are lined up, jackets hung, gloves and mitten placed, and scarves kept.

Talk about everything! Remember the wonderful African proverb, "Talking with one another is loving one another."

VISUAL ARTS TIMES

Look at the paintings in museums and galleries that are not landscapes, seascapes, nudes, or abstractions, and chances are you'll see a study of clothing. Flip through most magazines and newspapers and pages featuring fashion, and clothing will dizzy your eyes. The textures, colors, designs, and shapes of clothing have fascinated artists throughout the centuries. Because of the work of countless artists, we have an idea of how people dressed throughout history and around the world.

Young children love the fads and fashions of their world as well as the old-fashioned or exotic clothes of other times. These are adventures in history and imagination.

If there is a continuous emphasis on using powers of observation, comparison, and language enrichment, the children will sharpen their abilities to notice how things look and how they relate to each other. So much of the enjoyment of art is the awareness that precedes and accompanies activities.

As you read through the visual arts suggestions (just small samplings of what is possible), be creative and flexible. Arrange and rearrange them according to your own perspective and the special individuals who spend time learning with you.

Clothes collage For general awareness of the variety of clothing people wear, ask the children to cut out pictures of people wearing any kind of clothing. After all the pictures are pasted on a large sheet of paper, add labels that the children suggest, such as pants, shirts, and shoes.

A variation of this idea is to focus on one kind of clothing and encourage the children to cut out pictures for a shoe collage, winter clothes collage, summer clothes collage, jeans collage, and so on. Many teachers find that small groups of children like to work together on their own special interest, so instead of one large collage, your class may want to make three or four different collages.

Make your own smock Because yours is an active class, the children will need smocks to wear over their regular clothes while they are painting, constructing, gluing, and generally "working." Old, loose-fitting cotton shirts make excellent smocks. The children enjoy designing, decorating, signing their shirts with colorful permanent markers, then hanging them on clothes hooks or, as some classes feature, smock hooks!

Class cut-outs One of the most beloved of children's activities is to play with and dress characters, whether dolls, stuffed animals, or felt or paper cut-outs. Make two large cut-outs, a boy and a girl. Many teachers use the children's own life-size cut-outs for this project. Using the basic body shapes, cut out simple shirts, pants, skirts, hats, mittens, coats, shoes, and other articles of clothing. The children fill in the clothing shapes with colors and designs. Encourage them to add button and zipper shapes.

Keep all the clothing shapes together in a "closet" (special box or drawer). Each day, tape up two large children's cut-outs and ask the children to take turns dressing them. Masking tape makes dressing very easy.

Small cut-outs This is a variation of class cut-outs, but in this instance the children use their own smaller cut-out people (cardboard figures or tongue depressors work very well). They can design a family or friendship group and keep their characters and wardrobes in their own boxes. When Mary Rumm[24] shared this idea with children, they responded with great enthusiasm. Mary described the session: "We cut out and designed original items of clothing to paste or clip to the figures. Susannah wanted to make a family, so she had three figures: a mother, a father, and a child. She thought in threes and made long pants, medium pants, and small pants. The children learned about sizes as well as seasons. In summer, we added bathing suits; in winter, mittens, boots, and hoods. The children loved playing with the dolls and rearranging their wardrobes."

Paintings that feature clothing If you want to know how Dutch people dressed in the seventeenth century, look at the paintings of Rembrandt and Ver Meer. Gaugin painted the colorful people and clothing he saw in Tahiti in the nineteenth century. The Impressionists (Renoir, Monet, Degas, and Manet, to name a few) painted the people and clothing of France in the early 1900s. Cassatt, Bellows, and Prendergast painted feasts for your eyes of American styles and people a hundred years ago. For a look at how people dressed in the days of the Wild West, don't miss the works of Catlin, Remington, and Russell. Contrast those canvases and prints (I use postcards) with the paintings of Mexican people by Diego Rivera and Frida Kahlo. The vibrant colors and designs of urban African-Americans are caught in the paintings of Jacob Lawrence and Vincent Smith. With your children, honor the artistic works of painters of all times and backgrounds. The resource books from libraries featuring paintings are plentiful. Choose those *you* like! Share the enthusiasm. Let the paintings inspire the children's own works. Give them titles and, of course, exhibit them in your own galleries.

Portraits of myself in favorite clothing Encourage the children to draw pictures of themselves dressed in their favorite clothes. Talk about specifics like color, length, design, and buttons before the drawing or painting begins. Awareness influences children's works. Ask the children to give their pictures titles. Accompany the pictures with stories inspired by such questions as: "Where are you going in your favorite clothes?" "What are you doing in your favorite clothes?" and "How do you feel while you're wearing these clothes?" Write the children's comments on paper to be displayed beside or under their pictures. Of course, if the children are writing, encourage them to do their own.

Make your own wardrobe

   Mittens The children's hands are outlined on construction paper. Double the paper if you want real mittens the children can slip their hands into and wear. When the mittens are cut, put a few pieces of tape around the top and sides to hold them together. The children enjoy coloring and wearing their mittens. Turn this activity into a "find the matching mitten" game.

Shoes Children's feet are traced on construction paper or cardboard. Cut out the shapes for each child to design and color. If the child wants shoes with laces, paint or color little dots for eyelets.

After the children play with their shoes, dress their class cutouts in them, mix and match them, or display the pairs on a bulletin board or wall. I saw one such display labeled "Shoe Place." The children eagerly showed me their shoes with their names underneath.

Hats! Hats! Hats! Loosely outline shapes of hats such as rain hats; western hats; police officer, fire fighter, and letter carrier hats; derby hats; bonnets; astronauts' helmets and clowns' hats. Each of these calls for discussion and play involving the kind of hat chosen. Hats, more than any other article of clothing, correlate with careers, weather, special occasions, and special characters.

At one of the national conferences of the National Association for the Education of Young Children, many teachers enjoyed creating wildly original and colorful hats out of papier-mâché, newspapers, flowers, flags, and balloons. They caused a stir in New Orleans! Invite children to the fun of making their own wonderfully imaginative hats. Wear them—build characters around them—sing about them—celebrate them.

For free-spirited, funny ideas for way-out hats, share the very silly *Mrs. Honey's Hat*[25] with the children. They'll love the delightful illustrations and the outrageous plot, which decorates her hat with such items as seaweed, bubble gum, and cobwebs.

Many cultures feature special headdresses or hats for storytellers. With your children, create a colorful, magical hat that can be worn only by a person telling a story. Remember, storytelling is sacred in the traditions of many peoples.

T-shirt day Ask the children to wear their favorite T-shirt. Have extras on hand in case a few children forget. Give the children a paper T-shirt shape and suggest that they try to reproduce the color and design of the T-shirt they are wearing. Many delightful activities develop from this project, such as: "Find Juan's paper T-shirt!" "Let's put all the T-shirts that have the color yellow on this side of the wall!" and "Everyone who has more than one color on his or her T-shirt, hold it up and show us." When you are finished, display all the T-shirts.

Design your own T-shirt Send a note home asking families if they have an old white T-shirt for the children to use. Scrounge for extras in case you need them.

The easiest way to make an original shirt is to use fabric flow pens, but many teachers claim colorful markers do just as well. The children lay their shirts flat on tables or desks and choose their favorite colors to draw designs on the shirt. Encourage them to draw things or people they really enjoy. If children can write their own names, ask them to write them somewhere on their shirts. If they cannot, write the names for them.

The pleasant feature of this activity is that the children can wear the shirts immediately; they do not need drying. Play lively music and have a parade celebrating the wonderful new shirts. Have a fashion show!

Pick a pocket Pockets amaze and delight young children. There is something magical about them. "All this stuff was in my pocket and you couldn't see it!" six-year-old Brian explained proudly as he displayed the contents of his pocket.

Cut various-sized pockets out of felt scraps or construction paper for the children to design and color. The children decide where they want to place their pockets—on pants, shirts, sleeves; on the front or back. Use masking tape or Velcro to attach the pockets to their clothes for a Pocket Holiday.

Roxanne Demeter[26] and her first graders talk about such ideas as: "What will be in our pockets?" "What if we had only a tiny pocket?" "What if we were giants and had giant pockets?" "What if our pockets were magic?"

Scraps and snips, buttons and bows This kind of scrounging is fun. Ask families to send in odds and ends of material; buttons; old, inexpensive jewelry; ribbons; snaps; feathers; laces; and so on. All sizes, colors, designs, and textures are welcome.

Each child is given a person-shape outlined on construction paper or cardboard. The children paste bits and pieces of the scrounge material to their cardboard person to complete features and clothing. Samantha (Sammy), not quite five years old, pasted a most incredible white fur coat made of cotton puffs on her friend, "Vicki." She explained, "Vicki's all dressed up to go to the palace!"

Paint a button Young children have a marvelous time painting original designs and colors on plain buttons. The children use bright enamel paint. The buttons can be sewed on clothing for practical or decorative reasons or used for jewelry, sculptures, and collages.

Appliques for special days and times Americans enjoy the colorful skirts, shirts, and vests of appliqued felt and cotton made in Central America and Southeast Asia. Scenes, symbols, and stories are highlighted on basic articles of clothing by the beautiful cut-out shapes sewn or taped to the material.

The children can become "theme dressers" by creating appliques for holidays, seasons, and events. Go beyond familiar holiday symbols and create holidays that need special clothing: Animal Day? Flower Day? Alphabet Day? Rainbow Day? Friendship Day?

Clothesline Stretch a string or rope across your room or along a wall. After the children cut out, color, paint, and paste scrounge materials on articles of clothing, they hang them on the clothesline for everyone to see!

Dashikis African children wear loose, comfortable, colorful shirts called dashikis. American children enjoy making and wearing these shirts. The easiest way is to cut a sheet or any large pieces of scrounge material into rectangles, folded in half. Cut a semicircle from the material along the folded edge, for the child's head to pass through. The children sew or tape the sides, or leave the sides free. Use markers and crayons (iron the shirts after the crayoning for a tie-dyed effect) to create bright designs.

Jewelry People the world over decorate themselves with beautiful and unusual jewelry. To make necklaces, bracelets, rings, and belts, the children run string, thread, or shoelaces through assorted buttons, beads and shells (with tiny holes in them), and cutout cardboard shapes (punch holes in them). Glue bits of plexiglass, wood chips, tiny stones, sand, sparkly stars, feathers, fuzz, and scraps of satin, lace, and silk to buttons and cardboard shapes (fruit shapes, animal shapes, alphabet letters, numbers, abstracts) to make pins. Glue safety pins to the back of the button or cardboard.

Clothes mobile Wrap clothes hangers in colored yarn. The children cut articles of clothing out of cardboard or construction paper and color them. Laminate, if possible. Tie pieces of string to the hanger and attach each piece to an article of clothing. Some children enjoy making a clothes mobile of one kind of clothing. Marcie's "sweater mobile" was really outstanding.

Combine the mobile with weather and include a cutout person dressed for that weather. A group of kindergartners made sun mobiles. One of the children's hangers featured a brilliant, smiling yellow sun, a large red flower, and a cardboard girl dressed in a gorgeous blue and purple bathing suit.

Story illustrators Young children enjoy listening to stories or making up their own and then illustrating ideas from the stories. Laurent de Brunhoff's *Babar* books featuring elephants clothed in magnificent wardrobes inspire children to create their own wardrobes for Babar and his friends and family. Books with contrasts in clothing styles like *Masai and I* and *I Visit My Tutu and Grandma*[28] encourage the children to think about uniqueness and distinctions. In *Masai and I,*[29] an African-American urban child learns about the Masai people of East Africa. The child lives in an apartment house on a crowded street and dreams of what it might be like to be a Masai child living in a village. Your children will love the challenge of painting American kids in their clothing and Masai children in tribal dress. Nancy Mower's story, *I Visit My Tutu and Grandma,* is about a child with two grandmothers; one is Grandma, a Caucasian woman, and one is Tutu, a Hawaiian woman. The child who is part of them both enjoys the food, customs, and clothing of each culture. With Tutu, she wears colorful aloha prints; with Grandma, she wears more familiar styles. Both of these books are excellent resources for music, movement, and drama. The children's illustrations of Hawaiian and Mainland American clothing will delight everyone.

The children's artistic responses to stories are always revealing and engaging. Even if their interpretations differ from your feelings about a story, accept and respect their work. Enjoy it and celebrate it!

MUSIC TIMES

Improvised songs that feature children's clothing Nothing starts off the day more brightly than singing an easy-to-follow, familiar-sounding song naming every child in your room and a special article of clothing. We have used dozens of variations such as the following:

Good morning to Taisha's shirt,
Good morning to Bob's tennis shoes,
Good morning to Shana's pink belt,
Good morning to Merry's hat . . .
(to the tune of "Good Morning to You")

Igor's wearing Barney socks,
Barney socks, Barney socks.
Igor's wearing Barney socks
This sunny Wednesday.
(to the tune of "Mary Had a Little Lamb")

Just look around the room at each child and lyrics will come easily.

It's easy to combine children's names, clothing, counting, and colors in hang-loose songs:

One little, two little, three little shoes,
Four little, five little, six little shoes . . .

until every shoe on every foot is counted.

Turn "Frère Jacques" into a riddle by singing such improvised lyrics as these:

Where are Tamica's blue jeans?
Where are Tamica's blue jeans?
Here they are (children point to blue jeans)
Here they are.
Let's hear it for Tamica's blue jeans.
Let's hear it for Tamica's blue jeans.
Rah! Rah! Rah!
Rah! Rah! Rah!

Sheila Sokol[30] made up a special stanza for each of her six- and seven-year-olds to the tune of "Yankee Doodle." Here are two samples.

Melissa has a brand new jersey.
It's red, it's white and then it's blue.
She got it special for her birthday.
It really fits her nicely, too.

Chorus:
Every child in this room
Looks so very neat today.
Now we'll move to the next kid
And here is what we'll say.
Susie's got a yellow T-shirt.
It's got a turtle on the sleeve.
She wears it with her yellow tennis shorts.
The turtle's sitting on a leaf.

Old favorites like "Oh You Can't Get to Heaven" or Woody Guthrie's "Hey Lolly Lolly Lolly" are excellent for improvisation.

Oh you can't get to heaven
(repeat)
On Stevie's pocket
(repeat)
'Cause Stevie's pocket
(repeat)
Is not a rocket
(repeat)

The sillier the lyrics, the better they are. Children have zest for the ridiculous. Just be sure to include everyone.

Songs that highlight clothing and dressing The younger the children, the more open they are to all kinds of musical experiences. Dip into your knapsack of songs and music and discover the resources ready to be tapped. There are many songs about clothing that are enjoyed by children of all ages and that can be improvised. Here are just a few suggestions.

"I Got Shoes, You Got Shoes, All God's Children Got Shoes"
"Button Up Your Overcoat"
"Buttons and Bows"
"My Hat It Has Three Corners"
"Itsy Bitsy Teeny Weeny Yellow Polka Dot Bikini"
"Second-Hand Rose"
"Blue Suede Shoes"
"In My Easter Bonnet"
"In Her Hair She Wore a Yellow Ribbon"
"I Feel Pretty (*West Side Story*)"
"I've Got Something in My Pocket"
"Mary Wore Her Red Dress"
"Jenny Jenkins"
"Miss Mary Mack"

The old camp song "I've Got Something in My Pocket That Belongs Across My Face." (a smile) inspires not only the singing but also the playful movement and expression changes that accompany taking an invisible item out of a pocket and spreading it across faces. Smiles brighten up a room!

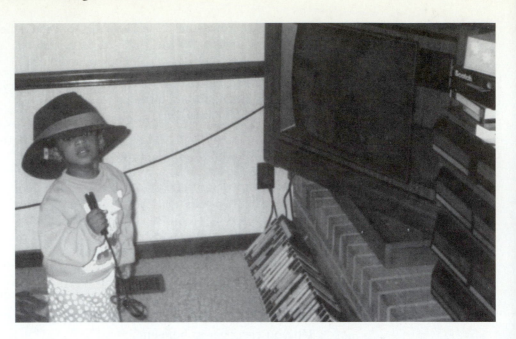

Thomas Moore's delightful "Pockets"[31] turns pockets into a guessing song with clues: "I've got a pocket/What is in my pocket?/They're lumpy and sticky and oh so good to eat/They're dried by the sun and a quite nutritious treat/What do you think it is? Raisins, raisins, raisins in my pocket."

The children love to make up their own verses as the contents of their pockets grow more fanciful and outrageous! "What do you think it is? A dinosaur, dinosaur, dinosaur in my pocket!"

Practice playfulness! Imagination feeds on the playful celebration of ideas. Enjoy language explosions daily!

Sole music for shoes Teachers like Roxanne Demeter can spend weeks exploring the ways shoes move us and the places they take us. She finds music to accompany her first graders' exciting discoveries. She usually plays "whatever is around," and miraculously it fits!

Sing or play lively folk music like "This Land Is Your Land" or "I'm on My Way" for traveling shoes; music with a steady beat for marching shoes; jazzy Scott Joplin tunes for tap-dancing shoes; Appalachian round dances for running shoes; lullabies for tiptoe shoes or bedroom slippers; lively percussion arrangements for clowns' shoes; drum beats for moccasins; square-dance music for Western boots; rainy songs for boots and galoshes (see weather songs); and lyrical music for ballet slippers.

Special clothes for musicians You would not expect a symphony orchestra to dress in cowboy and cowgirl hats and boots, and you would not expect a bluegrass band to dress in tuxedos and gowns. Talk about differences in musicians' dress with your children. Show pictures or photos (album covers often have excellent illustrations) that demonstrate the relationship between the dress and the kind of music played.

Country and western band Make western style hats and boots out of construction paper and tissue-paper scarves for a country and western band. Use rhythm instruments to create original music, or play a country and western album and have the children accompany the recorded music with their own instruments.

Symphony orchestra Across the country, teachers who love classical music share their favorite selections with their students. Young children are interested to know, for example, that Mozart, one of the world's greatest composers, began his musical career at the age of five. The kids are interested in the special way musicians in a symphony orchestra dress for a concert.

Doilies make excellent puffed shirtfronts for the boys. Bow ties of black construction paper, taped to the top of their "shirts," complete the outfit. The girls swish crepe-paper skirts or long skirts scrounged from the clothes box. The children seat themselves and pantomime the beautiful instruments of the orchestra as the music plays. They also enjoy playing their classroom instruments.

Rock and hip-hop bands   American children are familiar with rock groups and rap groups and their sights and sounds. The children raid the scrounge box for wild shirts, pants, shoes, and skirts. When they are ready, turn on a zesty rock album and let them pretend to be the performers. Use real rhythm instruments to play along with the record, or pantomime. Reggae bands and mariachi bands are some other examples of the variety possible.

Singing and doing   Children learn everything better with a song. They practice practical skills through play songs that involve movement and sequences. Many songs lend themselves to action. Just change a few words here and there and you have perfect lyrics for helping children learn to dress themselves and take care of their clothes.

Taking care of clothes   A group of four-year-olds enjoyed singing and moving to improvisation of "This Is the Way We Wash Our Clothes":

> This is the way we wash our clothes . . .
> This is the way we dry our clothes . . .
> This is the way we fold our clothes . . .
> This is the way we hang our clothes . . .
> This is the way we wear our clothes . . .

Each sequence was repeated four or five times. The children chose clothes from their "clothes closet" to use in the song. They learned a lot about folding and hanging through singing.

Dressing   I enjoyed teaching children about dressing themselves with what seemed like hundreds of variations of "There's a Hole in the Bottom of the Sea." For example:

> There's a hole in the top of the shirt.
> There's a hole in the top of the shirt.
> Put your head through. Put your head through.
> Put your head through the hole in the top of the shirt.

> There's a zipper on the front of your coat.
> There's a zipper on the front of your coat.
> Zip it up. Zip it down. Zip the zipper on the front of your coat.

We also used "Row Row Row Your Boat" to help the children practice zipping.

> Zip, zip, zip your coat
> Gently up and down.
> Zippity zippity zippity zippity.
> Now you can go to town.

Songs about making clothes

Cotton   Lots of clothes are made of cotton. Where do we get cotton? Throughout history, people picked cotton. People who picked cotton worked very hard. But they also sang. Many of our folk songs come from cotton fields—for example, "Jump Down, Turn Around, Pick a Bale of Cotton." It is good for young children to know that people doing important, strenuous work sing as they work to make the time go faster, to feel closer to each other, and to find a way to enjoy the labor. The children pantomime picking cotton and sing songs with a steady beat, such as "I've Been Workin' on the Railroad" (substitute "cotton field" for "railroad"), "Here We Go 'Round the Mulberry Bush" (substitute "cotton field" for "mulberry bush"), and "Pickin' Up Paw Paws, Put Them in Your Pocket" (substitute "cotton balls" for "paw paws").

Silk Silk comes from silkworms spinning threads for their cocoons. Imaginative teachers share this phenomenon with their children through songs. One group of first graders and their teacher changed the popular song "Glow Worm" into "Silkworm."

> Spin, little silkworm, faster, better.
> We need silk to make a sweater.
> We need silk to make a gown
> So we can wear it all 'round town.

Another class of second graders followed a talk time session about materials for clothes with an adaptation of "Inch Worm" (from the film *Hans Christian Andersen*).

> Silk worm. Silk worm.
> Spinning your silk cocoon.
> Making scarves and blouses
> For people to wear.

Weaving The over-under pattern of weaving, common in the making of so many materials, is easier to understand when turned into a song. Here is how a group of five-year-olds practiced the weaving idea of over-under (to the tune of "Have You Ever Seen a Lassie?").

> Have you ever seen wool go over,
> Go under, go over, go under?
> Have you ever seen wool
> Get woven today?

Wool Where did the wool come from that is in our sweaters, hats, mittens, and scarves? Lambs! Which brings us to that old favorite, "Mary Had a Little Lamb." What color was its wool? "White as snow." "Baa, Baa, Black Sheep" can be easily turned into a song. In this case, our wool is black.

A group of kindergartners sang "Mary Had a Little Lamb" and "Baa, Baa, Black Sheep" after a discussion about wool and clothing. One of the children exclaimed, "Mary's lamb and Baa Baa make us black-and-white sweaters!"

Songs about weather Teach your favorite songs about weather and seasons to the children. Pantomime dressing in appropriate clothing for the weather in the song; draw pictures showing special clothes; dress paper dolls or real dolls with special weather gear; and improvise puppet shows to go with the songs. Here are just a few suggested songs.

> "Rain, Rain, Go Away"
> "It's Raining, It's Pouring"
> "Raindrops Keep Falling on My Head"
> "You Are My Sunshine"
> "Good Morning Merry Sunshine"
> "Blue Skies"
> "Here Comes the Sun"
> "I Got the Sun in the Morning and the Moon at Night"
> "June Is Busting Out All Over"
> "School Days"

"Let It Snow"
"Summertime"
"Falling Leaves"
"April Showers"
"Winter Wonderland"
"Frosty the Snowman"
"Stormy Weather"
"Jingle Bells"
"Singin' in the Rain"
"Let a Smile Be Your Umbrella"
"On the Sunny Side of the Street"
"Zippity Doo Da"

Weather rhythm bands For activities celebrating different kinds of clothing, why not set the mood with original music expressing snow, rain, hail, and sunshine? Encourage the children to experiment with their instruments until they find a rhythm or melody that fits the weather. Once they hear the storm through their own music, they will create more vivid artwork and dramatic improvisations. They will even pantomime dress or practice dressing with more authenticity. Such challenging questions as "How can we reproduce the sound of thunder?" "What kind of sound can we make for snow falling?" and "Let's make the wind blow with our instruments—doesn't that sound cold and snowy?" help the children as they explore musical possibilities.

Make your own rainstorm This is a delightful body-rhythm activity that begins with gentle rain and develops into a storm. (Of course, no one can go out in a rainstorm without raincoats, boots or galoshes, rain hat, and umbrella!)

Ask the children to hold up one hand as if they are about to clap it. Tap the palm of that hand with one finger of the other hand. Listen. After a little while of listening to the gentle tapping and a few choice comments ("Hmmm . . . what does that sound like to you? Sounds like rain to me, too. Gosh, hope it doesn't storm!"), build suspense. Now the children tap their palms with two fingers. The raindrops sound louder. Go on to three fingers. "Uh-oh, the rain is definitely coming down harder!" By the time five fingers are slapping palms, it is pouring. Clap harder!

Add feet stamping. "Is that thunder we hear? How can we make the sound and fury of thunder with our bodies?" Boom! Jump in air, arms outstretched. Lightning jags. Sharp elbows, arms, and legs fly out and cut the air. Wind blows. Bodies sway and turn. "What a storm! Maybe the storm will blow over." Four fingers hit palms, three fingers, two fingers, one finger. Just a tiny sprinkling. The storm is over. "Maybe the sun will come out. Maybe we'll see a rainbow."

"Sing a Rainbow" is a perfect song to play or sing. Now the sun is out. "We don't need our raincoats anymore!" Pantomime taking off rain gear. "We can go play in our shorts and T-shirts. What a wonderful day!" Combine with art, movement, puppet shows, and story telling.

All-weather classics Symphonic music lends itself to interpretations of weather, such as clear sunny mornings, howling winds, snow gently falling, storm clouds gathering, and autumn leaves blowing. What better way to convey the most basic need for clothing (protection from the elements) than to play a piece of music that suggests powerful weather conditions? With that musical experience, art, drama, movement, talk, stories, and poetry evolve.

I have used a variety of music with young children of all ages. Some of my favorite compositions are Grofé's *Grand Canyon* Suite, Stravinsky's *The Firebird* Suite, Copland's *Appalachian Spring*, Tchaikovsky's *Nutcracker Suite,* op. 71a, Grieg's *Peer Gynt* Suites no. 1 and no. 2, Sibelius's Symphony no. 5 op. 82 ("Finlandia"), Debussy's *La Mer,* Mussorgsky's *A Night on Bald Mountain,* Khachaturian's

Gayaneh Ballet Suites, Debussy's *Clouds* and *Mists,* Rossini's "The Storm and the Calm" from *William Tell* Overture, Chopin's *Raindrop* Prelude, and Vivaldi's *The Four Seasons.*

It is important for you to find the music you enjoy and listen, move, paint, write, and play to it with your students. Two highly recommended reference books that correlate music with ideas such as rain, wind, and storm: *Recorded Bridges, Moods and Interludes,* edited by Henry Katzman (BMI, 1953); and *Music for Pictures* by Erno Rapee (Arno, 1970). Remember, most public libraries lend tapes, cassettes, and videos.[32]

MOVEMENT AND PLAY TIMES

Dressing up is one of the most popular kinds of dramatic play that young children *need* and enjoy. Children are the true magicians: a throw-away ribbon becomes a crown for a princess; a towel draped over a four-year-old's shoulders turns the wearer into a super-hero; a plastic cooking bowl plunked on a small head changes a little kid into a muscular construction worker.

Every room where young children learn and play (learn through play) must have an area where different kinds of clothing are accessible. Here are just a few examples seen in classrooms around the country:

Clothes Place (a special corner)
Clothes Store (specially designated shelves)
Hooked on Clothes (a wall of clothes hooks)
Clothes Trunk
Clothes Closet (portable, cardboard closet)
Clothes Basket
Hat Rack
Shoes/Hats/Shirts
Costume Box

In some rooms, separate boxes are labeled ("mittens," "shoes," "hats," and so on) and are used not only for play but also for learning games like categorizing, finding similarities and differences, and matching. Many teachers make use of the large containers discarded by ice-cream stores. (Wash them thoroughly and dry carefully.)

Ask the families of your students as well as your own family, neighbors, and friends to scrounge in their homes for clothes of all sizes, styles, colors, and shapes to donate to your class. This should be one of the first and most important "scrounge notes" you send.

In addition to clothing for the children, encourage families to send in cast-off baby clothes for dolls and large stuffed animals. Set aside a special box or shelf for the baby clothes. Because yours is a safe place where children and their possessions are respected and cared for, children will not hesitate to bring their beloved dolls and toy animals into the classroom.

Which comes first, the clothes or the game? It is probably fifty-fifty. Children often decide what they want to wear and who they want to be, and the story flows from the clothes. Other times, they make up games and stories and choose clothes accordingly.

Most play activities involving clothing will proceed beautifully *without you!* As long as there is a fine selection of clothes and enough time to play, the children will continue until they are stopped by adult schedules.

The following suggested activities are above and beyond the children's own, very important, self-initiated games. We know that most young children are so rich in creative energies and ideas that our part in their play is that of delighted observers

who enter their magic stories only to introduce a relevant theme, to encourage the inclusion of a child who is left out and who wants in, or to gently steer action away from a negative or hostile direction.

For every idea suggested, dozens are not. Your own take-offs are the best. When you are excited about an activity or an idea, the feeling is contagious. Children are susceptible to teachers' enthusiasm. Don't hesitate to dramatize a concept or introduce a character. Children want to see their teachers "hang loose" and jump into the fun!

Dress the weather person The weather person can be a real child or a felt or paper cutout. Each day the class decides, based on the weather, how to dress the weather person. The children take turns dressing the weather person. Add dialogue.

Find the mate The children make many pairs of colored mittens and shoes from plain construction paper. They scramble to find two of a kind, then fit their hands to a left and a right mitten or correctly set their feet on a pair of shoes. The children love the challenge!

Find your name Label different articles of scrounge clothing in the room with children's names (and/or photos) before they arrive in the morning. The game is: "Find your name and wear those clothes for the day."

Hats are tops Creative teachers are gatherers of hats! For example, Karen Wyerman's students have many kinds of hats to choose to play with: chefs' hats, hard hats, graduation caps, Mickey Mouse ears, ladies' straw hats, western hats, and fire fighters' helmets. Sometimes the children sit in special chairs, close their eyes, and receive hats. When a mirror is held up to them, they are encouraged: "Look at yourself in the mirror. Turn yourself into the person wearing this hat. Who are you? What are you doing? How does it feel? What is your name?"[33]

Give children the opportunity to wear different kinds of hats. Don't designate on the basis of sex. Girls enjoy wearing airline pilots' hats, and boys demonstrate digging and planting under straw gardening hats.

If your dress-up center doesn't feature many kinds of hats, find a book like *Ho for a Hat!*[34] Every page suggests delightful movement, dialogue, and dramatic interpretation. Share the book with the children and ask them to demonstrate the ideas on every page! For example, "A hat to wear cocked on the side of your head, to throw in the air, to toss on the bed . . . to hang on a hook, to have and to wear. . . ." Turn the title, *Ho for a Hat!* into a song, cheer, or chant. Be sure to spend time on the magician's hat and the hats from outer space!

Shoes and scarves Leslie Zak,[35] in her creative dramatics work with children, uses hats to begin activities. But, Leslie admits, she has a grand time trying on different kinds and sizes of shoes with the children. As the children try on shoes, she asks them challenging questions such as: "How do these shoes make you feel? Show us." "Are you big or small in these shoes? Let's see." "Do these shoes make you take giant steps or tiny steps? Do they make you walk on tip-toe or skip? Show us how your shoes make you want to move."

Scarves are magical articles of clothing. They can be as dainty as handkerchiefs or as long and wide as saris. They can fit in pockets, on heads, around waists, over shoulders, across chests, into sleeves, and over faces. Scarves change children into wizards, goblins, elves, fairies, kings, queens, cowhands, pirates, clowns, trees, rainbows, wind, waterfalls, waves, circles, and snowstorms.

In a safe, warm climate of joyful exploration, you will be surprised at the many scarf ideas that pop like firecrackers and materialize like streamers in the air. Accompany scarf celebrations with a variety of music to reflect different moods and rhythms.

Pantomime dressing Getting dressed is a popular theme of mimes and young children. Improvise a story to accompany a pantomime. "This is how these terrific boys and girls get dressed every day." (The children demonstrate through pantomime.) Ask them to continue the story. "What do they put on next? How do they do it?" Simple songs like Woody Guthrie's "Wake Up" are easily adapted to songs to pantomime dressing by.

We had a fantastic time with a group of first and second graders in Michigan changing "Dem Bones, Dem Bones, Dem Dry Bones" into a song to pantomime dressing. Our version went something like this:

Oh, your hats connected to your hairy head.
(repeat)
Now, here's the way we dress.
Oh, your sleeves connected to your two arms.
(repeat)
Now, here's the way we dress.
Oh, your shoes connected to your ten toes.
(repeat)
Now, here's the way we dress.
Oh, your shoes connected to your two feet.
(repeat)
Now, here's the way we dress.

A playful getting-dressed book that has the children laughing as they follow the simple, silly illustrations and mixed-up directions to dressing is *How Do I Put It On?*[36] As the little bear figure proclaims that he/she can get dressed all by "myself," the mishmash begins with the shirt going over his/her legs like pants and the text, "Do I put it on like this?" Each silly mix-up is followed by a blank page with the word "No!" The kids love to demonstrate the topsy-turvy method, shouting "No!" and then demonstrating the appropriate method.

In the book *The Philharmonic Gets Dressed*[37] the children follow all the steps: "first they get washed," then put on clothes, from underwear to the dignified black tuxedos for the men and black gowns for the women, and they finish with the performance of the orchestra. As the children pantomime and improvise the many dress-up steps in this delightful book, excitement mounts as the concert draws near.

Play your grandest selection of orchestral music for the children as they bow, take their seats, and play their imaginary symphonic instruments in their beautiful black and white clothes. Give everyone a turn to be the conductor!

A delightful story that begins with a philharmonic orchestra in concert then loosens up, dresses down, and takes to the streets for music making and dancing is *I Like The Music*.[38] With easy-to-move-in clothing, the kids will dance out such words as "I like the beat/of my feet/when my shoes hit the street/and rapa-tapa-tapa on the hot concrete." The clothing illustrations on the action-packed people are jazzy and flashy. Try it!

Dress class dolls and animals This is where the collection of baby clothes comes in handy. Baby clothes are full of snaps, ties, buttons, and zippers. Young children need practice to master these skills.

If you have class stuffed animals, puppets, or dolls, let the children take turns each day dressing them. If possible, encourage them to dress their "friends" according to the weather: sweaters or jackets for cold weather; shorts and cool shirts for warm weather.

The class can decide on situations for these special friends. Are they going to a party? To the playground? Should they dress for an occasion that the class creates? Include dressing these "friends" as part of daily assignments.

"Dancing Pants" and some other clothing poems to move to. Poems like Shel Silverstein's "Dancing Pants" are perfect for turning into dances. As the poem is read (children usually join in the reading), the children bounce to the rhythm of the words.

Play a lively jazz, Dixieland, rock, rap, or folk album and encourage the children to "Whirl, and twirl, and jiggle and prance." Join them in the fun. You have dancing pants, too!

With hundreds of young children, we have expanded Shel Silverstein's idea of "dancing pants" to "dancing shirts," "dancing shoes," "dancing sleeves," and so on. Once children get hold of an idea, there is no limit to how far they can go with it. Give them time to design and exhibit their own illustrations of their "dancing pants."

Let me indulge my whirly brain for a moment to play with the idea that there's no end to ideas. For example, why can't the "dancing pants" dance around the world, around our country, through many cultures? Using the verbs in the poem as choreographic suggestions, celebrate the "dancing pants" in Miami's pulsing Cuban rhythms, in San Diego to lively Mexican beats, or in San Francisco's Chinatown to lead the Chinese New Year's procession. What about the dancing pants for characters in stories like the Three Billy Goats Gruff—imagine them bouncing, prancing, and whirling as they cross the bridge! Of course, the pants will have to come in different sizes!

Pantomime waterproof dressing and strutting through the rain. "How do you walk over puddles? Through puddles?"

Rhoda Bacmeister's "Galoshes" captures the sloshy stomps and movement of snowy and rainy day clothing. Your children will have so much fun creating original movement interpretations.

Galoshes certainly make us move differently from sandals or bedroom slippers. Explore the differences. Substitute your children's names for the "Susie" in the poem.

Stories about clothing will move you Without your directing the activity, children naturally "act out" stories they enjoy. The characters and plot engage their imaginations and they need no prodding to make a play (improvisation) about the story. In a story they already like, you can raise awareness of clothing by asking, "What kind of clothing are you wearing?" or "Do you think Mr. Smith needs a hat?" or any other reminder. Some stories deal directly with clothing and are delightful for the children to improvise as you read the story to them or afterward.

Charlie Needs a Cloak[39] a brightly illustrated tale of Charlie, a shepherd boy who needs a cloak. The story is basically the sequence of steps Charlie takes to make a cloak, beginning with the shearing of his sheep. He washes, cards, dries, dyes, and weaves the wool into cloth. He cuts, pins, and sews it and is ready with a beautiful new cloak when winter comes. The children learn a lot about clothing as they go through each activity in the making of the cloak.

I must warn you: every time I "play" *Charlie Needs a Cloak* with young children, the first scene of shearing the sheep is the longest, because all the children want to be the sheep and be chased, caught, and gently sheared.

Following the same rhythmic, cumulative pattern as "There's a Hole in the Bottom of the Sea," Shirley Neitzel's *The Jacket I Wear in the Snow*[40] will have the children chanting, dancing, moving, and showing you as they begin with "This is the zipper that stuck on the jacket I wear in the snow." The story goes on and on, gathering items such as: "These are the boots, too big for me, that cover the jeans stiff in the knee, that go over the sweater all itchy and warm. . . ." Illustrations, colorful words, and bouncy rhythms inspire the children recreate the story.

Children have to move to books like *Shoes*.[41] Open to any page and *do* it! Imagine the children's joy to demonstrate, "Shoes to skate in, shoes to skip in, shoes to turn a double flip in. . . ."

Our young friend wearing the Red Dancing Shoes will inspire the children to demonstrate their own talents. Any page will start them moving:

> "That's some fancy footwork there, girl!" Miss Eva said.
>   "New shoes?" asked Mr. Tony, leaning over the counter.
>   "They're my dancing shoes," I told them. "Watch me."
>   I did the Mashed Potato. I did the Jerk.

What dances can your children do in their dancing shoes?

Jack Kent has so many marvelous activities in his lively *Hop, Skip and Jump Book*.[42] Young children enjoy pantomiming or actually trying each of the seven funny pictures titled "Put On," "Button," "Zip," "Buckle," "Tie," "Brush," and "Comb." Turn the ideas into riddles. Have the children show any of them and ask the class to guess which one they are demonstrating. Play easy-to-move-to music and practice each of the seven movement ideas.

Lost and found game This is a popular game that gives children experience in recognizing, naming, matching, differentiating, selecting, and comprehending. If you share *The Mystery of the Missing Red Mitten*[43] with your children, this game is a natural follow-up.

Use a real article of clothing as the lost item. Describe it vividly. Perhaps it is the mate of a glove, sock, shoe, or mitten that can be held up as a clue. Try to hide the item in an interesting place, such as on a doll or a stuffed animal, on the bulletin board, hanging from a mobile, or buried in the sandbox. Give hints sometimes. When the item is found, celebrate, and acknowledge everyone's cooperation in the search.

Folding, changing, rearranging The poet Theodore Roethke advised: "Reject nothing, but re-order all." Those are excellent words about creativity, which stresses flexibility, change, experimentation, and openness to new experiences.

After a few months, why not rearrange your room? With the advice of your students, designate a new place for clothes and costumes. If the clothes and costumes are going to be moved to a new place, it will help to organize them, especially if they are "messed up," as clothes places tend to be after so much playing. Divide the class into small groups and ask each group to be responsible for gathering up particular clothing items and folding them or laying them neatly in their boxes or on shelves.

Children want so much to help and have their contributions be of value that they take this game seriously. They are conscientious about it and learn important lessons in caring for clothes. I watched a kindergarten class work on this project for almost an hour. Everyone was busy. The children on the "shoes committee" grunted and groaned as they moved the ample collection of shoes, boots, galoshes, and moccasins. "I think ours is the hardest," flushed-faced Kenny explained. "You know, shoes weigh more than socks!"

Puppets By now you know that puppets are "friends" to most young children.

Puppets give directions and information Puppets can give directions on how to button, hang up clothes, fold shirts, tie shoes, zip, put on shoes and gloves, and tell right from left. For some reason, when puppets play teacher, children do not become as tense or anxious about the lesson. Children need to hear instructions and information many times, in many different ways. They need plenty of practice. Let puppets teach as often as possible and give yourself a break!

Puppets get mixed up On the flip-side of the puppet experience, children enjoy watching and correcting a puppet who "doesn't get it." They can easily identify with the character, and there is a lot of compassion as they correct (with humor) a mixed-up "friend." Laughter is a sign that we understand. It is another way of knowing. So when children burst out laughing at the antics of a puppet who puts socks over shoes, belts around legs, or coats on backwards, they are not only finding amusement but also discovering that they know a lot about dressing.

This activity is an excellent way to help children learn to accept and respect those who may not be as fast as others. We all learn at our own pace. If a puppet can communicate that message painlessly, with warmth and humor, then a valuable lesson has been taught.

For example, meet Sloppy and Neat-O, puppets in an improvised show.

The story was that Sloppy just dropped her clothes everywhere in big piles, jumped on them, walked on them—in short, made a mess everywhere. Neat-O, on the other hand, picked up his clothes as soon as he undressed and folded them, hung them up, or put them in the hamper. Neat-O was always ready for everything—the zoo, ice cream, parties. He never had to stay home because his clothes were messy. In contrast, Sloppy kept missing out on all kinds of fun because she had to pick up her clothes.

The children laugh uproariously as Sloppy's mess is exaggerated (at one point the puppet was buried under the clothes). But they got the message, and from them on, the children made an effort to take better care of their clothes, often referring to the puppets in their daily play and clean-up.

Magic pockets After singing some of the songs about pockets and talking about pockets, celebrate pockets. Celebrate imaginations! Ask the children to come in with a pocket or pockets on their jackets, coats, shirts, and pants. Have extras ready for children who may forget or are unable to come prepared. "How many pockets do we have?" Children love to be included in everything. Go around the room, stop at each child, and count the pockets aloud. A group of first graders was astonished to discover fifty-two pockets on the clothes they were wearing.

Start a storytelling, creative drama-movement session on "magic pockets." "What could be in your pocket that's special? Surprising? Exciting? Mysterious? Don't tell us—show us and we'll try to guess!" We had a marvelous time with a family grouping of second and third graders as they took turns giving movement hints about the contents of their pockets. When they were finished sharing their magic pockets, we made a giant dance out of all the contents. Enjoy the story and you will be able to imagine the dance: Shannon had a baby chick in her magic pocket; Ali had a basketball; Ella had a new baby brother; Marlon had a new pair of tennis shoes; and Joy had a bunny. We used a disco record that repeated the same beat for about ten minutes, enough time for Shannon to lead the group in baby chick movement, for Ali to lead basketball dribbling movement, and so on. Expand "magic pockets" into art activities: "Draw a picture of what's in your pocket."

Costumes and dances   When children make or wear clown hats, of course, they want to make up a clown dance. "What about a cowhand hat? What kind of dance does that hat want you to make? Do you need a horse? Do you want to gallop?" Play some square-dance music and gallop away. "What about a pilot's cap? What do pilots do? Fly? Can we turn ourselves into airplanes? Arms out? Full speed ahead." Find music with a speedy, steady beat—music to fly to. Ah, red handkerchiefs for magicians. "What kind of dance can magicians do?" Abracadabra—surprise! Every costume has movement possibilities. Ask questions that suggest ideas. Be open to all responses.

Traditional dress and dances of children around the world   Young children are fascinated by the *traditional* clothing of other cultures. Caps, aprons, and wooden shoes are worn by Dutch children; embroidered shirts and high boots by children from Russia, Poland, Hungary, and Rumania; wide-brimmed hats, colorful scarfs, and white shirts by Mexican children; headbands, feathers, fringed-bottom beaded shirts, and moccasins by Native American children; and colorful shirts, flower leis, and grass skirts by Hawaiian children.

Each culture is a study in color, texture, and style. Celebrate any of the traditions with a clothing item that every child can wear, such as a sash around the waist or a scarf around the neck. Play folk music from that culture as you and your children form a circle and improvise a folk dance. Add food and classroom visitors to the festivities. In their daily lives, people around the world often dress very similarly to Americans—jeans, T-shirts, tennis shoes, and so on. But, in every culture, there are occasions (holidays and festivals) when people honor their traditions by dressing in their historically distinct fashions. We are all a mix of contemporary and historical influences!

Clothing party   Distribute different kinds of clothing in specified places around the room. Use categories such as long-ago clothes, party clothes, work clothes, sports clothes, fairy tale clothes, and grown-up clothes. Introduce the children to the different types of clothing and encourage them to play in the clothes that most interest them.

A variation of this activity is to give each area a color or design symbol and hand out cards with the same color or symbol to the children. The children find the area that corresponds to their card and that is where they play.

This activity encourages the children to experiment and to try on clothing with which they may have little experience.

CLASSROOM VISITORS AND FIELD TRIPS
Classroom Visitors

Suggestions have been made throughout this book for tapping the rich resources of families, neighbors, and community members as classroom visitors.

Athletes, dancers, mimes, chefs, police officers, fire fighters, servers, letter carriers, supermarket cashiers, and construction workers all bring awareness of special clothing as part of their work, hobbies, and skills. Clothing need not be the reason for a visit, but should be integrated with the experience of meeting these interesting people who are kind enough to share some of their experiences with young children.

Because America is a land of immigrants (except for Native Americans), our people represent a cultural diversity rich in possibilities for understanding and appreciation. In addition to foods, crafts, music, and dance, people from different cultural backgrounds offer special clothing. Be sure to include clothing as part of visitors' agendas.

Costume designer Most communities have a theater group associated with a high school, church, or university. If the group is small, its costume collection is probably the right size to bring into the classroom, along with a friendly member of the costume crew to show the children the different items and explain how important costumes are to the success of a play.

Doll collection Many community people from different ethnic backgrounds treasure dolls dressed in the fashion of their cultures. You may be lucky enough to live in a community where such collections are shared.

Representatives of different cultures Check the resources in your community such as churches affiliated with a culture; for example, Russian, Armenian, Greek Orthodox, Serbian, and Macedonian churches. If you are near a university or hospital, find out if there is an international student organization. Also, children of professors, students, doctors, military officers, missionaries, and government service workers are likely to have a special wardrobe of traditional clothes from their countries and are usually willing to meet your class and share their songs, games, foods, and costumes.

When Sarni Dickerson[44] visits children, she talks to them about growing up in a Muslim tradition in a culture rich in customs from India. She demonstrates the wrapping of beautiful saris and wears her punjabi (pants/dress/scarf). The children sample curry, spices, and breads, and listen to sitar music. Their beautiful pictures, thank-you letters, and poems demonstrate their appreciation.

Emma Bailey[45] and Bess Haile[46] visit children in classrooms and show them the exquisitely embroidered designs on their Native American traditional clothes. You should always encourage the children to participate in a related activity, such as designing bead patterns for shirts.

The meanings and stories of the intricately woven colors of Kente cloth are explained and demonstrated to children around the country by members of the African-American community.

Every classroom visitor brings a multitude of gifts.

Magicians/Clowns Two occupations fascinating to children and dazzling in clothing associated with their work are magicians and clowns. Even the smallest town often has a person who performs magic and a clown who appears at parties and parades. Invite them to your classroom and watch your children's faces light up with attention and astonishment at the combination of trickery, clothing, and entertainment. Keep your eyes on pockets, scarves, gloves, and hats! Circus and magic shows will be high on the children's list of favorite games to play after the visits.

Yourself as a classroom visitor Turn yourself into a character from a story, from another time, from a faraway country by dressing up in the style of the idea. Why not greet the children one day as Mother Goose or Mother Nature or Father Time? You'll more than attract the children's attention. You'll ignite their imaginations! The children won't need persuading to dress themselves as storybook characters.

Field Trips

Clothing store Children are fascinated by the display of different styles, colors, sizes, and patterns, but they are even more interested in how people try clothes on, how clerks help them find their sizes, how clothing is wrapped and handled, and the interplay between customers and clerks (observation of manners and courtesy). As with all trips, when you return to the classroom, expand the experience into talk, art, music, drama, and movement activities, and write thank-you notes. Your kids will play store for a long time!

Dry-cleaning business Kay Callander brings all her classes to Callander's Cleaners.[47] Don Callander is familiar with young, curious, fascinated faces looking at the machines, the clothes hanging up, the trucks waiting to deliver clothes, the customers waiting their turns, the pressers, and the steam coming from the cleaning process.

Coin-operated laundry Because clean clothing is important, children should see that people, even if they do not have their own machines at home, take time from their work or school to take care of clothes. In a coin-operated laundry, people often read or study while they wait, and many fold their clothes there.

Seasonal walk Take a walk around the neighborhood to look at clothing, or make this interest part of a regular walk. The children are dressed for the weather, and as you walk together, notice that everyone in the street is dressed in similar outerwear. Point out the special clothing of community helpers you pass, such as delivery people, letter carriers, grocery clerks, service station workers, crossing guards, police officers, and landscape workers.

Tailor or dressmaker shop People who make clothes show children patterns, bolts of material, sewing machines, thread, zippers, and buttons. They explain how important measuring is. Children usually return to the classroom eager to measure themselves. This is a good introduction to topics of numbers, growing, and measuring.

Shoe repair shop If your community has a shoemaker or shoe repair shop, your children will enjoy the smell of leather; the sound of the metal; the sight of the scraps of heels, soles, and laces; and the feeling of pride in workmanship that most shoemakers still have.

Antique shop In addition to old furniture, books, and jewelry, clothing is a feature of many antique shops. Children, who have their own sense of time, need concrete images so they can more vividly imagine "long ago," "great-great-grandmother's time," and, "how we would have dressed."

Clothing mill or factory If you live near a clothing mill or factory, this field trip will contribute to an understanding and appreciation of the resources and skills needed to manufacture clothes.

Museums/Art galleries As you walk through museums and galleries, talk about the clothing worn by subjects in paintings, sculptures, and exhibits. Encourage the children to turn their powers *on*. Notice everything! Children are usually surprised at the magical ways artists make their subjects as real as life: shiny satins, flouncy ruffles, and rich velvet. Invite them to paint their own masterpieces. Of course, their artworks will be celebrated with a special exhibit!

They may also want to return to the classroom and create their own museum of shoe box scenes featuring people and clothing from different places and historical eras.

Ballets/Circuses/Theaters Millions of children enjoy special events and performances in communities. With the help of PTAs and area businesses as well as arts councils, busloads of children are becoming audiences for symphonies, ballets, theatrical productions, circuses, and festivals. Each event has its own wardrobe. That aspect is most interesting to the children. Leave time back in the classroom for children to discuss and react to not only the plots and programs, but also to the clothing worn by the characters. Be ready for myriad spin-off activities inspired by such special events!

IT ALL COMES TOGETHER

As you know, it all comes together all the time (unless you think in compartmentalized ways in which everything is isolated and disconnected). Just in case you need an extra perk to remind you of how easy it is to integrate learning, met Art Isennagle.[48]

From day one, Art's second-third split, which he calls his "multi-age family group, my learning family," knows that this will be a very different year! In Art's words:

> From the moment the kids walk in they know they have a crazy teacher! I tell them we're going to places on our magic carpet, the magic carpet of imagination, that allows us to have fun, be creative, do extraordinary things (above and beyond normal, extra special). All year we'll ride the magic carpet of imagination!
>
> Oh, you can start with any piece of clothing. I like to start with a hat and a story. One of my favorite ways to start off is to share *Caps for Sale*[49] and *Stone Soup* (I like the Marcia Brown adaptation). Both are about the gaining of something. Both are about working together.

My Love of learning
comes over me like
a strong wind
how great a debt we owe
to the great learners
who went before us
though
the ABC's of learning
I am willing
to not stop learning.

After we read the stories, we talk about the themes: all those delicious ingredients added to the stone and water to make a delicious soup; all the hats on the peddler's head that the monkeys take, play with, then return.

We take a little break and I put on a hat—a black, three-cornered pirate's hat. The kids always look surprised. I ask them, "What does the hat make you think of?" Oh, the kids immediately think of the soldiers in *Stone Soup*. "OK," I'll ask, "What else can you think of? I'm open to any answer." Ideas will flow: pirates, Captain Hook, George Washington, Paul Revere, Treasure Island, olden days. . . .

I keep prodding them—"What would a person wearing this hat feel like, look like, move like? What kinds of ideas would a person wearing this hat have?"

Now the kids are very excited. Pass the hat and show me the dance your sailor does. Ah! It's a jig! Yo Ho Ho and a bottle of rum! We have a wrestling mat in our room. I tell the kids to use the mat to show their ideas in pantomime and movement. We turn ourselves into pirates sailing on our ship on the rough ocean. We play Sea Shanties, make up our own songs, poems, dances, stories.

By the end of the session the children have learned a lot.

But, most important, we talk about the biggest lesson—that we can pretend to be anyone or anything with our imaginations. Because I started with one hat, I became many different ideas and people. This one hat connected to so many other suggestions. This silly hat allowed us the opportunity to go places like a pirate's ship, like the ocean, like Paul Revere's horseback riders, like the soldiers in *Stone Soup*.

We take our experiences and translate them into art works, into creative writing, into drama, into music.

Our class motto is "Committed To Learning," and all year we ride the magic carpets of our imaginations to great adventures.

Art had a copy of a letter written during the Civil War about "My Love of Country." His very appreciative and enthusiastic students adapted that letter into an original poem to Art called "My Love Of Learning" and presented it to him at the end of the school year.

May *your* students always be willing to learn and always feel full of love of learning!

NOTES ♥♥♥♥♥♥♥♥♥♥♥♥♥♥♥♥♥♥♥♥♥♥♥♥♥

1. Push Pin Graphic, *Why We Dress.* 67 Irving Place, New York, NY 10003.
2. Lila Pearl, illustrated by Leslie Evans, *From Top Hats to Baseball Caps, from Bustles to Blue Jeans: Why We Dress the Way We Do.* New York: Clarion Books, 1990.
3. Ibid. pp. 43–44.
4. Marion Sickel, *Japan.* New York: Chelsea House, National Costume Reference Book, 1987.
   Ronni Cummins, photographs by Mercedes Lopez, *Children of the World—Cuba.* Milwaukee: Gareth Stevens Children's Books, 1991.
5. Pearl, pp. 21–22.
6. L. Rowland-Warne, *Eyewitness Book, Costume.* New York: Knopf, 1992.
   Jacqueline Morley. *Clothes: For Work, Play and Display.* New York: Franklin Watts, Timelines series, 1992.
7. Peter Copeland. *Everyday Dress of the American Revolution.* New York: Dover, 1975.
8. Nancy Van Laan, illustrated by Nadine Bernard Westcott, *People, People Everywhere.* New York: Knopf, 1992.
9. Gene Zion, illustrated by Margaret Bloy Graham, *No Roses for Harry.* New York: Harper & Row, 1958.
10. Denise Lewis Patrick, paintings by James E. Ransome, *Red Dancing Shoes.* New York: Tambourine, 1993.
11. Ann Grifalconi, *Darkness and the Butterfly.* Boston: Little, Brown, 1987.
    ——— *Osa's Pride.* Boston: Little, Brown, 1990.
12. Steven Kellogg, *Pecos Bill.* New York: Morrow, 1986.
13. Arnold Adoff, illustrated by Karen Barbour, *Flamboyan.* San Diego: Harcourt Brace Jovanovich, 1988.
14. Bill Martin, Jr., and John Archambault, illustrated by Ted Rand, *Knots On A Counting Rope.* New York: Henry Holt, 1985.
15. Miyoko Matsutani, illustrated by Chichiro Iwasaki, translated by Alvin Tresselt, *The Crane Maiden.* New York: Parents Magazine Press, 1968.
16. Marie Louise Allen, "The Mitten Song," *Read Aloud Rhymes for the Very Young,* selected by Jack Prelutsky, illustrated by Marc Brown. New York: Knopf, 1986, p. 74.

17. Karla Kuskin, "Snow." p. 77. See *Read Aloud Rhymes,* above.
18. Judi Barrett, illustrated by Ron Barrett. *Animals Should Definitely Not Wear Clothing.* New York: Aladdin, 1970.
19. Jill Murphy, *All in One Piece.* New York: Putnam, 1987.
20. Margaret Miller, *Whose Shoe?* New York: Greenwillow, 1991.
    ———, *Whose Hat?* New York: Greenwillow, 1988.
21. Ron Roy, photos by Rosemarie Hausherr, *Whose Hat Is That?* New York: Clarion, 1987.
    ———, *Whose Shoes Are Those?* New York: Clarion, 1988.
22. Paul Rogers, illustrated by Jane Johnson, *From Me to You.* New York: Orchard, 1987.
23. Patricia Polacco, *The Keeping Quilt.* New York: Simon and Schuster, 1988.
24. Mary Rumm is a poet who helps children integrate the arts in Columbus, Ohio.
25. Pam Adams, *Mrs. Honey's Hat.* Wilts, England: Child's Play International, 1980.
26. Roxanne Demeter shared these ideas with her students at the Glendening School, Groveport Madison Schools District, Ohio.
27. Kate Spohn, *Clementine's Winter Wardrobe.* New York: Orchard, 1989.
28. Nancy Alpert Mower, illustrated by Patricia A. Wozniak, *I Visit My Tutu and Grandma.* Honolulu: Honolulu Press, Pacifica, 1984.
29. Virginia Kroll, illustrated by Nancy Carpenter, *Masai and I.* New York: Four Winds, 1992.
30. Sheila Sokol now makes up special songs for Gabriella in Columbus, Ohio.
31. Thomas Moore, "Pockets" from *Songs for the Whole Day.* Thomas Moore Records, #1000, 4600 Park Road, Charlotte, NC 28209.
32. Thomas Heck made these recommendations when he was the head librarian of the music and dance library at Ohio State University.
33. Karen Wyerman shared these ideas with children in the Groveport Madison School District, Ohio.
34. William Jay Smith, illustrated by Lynn Munsinger, *Ho for a Hat!* Boston: Little, Brown, 1989. .
35. Leslie Zak is director of Days of Creation Arts For Kids, Columbus, and participates in the Greater Columbus Arts Council's Artists-in-the-Schools Program.
36. Shigeo Watanabe, illustrated by Yasuo Ohtomo, *How Do I Put It On?* New York: Philomel, 1979.
37. Karla Kuskin, illustrated by Marc Simont. *The Philharmonic Gets Dressed.* New York: Harper & Row, 1982.
38. Leah Komaiko, illustrated by Barbara Westman, *I Like The Music.* NY: Harper & Row, 1987.
39. Tomie de Paola, *Charlie Needs a Cloak.* Englewood Cliffs, NJ: Prentice-Hall, 1973.
40. Shirley Neitzel, illustrated by Nancy Winslow Parker, *The Jacket I Wear in the Snow.* New York: Greenwillow, 1989.
41. Elizabeth Winthrop, illustrated by William Joyce, *Shoes.* New York: Harper & Row, 1986.
42. Jack Kent, *Hop, Skip and Jump Book.* New York: Random House, 1974.
43. Steven Kellogg, *Mystery of the Red Mitten.* New York: Dial, 1974.
44. Sarni Dickerson is well known in the Columbus area for her deep commitment to children and education.
45. Emma Bailey shares her Blackfoot traditions with central Ohio children through Days of Creation Arts for Kids and the Greater Columbus Arts Council's Artists-in-the-Schools program.

46. Bess Chee Chee Haile is a widely respected educator and influential member of the Shinnecock Nation in South Hampton, New York.

47. Callander's Cleaners is well known in Columbus.

48. Art Isennagle teaches at Olde Orchard Alternative School in the Columbus Public Schools. Art received the Walt Disney American Teacher Honoree Award in 1992 as a representative of the best teaching in the country.

49. Esphyr Slobodkina, *Caps for Sale*. Reading, MA: Young Scott, renewed, 1968.

BOOKS FROM MY KNAPSACK FOR CHILDREN

Border, Louise. *Caps, Hats, Socks and Mittens*. Illustrated by Lillian Hoban. New York: Scholastic, 1987.

Cobb, Vickie. *Getting Dressed*. Illustrated by Marilyn Hafner. New York: HarperCollins, 1989.

Corey, Dorothy. *New Shoes*. Martin Grove, IL: Albert Whitman, 1985.

Hest, Amy. *The Purple Coat*. Illustrated by Amyu Schwartz. New York: Macmillan, 1986.

Howard, Elizabeth. *Aunt Flossie's Hats (and Crab Cakes Later)*. Illustrated by James Ransome. New York: Clarion, 1991.

Hughes, Shirley. *Two Shoes, New Shoes*. Illustrated by Shirley Hughes. New York: Lothrop, Lee & Shephard, 1986.

Hurwitz, Johanna. *New Shoes for Silvia*. Illustrated by Jerry Pinkney. New York: Morrow, 1993.

Kahlman, Bobbie. *18th Century Clothing*. New York: Crabtree, 1992.

Lindbergh, Anne. *Next Time, Take Care*. Illustrated by Susan Ramsey Hoguret. San Diego: Harcourt Brace Jovanovich, 1988.

Marshall, Janet Perry. *Oh My Gosh! My Pocket*. Homesdale, PA: Bell, 1992.

Miller, Margaret. *Whose Shoe*. Illustrated by Margaret Miller. New York: Greenwillow, 1991.

Morris, Ann. *Hats, Hats, Hats*. Photographs by Kevin Heyman. New York: Lothrop Lee & Shephard, 1989.

Patrick, Denise Lewis. *Red Dancing Shoes*. Illustrated by James E. Ransome. New York: Tambourine, 1993.

Peek, Merle. *Mary Wore Her Red Dress*. Boston: Houghton Mifflin, 1985.

Perl, Lila. *From Top Hats to Baseball Caps, from Bustles to Blue Jeans: Why We Dress the Way We Do*. New York: Clarion, 1990.

Pragoff, Fiona. *Clothing*. New York: Doubleday, 1992.

Ransom, Candice. *The Big Green Pocketbook*. Illustrated by Felicia Bond. New York: HarperCollins, 1993.

Rice, Eve. *Peter's Pockets*. Illustrated by Nancy Winslow Parker. New York: Greenwillow, 1989.

Roy, Ron. *Whose Shoes Are These?* New York: Ticknor, 1988.

Serfozo, Mary. *Benjamin Bigfoot*. Illustrated by Joseph A. Smith. New York: Margaret McElderry, 1993.

Smith, William. *Ho For a Hat*. Illustrated by Lynn Munsinger. Boston: Little Brown, 1989.

Spohn, Kate. *Clementine's Winter Wardrobe*. Illustrated by Kate Spohn. New York: Orchard, 1989.

Stinson, Kathy, and Collins, Heather. *The Dressed Up Book*. Canada: Annick, 1990.

Watts, Bernadette. *Tattercoats*. Illustrated by Bernadette Watts. New York: North-South, 1989.

Winthrop, Elizabeth. *Shoes*. Illustrated by William Joyce. New York: HarperCollins, 1986.

———. *Sledding*. Illustrated by Sarah Wilson. New York: HarperCollins, 1989.

Part 4

The Shapes of Things

A World Full of Colors

The Gifts of Language

We Count!

Chapter 10

The Shapes of Things

We made these little gray houses of logs that you see, and they are square. It is a bad way to live, for there can be no power in a square.

You have noticed that everything an Indian does is in a circle, and that is because the Power of the World always works in circles, and everything tries to be round. . . . The wind, in its greatest power, whirls. Birds make their nests in circles, for theirs is the same religion as ours. . . . Our tepees were round like the nests of birds, and these were always set in a circle, the nation's hoop, a nest of many nests, where the Great Spirit meant for us to hatch our children.[1]   Black Elk

THE BASICS

As this chapter is being written, the first blustery winds of autumn are blowing leaves from the trees, baring silhouetted branches against deep blue September skies. Yellow school buses clog the traffic on crowded streets.

Callie Rose turns eight months old today. She sits in the midst of her toys choosing her favorites: Elmo (her Sesame Street stuffed animal) and her barrelful of colorful plastic triangles, circles, and rectangles. She tastes each of them and finds them delicious. She looks up to see her mommy opening a jar of baby food and squeals with anticipation. After lunch, she and Mommy walk to the park. It's such a beautiful day that Callie's mom decides to stroll a while before swinging Callie. As they pass the swings, Callie cries in agitation. She is "telling" her mom NOT to pass the swings. Swings are among Callie Rose's favorite things.

Callie's friend, Pnina Berk, is fifteen months old. She's not talking much yet, but she understands just about everything said to her. According to her mother, Pnina is at the "fetching" stage. "Fetching is a game but it's also about being a helper, being needed." Ask Pnina to please bring you a stone, an apple, a leaf, a ball, a spoon, a dish, a book, or a specific toy and she springs to action. See how proudly and accurately she delivers the exact item requested!

Twenty-three months old today, Len has a world peopled and shaped by his favorite things: bats, balls, garbage trucks, fire engines, airplanes, helicopters, trains, musical instruments, puzzles, balloons, animals (especially dogs, horses and ducks), sun, moon, and stars. Every day he learns the name of another object and matches the name with its shape in his ever-expanding world. Ask him about it—he'll tell you!

Kimani and his "big" friends just starting kindergarten know it all! They are *not* the toddlers who ask, "What's that?" They are the "elders" who answer the younger questioners. Kimani and his friends know the names for almost everything around them, at home, outside, in stores, on TV, at school, and in the playground. As they make sense out of the world, their language develops at an impressive rate. Their powers of observation and perception are sharp. They hardly miss a trick!

A lifetime exercise that begins immediately after we are born is to bring order out of chaos, to begin to organize the kaleidoscope of impressions that dazzle our senses. We start collecting information about our new world. We see, touch, smell, hear, and taste. What are the objects of our attention? And how do we comprehend them?

We move from the unfamiliar to the familiar, from vague generalizations to specifics. Slowly, in bits and pieces, our world takes shape. That warm, soft, gentle blob becomes "Mother"; that noisy, furry, bouncy shape is "dog"; that delicious, warm, white liquid is "milk"; and that round, bright sphere is "ball."

As we learn these and thousands of other objects, we discover that they are not interchangeable. We begin to differentiate, compare, and organize. We want to give things names and fit them into our expanding framework. This process of sorting, categorizing, labeling, and filing is part of the thought process.

E. H. Gombrich, in his brilliant book *Art and Illusion,*[2] offers a fascinating study of the psychology of perception. He compares the progression of learning to the game of "Twenty Questions." An object is explored through a series of categories until, through the process of exclusion and inclusion, we find the correct answer. We ask such questions as: "Is it big? Is it small? Is it alive? Is it dead? Is it an animal? Is it a person?" Once we know and name the object, it is ours.

Beware of oversimplification! The brain's phenomenal ability to observe, recognize, perceive, comprehend, remember, and imagine visual images is immensely complex. Researchers like Dr. Stephen Kosslyn,[3] pioneering in the field, are attempting to understand the many systems in the brain that enable Callie at eight

months old to not only recognize the shape and image of the swing, but also to know its meaning and understand that she is being deprived of something she likes by walking past it instead of being placed in it. We still can't fully explain how mental stimuli like words, melodies, smells, tastes, or memories can trigger clear images of specific objects or events as vividly as if we directly perceived them.

So when the young teacher said, "Shapes? Oh, we do our basic circles, squares, and triangles in the first month of school. We get it over with fast, then on to more exciting subjects!" I worried about *wonder* getting squeezed out of our curriculum, wonder shrinking before our eyes!

Creative teachers can never "get it over with fast." Shapes are basic to our lives, to everything we experience in this world.

Our children are ready and waiting to be fascinated. We learn from them to remember the power of fascination. As they look at and think about everything around them, moving way beyond "our basic circles, squares, and triangles," they will teach us about the way they construct their worlds. Even as our knowledge increases, the children will remind us to keep the wonder.

When we study the shapes of peoples' features, we can never say that all people of a certain race or nationality look alike. When we study bird nests, we see the similarities and differences between, for example, a wren's nest and a robin's nest. When we look for circles, we can find at least a hundred of them in no time at all. When we follow a cause, we recognize it by the shape of its symbol—an eagle, a cross, a star, a hammer and sickle, a statue of liberty. When we care about friends and family, we read the shapes of their bodies for clues to their feelings. When we go beyond simple observation and identification, we find meaning in specific shapes and may even attribute special qualities to them, as did Black Elk, holy man of the Oglala Sioux, when he spoke of the power of a circle. With all this in mind, how can we "get it over with fast"?

Good teachers know that learning is a process of integrating new information with what is already known. Susan Hendrickson[4] always relates and integrates ideas: "Everything reinforces! We talk about shapes in relation to seasons, numbers, letters, clothes—everything."

Shirley Davis echoes Susan's approach.[5]

> We try to include all the concepts we are learning in everything we do so that they are related to each other. Here's an example. We painted a carton and decorated it as a robot. We talked while we worked about its shape; the shapes, colors and numbers of things we were using for decorating; the letters R-O-B-O-T, what else starts with R, and so on. You would be surprised at how many different ideas young children are able to play with at the same time and how excited they are when they can use familiar concepts in new situations.

Shirley and her lucky students also make shapes part of their everyday conversation: "May I have the rectangular box of chalk?" "Let's sit on our carpet squares." "How about playing with that round, red ball?"

As we help children discover the shapes of things, we stamp those lessons with our own philosophy and attitudes. When we limit the learning to "Oh, let's get our basic circles, squares, and triangles over with fast," we are missing numerous opportunities to nurture imagination and intelligence. In his inspiring essay, "The Misunderstood Role of Arts in Human Development," Elliot W. Eisner discusses the values of a society in relationship to the teaching of the arts.[6] He reminds readers that "in the beginning was the image. It is the image that gives meaning to the label. The information of the image is a cognitive event." In so many instances, we separate form from content. Eisner writes, "Form is regarded as the shape something takes and content is the meaning something conveys." When we think in simplistic, closed-ended ways, we assign labels to things, categorize them, and too often, smugly think that we know them and that no other discoveries about them are needed. When we stop looking at them, we stop exploring their uniqueness.

Young children and most artists teach us to keep looking, keep making discoveries, keep sharpening our perceptions and widening our range of wonder and appreciation.

American educators are making pilgrimages to a small town in Italy, Reggio Emilia,[7] which was described earlier in this book. Because the community of Reggio Emilia is solid in its belief in the importance of the arts and in the way children best learn, they have put their beliefs into action. In this remarkably supportive environment, the "centrality" of the children is articulated and demonstrated. The young children of Reggio Emilia have the opportunities to enjoy total immersion in the arts, to develop ideas over a long duration, and to follow the winding journey of creative adventures as they develop works enriching thematic projects. The visual works created by the children are featured in an exhibit under the title, "The Hundred Languages of Children."

If you can't afford a trip to Italy, look around at the creative, imaginative early childhood programs surrounding you. Visit the Yew Chung International Children's Campus in South Bend, Indiana,[8] and listen to the director, Dr. Helen Lewis, and the head teacher, Blanca Palomo Bandera, describe with enthusiasm their new Art Barn, which is a special place for the children to work in wood, clay, paint, sand, water, textures, fabrics, straw, and Styrofoam—"all the messy stuff." The Art Barn, as beloved a place in the school as the playground, is painted, decorated, and splashed by the children. It's a place to experiment with shapes, designs, materials, and ideas. Yes, you'll see your basic circles, squares, and triangles, but you'll also see much, much more!

Let's get into shape for this chapter! Let's study the shapes of everything we see, notice details, make connections and comparisons, share observations, and express feelings. The activities in this guide will get you started. You'll like the shape of these suggestions!

DISCOVERY TIMES/WONDER TIMES

- We live in a world of shapes. Everything has a shape!
- Basic shapes include circles, squares, rectangles, ovals, and triangles.
- Circles are round.
- Squares have four equal sides and four corners.
- Rectangles have opposite sides of the same length and four corners.
- Ovals are egg-shaped.
- Triangles have three sides and three corners and are pointy.
- Some shapes are flat, have length and width, and are two-dimensional.
- Some shapes are solid and take up more room in space. They have length, width, and height or depth; they are three-dimensional.
- Objects usually keep their shapes. That is how we identify them. We get a lot of ideas from learning about the shapes of things.
- Sometimes shapes change, as when a piece of ice melts, a leaf hardens and shrivels, and a bud opens into a flower.
- Some things change shape dramatically, as when tadpoles become frogs and caterpillars turn into butterflies.
- We put similarly shaped things into categories, such as animals, houses, cars, people, and books. If we stop at the category, we won't explore the many variations with it—for example, imagine all the different kinds of flowers under "flower"!
- Shapes are often associated with special occasions, holidays, events, or ideas. We call them "symbols." Think about hearts for Valentine's Day, cats and pumpkins for Halloween, doves for peace, and the Statue of Liberty for America and for freedom.
- Bodies have shapes. Bodies can change shapes.
- We can usually tell how people feel or think by their posture and facial expressions.
- It is fun to make and rearrange shapes with crayons, paint, clay, and building materials.
- When we use our imaginations, we can see shapes in clouds, stars, stones, and clay.
- Artists train themselves to notice many things about shapes that most people miss because they do not look carefully. Children are very good artists.

SUGGESTED VOCABULARY

shape	zigzag	bird	combine
form	dim	fish	change
outline	hard	toy	touch
shadow	soft	heavy	feel
silhouette	wobbly	light	grow
size	narrow	strong	change
circle	wide	weak	freeze
square	curly	scary	slouch
triangle	sharp	large	droop
rectangle	pointy	small	crumble
corners	thick	funny	whirl
space	thin	silly	melt
angles	still	happy	shrink
sides	moving	sad	paint
oval	open	friendly	carve
sphere	closed	unfriendly	sculpt
things	round	sick	build
objects	curved	healthy	compare
posture	flat	different	statue
facial expressions	smooth	same	sculptor
still	rough	clear	architect
moving	leaf	look	artist
big	tree	see	designer
small	animal	symbol	choreographer
straight	flower	sign	pattern
crooked	person	pattern	design

As in all the lists of suggested words, different categories emerge. Here are words that describe and qualify shapes, words that enrich vocabulary as well as observations. Each adjective provides another ticket to looking and helps us notice qualities we may have otherwise missed.

Feelings words are included in this list because we respond to shapes emotionally. We are affected by the contours and patterns of the world around us.

Think of the words as resources for activities, as starting points for new experiences. Every word is a universe of possibilities!

SOME STARTERS

Start with the real thing! The most ordinary objects are the most effective in starting children thinking about basic shapes. Doughnuts, bagels, wedding bands, paper plates, and tambourines are guaranteed to inspire conversations about circles. Try shoe and cereal boxes, doors and windows to demonstrate squares and rectangles. Hard-boiled eggs are excellent examples of oval shapes. Turn the kids into scientists reporting on what they see. Invite them to become artists, documenting the visual stimuli on paper. Once the children have looked deeply into the different basic shapes through direct encounters with real objects, they will become fascinated by other objects and their combinations of shapes. And there's no end once you start!

Start with a search-and-find game Most young children love challenging games like, "How many circles can we find in this room?" or "I see five triangle shapes in this room. How many can you find?"

Start by wearing a shape badge Children cut out construction paper in the shapes of circles, squares, triangles, or rectangles and pin or tape them to their shirts. The badge reminds the group to focus on a shape and find objects of that shape during the day.

Start with "What if . . . ?" Young children enjoy jokes, riddles, and challenges. "What if wheels were square? What if ladders were round? What if we blew triangular bubbles? What if hens laid square eggs? What if oranges were shaped like bananas? What if we had pointy heads?"

Note: Children's senses of humor change as they develop. If the children do not respond enthusiastically, either they do not comprehend or they are not quite ready for this kind of play. In addition, each group of children has its own dynamics. Experiment. There are no formulas.

In order for children to understand and enjoy the craziness of "What if wheels were square?" they must understand that wheels are round and that only circles can roll smoothly. As Theodore Roethke observed, "The nuttier the assignment, the better the result."[9] Enjoy and experiment.

Start with a close-up study of a painting Such artists as Henri Matisse, Alexander Calder, Paul Klee, and Pablo Picasso painted works characterized by basic shapes. Browse through art books and catalogues and find a variety of artworks for the children to observe and discuss.

Start with "bugs on a log" and other shapely snacks Susan Hendrickson says that "bugs on a log" are excellent snacks for introducing shapes. She and her prekindergartners stuff celery with peanut butter and add raisins. Before they eat this snack, they look at the lines in the celery, the cylindrical shape of the celery, and the wrinkled and oval raisins.

Cookie cutters are of many sizes and shapes. Bake cookies with your children in the shape of circles, squares, stars, and so on. Before the children eat the cookies, ask them to name the shapes.

Start with mail Think about a letter or greeting card. The envelope is usually square or rectangular, as is the stamp. The postmark is usually round.

Start with marking the floor With masking tape or chalk, make a large circle, square, and triangle on the floor. The children will be surprised and fascinated the moment they come into the room. See "Movement and Play Times" for activities to fit these shapes.

Start by sitting *in* a circle and a square Sit in a circle of children, without leaders, without beginning or end. Then change the circle to a square. How does sitting in a square feel compared with sitting in a circle? Talk about it with the children.

Start by sitting *on* a circle and a square Most classes have carpet remnants, sometimes called "sit-upons." Cut sit-upons for each child in the shapes of squares and circles. Now you can play such games as: "Maria, will you pick out a red square sit-upon?" and "Chana, can you find a green circle sit-upon?"

A variation of this idea is to mix and match shapes. Form a circle and sit on circles or squares; form a square and sit on squares or circles.

Start with a silhouette game Cut dark-colored felt or construction paper in different shapes like a rabbit, a horse, a house, a tree, and a person. Ask the children to identify each one. Go one step further and ask, "How do you know?" You are on your way to talking about the idea of shapes.

Start with fingers Finger plays are popular activities. Try making circles, squares, and triangles with fingers. Make up poems to accompany finger works.

Here is an excerpt from a finger-play poem improvised by a group of five-year-olds.

> First we make a circle.
> Then we make two.
> Turn them into glasses
> And look right through!

Start with shadows What is more dramatic for young children than their own shadows following or leading them along the ground? Children are intrigued to discover that their shadows imitate their bodies as they change shapes.

For an enjoyable variation, try a shadow play with a white sheet for a screen and a light behind it, or with a clear section of the wall that is bright with light and catches the silhouette of a shape held in front of it. Children use their hands and bodies or hold up dolls, toys, cars, puppets, or cutouts to tell a story that introduces the idea of shapes.

Start with a shape day For every day of school, you can have a special celebration.

On "shapes days," Shirley Davis and her children label the room by taping construction paper shapes to objects that correspond to the shape of the day. Susan Hendrickson launches a shape day by cutting easel paper in a circle, square, or triangle and placing it on the easel. As soon as the children arrive, they know something is in store for them. All day, art, music, movement, games, snacks, stories, and songs reinforce the concept.

Books come in all shapes, sizes, and contents Almost as vivid as real objects are the images in books illustrated by such artists as Tana Hoban, Chris Van Allsburg, Ezra Jack Keats, Brian Wildsmith, and Eric Carle. Brilliantly illustrated books in contemporary children's literature are astonishing in their variety and high quality. Space limitation confines the number of suggestions. With your children, explore the clarity and textures of the illustrations. Hoban's powerful photographs, Keats' colorful images, Wildsmith's poetic pictures, Van Allsburg's almost supernatural, reach-out-and-touch black-and-white dramatic scenes, and Carle's immediately recognizable story lines are examples of books that can start children thinking about the shapes of things.

If we had time and space, we could easily demonstrate how a single raindrop, a blade of grass, a polka dot, a Band-Aid, and—we won't forget—a grain of sand can start you off on a journey exploring the shapes of things.

TALK TIMES/LISTENING TIMES

Because conversations about shapes can be all-inclusive, they are difficult to end. Conversations about shapes inevitably involve comparisons and contrasts, careful observations, and telling details. Conversations about shapes are also important avenues for expressing emotions.

Favorite shapes Dawn Heyman and her student teacher, Tracy Skistimas,[10] were amazed by their students' spirited responses to the question, "What are some of your favorite shapes?" Here are excerpts from that discussion:

> **Shawn:** *Car bodies. Also, ovals, because ovals make me think of moving spaceships.*
>
> **Turhaan:** *Twinkling stars, because they change shape.*
>
> **Tracy:** *Some shapes have the idea of feelings. What do you think are happy shapes? Sad shapes?*
>
> **John:** *A happy shape is a running horse.*
>
> **Kenita:** *Love is a heart shape, but sadness is a torn heart shape.*
>
> **Frankie:** *This is the saddest shape. (He drew a paddle for spanking.)*
>
> **Jeff:** *A mountain struck by lightning—that's the saddest shape.*
>
> **Tracy:** *A sad shape is a teardrop.*
>
> **Saunjia:** *A sad shape is a dying, drooping flower.*
>
> **John:** *A sad shape? A circle cut in half and turned upside down—that's a sad shape.*
>
> **Shawn:** *A shaking wire is a nervous shape.*
>
> **Doug:** *A nervous shape is a red square pierced by a black triangle.*
>
> **David:** *A tire is a happy shape.*
>
> **Doug:** *You know what a proud shape is? Many gold and yellow circles.*
>
> **Carmen:** *A sad and scary shape is a rundown picket fence. The shape of a person's mind is wisdom.*

Note how easily children expand their thinking when they are familiar with basic information. Doug's image of a red square pierced by a black triangle as a "nervous shape" shows the development of imagination and symbolism that proceeds from an understanding of the concepts.

When the children's activities are based on their own feelings and suggestions freely expressed, the experiences become more meaningful and relevant. Imagine, for example, a class collage featuring twinkling star, running horse, mountain struck by lightning, teardrop, drooping flower, and gold and yellow circles. A stimulating exercise for the children is to paint a picture of the shape of a person's mind. "How can we show the shape and design of wisdom?"

Getting to the shapes of things Even very young children have much to say about the fascinating topic of shapes. Patti Link[11] and her children enjoyed a lively discussion that demonstrated remarkable understanding of shapes, objects, and ideas. Enjoy eavesdropping!

> **Laura:** *Books are rectangles, but there are some round books, too.*
>
> **Eric:** *If you had a round book for colors, it would be a rainbow.*
>
> **Patti:** *Does everything have a shape?*
>
> **Ben:** *No, air doesn't.*
>
> **Eric:** *Hair doesn't.*
>
> **Patti:** *What shape is hair?*

Children: *Lines . . . lines are shapes.*

Ben: *Soap doesn't have a shape.*

Children: *Yes, it does!*

Ben: *No, liquid soap doesn't have a shape!*

Patti: *Faces have different shapes. Look around.*

Children: *Ovals, triangles, squares.*

Patti: *What's a sad shape?*

Bill: *An upside-down smile.*

Eric: *An upside-down rainbow.*

Laura: *A banana shape. An arc.*

Steve: *A flat tire is a sad shape.*

Jill: *A shoelace is a happy shape.*

Eric: *So is a clown.*

Laura: *My finger is a rectangle with a little circle (nail) at the end of it.*

The younger children are still working with the technical aspects of shapes. They are very specific and insist on using basic terminology, as demonstrated by Laura, described the shape of a banana as an arc. Here again, we see that children enjoy going beyond simple observations to more imaginative levels. All they need is a little encouragement.

A wonderful way to develop excellent listening habits is to suggest to the children as you begin a talk time that something special is going to happen at the end of the discussion, so they need to pay careful attention. Try playing a guessing game by asking such questions as: "Who said a tire is a happy shape?" "David!" "Who said a teardrop is a sad shape?" "Tracy!" Or you can ask the children to draw a picture of a shape they remember talking about. When the pictures are finished and shared, encourage the children to remember who suggested them.

Look, compare, talk, and discover Teachers like Ken Valimaki[12] fill their rooms not only with objects and pictures, but also with the buzz of conversation. Active listening, total participation, and the free exchange of ideas enrich understanding. Ken describes the kinds of learning experiences he and his children develop: "I always present alternatives. When we talk about, say, circles, we don't look at just one circle but at circles of different sizes and colors. We talk and look at many examples. We compare. We explore the room, the school, the neighborhood. We ask a lot of questions and make observations. We try to see relationships, see how other ideas fit with this new one. We use nature a lot. We're open to discovery. It's crucial to do things that excite the kids! We talk about the shapes of everything—traffic signs, rocks, trees, mountains, houses, animals, machines. . . ."

Imagine how ready the children are to follow such dynamic discussions with writing, art works, stories, movement, and songs. Talk times fuel creative energies.

The shape of imagination Always be open for the provocative, imaginative questions of children. Harrison, age 5, asked his mother, "Mommy, what shape are voices?" His mom hemmed and hawed and mumbled a vague response. Harrison thought for a moment then told her, "They're in circles!" His mom asked why. "Voices come out in circles," Harrison informed her, "because in books and everything, they draw circles around voices."

Invite all questions and observations, even when you have no answers. With the children, explore possible solutions!

Close-Ups, wide angles, and hidden pictures—How much can you see? Young children are intrigued with challenging invitations. *Look Closer*, Peter Ziebel's close-up photographs of such familiar objects as shredded wheat, shoelaces, zippers, and sugar, combined with guessing the identity of the subjects, forces children to take a closer look at things.[13] The more we look, the more we see. *Anno's Journey* begins with a single person rowing a tiny boat on a vast sea.[14] Page by page, image by image, shape by shape, the world widens. Houses, streets, roads, churches, and schools pack the expanding scenes. This kind of story inspires children to begin with a simple, single shape of an idea and help it develop. Always encourage the children to "keep looking—what *else* do you see? Let's talk about it!" Talk leads to action!

Brian Wildsmith's *Puzzles*[15] is an example of a book that urges the children to look deeper and closer as they discover answers to such questions as: "How many animals can you see in this picture?" Every page will evoke lively talking/listening responses.

Talking about everything This is a theme that can't be contained in a limited session or two. It is pervasive. Once children are tuned into the idea that everything has a shape, they will notice, share observations, and spin off ideas into movement, drama, play, music, and arts. I find children gathered around talking about such delightful old and new books as *The Shape of Me and Other Stuff; Red Bear's Fun with Shapes;* and these three books about basic shapes, *The Circle Sarah Drew, The Square Ben Drew,* and *The Line Sophie Drew.*[16] The children's conversation is so loud they are shushed by the librarian. They ask for paper and pencil to draw their own pictures about shapes. They love all the ways circles find themselves, all the different meanings. They love guessing Sophie's lines and finding them in different scenes. They want to write and draw their own books called *The Shape of Me and Other Stuff!*

VISUAL ARTS TIMES

A focus on shapes is about noticing everything around us. In learning communities that offer abundant, inviting materials mixed with ample time for delightful exploration, visual arts times will be most of the time! Just as those fortunate children in

Reggio Emilia, Italy, experience joyful immersion in the arts, so numerous American children participate in dynamic, holistic programs. For example, Dr. Rebecca Kantor shares feelings and ideas about the Sophie Rogers Early Childhood Lab School at Ohio State University.[17] Dr. Kantor and her staff are gatherers and presenters of varieties of materials, supporters, and guides, helping the children develop concepts and confidence. Because the children spend so much time exploring materials of all sizes and shapes, learning meanings and how they combine and change, they can expand to more complex adventures. For example, the children at Sophie Rogers talked about, walked about, and read stories about cities. From their interest and information, they were inspired to launch a tremendous undertaking—to build their own city! Dr. Kantor and her staff strongly believe that the children's ideas are at the beginning of curriculum. The kids enjoyed deep and direct experiences with materials—learning to understand and manipulate basic shapes, exploring, constructing, and playing with shapes. Because of those vitally important experiences, they were able to move on to the grand scheme of building a city. And the amazing phenomenon discovered by the adults was the length of time the children stayed excited and involved. Their city developed over *weeks!* It grew in intricacy. Using basic shapes, the children constructed buildings, streets, transportation, signs, trees, and animals. Materials, time, free flow of ideas: Go!

Big shapes, little shapes   Ken Valimaki shares one of his most popular activities: "I like to start kids off thinking about shapes with big shapes and little shapes. We talk, demonstrate, look around the room, and look at books to gather ideas. Then we go to our easels and paint or color big and little shapes. We put them in rows, overlap them, put them in circles, combine them with special colors, and make collages."

Tear a shape   This activity is popular with Ken's young students, who need lots of opportunities to cut, tear, paste, and make patterns. Ken and his students work with great satisfaction in creating irregular, rough-edged shapes; tearing frees them from the more concise expectations of cutting. They talk about what they see in their shapes. Walking and talking, they find irregular shapes in nature. They gather twigs, leaves, wood clumps, and stones and bring them back to the classroom to study and compare with their own torn shapes.

Tree full of shapes   Shirley Davis and her three- and four-year-olds grow shapes instead of leaves on their construction paper or real tree. Shirley often designates different shapes for different branches and asks the children to fill the tree with a branch of circles, of squares, and of triangles, usually correlated with special colors and numbers so the lesson is multifaceted. For example, Shirley suggests: "Let's put five green circles on this branch."

As part of your attention to basic shapes, children enjoy creating books (illustrations and words) cut in the shape of squares, circles, triangles, and rectangles. Be as expansive as possible as you and the children discuss ways to celebrate their shapes books. Old favorites like *A Kiss Is Round*[18] inspire many ideas, for example, "A kiss is round and so is a hug . . ." and "Nests are round little homes for sparrows. . . ." What else is round or square or triangular? Share ideas. Write about them. Illustrate them.

Shapes Are for Touching   Children's hands need to trace the journey of lines, the roundness of spheres, the corners of squares. This study of shapes is a hands-on process. The children will want to put their hands in mud, clay, sand, shaving cream, and playdough and create and re-create their own understandings of shapes. Be ready for surprises. Books like *Mudworks*[19] will help you keep your materials and ideas plentiful.

Going-around-in-circles mobiles   Children color and decorate different-sized circles and attach them on strings to a simple wood or hanger mobile. When the room is dotted with circles, enjoy talking about how that design makes everyone feel.

Do not limit your mobiles to circles. After you have studied all the shapes, fill the room with combinations of interesting mobiles.

Weather shapes With your class, design special shapes for particular weather conditions, such as rain, fog, sun, snow, wind, and storm. Be sure to make them on heavy construction paper; laminate them if possible. Use them every day as "weather helpers" to show and tell the weather report.

Funny people shapes Another of Shirley Davis's most popular activities is to have the children cut pictures of people from magazines and put heads on one paper plate, arms on another, and legs on yet another. The children use body trunks of construction paper and glue on different heads, arms, and legs to make funny-looking people. Shirley's classes also enjoy arranging circles, triangles, squares, and rectangles to make people.

What you can make from shapes Cut out an ample supply of basic shapes from brightly colored paper. Encourage the children to discover what surprises lie in store as they make patterns and experiment with the shapes. When they find combinations they like, they glue or paste the shapes to their papers.

This is a marvelous way for children to find out (without the aid of ditto sheets or workbooks) that a circle and a triangle make an ice-cream cone, a clown with a party hat, a bird's head, and a little sailboat; a square or rectangle and a triangle make a house, a building, a rocket ship, and a pencil; a face with eyes, nose, and mouth can be easily composed of circles and triangles; and trains, trucks, and cars are fun to make from circles and squares or rectangles. Always ask, "What else?"

Ovals and self-portraits Talk is an important part of understanding. Talk about what makes up a face and its expressions. Start with ovals and ask the children to add features to make self-portraits. Mirrors are helpful in this activity.

Ken Valimaki adds an idea to this activity. Before the children use mirrors in creating self-portraits, he asks them to draw themselves as they think they look. The children make stimulating observations about the two self-portraits.

Still life of different shapes Young children practice the art of careful looking as they study a group of different shapes and try to represent their special qualities. Encourage the children to experiment with thick, thin, dark, and light lines as they work. Some children especially like to work with large crayons. Susan Hendrickson offers her students an array of materials: "Some kids like Magic Markers. Others prefer crayons or paints. Still others like to build the idea with blocks. Then there are the kids who favor using felt and other textures."

Scrounge shapes for collages, montages, and sculptures Scrounge buttons of all sizes and colors; Popsicle sticks; twigs; magazine pictures; parts of toy cars, trucks, and planes; greeting cards; playing cards; bubble wrap; Styrofoam; confetti; pieces of jewelry; pie tins; paper cups; spools; and baby food jars. Encourage the children to experiment with these materials and see what new patterns they create.

Make something stand. Ken Valimaki introduces young students to three-dimensional shapes by handing out construction paper and paste or glue and instructing them to "Try to find a way to make the paper stand by itself." The children twist, fold, roll, tear, and pinch their papers until—presto—they have standing forms. Their paper sculptures can be looked at from every side, and they learn the difference between two- and three-dimensional shapes.

Shapes and feelings Children easily relate feelings to shapes and, going a step further, create images that give shapes to feelings. With whatever materials they choose, children respond enthusiastically to the suggestion that they paint, color, draw, or sculpt a happy shape, a sad shape, an angry shape, a silly shape, a shy shape, a proud shape, a friendly shape, a strange shape, and a new shape. As often as possible, ask the children to tell you something about the shapes they create.

One kindergartner showed me a flattened-out strip of clay and explained, "When I'm sad, I just lie down and wait till it's over. That's the lying-down part of sad."

Shapes for the Seven Dwarfs Snow White's friends, the Seven Dwarfs, correlate marvelously with feelings and shapes. Talk about the dwarfs, their names, and their special qualities. Enrich the discussion with movement activities (see movement section). The children may choose to celebrate one dwarf with a special design, picture, or shape, or they may choose several, even all seven.

Divide the walls into seven sections, one for each dwarf's pictures, and label the sections. Turn the shapes into badges that the children can wear to express their feelings. Write stories and songs about the dwarfs.

These activities provide an excellent opportunity to discuss shapes and facial expressions and how one little change of a line or curve can turn a happy face into a grumpy face. One group of children created all seven dwarfs using only circles, squares, rectangles, ovals, and triangles.

Favorite shapes After you and your class have studied and talked about shapes for a while, it is time to gather ideas, write or illustrate them on the board, and ask the children to choose a favorite shape. Now they are ready to concentrate on how to celebrate their favorite shapes in patterns.

Some children fill a sheet of construction or drawing paper with their shape in different sizes and colors; other children experiment with their shapes overlapping or exploding from a central point. Kelly chose birds as her favorite shape and used markers to draw a flock of migrating birds. Ariela designed a pattern of hearts, beginning in one corner of the paper with a tiny red heart and ending in the opposite corner with a large red heart.

This activity can be an effective way for children to learn about perspective. They look at their papers and see that some of the shapes appear far away, while others seem near. Discuss and display their discoveries.

Collectible shapes With your students, scrounge large cardboard boxes from your local supermarket and designate a different shape to be collected for each box. One group of first graders lined seven boxes along the wall, each labeled and decorated. The children, over a period of weeks, collected boxes of circles, squares, triangles, rectangles, leaves, animal shapes, and people shapes. The boxes were filled with such items as magazine pictures, cutouts, coloring book pages, bits and pieces of games and toys, snaps and knobs and buttons, plastic tops of cans, geometric patterns, and paper dolls.

This assignment had the children on their toes in seven ways for weeks, because they were on the alert for samples of the seven types of objects they had decided to gather. As they played with the contents, they marveled at how their boxes filled.

As a follow-up activity, the children were asked to choose one or more of the items gathered and make an arrangement or sculpture. Interestingly, a few children chose only one or two kinds of shapes and worked intently. Only two or three children chose to work with all seven ideas. Their works had titles such as "Jason's Study of Triangles," "Leaves and Squirrels," and "Cheryl's Study of People, Circles, Leaves, and Cats." The exhibit of all the art was enthusiastically received by the children, other classes, and parents.

Turn yourself into a shape The children design shapes that represent them. Record their shapes on a chart next to their names. After a while, the children learn their classmates' shapes. Play such games as: "When I draw your shape on the board, please stand," or "Guess whose shape I'm coloring." Use their shape symbols as often as possible for helper assignments, game positions, activities designations, buddies, and play groups.

Your name is a shape Probably the first word children learn to recognize and spell is their own name. Print or have the children print their names in their favorite colors on a sheet of paper. Encourage them to make designs or shapes out of their names by outlining the letters, coloring them, and creating patterns around them. Use these pictures alone or combined with the children's photographs, symbols (see above), or self-portraits. Remember—each letter and number is an important shape!

Field guides Michael Joel Rosen's *Kids' Best Field Guide to Neighborhood Dogs,* which accompanies his *Kids' Best Dog Book,*[20] is guaranteed to inspire children to illustrate their own field guides about the animals, plants, flowers, and trees they like the best. As you share Michael's *Field Guide,* which features more than seventy kinds of dogs, you and your children will sharpen your powers of awareness and perception. How are these dogs different? What special qualities do they have? What particular features do we notice? The children's artworks will reflect this deeper, closer look.

Shapes around the planet Mesas, mountains, canyons, cacti, hills, fields, and forests—these are the designs, landscapes, and shapes given to us by nature. Books like *The Seashore Book,*[21] beautifully illustrated by Wendell Minor, will validate the experiences of children who know the shapes of seashore and will nurture the imagination of children who have never seen the sea. Having read about gulls overhead, sailboats on the horizon, water lapping the sand, and a full moon shining on seaweed and shells, children are ready to contribute their own images of seashore. Sand dunes, camels, donkeys, and vast, graceful fields of sand introduce new images of land shapes and designs to young children. *Deserts*[22] gives children ideas to create their own earth shapes, landscapes, and seascapes.

Snow shapes Snow is an excellent background for showing off shapes. The contrast of line, color, texture, depth of objects, and people against a splash of snow is exciting. Children who live in snowy climates can create snow collages of shapes and images in real snow! Pour soap flakes in a box or on a plate for an inside project. Cotton puffs glued to paper or cardboard make excellent snow scenes. Snow books like *First Snow, Snow,* and *Snowy Day*[23] help children clearly see the power of sled lines, roundness of snowflakes, and crystal-clear outlines of myriad objects and people set against the snow. Their own artistic works will snowball!

Sky shapes Stars, moons, suns, and planets—these are among our most beloved images. Children love to cut them out, paste them, create collages, murals, T-shirts, posters, and sculptures, honoring these universally honored shapes.

In stunningly illustrated picture books, children find images and stories that inspire their own stories and pictures. In Charlotte Zolotow's *The Moon Was the Best*[24], with powerful photographs by Tana Hoban, a mother tells her little girl all the special sights she enjoyed in Paris. Each page/memory is more beautiful than the previous. Each page will have the children almost able to walk into the vividly conveyed scenes. Which sight was the best of all? The moon! Crescent Dragonwagon's lovely story, *Half a Moon And One Whole Star,*[25] is another example of a poetically narrated story about the coming of night, heralded by half a moon and one whole star and a little girl dozing in her bed as the animal and plant world prepare to sleep and the people in the city and on ships make their night music and do their night work. So many things are happening as that one whole star and half a moon rise in the night sky! We are so fortunate to have so many excellently written and illustrated children's books. Every page is an experience of exploration discovering shapes, images, colors, and meanings.

Children enjoy creating night pictures and day pictures. Under their huge sun shapes, they add daytime ideas of work and play. Under their star and moon shapes, they create their night images.

Changing shapes One of Barbara Chavous's favorite explorations with children is to give them ten sheets of paper and ask them to draw a tree or a flower or a circle (any familiar shape) on the first sheet of paper. After one minute, she instructs the children to stop and turn to the next blank page: "Please draw a tree on this page." After a minute, she stops them again and they go on to the next page with the challenge of drawing the same idea. When the ten pages are finished, the children share the excitement of displaying their ten different trees, circles, and flowers (whatever

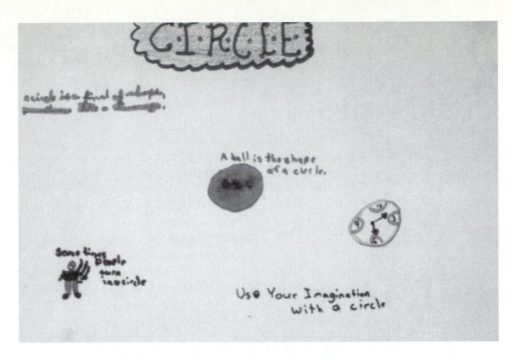

the image). No two of their pages are ever exactly the same. A child's ten trees or ten circles convey life and energy as you flip through the pages.

Seasonal changes, metamorphoses, weather variations, bodies growing, folding and unfolding, and seeds to flowers—children are fascinated by the dynamics of life. Even mountains erode! Children illustrate these ideas on strips of paper divided into sections, on accordion pages, and on flow charts. With scrounge materials they construct cocoons, constellations, and seasons. Changes are exciting!

Everything in the whole wide world and other stuff One of my favorite books is *Grover and the Everything in the Whole Wide World Museum*,[26] a wild and wacky story that tries to categorize everything in the whole world with labels like "tall things," "underwater things," and "very light things"—well, you get the point and can probably imagine the many categories for things in the whole wide world that you and your children can organize! With every kind of material from crayons to paints to tossed-away fast-food containers to cardboard and spackle, glitter and glue, children honor and categorize the shapes they love. Build them, mount them, exhibit them, hang them, label them, describe them, and spread them across tables, shelves, walls, and boards! Surround the children with inspiring books to get them going in case they need an extra push. Children enjoy books that present the shapes of things in vivid ways. Examples of excellent resources are: *Wheels;*[27] the hilarious spirit of *Roger's Umbrella;*[28] the bold images of *Ducks Fly;*[29] the mysterious and exotic images of *Dragon Kite of the Autumn Moon;*[30] the whirly images from countries around the world in *Henry's World Tour;*[31] and the beloved Max in *Where the Wild Things Are,*[32] presenting a study of shapes with triangles for ears and crown, circles for buttons, and semicircles for mouths.

In your gathering of Everything in the Wide World for your own museum, be sure to include shapes from memory, imagination, and tactile encounters. Talk times and listening times generate images in the mind. Don't limit the children's experiences to the pages in books or pictures on a wall. Their minds are full of pictures, shapes, and images.

These are but a few suggestions of countless possibilities at your fingertips. We didn't have time or space to go into detail about hand shapes, sign language and gestures, geometric shapes of indigenous designs, and symbols—jewelry, charm

bracelets, closets of shapes, clotheslines of shapes. . . . I warn you, you will not have room in your notebook for all the ideas waiting right before your round or oval eyes and under your triangular nose. Keep filling those pages!

MUSIC TIMES

At a break during a staff development program, I spoke to a few classroom teachers who wanted to know how my book was coming along. When I told them I was beginning a section on shapes and music times, a few teachers nodded enthusiastically. One teacher looked puzzled and asked, "How on earth do you see a connection between shapes and music? Isn't that stretching it?"

The more we think about shapes, the more that "everywhere" theme relates to everything, including music times. This little subsection is dedicated to all skeptical souls who may not even realize that the design of a question mark is an interesting shape that changes the music of our conversation. Right?

Shapes of musical instruments Musical instruments, so magical in their powers, have distinct shapes as well as generically recognized patterns, like circles in tambourines, drums, bells, rattles, cymbals, and so on.

Susan Hendrickson describes one of her most enjoyable ways to combine musical instruments and shapes. "When I teach the children about Native Americans, I get out the drum and announce that I'm the Chief. I beat the children's names rhythmically and call them to form a circle. We talk about the drum having a circle shape and about our circle of friends around the drum."

Each instrument has a shape and design that children find fascinating to study. They learn to recognize and name instruments by their shapes. When your students listen to different kinds of music, show them the instruments, or pictures of the instruments, that are making the music.

Begin this yearlong activity with instruments the children already know from home and school. Move from the familiar to the new.

Follow the shape of the instrument One way to conduct your rhythm band is to show a picture or drawing of the instrument to be played. Some teachers make a chart showing all the instruments, and the leader points to the instrument that begins the music.

The shape of music Children relish the challenge of listening to different kinds of music and imagining the shapes they hear. Give the children the opportunity to use the art materials they prefer as they listen to a variety of short musical selections and fill their papers with shapes inspired by the music.

A first grader explained the dark triangles on his jazzy paper: "That music kept popping up like rockets, with pointy notes." A kindergartner clarified his picture of circles tumbling across the paper as his response to a cowboy song: "The music is full of wheels rolling along." And a second grader drew lively stick figures to music by the Ohio State University Marching Band. "This music makes you do gymnastics," she explained.

Parade of musical shapes After the children have studied the shapes of musical instruments, organize a parade according to families of shapes. Instruments that are circular and spherical cluster together. Here come the tambourines, bells, drums, and maracas! Next are rectangular and cylindrical instruments such as flutes, horns, and pipes. Don't forget the triangles!

You may want to organize the parade of musical instruments into categories like big instruments (guitars and banjos) and small instruments (bells, triangles, or whistles). Another idea is to ask the drum majors or cheerleaders to hold up pictures of each instrument in the parade followed by the children playing those instruments.

Compose cheers and rhythms for each instrument or group of instruments.

The shapes of musical notes You need not be so technical about musical notes that young children lose interest, which is often the case. Children have no trouble learning that music has its own language and that the language helps us to sing and play songs. The shape of the language is very interesting and easily recognizable.

The staff has five parallel lines; the treble clef "is all swirly," as five-year-old Jackie observed; and the bass clef looks like "a question mark with two little dots," Boris told his first-grade friends. "To me, it looks like a fish's face. See his eye. And the two dots are two little bubbles!" Juan added. "The notes are little ovals with thin lines connected to them," Jeffrey told his kindergarten colleagues. "When the notes go up the lines in the staff, you sing higher and higher," Marcos explained. "Like climbing a ladder. The notes tell you that. You have to watch them," Kira piped in.

As you can see from these fragments of children's discussions about the language and shape of music, imagination, sharing ideas, and enjoying discovery are more important than a short-answer quiz in notation.

Try turning musical notes into happy faces when simple, happy songs are sung, such as "Good Morning to You" and "Pop Goes the Weasel." A few curves and lines give musical notes sleepy faces when lullabies are sung. This activity also provides the opportunity to review the power of shapes in conveying facial expressions and feelings.

Animal sounds and shapes Children are knowledgeable about animal shapes. Even urban children, whose firsthand experiences with animals may be limited to squirrels, pigeons, dogs, and cats, can recognize and name many different animals by looking at their pictures or outlines.

Every animal has its own sound. Give children the chance to identify an animal from a picture or an outline, then demonstrate its sound. This idea can flow in many directions. Here are just a few suggestions.

Divide the children into animal groups. When their animal's shape is held up, they make that animal's sounds. Give the group time to practice the sounds so they can work them into patterns and rhythms.

What happens when two different pictures are held up at the same time? Which two animals make the "best music" together? Listen to all the combinations and decide which sound the best. Use the animal pictures to set the sequences and arrangements.

Encourage the children to use their imaginations to create sounds for such animals as fish, caterpillars, butterflies, ants, ladybugs, giraffes, and lizards.

Move from verbal and body sounds to musical instruments. "What instruments and rhythms shall we use to produce bird songs? What instruments shall we choose to make the croaking song of frogs?" Develop a symphony of animal shapes and sounds. Correlate this activity with movement, drama, creative writing, and visual arts.

"What is the shape of a cat's meow?" After looking at animal shapes, identifying them, and listening to and talking about their sounds, ask the children to draw, paint, and color the "shape of their sounds." The results are remarkable. Be sure to label pictures with the children's own titles. Four-and-a-half-year-old Carlita proudly showed her paper covered with tiny, colorful dots. The title of her picture was "A Baby Bird Cheeping."

Music for basic shapes Rhoda Linder[33] and Wendy Wohlstein's class of three-and-a-half-year-olds[34] enjoyed a day devoted to celebrating squares. Wendy decorated herself in colorful squares pinned and taped to her clothing. She wrote a sing-song poem that she sang to and later taught the children.

I'm Sarah Square
And I don't care

If the shapes on my skin
Tickle my chin, pinch my nose
Or scratch my cheek.
No—I don't care—this is Shapes Week.

I've got green ones, orange ones, red ones and blue.
I know what the shape is today, do *you?*
It's not a rectangle, no, not at all.
Not a circle, not shaped like a ball.
Not a triangle, in case you care,
The shape of my body is a
          SQUARE!

When Susan Hendrickson and her students dedicated a day to round shapes, Susan composed a poem-song for the celebration:

Round is a doughnut,
A penny, a hug.
Round is a cookie,
A kiss and a bug.
Round is whatever you feel outside
When your inside smiles up
And sings to the sky.

A group of kindergartners who spent the day celebrating squares talked about the kind of music that fits the shape of squares. After experimenting with different kinds of music, the children chose marching music. Why? "Because we march in straight lines and turn sharp corners!" "And we're real even, like squares are even all around."

In trying to decide what kind of music reflects the special qualities of circles, a class of first graders listened to about five offerings and voted for "The Children's March" from Rogers and Hammerstein's *The King and I*. They did so "Because it sounds like somersaults and somersaults are circles rolling."

On Triangles Day a group of four-and-a-half-year-olds thought the 1–2–3 Latin-American rhythm of a conga fit the three angles and three lines of a triangle. If you were a triangle, wouldn't you want to listen to and do the conga? No question about it!

Shape up your rhythm band Why should your young musicians sit or march randomly when they can form a circle, square, triangle, or rectangle and play their music? "Ladies and gentlemen, we present a square of fine musicians!"

If the group decides to become a marching band, a circle of musicians will march in a circle, a square of musicians will march in a square, and so on.

Combine these activities with the children's interpretation of special music for their special formations. Have fun exploring these challenges.

Shape up your conducting Orchestras and music makers need conductors. When conductors' minds are filled with basic shapes, they are able to use those shapes as they conduct.

Give the children chances to take turns conducting taped and live classroom music. Encourage them to lead with the body language of shapes. Their skillful hands and arms draw imaginary shapes in the air as they direct the music. Take a turn yourself.

Next time you watch great conductors at work, notice how many circles, squares, triangles, and spirals they draw in the air with their hands and batons.

Travel the world through shapes and sounds Even our youngest children soon learn to associate specific images with specific places. For example, balloons go with parties and clowns with circuses; serapes, sombreros, and donkeys might convey images of Mexico; hula dancers, palm trees, ocean, and beaches could say Hawaii. Go one step further. Recognize the shapes and the images of a place or an event and add music that enhances the idea. Yodeling songs could accompany a scene of snow-capped Alps; bagpipes could bounce young Scottish dancers dressed in plaid kilts; whistles, flutes, and drums and percussion instruments could enliven pictures or posters of colorful West African festivals. Look at a photograph of a city's skyline and think together about the music that could enrich the idea of "city." As you blend images with music, you are giving the children many opportunities to learn to appreciate the rich diversity of the peoples and places of the world.

But beware of stereotyping! Even as you and your children enjoy the process of matching and making music to enrich appreciation of specific shapes and images, remind them that many, many combinations are possible—no one association is the only association. Who knows? Perhaps the music rising from the snow-capped Alps is country and western or reggae! When Billy married Mary Jane, the ceremony was highlighted by the joyful playing of Hava Nagila with bagpipes! In this ever-shrinking world, people are making new and surprising connections. Keep minds and hearts open at all times!

Shapes and songs As often as possible inspire the learning and singing of a favorite song with an appropriate shape. Check resources at your fingertips, such as books, magazines, and record covers, to help children make connections. Create your own images out of felt or construction paper.

Inventive teachers across the country find railroad trains to roll along with railroad songs, rivers to flow with songs about rivers, sun to warm the vocal cords for songs about sunshine, ships to sail along with songs about ships, rabbits to hop along with songs about rabbits, and umbrellas for rain songs.

Skinny songs, fat songs A group of first graders talked about the thin and thick qualities of lines and shapes. About a half hour after the discussion, the children had a singing session. They took turns singing lines alone, and the whole class joined in for the chorus. One of the girls observed that "When one person sings, it's a skinny sound; and when everyone sings, it's fat!" Children teach us to apply new knowledge and make unexpected and often captivating connections.

Fast, slow, high, low, big, small! Comparing, contrasting, perceiving specific qualities—all of these are part of developing comprehension. As we learn about the shapes around us, we enrich our understanding by combining meanings. Musical elements like melody, tone, and rhythm that convey pitch, timbre, and dynamics like loudness and softness are easily related to shapes. A simple book like *How Big? How Fast? How Hungry?*[34] is about different qualities of cats. A cheetah is faster than a house cat. When the children talk about and look at pictures in the book of cheetahs, the music they create will be *fast!* The house cat's music will be much slower. *Polar Bear, Polar Bear, What Do You Hear?*[35] highlights bold and colorful animal images of different shapes and sizes with excellent sound words for musical cues like "hissing," "yelping," "bellowing," "whistling," and "fluting." The images and shapes are full of contrasts. The music accompaniments the children compose will help them see the varieties of sounds, melodies, rhythms, and dynamics possible to create. Amazing discoveries! Add music to the text. Sing the words! As children learn to recognize the shapes of their world, they naturally add ideas to their understandings. Music is always an excellent idea to add to everything! A book like *In the Tall, Tall Grass*[36] is rich with recognizable shapes of caterpillars, bees, birds, and snakes hiding, living, and moving in the thick green grass. Each page features wonderful words for singing, moving, and imagining. Heavy words like "lug" and "tug" need heavy sounds. Moles make small, scratchy sounds. Beetles make fast sounds like "skitter, scurry, hurry." The children enjoy exploring a variety of music and movement interpretations inspired by the shapes of creatures on the colorful pages.

Musical notes are made of circles and lines. Instruments come in rectangles, triangles, squares, and circles. Every "thing" and "being" has its shape and language of sounds, its own music.

When Leslie Zak[37] sings with children sitting in the sacred circle, they sing "circular songs." Those are songs that if you didn't deliberately end them would just keep going like a circle! Shall we sing a "round"?

MOVEMENT AND PLAY TIMES

Remember that movement and play are the ways children learn. Wherever children live they will play. If they don't have toys, they will improvise toys of boxes, tubings, containers, pots, pans, and dishes. The ironic twist is that most children enjoy playing with the packing boxes complicated toys arrive in rather than the battery-operated, flashing, flashy toys themselves! Len, the Muffin Man, at twenty-three months old, loves anything that's round—balls of all sizes, balloons, basketball hoops, the sun, hula hoops. . . . Callie, at eight months old, is all hands, reaching, grabbing, twirling, touching every interesting shape that she encounters. Kimani and his buddies build intricate civilizations of blocks, boxes, construction sets, and scrounged materials.

Ask toddlers to show you "how big?" and their arms will stretch out. Ask toddlers to show you "how small?" and they bend down with lowered hands. Moving and playing, they shape their world! The following are but a few ideas to encourage them in their journey. Keep adding, rearranging, and playing with your own ideas!

Singing games/Changing shapes Familiar children's games take on special meanings when they become part of a focus on shapes. In "Ring Around the Rosy," children sing two words, "ring" and "around," that reinforce their understandings of circles. When children circle around for "Have You Ever Seen a Lassie?" encourage the child in the center to make interesting body shapes "this way and that way." Good old "Old MacDonald" could have a farm of shapes. Children enjoy choosing shape badges to wear or hold. Combine them with colors. Now, Old MacDonald can sing,

> On the farm, he had some circles . . .
> On the farm, he had some blue squares . . .
> On the farm, he had some triangles . . .
> On the farm, he had some birds/fish/trees . . .

All circle games help children understand the concept of "circle." Think of all the times you sing "around" with the kids, from "Mulberry Bush" to "Comin' Round the Mountain" to "The Wheels of the Bus Go Round and Round"! Highlight the shapely ideas.

"Let's give those kids a round of applause!" Spark your demonstrations of appreciation (which I hope are frequent) by clapping for yourselves. It's good for circulation and celebration. Instead of the usual hand clapping, try clapping in a circle shape—a *round* of applause. Clap in a square pattern: "Let's give ourselves a *square* of applause!" Clap in a triangular pattern: "Let's give these kids a *triangle* of applause!" In all of our classes, this has become a way of rejoicing with each other.

Show-me games These games are modified by innovative teachers to fit whatever theme they are highlighting. "Fernando, show me something in the room that's square." "I'm thinking about something in the room that's a red circle. Can you point to it, Danny?" "I see three green squares of different sizes. Can you find them, Katia?"

The children enjoy being the "instructor" in this kind of game and directing challenges to their classmates. Nothing is more satisfying to young children than to be able to relate different areas of learning as they demonstrate their cumulative knowledge by identifying objects by number, color, and shape!

Floor shapes So many discoveries about shapes are made through mind and body working together. Here are some of the challenges given to young children as they looked at the floor clearly marked with a large circle, square, and triangle. "Can you find a shape that has no straight lines and step inside it?" "See if you can find a shape that has corners and walk around it."

One of the children began walking around the circle shape. A few of his classmates shouted corrections to him. One of them explained, "There are no corners in a circle!"

"Find a shape with three sides, hop around it, and call its name!" "Find a shape with four corners, shout its name, and march along its sides."

After the children have had lots of time to experiment with the floor shapes, expand their new understanding to art, poems, stories, and songs.

Going around in circles These activities involve a series of developmental steps.

> Can you make a circle with your fingers? With your hands? Show me!
> Are there circle shapes on your bodies?
> Are you wearing circles on your clothes?
> Look around the room. Where do you see circles?
> Can you shape circles in the air with your arms and hands—above you, below you, around you?
> What kind of body shapes and movements tell something about circles?
> Let's draw circles on the floor with our feet. Circles in the air with our elbows, our heads, our hips.

After this exercise with circles, the children are ready to expand their thinking. "What are some bigger things you see or can do that remind you of circles?" Children have enthusiastically suggested ferris wheels, three-ring circuses, juggling balls, pizza pies, and carousels.

My memories of these experiences are bright, but one incident stands out. With a group of preschoolers (four-and-a-half-year-olds), we concluded our study of circles by enacting a merry-go-round. The children were horses, poles, riders, and ticket-takers. They placed themselves inside a large imaginary circle designated as the merry-go-round. Everyone had a part in the merry-go-round (self-determined, of course), everyone except Normie, who simply watched.

My always-ready, bouncy music was waiting on the phonograph. (I still use records!)

"Gosh, we need someone to turn on the merry-go-round," I said. "Normie, will you start us off?" Normie just looked up, open-mouthed, hardly moving. "Thanks!" I gushed and turned on the music.

The horses bobbed up and down, the poles stood straight and still, the riders swayed up and down and back and forth, and the whole group slowly moved within the circle. Normie was ecstatic! Did he *really* turn on a merry-go-round? Another example of Edwin Markham's poem came to life:

> He drew a circle that shut me out
> Heretic, rebel, a thing to flout.
> But Love and I had the wit to win
> We drew a circle that took him in.[38]

The pictures, sculptures, songs, stories, and poems that flow from these movement experiences are characterized by unusually rich images and feelings.

Bounce a ball, throw a snowball The idea of circles and spheres becomes clearer when you bounce, throw, and catch balls. On snowy days, make snowballs, igloos,

and snow people. Remember to make square forts and snow triangles as well. When the shapes melt, you can talk about why and how shapes change.

Mystery box of shapes to show and guess Kay Callander filled a mystery box with clearly defined pictures of objects or the objects themselves.[39] The children take turns reaching into the "mystery box," looking at the picture or object, and demonstrating it through pantomime and improvised body movement for their classmates to guess.

A variation of this activity is to fill the "mystery box" with objects only, and ask the children to take turns identifying them by touch alone.

Body shapes There are so many excellent ways for children to develop understanding and appreciation of shapes through body movement. Only a few ideas are presented here.

Challenge shapes Moira Logan's[40] young students responded with their bodies to "movement questions" such as the following:

> Let's change our bodies into tired, silly, strong, weak, straight, crooked, lumpy, heavy, light, smooth, and curvy shapes. (One at a time, of course.)
> Let's make shapes with our bodies that have windows, spaces, or holes.
> Let's close our shapes . . . open them.
> Let's make zigzag shapes, round shapes, angular shapes.

Moira reminds the children that they are in one shape or another *all the time*.

Change shapes, hold shapes Children really feel their powers with this exercise. Ask them to hold their shapes—freeze! Give them a drumbeat, tambourine shake, or hand clap to change their bodies to another shape.

Hold! Freeze! Change again. . . .

Grow shapes Begin with low-to-the-ground, closed-up bodies. Slowly expand and develop body shapes, one at a time. When the children have grown to their tallest, widest, and strongest, ask them to hold that shape for ten counts. Then shake out or do the following movement.

Shrink shapes Slowly, almost imperceptibly, the children begin to shrink their body shapes. The exercise ends with bodies as small and formless as when they began the growing process described above. Charge imaginations by talking together about things that grow and shrink and change.

Group shapes Groups of children combine body shapes to form a circle, square, triangle, and rectangle; a sad shape, happy shape, flat shape, zigzag shape, wide shape, and narrow shape; an animal shape, a machine shape, and a shape from nature; and a closed shape, an open shape, a moving shape, and a still shape.

Body shapes for stories and poems Discover how easily children learn shapes through movement interpretations of their favorite stories and poems.

Some stories The Seven Dwarfs have distinct shapes and movement patterns determined by their names. Encourage the children to develop special walks, postures, dances, games, sounds, and dialogue for each dwarf.

The Tin Man, Scarecrow, Cowardly Lion, Dorothy, Toto, Munchkins, Flying Monkeys, Good and Bad Witches, and Wizard inspire children to explore body shapes that express the qualities of these characters from *The Wizard of Oz*. Children also learn important aspects of shape, such as loose, tight, crooked, and straight.

A. A. Milne's beloved characters are recognized by their shapes and personalities. Kanga, Tigger, Eeyore, Rabbit, Owl, Winnie the Pooh, Christopher Robin, and Baby Roo stimulate imaginative demonstrations introducing characters by their shapes and movements.

Nursery rhymes like "Humpty Dumpty" provide rich material for children to interpret. Humpty Dumpty is a stout, oval-shaped character. How do bodies feel demonstrating that kind of shape? Humpty Dumpty falls off the wall. Falling down is usually the children's favorite part. Here come the king's horses and men, clippity-clop. Bodies change to this shape and movement. Oh, no. They can't put Humpty together again! Some children keep their broken shapes, while others try to fix Humpty's splattered form.

Children love any games that have to do with hiding! *Pigs in Hiding*[41] is a wacky story of mischievous pigs who hide behind or against objects in different rooms of the house while a character searches for them. At the end of the story, the searcher leaves a tray of refreshments that entice all the pigs out of hiding. Play the story with the children. You'll be surprised at the many imaginative ways they choose shapes in the room to hide against! Giggling may give them away! Animals of every kind and size hide in forests, plains, and river backgrounds in *We Hide, You Seek*.[42] Inspiring illustrations will launch your children's own hiding game. Invite the kids to choose their own animals to express with body shapes.

Two examples of books that help children build a world of shapes, from one to many, are *The House That Jack Built* and *The World That Jack Built*.[43] Set in the Caribbean, the colorful illustrations in *The House That Jack Built* will inspire your children to form house, rat, dog, cat, cow, rooster, man, and woman shapes that fill your room. *The World That Jack Built* begins with a house and a cat and expands to trees, stream, meadows, hills, forests, and, lastly, a factory. As the shapes of Jack's world multiply, a lesson in environmental protection is added as an important surprise. How are we shaping our world?

An old delightful book that prods children to "look around" is *Calico Cat Looks Around*.[44] Calico Cat looks around and sees rectangle windows, a circle of stones, ice-cream cones of half-circles and triangles and delicious flavors. Your kids can play, improvise, illustrate, and write their own "look-around" games, songs, and books. What do *they* see?

A poetic, sensitive book, *Sometimes I Dance Mountains*,[45] contains images, such as rain, wind, thunder, and mountains, that help children express feelings and moods through body shapes.

Some poems Pick up any collection of poems and merely read the titles, for example, "The Little Turtle" (Vachel Lindsay), "Little Black Bug" (Margaret Wise Brown), and "The Elephant" (Hilaire Belloc). Every title, every poem is a resource for shaping in gesture, pantomime, movement, and choreography. Always see the movement connection!

Many poems are *about* shapes, but all poems can be shaped up for extra enjoyment and appreciation.

A. A. Milne's "The Four Friends" presents four animals of different sizes and personalities. Children listen to the words and decide which animal they want to show with their bodies. The first stanza gives an idea how the children must understand the concepts in order to interpret the poem through body movement.

> Ernest was an elephant, a great big fellow,
>   Leonard was a lion with a six-foot tail,
> George was a goat, and his beard was yellow,
>   And James was a very small snail.[46]

Through the rest of the poem, each animal has a distinctive description and action in every stanza.

Children's original poems, chants, cheers, raps, and jingles are excellent resources for their own movement accompaniment. Here are a few examples from my knapsack:

A Kindergarten Cheer for Shapes
Hooray for shapes!
Hooray! Hooray!
Circles! Squares!
Put a ball in a box.
Circles! Squares!
Hooray! Hooray!

A first grade's notes for a "rap" song/poem/chant
One day I walked around around—
Circle to the right. Circle to the left.
Around is round. Circle is round.
Spin around. Dance around. Circle round.
Round we go—around around.

Chant it! Sing it! Dance it!

Shape up! Our body shapes tell stories. Proud, straight, and tall bodies convey strength and confidence. Slumped, bent, diminished postures convey a lack of self-image. Always encourage strong, proud body shapes!

Square dances and round dances On a day of celebrating squares, enjoy a simple square dance. If you do not know one, experiment with one such as the following.

Help the children form a square. Those on opposite sides (two sides at a time) skip toward each other, bow, and skip back. Opposite sides move toward each other, clap hands, and move back. Again, the sides move toward each other and rub

noses, touch elbows, do jumping jacks, stamp feet, or shake fingers and move back. Each pattern is done twice so that all sides have the chance to enjoy it.

Choose traditional square-dance music or any music with a steady, lively rhythm.

On a day of celebrating circles, enjoy a simple circle or round dance. All join hands and circle around. Skip, slide, run, gallop, jump, or walk around the circle. Change directions to make it more interesting. Use music from around the world!

Bubble bubble! One of Viki Rogers's favorite ways to celebrate circles with her students is with a bubble party.[47] Children love to blow bubbles, and a room full of colorful bubbles is another cheerful way to learn about circles. Viki shares her giant bubble recipe:

Two cups of Joy dishwashing liquid
Two-thirds cup thick Karo syrup
Six cups water
Fill a baking pan (don't shake it up)
Wave a large bubble wand through the mix and presto! Gigantic, colorful, thick bubbles will appear for stories, songs, bubble adventures, games, and inspired observations.

Books like *Soap Bubble Magic*[48] and original Bubble Books that your children create enrich the whirly experiences.

Shadows, tracks, and clouds Keep those senses sharpened! Every day we are presented with numerous opportunities to develop greater cognitive skills. Language, perception, self-esteem, and cooperation are among the many things to be learned from simple, ordinary (extraordinary) experiences like:

Discovering shadows: On sunny days, take the children out and help them find their shadows. As they stretch, jump, run, walk, dance, and race with their shadows, they learn a lot about shapes and changes, sizes and qualities of movement. Poems like "Hide-and-Seek Shadow" or "Poor Shadow"[49] that remind children that everything has a shadow—mountains, birds, balls—are fun to recite or sing-song along as shadows and children play together. Shadow pictures and illustrations are exciting challenges for the kids to create.

Following tracks Our youngest children who recite the names of every prehistoric dinosaur without hesitation are gifted in learning the designs and configurations of footprints and tracks. As they share information and practice recognizing such tracks as bird, rabbit, deer, and horse, choreographic ideas abound. Follow the tracks and dance the animal! Turn the tracks into riddle games, follow-the-leader animal dances. Keep track with books such as *Whose Footprints?* and *Let's Look at More Tracks*[50] and invite the children to create their own arrangements of footprints and track shapes.

Cloud shapes Beyond your windowpanes are skies of clouds waiting to be investigated by you and your children. What do you see in the clouds? What shapes emerge from the clouds? Tell us. Show us. Illustrate your ideas. Put your observations and imaginings in words! Play with the shared suggestions.

Cloud watching is an everyday happening! Children enjoy hiding shapes in cotton or painted clouds against blue skies. The children's original books are well used as are such imaginative books as *Hi, Clouds, Hello, Clouds!, It Looked Like Spilt Milk,* and *Dreams.*[51] On rainy days, these kinds of books will encourage the children to see the shapes in imagined clouds, to show and move and dance the shapes. Every page in any one of these books is a launching pad for integrated arts experiences, playfulness, dreamy conversations, silly observations, and the feeding of wonder.

Because our daily lives are composed of shapes, movement and play ideas that extend basic concepts can be gathered readily. Consider the following possibilities:

Pass a shape Leslie Zak enjoys sitting with kids in a circle and passing imaginary shapes around. As each person receives the "shape," indicated by hands/arms/body movement, it is changed and passed on to the next person.

Shapes for all seasons Winter shapes are different from spring shapes! How does a leaf change its shape from summer to autumn? What about tree branches? Hibernating bears?

Shapes for places and objects How can you show the shape of a bridge with your bodies? A building? A wall? A mountain? A fountain? A well? A road? A box?

Shapes for toys Turn your bodies into the shape and movement of bouncing balls, wind-up toys, robots, trains, planes, stuffed animals, dolls, and so on.

Shapes that change Explore the way bodies change to convey the ideas of a tadpole changing into a frog; water steaming, then freezing, melting, and evaporating; snowflakes forming into a snowball, into a snowshape. . . .

Shapes that move Spin yourself like a top, a dreidel, or a hula hoop. Crawl with your circular turtle shell along a rectangular path. Turn yourself into an expanding balloon; keep that big circular shape and float around the room.

Shapes of adjectives Show us the shape of tall, wide, pointy, round, flat, straight, crooked, big, and small. Each word will inspire a change of body design and will reflect the comprehension of the dancer!

Museum of statue shapes Create shapes for pioneers, Native Americans, astronauts, animals, scientists, festival dancers, elves, giants, witches, trolls, Paul Bunyan, Johnny Appleseed, George Washington, and Dr. Martin Luther King, Jr. Offer action verbs to go with the nouns, such as "Johnny Appleseed *planting*" or "Dr. Martin Luther King, Jr., *persuading*." Freeze that frieze!

Shapes of welcome/greetings Play with the many variations possible (combine and rearrange) for "welcome" and "hello."

How do we say "goodbye" to this section, which has no ending? We stop because of the shape of the hands on the clock and the limitations of rectangular sheets of paper!

CLASSROOM VISITORS AND FIELD TRIPS
Classroom Visitors

Artisans Invite persons such as woodcarvers, basketweavers, glass blowers, ceramicists, potters, jewelers, toy makers, furniture makers, quilt makers, and rug weavers to visit you and talk about the kinds of shapes and designs that are most appealing to them. Ask them to bring samples or to give demonstrations. Encourage the children to ask questions, to try an activity.

Actors and actresses Invite a group of community theater members, older students, or university thespians to do improvisations about shapes and shadow plays using silhouettes behind a white sheet; to recite poems about shapes; and to create plays and stories about shapes. Again, the involvement of your students will guarantee success and enjoyment.

Face painters In the last chapter, make-up artists like Leslie Zak were suggested as excellent visitors. Children's understanding of the effects of shapes on feelings and experiences is reinforced as they watch a face turn from sad to glad with the stroke of a make-up crayon. Be sure that all the children who want to, have their faces made up.

School custodian Ask this skilled staff member to share tools with the children. The shapes of tools are distinct; nails, screws, nuts, and bolts help the children see and feel circle and square shapes.

Jewelry maker Bracelets, necklaces, and rings are round. Beads are round. Pins and earrings combine a mix of shapes. Don't forget to involve the children in active jewelry-making.

Tailor Buttons, belts, collars, hems, and sleeve cuffs are round. Thimbles, pinheads, and spools are also round. Pockets come in all shapes. Zippers are linear. Patterns are a combination of shapes.

Clown/Magician Some clowns and magicians shape balloons. Some juggle balls. Under their circular magicians' top hats hide tricks of all shapes! Clowns ride unicycles and do somersaults and cartwheels. "Circus" comes from the Latin word meaning "circle." Talk about and demonstrate three-ring circuses!

Opticians Eyeglasses come in a wide variety of shapes. Eyeglasses as a fashion fad for even our youngest children (note how many toddlers wear sunglasses!) are fascinating. After an interesting visit with an optician, the children will want to design their own eyeglass illustrations.

Origami artists Paper has amazing powers, especially in the hands of an artist who shares the rich tradition of Japanese origami with children. Yasue Sakaoka demonstrates and teaches children to create imaginative shapes with paper.[52]

Note: Almost every hobby, occupation, and profession includes certain inherent objects describing basic shapes. As you invite community resource volunteers, family members, colleagues, and neighbors to visit with you, add the element of shapes as part of every theme. From bakers' rolling pins and pots to potters' dishes, cups, and bowls to Aminah Robinson's amazing button-rich sculptures, to quilters' patches to designers' swatches, children continue to develop awareness and knowledge of the world of shapes.

Field Trips

Your own room Turn your room into a field trip! If your room is full of colorful displays of children's work, photographs, paintings, murals, and sculptures, it merits special attention. You may even want to sell tickets (in the shape of circles, squares, or rectangles). Guide the children around the room so they look at familiar surroundings in new ways. Ask them to find objects and images that are circles, squares, rectangles, triangles, spheres, cylinders, and other shapes. Combine with counting. Extend this in-house trip to other rooms.

Shapes walk As you walk, correlate shapes with other topics. In autumn, for example, children in the Midwest and the Northeast pick up round brown buckeyes and red berries. Most children will note the special shapes of traffic and street signs, the round street lamps, triangular rooftops, rectangular buildings, square and rectangular doors and windows, and round wheels of cars, buses, and trucks. When you return to the room, translate the shapes you gathered into pictures, poems, sculptures, songs, and games.

Food stores and supermarkets Be sure to include observations and discussions of the shapes of products and produce during your trips to stores. Note with your children that cans are round, boxes are square or rectangular, peas are round, and potatoes are lumpy and bumpy. These descriptive words become part of the way children look at things. What fruits and vegetables are round?

Sculptor's studio—The shape of hope Because children are natural sculptors, always forming shapes out of whatever material is at hand, they are fascinated by the art and intensely interested in the sculptor's ideas, feelings, and experiences. Ask the sculptor to talk about and, if possible, demonstrate such concepts as positive and negative space (open and closed forms), the wide range of materials used for sculpting, some of the tools needed, where ideas come from, and how a shape emerges from the material.

Learn the excellent resources waiting for you in your community. Central Ohio children are fortunate to have Alfred Tibor living in the area.[53] Alfred's sculptures are known internationally and are often dedicated to important causes and clearly expressed themes. His powerful sculpture *Hope* was commissioned by the Arthur James Memorial Cancer Hospital at Ohio State University. What is the shape of *hope*? Children are inspired to think about how they would shape beliefs, feelings, and wishes into materials like wood, clay, metal, sticks, and stones. How can shapes convey ideas like hope? Love? Peace? Friendship?

Florist, nursery, garden, and park These kinds of trips help children to appreciate the diverse shapes of nature. If possible, take crayons and paper and encourage the children to write and draw their impressions. Otherwise, follow up in school as soon as possible with enriching visual arts activities, talk times, music times, and creative writing times.

Sporting goods store What better place to see round, oval, spherical, and cylindrical shapes, such as basketball hoops, balls of every size, racquets, paddles, and cans of balls?

Bakery Cakes, doughnuts, bagels, pies, and certain breads are circular and spherical. Cookies come in many different shapes. How many shapes of delicious-smelling baked goods can your children identify?

Wallpaper and floor covering store The designs and colors of wallpaper, rugs, and tiles are fabulous. Children easily spot basic shapes and marvel at how cleverly they are combined with other shapes and with colors. Design your own rugs, wallpaper, and tile when you return to the classroom.

Art gallery or art museum Focus on shapes as part of your students' experience at an art museum, gallery, or studio. Here they may also discover the phenomenon of optical illusion. "Are those circles moving?" "Is that square bigger or smaller than the others?" "Are those lines waving?"

Responses to paintings and sculpture can be readily combined with movement activities, art, drama, song, and creative writing. Here are a few examples of how easy it is to ask children to connect ideas and express themselves. "Use your super eyesight. In this room are three paintings that feature circles. Draw an imaginary circle with your hands in front of each of those paintings." Again, "Look around the room. When you see a painting of a large, rectangular purple house with a green triangular roof, stand in front of it and show the roof's shape."

The town square and other shapes of interest Most towns and cities have a central place identified by its distinct shape. A. A. Milne's Christopher Robin "takes his penny to the market square." Ohio State University students meet at the Oval, the center of campus. New Yorkers double their shapes by going to a play at the Circle in the Square Theater. A baseball field is diamond-shaped; a tennis court is rectangles; and a circus has three rings. Check your area and find places that are clearly defined, perhaps even named by their shapes.

Throughout this book you will find many ways to include shapes in visits and field trips. People, places, things, animals, indeed everything in the whole wide world, helps us make comparisons, discern patterns, discover relationships, categorize, name, and identify. As five-year-old Davie, whose class was studying shapes, noted wearily, "It's getting so I can't go a step without noticing everything's shape. I even dream about it!" My dreams are in circles. How do yours shape up?

IT ALL COMES TOGETHER

When you visit Alpine Elementary School you immediately know you are entering special grounds![54] As you walk toward the school, your attention is caught by the beautifully designed gardens brightening the path. Stop and look at the colorful, carefully patterned arrangements of plants and flowers. Before you take another step, stand astonished at the four large sculptures on the front lawn, each of them distinct, each of them beckoning you to come closer.

Glowing with enthusiasm, Lois Arend, Alpine's principal, gives you a guided tour. She talks about the close relationship between the community and the school. Alpine's PTA is formidable and totally committed to enriching the learning environment of the children. Lois is eloquent about values and beliefs. (Don't our beliefs, our values, generate action? As we believe, so we teach!)

"We want to involve all the children in the whole school in creative adventures," she says. "Every year, we want our children to create something permanent to leave as a gift to the school, as a way to honor the arts, to honor our collective efforts. We want the children to come in and say, 'I had something to do with this . . . garden or this sidewalk. . . .' "

We step on the sidewalk, which features panels of patterns designed by every grade in the school. Each panel is composed of four squares with repeated designs and words. Family members and community neighbors volunteered materials and labor consultation.

We walk toward the exquisite garden. Lois explains that the children, inspired by the international flower show, AmeriFlora, held in Columbus in 1992, wanted to design their own garden. With input from all the classes and professional advice

from landscape artists, the children designed the garden. Every child in the whole school planted either a shrub or a bulb. The garden belongs to every child in the school!

We admire the four "site pieces" in front of the school. Coordinated by Carol Cruikshank, Alpine's art teacher, and inspired by the natural-material sculptures children created during a Days of Creation Arts for Kids summer program during AmeriFlora, the four pieces took form. Four sculptors were invited to work closely with the children of the school. Four very different shapes emerged. With Gretchen Cochran, the children created a larger-than-life-size topiary shape for their interpretation of Mother Earth. With Yasue Sakaoka, the children created a large wood sculpture featuring the beauty of faces from around the world. Every Alpine child contributed to the sculpture. San Antonio sculptor Michael Rodriguez shared his Mexican-American heritage with the children. They especially like the picture story of "La Chalupa" from the Mexican picture-card game, Loteria. Chalupa is a woman who brought food into Mexico City by boat. The children and Michael created a large, brilliantly painted boat, woman, oar, and food. It sails on a river of grass in front of the school. Barbara Chavous encouraged the children to think of symbols and shapes with special meanings to them to build into a large totem. They made beads out of clay, firing and painting their creations. Look closely at the totem and you will see the shapes of the sun, stars, moon, and flowers.

Stories, creative writing, drama, songs, letters, posters, pictures, quilts, mosaic walls, mobiles, and puppets spring from gardens, patterned walkways, and outdoor sculptures. At the school's annual spring Gallery Hop, hundreds of people from the community come to celebrate with the children.

"The shape of our school changes every year," Lois explains. "I guess you could say that we continue to try to shape our world. Is there a way to shape the spirit in our school?"

What do *you* think?

NOTES ♥

1. John G. Neihardt, *Black Elk Speaks*. New York: Simon and Schuster, 1972, pp. 164–166.
2. E. H. Gombrich, *Art and Illusion*. Princeton: Princeton University, Bollingen Paperback Edition, 1972.
3. Dr. Stephen Kosslyn is a psychiatrist at Harvard University. He has been interviewed many times by newspapers around the country.
4. Susan Hendrickson teaches at First Community Church Early Childhood Program in Columbus, Ohio.
5. Shirley Davis teaches at the Jewish Center Childcare Program in West Bloomfield, Michigan.
6. Elliot W. Eisner, "The Misunderstood Role of the Arts in Human Development," *Phi Delta Kappan*. April, 1992, pp. 591–595.
7. For a wonderful resource about the programs of Reggio Emilia, see *The Hundred Languages of Children: Narrative of the Possible*, the book documenting the unforgettable exhibit of works. The exhibit is traveling around the United States. Or see C. Edwards, L. Gandini, and G. Forman, *The Hundred Languages of Children: The Reggio Emilia Approach to Early Childhood Education*. (Norwood, New Jersey: Ablex, 1993).
8. Dr. Helen Lewis is one of the coauthors of *Clay in the Classroom* (New York: Teachers College, 1988). Inspired by the creative and challenging Yew Chung program for young children in China, Dr. Lewis began her American adaptation of the program in South Bend, Indiana. She teaches in the College of Education in the University of Indiana, South Bend.
9. Theodore Roethke, *Straw for the Fire*. New York: Doubleday, 1974, p. 234.
10. Dawn Heyman and Tracy Skistimas talked with children at the McGuffy School in Columbus, Ohio.
11. Patti Link talked with her children at the First Community Church's Early Childhood program in Columbus.
12. Ken Valimaki, an award-winning sculptor whose work is widely known, teaches art in Ft. Hayes High School, Columbus Public Schools.
13. Peter Ziebel, *Look Closer*. New York: Clarion, 1989.
14. Mitsumasa Anno, *Anno's Journey*. New York: Philomel, 1978.
15. Brian Wildsmith, *Puzzles*. New York: Franklin Watts, 1970.
16. Theodore Geisel, *The Shape of Me and Other Stuff*. New York: Random House, 1973.
    Bodel Rikys, *Red Bear's Fun with Shapes*. New York: Dial, 1993.
    Peter and Susan Barrett, *The Circle Sarah Drew*. New York: Scroll, 1972.
    ———, *The Square Ben Drew*. New York: Scroll, 1972.
    ———, *The Line Sophie Drew*. New York: Scroll, 1973.
17. Dr. Rebecca Kantor is the director of the Sophie Rogers Lab School at Ohio State University as well as associate professor of Family Relations and Human Development. In visiting and studying the programs in Reggio Emilia, Dr. Kantor constantly reminds teachers and university students that there are no formulas, no recipes. Every program is unique and shaped by the individuals who are involved in the creative process. She urges students to adapt any ideas they like in the building of programs that reflect their own individuality and the qualities of the children.
18. Blossom Budney, illustrated by Vladimir Bobri, *A Kiss Is Round*. New York: Lothrop, Lee and Shepard, 1954.
19. Mary Ann F. Knoll, illustrated by Kathleen Kerr, *Mudworks: Creative Clay, Dough and Modeling Experiences*. Bellingham, WA: Bright Ring, 1989.
20. Michael Joel Rosen, *Kids' Best Dog Book*. New York: Workman, 1993.

21. Charlotte Zolotow, paintings by Wendell Minor, *The Seashore Book*. New York: HarperCollins, 1992.

22. Norman Barrett, *Deserts*. New York: Franklin Watts, 1989.

23. Emily Arnold McCully, *First Snow*. New York: Harper & Row, 1985.
Isao Sasaki, *Snow*. New York: Viking, 1980.
Ezra Jack Keats, *The Snowy Day*. First published New York: Viking, 1962; numerous editions and reprints.

24. Charlotte Zolotow, photographs by Tana Hoban. *The Moon Was Best*. New York: Greenwillow, 1993.

25. Crescent Dragonwagon, illustrated by Jerry Pinckney, *Half a Moon and a Whole Star*. New York: Macmillan, 1986.

26. Sesame Street, *Everything in the Whole Wide World Museum*. New York: Random House, 1974.

27. Byron Barton, *Wheels*. New York: Thomas Crowell, 1979.

28. Honest Dan'l Pinkwater, illustrated by James Marshall, *Roger's Umbrella*. New York: Dutton, 1982.

29. Lydia Dabcovich, *Ducks Fly*. New York: Dutton, 1990.

30. Valerie Reddix, illustrated by Jean and Mou-Sien Tseng, *Dragon Kite of the Autumn Moon*. New York: Lothrop, Lee and Shepard, 1991.

31. Robert Quackenbush, *Henry's World Tour*. New York: Doubleday, 1992.

32. Maurice Sendak, *Where the Wild Things Are*. New York: Scholastic, 1974.

33. Rhoda Linder and Wendy Wohlstein celebrated ideas with children at the Leo Yassenoff Jewish Center's Early Childhood Program in Columbus.

34. Barney Waverly, illustrated by Steve Henry, *How Big? How Fast? How Hungry? A Book About Cats*. Milwaukee: Raintree, 1990.

35. Bill Martin, Jr., illustrated by Eric Carle, *Polar Bear, Polar Bear, What Do You Hear?* New York: Henry Holt, 1991.

36. Denise Fleming, *In the Tall, Tall Grass*. New York: Henry Holt, 1991.

37. Leslie Zak, director of Days of Creation Arts for Kids in Columbus, is a drama and music specialist spending time with children in a variety of settings, including programs under the Greater Columbus Arts Council's Artists in the Schools.

38. Edwin Markham, "Outwitted," *Modern American Poetry—Modern British Poetry*. Combined Mid-Century Edition, ed. by Louis Untermeyer. New York: Harcourt Brace Jovanovich, 1950, p. 106.

39. Kay Callander was a classroom teacher and a drama specialist in the Columbus Public Schools for many years.

40. When she was assistant professor of Dance at Ohio State University, Moira worked in creative movement with children of all ages.

41. Arlene Dubanevich, *Pigs in Hiding*. New York: Scholastic, 1983.

42. Jose Aruego and Ariane Dewey, *We Hide, You Seek*. New York: Greenwillow, 1979.

43. Jenny Stow, *The House That Jack Built*. New York: Dial, 1992.
Ruth Brown, *The World That Jack Built*. New York: Dutton, 1991.

44. Donald Charles, *Calico Cat Looks Around*. Chicago: Children's Press, 1975.

45. Byrd Baylor, *Sometimes I Dance Mountains*. New York: Scribners, 1973.

46. A. A. Milne, "The Four Friends." *The World of Christopher Robin*. New York: Dutton, 1958, pp. 16–18.

47. Viki Rogers teaches in a bubbly way at Montrose School in Bexley, Ohio.

48. Seymour Simon, illustrated by Stella Ormai, *Soap Bubble Magic*. New York: Lothrop, Lee and Shepard, 1985.

49. Margert Hillert, "Hide-And-Seek-Shadow," *Read-Aloud Rhymes for the Very Young*. Selected by Jack Prelutsky, illustrated by Marc Brown. New York: Knopf, 1985, p. 25.

Ilo Orleans, "Poor Shadows." Ibid., p. 25.

50. Masayuki Yabuchi, *Whose Footprints?* New York: Philomel, 1985.
    Ann Kirn, *Let's Look At More Tracks.* New York: Putnam, 1970.

51. Carol Greene, illustrated by Gene Sharp, *Hi, Clouds.* Chicago: Children's Press, 1983.
    Dalia Hardof Renberg, illustrated by Alona Frankel, *Hello, Clouds!* New York: Harper & Row, 1985.
    Charles G. Shaw, *It Looked Like Spilt Milk.* New York: Harper & Row, 1947.
    Peter Spier, *Dreams.* New York: Doubleday, 1986.

52. Yasue Sakaoka shares many of her traditional Japanese art forms such as origami, kite making, and paper sculpture with children through Days of Creation Arts for Kids and Greater Columbus Arts Council's Artists in the Schools programs. Yasue's work has been exhibited throughout the country.

53. A life-affirming Holocaust survivor who came to America from Hungary, Alfred Tibor has dedicated his deeply felt sculptures to the highest values—hope, freedom, and love—and to children. His pieces have been commissioned by institutions and individuals around the country.

54. Alpine Elementary School is part of the Columbus Public School District. It thrives as a reminder to all that outstanding creative education happens in nonalternative (nonmagnet) schools as well as in magnet schools. Alpine is one of the ordinary, extraordinary schools flourishing in every city and town in America.

BOOKS FROM MY KNAPSACK FOR CHILDREN ♥ ♥

Brown, Margery W. *Afro-Bets Book of Shapes.* Illustrated by Culberson Brown. New Jersey: Just Us Books, 1990.

Crews, Donald. *Freight Train.* New York: Greenwillow, 1978.

———. *Light.* New York: Greenwillow, 1981.

Demi. *Find Demi's Sea Creatures.* New York: Putnam and Grosset, 1991.

Editors of Klutz Press. *Face Painting.* Palo Alto, CA: Klutz Press, 1993.

Ehlert, Lois. *Color Farm.* New York: HarperCollins, 1990.

——— *Color Zoo.* New York: HarperCollins, 1989.

Fisher, Leonard Everett. *Look Around! A Book About Shapes.* New York: Viking, 1987.

Henrietta. *A Mouse in the House.* Photographs by Tim Ridley. New York: Dorling Kindersley, 1991.

Hill, Eric. *Spot Looks at Shapes.* Illustrated by Eric Hill. New York: Putnam, 1986.

Hoban, Tana. *Dots, Spots, Speckles, and Stripes.* Photographs by Tana Hoban. New York: Greenwillow, 1987.

———. *Spirals, Curves, Fan Shapes and Lines.* Photos by Tana Hoban. New York: Greenwillow, 1992.

Hughes, Shirley. *All Shapes and Sizes.* Illustrated by Shirley Hughes. New York: Lothrop, Lee & Shephard, 1986.

Jonas, Ann. *Round Trip.* Illustrated by Ann Jonas. New York: Morrow, 1983.

Lillie, Patricia. *Everything Has a Place.* Illustrated by Nancy Trafuri. New York: Greenwillow, 1993.

Mariotti. Maris. *Hanimals.* Photographs by Robert Machiori. New York: Green Tiger, 1982.

Marzollo, Jean. *I Spy, a Book of Picture Riddles.* Illustrated by Walter Wick. New York: Scholastic, 1992.

McMillan, Bruce. *Fire Engine Shapes.* Photographs by Bruce McMillan. New York: Lothrop, Lee & Shephard, 1988.

————. *Mouse Views: What the Class Pet Saw*. Photographs by Bruce McMillan. New York: Holiday House, 1993.

Rogers, Paul. *The Shapes Game*. Illustrated by Sian Tucker. New York: Henry Holt, 1989.

Rose, Agatha. *Hide and Seek in the Yellow House*. Illustrated by Kate Spohn. New York: Viking, 1992.

Tafuri, Nancy. *Follow Me*. Illustrated by Nancy Tafuri. New York: Greenwillow, 1990.

Testa, Fulvio. *If You Look Around You*. Illustrated by Fulvio Testa. New York: Dial, 1987.

Van Fleet, Matthew. *Match It—A Fold the Flap Book*. New York: Dial, 1993.

Wilmer, Diane. *Big and Little*. Illustrated by Nicole Smee. New York: Macmillan, 1988.

Chapter 11

♥♥♥♥♥♥♥♥♥♥♥♥♥♥♥♥♥♥♥♥♥♥♥

A World Full of Colors

These four ribbons hanging here on the stem are the four quarters of the universe. The black one is for the west where the thunder beings live to send us rain; the white one for the north, whence comes the great white cleansing wind; the red one for the east, whence springs the light and where the morning star lives to give men wisdom; the yellow for the south, whence come the summer and the power to grow. . . .[1]   Black Elk

THE BASICS

De colores se visten los campos
En la primavera
De colores son los parjaritos
Que vienen de afuera
De colores es el arco iris
Que vemos lucir
Y por eso los grandes amores
De muchos colores me gustan a mi. . . . (Loosely translated: The country fields dress in spring colors. The little birds and the shining rainbow are fitted with colors. I love seeing all the colors.)

Even though it is not spring, but autumn, I am enjoying one of my favorite songs, a traditional Spanish folk song about colors, as I look out on this spectacular midwest October day and admire the bright red berries of firebush and firethorn; mums as sharp and clear as the colors of saltwater fish; oaks, maples, and sycamores with their leaves of fiery gold, rust, and burgundy; ripening green, yellow, and red apples; and pumpkins, gourds, and squashes of every size, shape, and shade. Autumn colors are dramatic and exhilarating to me.

But not everyone would agree about the beauty and excitement of this season's colors. We perceive the world with different lenses. As I am singing my little song, admiring the magnificent mix of colors, you might be witnessing the same scene and feeling depressed about the end of summer, anxious about the coming of the shorter, darker days and frustrated about the passing of time. We share our world from our own unique perspectives!

Colors affect our lives in so many ways. They describe and define the physical world; they influence behavior; they evoke emotional responses; they trigger multi-dimensional sensory impressions; and they are replete with symbols, signs, and metaphors. Our language is rich with colors! We move at the green light; our bank balance is in the red; she is green with envy; he turned white with fear; I've got the blues because I was handed a pink slip on a gray day.

Color consciousness begins at early ages. Callie Rose at nine months consistently reaches for the color orange in toys, books, and dolls. At a year and a half, my friend Ben Rosen knew to pick only the red cherry tomatoes in the garden. Enjoy a few minutes of eavesdropping on a color-full conversation between Maddie Botnick Fireman and Jackie Reedy Griffin, two four-year-olds jabbering away as they try on each other's clothes.

Maddie: *I'm for blue and pink.*

Jackie: *I'm for blue and pink and yellow and red and orange.*

Maddie: *I'm green, yellow, pink, orange, purple, gold, and silver.*

Jackie: *Oh, I'm for gold and silver, too.*

I wonder out loud: *Where did colors come from anyway?*

The girls confer, agree, and explain: *"We really got colors from the rainbow!"*

Colors symbolize country, school, class, caste, clan, and cause. Be careful of colors! They can be dangerous! One of my husband's most frightening experiences was attending a soccer game with friends in Brazil. Inadvertently, their seats were in the section of the stadium that was rooting for the team in red. Unfortunately, Howard was wearing a blue jacket, the color of the opposition's uniforms. Curses, threats, fists, bottles, and stones were angrily aimed at this innocent person, who had no allegiance to either team! Bringing it closer to home, Heaven help the misguided University of Michigan football fan who waves a blue-and-gold banner or

wears a blue-and-gold cap, scarf, or sweatshirt in the midst of the fanatic scarlet and gray Ohio State University cheering section!

Colors have meanings on many levels. Doretha Holland is finishing her dress for the Native American Pow Wow. Consistent with her Cherokee traditional colors, she is hemming bands of red, black, and white around the skirt. Even though these are important Cherokee colors, Doretha infuses them with personal significance. The red, black, and white ribbons represent the races in her family. Doretha is a child of three racial groups. She wears her colors with pride! Red, black, and white *are* beautiful.

Colors have great importance in the cultures of indigenous peoples. But just because the same color may be honored by different cultures, tribes, or nations, that doesn't mean that there is an objective symbolism that they all agree on. Red may mean strength to one group, wisdom to another, and stubbornness to a third. The same color may tell many stories and may have strong and varied meanings.

What are *your* colors? What symbols and signs, loyalties, and statements are mixed with the colors on your palette? Chances are that your children will soon know your favorite colors! Our young children are very alert observers. Teacher-watching is one of their most notable characteristics!

Our earliest ancestors celebrated colors. They discovered that natural pigments existed in minerals and plants. The stone lapis produced the color blue. Crushed animal teeth and bones, when roasted, became rich black "paint." Irises and elderberries also yielded blue. Madder roots and the inner bark of birch trees produced red. Clay, coal, iron, fish, and insect shells were all found to produce colors.

An experience similar to one that our cave-dwelling relatives probably enjoyed thousands of years ago was repeated by a group of children at summer camp.[2] The children and their counselors spent the morning sloshing barefooted through the cool waters of a creek. A shout rang out as one of the children found that a stone he had lifted out of the creek "wrote blue" when he scratched it on a large flat rock. The adventure continued through the afternoon as the children found stones that produced blues, reds, yellows, grays, blacks, and greens on rock, paper, and themselves.

Look around your neighborhood, street, city, and countryside. What colors do you see? The palette of the Southwest contrasts sharply with that of the New England coast, and the colors of New York City clearly differ from those of Albuquerque. Consider how these colors change at different times of the day and the year. Too often we are an unappreciative audience of this fantastic light and color show.

The late Ed Jacomo,[3] one of the nation's most colorful teachers, spoke "passionately" about colors and young children. Teachers, Ed believed, do not teach children color, because the children already know it. "Teachers," he said, "facilitate learning, help kids affirm what they already know, and help heighten perception."

Ed sent letters to his students' families that encouraged them to participate in celebrating colors. Here is an example of one of his letters:

Dear Parents,

Throughout the school year, we will be adding color words to our vocabularies so that we can describe the things we see. You can help your children add new color words and use those they already know. Here are some suggestions:

1. As you help your children select clothes for school, talk about the blue dress, green slacks, and red socks rather than just the dress, slacks, and socks. This is a good time to show children how some colors go together better than others.

2. As you take a walk or ride with your children, play guessing games with color. You can say, "I spy something yellow" (or red or blue or orange), and let the children continue guessing until they name the object. When they guess it, let them choose something and give its color. Then you guess what it is.

3. Look at color photographs or magazine pictures and pretend that you and your children are walking into the pictures together. As you walk along, what colors do you see? Take turns describing the colors of things in the pictures.

4. Look for books in the library that tell about colors. One of the following may be in your library: *Is It Blue As a Butterfly?*, by Rebecca Kalusky; *The Color Kittens*, by Margaret Wise Brown; and *What Color Is Love?*, by Joan Walsh Anglund.

5. Look at things through pieces of brightly colored cellophane or colored glass.

Sincerely,

Ed Jacomo

Ed's letters usually included a poem rich with color images to further encourage and inspire children and their families.

The most imaginative teachers have trouble separating color activities from other activities. They think color all the time!

On the palette of creative teachers, pigments, words, and experiences are mixed together. As children grow in awareness of the colors of the world, their vocabularies are enriched. When we teach to imagination, our "lessons" are enhanced. We can *hear* colors in music, in voices, in sounds, and in bird songs. We can *perceive* colors with all of our senses, not just our eyes. Young children, sensitive adults, and most artists experience this synesthesia.

This phenomenon occurred when I gave each child in a kindergarten class a seed and asked the children to close their eyes and feel the seeds in their hands. Then we smelled the seeds and finally, opened our eyes to look at the seeds. I asked:

"What does the seed smell like?" "Can you see the flower in your seed?" "What color will it be?"

The children quickly responded: "My seed smells like oranges"; "My seed has a red flower in it"; "My seed smells like pine trees"; and "My seed is full of a yellow dandelion!" The stimulus of a seed evoked responses from several senses.

Think about people who have never seen colors. To visually impaired people, colors are words and concepts that they must shape in their minds on the basis of cues from other senses. Through their imaginations, such people give life to colors.

What is the impact of color on people who, spontaneously or through surgery, regain or gain their sight after years of blindness? In *Pilgrim at Tinker Creek,* Annie Dillard relates the findings of Marius von Senden, who studied such individuals.

> In general, the newly sighted see the world as a dazzle of color patches. They are pleased by the sensation of color and learn quickly to name the colors, but the rest of seeing is tormentingly difficult. Soon after his operation, a patient generally bumps into one of those colour-patches and observes them to be substantial, since they resist him as tactual objects do. In walking about, it also strikes him . . . that he is continually passing in between the colours he sees. . . .
>
> A twenty-two-year-old girl was so dazzled by the world's brightness, she kept her eyes shut for two weeks. When, at the end of that time, she opened her eyes again, she did not recognize any objects, but the more she now directed her gaze upon everything about her, the more it could be seen how an expression of gratification and astonishment overspread her features; she repeatedly exclaimed: "Oh God! How beautiful!"[4]

Those who take the gift of sight for granted do a disservice to their students. How can we help young children learn to appreciate the wonders of life if we fail to see, observe, think, and feel?

Many people *with* sight are shortsighted or use limited vision. Who is visually impaired: the person who is labeled "blind" but has a rich imagination full of colors and sensory awareness, or a person with no obvious impairments who is able to see, but doesn't see? Which is the truly impaired person?

The late singer-composer Harry Chapin wrote a poignant song called "Flowers Are Red."[5] It is about a little boy who wants to use all the colors in his crayons to draw flowers. His teacher, a narrow-minded person, corrects him and tells him the "right way" to look at colors. She sings:

> Flowers are red, young man.
> And green leaves are green.
> There's no need to see flowers any other way
> Than the way they always have been seen.

The little boy responds:

> There are so many colors in the rainbow.
> So many colors in the morning sun.
> So many colors in the flowers,
> And I see every one.

The teacher considers the little boy a troublemaker, and he is kept inside to work on the color lesson until he gets it right. All his classmates are playing outside and he wants to join them, so he agrees to the lesson of the day.

After some time, the child moves to another place and goes to another school. In that school,

> The teacher there is smiling.
> She said, "Painting should be fun.

There are so many colors in the flowers,
So let's use every one."

But it is too late. The little boy has learned his lesson well. No, he tells the new teacher,

Flowers are red.
And green leaves are green.
There's no need to see flowers any other way
Than the way they always have been seen.

In our fast-paced, mechanized, computerized society, children learn at young ages to "turn off," be cool, and keep a low profile. Astonishment, excitement, and joy are diminished, even extinguished. This book is dedicated to preserving spirit and imagination by encouraging young children to use and enjoy their minds, appreciate their senses, and express curiosity and wonder as they journey through this world rich with colors.

DISCOVERY TIMES/WONDER TIMES

- We live in a world of colors. Nature is full of colors.
- Colors make the world a beautiful and more interesting place.
- Colors change depending on time, weather, and season.
- Sometimes colors give us messages, like red lights and green lights.
- We recognize things by their colors: white milk, orange juice, lilacs, goldfish, redbirds, and evergreens.
- Colors can be symbolic: the Red Cross; the white dove of peace; and the colors of weather flags for ships at sea.
- We need light to see colors.
- All of the colors we see have names.
- Black absorbs sunlight and white reflects it, so we often wear light-colored clothes in summer and darker clothes in winter.
- Red, yellow, and blue are called primary colors. All other colors result from mixing two of the primary colors: red and yellow make orange; yellow and blue make green; blue and red make purple. It's like magic!
- When black is added to a color, it darkens the color; when white is added to a color, it lightens the color.
- When black and white are mixed, gray results.
- Some colors are bright and clear, others are dull.
- It is fun to mix and use colors in our pictures.
- All over the world, throughout history, people have found ways to mix colors and paint pictures.
- Painting pictures is special to the "people family." Only people know how to use colors in different kinds of arrangements and designs, always making up new patterns and combinations. People are very creative!
- The human family is colorful—we have many colors of eyes, hair, and skin. The colors of people are beautiful and should be respected and appreciated.
- Visually impaired people use their imaginations to picture colors.
- People with eyesight should use all of their powers to see and appreciate the many colors in the world.

SUGGESTED VOCABULARY

colors	paintbrush	grass	fruits
rainbow	crayons	flowers	candy
eyes	chalk	flags	cake
see	picture	stamps	sunglasses
sun	painting	wallpaper	cellophane
sunset	artist	carpets	tissue paper
sunrise	mix	rugs	wrapping paper
red	add	books	greeting cards
yellow	parades	picture books	scarves
blue	clothing	holidays	curtains
primary colors	skin	St. Patrick's Day	beach towels
orange	people	Valentine's Day	spring
green	eyes	Thanksgiving	autumn
purple	hair	opaque	winter
violet	balloons	translucent	summer
gray	spectrum	light	fish
black	reflection	dark	birds
white	circus	bright	ocean
lavender	vegetables	dull	forest
pink	bubbles	clear	ice-cream flavors
navy blue	kaleidoscope	muddy	animals
light green	prism	colorful	designs
dark red	magic	transparent	toys
turquoise	dye	party hats	books
palette	stained-glass windows	birthday	magazines
easel	sky	candles	

Many words in the above list were contributed by children during conversations about "colorful things." Words like circus, ice-cream flavors, balloons, flowers, birds, and fish convey colorful images known and loved by young children.

Some of the words on the list may seem technical or too advanced for your students. But most children will surprise you with how easily they learn new vocabulary. Do not hesitate to use such words with young children.

As you talk about or become involved with your surroundings through activities, specify objects by their colors as often as possible. Ed Jacomo's letter directed families to refer to clothing by colors. Expand that kind of awareness to everything around you. Label and describe the colors in your room so that children continue to relate colors to objects and places. Because you are helping the children to see and connect colors in everything around them, they will learn to appreciate and enjoy this amazing world.

SOME STARTERS

From day one, children will learn with you that colors are part of everyday experiences. They may not be the focus or the subject but they will be inextricably connected to every object, activity, and discussion. Enjoy these few starters to get you thinking about teaching in a colorful way.

Start with the children's clothing As we know, clothing is very important to young children, and giving each child many opportunities to be highlighted is a way of celebrating. It's so easy to take a few minutes to say or sing the children's colors (leave *no* child out!). "I see Yuri's green shirt, I see Quinetta's yellow belt, I see Devonne's black shoelaces. . . ." Turn the little welcome into a song, a game, or a chant.

Start with any colorful book As we have continually noted, children's literature abounds with beautiful illustrations. Almost every fine children's picture book is an experience in color appreciation. The topic of the book doesn't need to be *about* colors. For example, I pick up Faith Ringgold's *Tar Beach*.[6] The story is about a little girl named Cassie who flies over her neighborhood in New York City, over her favorite bridge, the George Washington Bridge, and transforms her memories into dazzling, colorful, family, and urban scenes bordered on every page by quilt designs.

Lois Ehlert's magnificent books are about animals, plants, vegetables, and fish, but every one of them is an amazing experience in color celebration. Here is *Feathers for Lunch*,[7] a beautiful book honoring birds and flowers. Stop. Look. Listen to the colors on every page. In the sunny, oceanside colors of *Beach Ball*,[8] a multicolored beach ball bounces and flies over lively, crowded beach scenes. Every page playfully challenges readers to find hidden letters, numbers, shapes, animals, and opposites. As the children search through the colors, a natural and playful way to guide them or urge them along is to model clues like, "I think I see two blue and white umbrellas. Can you find them?" The children will want to create their own colorful works inspired by such outstanding illustrators. I can't imagine anyone sharing books like these with children without spending time admiring, appreciating, and discussing the outstanding use of colors in the pictures telling the story. What color-drenched book is in your hands right now?

Start with any colorful look What's the weather? What's the season? What's the time of day? Be alert to the changes of colors day by day, hour by hour, week by week. On rainy days, colors have different hues. Use descriptive words with your children so all participants enjoy rich language stimuli. Sharing books like *The Umbrella Day* and *Anna's Rain*[9] add opportunities for observation of muted colors, rain-washed colors. Be open to all teachable moments!

Start with a color walk Walk and talk around the room, school, schoolyard, street, or neighborhood. As you walk, stop and look. "What colors do we see? How many colors can we name? Which colors do we like the best?"

Start with a display table Barbara Kienzle's favorite way to launch a focus on color[10] is to fascinate children with such hard-to-resist items as prisms, kaleidoscopes, sunglasses, magnifying glasses, plastic "stained-glass" strips, colored tissue paper, and cellophane. She encourages the children to see, touch, experiment with, and talk about light and color.

Start with a rainbow A real rainbow is preferable, but if nature does not cooperate, a book about rainbows, such as Don Freeman's *A Rainbow of My Own* or *Rainbow Rider,* or a beautiful photograph or painting of a rainbow, is irresistible.

Start with darkness Turn off the lights and pull down the shades. Ask the children to close their eyes and hide their faces behind their hands (like peek-a-boo). "What do you see in a dark room with your eyes closed and your face hidden?" Nothing! But what colors can they *imagine*? Then, ask the children to take their hands from their faces and open their eyes. "What do we see?" Shapes and colors in the dim room. Lift the shades, turn on the lights, and ask the children to *really* look at the room. "Now what do we see? Are the colors brighter, the shapes clearer?" This is an effective way to begin thinking about colors and light.

Start with a color buddy search Here is an example of a buddy activity that starts a focus on colors. Give each child a design or card of a distinct color. Ask children to hold up their cards and walk slowly around the room to find friends who have cards of the same color. When they find their "color buddies," they form a small group.

This project can be easily expanded. For example, each color group has a special activity for the day, which is written or pictured on a large colored card. The children match their colors to the activity cards.

Each group can also lead an exercise. The yellow group, for example, decides to do jumping jacks; when the yellow card is held up, everyone does jumping jacks.

Start with a challenge Young children usually respond to challenges with enthusiasm, for example: "Let's see if we can find ten blue things in our room"; "Let's look out the window and see if we can count five different colors"; or "How many things can you find in our room that match the color of this red book?" Invite the children to turn on their bright lights and press their alertness buttons. It's so easy to begin! Songs, puppets, games, stores, art projects, sharing times, riddles, costumes, and food are excellent ways to start journeys. Keep your colorful eyes open for opportunities to mix color with every aspect of your time.

Start with a color day Fun-loving, dynamic teachers across the country experiment with variations of this idea. Celebrate one color. Have a Red Letter Day, or a Blueness Day, or a Green for a Day Day.

The children celebrate the color many ways: they wear ribbon or patches, or construction-paper hats, headbands, armbands, bows, or bowties in the color; make up songs and poems about the color; name things defined by the color; draw, paint, and color pictures and designs in the color; connect the color to feelings and ideas ("This color makes me feel . . ."); play music that expresses the color; make up puppet shows about the color; make up games and riddles about the color ("I'm thinking of something way above our heads, high above us, very wide and high that often shows our special color." Answer: The blue sky!); correlate the special color with letters, numbers, and shapes; make tissue-paper flowers of different shades of the color; and read books and find pictures that feature the color of the day. There are more ideas of this kind later in the guide.

Start with a famous painting Nothing is more dramatic for children than discovering that artists begin with blank canvas and, by adding colors, shapes, and lines, create images and scenes that satisfy senses and emotions. Children are dazzled by the colors of Van Gogh's *Sunflowers* and *Starry Night,* Monet's *Gardens at Giverny* and *Waterlilies,* Gauguin's South Seas landscapes and villages, Homer's seascapes, Cassatt's *The Boating Party* and *Children at the Seashore,* Degas' dancers and horses, Renoir's children and parks, and Chagall's circuses and villages. Browse through the art catalogues and prints in your local library and borrow the paintings you enjoy, and introduce your students to them. Your room reflects *your* interests, values, and hobbies. Share the works of art you most enjoy with your students. Joan Kalb's students are the fortunate recipients of Joan's passionate love of art.[11] Prints, posters, paintings, and art books are everywhere in her room. The children learn about people, places, nature, design, and events through studying and enjoying the varied artists and arts offerings surrounding them. Any one reference to any one of the many works on walls, shelves, pages, and tables can launch a dynamic focus on colors. Folk artists of every culture use colors in powerful ways.

Start with eyes and hair Children are fascinated by the colors of their eyes and hair and those of others. Look in mirrors. Look at each other. Say each child's hair and eye colors. Marvel at the diversity. Start the children thinking about how boring it would be if everyone had exactly the same eye and hair colors.

Go from eyes and hair to the mind-boggling varieties of flowers, sunsets, animals, fish, birds, seashells, vegetables, leaves, and stones. These are nature's marvelous colors. Also consider the variety of colors that people choose for their homes, rooms, clothes, cars, and toys.

TALK TIMES/LISTENING TIMES

Ed Jacomo said, "Colors last all the year. Color is all the time." Children never tire of talking about colors. Remember, they are in the process of learning colors, and the spectacle of daily life is a constant source of discovery, amazement, and joy of recognition.

Integrate color consciousness in every topic! Be ready with sharing and questions. For example, "My dog is black and white. What color is your dog?" or "My neighbor got a new yellow ball. What's your favorite colored ball?"

Imaginative teachers always teach in color-connected ways. You probably are already sharing technicolor education with your students. Consider these suggestions as more flavors to add to your list of delicious ideas!

Classes of colors Through the years, the children who came to school under Muriel Hampton's programs[12] worked and played in a world of colors. "Even our chairs are painted different colors," Muriel explains with a twinkle in her eyes, "so we can casually say, 'Let's skip to a red chair' or 'Michael, could you please carry the yellow chair over to the green table. Thank you!' "

Talk times/listening times in Muriel's rooms are very casual and natural. "We don't quiz the kids," she says. "We don't test them all the time. But when the children tell us they need more paint, we'll say 'Sure, what color do you need?' We play games with color wheels, tell stories with colors in them; for instance, just what colors were the mittens of the three little kittens?" Because the children are constantly involved in enjoyable activities, there is a buzz of conversation underlying the action in Muriel's rooms. "When we put just red and orange out, or just blue and yellow, for the children to experiment with, there is so much discussion about those colors and how they change."

In rooms full of toilet paper tubes with colored cellophane taped over the ends, rainbows made of scarves, papers, and streamers of real and crafted flowers, Muriel's children "talk all the time" about the colors around them.

Colorful conversations Colors brighten all conversations! Carol Price and her children[13] enjoy discussing the colors of football, baseball, and soccer games and cheerleaders' uniforms; the colors of traffic lights and what they mean; how some animals like snowshoe rabbits, wolves, and salamanders change colors to protect themselves; the colors of seasons; how dull our lives would be without colors; how colors affect our lives; how colors change in different kinds of light; how some colors make us sleepy and some make us bouncy; why certain colors are our favorite colors; how we can imagine colors in our minds; how everything has its own colors. As often as possible, write the children's names and ideas on a Talk Charts/Conversation Bulletin Boards/Great Ideas wall. Think of all the extended activities that can flow from these initial conversations!

Color "talks" into poems When Joan Kalb and her children talked about *their* colors, in her room full of colorful paintings and objects, ideas exploded like fireworks. They listened intently to each other, appreciating and sharing feelings and experiences. Their words wanted to become poems. With high motivation, the children recorded their ideas on paper. Here are a few samples from that colorful session:

> Colors are so nice today.
> Go out and see the beautiful
> blue sky and the lovely
> green grass on the world's floor.
>
> Ryan Stevens, age 8

The children talked about the many shades of one color. We might call the color "green," but green doesn't always look the same. Colorful poems emerged from sharing ideas.

Talk about a birthday rainbow It was Todd's eighth birthday. We talked about doing something special for a person on his or her birthday. We talked about creating a special birthday story for Todd. Ideas came fast and furiously. I wrote story lines on the board as they were suggested. Here is Todd's classmates' talk/story gift to him on his eighth birthday.

> I flew up to the sky. The stars flickered their lights around me. I turned invisible. It rained and I washed out into the rainbow. I ran around the colors. It smelled like strawberries. I heard the song of the rainbow:
>
> **The Song of the Rainbow**
> Happy birthday to you,
> You live in a rainbow.

Colors

Green, there are many different shades of green like jungle-green, yellow green, sping green, emerald green, sea green, green, olive, and slime green and last but not least pine green.

There are also many things that are green like grass, snakes, dinosaurs, frogs, trees, alligators, crystals, lilly-pads, bushes, poison ivy, poison oak, poison sumac, sea weed, coral, fish, eels, teddy bears and birds, paper, book covers, blankets and more lots more so now you know a little more about the color green bye bye.

By: Kara Age 8.

I give you blue.
I give you orange.
I give you pink.
I give you red.
I give you purple.
I give you yellow.
I give you green.
I give you brown.
I give you autumn leaves.
I give you a closet of rainbow clothes.
I give you a forest of wildflowers.
I give you a school full of colorful kids.
Happy Rainbow to You!

Leading questions spur children on. Todd's rainbow story was developed and enriched when, during pauses in the children's suggestions, questions were asked, such as: "What happened when you flew into the sky?"; "What did you do in the rainbow?"; and "What did you smell? What did you hear?"

Color wishes Steven Conkle[14] and his second graders shared ideas about wishes and colors. Steve encouraged the children to suggest a color in every wish. They talked together about their wishes and colors and finally collaborated on a group poem based on their suggestions. Here is an excerpt from that work:

> I wish I had a blue fish in my home
> brown puppy in my backyard
> red and white rabbit in a fish tank
> polka-dotted monkey in my mouth
> black and blue cat in my bed
> blue and white bird in my desk . . .[15]

Every activity in this book is accompanied or inspired by "Talk Times." So keep talking.

VISUAL ARTS TIMES

In rooms where color is an everyday topic, children enjoy a variety of arts experiences, constantly building on what they did before and combining new ideas.

Innovative teachers scrounge color chips, color swatches, purple and green dividers from apple crates, crepe paper, waxed paper, newspaper, old plastic squirt bottles, shoe-polish applicators, sponges, food coloring, ribbons and bows, medicine droppers, tongue depressors, swabs, crayons, finger paints, colored chalk, charcoal, buttons, tempera, watercolors, stones that produce colors, catalogues, magazines, greeting cards, and clay.

Innovative teachers are open to the countless opportunities that lend color to our lives! Excitement, exploration, and experimentation (the three E's) are blended in the mix. Warning: nothing is guaranteed, not even such a colorful theme as colors! Narrow-minded, humorless, unimaginative, and authoritarian adults can easily kill the theme of colors for children (remember "Flowers Are Red"). So, whatever the materials and ideas, share them with joy and playfulness. Be flexible. Adapt them to your special mix of unique children.

A color-splashed room Posters, pictures, displays, bulletin boards, borders, windows, walls, and doors are surfaces waiting for colors! Color charts/color wheels featuring the children's names connected to their favorite flower colors, vegetable colors, or animal colors are examples of colorful child-centered materials that enrich learning with images and words. Keep all ideas generated by your children prominently displayed in colorful ways.

Creators of colors All of the arts fill empty spaces, blank places, and silence. With your children, talk about the wonder of how colors began—legends and stories of how colors came to the world are inspiring and stimulate the children's own ideas. Our old and beloved friend, Frederick[17]—the little mouse who collects warm images, words, and colors to brighten cold winter nights—motivates the children to turn themselves into Frederick and paint their own warm, bright colors and words for cold times. Tomie dePaola retells a Native American legend in *The Legend of the Indian Paintbrush*.[18] It's about a boy who is given a pure white buckskin and told to keep it and "one day you will paint a picture that is as pure as the colors in the evening sky." The story will dazzle the children's imaginations, especially if you give them a beautiful sheet of white paper ("pure white buckskin") and invite them to paint their own picture of the beautiful sky or trees or flowers. Ask the children,

"How did you feel when you were painting this?" or "Tell me about your picture." Add words!

Eric Carle's *Draw Me a Star*[19] catches the true excitement of the creative process as the artist paints stars, rainbows, flowers, birds, and clouds on blank pages. The children discover that they, too, are artists who can magically add marvelous colors to empty spaces.

One color at a time Theresa Gelonese[20] likes to start out with the color white. The children look at pictures of white; color, chalk, and paint with white; and talk about ideas and feelings evoked by the color white. Words and pictures are combined. Then Theresa adds, one by one, the primary colors red, blue, and yellow. The children paint with each color so they get specific feelings from the color. Later, the three primary colors are offered at the same time. Theresa encourages the children to experiment and make their own discoveries when they mix the primary colors. An old favorite, *Little Blue and Little Yellow,*[21] is an example of an excellent story way to enrich the children's explorations in mixing primary colors. I visited one school where the primary children had re-created their own illustrations interpreting the story. Their colors were prominently spread across an entire wall.

Let's paint the "shapes and colors of joy" Children need to talk about joyful times, events, people, and feelings in their lives. Gather ideas. Brainstorm together about how we can paint joyful, cheerful colors and designs. Sing happy songs. Listen to merry music. Read inspiring stories like *Matthew's Dream,*[22] which is about another little mouse who discovers the beautiful paintings in a museum and dreams that he and a friend walk hand in hand into a fantastic painting. "As they walked, playful patches of color shifted under their feet, and all around them suns and moons moved gently to the sound of distant music." But that wonderful experience was a dream, and when Matthew awoke, he was back in his dreary corner. He decided he would become a painter, and he painted "large canvases filled with the shapes and colors of joy." The children love to turn themselves into Matthew and paint their own "colors and shapes of joy." Children need to be reminded of the positive aspects of their lives.

Color trays Ask the children's families to save the Styrofoam packing trays from the market. When you have enough, give one to each child. The children choose their favorite colors of markers and fill their trays with bright, beautiful colors. The trays are easily attached to the wall with masking tape, and they make a fine display of color.

Scratch a color This activity takes muscles. The children fill a sheet of paper with crayon blobs of their favorite colors. Be sure they press as hard as they can so the colors are solid and pure. When their paper is filled with a design of different colors, suggest that they color their papers with black crayon and that they press hard so that the colors underneath are hidden.

Now you are ready for the magic. With hairpins or toothpicks, the children scratch out shapes (for example, circles, rectangles) or drawings on their papers. Wherever they scratch, the black crayon is cut away and the bright colors underneath show beautifully.

Show the colors Our youngest children soon recognize the American flag waving in every classroom. The flags of the world are colorful and fascinating, with symbols and designs in crystal-clear color patterns. As you and your children grow to know each other, you will learn that many of your families come from diverse backgrounds. The flags representing the countries of origin of your students present new color schemes and symbols for your children to learn. On paper or material, encourage the children to create an assortment of flags. When Pierre came to kindergarten from Canada, the children learned to recognize the red and white Canadian flag, which features a large red maple leaf in the center. Saito, from Japan, proudly showed his classmates a picture of his white flag with a bright red sun in the center of it. The children enjoyed painting flags and flag pictures. They especially loved creating their own flags! Be sure to raise all the flags, march with them, show the colors. Even though it's not up to the latest changes in boundaries and countries (is anything?) *The Guide to the Flags of the World*[23] is a book children use with enthusiasm for ideas of colors and symbols. Find music to accompany the different flags.

"Glorious trash" color pictures One of the late Ed Jacomo's favorite art activities began with gathering things the children liked that had especially attractive shapes and colors.

> We arrange the things on a big piece of paper and spend time just looking at them and enjoying the different colors and textures. Maybe we'll have a yellow pencil, a brown flowerpot with a red flower in it, a white napkin, a pink mitten, a white baseball. Then we remove one of the items and paint or crayon its shape and color in the empty spot. One by one, we replace the objects with their colors and shapes on the paper. Finally, all the "glorious trash" is gone, but the color patterns on the paper are reminders of it. We hang our unusual art on the wall and admire it for a long time.

Turn yourself into a famous artist Artists use color in amazingly diverse ways. Their techniques offer examples of possibilities to young children who are known for their openness and willingness to experiment.

As often as possible, choose paintings to study and celebrate. Encourage the children to really look at the way the artist used color. Is the color pure or mixed or blended with other colors? Did the artist make little dots of color or large, thick strokes? Are there dark and light areas in the painting? Do the images in the paintings look very accurate, or are they kind of dreamy and imaginative? Are they mostly shapes and designs, or are they recognizable subjects? Children enjoy finding Chagall's favorite images, present in most of his paintings but sometimes hidden. A

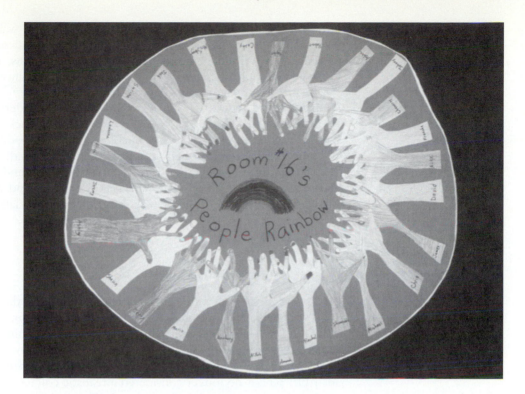

group of kindergartners had a marvelous time painting Chagall-inspired pictures with their own hidden images and dreamy colors. Large and small motor skills were exercised to new levels as children turned themselves into the ancient Chinese painter/poet Li Po, who, in the tradition of his culture, painted with a delicate brush. In a contrast of colors and concepts, children then turned themselves into Van Gogh, painting swirling stars and clouds and waving grass.

Children need to learn that there is no "right" way to paint or to use colors. When they practice many different ways, inspired by the works of many different artists, they learn coordination and confidence as well as openness and appreciation.

Color books Gifted artists and writers, young children create delightful and beautiful books about colors. Depending on their interests, they feature one color and illustrate all the images that come to mind featuring that color. An example of a book all about one color is *Seeing Red*.[24] Most of us have trouble picking *one* color to feature, so be open to two or three or more! *Thinking about Colors*[25] invites children to create their own books, highlighting a page for every color to be honored with words and pictures displaying the colors. In this bright and cheery book, the children even think in dialogue bubbles of colors. In *Samuel Todd's Book of Great Colors*,[26] the child artist writes: "In my book, the great colors come in this order: Orange/Green/Purple/Yellow/Brown/Red/Blue/Gray/Pink/Black and White." And those colors are honored in that sequence. Invite children to create their own books of great colors with their own lists.

Class color books make enjoyable collaborative ventures. Each child contributes a page or pages to the book. Be sure to celebrate the class color book with a colorful party. Toss confetti in the air!

Colors for all seasons With all your senses, explore the seasons. Around the country, teachers and children decorate classroom trees with autumn leaves (sponges dipped in tempera colors on cardboard leaf shapes is a popular method) of every autumn color. Buds, blossoms, flowers, and fruit appear as the seasons change. Winter shapes and figures, colors, and designs on white backgrounds show clear contrasts. Spread large mural paper across the wall and invite the children to contribute every shade of green for lush spring and summer landscapes. Use scrounged materials to create three-dimensional gardens, forests, and fields. Add words of description and inspiration. Read colorfully illustrated books like *Rain, When Autumn Comes, When Winter Comes,* and *Changes*[27] for further enriching.

A show of hands. Rose Stough[28] and her third graders had a lively discussion about skin colors. They described their own colors as black, tan, reddish, brown, orange, Indian, light blue, "all kinds of colors." Rose flipped her wrist and noted that her palm was lighter than her hand. The children flipped! They were amazed that their bodies were composed of different colors—darker and lighter. Rose read them poems from Arnold Adoff's *All the Colors of the Race* and *Black Is Brown Is Tan*[29] inspired by his own interracial family. The children especially loved the refrain,

> Black is brown is tan
> is girl is boy
> is nose is face
> is all the colors of the race.[30]

Rose and the kids put their hands together to see their own beautiful colors. They arranged and rearranged their hands so the colors and patterns changed. They loved the colors of their hands together and loved outlining, cutting, coloring, and pasting their handprints together in a "People Rainbow." (Isn't it interesting to note that many crayon manufacturers now offer a diversity of colors for "skin colors"? Off-pink is no longer considered a realistic color to depict skin.)

We are always learning from the children. This touching story came from a mother whose five-year-old son finally asked his new best school friend to come visit. After the friend played and left, Mom spoke to her son, "You didn't tell me that your friend, Dominick, is black." The child looked at her in puzzlement and answered, "He's not black, Mom, he's beige!"

What blend of colors describes your skin?

Words and colors Every color creates its own vocabulary. Colors evoke vivid images, and children enthusiastically respond to the challenge of thinking of words inspired by specific colors. There are many ways to celebrate the fusion of words and colors. Here are a few samples.

Color frames On sheets of white paper, paint, crayon, or paste strips of colors around the borders. In the center of the paper, words are written in the same colors as the borders.

Color-word explosion On a large sheet of white paper, the name of a color is written or printed in large letters. Ask the children to embellish the name with paint, crayon, or chalk so that it really stands out. Fill the rest of the paper with words and pictures that are suggested by the color word. The final pictures explode like color-word fireworks.

Color-word posters The children celebrate their favorite colors with a composition of pictures and words expressing their feelings about that color.

Color-word picture montage Children enjoy working on these projects individually or in small groups. Using magazines, catalogues, and greeting cards, children cut out pictures of objects in the color they are featuring. The pictures are pasted on a large sheet of paper. Many teachers write the name of the color in large, wide poster letters. All the pictures are then pasted inside the outlines of the letters of the word.

Word-color balloons Draw large circles on a sheet of paper or one circle on a smaller sheet. Ask the children to press hard on their crayons to present the color as strongly as possible. If they are using paints, ask them not to dilute the paints with water; the colors should be as pure as possible. When the balloons of colors are finished and dried, fill the balloons with words triggered by the colors. A blue balloon in a kindergarten class carried the words "sky," "water," and "my eyes."

Colorful poems Poems are already word illustrations of the power of imagination. Poetry and colors blend naturally. Many collections of poetry are beautifully illustrated by the nation's finest artists. Children need daily doses of poetry and colorful pictures! They will be inspired to create their own collaborations with classmates, illustrating the poems of others as well as their own, when they read books like *Sing to the Sun, In for Winter, Out for Spring, High in the Mountains, Sky Songs, Listen to the Rain*, and *Black Is Beautiful*.[31] Each of these uniquely designed books will encourage your children to use their original powers to write and illustrate their own poems. It's a cause for celebration!

Construction-paper mosaics Children can spend hours cutting, pasting, and arranging colorful shapes. Cut sheets of brightly colored paper into small squares, circles, triangles, rectangles, and other shapes. The children cover sheets of paper with glue and affix the shapes. Unless you are working on a specific assignment combining counting, colors, and shapes, encourage the children to create their own patterns with the small, colorful shapes.

Tissue- and waxed-paper stained-glass windows Cut out brightly colored shapes of tissue paper. Smear sheets of waxed paper with glue or paste. Encourage the children to paste the tissue-paper shapes on the waxed paper. Press the different colors of tissue paper down firmly. When they dry, tape them to the windows and enjoy the way the light shines through each color.

A delightful variation of this activity is one of Lynn Salem's favorite ways to make stained-glass windows. She cuts sheets of black construction paper into shapes of window frames and gives one to each child. The children choose their favorite colors of tissue paper and paste them to the black frames. When all the window frames are hung in the classroom windows, the result is spectacular.

Coffee-can-lid stained-glass windows Ed Jacomo made stained-glass windows by scrounging the plastic lids from coffee cans. He gave one to each child. The children brushed one side with liquid laundry starch and lay colored tissue paper on the starch. They were encouraged to overlap colors and shapes. When the lids dried, they punched holes in them and hung them on the window.

Chalk it up Jean Williams experiments with ways to make colors. She encourages her kindergartners to discover the variations in color when they use different parts of crayons or chalk. "We color with the point, the side, and the blunt end," Jean explains. "We paint every day; painting is part of everything we do. We use tempera, watercolor, crayons, and chalk." Her children like to fill manila or construction paper with colored chalk designs. They try wet chalk on dry paper, dry chalk on wet paper, white chalk on black paper, and every possible combination. What better way to practice creativity?

Note: Gently spray chalk pictures with one push-button of hair spray to set the colors and keep them from smearing.

Night and day colors Children have a lot to say about the dark and how it's hard to see in the dark.

"I never see colors in the dark," a kindergartner said.

"But if you turn lights on, you see colors," a classmate reassured the first.

When children create night pictures, it helps diffuse the mystery and often the fear of darkness. Here is a chance for the kids to use their silvery and gold colors to twinkle the stars and shine up the moon! Night clouds look soft and white against dark skies. Colors are muted in the dimness of night. Monet stood outside painting his cathedral at all hours, from bright noon to dusk, to catch the color changes. With the children, note sun and shadows, brighter and duller colors. *Night in the Country* and *Sun Up*[33] are examples of two books of simply told stories with effective illustrations that will reinforce the children's observations as they create their own pictures with paints, crayons, and markers. It's fun to divide a board into two large sections titled "Night" and "Day" and invite the children to contribute colors and images for each section.

More colorful ideas to celebrate Certain ideas are packed with colors! Ask your children their suggestions about colorful places, people, events, animals, and things, and they will provide you with enough material to go on for months.

Rainbows of colors Rainbows are a popular subject with young children. Rainbows come in all sizes and varieties. Here are just a few. Draw them on T-shirts with markers; paint them on waxed paper and tape them to windows for stained-glass rainbows; color rainbow badges, one for every child; create a huge rainbow, as big as a wall, to which every child makes a colorful contribution; paint or write rainbow books cut in an arc shape and with a different color of the rainbow for each page, and combine with words for each color of the rainbow. Go further! Rainbows don't just hang in the sky with their beautiful curved arc shapes. Where do they appear? Over forests? Fields? Farms? Share ideas for images to add to your rainbow pictures. Ruth Craft's boldly illustrated book, *The Day of the Rainbow*,[34] tells a magical story of city folks on city streets on a hot summer day and what happens when they see "a swerve of red, orange, yellow, green, blue, indigo and violet making a wobbly curve. . . ." You and the kids will enjoy creating landscapes and cityscapes for rainbows to brighten.

Circus of colors Talk about clowns, elephants, balloons, jugglers, horses, acrobats, costumes, lions, tigers, tightropes, parades, monkeys, dogs, dancers, three rings, seals, and crowds of people. Turn your room into a circus tent. Each day work on one circus idea. For example, one day everyone colors a beautiful balloon. Tape the balloons to the walls or hang them on mobiles. The next day, work on clowns. Encourage the children to use the brightest, most delightful colors for clowns' hats, faces, and costumes. Add the clowns to the scene. By the end of a week, your room will be a circus of colors. Play circus music! Have a parade!

Other colorful celebrations The following are examples of colorful images gathered around a central idea suggested by the children. There's no time limit on these kinds of experiences—they continue to evolve, moving through time and brightening space. Imagine the throbbing colors and shapes for "garden" (flowers, grass, birds, vegetables, and butterflies), "birds" (in the sky, on the farm, in the city, in Antartica, and in the rain forest), "peacock" (every child contributed a beautifully colored feather to create a fan of peacock feathers that dazzled the room), and "ocean" (Ed Jacomo played "watery music," poured blue dye into clear fishbowl water, talked about where the water was lightest and darkest and how it moved). Excited about ocean ideas, inspired by the blue water and music, the children created their own ocean with colorful fish, coral, and treasure!

With your kids, continue to share observations honoring the technicolored creativity of nature. Just as nature combines colors and designs in endless varieties, we artists can continually explore new combinations and patterns. With your encouragement, your children will feel confident and joyful as they freely and playfully take their rightful place in the creative process by adding their own colors to fish, flowers, trees, balloons, or birds, whatever your special focus, whatever your "theme."

Visual arts projects are part of all activities. A word, a song, a game, a story flows into and from visual arts experiences. Spin your color wheels: paint everything green or red or orange; choose your colors! Join Mary O'Neill's colorful questions such as "What is yellow?" "What is orange?"[35] in her newly illustrated, beloved *Hailstones and Halibut Bones*. Encourage the children to illustrate and write their own color poems! Continue to correlate ideas, discovering how they overlap and how they are inseparable. Think color! Splash colors on everything. Add a little color to your daze!

MUSIC TIMES

In the unlikely possibility that you do not immediately see the connections between colors and music, think of the terminology associated with both subjects. The elements of music and color are discussed with such words as "tone," "harmony," "mixture," "tone color," "dynamics" (loud/soft), and "rhythm" (regular/irregular/accent). We could go on! Colors and musical notes can be complementary, harmonious, or dissonant. Each instrument and each voice, like each color, has its own languages. Blending and separating colors and blending and separating voices and instruments are similar experiences. What color is your voice? Does it change colors? When?

Learning the names of colors, recognizing colors, and becoming more aware of colors are ideas worth singing about. Think color as you and your children make up songs, chants, raps, hums, and symphonies!

Improvised songs that celebrate the children's colors Clothing, eyes, hair, and names are favorite topics in early childhood classes. Here is a brief excerpt from a long series of color verses, improvised for each child, sung to the tune of "Mary Had a Little Lamb."

Bob is wearing a yellow shirt,
A yellow shirt,
A yellow shirt.
Bob is wearing a yellow shirt
On this Wednesday morning.

Laura's wearing a red and blue skirt,
Red and blue skirt,
Red and blue skirt.
Laura's wearing a red and blue skirt,
On this Wednesday morning.

Each child was featured in a stanza. Afterward the children colored pictures of their special clothes.

If your children know their colors and are ready for lots of ideas at once, expand the "Mary Had a Little Lamb" tune to include more observations such as:

Erika has such brown brown eyes,
Brown curly hair,
Tan western boots.
Devonne has on his green turtle shirt
On this Wednesday morning!

What a way to start the day with eyes open and minds sharp.

The old folk song, "Mary Wore Her Red Dress" (which I've heard sung in ten different ways with a dozen different melodies) turns into a musical, colorful game/song. Clap, sing, bounce along with such verses as "Henry wore his green sneakers, green sneakers, green sneakers. Henry wore his green sneakers all day long. . . ." Delightfully adapted and illustrated by Merle Peek in a picture book, *Mary Wore Her Red Dress/And Henry Wore His Green Sneakers,*[36] the song celebrates children, colors, and clothes. Improvise the lyrics with the names of your own children and their colors and clothes!

Original songs, cheers, and chants about colors A group of prekindergartners celebrated a Yellow Day. They wore something yellow, made yellow Jell-O, painted yellow pictures, tied yellow ribbons and strings on their arms, and made up a song about yellow to the tune "For He's a Jolly Good Fellow."

For it's a jolly good yellow
For it's a jolly good yellow
For it's a jolly good yellow
That nobody can deny!

Here is a rhythmical cheer celebrating the color blue, created by a class of second graders.

Blue for the sky (clap/clap/clap)
Blue for our jeans (clap/clap/clap)
Blue for blue eyes (clap/clap/clap)
Blue for blueberries (jump/jump/jump)

Listen to the music of the colors Because humans have the gift of synesthesia, we can close our eyes, listen to music, and let the music evoke vivid images in our minds. One sensory stimulus triggers another sensory response. Synesthesia is a celebration of the senses! I smell strawberries and I can imagine their taste and clearly see their shapes and colors in my mind. A colorful seascape touches my ears, and I hear the crashing of waves, the squawk of gulls. I smell the salt air. I feel the sand.

Give the children opportunities to listen to a variety of music and ask them to respond in challenging ways, such as: "Listen to the music. What pictures do you see? What colors does this music make you imagine?" Pass out papers, crayons, paints, chalk, and markers. Ask the children to listen to the music and, as they listen, to cover their papers with the colors and designs that the music evokes. Remember, all interpretations should be accepted and respected.

These are also opportunities for you to discover the creative talents of children who may be visually impaired. As they listen carefully to musical selections, you may notice that they press their crayons on paper with heavier strokes in response to loud sounds; swirly, graceful lines often accompany more lyrical pieces. Listen for gentle sounds, for boisterous, merry-making sounds, and for music with clearly contrasting themes. The children's colorful interpretations will be loyal to the music. Encourage all the kids to tell stories, make poems, share feelings, and create titles for the different colorful musical moments.

Experiment with different rhythms. Be on the lookout (and listen-out) for music from around the world. Children's paintings and drawings responding to Arabic music will be different from their interpretations to Chinese or Andean music. When you use music that *you* love, the enthusiasm will be contagious.

Our own country is a world rich with diverse musical rhythms, from gritty blues to hip-hop, from rockabilly to rhythm and blues, from country and western to Cajun, from Hispanic pop rock to Appalachian mountain music. I repeat: when you use music that *you* love, the enthusiasm will be contagious. Color all the musical patterns!

Scrounge your own, your neighbors', and the libraries' collections for examples of music that express different moods. Through the years, I have shared a wide range of musical selections with young children. Their artistic interpretations and expressions are always highly original.

Colors of musical instruments Listening with sensitive ears to the sounds of specific instruments is a valuable and enjoyable experience for young children. Correlate such listening with art and ask the children to imagine the colors and designs each instrument or family of instruments evokes. Children of all ages have listened to and painted the colors of such diverse instruments as Pete Seeger's banjo; Ravi Shankar's sitar; Carlos Montoya's flamenco guitar; Clarence Clemons's saxophone; Montego Joe's African drums; and Orff's percussion instruments, bells, and flutes.

Label the pictures with titles and stories the children suggest. A six-year-old added these feelings to his bright red picture of the sound of gypsy violins: "These violins are red because the sky turns red at night when you hear their music."

Musical sky colors Many musical selections suggest images of skies and weather. Grofé's *Grand Canyon* Suite inspires sensitive pictures of sunrises and of sudden rains; Debussy's *La Mer* is all clear sky and ocean; Mussorgsky's *A Night on Bald Mountain* helps children paint the dramatic colors of thunderstorms; and Brahms's *Lullaby* is a perfect palette of sunset colors. Native American flute music paints soft colors of dusk and dawn. Richie Havens's interpretation of The Beatles's "Here Comes the Sun" is a palette of musical colors! Catch a flurry of exciting colors in the African drums of Montego Joe.

Color-cued rhythm bands Designate a different color for each group of instruments in your class rhythm band. Make a color chart of the instruments and their color cues. Paint or color large cue cards; use any design or outline of instruments. Now the children are ready to take their musical cues from the cards.

A delightful variation of this activity is to use dark and light shades for each instrument. For example, when light blue is held up, the drums are played softly; when dark blue is the cue, the drums are played with gusto.

Ed Jacomo carried this idea a step further. He correlated shades of colors with numbers of instruments played. "When yellow is very very pure, all eight tambourines play," he instructed his youngsters. The children had to look carefully at the cards to distinguish the degree of brightness and respond with the brightest sounds.

Musical rainbows Expand on the above activities. Assign different families of instruments to colors of the rainbow. For example, the triangles are purple. All the children playing triangles wear purple ribbons, string, or scarves; or purple paper taped to their shirts; or purple hats. They stand to form an arc. Behind them, in another arc, stand children with another color and another group of instruments. Continue this pattern to form a rainbow. Now all the colors of the spectrum are celebrated by their own musical sounds played by a rainbow of children. Have a rainbow parade. Read rainbow poems and stories. Play rainbow music.

Musical backgrounds to colorful stories Children's picture books are often brilliantly illustrated by outstanding artists. Choose books that offer colorful illustrations and ask the children to decide what kind of music or sounds could accompany specific pictures.

Arnold Lobel's *The Great Blueness and Other Predicaments*[37] is an example of a good book to set to music. As the Wizard paints everything one color and the world turns into that color, children enjoy creating the sounds of the world turned blue, turned yellow ("the Great Yellowness"), and turned red ("the Great Redness"), until a symphony of instruments expresses the fabulous finale when all the colors are celebrated in a world that is "too beautiful ever to be changed again."

A wonderful picture book like Brian Wildsmith's *The Circus*[38] inspires bouncy, cheerful circus music that children enjoy creating and moving to as each of Wildsmith's circus images spurs a new musical interpretation.

Gerald McDermott's *Arrow to the Sun,*[39] based on a Pueblo Indian story, is enjoyed for its unusual dramatic colors, inventive illustrations in which all the characters are different shapes, and musical language. Children play drums, bells, and tom-toms in Native American rhythms to accompany each illustration. A delightful, playful book by Bill Martin, Jr., *Brown Bear, Brown Bear, What Do You See?*[40] invites children to mix colors, animal sounds, movement and specific music for each animal. Think of the symphony of sounds, colors, and animals you'll have when the children build to an exciting finale of brown bear, red bird, yellow duck, blue horse, green frog, purple cat, white dog, black sheep, and gold fish!

Red light, green light The children play their favorite instruments to familiar or improvised music. Hold up a bright red circle to signal "stop the music." Hold up a bright green circle to signal "start the music." The children learn those important signals as they discover something about silence and sound—the dramatic pause.

Expand this activity with other color symbols and by signalling faster, slower, louder, and softer responses.

National flags and ethnic music The children learn that countries have their own flags with special color combinations. Correlate flags with music. Teach the children countries and their flags, one at a time. Begin with the American flag. The children color flags on sheets of paper or white scrounged material. As the flags are displayed or waved, play music representative of the country.

We learn important lessons through music and songs. After my mother and her family emigrated from Rumania and came to America, she lived most of her life in New York City. One day, she and my father decided to spend an afternoon at Rockefeller Center. When she saw the splendid array of the world's flags, she wanted to look for the Rumanian flag. But, alas, she had forgotten the colors of that flag. She recalled the little song all Rumanian children learn with the words to the colors of the flag (phonetic pronunciation: "rosh," "galban," and "albostru"). More than seven decades after she learned it as a child, my mother sang the song to herself and found the Rumanian flag—red, yellow, and blue. Because she remembered the song, she remembered the colors!

Songs with color words Many colorful songs are waiting in your knapsack to be shared with your children. Start a list of songs about colors and you will be surprised at how many you know. At a recent workshop, teachers made lists that included "Blue Skies," "Around Her Neck She Wore a Yellow Ribbon," "Scarlet Ribbon," "White Christmas," "Black Is the Color of My True Love's Hair," "Red River Valley," "Red Sails in the Sunset," "Follow the Yellow Brick Road," "The Rainbow Connection," "Yellow Submarine," "I Can Sing a Rainbow," "Greensleeves," "Five Foot Two, Eyes of Blue," "The Green Leaves of Summer," "Mary Was a Redbird," "Mary Wore a Red Dress," "White Coral Bells," "Miss Mary Mack," and "It's Not Easy to Be Green."

Improvised songs about colors Teachers like Carol Price enjoy making up their own songs, as well as teaching children songs composed by others. Carol's kindergartners enjoyed her original song "Traveling Rainbow," which has a melody similar to "Hi Lili, Hi Lili, Hi Lo," from the film *Lili*.

> **Traveling Rainbow**
> I found me a traveling rainbow
> On a happy and warm summer day.
> I found me a traveling rainbow
> With colors so bright and so gay.
>
> I touched it and it felt like sunshine
> With wings soft as cobwebs and lace.
> I touched it and it felt like sunshine
> With sprinkles of dust on its face.
>
> But, I can't keep this traveling rainbow
> It's part of the blue summer sky.
> I can't keep this traveling rainbow—
> For it's really a butterfly.

Add music to colorful celebrations A list of suggestions for colorful celebrations was presented in "Visual Arts Times." Add music to those themes. Music adds another dimension to any experience. As the children paint, color, or sculpt circus ideas, play circus music; as they paint bright colors on their rain forest birds, play African folk music and Caribbean rhythms.

A variation of this idea is to encourage the children to create original music and sound effects for their celebration. Tape their music and play it to accompany the various activities of their celebration.

Colorful birthdays and other special parties What is your Birthday Child's favorite song? What music does your Child of the Week want to play or sing? Listen to, play, or sing the child's favorite music during the party. Make flags of the child's favorite colors and wave them as you sing and play music.

Music for the colors of outer space Children are familiar with the adventures of space journeys, the blast-off of rockets, and the strange rhythms of space exploration. What color is outer space? The children paint and draw pictures and murals and make mobiles of planets, stars, suns, and comets. What are the sounds of outer space? The children create their own space music with instruments, objects, bodies, and voices, or choose music like that of *Star Wars* to be played as they improvise space trips.

Sounds for colors Here is an opportunity to encourage imagination and experimentation. Ask the children to imagine the sounds of a color. The children usually begin with words like "loud," "soft," "scary," "fast," "bouncy," "tinkly," "lazy," and "peaceful." Write down all their words, but keep going.

Then ask the children to try making the sounds of the color with their voices, bodies, instruments, and anything else in the room that makes sounds. Children discover that they can make musical sounds by tapping two pencils together, shaking a jar of paper clips, clinking spoons against each other or a tabletop, and waving paper. An imaginative second grade decided that blue had the sound of wind—"blowy" and "airy." They worked out an extraordinary symphony of sounds and melodies to express music of blue.

Here is a chance to make another musical rainbow as groups of children work on the sounds of different colors of the rainbow. Give each group a chance to share their color's sounds by themselves; then go around once more, adding each color's sounds to the others as all the colors of the rainbow are played together.

Colorful conductors Brightly colored streamers, ribbons, banners, and scarves spark musical conducting activities. As children listen to music of different types, they choose colors that they feel express the feeling of the music. Play with variations. For example, children take turns being the conductor; small groups of the "orchestra" feature specific colors; or each child has an individual color. Be playful and flexible. Encourage the children to *really* listen to the music. In one kindergarten class, a few children automatically swirled red scarves to a violin solo. The reds stopped as the music proceeded. Why? "Red's too loud for this part!" When all the banners follow the music with their whirly, swirly movements, your room will be turned into a dance of colors, a symphony of colors. What colors do you see when you hear music?

MOVEMENT AND PLAY TIMES

Here is a reminder that we don't teach children to move and play; this is what children *do!* Our responsibilities and sacred commitments are to help create bright, encouraging, loving, and colorful environments that nurture the natural ways children best learn.

As I travel around the country, I am happy to see colors blended with every aspect of learning communities. For example, activities are printed on brightly colored cards held together by colored clothespins or stored in colored envelopes. Children's names are prominently displayed in living colors. Cubbyholes are painted in bright colors. Colors are used constantly as identification, reference, instruction aids, and celebration. Color is part of everything these fortunate children do.

Think about children spending their days in colorful surroundings integrally connected with their activities as you enjoy a few suggestions to keep things moving and playful.

Color magicians Doug Henning, an outstanding magician, believes that the real magic is everyday life and the best tricks are the ordinary events we take for granted. Because we have all become so "cool" and contained, we need magicians to jolt us into the feelings of astonishment that we forget we have. Henning believes that once these feelings of astonishment and wonder have been revived, we will be able to use them in appreciating the miracle of our daily lives.

Fortunately, young children have not yet lost the gifts of wonder and amazement. Perhaps we can help them (and ourselves) preserve that spirit a little longer. For that reason, many imaginative teachers add a touch of magic when they demonstrate the mixing of colors.

Change children into magicians Young children are easily turned into magicians with a few words of wonder from you, a little story, a magic wand, or a spray of magic dust. Once the children are turned into magicians, they demonstrate the following "tricks" with authority, excitement, and pride.

Soufflé cups and crepe paper This is a magical way to show the mixing of primary colors. Each "color scientist" receives three soufflé cups. The soufflé cups are filled with water. Each child receives pieces of yellow, blue, and red crepe paper. When the children dip the yellow crepe paper into one of the soufflé cups, the water turns yellow. Shazzam! Then they dip, into the same cup, a piece of blue crepe paper. Abracadabra, the yellow turns green. What a fabulous trick! The children continue with the other two cups to discover other mixtures. Mix this trick in with magic shows!

Food coloring and jars of water Probably the simplest and most popular way to show what happens when two primary colors are mixed together is to fill three large clear plastic soda bottles with water. Be sure to remove the labels. As the "color magicians" look at the three bottles, encourage them to turn on their magical powers.

Release a single drop of red, yellow, or blue food coloring into one of the bottles. Observe what happens to the water. Give the children turns to drop more of that color into the bottle. "Is everyone ready for the magical happening?" Make it dramatic. Into the bottle of red water, with your magicians' help, add drops of yellow (to make orange) or blue (to make purple). Say the magic words!

Finger paints and Formica tables Marilyn Cohen[41] and her kindergartners first make their finger paints out of liquid starch, Ivory Snow flakes, tempera, and water. They start with blue or yellow. First they finger-paint one color on a Formica table. They press pieces of paper on the table and make prints of their designs. Then they mix the second color with the first on the table. Presto! The blue and yellow finger paints turn green. They press more paper and print green designs.

Napkin batiks Another of Marilyn's most effective tricks for her color magicians is to give each child a white napkin. The napkins are opened all the way. The children fold them any way they want to and fasten the folding with a pin or a paper clip. They dab drops of red, blue, and yellow food coloring on the napkin, and the colors flow through. When they open their napkins, beautiful batiklike designs appear. The children mount their napkins on wallpaper for place mats or on construction paper for wall hangings.

Colorful clay Suzanne Raymo,[42] who was been nicknamed Ms. Rainbow by her students, uses clay and paint to help children see the drama of primary colors mixing together. The children make interesting clay shapes. They paint their shapes with a primary color in tempera or thick watercolor. They choose another primary color to paint over the first one. Before their eyes, the clay turns color. They turn themselves into wizards, magic-makers, and rainbow magicians.

However you choose to show children how primary colors mix to form secondary colors, do it with pizzazz. Mix it with wonder. Be playful.

Rose-colored and other colored glasses Color magicians have many wonderful ways to look at the world, including rose-colored glasses. Scrounge eyeglass frames or make frames out of the round plastic holders used for six-packs of beer or soda by cutting out two holders and fastening them around the children's heads with string or strands of wool. Tape different colors of cellophane to the frames.

When the children wear the glasses, everything looks different to them. Make up a game like, "Color Magicians, what do you see through your magical colored glasses?" The children make lively observations, such as: "I see yellow paper towels, yellow water in the fish tank, yellow windows!" or "Through my magic red glasses, I see red cookies! I see red milk! Marcie's face turned red!"

Colored glasses help children play the imagination-triggering game, "what if?" "What if everything was *one* color? What if the sky, the grass, the water, the clouds, all the flowers, *everything* was yellow? Or blue? or red?" Play with that intriguing idea. A delightful song like "The Easel" by Thomas Moore[43] in simple call-and-response style reminds the children that at the easel, they can choose any color they want. In stanzas highlighting red, yellow, blue, and green, they paint the house, dog, sky, and grass *one* color! With a twinkle in their eyes, they sing, "Today, I must like red (or yellow, blue, or green)." The Rainbow Magicians—with their magician's hats and capes (scrounged or improvised), colorful tricks, and "abracadabra" (or an original chant)—squeal with mischief as they turn the world one color!

Magic color wands Marilyn Cohen's color magicians have marvelous color wands. They are made by cutting cardboard paddles with a hole in the middle and covering each paddle (wand) with a layer of cellophane in one of the primary colors.

When the children look through their magical wands, the world changes color. Put two different-colored wands together and look through them. Zingo! The world turns a new color. Play mysterious music as the children perform this color wand feat. Use the color wands in stories, songs, puppet shows, and improvisations.

How are they alike? Jean Williams enjoys making up games. Here is one of her favorites. She calls children to the front of the room and asks the rest of the group to look at them carefully. "How are they alike?" she asks. She makes groupings, such as three children with blue eyes, six children wearing blue jeans, four children wearing the color white, and two children with green name tags.

Her classes quickly learn that they must go beyond obvious answers, such as "They all have hair on their heads," or "They all have noses!" When children offer these responses, Jean smiles and replies, "How else are they alike? Keep looking!" Invariably, the children guess correctly.

Try the same game with objects, plants, and pictures.

Colorful movement and mime for special days This is a variation of "Turn Yourself Into . . ." that celebrates ideas inspired by colors. Correlate these activities with Color Day celebrations or simply use them throughout the year.

Talk first, then move. "Let's talk about the color red. What are some red objects that we think of immediately?" "Fire engines." "Fires." "Robin red breast."

Start off by asking the children to turn themselves into a bright red fire engine, zooming around the room (everyone moving in the same direction, of course!). Stop. Shake out the fire engine. Ask the children to turn themselves into a red fire, flaming and smoking. Half the class can be the fire; the other half can be the fire engine. Whoosh. The fire hoses put out the fire. Children show the fire going out. You will probably have to do this twice and give children a chance to be both fire and fire engine.

Shake out those two red ideas and try the third suggestion, robin red breast. The last time we did this activity, the children tapped their chests and said, "Mmmmm. Beautiful red!" Some of them wanted to tape red construction paper to their shirts. We fluttered and pecked and slept with our heads under our wings.

Expand this activity into color books, murals, poems, charts, and collages with red pictures of fire engines, fires, robin red breasts, and other red ideas the children may have. Move to all suggestions!

Color dances First look at and talk about a color. Then share ideas about what that color makes you think, how it makes you feel. From these suggestions, select one or two images to experiment with in movement.

Here is an example from a recent session with first graders.

Child: *Blue, I think of the sky.*

Child: *I think of blue, blue water.*

Teacher: *Maybe we can think of movement to express sky and water.*

Child: *Sky is high. We can stretch way up.*

Child: *It's all over above us—we can wave our hands over our heads to show how big it is.*

Teacher: *Let's try that. First stretch as high as you can stretch. Now wave hands and arms over our heads, above us. That looks beautiful! Shall we keep that and remember it for our blue movement?*

Children: *Yes!*

Continue with other colors. For each color, think of ideas. From the ideas, develop one or two movements. The children learn and perform them when the color is mentioned or shown.

All kinds of music can be used for accompaniment. Color cards or posters can be used to direct the sequence of dances. Give the children opportunities to rearrange them.

After a group of kindergartners learned four "color movements" the children planned to take turns deciding the order. One girl placed the color cards in the pattern blue, red, white, and black. When the children finished performing the colors in that order, another child had a turn to rearrange the cards. He decided to keep the same order. "Don't you want to try changing it around?" I asked. "No. It's perfect this way!" he announced. And that was the way the class decided to keep it.

Color exercises Ask the children to name their favorite exercises. Write them on the board. Then ask the children to name the same number of colors. Write them on the board. Decide, with the children, which exercises match which colors. Make a chart on which each exercise is printed in a special color, or make exercise cards, each one a different color. Add stick figures to the cards or chart. Each day, assign different children to select exercises to lead. After a while, they will be able to announce the exercises by their colors alone.

"Old MacDonald Had a Farm" of colors Add colors to the beloved children's singing game "Old MacDonald." Give each child a picture of a fruit or vegetable. When the fruits and vegetables are called into the game, describe them by color, for example, "And on his farm he grew *green* cucumbers." "*Orange* pumpkins." "*Green* peppers."

Colors "Hokey Pokey" Celebrate the children's clothing colors or invite the children to choose their own color badges or symbols. Play with the old "Hokey Pokey" song:

> We put purple in, we put purple out.
> We put purple in and shake it all about. . . . Do the hokey pokey and turn yourself around.
> That's what it's all about.

Try calling in more than one color at a time. Be sure all the children are called into the circle many times.

> We put brown hair in, we put black hair in
> We put blond hair in and we shake it all about!

or

> We put green eyes in, we put blue eyes in.
> We put brown, black, or gray eyes in and we shake them all about!

Always include everyone! Put everyone *in*!

Find the color celebration! Children are excited when they learn to identify and recognize colors. They need many opportunities to demonstrate their newly acquired knowledge. Challenge the kids with such playful instructions as: "Look around the room. Find the color red five times!" Before the sentence is finished, the children will be pointing and chiming, "My shirt!" "The balloon picture!" "Kalia's belt!" "The elf's hat!" "Tracy has red in her flowers on her blouse!" That's five! When everyone has seen five "reds," do "high fives" and five jumps or five jumping jacks. Then go on to another colorful challenge, culminating in a favorite exercise or movement.

Colorful clowns As part of your circus celebration, make cardboard clown hats (from triangles and circles); or scrounge colorful pompons, ribbons, bows, crepe paper, and yarn. Let the children choose their favorite colors for hats or pompons. Now they are part of the World Famous Color Clowns, known far and wide for their sensational tricks and dances.

Call the children by their color names and give each one a chance to show special routines. "Ladies and Gentlemen. Here are two of our fabulous Color Clowns to do their circus trick for you! Todd Red Clown and Tia Purple Clown! Here they go!" The "acts" will probably take about 20 seconds and will range from hopping on one foot to doing somersaults. Applaud all the children, even the color clown who does a standing-still, sucking-his-thumb act.

When the clowns form a circus parade to bouncy music, encourage them to move in a variety of ways according to colors. "Wow! The Blue Clowns are playing drums in the parade! The Yellow Clowns are twirling batons! The Red Clowns are riding horses!" Keep changing ideas as the parade continues so the children have many opportunities to follow new directions and enjoy new movements.

Children love to create their own clown dances: silly, funny, and full of tricks. They will have many ideas to demonstrate and describe. In case you need an extra push, find a book like *Today I Am . . . A Clown*.[44] It is full of lively colors, and its text is rich in movement suggestions: "I can do lots of cartwheels . . . ," "I trip over my toes . . ." (young children adore tripping and falling!), and "I jump about. . . ." Everyone claps and waves! Take a bow, clowns!

Rainbow machines Lynn Salem's first graders are rainbow-crazy. They read about, write about, paint, color, and dance rainbows. One of her most enjoyable experiments is to challenge the children to invent a rainbow-making machine. They can draw it, make it out of scrounge materials, or show it with their bodies.

Machines are excellent movement ideas, because all the parts must work together for it to succeed. There is no right way or wrong way to make a rainbow machine; encourage the children to try as many body combinations as possible before they decide how they want their rainbow-making machine to work.

Color dress-up time Spread out the clothes in your clothing collection so they are easily seen. The "game" is to ask a child at a time to put on one of the items that you describe by its color. "Dominique, will you put on the black hat?" "Janina, will you put on the brown shoes?" Encourage the children to move and play in the clothes for a few minutes, look in the mirror, and exchange clothes (if time and spirit permit).

Stories, folk tales, nursery rhymes, poems, and songs to improvise Here are just a few suggestions to start you thinking about movement and play possibilities in story and song. Even when a story is not *about* color, it usually contains enough references to color to be useful. Add color!

Stories and folk tales An old favorite, Don Freeman's *A Rainbow of My Own*[45] is the story of a little boy who sees a rainbow so beautiful that he wants to catch it for his very own. Since that is impossible, he imagines having his very own rainbow that follows him and plays with him. He has a delightful time with his beautiful rainbow, and when he goes home, he finds that the sun shining through the water in his fishbowl beams a rainbow on his wall.

This is such a lovely story to improvise, especially if you give the children strips of brightly colored crepe paper stapled together at one end to hold and let trail behind them as they run. In this way the children really have rainbows of their own that follow them, swirl around them, and become rainbow capes, rainbow tails, and rainbow wind.

Marilyn Cohen puts a mirror in a dish of water. When the sun shines on the mirror, a rainbow is reflected on the ceiling of the room—a perfect ending to the children's adaptation of *A Rainbow of My Own*.

On a Red Day when all the children come to school dressed in something red (and you are ready with something red to pin on or add on in case a child forgets), a likable story to share is *I Dance in My Red Pajamas*.[46] This is another example of selecting parts of a story (or poem or song) that lend themselves to movement and play improvisation. Many times the text of materials provide choreographic and dramatic materials without your having to do anything but follow along! When the lively little girl in the story visits her grandparents, she wears her red pajamas. She dances in her red pajamas, clapping, stomping, and swinging around. Play any bouncy music and enjoy clapping, stomping, and swirling around in "red pajamas"! As often as time permits, spin off, expand ideas, and explore ways to create individual interpretations. For instance, what if the children could make up their own story dances and improvisation to such extensions as "I Dance in My Blue Snowsuit!" or "We Dance in Our Green Swimsuits!" or "We Dance in Our Black and White Jogging Pants!" Imagine how different each of those movement patterns, stories, and illustrations would be!

Lunch boxes are favorite objects to young children. The shapes of lunch boxes are easy to draw, cut, color, and design. Jeannette Caines's *I Need a Lunch Box*[47] is a story about a little boy who wants a new lunch box but his mom says he can't have a lunch box until he starts school! He dreams about new lunch boxes: five new lunch boxes, a different color for each day! His dreams are in the color of the special day. Colors and dreams are natural fusions. Children enjoy talking about, sharing ideas, and playing and moving to the story of the colorful dream lunch boxes and the colorful dreams. "What are green ideas? How does green make you want to move? What kind of music shall we play for *green*? Let's put our green lunch box shapes or symbols in the middle of the room while we do our green dream-dance around them!" There is no end to the possibilities.

A simple little book like *The Green Queen*[48]—the queen lies in her red bed, puts on blue shoes and a black jacket and wraps a yellow, pink, turquoise, brown, orange, and indigo scarf around her neck—is a colorful and easy book to play with. Change the Green Queen into the Green Queen and King and play the story with cut-outs of blue shoes, black jackets, and multicolored scarves or color badges (masking tape) to add to clothing as the story progresses. Just read the story and invite the kids to *do it!*

A beautiful Lenape legend, *Rainbow Crow*, retold by Nancy Van Laan,[49] is a fascinating story for the children to improvise in movement, drama, poetry, visual arts interpretation, and music. According to the Lenape story, Crow once had rainbow-colored feathers and a beautiful song. But long, long ago, the earth grew icy cold. The animals huddled together, screeching and howling because they couldn't decide who should visit the Great Sky Spirit to ask him to stop the snow. (Imagine your children huddled and screeching as they "argue" about a plan!) Soon the snow was so deep that the small animals disappeared in it and had to climb to higher places to keep from getting lost forever in the snow. (Children love to do climbing movements.) The most beautiful bird on Earth, Rainbow Crow, offers to fly to the Great Sky Spirit. All the animals praise Rainbow Crow. (What a wonderful dance and song you and your children can create for this idea!) Rainbow Crow (everyone can be Rainbow Crow) flies higher and higher. He sings to the Great Sky Spirit. The beautiful voice of Rainbow Crow moves Great Sky Spirit, who gives Crow a stick with fire on the end of it and tells him to fly down to Earth and bring fire. As Rainbow Crow flies back to Earth, the sparks darken his bright feathers and the smoke cracks his beautiful voice. By the time he reaches the animals, Crow's song is a croak and his rainbow feathers are black. Rainbow Crow is very sad. Great Sky Spirit praises Rainbow Crow for his unselfishness and bravery and tells him that if he looks closely, he will see that in the black feathers, all the colors on earth are reflected. (If you look closely at a crow in the sunlight, you will see "shining feathers full of tiny rainbows.") Because Crow's voice turned croaky and harsh, no hunters came after him. He became a bird who flew freely!

This is a story full of colors, full of the possibilities of song, dance, drama, movement, poetry, and illustrations.

An Oriental legend is adapted and illustrated by Marilyn Hirsh in her book *How the World Got Its Color.*[50] Once the world had no colors except for a set of paints given to an artist by the gods. The artist's young daughter, Miki, watched her father paint every day with the beautiful colors. One day, when her father went away, Miki took his paints outside and painted everything she saw. When her father returned, he scolded her fiercely, but the gods who had made the world were pleased and liked the colors. They smiled, and everything that Miki had not already painted was filled with color. We have had colors ever since.

One of many ways to expand this story is to tell it with puppets. The children have so many ideas for dialogue as their puppets decide what to paint: "I think I'll paint those flowers purple and red!" "Let's paint the snow white!" "Oooh, we need to paint these cars!" Puppets love to lose their tempers. What a wonderful opportunity for the puppets playing Miki's father to have magnificent tantrums.

Nursery rhymes and poems Colorful nursery rhymes can be moved to, mimed, improvised, turned into puppet shows, or transformed into games. A simple nursery rhyme like "Baa, Baa, Black Sheep" can become a delightful movement game by changing the color word; for example, "Baa, Baa, Green Sheep."

A familiar rhyme like "Little Boy Blue" easily becomes a new game. Give children turns to be Little Boy or Girl Blue by taping blue badges to their clothes, tying blue crepe paper strips around their waists, or making blue paper hats. The rest of the children turn into sheep and cows, munching grass in the meadow. Little Boy or Girl Blue finds a nice cozy spot and falls asleep.

It is fun to embellish the poem by interspersing lines such as: "Now where can that Little Boy/Girl Blue be? Sheep, have you seen him/her? Cows?" Nothing is more exciting for young children than to be found. When sleeping Blue boys and girls are awakened, what do they do? Blow their horns (pretend or real).

Poems like Rachel Field's "Taxis" are packed with colors. Here are a few lines from this vivid poem.

> Ho, for taxis green or blue
> Hi, for taxis red,
> They roll along the Avenue
> Like spools of colored thread!
> Jack-o-Lantern yellow,
> Orange as the moon,
> Greener than the greenest grass
> Ever grew in June.[51]

The children can play this poem many ways. Here are just two ideas. Each child can roll one of the toy cars from the class garage along the avenue. Correlate the traffic with red and green traffic lights. When all the cars are moving together, the children enjoy reciting these lines from the poem: "Don't you think that taxis/ Make a very pleasant sight?"

Even more than rolling toy cars, children enjoy pretending to be cars themselves. Ask the children to listen to the poem and take a sheet of construction paper that is one of the colors mentioned. Tape the colors to the children. They become taxis and create traffic. Control the flow of traffic with red and green lights.

The Trees Stand Shining[52] is a beautiful collection of poems by Native Americans. Many of these simple yet powerful poems have color images and ideas that children enjoy listening and moving to. The following Papago poem is a perfect example of how naturally a poem can turn into a dance, with children wearing something yellow.

> A little yellow cricket
> At the roots of the corn
> Is hopping about and singing.[53]

Keep improvising this haikulike poem by changing the color and asking the children to tape or tie the matching color symbol to their clothes.

The following Nootka poem is inspiring for young children. They dance it with gentle movements that seem to touch everything.

> You, whose day it is,
> Make it beautiful.
> Get out your rainbow colors,
> So it will be beautiful.[54]

After the children hear the poem, they easily imagine their power to make the world beautiful, to cover it with rainbow colors. Ask them to show with their arms, legs, and heads how they would paint the world with rainbow colors. Play Native American or any tribal chants or songs to accompany the dance.

Remember, there is no one way to interpret the poem. Accept and encourage the children's own movement patterns.

Navajo songs and chants An effective way to keep children alert to colors around them is to adapt the perspective of many Navajo prayers and songs. These repetitive chants express traditional Indian feelings of harmony with the universe:

> With beauty may I walk.
> With beauty before me, may I walk.
> With beauty behind me, may I walk.
> With beauty above me, may I walk.
> With beauty below me, may I walk.
> With beauty all around me, may I walk.[55]

Ask the children: "What are the colors before you? Look behind you, what do you see? Look above you, what colors do you see? Look below you, what do you see? Look all around you, what colors do you see?" Here is a segment from some first graders' explorations on a lovely spring day.

> Above us, white clouds.
> Below us, brown dirt.
> Before us, yellow school bus.
> Behind us, green trees.
> All around us, yellow dandelions.

These ideas are easily interpreted in movement as children experiment with ways of demonstrating the concepts of above, below, before, behind, and all around.

Songs Children enjoy moving to songs, especially soft, soothing songs in living color, such as "I Can Sing a Rainbow" or "Somewhere Over The Rainbow." I like to call dances to these kinds of songs "color dreams." Imagine how easy it is to invite the children to "float" around the room and brush colors with their fingertips. Add verses about other colors you see. Sweep the colors in the gentle arcs of a rainbow.

Color songs that help children care about each other and the environment Young children have no trouble understanding that when chemicals, oil, and sewage enter clean water, when cigarette smoke and industrial smoke mix with clean air, and when litter is thrown on streets and fields, our earth, as one six-year-old put it, "gets junked up!" What happens to the beautiful colors of the earth when we fail to take care of the earth?

Tom Paxton's "Whose Garden Is This?" is a powerful song with an important message. Even if young children comprehend only part of it, the song has value for them as they begin what we hope is a lifetime of concern. With a group of first and second graders, we made up a story about how people neglected the air, water, and land. The air was full of chemicals and dark smoke; the rivers were full of garbage; and the land was full of litter. We pretended we were walking through this sad scene, and Tom Paxton's song helped the children respond to each element. (Tragically, in many places this activity could be a real, not an imaginary, field trip.)

Pete Seeger's song "My Rainbow Race" gives the children a chance to bring all their colors together, join hands, walk in a circle, and feel part of a group. After all, the children are a special family—"the rainbow race," a family of beautiful colors.
Fancy dancin' marchin' flag wavers Ask the children, "What are your favorite colors? What colors would you like in your own flag about yourself?" Color, cut, and design simple flags out of paper or material expressing the favorite colors of the children. Have a parade of bouncy, fancy, dancing marchers proudly displaying their talents and their colors.

Color and wave flags for the earth (what colors do we want on our Earth flags?), or for the sky, the seasons, or class groupings. I visited one kindergarten class and found the children at tables defined by specific colors. I asked the children at the orange table why they displayed the color orange. They had chosen the color for themselves. Why? "Oh," they explained, "we're brighter than the sun!"

Brighten every game, play, dance, song, poem, story, and discussion with color combinations! It's so easy. Take out your blue plan book, sharpen that yellow pencil, and jot some colorful ideas on those blank white pages. You'll feel in the pink! No more blues as you sail your red sails in the sunset colors of the curriculum.

CLASSROOM VISITORS AND FIELD TRIPS
Classroom Visitors

I hope that you and your children enjoy many classroom visitors throughout the year, celebrating themes and ideas across the curriculum. Each visitor can be welcomed by flowers/hand leis of lovely colors or greeting and thank-you cards of bright colors and designs. Combine common courtesy and friendliness with colors, shapes, names, poems, letters, pictures, songs, and dances.

Note the colors of clothing, objects, and props of all visitors as part of general awareness. Many guests are extra colorful, such as the following examples:
Friends from diverse cultural backgrounds When Baba Jubal Harris[56] visits a school or classroom with his unusual drums and percussion instruments and his traditional stories, songs, and dances from West African cultures, the first words he usually speaks are, "How do you like my colorful clothes?" And he presents himself, sharing his beautifully printed tunics, robes, pants, and hat to the delight of the children. He begins his sessions with honoring the beautiful colors of the peoples of Africa—the colorful way they see the world.

From traditional colors representing regions of countries to family crests and clan designs, the cultures of the world often show themselves in recognizable color schemes and patterns. Many times, we recognize cultural identity by the colors and designs of clothing and costumes. Be sure to ask Native American and African guests to talk about the meanings, messages, and symbolism in the carefully selected colors of bead designs and clothing patterns.

Florists, gardeners, and groundskeepers Colors and flowers and plants go together. The variety of colors produced by nature is mind-boggling. Help nurture the children's wonder and awareness by asking such classroom visitors or field trip guides to mix colors with every presentation. Leave time for the children to create their own floral arrangements, either on paper or in three dimensions.

Artists, designers, and photographers Whether they use palettes, paintings, sketches, or photographs, those working in the visual arts have many important things to share with the children about the power of colors.

Magician Every community has at least one magician willing to dazzle young audiences with brightly colored scarves, flowers, hats, and juggling balls—the tricks of the trade.

High school or college cheerleaders, athletes, and band members Teenagers like to visit young children and show their school colors. Uniforms, pompons, flags, and caps, combined with cheers, music, and warm-up exercises, make an enjoyable classroom visit.

Clowns Clowns wear cheerful, colorful costumes. Their makeup and wigs are wonderful to behold.

Color characters Parents, colleagues, friends, family members, and neighbors can be imaginative classroom visitors, such as Mrs. Rainbow, Mr. Green, Ms. Blue, and Mr. Purple. It is fun to dress up and enjoy demonstrating colors in delightful and original ways. Wonder what Mr. Purple has in his purple pockets? Add poems, songs, and games.

Yourself as a color character Carol Price surprises her kindergartners by dressing from head to toe in whatever color is being celebrated. She becomes, for example, the Red Lady or the Green Lady. "After we've celebrated a lot of different color days, I come in wearing my clothes of many colors with my rainbow wig and introduce myself to the children as the Rainbow Magic Lady!" I wonder what colors Mother Nature wears.

Field Trips

Seasonal walks The colors of the seasons always beckon. On a clear day, walk with your children through autumn leaves, softly falling snow, blankets of spring grass, or budding flowers. Stop. Look. Look again. When you return to the classroom, celebrate with song, art, movement, and story.

Poems like Arnold Adoff's "A Song" enrich the meaning of a color walk.

A Song
I am of the earth   and the earth is of me.
I am all the colors of the corn field,
                    and the corn field
        is all the colors of me.
I am all the colors of the plowed-up garden,
                    and the plowed-up garden
        is all the colors of me.
I am of the earth   and the earth is of me.
We are together   under the blue sky.
We are together   under the yellow sun.
We are together   under the gray clouds.
We are together.[57]

Sky walks Each day, the sky offers a show of color changes. Take a walk. Find a comfortable place to stand or sit as you focus on the colors of the sky. Talk and look. Bring paper, crayons, and markers to catch the colors, or return to the room, paint sky pictures, and make up sky stories, poems, dances, and songs.

One-color walks Focus on one color. See how many places and in what shapes or things that color exists. Share observations and ideas. Add a touch of fun by giving each child a balloon in the special color to carry on the walk. Create a collaboration of one-color celebrations.

Vegetable store, fruit stand, or supermarket Fruits and vegetables are beautifully shaped and colored. Manufacturers know the importance of packaging their goods in bright, attractive colors. Children enjoy walking through the aisles of stores to see the variety of colors and designs.

Clothing or department store A wealth of textures, materials, designs, and colors are featured in this kind of store. Look at scarves, shirts, dresses, suits, socks, hats, shoes. What are the most popular colors seen? What color combinations are the children's favorites?

When you return from a field trip such as this one, send thank-you notes, poems, and pictures to the proprietors. Expand upon the experience with classroom activities.

Florist, greenhouse, or conservatory Pictures and talks about flowers are valuable but do not match the experience of seeing and smelling the amazing array of plants and flowers of every possible color combination.

Designer or interior decorator's studio Here people work with color charts, carpet samples, and swatches of fabric and wallpaper. Children appreciate the study and arrangement of colors.

Stained-glass windows of churches and synagogues Many places of worship have beautifully designed and crafted stained-glass windows. Following the field trip, make stained-glass designs to brighten your room.

Art gallery or museum Children respond with enthusiasm to a walk through a gallery or museum to see how artists colored canvas with people, landscapes, weather, and abstract designs.

Artist's studio or art class Check your community resources to learn about artists who welcome visits from young children. If there are artists working in glass,

your class will be fascinated by the pure, glowing colors of glassworks. A visit to an art class at a high school, college, or recreation center is an opportunity for your young artists to discover new ways that people work with colors.

Throughout this book are excellent ideas for field trips mixed with color. Add color to trips to pet stores, zoos, fire departments, restaurants, factories, houses, farms, libraries, aquariums, apple orchards, and pumpkin patches.

Always remember to look for, smell, touch, taste, listen to, talk about, sing about, notice, move through, and wonder about *colors!* Keep the color connection!

IT ALL COMES TOGETHER

My original plan for this last little reminder of how "it all comes together" (all the time, unless we compartmentalize and isolate ideas) was to highlight a sunny sampling from "You Are My Sunshine: A Thematic Unit for Early Childhood" by Rose C. Merenda.[58] The article describes an exciting process beginning with a splash of brainstorming suggestions with children as they sat in a sunny spot around a sun-centered chart paper. Shining with enthusiasm, they converted the entire classroom into a "sparkling sunshine-yellow environment" blending every component of the curriculum into the celebration of learning and culminating with a "sun party" featuring such snacks as yellow cheese on circle crackers, lemonade-pineapple punch, and a "sun salad." Of course, everyone wore sunglasses and sun hats and sat under a sun umbrella!

But, as all plans are made for changing, I invite you to enjoy reading about those "sun-sational" experiences while I share another offering with you.

The theme for the 1993 British Columbia Primary Teachers Association's fall conference was "Let's Lighten Up!" When I arrived at the convention center in Victoria, hundreds of teachers were browsing in the large exhibit hall, checking out the latest resources for young children. Bigger crowds, however, were gathered along the walls of the hallways, pointing and admiring. From a distance away I could only see the throngs of people and walls pulsating with colors. As I made my way closer, I joined the astonishment and admiration, for the hallways were covered with banners and hangings representing the works of thirty-three elementary schools in Victoria. Many teachers of the children who created these outstandingly beautiful, imaginative, and colorful works were sharing incidents from the creation of the hangings. Eavesdropping, I heard them say: "This song . . ." "This game was perfect!" "These books gave the children so many ideas!" "Poems like . . ." and "Our trip to. . . ." I noted the diversity of color-splashed ideas interpreting "Let's Lighten Up!" In fabrics, paint, glitter, markers, sculptures, ribbons, feathers, quilts, and prints, the children had created dazzlingly bright scenes of fish, birds, zoos, clowns, farms, schools, rainbows, hot-air balloons, smiling children, flowers, and trees. One of the hangings measured thirty-seven feet long, stretching from the balcony to the water two stories below! It was a brilliant tribute to the artist Matisse. They called it "Matisse-like Magic."

I walked along with Audrey Van Eerden,[59] one of the coordinators for the conference. She had been instrumental in asking every school in Victoria to create a large wall-hanging or banner expressing the theme, "Let's Lighten Up!"

Audrey's enthusiasm was contagious. Here are some of the things she had to say as we walked along the walls of colors:

"Because we left the instructions open-ended, the children and teachers had free reign to interpret, to express our theme however they chose. We trusted them. We expected a variety of interpretations, but the numbers and diversity more than surprised us! It's funny, we *never* used the word 'color,' but everyone burst with colors!"

Now, we stopped before a hanging of a farm next to one celebrating clowns. Audrey said, "When you see these hangings, close your eyes and you can hear the brainstorming that went into them. Oh, the children and teachers had so many ideas before they settled on these! They brought in books, stories, songs, paintings—they practiced K–W–L. What do we already Know? What do we Wonder? What have we Learned? That covers just about everything possible to cover, don't you think? These aren't just objects, just artistic products, are they?" Audrey summarized her feelings:

"One key thing—go simple! This concept had room for *everything* to happen! And then, let everything happen!" She thought for a moment, then added, "What if we had sent instructions with specific, preset expectations and very structured directions leaving little room for free-spirited interpretations? We would have had garbage!"

We laughed together. Audrey's eyes brightened. She added, "The children caught the spirit. They really *understood* how to remind us to 'lighten up!'" The colors held us and cheered us.

NOTES ♥♥♥♥♥♥♥♥♥♥♥♥♥♥♥♥♥♥♥♥♥♥♥♥♥♥

1. John G. Neihardt, *Black Elk Speaks*. New York: Simon and Schuster, 1972, p. 2.
2. This colorful morning is still remembered years later by children who participated in a Days of Creation Arts summer program in Columbus, Ohio.
3. Ed Jacomo was one of the country's most beloved spokespersons for Arts Education. His last assignment was at Western Michigan University in Kalamazoo, Michigan. He received the state of Michigan's highest honor for his work in Arts Education.
4. Annie Dillard, *Pilgrim at Tinker Creek*. New York: Bantam, 1975, pp. 28–29, 30–31.

5. "Flowers Are Red" was first issued on Electra/Asylum Records on the album, *Living Room Suite,* 1978.

6. Faith Ringgold, *Tar Beach.* New York: Crown, 1991.

7. Lois Ehlert, *Feathers for Lunch.* San Diego: Harcourt Brace Jovanovich, 1990. See also *Fish Eyes, Planting a Rainbow,* and *Color Zoo.*

8. Peter Sis, *Beach Ball.* New York: Greenwillow, 1990.

9. Nancy Evans Cooney, illustrated by Melissa Bay Mathis, *The Umbrella Day.* New York: Philomel, 1989.

    Fred Burstein, illustrated by Harvey Stevenson, *Anna's Rain.* New York: Orchard Books, 1990.

10. Barbara Kienzle teaches at Hamilton Alternative School in Columbus, Ohio.

11. Joan Kalb teaches in Woodward School in Delaware, Ohio.

12. Muriel Hampton is Director Emerita of the Canfield Methodist Pre-School in Canfield, Ohio. Muriel was honored for her inspiring work with young children by being named Teacher of the Year by the Ohio Association for the Education of Young Children.

13. Carol Price is principal of Colonial Hills School in Worthington, Ohio. Colonial Hills School, Carol, and her staff and students were highlighted in my article, "Flamingos in the Bathroom, Love in the Classroom," *Phi Delta Kappan,* Kappan, January 1993, pp. 413–414.

14. Steve Conkle worked with children writing poetry in the Ohio Poets in the Schools program.

15. "I Wish," *Good Old Poems/I Love Them.* Columbus: Ohio Foundation on the Arts, 1979, p. 49.

16. Jean Williams teaches at Douglas Alternative Elementary School in Columbus.

17. Leo Lionni, *Frederick.* New York: Pinwheel, 1973.

18. Tomie DePaola, *The Legend of the Indian Paintbrush.* New York: Putnam, 1988.

19. Eric Carle, *Draw Me a Star.* New York: Philomel, 1992.

20. Theresa Gelonese added colors with children at the Immaculate Conception School in Columbus.

21. Leo Lionni, *Little Blue and Little Yellow.* New York: Astor, 1959.

22. Leo Lionni, *Matthew's Dream.* New York: Knopf, 1992.

23. Mauro Talocci, edited and translated by Whitney Smith, *Guide to the Flags of the World.* New York: Quill, 1982.

24. Robert Jay Wolff, *Seeing Red.* New York: Scribners, 1968.

25. Jessica Jenkins, *Thinking about Colors.* New York: Dutton, 1992.

26. E. L. Konigsburg, *Samuel Todd's Book of Great Colors.* New York: Atheneum, 1990.

27. Robert Kalan, illustrated by Donald Crews, *Rain.* New York: Greenwillow, 1978.

    Robert Maas, *When Autumn Comes.* New York: Henry Holt, 1990.

    ———, *When Winter Comes.* New York: Henry Holt, 1993.

    Marjorie N. Allen, photographs by Shelly Roner, *Changes.* New York: Macmillan, 1991.

28. Rose Stough teaches at Moler School in Columbus.

29. Arnold Adoff, illustrated by John Steptoe, *All The Colors Of The Race.* New York: Lothrop, Lee and Shepard, 1982.

    Arnold Adoff, illustrated by Emily McCully, *Black Is Brown Is Tan.* New York: Harper & Row, 1973.

30. Ibid. P. 30.

31. Ashley Bryan, *Sing to the Sun.* New York: HarperCollins, 1992.

    Arnold Adoff, illustrated by Jerry Pinkney, *In for Winter, Out for Spring.* San Diego: Harcourt Brace Jovanovich, 1991.

Ruth Yaffee Radin, illustrated by Ed Young, *High in the Mountains*. New York: Macmillan, 1989.

Myra Cohn Livingston, illustrated by Leonard Everett Fisher, *Sky Songs*. New York: Holiday House, 1984.

Bill Martin, Jr., and John Archambault, illustrated by James Endicott, *Listen to the Rain*. New York: Henry Holt, 1988.

Ann McGovern, photographs by Hope Wurmfeld, *Black Is Beautiful*. New York: Four Winds, 1969.

32. Lynn Salem taught in technicolor at Immaculate Conception School in Columbus.

33. Cynthia Rylant, illustrated by Mary Szilagyi, *Night in the Country*. New York: Bradbury, 1986.

Alvin Tresselt, illustrated by Henry Sorensen, *Sun Up*. New York: Lothrop, Lee and Shepard, 1991.

34. Ruth Craft, illustrated by Niki Daly, *The Day of the Rainbow*. New York: Viking Krestrel, 1989.

35. Mary O'Neill, illustrated by John Wallner, *Hailstones and Halibut Bones*. New York: Doubleday, 1989.

36. Merle Peck, *Mary Wore Her Red Dress/And Henry Wore His Green Sneakers*. New York: Clarion/Ticknor and Fields, 1985.

37. Arnold Lobel, *The Great Blueness and Other Predicaments*. New York: Harper & Row, 1968.

38. Brian Wildsmith, *The Circus*. Oxford: Oxford University Press, 1980.

39. Gerald McDermott, *Arrow to the Sun*. New York: Viking, 1974.

40. Bill Martin, Jr., illustrated by Eric Carle, *Brown Bear, Brown Bear, What Do You See?* New York: Henry Holt, 1983.

41. Marilyn Cohen teaches at the Bet Shraga Hebrew Academy of the Capital District in Albany, New York.

42. Suzanne Raymo played with children, paint, and clay at the University Liggett School in Grosse Pointe, Michigan.

43. Thomas Moore's "The Easel" can be found on "I Am Special Just Because I'm Me!" Record number 1000, 4600 Park Road, Charlotte, NC 28209.

44. Jane Bottomley, *Today I Am a Clown*. Nashville: Ideals Children's Books, 1989.

45. Don Freeman, *A Rainbow of my Own*. New York: Viking, 1966.

46. Edith Thacher Hurd, illustrated by Emily Arnold McCully, *I Dance in My Red Pajamas*. New York: Harper & Row, 1982.

47. Jeanette Caines, illustrated by Pat Cummings, *I Need a Lunch Box*. New York: Harper & Row, 1988.

48. Nick Sharratt, *The Green Queen*. Cambridge, MA: Candlewick, 1992.

49. Nancy Van Laan, illustrated by Beatriz Vidal, *Rainbow Crow*. New York: Knopf, 1989.

50. Marilyn Hirsh, *How the World Got Its Color*. New York: Crown, 1972.

51. Rachel Field, "Taxis" from *Anthology of Children's Literature*, 3d edition. Edited by Edna Johnson, Evelyn R. Sickels, and Frances Clarke Sayers. Boston: Houghton Mifflin, 1959, p. 1043.

52. Hettie Jones, ed., paintings by Robert Andrew Parker, *The Trees Stand Shining: Poetry of the North American Indians*. New York: Dial, 1971.

53. Ibid.

54. Ibid.

55. George W. Cronyn, ed., *American Indian Poetry: An Anthology of Songs and Chants*. New York: Ballantine, 1962, p. 93.

56. Baba Jubal Harris works with children of all ages, passing on his rich traditions under such programs as Ohio Arts Council's Artists in Education,

Greater Columbus Arts Council's Artists in the Schools, and Days of Creation Arts for Kids.

57. Arnold Adoff, illustrated by John Steptoe, "A Song," *All the Colors Of the Race*. New York: Lothrop, Lee and Shepard, 1982, p. 44.

58. Rose C. Merenda, "You Are My Sunshine: A Thematic Unit for Early Childhood." *Day Care and Early Education*, Winter 1992, pp. 17–18.

59. Audrey Van Eerden teaches at Rockheights School in Victoria, British Columbia.

BOOKS FROM MY KNAPSACK FOR CHILDREN ♥ ♥

Adoff, Arnold. *Greens*. Illustrated by Betsey Lewin. New York: Lothrop, Lee & Shephard, 1988.

Dodds, Dayle Ann. *The Color Box*. Illustrated by Giles Laroche. Boston: Little, Brown, 1992.

Ehlert, Lois. *Nuts to You!* San Diego: Harcourt Brace Jovanovich, 1993.

———. *Painting a Rainbow*. San Diego: Harcourt Brace Jovanovich, 1988.

Emberley, Ed. *Go Away Big Green Monster*. Boston: Little, Brown, 1992.

Jenkins, Jessica. *Thinking about Colors*. Illustrated by Jessica Jenkins. New York: Dutton's Children's Books, 1992.

Jonas, Ann. *Color Dance*. Illustrated by Ann Jonas. New York: Greenwillow, 1989.

Kunhardt, Edith. *Red Day, Green Day*. Illustrated by Marilyn Hafnew. New York: Greenwillow, 1992.

Leonni, Leo. *A Color of His Own*. Illustrated by Leo Leonni. New York: Knopf, 1975.

Martin, Bill, Jr. *Brown Bear, Brown Bear, What Do You See?* Illustrated by Eric Carle. New York: Henry Holt, 1983.

Maxner, J. *Lady Bugatti*. Illustrated by Kevin Hawkes. New York: Lothrop, Lee & Shephard, 1991.

McMillan, Bruce. *Beach Ball Left Right*. Illustrated by Bruce McMillan. New York: Holiday House, 1992.

Pragoff, Fiona. *What Colors?* New York: Doubleday, 1989.

Remkiewicz, Frank. *The Last Time I Saw Harris*. New York: Lothrop, Lee & Shephard, 1991.

Serfzo, Mary. *Who Said Red?* Illustrated by Keido Narahaski. New York: Aladdin, 1992.

Sharratt, Nick. *The Green Queen*. Illustrated by Nick Sharratt. Cambridge, MA: Candlewick, 1992.

Tilde, Michels. *What a Beautiful Day*. Illustrated by Thomas Muller. Minneapolis: Carolrhoda, 1992.

Walsh, Ellen Stoll. *Mouse Paint*. Illustrated by Ellen Stoll Walsh. San Diego: Harcourt Brace Jovanovich, 1989.

Williams, Vera B. *Cherries and Cherry Pits*. Illustrated by Vera B. Williams. New York: Mulberry, 1991.

Wu, Norbert. *Fish Faces*. Illustrated by Norbert Wu. New York: Henry Holt, 1993.

Yorinks, Arthur. *Hey, Al*. Illustrated by Richard Egielski. New York: Farrar, Straus & Giroux, 1986.

Young, Ed. *Seven Blind Mice*. Illustrated by Ed Young. New York: Philomel, 1992.

BOOKS FROM MY KNAPSACK FOR TEACHERS ♥ ♥

Cole, Alison. *Color—Eyewitness Art*. London: Dorling Kindersley, 1993.

Chapter

♥♥♥♥♥♥♥♥♥♥♥♥♥♥♥♥♥

12

The Gifts of Language

In Praise of ABC
In the beginning were the letters
wooden, awkward, and everywhere.
Before the Word was the slow scrabble of fire and water.

God bless my son and his wooden letters
who has gone to bed with A in his right hand and Z in his left,
who has walked all day with C in his shoe and said nothing,
who has eaten of his napkin the word Birthday,
and who has filled my house with the broken speech of wizards.

To him the grass makes its gentle sign.
For him the worm letters her gospel truth.
To him the pretzel says, I am the occult
descendant of the first blessed bread
and the lost cuneiform of a grain of wheat.

Kneading bread, I found in my kitchen half an O.
Now I wait for someone to come from far off
holding the other half, saying,
What is broken shall be made whole.
Match half for half; now do you know me again?

Thanks be to God for my house seeded with dark sayings
and my rooms rumpled and badly lit
but richly lettered with the secret raisins of truth.[1]   Nancy Willard

THE BASICS

In the midst of intense sessions of professional educators working tirelessly to mold an early childhood program to meet a state initiative, one of the key participants felt the terminology, the competition of theories, the articulation of strategies, the choice of directives and resources, the list of outcomes, and the selection of assessment mechanisms close in on her. She excused herself, and drove across the city to the early childhood program she had taught in and administered before she joined the state education staff. She watched the children play and listened to the children laughing, talking, and singing. They were so involved in building structures of blocks, dressing up themselves and their dolls, preparing play food, painting, drawing, pasting, and puppeteering that they hardly noticed her. For two hours, she breathed in the joyful energy of the children, warming herself in the bright light of engaged, active learners. Refreshed, renewed, reminded (the *real* Three R's!) of the *centrality* of the children in the schemes, initiatives, and directives of adults, she returned to the offices of the state education department.

This incident parallels the atmospheric pressures on the educators of our country. The turbulence of "The Never-Ending Debate"[2] storms around us. How do children best learn? What *is* learning anyway? What is "authentic" learning? How do children learn to read most successfully? How do children learn to read anyway? What do we know about language acquisition? Shall we go with phonics as *the* method? Shall we join the whole-language movement? Is the literature-based curriculum the best? Shall we maintain our traditional philosophy, which features external punishments and rewards and which relies on teacher-directed, highly structured materials, methods, and stated outcomes? Is there such a thing as a purely traditional classroom? A purely "whole-language" environment? Where do the skills fit in? What about individualized learning styles? Is learning a solitary endeavor or a social activity? Shall we emphasize the rules of the language, breaking down the components of language into compartmentalized lessons, or shall we view language learning as a lifelong process beginning in our mothers' wombs and continuing in the making of meanings throughout our years?

We must try to keep up with the research literature. What can we learn from early intervention programs like Reading Recovery?[3] We must know what Developmentally Appropriate learning practice is all about.[4] What is the importance of *play* in the lives of young children? How do children interact with materials, ideas, and each other? Are young children capable of making choices, of initiating self-directed learning? What is the teacher's role in such interactive learning environments?

Immersed in stimulating resources,[5] we try to create our own styles or philosophies. Gerald G. Duffy, in his article, "Let's Free Teachers to Be Inspired,"[6] challenges teachers to use various philosophical and theoretical ideas in intelligently selected combinations. He encourages teachers to become empowered, adventuresome, and creative as they adapt their professional knowledge to what students need. Inspired teaching, Duffy believes, "lies within the teacher who assesses the particular demands of the situation and creates an instructional mosaic that is at once conceptually coherent, responsive to students and reflective of a broad range of professional knowledge." Remember that all methods work sometimes and at other times don't work at all. Our reverence should never be for the "method" but for the sacred spirit of the child who is always learning no matter our stated methodology!

The passion and brilliance of ideas and philosophies can be overwhelming. Like our friend in the state education office who had to break away and return to her old preschool, I feel a need to break (we should always brake for children) from this room heavy with journals, books, and papers and see what the children and their friends are up to. Come with me!

The kindergartners are gathered at the far end of the playground. We can hear their clapping, stamping, and singing across the field as they chant their current favorite recess "song," complete with intricate choreography and rhythms. They chant:

This train goes
Down, down baby
Down by the roller coaster
Sweet, sweet baby
I don't want to let you go
Shimmy, shimmy, cocoa pop
Shimmy, shimmy, raaah
Shimmy, shimmy, cocoa pop
Shimmy, shimmy, raaah

Mama mama sick in bed
Call the doctor and the doctor said:
Let's get the rhythm of the head—ding dong
We've got the rhythm of the head—ding dong
Let's get the rhythm of the hands—two claps
We've got the rhythm of the hands—two claps
Let's get the rhythm of the feet—two stamps
Let's get the rhythm of the hoo-ot dog (circle the hips)
We've got the rhythm of the hoo-ot dog (circle the hips)
Put them all together and what do you have?

Hoo-ot dog
stamp stamp
clap, clap
ding dong!

Let's now visit Patrick Muccio. In the middle of a room noisy with kids and toys, twenty-two-month-old Patrick cheerfully adapts any name to the tongue-twisting, playful jingle that he has mastered:

Pat Pat Bo Bat
Banana Fanna Fo Fat
Me My Mo Mat
Pat!

Tracy Tracy Bo Bacy
Banana Fanna Fo Facy
Me My Mo Macy
Tracy!

Want to suggest any more names for Patrick to rhyme?

Another toddler, twenty-five-month-old Dylan Telerski, interrupts my research gathering in the children's department of a nearby library. Stopped in front of shelves of well-used, obviously loved series books such as *Curious George, Jafta, Madeline, Frog and Toad, Nate the Great,* and *Amelia Bedelia,* I note the titles as well as the phenomenon of children's loyalty to stories that especially hit them. Dylan's toddler voice calls in a demanding, decisive way, "I want Tom and Pippo!" Her mother tries in vain to convince her to choose a different book: "You've read every book in the series over and over!" Dylan's tiny hand pulls out one of the Tom and Pippo books, *Tom and Pippo See the Moon.*[7] She flops to the floor and sits with her head bent over the familiar and cherished pages. Her semiexasperated mother

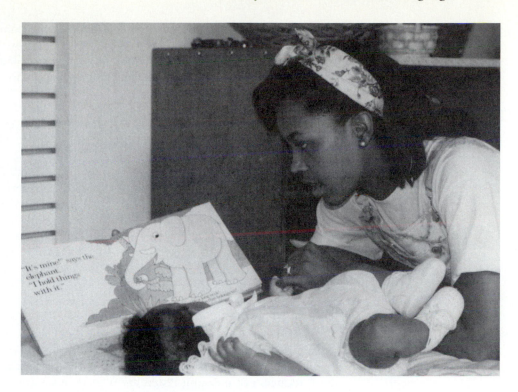

explains, "She knows every book on the shelf, every story. She really relates to these stories. She even got into potty training because she saw Tom sitting on the potty looking at the moon. The potty isn't even mentioned in the story, but because Tom did it, she asked to sit on the potty! She's hooked on Pippo!"

Spend an hour with Pnina Berk at sixteen months old and you'll see her scribble-scrabble with crayons and pencils on paper, turn pages of magazines, rummage through her toy box to find her favorite books, *Good Night, Moon* and the multi-sensory delight, *What Does Boots Hear?* Eric Carle's *Very Busy Spider* is always at the top of her list. Pnina loves books with animal sounds, with textures to touch, with lots of familiar images to identify.

Yuri, the ten-month-old infant sitting on his mother's lap next to me on the plane, spent most of the journey totally involved in writing and reading. Pressing a crayon on paper spread on the tray, he was the perfect poster child for Writer At Work! As his mom read the magazine, he turned the pages, making conversational sounds as he pointed to the pictures. Our very youngest children are readers, writers, conversationalists, and artists!

Being with the children refreshes, renews, and reminds me about an important aspect of learning: *learning is a human activity happening all the time.* Children learn to talk by listening to and responding to people who talk to them. Children learn about reading and writing by being read to, and by using, being near, and seeing pencils and pens in hands moving across papers. The gifts of language given as the birthright of every child can't be learned in isolation. Frank Smith urges us to remember that learning is social and developmental. "Tremendous but unsuspected amounts of learning are accomplished . . . from others . . . from the people who interest us and help us to do the things they do."[8] I am thinking of our youngest children who listen, imitate, begin to understand, communicate feelings, and express wishes and needs. I like to tell kindergartners, "Imagine when you were a newborn baby. You had *no* words! You didn't come home from the hospital and greet the family: 'Hi, I'm your new baby. I'll be living with you now. Where's my crib? What's for supper?'" The children go into gales of laughter. They beam when I inform them that they now, in kindergarten, have thousands and thousands of words. Their mouths make large O's! Thousands and thousands of words? How could that be possible? We talk about all the words they know, the books they love, the letters and words they recognize, the lyrics they sing, everything inside, outside, and around them that they can recognize and identify. They agree. We do know thousands and thousands of words.

Thinking about the children and their wealth of vocabulary and comprehension, I return to the desk, heavy with journals, position papers, curriculum guides, and textbooks. On my way into the room, I see two of my oldest and dearest friends from A. A. Milne's "Rabbit's Busy Day."[9] What are they up to? Why, it's Piglet and Eeyore! Grumpy old Eeyore is looking at three sticks on the ground. Two of the sticks touch at one end but not the other, and the third stick lies across them.

Eeyore asks Piglet if he knows what the sticks are. Piglet, flustered, does not know. Eeyore explains, "It's an A." "Oh," says Piglet. "Not O, A," says Eeyore severely, then adds, "Christopher Robin said it was an A, and an A it is until somebody treads on me."

Now Eeyore is asking, "Do you know what an A means, Little Piglet?" Of course, Piglet does not. Eeyore explains, "It means Learning, it means Education, it means all the things that you and Pooh haven't got. That's what A means . . . to the Educated, not meaning Poohs and Piglets, it's a great and glorious A. Not just something that anybody can come and breathe on!" Eeyore's "great and glorious A" pulls my mind away from the playground children, from Patrick, from Dylan, from Pnina, from Yuri, to a journey back through history, remembering the times before A, perhaps 50,000 years ago when our ancestors painted pictures on the walls of their caves and on nearby stones and rocks. Their pictures marked events, told stories, had magical powers, and recorded information.

Through the ages, people expressed themselves not only in paintings but also through language and movement—speech, song, and dance. Unwritten stories, myths, chants, prayers, and ballads were passed from generation to generation, from mouth to ear.

Ancient peoples painted images that represented objects. They painted a fish to mean "fish," a bird to mean "bird," and a mountain to mean "mountain." This kind of writing is known as a "pictograph" or "hieroglyph." Hieroglyph means "sacred writing." But there were feelings and qualities that could not be expressed by simple pictures, such as the passage of time, the peacefulness of a sleeping baby, and the sweetness of a grape.

To meet this need, "ideographs" evolved. The Chinese, for example, combined the symbols of sun and moon to say "bright." A lion became the Egyptian symbol for power. Images changed from simple representations to more abstract designs that conveyed meanings understood by all members of the community.

In the middle East, one of the world's most culturally fertile regions, soft clay tablets were marked on. The tool used was a stylus, and it produced wedge-shaped marks—a form of writing that became known as "cuneiform." When the tablets were covered with symbols, they were baked and preserved. The tablets were filled with legends about the Great Flood, Creation, and the epic adventures of King Gilgamesh. These Sumerian tablets are considered among the oldest evidence of such writing and date back approximately 5,500 years.

As sailing, trading, bartering, conquering, and governing—the stuff of cultural exchange—accelerated, people borrowed ideas from one another and adapted them to their own needs. Writing systems were evolving with specific symbols for images, sounds, and syllables. Many of the word-symbols for picture ideas were shared by diverse groups. For example, both the Phoenicians and the Hebrews had a symbol and a word for "ox." Their word was "aleph." Another symbol they shared was for "house." Their word for "house" was "beth."

These two symbols and words, aleph and beth, traveled with Phoenician sailors to Greece. The Greeks adopted the shapes of the letters and changed their original Phoenician and Hebrew names just a little. Aleph and beth were called "alpha" and "beta," which became the first two letters of the Greek alphabet. Say alpha and beta together and you say alphabet. In French, the word for illiterate is "analphabete," or "without alphabet."

These and other letters of the Greek alphabet were adopted by Roman conquerers, but not before the Romans adopted their written symbols as well as some of their ideas in art and sculpture. Handed down from Phoenicians, Hebrews, Greeks, and Romans, alpha and beta became the letters A and B in the English alphabet.

The impact of written language upon the peoples of the world was immeasurable. They could write letters to each other, keep journals, publish books and newspapers, post announcements, carry proclamations to distant places, scrawl graffiti on the walls of buildings, and share poems and stories with people living in different times and places. They could keep records of their transactions, write inscriptions on tombstones, advertise products and services, make shopping lists, and write prayers. Written language was considered so great a gift to human civilization that most ancient cultures believed it came from the gods. The designs of written languages are art forms. Wallpaper your room with images of print!

Henry Wadsworth Longfellow's Hiawatha learned not from books but from his grandmother, Nokomis, who sang, showed, and told him how to recognize the signs of his world. He learned to "read" many things, such as the patterns of stars, the meaning of comets and rainbows, the whispering secret of pine trees, the dance of the firefly, the message of wild flowers, deer prints, and the rustle of wind. From Nokomis he learned the names of birds, trees, plants, and animals; the paths in the woods; and the directions of stars to lead him home.

Modern-day Hiawathas do not rely on grandmothers and legends alone to help them read the world. Rather, they go to bed with A in their right hand and Z in their left hand, so beautifully described by Nancy Willard in her poem "In Praise of ABC." The letters of the alphabet are as integral a part of their world as were animal tracks and the marks on trees in Hiawatha's world.

The alphabet song is one of the first songs children learn. An unforgettable message on our answering machine was the baby voice of Len, the Muffin Man, not yet seventeen months old at the time. He sang, "A B C D, Pa!" for us to enjoy.

Which brings us back to our kindergartners chanting on the playground, Patrick rhyming names, Dylan choosing her *Tom and Pippo* books, Pnina making animal sounds and touching textured pages of her current favorite stories, and all the infants pressing crayons and pencils on paper and turning pages of magazines, newspapers, and books.

Here come the children! The playground chanters line up and return to their various classes. Soon Patrick, Dylan, Pnina, and Yuri will also be students. Their experiences in school will reflect the ways teachers interpret and synthesize philosophies and methodologies. Will the playground movers and shakers, dancers and singers stifle themselves, sitting passively at desks waiting for instructions on their latest ditto, their latest worksheet? Will they have a teacher who explains, "We won't have language arts today because of our guest"? Will they "wait" to begin oral language until "the talking stops"? Will they learn to fear reading and writing because they don't always have the right answer or the right response? I don't believe in "strategies." I believe in life and death. Call them what you will. Teachers who believe in life-affirming education create environments of trust, warmth, respect, and encouragement where children are challenged, inspired, and reassured.

Their environments are language-rich learning communities. Their lives in and out of school are "drenched" in language. They are not only immersed in language, they also swallow it, drink it, and splash in it. They dream it! They eat it!

Do we wish for all children to live in loving homes where cuddling on laps to read favorite books is a peak activity of every day? Of course. But reality doesn't always guarantee our wishes. Millions of our children come from homes where no one talks to them, reads to them, or plays with them. Our schools must be cities of refuge for so many of our children. The friends our children meet in school crisscross ages and occupations, cultures and religions. With their classmates, they find friends in stories and poems, songs, and games. When they meet Eeyore, Piglet, and Pooh, they make friends forever. When Dylan sits on the potty looking for the moon, she reaffirms her friendship with Tom and Pippo! At two years old, Len, the Muffin Man, stakes his claims: "*My* Baby Beluga!" "*My* Curious George!"

Becky Moore has spent her life with children and books.[10] Her observations and experiences concur with the studies and writings of the major scholars in the field. When children are read to often and with a loving feeling, they learn to read more quickly and easily than children deprived of such experiences. They have a sense of story, a sense of print on page, of knowledge that we read from left to right and we turn the page and begin again on the left-hand side. They recognize print, how print is called letters and words, and how words carry messages. Becky tells teachers to show the children (with their fingers) as they read how print progresses on the pages. Take time to stop, look at pictures, and talk about the story and the pictures. Read every way! One to one. Small groups. Partners. The whole class. Ask the children to retell the story, to "read" it back to you, and to "read" it to dolls, puppets, pets, and friends. Don't be afraid to use books with expanded vocabularies.

Young children understand many words, even complicated ones. Although most children begin with their ABCs, learning individual letters first, some teach themselves to read without even knowing the names of letters. The words that mean the most to children are the words they want to learn how to read and write.

Because children know the names of letters does not necessarily mean that they will learn how to read. They need a concept of print and story. Children learn best when teachers and families are accepting of early attempts, when stories are stressed, and when children are encouraged to use their own language to talk about the stories. Becky has a challenging observation:

> Isn't it interesting that children learn how to walk and talk in a loving, accepting atmosphere, but when it comes to learning to read, the environment too often gets hostile? Parents become tense and anxious. They demand programs that lock children in patterns. (We know children don't learn that way!) In too many environments, the tension over reading creates emotional problems that block learning.

Ideas come from everywhere. When our hearts and minds are open, we learn from everyone. On my wall is a Native American saying, "May all the paths recognize each other." Today I learned a lot from Tobie Sanders.[11] In addition to her work with university students, she directs an exciting program, The PARTY Project (Participate Actively in Reading Throughout the Year). She liked the "drenching" image to add to "language immersion." She and her students of all ages "play in the puddles of language, shower with language!"

"Connections" is a key word, Tobie believes. Listening and talking are interwoven strands of the fabric of language. She encourages her students and families to have *real* conversations. Talk to and listen to each other. Language, like the arts, connects generations and cultures.

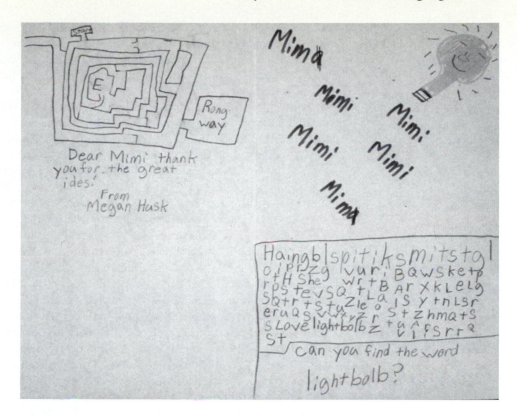

Tobie's students have many opportunities to listen to the beauty of all kinds of languages. Together, they learn to appreciate the sounds, rhythms, and feel of languages.

"We give the gift of words like the words for 'love,' 'welcome,' 'friends,' in many different ways, including gesture and Sign Language. It helps us remember that despite diverse backgrounds and languages, all peoples have vocabulary for these basic relationships and feelings," she says.

In all her programs and classes, Tobie focuses on sharing literature from many cultures. "This is as important for teachers as for children! Especially mainstream teachers who have not had broad experiences with children from diverse cultures. Sharing rich literature representing the treasures of many cultures expands sensitivity to others. It broadens us, as teachers and as people. Even the process of finding these kinds of excellent resources is exciting—like finding a new person, a new friend. Good teachers are always open to good materials all the time! Our 'differences' are a vital resource!"

Meaningful, authentic activities involve the children who learn with Tobie and her student teachers.

"I'm not big on labeling everything," Tobie says. "I like to see *real* language— gifts of language, notes, letters, posters. For example, if you know a child's interested in, say, a specific topic like horses and you find a picture or cartoon of a horse, why not put it in a little note and write, 'I saw this in the paper and knew you'd love it' and give it to the child.

"I like to keep a class book. Someone writes in it every day, like a ship's log. The youngest children dictate the news. We keep interesting items like 'Jamie's mom visited with their new baby' or 'We worked hard on our invitations to Open House' or 'We went for a walk and found a bird's nest.' We don't write this 'log' on big chart paper but more in a special book like a real journal book. Every day we begin by reading from the day before. . . . During the course of a day, the children share poems, songs and stories on every relevant theme: new shoes, loose teeth, moving, new babies. . . . We read and reread our old favorites. Our story and poetry list accompanied by the children's pictures goes into the hundreds and hundreds by the end of the year!

"You know, most children believe they can write. When you ask even a very young child to write, you'll see 'writing'! Remember, those scribble scrabbles become letters and words. . . . There are so many opportunities for children to write, to make connections between home–school–print! For example, just bringing in tossed-away envelopes showing different kinds of handwriting, postmarks, addresses, and stamps is a wonderful learning experience. When Damien learns that Grandma writes to me from far away and Mom reads me the letter, I can almost hear Grandma talking in my mind! We're always writing letters and notes, taking orders for our play restaurant, role playing. . . ."

Tobie's years of experiences taught her something important: "Little kids learn big things before they learn the little things! As adults, we think it's logical that children learn little things like sounds and letters, but Damien is learning that the language on the envelope and in the letter Mommy reads connects him with his Grandma. That's a *big* concept! When children feel safe in a trusting environment to expand ideas in extended conversations they have so much to contribute. When you're doing patterns—in music, art, games, dances, you're learning language, because children are recognizing patterns in the environment around them. Writing happens all the time in these kinds of classes. We don't worry about correct spelling with our young children. Children's invented (and inventive) spelling is very important to collect and know. It ties back to kids learning *big* things. They're following rules they understand, recording sounds they hear to correspond with letters they are recognizing. Through invented spelling stories and poems, the children express their knowledge at the moment!"

They are communicating to you their attempts to grasp the often complicated, contradictory rules of the language. Tobie's favorite invented spellings can teach us about the spellers' levels of skills and comprehension. For example, can you read the following words?

gusy (juicy)
uspesle (especially)
dreasions (directions)
Jmone (Germany—note the capital J)
wuzu (was a)

Josh Appelbaum is in kindergarten.[12] This is his first written story, which he typed on the computer:

i went to my soccor game.
ne kick the ball.
ever 1 was yelling.
we hadd so much fun!

As we ponder over philosophies and research, trying to make sense for ourselves about this amazing phenomenon of learning, these gifts of language that are nothing less than astonishing, try to keep sane in the midst of the swirl of ideas. I like Frank Smith's warning: "People who do not trust children to learn—or teachers to teach—will always expect a method to do the job."[13] He also reminds us, "Not all children will learn what we want them to learn when we want them to learn it, no matter how understanding and collaborative their teachers might be. Children are individuals, no more capable of being standardized than are adults."

The philosophy that generates the life of your classroom will reflect your personality, experiences, instincts, memories, goals, commitments, and spirit. No one method provides identical programs for all children. A whole-language class in Room 230 with Maureen Reedy may be a totally different kind of environment from Room 231 with Tom Griffin. The bottom line is: What do you believe? What do you *do?*

Remember, children do not always fit into learning schemes. Some children save you the trouble and teach themselves to read at the age of four; other children defy every approach and program.

Reading, writing, talking, and listening go hand in hand. Remember that our children play at writing long before they learn their first letter. They "talk" before they learn words! Children should be encouraged to write every day—their names, titles for pictures, stories, poems, songs, directions, and labels. As often as possible, display their writing and make books, anthologies, newspapers, and letters to families. Talk and sing their words.

Do not belabor spelling skills with young children. Never allow anxiety about correct spelling to block children's desire to write. Spelling skills will develop each day as you talk about, read, and display words. The freedom of spirit necessary to enjoy writing is fragile and can be easily broken by too heavy concentration on perfecting spelling and handwriting. Talk about everything.

Read! Read! Read! Right? WRITE. The more children write, the easier and more satisfying writing becomes. When writing is part of their everyday activities, it ceases to be a foreign and formidable exercise that arouses tension and fear. Pnina and Dylan *can* read and write. The key words are *eclectic, flexible, encourage, share,* and *read and write together.* As one first grader advised, "The way to teach us to read and write is to love us kids."

DISCOVERY TIMES/WONDER TIMES

- A way of understanding each other is called language.
- Listening, speaking, reading, and writing are important parts of the way we express and understand our language.
- Gestures, facial expressions, body movement, pantomime, and voice tone are some other important ways we express ourselves.
- Language is a fascinating and amazing aspect of our human family.
- While our primary language in America is English, many people in our country speak more than one language.
- Throughout the world, thousands of languages are spoken.
- Some people in our own class may speak more than one language or a language other than English.
- It's an amazing thought that any baby is capable of learning any language. If we were born in Greece, we would speak Greek. If we were born in Spain, we would speak Spanish. If we were born in Tanzania, we would speak the Bantu language of Swahili.
- Some people know ten languages!
- Words are the most important part of language.
- Words have meanings that people agree on. Some words have more than one meaning.
- All words are made up of letters.
- In the English language there are twenty-six letters. Imagine, all of our words are made up of only twenty-six letters!
- Every letter has its own shape and sounds.

- Words have their own shapes because of the combination of the letters that form them.
- Our language helps us to think about so many things. We have words for almost everything in our lives and our world.
- Scientists are still learning about language and how human beings use and understand language.
- We wonder about the language of animals. Scientists are studying about the ways animals communicate with each other.
- A word is a thought in our minds, a written symbol, a sound, or a shape. We can say our words, think our words, write our words, listen to our words, draw pictures to show the meanings of our words, act out our words, or sing our words.
- We can enjoy stories, poems, songs, and information that other people shared, even people who lived long ago and very far away from us.
- People are so inventive! We can even communicate by touch with friends who are visually impaired, using a language called Braille. We have Sign Language for people who are hearing impaired. We have interpreters to help people who speak different languages talk together.
- When we learn how to read and write, others are able to read our words and write to us!
- When we pay attention, we notice that words are all around us. We are always learning our language!

SUGGESTED VOCABULARY

sounds	sign	computer	translate
words	read	plays	posters
letters	talk	puppet shows	signs
alphabet	speak	nursery rhymes	author
ABCs	tell	fairy tales	writer
names	listen	folk tales	playwright
questions	recite	legends	journalist
answers	page	movies	poet
people	print	TV shows	editor
places	books	journals	question mark
things	newspapers	diaries	comma
feelings	magazines	calendars	sentence
ideas	posters	lists	capital letter
imagination	mail	notebooks	small letter
information	postcards	chalkboard	handwriting
news	telephone book	chalk	exclamation point
reports	dictionary	paper	notes
meanings	stories	pencil	message
understand	poems	pen	communication
write	riddles	crayon	character
sing	songs	typewriter	

In his book *Straw for the Fire* (Doubleday, 1974), the late poet Theodore Roethke shares wit and wisdom about language. He writes: "In this first assignment, just care about words. Dwell on them lovingly."

Words have power. They affect the way we see and react to things. They are the stuff of our ideas and imagination. They enrich our experiences and help us to know one another. There is no end to what we can know about words.

SOME STARTERS

Start with the children's names What more wonderful and important group of letters than those in our names? Across the country, imaginative teachers welcome children into their rooms on Day One with prominent displays of their names accompanied by colors, designs, and symbols. Older children are immediately invited to honor their names with name tags, posters, and displays. Many teachers take Polaroid snapshots the first day of school so names and faces are seen together.

Start with day, date, and a welcome Children love rituals. Many teachers begin each day with special greetings and the reciting and writing of the day and the date on the board or on a chart. "Good morning, friends" and "Welcome, friends" are warming words to start a new day.

Start with the idea that everything we say and sing can be written Even the youngest children learn that the words they speak are sounds we recognize, and that the words are also language that can be written and read. They may not yet be able to read the words, but they know that when their teacher writes on the chalkboard or on a chart that "Jamil has something to share today" or "Later we will sing the Sunshine Song," it means their words have shapes that can be read. They are proud and excited to see their spoken words honored in print.

Start with a song Many children learn to sing before they learn to talk. Be sure that every song the children enjoy is written on a song page for an ever-expanding collection of songs. Our youngest children know the lyrics to numerous songs.

Start with delivering a letter A delightful way to begin your yearlong study of letters and words is to give each child a letter of the alphabet cut from cardboard, construction paper, or felt. Add excitement by asking the children to close their eyes while you give them their special-delivery letter.

Start with admiring a letter Many of Wendy Sample's students are from Arabic backgrounds and English is their second language.[14] Wendy and her students look at the letters of the alphabet as if they were works of art. "We talk about which directions the shapes are going, how they are connected, and whether they have curved or straight lines."

Start with the word of the day Tape it to your clothes; tack it to the bulletin boards; tape it to the children's backs. Border the room with the words you celebrate, adding a new word each day. Encourage the children to choose the special words.

Start with a red-letter day Adapt the above idea to introducing a new letter instead of a word. Cover yourselves and your room with that letter. Combine it with a color. Imagine the children's delighted response to walking into a room covered by red, yellow, or blue S's.

Start with an alphabet puppet Assign one of your puppets or stuffed animals the job of introducing new letters and words. On the day of a new letter or word, your alphabet puppet is dressed head to toe in the design of that letter or word. Sometimes the puppet can be the questioner. "What's this?" the puppet can ask, pointing to a special letter.

This activity lends itself to variations. Here are just two: a different puppet for each letter of the alphabet, such as Albert for A and Bobby for B; and animal letter puppets, such as a cat puppet for C and a dog puppet for D.

Start with a letter search Children enjoy seek-and-find games. Give them opportunities to look for letters in books and magazines and around the room. See how many occurrences of a letter the children can find in just a short time.

Start with name-tagging everything in the room At the beginning of the school year, after the children have received their name tags and are accustomed to wearing them, encourage the children to help you tape name tags to areas and objects in your room. After a while, the children will learn to read all the names. How will you know? Mix them up and see what happens! Or make new tags, remove the old ones, and ask the children to tape the new ones to the matching objects or places.

Start with a missing letter Make alphabet cards and show them to the children, beginning with A. "Uh-oh! A letter is missing! Darn! Which one is missing? What does it look like? Where could it be?" Be sure it is hidden in an interesting place. "Could the Alphabet Puppet be sitting on it? Hmmmmmm. It might be hidden on an object that begins with that letter." You never can tell where missing letters are hiding!

Start with a letter or word in your pocket Pockets are popular with young children. Designate or sew on a special pocket that is full of surprises all year long. Sometimes the surprises are letters or words to celebrate all day.

Start with a favorite-words chart Clearly print your children's names on a large chart and leave space after each name. Talk about favorite words. Ask the children, one at a time, to tell you their favorite words. Next to each of their names, print one or more of their favorite words. Talk about them, draw them, act them out, make games and riddles out of them. Children like to see their names in print and easily learn to recognize words associated with their names.

Start with a delightful story about letters of the alphabet Bill Martin, Jr., and John Archambault's *Chicka Chicka Boom Boom* is an example of a playful, immediately likable story featuring the letters of the alphabet that children love to recite.

Chris Van Allsburg's *The Z Was Zapped*[15] intrigues the children and reinforces letter recognition as they study each of the black-and-white pictures, which show the letters of the alphabet vanishing, melting, growing, and being flattened. What if Z were missing? See *The Story of Z!*[16]

Start with letters, laughs, and riddles Young children love to be silly, delight in riddles, and need successful experiences in generous daily doses. Illustrations in Robert Lopshire's *ABC Games*[17] accompany each alphabet letter with a page of silly options for simple riddles about the alphabet. The children can't miss guessing the "right" answer in between giggles and sharing their own jokes and riddles. Make time for laughter.

Start with a poem Bill Martin, Jr., told of a friend of his who taught first grade and spent fifteen minutes a day sharing poetry with his students. Some poems were read ten times, some even more. Bill said, "The children say the poems together and have the poems in their long-term memory forever. All the poems shared are written down (as are song lyrics). The children know the poems inside out and upside down. By the end of the school year, those children know over a hundred poems."

My favorite poem to start the children thinking about the power of words is "Take Sky" by David McCord.[18] This poem inspires children to really think about words and their sounds, meanings, and power. From the beginning of the poem,

Now think of words. Take sky
And ask yourself just why—

> Like sun, moon, star and cloud
> It sounds so well out loud. . . .

until the last thought, featuring the most important word of all—*wonder*, children hear the sounds of beautiful words. Every word spoken in the poem can be illustrated and demonstrated. Begin gathering words you and your children especially love. Display those words, accompanied by illustrations. Watch the collection expand and cover your walls!

There is no end to Starters! With our first gesture or word on that first moment of the first day of school, we have launched our language curriculum. Be sure it's a curriculum of Life!

TALK TIMES/LISTENING TIMES

It is difficult for me to imagine that even today as this page is being written, thousands and thousands of our young children "learn" in silent classrooms. Learn what? A recent incident provided another reality check. Caring, anxious, wanting only the best for their four-year-old, the parents sent the child to a highly structured, "back to the basics" early childhood program that *guaranteed* that each child would become a successful reader by the end of the year. For over a month, the little boy came home from school with nothing to report or share. Finally, he ran into the house excitedly to tell his mother, "Mommy, Mommy! I have a new friend!" The mother was practically moved to tears in joyous relief. She hugged her son, saying, "Wonderful! What's your new friend's name?" Her son's shining eyes dimmed as he explained, "I don't know, Mommy. We're not allowed to talk."

Alice Sterling Honig has written many excellent articles and books about the importance of oral language in the healthy, Developmentally Appropriate education of young children. She writes, "We need to understand the functions of language and the development of competence, both in receptive and expressive language. We need to be aware of the ways in which oral and written language are related. . . . Effective teachers use the strengths of children, such as their oral fluency or their attentive listening skills to help them develop richer language fluency and skills such as storytelling, answering questions about a story, or learning to read for meaning. . . . Unconditional acceptance of the goodness of children helps them to open up and use talking in richer and more honest ways. . . ."[19] In the same article, Honig offers twenty tips for caregivers and educators that can help young children find "the pleasures and powers of language in their everyday world." These suggestions include humor, dramatic play, open-ended questions, music, chants, rhythms, making up stories, and listening to children.

When we think of the children, we think of countless ways to encourage talking and listening. Here are but a few suggestions to help you break the vows of silence.

Informational talks These daily necessary sessions help you catch up with news from the children. In environments of lovingness and safety, they will offer you information from the birth of babies to the death of pets, from reports of new items of clothing to reviews of TV programs or movies. Sometimes, we need to put everything else aside for the moment and invite the children to take turns sharing whatever is on their minds.

Daily schedule talks Many teachers begin their days with calendars, agendas, and overviews of the day's events. Children should feel welcome to ask questions or share ideas about these items. Their input is very important. Often, their suggestions are the best ideas to translate into activities.

Plans, rules, regulations, and programs Children have opinions about all aspects of their lives: field trip suggestions, classroom management systems, issues of fairness and behavior, proposals for special programs. Children's input is important and must be encouraged. As ideas are shared, write them on the board or on chart paper. Brainstorming sessions usually astonish the children with the plethora of suggestions generated. We teach by example. We teach by "doing it." When the children have a say in their own learning environment, they take ownership and responsibility.

Problem-solving talks Even in the most ideal classrooms, problems will arise. These are times for sitting together quietly, talking them through. Thoughtfulness, sensitivity, and empathy are important qualities of character strengthened through such conversations. Children become empowered when they discover that they can do something about difficult situations and difficult classroom relationships. When solutions are agreed upon by the group, print the conclusion on a chart and ask the children to sign their names if they agree with it. For example, following a bitter playground fight over the forming of teams for a game, the children talked through the problem. After a lengthy, valuable discussion, they agreed that when people get left out of games their feelings are hurt. The teacher printed on a large board: "Because we know how it hurts to be left out of games, we will try not to leave people out." Every child signed the board by the end of the day.

Playful, humor-filled talks Humor is another of our precious human "gifts." Studies show that young children laugh often during a day. Look for humor in everyday things, but never hurtful humor. Don't laugh *at* anyone, but always *with* them. Shared playful kidding, joking, and "noodling around" is excellent for language usage as well as comprehension. If you laugh with us, you "get it"; you comprehend. Cartoons, riddles, jokes, silly situations, and funny games and songs all help humor remain a constant delight in your room.

Talks for the Seven Dwarfs (feelings) Earlier in the book we highlighted the practicality and accessibility of inviting the Seven Dwarfs—Bashful, Sneezy, Sleepy, Dopey, Doc, Grumpy, and Happy, and any other feelings the children experience—into the classroom. Feelings top the list of the children's agendas and need to be attended to. In my early years of teaching, I remember a few children living through extremely traumatic circumstances. I know their times during that difficult period were softened because school was a comforting place where they could say without fear of criticism or rejection, "I'm sad today because. . . ." Once they shared that feeling, they could go on and experience friendship, community, and laughter as they let themselves become involved in their other life—*the life of the classroom*. When children don't have the opportunity to share important feelings every day ("Roberto, you must wait until Friday at 10:30 for our sharing time, and our list is already full. Sorry."), we guarantee that they will be "stuck" in the sad/angry/anxious state in which they arrive in the morning. Enchanted education is magical. It takes children on an exciting journey and helps them build a valid, vital aspect of their lives. Obviously, children who are suffering profound emotional problems need professional counseling. But our across-the-board open-heart policy is helpful for all children. Remember the "ear" in the center of "heart"!

Book talks Every story read, every word or image in any story, is subject to marvelous discussions. Don't just read through from beginning to end. Stop. Look. Listen. Observe. Ask questions beyond "How many porridge bowls are in the Three Bears' house?" Expand thinking by opening up imagination and expanding language possibilities: "I wonder what the porridge tasted like? Any ideas?" Books are conversation starters!

Magic vocabulary talks Mario loves karate! Jennifer always wears her Sesame Street clothing. Garth knows all the dance steps on MTV videos. Dylan loves Pippo. Observe and listen to the children. They'll "tell" you their favorite topics! They want to talk about them.

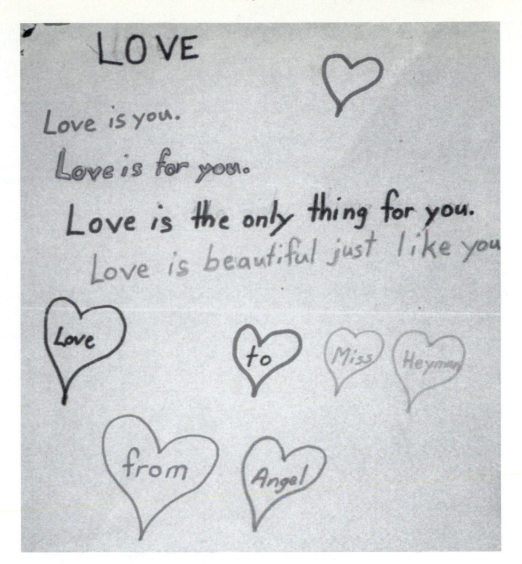

I call these special topics "Magic Vocabulary." We all have our own Magic Vocabularies, and tuned-in teachers constantly make room in the curriculum to connect these close-to-the-heart "words" like Pippo, karate, Bolivia, MTV, Sesame Street (what's on *your* list?) with every subject strand. They always connect!

Table talk/Busy talk/Play talk Most young children won't need your structured plan or strategy to get them talking. They will already be talking as they work and play. When children learn the "way it is" in your classroom, they know there are times when everyone is paying attention to the information being conveyed or to the speaker of the moment. But throughout the day, there are numerous opportunities for children to enjoy healthy communication as they play, eat snacks, and plan together. No one eats next to people in total silence. No one sits at tables with others in total silence. *Or do they?* I am sad to report that children still attend schools and programs where talking is *not* permitted until Oral Language time! If that time falls on a holiday or snow day, can you wait until next week?

"Talk story" The Chinese call telling stories and sharing memories "talk story." We call it storytelling. It is universal. There is no culture without literature, its stories, poems, and chants. Throughout this book, I have encouraged you to think about storytelling in the most reverent way. When we tell stories, we honor a unique gift presented to us at birth. Storytelling time should always be special, heralded in creative ways, participated in with heightened anticipation. Storytelling should never be hum-drum, ho-hum.

Wonder-full conversations Children have fascinating things to say about almost any topic. Open-ended questions evoke stimulating discussions. For example, young children are eager to tell you how they learned to read. The question was, "Learning to read is so complicated! I wonder if any of you remember how you learned?" Here are some sample responses:

Pammy: *My Aunt Patti sang the alphabet song to me. We looked at lots of books and played with magnetic letters. I like letters with lines the best. My favorite letters are E and F and X.*

Jessi: *I have a letter box. I teach letters to my dolls. I can write Y–E–S. Do you know what that spells? It spells* yes!

Cheryl Harbold asked her kindergartners a big wonder question: "How did we get letters and words?"[20] The children had, as always, a lot to say:

Eric: *They made words using your imagination. If we didn't have words, we could just move our mouth.*

Tanya: *When you say the ABCs, you sound them out and get letters and words.*

Annelyn Baron and Lori Selczer's prekindergartners considered the origins of letters and words.[21]

People made them out of plastic.
We get them from the letter store.
We got them from God.
They fell down from the sky.
We put letters together and that makes words.
We get letters and words from our house.
Words come from pencils.

Talking about and comparing alphabets is a fascinating topic of conversation for young children. Betsy Distelhorst recalls that when her son, Roy, was in prekindergarten, a Greek alphabet chart was brought into the class.[22]

The children were fascinated by the unusual symbols and were interested in comparing them to letters of the English alphabet. They talked about alphabets in general, their own alphabet, and that people around the world speak different languages. In their class were a few children from homes where Spanish, Portuguese, or French was spoken. One of the most amazing discussions centered on the fact that the Spanish, Portuguese, and French use letters of the English alphabet to make other languages.

Talking about the different alphabets and exploring the differences helped the children to understand the English alphabet clearly. One little guy was way behind the others in language development. In a short time he was able to differentiate among letters of the English alphabet.

More wonderful talk about language Because our country is so diverse, we don't have to look far for the immense inventiveness of the human family in divising so many language systems. Written languages are beautiful visual art forms in themselves. Yesterday, I had the opportunity to admire the designs of Arabic words written on posters displayed in a Middle Eastern restaurant. An English-Russian brochure distributed at a community center was fascinating in contrasting the

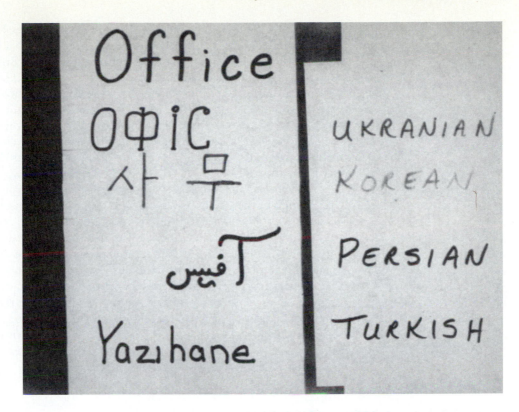

shapes of the two languages. In language-drenched rooms, children see many examples of print around them at all times. Especially in schools with few students from cultures other than mainstream America, children need to see the variety and diversity of written languages. In classes and programs where there is more multicultural representation, the languages of the teachers and children should always be honored in visual displays. It's exciting to be welcomed into buildings with words of welcome in Japanese, Swahili, Greek, Chinese, and German, as well as English. Even very young children will point out the "Welcome" spelled in English letters: "My language!" Imagine featuring your children's photos with their names displayed in English, Arabic, Hebrew, Chinese, and so on. What a dazzling wall of faces and languages that would be.

Books like *Jambo Means Hello—Swahili Alphabet Book* offer interesting Swahili words for every letter of the alphabet.[23] Excellent illustrations and explanations accompany each word. The children reinforce their knowledge of the English alphabet as they learn about another culture.

Another book that combines letters, information, and important concepts is *A Is for Aloha*.[24] Once again, using their own alphabet letters, the children discover many things about Hawaii's unique culture.

A more complicated book is *An Around-the-World Alphabet*.[25] Younger children enjoy talking about the images designed for each letter page. Older children note the richness of the combinations and the higher level thinking they are exercising to understand and talk about ideas such as K is for kettle, kangaroo, kepi, kale, and karate.

Pete Seeger's marvelous song, "All Mixed Up," spices up discussions about diversity expressed in our language. Pete sings: "This language that we speak is part German, Latin and part Greek, Celtic and Arabic all in a heap. . . . Choctaw gave us the word OK. Vamoose is a word from Mexico way. . . . I like Polish sausage, Spanish rice, pizza pie is oh so nice, corn and beans from the Indian sphere. . . . I think this whole world—soon Mama—my whole wide world . . . is mixed up!"[26]

Children eagerly contribute words that sound unusual or exotic to them, talk about them, wonder about them. Today Maya played with a set of pipe whistles from Bolivia. Maya, who is six, must have repeated the word "Bolivia" thirty-six times!

Always leave time for wonder and wonder questions. These are not short-answer quizzes. They are times for sharing and remembering how children remind us to explore topics that are often taken for granted. They are never afraid (unless we teach them to be) to offer explanations for the greatest mysteries.

Children don't learn their language in silence. Their talk is purposeful and meaningful. Their language develops in satisfying ways as they explore their worlds in their own words.

Important note: Our spoken language is very important to us. Be sensitive to the feelings of the children as they learn to express themselves in a safe and loving environment. Harsh correction for incorrect usage or pronunciation will surely frighten and tighten the children. Know that we have many languages. We speak a certain way at home, with strangers, at interviews, and on dates. The language your children bring into the classroom is *their* language. With you and their classmates, they are learning yet another language system. We are all multilingual! Unless children are using obscene or hurtful words (in which case the issue of inflammatory language becomes a problem that needs immediate solving, because it threatens the sense of safety in the group), it's best to teach gently, with love, with humor, and by example. Model the language you want to teach! Let the language spoken in your class reflect the spirit of the learning.

VISUAL ARTS TIMES

In *Harold and the Purple Crayon,*[27] the little boy, Harold, creates his entire world by drawing with his purple crayon.

Ever since the earliest days of human life on earth, people have left their marks on stone, wood, skin, and bone in purple and other bright colors. Carved and painted in the language of the time, experiences, history, news events, legends, superstitions, poems, and statistics were indelibly stamped for us to appreciate and to study. Visual arts times—in sand, on parchment, with feathers, with goose quills, on marble, on tablets, in clay, on all surfaces, with all available materials—were basic acts, essential to the cultural lives of all peoples.

Our young Harolds and their friends must be encouraged to use their purples, as well as all their materials and other colors, to make their marks. It's our turn to etch our words and images on our pages of history.

Here are a few suggestions for colorful challenges guaranteed to succeed (unless they are shared in rigid, uptight, or joyless ways).

Finger-paint letters Combine letter writing with favorite colors. Ask the children to use their favorite colors of fingers paints to write their letters and names. Dry and display all works.

Snowy letters and words If you live in a wintery place, bundle up and go outside on a sunny, snowy day so that the children can write in the snow with sticks, shovels, hands, feet, and elbows. If the weather stays cold, their letters will remain frozen and you will be able to see them every day.

Sand script Sandboxes and beaches are excellent places to write letters and words. Fill large cake tins with wet sand and make letter cakes.

What's in a word? Popsicle sticks, tongue depressors, toothpicks, pipe cleaners, twigs, pebbles, buttons, cut-out shapes, and Tinkertoys are a few examples of scrounge materials that can be glued, pasted, taped, and pinned together to form letters and words. Display the children's creations.

Playdough, clay, and mud letters Roll, pound, squeeze, and pinch letters out of Playdough, clay, and mud. Roll out the letters and bake them in the oven. When the letters are dry, the children paint them with tempera.

Mosaic letters Cut colored construction paper into small pieces; collect tiny pebbles; and save scraps of gold, silver, and glitter from greeting cards. Outline the children's names, letters, or favorite words on heavy construction paper or shirt cardboard. Cover the letters with glue or paste. The children fill in the letters with mosaic material.

It's fun to paint names on construction paper. The children go over each letter with a finger of glue. They attach twigs, cut straws, sand, glitter, and stars to their names.

Name and word collages The children's names or favorite words are printed in block letters on large sheets of construction paper. Ask the children to think about the meanings of their names or words. How they can show more meanings by cutting out, designing, and pasting pictures and textures on the block letters? Five-year-old Jake filled in the letters of his name with pictures of football players.

Connect the dots Dot letters, names, and words on paper. When the children connect the dots, they discover their initials, names, and favorite words. They enjoy going over the dotted letters with different colors, which not only gives them practice in writing, but also results in a room of bright and lively words. Illustrate the words.

"Alphabelts" When five-year-old Katherine explained language, she told about the "alphabelt": "That's your ABCs. You start at A and try to get to Z!" How do you do that? Katherine went on, "You rememberize. That's how you get from A to Z."

Katherine's word for alphabet is a delightful project. Cut out strips of heavy paper or an old white cotton sheet, long enough to fit around the children's waists. With crayons, or fabric markers, the children print all their letters, names, or favorite words on the length of the strip. Two paper clips hold the belt in place.

Rock letters On one of your walks, gather small rocks of different shapes and sizes. As a change from painting designs and faces on the rocks, suggest that the children paint letters and words on them.

Greeting cards for all occasions You cannot have enough reasons for writing letters and words. One very good reason is to make greeting cards that have not only beautiful decorations and pictures but also important messages. Be sure the cards are mailed or delivered personally. Children also enjoy making cards for classmates as part of friendship projects.

Make room for letters Divide your room into letters the children are learning. In those areas, the children draw, cut out, paste up, hang mobiles, and make collages showing words and things that begin with those letters.

Charts full of words we know Spread magazines, catalogues, greeting cards, and newspapers in a central place in the room. Ask the children to cut out *words they know how to read*. Scrounge poster-size paper and fill the posters with the children's words. Encourage the children, if they can, to paint or color their names under the words they contribute.

Go a step further by using the words for art activities, songs, movement improvisations, riddles, and games.

Catch the letter and spirit of words Talk about the spirit of the meaning of different words. The word "bird," for example, evokes images of colors, wings, sky, clouds, song, flight, and freedom. Clearly print words the children suggest on sheets of poster, tag, or construction paper, one word to a sheet. Ask the children to go over the printing of the word a few times with crayons or markers so the letters are clear and can be read from a distance. Encourage the children to illustrate their words in the most imaginative and liveliest ways possible.

A second grader put wheels on the bottom of each letter of his word, "car," and a third grader colored her paper blue-green and filled it with fish swimming around her word, "fish."

Cover a wall with the exciting display of words.

Special projects for special letters Celebrate every letter with a special activity. For the letter B, for example, sew beautiful buttons and beads on a burlap letter B. The wall hangings make a fine display. For the letter Z, scrounge zippers of all sizes and colors, and zip and unzip zealously.

Around the country, I have seen children make elephants for E day, puppets for P day, robots for R day, snow people for S day, beautiful quilts for Q!

Edible alphabet Marilyn Cohen believes that one way to children's minds is through their stomachs. She goes through the alphabet, from A to Z, making food that celebrates each letter: for example, cookies for C; and doughnuts for D. Her favorite is homemade pretzels shaped into special letters. The children design placemats of colorful letters, words, and pictures.

Name those T-shirts Ask families to send in old T-shirts and scrounge extras. The children decide what words they want to write and design on their T-shirts. Do not be surprised if the choices range from initials to names to whole sentences. One first grader wrote on his shirt, "I'm a Good Kid." The easiest method is to write with fabric or felt pen. Be sure that you make one, too.

Original alphabet books Many outstanding alphabet books, on a wide variety of themes, are available at libraries and bookstores. Be careful when you choose alphabet books, because some of them, though brilliantly illustrated, are confusing to young readers. They combine a picture of a noun with the letter of a verb, or they have so many unrelated pictures on a page that the meaning is unclear.

Surround your children with effective word and alphabet books to read and enjoy. After the children have become familiar with alphabet books and have started to study letters and words, they are ready to create their own alphabet books. Every page is devoted to a different letter and shows something that begins with that letter.

Greg Siegler[28] and his children used dividers with plastic tabs to make combination alphabet-address books. Every section has drawings, words, and pictures starting with the same letter, plus names and addresses of classmates whose last names begin with that letter. By the end of the school year, the children's books are filled with important ideas about each letter as well as important information about their classmates.

Throughout the country, children are creating alphabet books of favorite themes. Students work together to write and illustrate alphabet books honoring such themes as birds, food, zoos, flowers, names, places, nursery rhyme characters, rain forest environments, and exercises. Each letter is written in the style of the book's theme, for example, exercise figures make up the letters in exercise books.

There are so many outstanding alphabet books inspiring children today that naming them all would take pages and pages. John Agard's *The Calypso Alphabet*,[29] with its colorful, rhythmical text and pictures, is an example of how a simple alphabet book conveys information and material for movement, play, songwriting, and discussions. The children learn sounds and meanings of words from a different culture, learn about others and what we have in common, and generate their own ideas for their own books of colorful letters, words, and pictures. I especially like "W for Work-song—Sing it while you work-o, work-o." Imagine all the Work-songs you and your children can sing while you work-o, work-o during the day!

In books like *A B C E D A R—An Alphabet of Trees*[30] readers are treated to the leaves, trees, and letters from aspen to zebrawood. Beautiful hands of every color hold leaves of all colors. Children will want to create their own beautifully illustrated books (or pages for a class book) immediately!

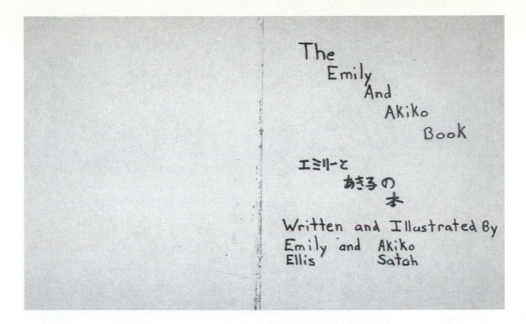

Word books A single word can electrify imagination! Donald Crews's fascination with the visual interpretations of single words like *Truck, Light,* and *Parade*[31] cannot help but motivate the children (and you!) to create their own fantastic books or pictures featuring print and illustrations. *Truck,* especially, focuses on the design of words interconnected with illustration. The children have many ideas to choose from using their own Magic Vocabulary list or the ever-expanding collection of class suggestions of favorite words.

Books of words and pictures High on his list of favorite books is (twenty-five-month-old) Len's very worn copy of *Sesame Street Word Book.*[32] Page after page highlights words and images from all the worlds of children, for example: playground, kitchen, school, park, zoo, and store. Here is an opportunity to invite children to contribute their own words and pictures in theme clusters to large colorful and collaborative works. What about your own class's *Big Book of Words and Pictures?*

Partner books (two by two) When children work together, combining talents and ideas, amazing things often happen. Emily Ellis and Akiko Satoh decided to celebrate their friendship by writing and illustrating *The Emily and Akiko Book*.[33] In their preface, they wrote: "Emily and Akiko are best of friends but they are different in ways. This book is about what they each like." In simple words and painted and textured illustrations, the children created a most original and beautiful book. Partners choose many themes to honor in words and pictures. I have enjoyed reading and admiring the artwork in children's books like *Our Pets, Our Day at the Circus,* and *Tashana and Kim and the Giant Snowman.*

Label all your works Sculptures of clay, wood, and scrounged materials, as well as paintings and drawings, need labels and signatures. Because the children's works are continually celebrated in your room, they must be treated with respect. Titles, notes, and artists' signatures should accompany each artwork. The children will want to name and describe their creations.

Masks, props, scenery, and symbols Every idea the children explore has a visual arts component. If they are playing a story featuring a fox, enrich the drama with a fox mask, symbol, puppet, stick figure, silhouette, or costume. Think "accessible." Projects don't need to be overcomplicated. Encourage the children to develop their ideas at whatever levels they choose or feel. Give them many opportunities to work with a variety of materials. Be open to surprise and delight.

A sampling of handwriting/picture-making activities Their own names are probably the first words that children learn how to write. As they become proficient in writing their names and practicing other letters and words, try some silly exercises that give them a chance to practice small muscle coordination, show their handwriting abilities, and use their imaginations.

Seven Dwarfs' handwriting Ask the children to pretend to be the Seven Dwarfs and write their dwarf names in the style of their personalities. Grumpy's handwriting will be surly; Sleepy's handwriting will be sooo tired; Dopey's handwriting may be a little hard to read; and Doc's handwriting will reflect his know-it-all mind. Do you think Bashful writes big or small? Uh-oh, what if Sneezy *sneezed* while writing his or her name? Well, Happy Happy Happy—how would you write?

Worst handwriting, best handwriting If you want to see your students puff up with pride and confidence, give them the opportunity to do a series of names or words, from their very sloppiest to their very best handwriting. Display all the papers. They make fascinating reading and designs.

Playful handwriting fun

Wizard of Oz handwriting Scarecrow's loose, swirly handwriting would contrast greatly with Tin Woodsman's rigid, tight print. Lion's courageous nature might expand his handwriting, but his cowardly streak would probably shrink it. The children love writing letters in the style of the characters. Expand the fun and ask them to turn themselves into the characters, signing "Tin Woodsman" or "Lion" and their own names in parentheses in the same style. Illustrate, of course!

Bears, billy goats, elves, and giants Baby Bear's pictures and handwriting most likely would reflect smaller paws and size, right? Talk about each character's special qualities and enjoy expressing them in writing and pictures. Elves' and giants' signatures and pictures would be very different (unless an imaginative child decides that elves can paint gigantic pictures and sign their names in huge letters! Be open to all possibilities!). Children enjoy designing posters, wallpaper, bumper stickers, buttons, and T-shirt logos for storybook characters using pictures and words to express their special personalities.

Let's use Goldilocks as an example. Wouldn't it be fun to ask the children to write invitations to their Goldilocks play, puppet show, or story-drama by turning themselves into one of the characters and designing the invitation from the character's style? Baby Bear's invitation certainly would contrast with Papa Bear's or

Goldilocks's! Imagine the Three Billy Goats and the Troll writing invitations to your Three Billy Goats Gruff play!

Name droppers Design a new flower. Name it. Write it. Design a new animal. Name it. Write it. Today's newspaper featured a report from Crayola Crayons on the results of a nationwide contest to name sixteen new colors. The winners ranged from age five to age eighty-nine. Some of the new colors are: tropical rain forest, denim, shamrock, purple mountain's majesty, robin's egg blue, Granny Smith apple, and tumbleweed.[34]

Sign here As often as possible, ask the children to sign their names to agreements, directions, and projects. This activity will teach them the importance of a person's signature, as well as give them practice writing letters and names. Use chalkboard, wall charts, bulletin boards, and doors.

One first-grade classroom featured a sign that read: "We want to go outside on the first warm day." Twenty-two children's names were signed below, in addition to one teacher's and one student-teacher's name.

Combine such exercises with colors: "Sign your name in red if you want to hear a story"; "Sign your name in your favorite color if you want to sing a song." Add pictures, symbols, and designs.

We are tops, from A to Z Tape two or three large sheets of paper together to make a huge alphabet chart. Each letter begins an adjective describing how wonderful the children are. Make room for all the children's signatures first, followed by:

We are:

Adorable	Natural
Beautiful	Original
Cute	Playful
Daring	Questioning
Educated	Responsible
Friendly	Silly
Great	Terrific
Happy	Unreal
Interesting	Valuable
Jumpy	Wonderful
Kissy	Exciting (children's suggestion)
Loving	Young
Musical	Zippy

Add bright, lively illustrations and self-portraits to the chart.

Create A–Z charts for topics such as animals, ice-cream flavors, story and TV characters, fruits, vegetables, seasons, earth, and people.

Words and pictures Constantly encourage the children to write stories, poems, journals, reports, and letters. If they are too young to write for themselves, volunteer family members and older children to take their dictation, or do it yourself. Read their works to classmates. Ask the authors and poets to illustrate their writing. Display. Share. Celebrate. Collect their pieces into individual books of writing, class books, murals, posters, and exhibits. Add words to everything!

MUSIC TIMES

As you have read throughout this book, music is a fundamental part of human language. Languages in themselves are musical; they have pitch, tone, rhythm, and melody. Contrast the sounds of people speaking together in German with the sounds of Chinese people talking together. Our voices have great ranges. Languages teach us the pitch and accent patterns inherent in those tongues. Human infants are capable of learning any language fluently. Music is a language common to all peoples. Every single culture in recorded history has its musical traditions and a wealth of songs, chants, and melodies. Musical instruments dating back thousands and thousands of years were found in caves. Many babies sing before they talk. Listen to the humming sounds of babies as you push them in strollers or carriages!

So it's no surprise that even very young children, our youngest students, come to our programs with rich resource materials ready to share. They are already singing their language. I spoke to some of my college friends who told me they know every world to the Preamble to the Constitution and the Declaration of Independence because they learned it as a rap in junior high school!

Remember the kindergarten teacher who sang a song with her children and made an apologetic face as she felt her voice was poor? One of the children hurried to her, patted her on the cheeks, and reassuringly said, "Don't worry! You did your best!"

The children don't expect you to be Pavarotti or Ella Fitzgerald! They just need you to be *you* doing your best!

Here are a few musical suggestions for enriching language experiences.

Talking drums All around the world, instruments communicate information and messages. Many indigenous peoples know the language of drums and respond to their vocabulary. Drums call for the people to gather, to warn of danger, to herald special events.

With your children, explore possibilities for musical messages using instruments in the classroom. Do bells signal story time? Does the tambourine remind us it's almost time to go home?

Posters and illustrations for poems, stories, and songs Highlight the words of poems, stories, and songs, selecting sections or lines that lend themselves most to visualization, and prominently print them on large poster paper and illustrate them. Use the words for the titles of the pictures. Any beloved text will do! Dylan is already at her crayons and paper with a picture interpreting, "I think Pippo and I will go to the moon one day."

Alphabet songs As three-and-a-half-year-old Jonathan explained, no one taught him the alphabet song; he simply "learned it in his bed." If your children have not learned this song in their beds, be sure to teach it to them. They never tire of singing it.

Make up your own alphabet songs as well, or songs for every letter of the alphabet. Sing them while you practice writing letters and words. Here is a song that a class of prekindergartners composed with their teacher after they studied the letters S and T. Try your own melody to the words.

S S S.
S is very curly.
T T T.
T is very straight.

Some of you may remember the old popular song, "A, you're adorable/B, you're so beautiful/C, you're a cutie full of charm. . . ." Sing it to your children and watch their faces brighten.

Spelling songs Can you spell M-I-S-S-I-S-S-I-P-P-I without singing it? Michael Joel Rosen learned how to spell "encyclopedia" through the Mickey Mouse Club's Jiminy Cricket's spelling song. Michael admits that occasionally he still sings the spelling in his mind as he writes the word.

Turn the children's names into spelling songs, or use the spelling of their favorite words as lyrics to original spelling songs.

Spelling cheers Each word should have its own cheer.

Gimme an F.   F!
Gimme a U.   U!
Gimme an N.   N!
What does it spell?
FUN!   Hip Hip Hooray!

Experiment with different rhythms and movements. Point to or show the letters as they are called.

Song cards As each new song is learned, print the name of the song on a special card. The children enjoy decorating or illustrating the card. Keep the cards in a designated place. Children select songs they want to sing by choosing the cards and holding them up for the others to see.

Correlate this activity with daily helpers' and song leaders' duties. After a while, your children will be able to recognize and identify the song cards and sing at the sight of the names.

Songbooks Collect the songs your class sings into a large songbook complete with clearly printed words and the children's illustrations. This book will be one of the most popular books in your class.

I watched a kindergartner hum and sing his way through a large book of class songs. His teacher explained that "Every day, during free play, at least one child chooses to read the songbook!"

Alphabet instruments Print name cards for every instrument in your room. Combine with shapes and colors. After the children are familiar with the name cards, deal them. The children receive their cards, find the corresponding instruments, and experiment with different sounds.

Sheet music Scrounge a white sheet. With markers, print the words to songs the children know, until the sheet is filled. Drape the sheet across a wall or hang it on a clothesline. The song leaders of the day point to the songs they want to lead.

Singing telegrams For special occasions, singing telegrams are a popular form of communication. In this activity, the children do the singing when the message is read to them. The singing telegrams contain simple, cheerful songs—"good morning" songs, "happy birthday" songs, and holiday songs.

Letter lyrics When the children know and recognize their letters, give each child a card with a letter printed on it. Ask them to make up a song about the letters on their cards.

Here are the words to Tanya's song about the letter M.

Mmmmmmmm Mmmmmmmm M M M.
Mmmmmmmm Mmmmmmmm M & M's.

Tanya associated her letter with one of her favorite kinds of candy and created a little song that became part of the class repertoire.

Musical notes and alphabet letters Musical notes are named after letters. The children cannot help but notice the relationship as they look through music books in the classroom. Even children who are not interested in the more technical aspect of music are fascinated by the idea that when musicians play and sing music, they read notes. Your youngest students will proudly recite the notes printed on a page of guitar or piano music.

Call-and-response songs An excellent way for children to learn is a form of singing known as call-and-response. The leader sings a word or phrase and the group echoes it. "Oh, You Can't Get to Heaven" is an example of this style.

Children respond enthusiastically to these songs, which are easy to make up as you work, talk together, greet each other, and walk along. Improvise spelling and alphabet songs in this style. For example, go down the alphabet and use a little melody:

TEACHER: A B
CHILDREN: A B
TEACHER: C D
CHILDREN: C D
TEACHER: E F
CHILDREN: E F
All the way to Z!

The children's names make excellent lyrics for call-and-response songs. Take attendance this way. As the children's names are sung, the class points to their names on a name chart.

Alphabetical parade After the children have learned to recognize the first letters and perhaps the words for the musical instruments in the room, organize the instruments for a parade according to their letters. For example, all the T instruments are grouped together; here come the triangles, tambourines, and tom-toms. There are even instruments for U (ukelele) and X (xylophone).

The children add to the theme by wearing alphabet letter cards around their necks or taped to their backs. They wave paper or cloth flags featuring letters of the alphabet.

Sing-along nursery rhymes Nursery rhymes are an excellent way to introduce children to the idea of rhyming words. Make up melodies to favorite nursery rhymes. As you sing together, listen to the rhymes. These are stepping stones to greater language awareness.

Sing-along limericks Children enjoy the repetition and silliness of most limericks. A group of second graders made up limericks for most letters of the alphabet. They sang them with twinkly eyes and mischievous grins.

> There once was a letter A.
> We found it in the hay.
> It fell over B
> And couldn't C
> And hid behind the D.

The music of language As you know, language itself is musical, rhythmical, and melodic. Every word can be played on an instrument, hummed as a melody, and used as a lyric in a song.

A group of first graders composed a lively musical interpretation based on days of the week. Monday through Friday and Sunday are two beats each, and the first syllable is stressed. Saturday is three beats, and the first syllable is stressed. The children experimented many ways before they decided on their favorite musical patterns. Here is the way they started.

> Monday—CLAP clap
> Tuesday—CLAP clap
> Wednesday—CLAP clap
> Thursday—CLAP clap
> Friday—CLAP clap
> Saturday—CLAP clap clap
> Sunday—CLAP clap

The days of the week were printed on the board so that the children remembered the order. In a short time, the children recognized the words by sight.

The children improvised basic clapping rhythms by interspersing softer, tapping sounds between each day.

> Monday—CLAP clap (tap tap tap)
> Tuesday—CLAP clap (tap tap tap)

They played with variations of loud, soft, fast, and slow.

Use the children's names, characters from books, and everyday vocabulary words as material for making music.

The sounds of the earth and other onomatopoeias Many words represent sounds, for example, hiss, buzz, drizzle, swish, bobwhite, brush, pop, snap, and flop. Challenge your children's imaginations and increase their awareness of sounds and letters by asking such questions as: "What are the sounds of snow falling? Of ice thawing? Of gentle, misty rain? Of a thunderstorm? Of boots walking on snow? Of sand blowing? What are the sounds of seeds growing? Of buds blossoming? Of leaves falling? Of wind blowing? What are the sounds of trees rustling in the breeze? Of water splashing? Of mud forming after the rain?" Then ask the children to suggest the letters needed to make the sounds into words. Write all their suggestions on the board.

Change "the sounds of the earth" into musical patterns played by classroom musicians using rhythm instruments and improvised sounds. In this way, a second grade composed a "Symphony of Four Seasons." One section developed a theme, from the almost imperceptible hush of seeds growing, to buds opening, to drizzle, to rainfall, to a thunderstorm.

Sing stories and poems In long-ago times, most stories and poems were sung by minstrels and troubadors who went from town to town sharing the literature of the culture. Many children's stories have repetitive lines, like choruses. They can be sung easily. Try it! Pat Hutchins's *Silly Billy*[35] is the silly story of the "nicest family of monsters ever." The youngest member of the family wants to be included in all the activities. As each situation emerges, the family members chant, "Let Billy have a turn, he's only little." Of course, by the end of the story, order is made out of chaos and Silly Billy's whole family chants the refrain together. It's very easy to sing! Eve Merriam's *Goodnight to Annie—An Alphabet Lullaby*[36] dazzles the eye with lush illustrations for each letter, along with poetic lines like "Grass is silently growing" and "Inchworms are inching, minching along." Hum along as you read the words. These are words that want to be sung by you and your children. Add movement interpretation. Nikki Giovanni's "The Drum,"[37] describing the world as a tight and hard drum and ending "I'm gonna beat out my own rhythm," is an example of a poem that is easy to chant and easy to accompany with drum rhythms. Every child needs a chance to create a drum song.

Songs from all the languages Long before "multiculturalism" ever became an "-ism" in educational vocabulary lists, Ella Jenkins (a national treasure) shared the hand-clapping, finger-snapping, foot-stamping songs of the children of the world with American teachers and children. Through the years, Ella sang, "The world is big and the world is small, so there's lots of room for the short and tall."[38] Making room for all languages and all children, she helped them learn about rhythms, melodies, the sounds of words, the rich music of languages, and the connectedness of the human family.

A minstrel who sings in sixteen languages, including Hindi, Seneca, Arabic, Hebrew, Japanese, Swahili, and Hungarian, is Leslie Zak.[39] She talks about the songs all cultures have in common—songs about children, animals, nature, stories, and relationships, as well as rhythm songs. How wonderful a way it is to help children learn language through songs! Leslie explains, "I ask kids to listen for words that sound like what they mean or sound familiar. For instance, in an Argentinian gaucho song, I ask them to listen for the word that sounds like a horse moving. When we get to 'galopando,' all the hands wave!" Leslie talks about universal songs featuring "sillies," heroes, and friendship. "We learn to listen carefully for sounds and rhythms. A lot of repetition, breaking down segments of sounds, feeling success as we learn words and melodies. It's fascinating that animal sounds in other cultures have a flavor of the language. For cats, we say 'meow' and the French say 'miaou.'" After one of Leslie's sessions, a boy told her, "How great it is to find out how we are all alike even though we're different!"

At a recent festival, the children in an elementary school chorus performed a group of songs in different languages. As they sang, signs were lifted by the children with the name of the language featured. It added a dimension of liveliness to the presentation. Write and illustrate words to spark the singing as you sing along. It's a delightful dimension in any language.

Signs and music for characters, action, and moods In the "olden days," before talking films, audiences learned about plot and character from written cues. How simple an idea it is for musical interpretations of stories. What if the children designed large language/picture cues for all the characters in *Peter and the Wolf*? Or *The Nutcracker*? Or your own original opera? Now we have fused story, music, visual arts, drama, and print. Comprehension underlies all of them.

Mirthful, playful, mess-around songs Imagine how language is enriched when children feel free to play with you and stir the lyrics of familiar songs with humor and imagination. Peter, Paul, and Mary had a delightful time adding on to "I Know an Old Lady Who Swallowed a Fly." Children have so much fun making up their own series of cumulative stanzas to songs like "There's a Hole in the Bottom of the Sea." Even the simple, beloved song "I See the Moon and the Moon Sees Me" is a key to expanding the world as children improvise with all their names—"I See Gabriella and Gabriella Sees Me . . ." as well as with animals, objects, countries, and natural forms. Always keep the language journey moving, from the familiar to the new, from old combinations to new patterns! I know that you are already thinking of new lyrics to "She'll Be Coming Round the Mountain When She Comes." Of course, add all the variations to your song collections!

There are some indigenous cultures that celebrate a time when young people arrive at a new level of understanding. Their community expects them to present their own song to the group. From then on, the song is known by the composer's name, and it belongs to that individual. All of our children have their own songs to sing. Let us always be the community that honors the songs of the children.

MOVEMENT AND PLAY TIMES

Movement probably is our oldest language, our first language of life. Just as children read wordless picture books and comprehend beautiful and powerful stories, so through the ages have people learned the stories and legends, the language of their cultures, through dance, movement, and gesture. If I asked you to "please stand up" and you didn't know the language, you wouldn't move. If I held up a sign that said, "please stand up" and you couldn't read, you wouldn't move. But if you understood my spoken words and could read the written words, no problem— you would immediately stand up! Movement is a way of expressing not only feelings, drama, stories, wonder, and relationships, but also of comprehending. When we say "show me," we invite children to demonstrate that they understand what we are saying. Movement is a vital component of "language arts." Many children learn best through movement (see Howard Gardner's multiple intelligences). How truly deprived are millions of American children who spend their days in passive, stifled, rigid environments with minimum action or interaction. (Aren't verbs "action words"?)

The following few suggestions to get you moving are offered to be mixed with fun, excitement, and success. When you discover that learning is a moving experience, you'll see listening skills, cooperation, following directions, organizing material, comprehension, vocabulary, large and small motor skills, learning patterns, and a few hundred more basic curriculum items strengthened. Keep moving!

Show-me games Children and teachers consider these games among their favorites. Children eagerly respond to such challenges as: "Show me the letter X"; "Find your name"; and "Point to the word 'Hi.' "

These games can be played a variety of ways. Call the children's names individually to point to a letter, picture, or word. Suggest that when they point to the object, they do something about it. For example: "Look for the letter A. When you find it, clap your hands."

"Call me by my initial" One day Jon, Josh, and Jason were full of energy. Their kindergarten teacher could not get their attention. "Jon! Josh! Jason!" their teacher scolded. They kept running. "Boys! Come here this minute!" They did not respond.

After a few more attempts, the teacher had an idea. "Will all those people whose names begin with the letter J come right to this circle!" In one great leap, the three boys joined the circle and listened intently to their teacher as she explained the upcoming activity.

Many teachers enjoy playing initial games with their students. "Will all those children whose names begin with the letter D start putting on their coats." "Today, the children whose names begin with the letter G will lead the singing." "Where are our children whose names begin with the letter T? Can you show us your favorite tricks?"

Initials and exercises A variation of the above activity is to go through the alphabet from A to Z, stop at each letter that begins the first names of children in your class, and give those children a chance to lead an exercise. In one group, the initials were A, B, L, J, and M. The A's led jumping jacks; the B's led sit-ups; the L's led push-ups; the J's led touch-toes; and the M's led twists. If possible, show the letters as you call them.

Alphabet activities Gather ideas for different activities for each letter of the alphabet. Here is an example of a few alphabet activities suggested for a second-grade class.

A   Act out an animal, ask a question, aerobics.
B   Build a sculpture, blow up a balloon, balance on one foot.
C   Cut an interesting paper shape, color a weather report, chant and cheer.
D   Draw a design, dress a puppet, demonstrate a body design.
E   Eyes to the window (What do you see?), ears to the room (What do you hear?). Exercise.
F   Feed the fish, fill the texture box, fancy footwork.
G   Gather interesting shapes, give a gift.
H   Houses and horses are fun to draw. How do horses gallop?
I   Ice-cream cones are interesting shapes. How many flavors can you draw? Imitate an icicle melting.
J   Jog in place, jump like a jack-in-the-box.

Always encourage and include your students' suggestions.

Pin the word on the object As part of labeling or name-tagging your room, adapt the popular game "Pin the Tail on the Donkey." Print word cards for all the objects in your room. The children pick a card, one at a time. Read it to them if they cannot read. They find the object the card describes and pin or tape the card to the object.

The game should be played in an atmosphere of fun and helpfulness, not competition or tension. When the game is over, your room is full of words that the children will soon recognize.

Alphabet trains Children enjoy making a train with their bodies. They form a single line, one person behind the other, with hands on the shoulders in front of them. Give the children (or have them pick out of a grab bag) a letter card to tape to their shirts or sleeves.

Duke Ellington called his great jazz piece "Take the 'A' Train," and what better way to start your train? "All aboard. We need our A car!" The child with the letter A hangs on behind you or starts the train. Go through all the letters until every child is attached. Now the train is ready to roll!

After a few runs, the train is ready to leave various cars. "Z car getting off!" or "A car getting off!" Continue until all the cars are scattered around the room.

Post office   Mark boxes, hanging pockets, or cubbyholes with letters of the alphabet. Encourage children to write notes, cards, and letters to their classmates. Many teachers suggest exchanging letters on "Buddy Day."

The children print or write the buddies' names on an envelope or on the outside of the note or picture. They put their greeting in the box whose letter of the alphabet corresponds to the first initial of their friends' names.

The "game" is played many ways. Here are just two variations. The children take turns finding their mail by looking for the box with their initials and thumbing through the letters until they find their own. Or the children take turns being the postal clerk who sorts their mail and gives it to them.

Alphabet fingers   Ask the children to show you a letter of the alphabet with their fingers. See how many letters the children can make. Name and celebrate each letter.

Alphabet bodies   If fingers can do it, why not whole bodies? Can you "turn your bodies into letters of the alphabet?" The children squirm, stretch, bend, and twist to form the letters, most of which are easily recognizable. Do as many as possible standing up; then try the whole alphabet lying down.

Encourage children to work together to form, for example, M, K, and A. The children are excited by this challenge, and before you know it, they are ready for the next activity.

A delightful spinoff is to turn the children into a can of alphabet soup, with each child a different letter. What happens to that letter when the soup is cooked? Let's see!

Body words   Working in pairs, children can form the words TO, IT, IF, and IS. Working in pairs or groups of three or four, children can shape their bodies into HI, LOVE, CAT, DOG, PAL, and FUN. In no time, the floor is covered with energy-filled words that are easy to read and recognize.

An enjoyable variation is to ask small groups of children to form the same word, but with different qualities. Groups of four first and second graders filled the floor of a gym with the word CATS. Each group was unique. There were fat CATS, skinny CATS, mean CATS, shy CATS, silly CATS, snobby CATS, and scary CATS.

Alphabet exercises and T parties   While the children are shaping their bodies into letters, offer them this opportunity. Using the letter T, for example: "If you were the letter T, what exercises could you do without losing your basic T shape?" The children try different ideas. Keeping their T shapes, they jump (legs held tightly together), twist, turn, tremble, tickle twirl, tiptoe, and tighten. It is amazing how many of these T tricks begin with the letter T!

Now "The letter T is going to a party." What kind? A T party! Play rhythmical music that helps the children move energetically. After a few minutes, stop the music and ask the T's to take a T bow and curtsy.

I like to play around with the children. Usually, I'll follow the T party celebration with, "Who's that coming to the T party? Why, it's Y!" (It's easy for T bodies to turn into Y bodies and do Y dances! Now we have T's and Y's dancing together! "Any other letters want to come to the party?") After you practice them all, ask the children to dance their favorites. Always encourage choices.

Follow this activity with art projects creating unusual letter and word posters and pictures—creative writing and songs.

Dance through the alphabet Choose an exciting word that begins with A and turn it into a dance. Continue through the alphabet.

Here are some of the A–Z dances enjoyed by young children. For A they danced alligators; B, birds; C, clowns; and D, dogs. Their favorite letter dance was R; they danced robots.

Use music, tambourine shakes, drumbeats, and hand claps. Follow with pictures, stories, poems, and songs based on the children's suggestions.

Alphabet trees Linda Goldsmith and Jo Ann Bell's kindergartners arrived at school one day to find their classroom tree covered with construction-paper upper- and lower-case letters, all mixed up. Linda challenged them to "find the little b and place it near the big B; find the little c and place it near the big C."

Shirley Davis tapes different letters to different branches. The children find a branch of A's, a branch of D's, a branch of Y's, and so on. They play games in which the children are asked to remove letters, one at a time, to spell a word or name.

Live alphabet books Like the most successful alphabet books, you and your students can combine letters with a theme. How about an alphabet circus?

The ringleader announces each circus act in alphabetical order. Children hold up the letter card and the card announcing each act: A for acrobats, B for bears, C for clowns, D for dancing dogs, and so on.

Experiment with such themes as alphabet zoo, alphabet pet shop, alphabet ice-cream flavors (the children play ice-cream store), alphabet restaurant, alphabet garden, alphabet supermarket, alphabet earth. Afterward, make alphabet books on the same theme.

Letter charade Fill a shoe box or shopping bag with word and picture cards. The children pick cards and pantomime their cards. The only "hint" they give the others is the beginning letter.

Clap for the special letter This is one of Shirley Davis's favorite games. She shows the children a letter, talks about words that begin with that letter, and explains that she is going to say words. Some of the words will begin with the special letter; others will not. When the children hear a word beginning with the special letter, they clap their hands.

If clapping hands becomes tedious, try snapping fingers, stamping feet, touching toes, blinking eyes, wiggling noses, or patting heads.

I often introduce a nursery rhyme or a story with letter challenges. I'll tell the children, "Today we have a terrific celebration of a favorite nursery rhyme beginning with the letters W W W. Think! Think! I'm going to try to trick you. Do you think W W W stands for (and I exaggerate the pronunciation) 'Mary Mary Quite Contrary'?" The kids usually shout "No!" or they demonstrate "no" in sign language or movement responses. By the time we get to 'Wee Willie Winkie,' they are so excited they are jumping in the air and cheering! The simplest ideas are the best.

Punctuation is a moving experience Think of it—punctuation is a way of emphasizing, stressing, and interrupting. Punctuation marks are like traffic signs. Periods say *stop*. Commas say *pause*. They flash their orange lights—slow down! Exclamation points say *wow! Stop or else!* Question marks change the music of our sentences. Children enjoy turning words and sentences into a flow of traffic with periods stopping the energy, with exclamation points jumping in the air, commas pausing the movement for a second. Invite them to explore the shape of punctuation marks with their arms, like conductors. Accompany with visual arts symbols. Without punctuation marks, the traffic of words would turn into a traffic jam!

Picture books, poems, and nursery rhymes Move to or mime every alphabet book in your room. Go through each book and ask the children to take the shape of every picture (or at least the ones you like best). Turn the shape into a dance! Be sure to introduce the picture by its letter and sounds.

If everyone is feeling silly, interpret *Dr. Seuss's ABC*. The children have hilarious times showing the Q page: "The quick Queen of Quincy and her quacking quacker-oo."

Gyo Fujikawa's *A to Z Picture Book*[40] features ample selections of pictures for each letter so that every child finds ideas to move to. Remember, there are no correct or incorrect interpretations. Encourage all responses to the ideas.

Shel Silverstein's delightful poem "Love" is fun to do by itself and to use as a basis of improvisation.

> **LOVE**
> Richy was "L," but he's home with the flu,
> Lizzie, our "O," had some homework to do,
> Mitchell, "E," probably got lost on the way,
> So I'm all of love that could make it today.[41]

With this poem is a picture of a little girl holding up a V all by herself.

We play this poem many ways. The most popular one is a row of four children holding up the letters L, O, V, and E. As the poem is recited, each letter leaves the line. Only the V is left.

Try your own variations. Here is one of our favorites. Four children held up letters forming PLAY.

> **PLAY**
> Peter held the P but he dropped it.
> Julie held the L but she lost it.

Jennifer held the A but it fell.
Y doesn't spell PLAY very well!

Because of their repetition and rhythm, nursery rhymes are excellent subjects for moving and playing while children learn letters, sounds, and words. "Jack and Jill" and "Jack Be Nimble" help children learn J's as they recite while tumbling down hills and jumping over candlesticks. And who says Jack jumps only to "American music"? How about jumping over candlesticks to music from around the world?

Almost every story or picture book the children enjoy can be expressed in movement. A very simple story like *Baby Says*[42] invites the children to demonstrate baby movement (which they love to do and need permission to do!) as they use familiar dialogue like "Uh-oh!" and "OK." Children also love sweet little stories like *Quick Chick*,[43] which is about a family of little chicks called Cute Chick, Sweet Chick, and Good Chick. The last little chick is the one who doesn't pay attention. By the end of the story, that little chick earns the name of Quick Chick. We don't choose parts. We dance all the parts together, inviting the children to create their own movement ideas as the story unfolds. No formulas! Experiment and find the ways most natural to you and your children.

Movement books *Jiggle wiggle prance*[44] is an example of a picture book guaranteed to move the children. The title alone is your choreography. Read it and do it!

As you enjoy the many delightful varieties of stories in your language-soaked room, stop at any of the verbs, any of the action descriptions, or any of the adjective-rich descriptions and translate those portions of the stories into movement.

Cue cards In our visually oriented society, children are accustomed to printed messages. Make cue cards for various activities, directions, and announcements. Say the words as you show the cards, and in a short time the children will respond to the cards alone.

Try variations. Have classroom puppets hold cue cards, or ask children assigned to special jobs to use the "Clean-Up Time" card or the "Get Ready for Snack" card.

Expand the idea of cue cards. If you and your children interpret Tchaikovsky's *Nutcracker* in movement, help the children remember the different ideas by showing them cards such as "Sugar Plum Fairy," "Russian Dance," and "Arabian Dance." A class of second graders were cued into their original movement patterns for Prokofiev's *Peter and the Wolf* with cards lettered: "Peter," "Grandfather," "Duck," and so on.

Say "Aaaaah." There is no end to this silly vowel-pronunciation activity. Ask children to "Open your mouth and say 'Aaaaah,' 'eh,' 'ih,' 'oh,' and 'oooh.'"

Because vowel sounds are breath sounds, body movement is easily added to express the different vowels. Ask the children to take a breath and, as they exhale, to say a vowel sound and let that vowel shape their bodies. "How does 'oh' feel in your arms and legs? How does 'eh' make your neck, back, and head want to move?" Try them all and surprise yourself with discoveries.

Original dances to original stories, folk tales, and legends Go back to the basics! With the beauty of movement enriched with masks, props, costumes, signs, symbols, music, song, dialogue, poetry, drama, and puppetry, children create dances that tell stories. Recently, Marlene Robbins's children presented a most exciting dance-story inspired by the Turtle legend of Native American Creation stories.[45] The highlight of another school program was the dancing of a young girl from Bangladesh. Every gesture, facial expression, and body shape had a meaning in the literary language of her culture.

As you and your children create your own dances to stories, ask them how they want to "show" such ideas as Mountain, River, Giant, Queen, King, Morning, Darkness, Light Storm, and Journey—words of enchantment. As you make decisions on the content, patterns, sequences, characters, and plot of your dance-stories, language is celebrated on many levels, connecting many vital strands of curriculum.

Streets and playground chants, raps, cheers, movement games Early in this chapter we eavesdropped on kindergartners singing in perfect rhythm—"This train goes . . . Down, down baby. . . ." Children, *without adult direction,* learn amazingly complex movement and language patterns in such action chants. Be aware of the talents of your children as major language resources. Jump-rope chants, cheers, rap songs (be selective), clap-songs (we've come a long way from patty-cake!) are but a few of the ways children demonstrate language knowledge and competency. Appreciate the language they share. Be aware of the connections between movement, music, oral language, listening skills, vocabulary, and usage. Honor those chants and cheers by including them in your displays and collections of written language.

Moving words from around the world Familiar "dance" words such as circle, square, partners, lines, skip, turn, hold hands, hop, jump, clockwise, forward, backward, clap, kick, slide, sway, and bounce are but a few examples of movement ideas common to cultures around the world. Every theme blooms with its own vocabulary. Play any music of the world. Choose any of the movement vocabulary words to incorporate into the choreography. Be playful! Children are our movers and shakers.

CLASSROOM VISITORS AND FIELD TRIPS

Your visitors have names, hobbies, talents, and careers. What are they? Write them on the board or on posters.

Colorful and imaginative invitations and thank-you notes show good manners and also help children learn how to write letters.

Questions and ideas about the guest or trip are important aspects of planning, doing, and evaluating. Write the children's suggestions on charts or boards. Their words have shapes that they will soon learn to recognize and read. This list of questions was printed on a first-grade wall chart in preparation for a trip to the airport.

1. Where do the planes come from?
2. Where are the planes going?
3. How do you get a ticket?
4. How do you know where to go to get on the plane?
5. Who flies the plane?
6. Where do you put your suitcase?
7. What if the plane is late?
8. Where do you go to meet people who are visiting from other places?
9. How can you get a job working on an airplane?

A guest or trip is more enjoyable if you brainstorm feelings, questions, and ideas before, during, and after the experience.

Classroom Visitors

Visitors from different cultures Always be on the lookout for members of the community who can help children learn about people from different backgrounds. Ask your guests, if possible, to show the children examples of words written in their language. The beautiful brush strokes of Chinese letters, the right-to-left order of Hebrew, and the flowing, beautiful curves of Arabic are fascinating to children who are just beginning to discover their own language.

Storytellers There are storytellers in every community waiting to be invited to share their art with young listeners. Encourage your guest to involve the children

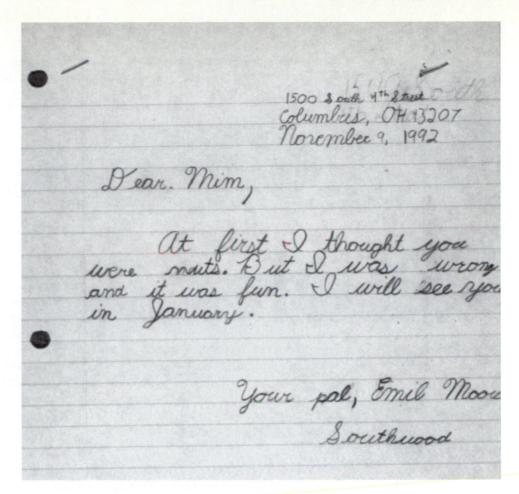

1500 South 4th Street
Columbus, OH 43207
November 9, 1992

Dear Mim,

At first I thought you
were nuts. But I was wrong
and it was fun. I will see you
in January.

Your pal, Emil Moore

Southwood

in the stories as much as possible by teaching them repetitive lines or choruses from the stories. Write down the lines to enjoy after the guest has left. Your students enjoy being storytellers. Give them every opportunity. Pass along the "talking stick" or the storyteller's hat or special prop or symbol.

Folk singers Most folk songs and ballads have choruses that children easily learn and sing. Children need to experience the richness of oral literature through stories and songs. Follow the visit with improvised lyrics for favorite songs, and with art, movement, and creative writing activities.

Writers, poets, journalists Children need to know that just as woodcarvers work with wood, potters with clay, and builders with stone and wood, writers work with words. Words are their raw material. Follow the visit with creative writing sessions.

Calligraphers Writing letters of the alphabet beautifully is an art called "calligraphy." Calligraphers are excellent classroom visitors because they can demonstrate their skills. After such a visit, children are inspired to practice handwriting as an art form!

Puppeteers Check your community resources for puppeteers. Ask your guests if they can improvise a skit in which letters and words are part of the plot. Encourage the guests to involve the children as much as possible. Follow the session with your own puppet shows.

Actors and actresses Be sure they bring their scripts along to show the children. It is important for young children to know that, except for some improvisational theater, actors and actresses begin with a script that they read and memorize. Ask your guests to read aloud from their scripts. Because their reading has feeling and power, your children will be inspired to read stories, poems, and plays with such expression.

Alphabet people Unusual and funny guests (you, your colleagues, family members, and good-sport neighbors) reinforce learning in entertaining ways. The alphabet person is dressed from head to toe in a letter of the alphabet, which is taped, pinned, or written on clothing, hands, face, and head. Some alphabet people are covered with words beginning with a particular letter, and some alphabet people speak only in words that begin with their letter.

Note: Every single classroom visitor is a language experience! People have names, backgrounds, reasons for visiting, ideas to share, information to communicate, and stories to tell. Encourage interaction between visitors and the children, so that language is always learned in dynamic ways.

Field Trips

Letters and words walkabout Take a walk and focus on letter shapes you discover along the way. Nature provides infinite varieties of shapes, textures, and designs—many of them in recognizable letter shapes. Books like *Arlene Alda's ABC* and *The Alphabet in Nature*[46] stimulate sharp observations. The children will find letter shapes in tree branches, in flying birds' formations, in twigs and leaves, in animals and telephone wires. Words are everywhere around us—children will point out auto licenses, billboards, store signs, graffiti, and skywriting! Take notebooks and sketchbooks along. Walk, stop, write, draw, and talk.

When you return to the classroom, write all the words and letters seen on the board. Use them as a resource for art, drama, songs, and creative writing projects. Here are a few excerpts from a class gathering:

> We saw doughnuts that looked like the letter O.
> We saw a window frame with an E shape.
> We saw a stone that looked like a Q.
> We saw a sign that said "Going Out of Business."
> We saw a tree in the shape of a giant Y.

Library, bookmobile, and bookstore Where can children find a greater celebration of written language? Be sure the children have the opportunity to experience the range of subjects and materials available. Give them time to browse and wonder. Try to coordinate your visit to the library with a storytelling program, often a feature of the children's room.

Newspaper The daily newspaper is part of most children's experience. But where do all those words come from? Who writes them? How do they get into the paper every day? When you return from the newsroom and the printer, you may want to publish your own class newspaper.

Outdoor advertising company These people are responsible for filling billboards with words and pictures. Find out if they have samples of advertisements and public announcements. The size of these items always amazes young children. The company may even give you some scrounge billboard-sized poster paper to use for your own giant letter-writing.

Graphic design studio or advertising agency The goal of these businesses is to catch your eye by the way they design words and pictures. Children will see how these people use letters in artistic, humorous, and unusual ways. The variety of print styles for letters is astonishing.

Computer graphics agency or word processing office Children are interested in modern technologies. They are curious about how a word processor arranges and changes words as fast as they can say them. They want to know how words seem to come out of smoke, out of animals' mouths, and out of mountaintops. Our children are computer smart!

Sign painter's studio "Sign painters have so much fun," a first grader observed after a visit to a sign painter's shop. "They get to write: 'Beware of Dangerous Dog,' and 'All the Pizza You Can Eat.'" After your visit, do not be surprised if your students spend the next few days painting their own signs.

Greeting card shops or stationery stores When children see so many ways of printing "Happy Birthday," "Get Well," and "Congratulations," the words will become familiar to them. Stationery stores also feature paper products with monograms and personal names. When you return to the classroom, the children will want to design their own cards and writing paper.

Airport, railroad station, or bus terminal These are exciting places for young children to visit. Schedules, cities, and codes flash on screens and display boards. Travel posters, ads for rental cars, and instructions for travelers' aid and luggage abound. The practical value of reading is conveyed in dramatic ways.

Note: Every single outing is a language experience! When you take children to farms, factories, stores, restaurants, plays, concerts, festivals, and orchards, they are soaking in language. Each visitor and each trip offers its own vocabulary. Don't think you *must* go to a bookstore to have a language experience. Even the budget cut or the failed school levy is a language experience!

With awareness you will find opportunities for language expansion and development every moment of every day. Sitting under a tree in the schoolyard watching the world go by is an excellent language experience. When you teach in the key of life, you are a person on whom nothing is lost! Your antennas are always high, and your bright lights are always on!

IT ALL COMES TOGETHER

Last summer, whenever we called our friends, the Ghodsizadeh kids, Raphaela (nine), Odelia (seven), and David (four), we were told they were busily reading. When we finally worked out a time to visit, the children excitedly shared their latest favorite books. Odelia and Raphaela got into reading the *American Girl* series, *The River That Gives Gifts, Riddles and Books That Make Us Laugh*—oh, there are too many favorites to list them all. Together, the girls read to their younger brother, who listened attentively to picture books, books about dinosaurs, and books about nature. The children talked about their best books and remembered how they learned to read. Odelia recalled that she was about four when she learned how to read. "I learned first 'and' and 'the' and 'horse' and 'parrot.' I got to be a good reader and writer when I was five. My kindergarten teacher read us a lot of stories."

Raphaela explained the flurry of activity as the children rushed around the house, showing us flyers, coupons, dinosaur scales, and book logs. "It's all happening at the library! We're putting scales on a giant dinosaur—it's an Apatosaurus! It's so much fun and we're reading so many books and. . . ."

A call to Nancy Smith, who works in the children's department of the library in Westerville, Ohio, was imperative. What's happening in this town? If these three Ghodsizadeh children were an example of reading as a major activity—a cause for celebration—I wanted to know the story!

Over the years, Nancy and her staff, along with children's librarians throughout the country, chose a summer theme as a motivating focus for children's reading. This particular summer the Westerville staff decided they wanted to do something "a little different than handing out tokens for every five books read and then applying the tokens to a mural." Laughing, Nancy noted, "The amazing thing about our choosing dinosaurs as our summer theme is that we made that choice before *Jurassic Park* ever came out! It was just coincidence!" With funding from community

businesses and the Jaycees and in garage space donated by community friends, artist Charles Doeble created the Apatosaurus out of papier-mâché around chicken-wire frames, with crumpled newspapers and carpet rolls wrapped with duct tape adding bulk. The finished Apatosaurus was 45 percent of actual size and stood twelve feet high from head to floor. "Our Apatosaurus was beautiful!" They sent out flyers about Dinosaur Days, which featured story times, craft days, family story times, puppets, songs, and games. Children from age three and above were invited to read, read, read. For every five books they reported in their logs, they received a dinosaur scale to add to their dinosaur's body. All participants received store coupons and little gifts. Raphaela received a *Jurassic Park* Travel Kit, Odelia a dinosaur egg with a little dinosaur in it, and David a can of dinosaur soup.

The children's summer was busy: listening to "Steggie stories"; admiring a six-foot dinosaur nest in the library with dinosaur eggs that were counted, speculated on, and imagined about together; making up puppet shows; creating "Dino-mite Crafts"; and having movement fun, "not just finger plays but big movement!"

"Community and family involvement was terrific," Nancy said. "We ran out of scales—the walls of the library were bordered with scales. . . . We were surprised at the response. Our actual participants ranged from eighteen-month-old toddlers to three sixteen-year-old boys! Oh, the children read books about everything—not just dinosaurs! Out of 2,000 kids who signed up for the summer, 1,300 participated—that's 65 percent, and that's pretty good! In all, 33,220 books were read and read to (younger children) in eight weeks! Our story times were packed. Our library was full of the excitement of singing, talking, sharing, imagining. It was fun!"

Could such a successful venture happen anywhere in the country? Without hesitation, Nancy responded, "Of course!"

NOTES ♥

1. Nancy Willard, "In Praise of ABC," *Carpenter of the Sun*. New York: Liveright, 1974, p. 15

2. Frank Smith, "Learning to Read: The Never-Ending Debate." Phi Delta Kappan, *Kappan,* February 1992, pp. 432–441. This provocative article, based on Professor Smith's speech, was delivered to the annual convention of the International Reading Association, 1991.

3. The work of Marie Clay inspired the Reading Recovery program in America. To learn more about this early intervention program, see: Marie Clay, *Reading Recovery: A Guide Book for Teachers in Training*. Portsmouth, NH: Heinemann, 1993.
   Diane E. Deford, Carol Lyons, and Gay Su Pinnell, *Bridges to Literacy: Learning from Reading Recovery*. Portsmouth, NH: Heinemann, 1991.

4. Every major educational organization has issued position papers describing Developmentally Appropriate practices in early childhood programs. Write to the National Association for the Education of Young Children, 1834 Connecticut Ave. NW, Washington, DC 20009, 800–424–2460, for its collection of position papers. Janice J. Beaty, *Preschool Appropriate Practices,* Fort Worth: Harcourt Brace Jovanovich, 1992, is an excellent source in addition to the position papers.

5. This focus is always current and controversial. Read across the spectrum of philosophies and approaches. At the moment, the books and journals at my fingertips are:
   Teacher Magazine, August 1991; theme: whole language.
   Instructor Magazine, November/December 1992; theme: whole language for the 1990s.
   Educational Leadership (Association for Supervision and Curriculum Development), April 1993, Vol. 50, #7; theme: authentic learning.
   Language Arts (National Council of Teachers of English), April 1993, Vol. 70, #4; theme: integrated arts instruction; December 1992, Vol. 69, #8; theme: oral language and language arts instruction.
   Jeanne Chall, *Learning to Read: The Great Debate*. New York: McGraw Hill, 1967.
   Marilyn Jaeger Adams, *Beginning to Read: Thinking and Learning About Print*. Cambridge, MA: MIT Press, 1990.
   Frank Smith, *Understanding Reading,* 4th ed. Hillsdale, NJ: Erlbaum, 1988.
   Yetta M. Goodman, ed., *How Children Construct Literacy: Piagetian Perspectives*. Newark: International Reading Association, 1993.

6. Gerald G. Duffy, "Let's Free Teachers to Be Inspired," Phi Delta Kappan, *Kappan,* February 1992, pp. 442–447.

7. Helen Oxenbury, *Tom and Pippo See the Moon*. New York: Aladdin, 1988.

8. See note 2, p. 434.

9. A. A. Milne, "In Which Rabbit Has a Busy Day, and We Learn What Christopher Robin Does in the Mornings," *The World of Pooh*. Illustrated by E. H. Shepard. New York: Dutton, 1957, pp. 231–232.

10. Becky Moore was a reading specialist in the Columbus Public Schools, worked with adults and students from other countries in community college settings, and helped organize the "knapsack books" sections of this text. She was one of the founders of Cover To Cover, a bookstore for children in Columbus, Ohio. She is the grandmother of Emily.

11. Tobie Sanders is associate professor of Education at Capital University in Bexley, Ohio. She is the director of the PARTY Project (Participate Actively in Reading Throughout the Year), which has earned wide acclaim for its success

in getting children to read. These excerpts have been selected from a lengthy conversation.

12. Josh Appelbaum is in kindergarten at Montrose School in Bexley.

13. See note 2, p. 441.

14. Wendy Sample is deeply involved in Art Education in the schools of Dearborn, Michigan.

15. Chris Van Allsburg, *The Z Was Zapped*. Boston: Houghton Mifflin, 1987.

16. Jeanne Modesitt and Lonni Sue Johnson, *The Story of Z*. Saxonville, MA: Picture Book Studio, 1990.

17. Robert Lopshire, *ABC Games*. New York: Crowell, 1986.

18. David McCord, "Take Sky" from *More Rhymes of the Never Was and Always Is*. Drawings by Henry Kane. Boston, MA: Little, Brown Dell, 1971, p. 3.

19. Alice Sterling Honig, "Talk, Read, Joke, Make Friends: Language Power For Children," *Day Care and Early Education*. Summer 1989, pp. 14–17.

20. Cheryl Harbold talked about the origins of letters and words with kindergartners in Hilliard Elementary School in Hilliard, Ohio.

21. Annelyn Baron and Lori Selczer talked about letters and words with children at the Leo Yassenoff Jewish Center in Columbus, Ohio.

22. Roy Distelhorst was introduced to a Greek alphabet chart at Indianola Alternative School in Columbus.

23. Muriel Feelings, *Jambo Means Hello—Swahili Alphabet Book*. Illustrated by Tom Feelings. New York: Dial, 1974.

24. Stephanie Feeney, photographs by Hellen Hammid, *A Is for Aloha*. Honolulu: University of Hawaii Press, 1980.

25. Jeanne Jeffares, *An Around-the-World Alphabet*. New York: Peter Bedrick, 1989.

26. Pete Seeger, "All Mixed Up." Stormking Music, Inc. 1964.

27. Crockett Johnson, *Harold and the Purple Crayon*. New York: Harper & Row, 1955.

28. Greg Siegler shared these ideas with children at the Miami Tutorial School in Miami, Florida.

29. John Agard, *The Calypso Alphabet*. Illustrated by Jennifer Bent. New York: Henry Holt, 1989.

30. George Ella Lyon, illustrated by Tom Parker, *A B C E D A R—An Alphabet of Trees*. New York: Orchard, 1989.

31. Donald Crews, *Light*. New York: Greenwillow, 1981.
———. *Truck*. New York: Greenwillow, 1980.
———. *Parade*. New York: Greenwillow, 1983.

32. Children's Television Workshop, illustrated by Tom Leigh, *Sesame Street Word Book*. New York: Western, 1983.

33. Emily Ellis and Akiko Satoh created their beautiful book when they were students at Northeastern Elementary in Bellefontaine, Ohio.

34. The article about the names of new colors appeared in the *Columbus Dispatch*, Nov. 10, 1993.

35. Pat Hutchins, *Silly Billy*. New York: Greenwillow, 1992.

36. Eve Merriam, illustrated by Carol Schwartz, *Goodnight to Annie—An Alphabet Lullaby*. New York: Hyperion, 1992.

37. Nikki Giovanni, "The Drum" from *Spin a Soft Black Song*. Illustrated by George Martins. New York: Farrar, Straus and Giroux, 1985.

38. Smithsonian/Folkways is the source for much of Ella Jenkins's music. Fred Koch, with Ella's blessing, honors her songs in *Did You Feed My Cow? Fred Koch Presents the Songs of Ella Jenkins*. Red Rover Records, P. O. Box 124, Lake Bluff, IL 60044.

39. Leslie Zak, director of Days of Creation Arts for Kids in Columbus also makes music and drama with children through the Greater Columbus Arts Council's Artists in the Schools program. She can be reached at 65 W. Como St., Columbus, OH 43202.

40. Gyo Fujikawa, *A to Z Picture Book*. New York: Grosset and Dunlap, 1974.

41. Shel Silverstein, "Love," *Where the Sidewalk Ends*. New York: Harper & Row, 1974, p. 95.

42. John Steptoe, *Baby Says*. New York: Lothrop, Lee and Shepard, 1988.

43. Julia Hoban, illustrated by Lillian Hoban, *Quick Chick*. New York: Dutton, 1989.

44. Sally Noll, *Jiggle Wiggle Prance*. New York: Penguin, 1993.

45. Marlene Robbins is the movement specialist on the Arts Impact team in Reeb School and Indianola Alternative Elementary School in Columbus, Ohio.

46. Arlene Alda, *Arlene Alda's A B C*. New York: Celestial Arts, 1981. Judy Feldman, *The Alphabet in Nature*. Chicago: Children's Press, 1991.

BOOKS FROM MY KNAPSACK FOR CHILDREN ♥ ♥

Ahlberg, Janet and Allan. *The Jolly Postman or Other People's Letters*. Boston: Little, Brown, 1986.

Amery, Heather. *The First Hundred Words*. Tulsa: EDC, 1988.

Anderson, Karen Born. *An Alphabet in Five Acts*. Illustrated by Flint Born. New York: Dial, 1993.

Arnosky, Jim. *A Kettle of Hawks and other Wild Life Groups*. New York: Lothrop, Lee & Shephard, 1990.

Bang, Molly. *Yellow Ball*. New York: Morrow, 1991.

Base, Graeme. *Anamalia*. New York: Dutton, 1987.

Birdseye, Tom. *Airmail to the Moon*. Illustrated by Stephen Gammell. New York: Holiday House, 1988.

Bond, Michael. *Paddington's ABC*. Illustrated by John Lobban. New York: Viking, 1990.

———. *Paddington's 1 2 3*. Illustrated by John Lobban. New York: Viking, 1990.

Bowen, Betsey. *Antler, Bear, Canoe: A Northwoods Alphabet Year*. Boston: Little, Brown, 1991.

Brown, Ruth. *Alphabet Times Four: An International ABC*. New York: Dutton, 1991.

Burningham, John. *John Burningham's ABC*. New York: Crown, 1964.

Butler, Dorothy. *Higgledy, Piggledy, Hobledy Hoy*. Illustrated by Lyn Kriegard. New York: Greenwillow, 1991.

Caseley, J. *Dear Annie*. New York: Greenwillow, 1991.

Catalanotto, Peter. *Mr. Mumble*. New York: Orchard, 1990.

Charlip, Remy, and Miller, Mary Beth. *Handtalk: An ABC of Finger Spelling and Sign Language*. New York: Four Winds, 1980.

Cooper, Edens. *The Glorious ABC*. New York: Atheneum, 1990.

Elliott, David. *An Alphabet of Rotten Kids*. Illustrated by Oscar de Mejo. New York: Putnam/Philomel, 1991.

Fisher, Leonard Everett. *The ABC Exhibit*. New York: Macmillan, 1991.

Grossman, Virginia, and Long, Sylvia. *Ten Little Rabbits*. Illustrated by Virginia Grossman. San Francisco: Chronicle, 1991.

Grover, Max. *The Accidental Zucchini: An Unexpected Alphabet*. Browndeer, 1993.

Hale, S. J. *Mary Had a Little Lamb*. Photographs by Bruce McMillan. New York: Scholastic, 1990.

Kennedy, X. J., and Kennedy, Dorothy M. *Talking Like the Rain*. Boston: Little, Brown, 1992.

Lear, Edward. *An Edward Lear Alphabet*. Illustrated by Carol Newson. New York: Lothrop, Lee & Shephard, 1983.

Lippman, Peter. *One and Only Wacky Wordbook*. Illustrated by Peter Lippman. New York: Golden Press, 1979.

Lobel, Anita. *Allison's Zinnea*. Illustrated by Anita Lobel. New York: Greenwillow, 1990.

Martin, Bill, Jr., and Archambault, John. *Chicka, Chicka Chicka Boom Boom*. Illustrated by Lois Ehlert. New York: Simon and Schuster, 1989.

McMillan, Bruce. *One Sun: A Book of Terse Verse*. New York: Holiday House, 1990.

Micklethwait, Lucy. *I Spy: An Alphabet in Art*. New York: Greenwillow, 1992.

Obligado, Lillian. *Faint Frogs Feeling Feverish*. Illustrated by Lillian Obligado. New York: Penguin, 1983.

Pallotta, Jerry. *The Victory Garden Alphabet Book*. Watertown, MN: Charlesbridge Publishers, 1992.

Paul, Ann Whitford. *Eight Hands Round: A Patchwork Alphabet*. Illustrated by Jeannette Winter. New York: HarperCollins, 1991.

Pittman, H. C. *Miss Hindy's Cats*. Minneapolis: Carolrhoda, 1990.

Prelutsky, Jack, ed. *A. Nonny Mouse Writes Again*. Illustrated by Marjorie Priceman. New York: Knopf, 1993.

———. *For Laughing Out Loud*. Illustrated by Marjorie Priceman. New York: Knopf, 1991.

Rankin, Laura. *The Handmade Alphabet*. New York: Dial, 1991.

Riddell, Edwina. *100 First Words*. New York: Barron's, 1992.

Rosen, Michael. *We're Going on a Bear Hunt*. Illustrated by Helen Oxenbury. New York: Macmillan, 1989.

Ryden, Hope. *Wild Animals of America*. New York: Lodestar, 1988.

Steptoe, John. *Baby Says*. Illustrated by John Steptoe. New York: HarperCollins, 1992.

Terban, Marvin. *In a Pickle and Other Funny Idioms*. Illustrated by Giulio Maestro. New York: Clarion, 1983.

———. *Mad as a Wet Hen and Other Funny Idioms*. Illustrated by Giulio Maestro. New York: Clarion, 1987.

———. *Superdupers: Really Fun Real Words*. Illustrated by Giulio Maestro. New York: Clarion, 1989.

Walls, Ruth. *A to Zen*. New York: Simon and Schuster, 1992.

Wilner, Isabel. *A Garden Alphabet*. Illustrated by Ashley Wolf. New York: Dutton, 1991.

Yolen, Jane. *An ABC of Elves*. Illustrated by Lauren Mills. Boston: Little, Brown, 1990.

Zutter, Hank. *Who Says Dogs Go Bow Wow?* Illustrated by Suse MacDonald. New York: Doubleday, 1993.

BOOKS FROM MY KNAPSACK FOR TEACHERS ♥ ♥

Cazden, C. B. *Classroom Discourse: The Language of Teaching and Learning*. Portsmouth, NH: Heinemann, 1988.

Chenfeld, Mimi Brodsky. *Teaching Language Arts Creatively*, 2d edition. San Diego: Harcourt Brace Jovanovich, 1986.

Cochran-Smith, Marilyn, and Lytle, Susan L., eds. *Inside/Outside—Teacher Research and Knowledge*. New York: Teachers College Press, 1992.

Colgin, Mary Lou, ed. *One Potato, Two Potato, Three Potato, Four!* Mount Ranier, MD: Gryphon House.

Dunn, Sonja. *Butterscotch Dreams—Chants for Fun and Learning.* Portsmout, NH: Heinemann, 1987.

Goodman, Yetta, and Freeman, D. *Whole Language for Second Language Users.* Portsmouth, NH: Heinemann, 1992.

Graves, Donald. *Writing: Teachers and Children at Work.* Portsmouth, NH: Heinemann, 1983.

Hiebert, Elfrieda H. *Literacy for a Diverse Society.* New York: Teachers College Press, 1991.

Livingston, Myra Cohn. *Poem-Making: Ways to Begin Writing Poetry.* New York: HarperCollins, 1991.

Marks, Alan, ed. *Ring-a-Ring O'Roses & A Ding, Dong, Bell: A Book of Nursery Rhymes.* MA: Picture Book Studio, 1991.

Mills, Heidi, O'Keefe, Timothy, and Stephens, Diane. *Looking Closely: Exploring the Role of Phonics in One Whole Language Classroom.* Urbana, IL: National Council of Teachers of English, 1992.

Paley, V. G. *Molly Is Three.* Chicago: University of Chicago, 1986.

Spodek, Bernard, and Saracho, Olivia N. *Language and Literacy in Early Childhood Education.* New York: Teachers College Press, 1993.

Strickland, Dorothy, and Morrow, Lesley Mandel, eds. *Emerging Literacy—Young Children Learn to Read and Write.* Urbana, IL: National Council of Teachers of English, 1989.

Thompkins, Gail E., and Yaden, David Jr. *Answering Students' Questions about Words.* Urbana, IL: National Council Teachers of English, 1986.

Chapter

13

We Count!

Arithmetic

Arithmetic is where numbers fly like pigeons in and out of your head.

Arithmetic tells you how many you lose or win if you know how many you had before you lost or won.

Arithmetic is seven eleven all good children go to heaven—or five six bundle of sticks.

Arithmetic is numbers you squeeze from your head to your hand to your pencil to your paper till you get the answer.

Arithmetic is where the answer is right and everything is nice and you can look out of the window and see the blue sky—or the answer is wrong and you have to start all over and try again and see how it comes out this time.

If you take a number and double it and double it again and then double it a few more times, the number gets bigger and bigger and goes higher and higher and only arithmetic can tell you what the number is when you decide to quit doubling.

If you have two animal crackers, one good and one bad, and you eat one and a striped zebra with streaks all over him eats the other, how many animal crackers will you have if somebody offers you five, six, seven, and you say No no no and you say Nay nay nay and you say Nix nix nix?

If you ask your mother for one fried egg for breakfast and she gives you two fried eggs and you eat both of them, who is better in arithmetic, you or your mother?[1] Carl Sandburg

THE BASICS

In 1911, Ishi, the last known surviving member of the Yana/Yahi people, whose history dates back 4,000 years in the mountainous lands of northern California, stumbled into civilization. Immediately adopted by anthropologists and ethnographers, he spent his remaining four years in the museum associated with the University of California in Berkeley. Here, Ishi discovered a new life in a new world. Social scientists and curious civilians discovered him. Fluent in Ishi's language, Dr. Alfred Kroeber and his staff communicated with this visitor from a Stone Age culture. At one point, they asked Ishi to count for them. He gladly did so but stopped at ten. When they asked him to continue, he responded, "No more. That's all."

In articles and lectures, the ethnographers mentioned this "astonishing culture loss," explaining that Ishi's limitations in counting were probably due to the years of isolation and meager existence and few occasions for Ishi to think past the number ten.

Months later, Ishi began performing custodial work in the museum. He was paid a small salary in silver half dollars in addition to room and board. Ishi saved his silver dollars in canisters. Each canister held about forty coins. Ishi put his canisters of coins in a safe. Once in a while, he asked for his coins and spread them on the table, delighting in them. One day, Dr. Kroeber noticed that Ishi was stacking the coins, dividing the piles and rearranging the numbers.

Dr. Kroeber joined Ishi at the table. "How much? How much money?" he asked, pointing to a full stack. Ishi answered at once and correctly: *daumistsa,* "forty." "The half stack?" Ishi replied *uhsiwai,* "twenty." On and on they went, halves, doubles, triples. It was obvious that "Ishi's numeral vocabulary and his knowledge of the full Yana counting system were undiminished."

You are probably wondering the same thing that Dr. Kroeber wondered. Why had Ishi counted only to ten and no more? Here is the explanation: "Counting in the abstract was something he was not accustomed to doing. He probably found it trying, and surely he found it pointless. Counting is for counting something tangible such as beads or treasure or the number of quivers in a case, or the number of arrowheads finished, or numbers of geese in flight, or salmon in a catch. Abstract numbers did not interest him as such, nor did they figure in philosophy in the Yana world view. Ishi's interrogators knew this as they knew also that the questionnaire form of putting a query may be expected every so often to yield misinformation, since the presumptions from which it arises may be unknown or meaningless to the person being questioned. . . . That their culpability should have come to light as the wild man was engaged in counting his civilized money in quite the manner of a bank teller was particularly humiliating."[2]

As bare trees pierce wintry skies, I warm myself with a few summer memories. With astonishment, Dr. Kroeber watched Ishi count his money way beyond ten! With delight, I watched toddlers Pnina, Len, Louis, and Ben pick, sort, and arrange numerous fallen apples from the Rosens' tree. They placed them carefully into the compartments of tray flats, pots, and cups. Seven-month-old Callie sat fascinated in her stroller. The children were busy "counting" their apples.

One hot August day, Kimani set up a lemonade stand with a sign advertising, "Lemonade—50 Cents." I challenged him, "Fifty cents? Hey, Kimani, give me a break! When I was a kid lemonade was a penny a glass, maybe a nickel!" Peering at me with serious eyes, Kimani explained, "Everything's more expensive nowadays!" Always ready to support fledgling enterprises, I plunked down my money and sipped slowly. In September, Kimani shared his lemonade-stand experiences with his kindergarten project, "Things I Did Last Summer."

Remember Raphaela, Odelia, and David reading hundreds of books, keeping their logs of five books, earning scales and prizes, and adding up their totals as they went along? It was impossible to have a regular visit with those kids. Their excitement and purposefulness dominated all agendas!

The visitor from the Stone Age, Ishi, along with Pnina, Len, Louis, Ben, Callie, Kimani, Raphaela, Odelia, and David, have a lot to tell educators about the way they learn. Listen to, pay attention to young children at play. Take notes. They might dictate ideas such as these:

> We're hands-on kids. We like touchy-feely stuff. Let us explore our world through direct experiences with concrete materials and purposes. We are problem solvers and creative thinkers. We like to take risks and make choices. We're open to new ideas and new experiences. We like to work hard at meaningful challenges. We're snoops. We want to know about everything. We've got lots of questions and sometimes a bunch of answers. We have great powers of concentration unless things are boring and passive and disconnected from our lives. Every day, when we play, we learn more and more. We experiment with sand, mud, water, dirt, blocks, colors, and stones—everything and anything! We like to make investigations, experiments. We all learn differently. Learning is fun! Watch us! Listen to us!

The good news is that educators *are* watching and listening to young children and doing something about it.

Caryn Falvey's energy and enthusiasm about holistic, Developmentally Appropriate, meaningful, authentic education for young children is contagious.[3] Caryn's beliefs and behavior are consistent with research findings; with the National Council of Teachers of Mathematics, Commissions on Standards For School Mathematics;[4] and with her observations and knowledge of young children in action. She would agree with Patte Barth, associate editor of *Basic Education,* the newsletter of the Council for Basic Education, who wrote, "The idea of putting small children in front of workbooks and asking them to sit at their desks all day is a nightmare vision."[5]

Caryn's students don't learn by memorizing facts. She says, "We don't learn our language by memorizing rules and underlining answers in workbooks!" Caryn's students, like thousands of other children around the country, are now learning math the way they are learning their language—by thinking it, using it, and playing with it.

"Math is a meaningful language when it's in context . . . there's math all around us: when kids are figuring out how many playing pieces in a game or do we have the right amount of cookies. . . . Kids have a natural sense of number, a natural sense of order about things. They can see relationships, recognize patterns, solve problems. . . ." Caryn's students are Grand Thinkers! They are graphmakers, survey takers, counters, and measurers. With children the nation over, Caryn's kids are brain-stormers, explorers, investigators, and journal writers. They use "Kwissle" charts to help solve problems:

What do we Know?
What do we Want to know?
What Strategies shall we use?
What have we Learned?
(KWSL, pronounced "kwissle")

Totally involved in active learning experiences, Caryn's kids work together, talk a lot, and use every kind of material—from rubber bands to pattern blocks, from coffee stirrers to linking cubes—in their process of discovery. Throughout the day,

Caryn's children make many estimates and offer many predictions. In everything they do, they are practicing a way of thinking, a way of learning. "I always ask, 'What do you think?' 'How did you come to that conclusion?' 'How many ways can we come up with to solve this problem?' " she says.

Laughing, Caryn shared one of her most successful learning adventures: nostrils! One day she wondered aloud, looking around the room, "How many nostrils are in this room at this moment?"

There was an instant roomful of smiles as the hands flew up with suggestions.

"Count each nostril."
"Count by twos. It's faster!"

Finally, Caryn introduced the idea of multiplying the twenty-four children by two nostrils each, plus Caryn's two nostrils. Fifty nostrils!

"The children's problems are even more funny sometimes!" Caryn explains. Anything goes except hurtful words or violent images.

Pick up any educational journal and you will find articles validating the spirit of learning practiced by teachers like Caryn. For example,

> Children who design their own investigations for the day have ownership of what they are learning. When children decide what to measure, survey and explore, they are pursuing activities that are interesting and relevant to them. A math activity that children help design is math that belongs to them. Math that is not confined to a math workbook or squeezed into 40 minutes of teacher-directed math class is whole math.[6]

Some children learn through their noses by counting nostrils, others like the smell and feel of apples. Howard Gardner, whose theory of multiple intelligences generated dynamic rethinking of the learning process and learners' processes[7] discussed "authentic learning" with Ron Brandt.[8] Gardner urged teachers to "provide what I call 'multiple entry points.' Kids don't all learn in the same way: they don't all find the same things interesting. . . . I'd say that you can approach almost any rich topic in a whole variety of ways. . . . We need to give kids a chance in school to enter the room by different windows so to be able to see the relationships among the different types of windows. . . ."

This dynamic time in education is happening on many levels and in many places. Halfway across the Pacific, in our newest state, Louise Bogart,[9] whose teaching is honed by years of Montessori training and study, found the National Council for Teachers of Math Guidelines consistent with Montessori math. "It's a constructionist approach," Louise explained. "It dovetails perfectly—children construct their own math concepts and knowledge from working with others in meaningful activities through cooperation, critical thinking, direct hands-on experiences. . . ."

Honoring Sylvia Ashton-Warner's belief that before we teach others, we must teach ourselves, Louise was awarded a significant grant to train the entire staff of a rural elementary school on the island of Kauai. At the sessions, the teachers strengthened their awareness that math is part of everyday living, not isolated into limited workbook drills or time slots. Based on their own classroom experiences, the teachers set the direction of the program, exploring concepts, creating their own materials, and working in collaboration and cooperation with others. It's hard to break with traditional methods. Some teachers found the informal, child-initiated, active approach somewhat threatening. In order for children to work in small groups on solving math problems chosen by themselves, straight rows of desks had to be rearranged into pods. After a while, one of the teachers found it too much of a hassle to keep changing the rows into pods for math so he maintained the pods and found it much easier and more fun for the children to learn across the curriculum in small groups. Louise felt happy about that outcome. "He didn't change because he was told to—he learned through his own experiences and from responding to the positive signals of the children. Children always tell you with their behavior how they are learning. Give them opportunities to work on their own so you can stand back, observe, reflect, learn from them. . . ."

The messages are going out to university students, in-service teachers, families, and community members. No child is born to fear math or to build anxiety over failure in math. Those negative lessons are learned in tightly structured, teacher-directed, passive, drill-centered, rote-learning environments where successful test taking is the major goal. How meaningful are such lessons when there is no connection to children's interests? In the current math education, children are learning in ways that distinguish between "achievement that is significant and meaningful and that which is trivial and useless."[10] We call "authentic learning" the kind of learning that features higher-order thinking, depth of knowledge, connectedness to the world beyond the classroom, substantive conversation, and social support for student achievement.[11]

As Ishi arrived at his conclusions through counting, comparing, combining, and manipulating materials and information, he demonstrated the idea of "authentic learning." He taught his teachers how he could count when there was something worth counting!

As you begin your days of numbers with dates, times, schedules, attendance, lunch money, snack portions, lists, and plans, count the ways math figures into your every moment. It's ticking away right now!

Measuring our time and space, we leave a few pages to talk about numbers and their fascinating story, which really is part of the language story.

Ask a toddler "How many?" or "How old are you?" and chances are you will be shown the correct number of fingers.

Numbers that could not be divided by another number were considered magical or divine by ancient peoples. Numbers like three and seven were full of mystery. If you think people have abandoned superstitions, just visit the casinos of Las Vegas or Atlantic City.

Numbers and ways to mark and count them became part of the language of ancient cultures. Because fingers were the first way people counted, the mark for *one* looked like a finger. The Latin word for finger is "digit." When you think of the word "digits," do you think of numbers or fingers? Some cultures used ten as a base number (ten fingers?), while others used five (one hand?). The Mayans used twenty (two hands and two feet?).

When people started to write symbols for numbers, they had a lot of writing to do. If they wanted to write one hundred, they had to mark one hundred 1's. Because this took so long, people figured out an easier way to count, one that is still used today: groups of four vertical lines cut by a fifth line. Eventually, all the ancient cultures created their own symbols for numbers. Some were pictures, others were designs, and still others were like letters of the alphabet.

Because Romans occupied a large part of the ancient world, their number system was widely adopted. Roman numerals were based on letters of the alphabet. In the early years of the Roman system, the numerals were written in any order. If people wanted to know what they stood for, they just added them all together. In time the Romans worked out a way to write the same number with fewer numerals. They agreed that when the first of two symbols stood for a higher number than the second, the first would be added to the second. Therefore, XI = 11. When the first of two symbols represented a smaller number, the first would be subtracted from the second. Therefore, IX = 9.

Meanwhile, in another part of the world, the Hindus in India had created their own system of numbers, very different from that of the Romans. Many scientists and philosophers believe that the Hindu system was the most brilliant of all. Sometimes it is called the Hindu-Arabic system and even our numbers are referred to as

Arabic numerals, but the Arabs adapted the Hindu system and used it for hundreds of years before Muhammed Al-Khwarizmi, a ninth-century Arab mathematician, wrote an important book describing and giving instructions for using the Hindu system. Al-Khwarizmi's book found its way into Europe and began affecting the way scholarly mathematicians looked at numbers. Because the book was written in Arabic, the Europeans called that number system Arabic.

What distinguishes the Hindu-Arabic number system is the importance accorded the position of each number. The system is based on 10, and each number has its own symbol. Any number can be represented by these numerals, just as all of the words of our language can be formed from the same twenty-six letters. From 1 to 9, one-digit numerals are used; from 10 to 99, two-digit numerals; from 100 to 999, three-digit numerals; and so on.

When a number is written, the numerals are not interchangeable. For example, 142 cannot be written 421 or 241, as was the case with early Roman numerals. In the Hindu-Arabic system, the place or position of a number indicates its value. In two-digit numbers, the digit on the right-hand side stands for numbers of ones, and the digit on the left-hand side stands for numbers of tens. The number 25 means there are five ones and two tens (twenty). In a three-digit number, the value of hundreds is added. That is, 425 means there are five ones, two tens, and four hundreds.

This system of "place value" greatly simplified notation, counting, and calculations. Consider, for example, the simplicity of "1994" compared with MDCCC-CLXXXIIII and MCMLXXXXIV.

The Hindus are also credited with one of the most profound and practical mathematical inventions—zero. Their basic number system was in use for thousands of years before they created a symbol for the concept of "none." Until this time, they left spaces between numbers (5 4 meant five hundred and four), then used dots (5.4). The zero, which means *nothing,* changed just about *everything.*

It took a very long time before people who lived under Roman rule changed to the Hindu-Arabic system. Most of the Roman Empire ended about 1,500 years ago, but the use of Roman numerals continued for about 700 years, until the introduction of the printing press helped spread the Hindu-Arabic system.

We cannot think about numbers without attending to one of their most important functions, measurement. We have come a long way from the days of measuring the passage of time by painting suns on animal skin or tree bark, or measuring distance with hands or forearms. Today our wafer-thin wrist watches provide time, date, temperature, jogging time, and times in other places of the world. Some watches have alarms or play music, some talk. We now have instruments of measurement from A to Z, from altimeters to zymoscopes, but most of the questions people ask are the same now as they were in earlier times: how long, how high, how wide, how fast, how far, how dark, how wet, how hot? How to make sense of this world?

How quickly children develop a recognition and understanding of numbers, like their general development, is highly individual. Their rate of development is influenced by many factors, including the quality of their environment; interaction with siblings and older children; socioeconomic factors affecting family life; the games they play and the TV programs they watch; the degree of verbal and nonverbal communication; and the diversity of learning experiences. It is important to recognize that although Len can recite his numbers, he may not understand what it means to count to thirteen. Because he holds up two little fingers does not necessarily imply that he knows what it means to be two years old.

Which brings us back full circle to the children, who must always be in the heart of our circular thoughts!

What kind of learning experiences are waiting for Len, Pnina, Callie, Ben, Louis, Kimani, Raphaela, Odelia, and David and their thousands of classmates when they enter *your* classroom is largely in your hands.

I hope with you, the children will become Grand Thinkers, problem solvers, risk takers, explorers, and investigators. With you, the children will learn to express opinions and ideas, make choices, discover concepts, and strengthen skills. Ken Goodman, an influential voice in the whole-language movement, had a simple explanation that applies to all learning, especially math learning:

> It's real and natural. It's whole. It's sensible. It's interesting. It's relevant. It belongs to the learner. . . . The learner chooses to use it. It's accessible to the learner. The learner has power to use it.[12]

DISCOVERY TIMES/WONDER TIMES

- Numbers are part of our everyday life.
- How did we get numbers, anyway?
- Numbers help us count things.
- Numbers have their own words and symbols.
- Numbers are called numerals. Numerals are one, two, three, four, five, six, seven, eight, and so on. They are also called cardinal numbers.
- Sometimes we talk about things in order: first, second, third, fourth. These are called ordinal numbers.
- Numbers tell us our age, height, and weight.
- Numbers tell us our telephone area code, our house number, and our zip code.
- Numbers tell us the temperature and humidity.
- Numbers tell us how much things cost.
- Numbers tell us about money: pennies, nickels, dimes, quarters, half dollars, and dollars.
- Numbers tell us something about sharing so that everyone gets an equal amount.
- We can count so many things: people, animals, books, toys, houses, years, weeks, days, hours, and minutes.
- Sometimes stories have numbers in them, for example, "The Three Bears" and "The Seven Dwarfs."
- It is fun to play number games.
- When we cook or bake, we use numbers to measure ingredients.
- When we join numbers (or similar things) together and count them, we count a higher number than the original separate numbers. This process is known as addition.
- When we have a number (or similar things) and we take some away, we count a lower number than when we started. This process is called subtraction.
- Zero means nothing.
- There is no end to numbers. If you try to think of the highest possible number, you can always add another number to it. Thus numbers are infinite, without end.
- Learning numbers is like learning letters of the alphabet.
- It is fun to learn to read and write numbers.
- Aren't we amazing to have so many words and numbers in our brains?

SUGGESTED VOCABULARY

low	fifteen	whole	dime
high	sixteen	half	quarter
large	seventeen	all	half dollar
small	eighteen	none	share
full	nineteen	some	count
empty	twenty	zero	add
numbers	thirty	score	subtract
time	forty	ruler	multiply
temperature	fifty	yardstick	divide
clock	sixty	measuring	take away
watch	seventy	tape	measure
calendar	eighty	scale	bunch
dollar	ninety	thermometer	group
coins	one hundred	pounds	herd
calculator	one thousand	inches	flock
recipe	one million	feet	crowd
score	infinity	date	stack
team	many	year	pile
one	few	minute	graphs
two	more	hour	surveys
three	less	second	speed
four	a lot	telephone number	speedometer
five	a little	address	circle
six	same	age	square
seven	different	how old?	triangle
eight	equal	how tall?	rectangle
nine	single	how heavy?	dots
ten	double	money	lines
eleven	triple	change	shapes
twelve	over	price	nothing
thirteen	under	penny	everything
fourteen	high	nickel	fraction

As you glance over these suggested vocabulary words, you probably realize how many of them you use every day. Words about numbers and number concepts are an integral part of our lives. How many people are we expecting? What's the temperature today? What time shall we have our snack? How many people will line up for a drink of water? What shall we do first? How many children are buying hot lunch today?

Because your room is full of conversation and nonverbal communication, your children will hear these words often and will be encouraged to understand and use them. When you say, "The *first* thing we will do today is sing our Rabbit Song," and follow that announcement with your song, the children begin to grasp the concept of order, or ordinal numbers. Say and do!

The activities in this guide are packed with vocabulary. Don't be the strong silent type! Children learn their language by using it and hearing it.

SOME STARTERS

Start with the date Even if your children are not yet reading or writing or counting, they will soon recognize the special words and numbers on the board or on a chart that signify the date. "Boys and girls, today is September 12, 1994." Each day is a new day with a new number, but the year stays the same for awhile.

Start with counting heads The first day of school is a fine time to find out just how many children are in your class. Children are fascinated by the counting process, especially if you gently touch each head as you count (every person is important in this process). Announce the grand total of children in your class. Write the number on a chart or on the board.

Start with treasure boxes At the beginning of the school year, many teachers send letters to families asking for a variety of scrounge materials for "treasure box" collections. Carol Price asks the children to bring in such items as bread tags, small lids or caps, seashells, pebbles, marbles, corks, wooden spools, buttons, nuts and bolts, and keys.[13]

Carol Price explains why this kind of gathering is one of her favorite ways to start things off: "I begin our math program! We cover boxes with contact paper and label each box according to its special items. The children put the seashells in the seashell box, the pebbles in the pebbles box, until all of our treasure boxes are full. We use them to learn counting, sorting, and comparing. They really are treasures!"

Start with ages Children's ages are important numbers in their scheme of things. Write all the children's names on a chart; next to their names, clearly write their ages as they tell you.

Start with heights and weights Measuring the children's heights and weights is one of the first things many teachers do at the beginning of the school year. Even the youngest children know the meaning of a mark, number, or color next to their names. "That's how high I am," a four-year-old explained as he showed his statistics on a bright yellow chart.

When this delightful activity occurs early in the school year and is repeated every few months, the children learn a lot about their own development, and about measurements, numbers, and addition.

At the end of the year, Lynn Salem[14] cuts height markings from the measurement chart and gives the children their own colorful strips showing how they grew.

Enjoy experimenting with ways to measure. More measurement suggestions are provided in this guide.

Start with a counting song Just as children love their alphabet songs, so they enjoy singing songs with numbers. Wherever I go in the country, young children are chanting "Five Little Monkeys Jumping on the Bed" or "This Old Man." Greg Millang and Steve Scelsa's popular "Number Rock" is simple and delightful. The children never tire of singing numbers. Make up your own counting songs.

At a recent Fran Avni concert, I jotted songs she sang that highlighted number concepts. Here are a few fragments from my notes: "There is always room for one more/maybe two or three or four/always space for another face/around our family table." "Jumping beans/jelly beans/1 2 3/Some in my pocket/Some in me/Jumping beans/jelly beans/1 and 2/Some for me/Some for you/Pass it on." When you read Fran's tape notes, catch the songs with numbers like: "Five Little Leaves," "Seven Silly Squirrels," "Three Little Pigs," and "Twogether."[15] Be a musical numbers gatherer!

Start with high fives Nowadays, very young children slap their five fingers to yours without hesitation. In a snap, they learn high tens! Try it! It's a way to celebrate and congratulate.

Start with a cheer "2 4 6 8, who do we appreciate? The kids! The kids! Yaaay!"

Start with a question How many people need a drink now? Do we have enough crayons for everyone in the class? How many cookies do we need so everyone has a cookie? Are there any extras? As you move through your days, you'll find more and more opportunities to integrate math awareness.

Start with an imaginative number story book Your room is no doubt filled with a variety of colorful, interesting books that are constantly in use. But children love *extra* challenges. Read, look at, and talk about books that motivate children to make careful observations and sharp conclusions.

Such a book is Maurice Sendak's *One Was Johnny*.[16] Beginning with "1 was Johnny who lived by himself," each page introduces another crazy character and drama until ten ideas have been counted. Then, one by one, the characters depart, leaving "1 was Johnny who lived by himself and LIKED IT LIKE THAT!"

As the children count up to and back from 10, they are laughing at the silliness of the plot. More importantly, they are thinking up their own silly stories that begin with a single idea and proceed to further adventures.

(Be sure to write the children's stories if they are not yet able to write themselves. Volunteers from the community or older children are eager to transcribe the young children's stories and poems. Illustrations are as important as words.)

Another challenging book children enjoy is *Willy Can Count*.[17] As Mother and Willy walk along, each page introduces a new scene and a new playful task: "I can count one brown cow," said Willy. "Good!" said Mother. "What can you count two of?"

On the next page, Willy counts two red birds, and Mother says, "Good! What can you count three of?"

This is an easy book for reading to and improvising with the children. They can adapt the idea for their own observations, stories, and books.

In the wordless *Anno's Counting Book*,[18] children learn to recognize sets (like things) by finding the right number of cows or houses or trees as the scenes grow increasingly more complicated. You will find your students returning to this book again and again to see if they missed anything.

Start with counting in other languages Children are the fastest language learners! They are gifted linguists who quickly learn words and numbers in languages different from their own. If you have children in your class who speak languages other than English, this is the time for them to share their numbers with their classmates. Make charts with the corresponding number words, symbols, and pronunciation and have them accessible at all times. Keep adding words and numbers. As often as possible, include the words and numbers of the other languages in your natural discussions, instructions, and games. Remember, our children are children of the world!

Start with absentmindedness Ina Mayer discovered a most enjoyable way to start her first graders on a math spree.[19] "I play dumb! I play absentminded. I deliberately count wrong or I write the wrong number on the board. The children gleefully correct the mistake. Oh my, sometimes we have so much to do, we just forget some things, don't we?" Ina twinkles.

Let me put in an extra word for a "making mistakes" game. When children know something, they need many ways of celebrating that knowledge. What more immediately satisfying and enjoyable way than to correct a mistake with humor and fun?

If you kid around and recite "One and one are three" and get no response, that will tell you something about what your students do not know. So be human once in a while. Make some fun mistakes and watch how exuberantly your students set them right.

If you feel self-conscious playing "absentminded," then delegate that responsibility to a puppet, perhaps the same puppet or a relative of the puppet who sometimes fails to understand letters and words and other important ideas.

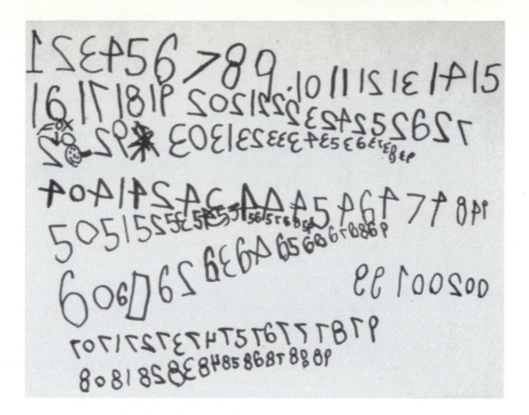

Start with first things first Young children need experience with the concept of ordinal numbers like "first," "second," and "third." As often as possible, use the terms and follow or accompany them with actions that demonstrate the principle. For example, when you say "Kira will be the first person in line today," Kira stands to lead the line. Or "We have three important things to do this morning: first, to hear our story about the snow; second, to finish our pictures; and third, to go outside and play." Then do those things in order, with reminders along the way. At the end of the day, it is fun to summarize. Ask the children, "Do you remember what we did first today? What did we do second?"

Many teachers complain that their students have trouble understanding and following sequences. The kind of scheduling described above is helpful in clarifying the idea of sequences. Even more effective are movement activities suggested in "Movement and Play Times."

Start with the special number of the day Colors, shapes, letters, words, children, holidays, animals—all are excellent causes for celebrations. So are numbers. Begin at the beginning with "good old number one," as Kenyatta introduced it to his fellow kindergartners. Talk about it. Write it. Count it. Draw pictures of the idea of it. Make up songs about it. Improvise puppet shows explaining it. Make mobiles of one item each. Cut out pictures and shapes demonstrating the idea of one unit of something. Correlate it with color. Dance it. Read books about it. Write poems and stories about it.

Here is a poem about the number one that was written by a class of kindergartners. I copied it from their colorful chart displayed on a wall filled with designs and illustrations.

Number One
Today is Number One's Day.
Here is Number One—1.
Number One is all alone.

One tree is number 1 and
One dog is number 1.
Today Number One is happy
Because it is Number One's day.

Start with a snack full of numbers Cookies, tiny pretzel sticks, and crackers are snack foods that are easy to distribute by numbers. "Today, everyone is going to have a special number of pretzels. Spread your napkins. Wait till all of us have our special number before we eat them. Let's count them first."

Add suspense and excitement by asking the children to close their eyes while the peanuts are distributed. Count them together. "Wow! We all have six pretzels each! That's a lot."

With one group of prekindergartners, we really had fun asking them: "How will you eat your pretzels? One at a time? Two by two? Three by three? Hmm-mmm?" Suggesting such possibilities was an important way to introduce number concepts. Be prepared for all the children to announce their choices. "I ate one at a time!" "I ate three at once!"

Start with a survey Nancy Roberts[20] and her first graders often conduct surveys. They record their findings on charts and graphs and in number stories. Their questions include the following:

How many boys are in our class? How many girls?
How many six-year-olds are in our class? How many seven-year-olds?
   How many eight-year-olds?
How many people in this class have pets?
How many people live in apartments? In houses? In tents? On boats?
How many children have a tooth or teeth missing?
How many class members have dark hair? How many have light hair?
How many children like winter best? Summer best? Spring best?
   Autumn best?

Every activity in this guide is an excellent starter. Once your imagination is in high gear, you will find possibilities in everything you see and do. Ideas multiply!

TALK TIMES/LISTENING TIMES

Children have so many questions, observations, impressions, and feelings about *everything* in their lives, including numbers. When Ariela was six years old, she and I sat together quietly, visiting. Her head was bent over a paper filled with numbers. She broke her concentration to share her feelings and, with a dazzling smile, observed, "Aren't numbers beautiful?" When Ariela's sister, Adina, was seven, her class talked about the idea of infinity. Adina burst into the house that day and told her mother, "Do you know what my favorite number is? Infinity. Because it goes on forever!"

Ask Lynn Salem and Nancy Roberts "What's there to talk about?" Their first graders had so much to say about numbers that their teachers had trouble recording all their ideas. They talked about lucky numbers, the biggest numbers they could think of, how numbers came about, and what they wanted to learn about numbers. Enjoy the following excerpts of conversations from both classes. As you read, imagine the sounds of curiosity and excitement, the music of "Talk Times."

Let's talk about our lucky numbers.

Bridget: *32. My mom's age!*

Kevin: *17. I'm 7, and 17 is just about like 7.*

Patrick: *100. Well, one hundred dollars! What else?*

Tarraine: *6. Because when I play games, I always roll 6 with the dice.*

John: *My lucky number is my birthday, 8.*

Nina: *2 is my favorite. When you're playing and you have a friend, that's 2 and that's nice.*

Let's talk about the highest number you can think of.

Several Children: *Infinity.*

Vanessa: *100. Because it takes a long time to count to 100.*

Molly (I): *If you can't write it, then that's the biggest number!*

Janie: *650 is the biggest. It's almost at the end of the numbers and that's how you know.*

Jimmy: *99 zillion 999. Well, it's higher than 100 and less than 1,000!*

How did you learn your numbers?

Rachel: *My Mom and Dad.*

Terence: *I tried to learn them myself.*

Jim: *I learned them by counting my fingers.*

What's the best way to teach little children their numbers?

Shean: *Show them your fingers.*

Molly (II): *Say the number first and they will say it after you.*

Kara: *Give them pencil and paper. Give yourself pencil and paper. Write the numbers and let the child copy them.*

How do you think numbers started?

Michael: *God thought them up and put them in people's brains and they taught other people.*

Jamie: *God sent Jesus down and he knew about numbers and he taught people about them.*

Jim: *One guy said, "There's one way or two ways to make numbers."*

Bridget: *Numbers got started when electricity started. If you didn't have electricity, you wouldn't have a clock. You wouldn't have numbers either. I think numbers really got started by George Washington and Abraham Lincoln because they're on the money.*

Jane: *One day someone went into the woods and there was a bear in a tree, two bears in another tree, three bears in another tree (all the way up to ten). They had to make up some numbers so they could count those bears!*

Molly (II): *Well, you know most people think that people like George Washington started numbers, but you're wrong. People started like gorillas. Well, one day, these gorillas started looking at their hands and they decided to do something with those fingers, so they counted them.*

Adam: *God could have put it in Adam and Eve's brain and they told other people like Cain and Abel and they spread it around.*

Mark: *Numbers came from shapes.*

Ben: *Just people think them up.*

Jim: *Maybe they had little dots and they started to count them.*

Kristen: *They would put people in a line and start counting them.*

Aspen: *If you didn't have letters, you wouldn't have numbers, 'cause number words are made out of letters.*

Everything counts! Teachers like Ken Gillies[21] and his children spend a lot of time singing and talking. "We talk about everything, and our talks lead to action and activity." Here are things they talk about:

Birthdays Whose birthday comes first? Which month has the most birthdays? Whose birthdays have the same numbers? We make graphs, poems, songs.

Sports and hobbies We talk about our favorite sports and hobbies. We think, "How would we draw our favorite interests?" We decide on symbols for each idea, maybe a bat and ball for baseball. I tell the children, "When you've arranged it, let me know and we'll glue down our symbols on big charts." We make graphs. How many kids have soccer as a hobby? How many kids are musicians?

Weather We add to our weather chart every day. How many think it's sunny? Cloudy? Rainy? One month we looked at our continuous weather graph and counted sixteen days of sun! We celebrated.

Lists and questions We're always making lists of things. We play with arbitrary numbers, open to change, such as nine questions for our speaker or seven suggestions for our color graph.

Puppet shows After we work on our puppet shows, we make our lists of things we want to do, like: 1. write invitations; 2. make posters; 3. plan a welcome/greeting song; 4. write thank yous; and 5. evaluate our program.

Ken's children demonstrate every day that they are becoming Grand Thinkers!

Wonder talks One of the gifts young children bring to us is the gift of wonder. When teachers go beyond right/wrong short answers and preset problems printed in workbooks that don't necessarily love the children, they discover the richness of imagination and high-level thinking.

The children and I were squealing with excitement at the notion of "adding one" to any number—the largest number they could think of. They even made up numbers like "one frillion, two shrillion, a hundred thousand billion . . . ," and we said, "Add one!" What a mind-blowing experience!

Children love the book *How Much Is a Million?*[22] It's packed with stimulating, imaginative text and pictures and can't help sparking clever suggestions and images. My favorite idea is, "How tremendous is a trillion? If a trillion kids stood on top of each other, they would reach way, way, way beyond the moon." At the end of the book is a note from the author explaining the "arithmetic journey" taken along with the calculations.

Children are always intrigued by eggs and the mystery and wonder of eggs hatching. *Seven Eggs*[23] will inspire counting and predicting, surprise and delight. Their own ideas are often more creative than any text, however outstanding! After the book is shared, they will want to make their own Seven Eggs (or any number eggs) stories and pictures. A good book to interpret in movement and drama. And what is the song coming from each of the eggs? Sshhh. Listen!

I like to introduce a song or story with a wonderful thought to pass on to the children.

"There are more stories/songs/poems in the world than there are . . . snowflakes in a snowstorm!" We pause to appreciate the immensity of that image. Then we say, "Wow!"

I continue, "There are more stories/songs/poems in the world than there are . . . fish in the ocean!" Pause, then: "Wow!"

After a while, it gets to be a game the children love to play. Their suggestions about possibilities for imagining vast numbers of numbers are marvelous: leaves on trees, grains of sand on beaches, and raindrops in storms. After we enjoy sharing those ideas I pause dramatically and say, "Now we are going to celebrate *one* story/song/poem!"

But then, not to leave anyone smug, we talk about how even though all of us are sharing *one* story doesn't mean that when we tell other people *that* story, all the versions will be exactly alike. So we explore the idea of twenty-nine people telling friends and family the *one* story and now we have twenty-nine little variations of the same story! Not one to leave well enough alone, I always have to add, "If every one of us—that's thirty people, counting me—told one other person the story by nightfall, how many people would be enjoying that original one story?" Things just keep going!

Problem-solving talks Every day is rich with opportunities for children to solve meaningful problems that involve math concepts and skills. Be open to all the solutions and strategies they may want to try. Challenging questions like "How much?" "How high?" "How many?" "How tall?" "How shall we divide these supplies? Snacks? Treats?" "What time is it?" "How much time do we have left?" "What shall we do first?" "Let's vote on it! Who will be our counters?" "How many days until . . . ?" "How many do we have left?" and "How many children are absent?" are all-the-time kinds of questions. You are not limited to: "Oh, it's 9:15, math time, so here are our math questions!" Math is happening all the time.

Children's concerns extend beyond the immediate classroom. They care about neighborhood, environment, nature, poverty, and peace. Talking, listing ideas, numbering suggestions, and charting solutions are relevant activities for valid topics.

Poems Poems like "Two Friends" by Nikki Giovanni[24] featuring Lydia and Shirley and a number of things they share like "two berets," "two smiles," "one bracelet," and "one good friendship" are fun to recite. They inspire the children to compose and recite their own poems about numbers and friends.

Poetic books like *The Twelve Days of Summer*[25] are spin-offs of the popular song "On The First Day of Christmas My True Love Gave To Me." Accompanied by summery illustrations, the poetic text begins with "On the first day of summer/I saw down by the sea/a little purple sea anemone." Each day adds a sight, increases the numbers, and summarizes the preceding ideas until by the twelfth day we see "twelve gulls a-gliding/eleven waves a-crashing/ten dolphins playing/nine seals a-barking" until we end with "a little purple sea anemone." Children enjoy the challenge of cumulative language and images, and they always surprise adults with how quickly they "get it" and how excited they are to recite it and chant it. Their own original "Twelve Days of . . ." or "Five Days of . . ." or whatever variation they decide upon are creative and demonstrate comprehension.

In a room filled with the dynamics of learning and sharing, numbers can turn out to be your number one topic of conversation. From the schedule of the day to directions for a new game, to how many cups of water are needed for a recipe, numbers are part of everything you do together. Do not miss opportunities to correlate numbers with all areas of interest. Be a number dropper.

VISUAL ARTS TIMES

Discussions and preparations for visual arts activities are excellent ways to reinforce the learning of numbers:

> Each child gets three pieces of paper for this project.
> Art helpers, please give everyone in the class two sponges and one cup of water.
> When the paper helpers come around, boys and girls, please tell them if you want a large or small sheet of paper.
> Boys and girls, in this project we have two important steps: The first step is to draw your design; the second step is to cut it out.

Art activities and numbers are so interrelated that we are often unaware of their connections. How many colors shall we use? How many flowers, trees, houses, people, and dogs shall we draw? How big? How small? Shall we cover our whole paper or concentrate on one area? Shall we make a picture of one idea or of many? How many buttons shall we glue to our collage? What if we cut our paper shapes in half?

As you grow more aware of the many ways math relates to art, you and your students will enjoy a diversity of experiences, deeper and more successful because different areas of understanding and imagination are combined. As often as possible, help your children discover relationships. When you do, you find not only the rainbow but also the pot of gold (and the gold pieces to be counted).

A word of caution. When you integrate ideas, do it smoothly. If you are heavy-handed and overly directive, you will turn every delightful art activity into a math lesson. A natural observation linking numbers to art might be: "Jason, I like the way you drew those two balloons in the sky." Easy does it.

Numbers are designs Just as children are fascinated by the lines, curves, and angles of alphabet letters, so they are enthralled with the configurations of numbers and are eager to design them in sand, fabric, mud, paint, dirt, snow, glitter, crayon, and scrounged materials. Include numbers as often as you can on titles for pictures, posters, and murals. I enjoyed reading the names of paintings in the museum in Taiwan. Chinese artists were very literal in their titles, for example, "Three Bucks Swim on the Narrow Stream," or "Two Blossoms Bloom on a Cherry Tree Along a Mountain Trail."

Pictures of ones, twos, threes As you celebrate different numbers, you will find your students responding enthusiastically to the idea of painting or drawing a picture of a particular number of things. Beginning with the number one, children may suggest one flower, one tree, one sun, one moon, one person, one dog, one house, one bike, one circle, one triangle, and one dot.

We did this with a group of six-year-olds. Missy proudly showed her bright green picture with a tiny brown speck on one side of the paper. "One seed," she explained.

Montage or collage of ones, twos, and threes A variation of the above activity is to encourage the children to cut out pictures from magazines and catalogues that show the featured number. The children paste their pictures to a large piece of paper taped to a wall.

Pictures of ones and twos and threes After children demonstrate their comprehension of numbers, they enjoy the following challenge: "Wouldn't it be fun to make a picture that has *one* thing in it and, if you have room, somewhere else in the picture draw *two* or *three* similar things?" Always take time to talk about ideas first so the children's minds are simmering with possibilities.

Give your students the opportunity to create their own progression pictures and choose their own sets of things. Vary the challenge by deciding as a class the numbers and sets and asking the children to make their own interpretations.

The first graders planned winter pictures featuring one tree, two Santas, three reindeer, and four snowflakes. Even though the pictures had these elements in common, every one was an original interpretation.

Find the lucky number in the pictures "How many ways can you show your lucky number in your picture? We'll look at your picture and try to guess the number you have in mind! Write your number on the back of the paper."

Among the drawings of a group of second graders, Jackie's clown had four balloons in his hand and four bright buttons on his costume. Around him, four little circus dogs performed tricks. In one corner of the paper, Jackie had drawn a poster for the circus that read: "Circus, May 4."

Mystery pictures Don't we all perk up when we see books or illustrations featuring hidden images? Tell the children, "Somewhere in this picture, four monkeys are hiding. Can you find them? Look carefully. Do you see the six butterflies hidden among the flowers?" Children will want to create their own mystery pictures of hidden images.

Numbers and shapes *Brian Wildsmith's 1, 2, 3's*[26] intrigues young readers (and old readers!) with the imaginative use of basic shapes and colors related to numbers. Combining triangles, circles, and rectangles, Wildsmith arranges designs to correlate with specific numbers. Children enjoy cutting out basic shapes, coloring or painting them, and arranging them in their own number books or pictures.

Lois Ehlert's *Fish Eyes—A Book You Can Count On*[27] inspires the children to choose one idea—like fish, flowers, balloons, or stars—and change the qualities of the single idea along with the numbers. Ehlert's pages feature spectacular illustrations of such offerings as five spotted fish, which have very different designs than eight skinny fish! Every idea has a little nondescript fish that is added into each scene—"plus me makes 9." Encourage the children to be imaginative in creating their illustrated numbers, descriptive words, and clear images.

Numbers on houses and apartments With blocks, scrounged materials, paint, sticks, or clay, invite them to construct houses, apartment houses, mobile homes, tents, igloos, and so on. Add numbers to the dwellings. The children can draw or construct their own houses or apartments and write their actual numbers of their address on signs or on the pictures themselves.

Designer clocks and watches Choosing any color scheme, theme, or pattern, children have fun creating their own images of watches and clocks. Include numbers on the faces of the clocks and watches.

Necklaces, bracelets, and belts What materials are older than beads? Children make intricate color patterns with different-sized beads, counting numbers, enjoying the designs they create. I overheard an intense artisan in first grade mumbling over his beads like a mantra, "Five blue, three green, one white. Five blue, three green, one white. . . ."

Colorful class calendars Divide a large piece of paper into the number of days for the month. Print the numbers clearly and leave room in each space for a picture. Assign each child to one or more days. The children draw their own little pictures and tape or paste them to their box or draw directly on the box. Talk about the season, month, and any holidays or special events.

A variation of this idea is to give each child a sheet of paper with the number of a day on it. Collect the papers and with the children make a flip calendar featuring one day at a time. That day belongs to all the children, but it especially belongs to the child who illustrated it. Be sure all the artists sign their works.

Count-up/count-down picture charts Excellent commercial versions of this idea abound, but children's original works are even more colorful and interesting. With your children, make large number charts and draw or paste the items they suggest on each number row. Combine with colors and stories. Children usually become more imaginative when asked to think about related ideas. Think themes!

A memorable count-up chart that hung on the wall of a first-grade class appears on p. 473.

Encourage the children to create count-up/count-down charts on their own themes.

A third grade created an Autumn Count-Down Chart with bright illustrations of ten autumn leaves/nine clouds/eight squirrels/seven birds/six pumpkins/five kids playing/four piles of leaves/three trees/two bird nests/one football.

Children's original books of numbers The easiest way for children to make their own books of numbers is for them to do one number at a time, one page at a time, beginning with one. On page one, one thing is drawn; on page two, pairs of things or any two items are drawn; and so on to ten. When the children are finished, ask them to make a colorful cover for their book. Staple or tape the pages together, and you have a library of books about numbers.

When children are immersed in good books, they are stimulated to create their own wonderful books of numbers. Adding words, titles, lyrics, descriptions, questions, and riddles to the illustrations enriches the experience for readers as well as creators. Tasha Tudor's gentle touch in *1 Is One*[28] begins with "1 is one duckling swimming in a dish" and progresses to "20 is twenty geese flying toward the dawn." Invite the children to create as many numbers as they want. Celebrate them all! Any one of the ideas is a movement, music, or drama suggestion. Just use those magical words: "Show me! Show the idea!"

One Crow—A Counting Rhyme[29] varies the idea of a numbers counting book by adding the element of seasonal change. Keeping the same correlation between images and numbers from 1 to 10, Jim Aylesworth presents two seasons, summer and winter, two sets of 1 to 10 sequences and contrasting ideas. In summer, "Eight sheep nibble/in the summer green/Air in the meadow/smells sweet and clean." But in the winter, "Eight sheep huddle/in the winter white/Air in the meadow/

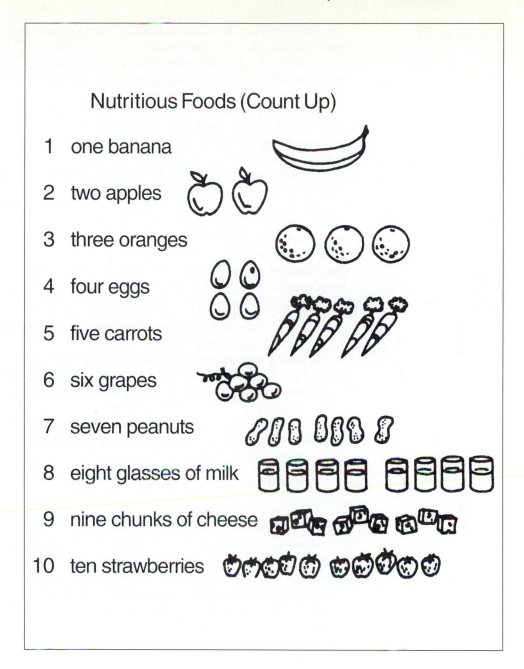

Nutritious Foods (Count Up)

1   one banana

2   two apples

3   three oranges

4   four eggs

5   five carrots

6   six grapes

7   seven peanuts

8   eight glasses of milk

9   nine chunks of cheese

10 ten strawberries

feels crisp and light." There is a lot to talk about, decide, and understand in these engaging combinations. The children's own imaginative images and numbers are exciting.

Sequential picture stories Most children are familiar with comic strips and the concept of following the action of a story from one space to the next. So many ideas can be expressed in sequence. Be sure to talk first and share ideas.

One group of first graders talked about chicks hatching, then depicted each step of the action in a series of boxes, comic strip style. They numbered the boxes as they went along:

(1) there is an egg; (2) inside, a little chick is growing; (3) the chick is growing bigger and bigger; (4) the chick wants to get out; (5) the egg cracks; (6) it cracks again; (7) the egg breaks; (8) here is the chick. Yaaaay.

First graders talked at length about what they did from the time they woke up until the time they went to bed at night. They listed activities such as brush teeth, get washed, get dressed, read a book, play a game, eat, and walk. On rolls of adding-machine paper, they chronicled their day and drew each scene in a box, beginning with getting up in the morning.

Follow any reading or story-telling session with a sequential picture summary.

Ten-speed "I Can" pictures Give the children large sheets of paper divided into ten spaces, and ask them to number the spaces from 1 to 10. In every space, draw a picture or paste on a cutout picture showing something they can do. Teachers can do ten things, too! Add words. Cover a wall with your pictures and watch your student's self-image and respect for others grow.

As this activity is shared, emphasize that all your students can do hundreds of things and that they are only selecting ten at a time. Encourage them to make as many sheets of "I can" ideas as they want to do, and remind them that they always have more to add.

Addition pictures Devote a whole wall to these ever-growing pictures. The children take turns contributing to the story as the plot thickens. Ideas for this activity are numerous. Here are a few suggestions for starters.

> A bird feeder with no birds. Each day a new bird arrives to eat at the feeder. Add a bird!
> A clown with no balloons. Each day a balloon is added.
> A beautiful ocean with no fish. Each day a different fish swims by.
> A barren plot of land. Each day a new plant begins to grow or a flower blooms.
> A zoo with no animals. Each day we add another animal.
> An ice-cream store with no ice-cream cones. Each day another ice-cream cone is shown.

Talk about your picture each day. Observe and count together as ideas are added.

Find fun ways for the children to discover when it is their turn to add to the picture. An easy way is to print the child's name on the board with the symbol next to the name. A complicated way is to ask the children to pick a piece of paper from a box or grab bag. On one of those pieces of paper, the idea is drawn. The child who picks the marked paper contributes to the class picture that day.

Special-number scrounge sculptures "How old are you? What's your favorite number? What's your lucky number?" Use questions such as these to prompt children to create a sculpture. "What can you make out of five (for your age) pieces of scrounge material?" Or "Your lucky number is seven. Pick seven things from the scrounge box and see what amazing shape you can make with them."

Remember, there are no rights or wrongs in this activity. Be accepting and encouraging of all products. It is the process that counts.

Mosaics, designs, and patterns Children are already fascinated by the shapes of things. They learn to distinguish variations and to recognize patterns, which are very important skills in understanding geometry! As they create repeating or progressive patterns for borders, wallpaper, notepaper, place mats, bulletin boards, and their own desk and tables, they discover numbers are as important as colors and shapes.

When they create tiles, mosaics, quilts, and sculptures of myriad materials, talk and thought are stimulated. "How many squares of yellow?" "How many circles of red?" "What colors are you using?" "I'll do mine in orange circles with one green triangle." "I'm going to use numbers in my design like 5! I like the shape of 5's!"

In projects with repeating patterns, whether the materials are paint, beads, braids, cut-out shapes, pasted-on designs, or fabric, the children are encouraged to think about number combinations as they select designs, colors, and textures.

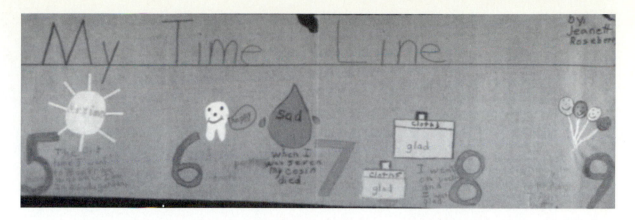

A second-grade class enjoyed a challenging art assignment. The magic number was ten, and combinations of numbers that added up to ten were encouraged. Some children strung bead necklaces, bracelets, and belts. One child was pasting color squares on a mosaic design. He chose an interesting combination of nine green squares and one yellow square. "Doesn't it look springy?" he asked.

When children design T-shirts, pins, quilts, drapes, belts, wallpaper, writing paper, greeting cards, calendars, weavings, wall hangings, invitations, masks, or totems, numbers can be featured. Be open to surprises.

MUSIC TIMES

Is music a mathematical experience? Think about all the connections. Music expresses time. It can be measured and counted. It has meter and scales. It has rhythm. It ticks. It tocks. It increases in volume and intensity—crescendo. It diminishes—diminuendo. It has vertical and horizontal lines. It has patterns and repeated sequences. Music helps children recognize relationships, number combinations, and the concepts of ordinal numbers.

Numbers are words in our mouth and lyrics for songs. After talking with a group of children about all the math references in the language of music, one of the boys offered this observation: "Music is noisy math!"

Songs and chants you can count on Children sing numbers as easily as they sing sounds and words. Each time they repeat or improvise lyrics to a familiar counting song, their knowledge of the numbers is reinforced.

After a workshop, a few teachers of young children pooled songs about numbers and counting that they had used successfully in their classrooms. Add to their list the counting songs that you have gathered from your own experiences.

"This Old Man"
"Three Blind Mice"
"Five Hundred Miles"
"Twelve Days of Christmas"
"Rock Around the Clock"
"Five Little Monkeys"
"Inchworm"

"Two Ducks on a Pond"
"My Hat It Has Three Corners"
"Hickory Dickory Dock"
"Sing a Song of Sixpence"
"Take Me Out to the Ballgame"
"One Elephant Went Out To Play"

Improvised numbers and counting songs Improvise familiar songs to use with numbers. The popular fingerplay "The Eensy Weensy Spider" evolved into an exciting counting experience for a kindergarten class. Instead of fingers, the children used their whole bodies to show the spider climbing up the water spout. They sang the song like this:

One eensy weensy spider climbed up the waterspout
Down came the rain and washed the spider out.
Out came the sun and dried up all the rain
And the eensy weensy spider climbed up the spout again.

Two eensy weensy spiders . . .

Three eensy weensy spiders . . .

The song continued until every child-spider was added to the song.

"Hickory Dickory Dock" became an imaginative numbers song when the children added such lines as:

The clock struck two
The mouse ran through . . .

The clock struck three
The mouse ran free . . .

"Three Blind Mice" is easily changed to "Four Blind Mice," "Five Blind Mice," and so on, until all your young mice show you how they run, sing, and count.

Second verse, same as the first A fine and fun way to help children understand ordinal numbers is to reinforce the idea of stanzas or verses. If you have ever been to summer camp, you know how children enjoy repeating lyrics, and more loudly each time.

A silly chorus that fits many songs helps children to sing more loudly while saying their ordinal numbers. I have heard it sung in many different melodies and rhythms, so feel free to create your own "loony tune" with your students. This is the chorus:

Second verse, same as the first.
A little bit louder and a little bit worse.

This idea has been used with such simple songs as "Row, Row, Row, Your Boat." Begin very softly, singing almost in a whisper. After the first singing, the chorus is chanted, and "Row, Row" is repeated, a little more loudly. With a group of four-and-a-half-year-olds, we stopped (for snacks) at this point: "Seventh verse, same as the first. . . ." By that time, the room was rocking with the volume of song.

Vary the activity by substituting the word "faster" for "louder," and begin your song very, very slowly. Try experimenting with the word "higher" for "faster"; begin in very low tones and move up the scale each time you repeat the song. Of course, as the children sing, they hold up the number of fingers that corresponds to the verse.

Count on musical signals and musical messages As we mentioned, many indigenous peoples used drumbeats to send messages. In numerous tribal cultures, only certain instruments were allowed to express specific feelings and ideas in ceremonies and rituals. Following these old traditions, your children will enjoy deciding on musical patterns for messages. Always encourage brainstorming. Which instruments shall we use for telling people to get ready for recess? To clean up? To sit quietly? A group of first graders chose five loud, slow drumbeats followed by five fast running beats as their signal to get ready for recess. Their musical signal for cleanup time was three claps of the cymbals, three counts of silence, and three more cymbal claps. It was dramatic!

Your students will work out interesting musical rhythms that will help language development, musical awareness, communication, and cooperation. Notice how their listening habits improve.

Unfortunately, concentration on numbers and counting often lends itself to tense situations. Avoid these at all costs. Enjoyment of the activity and encouragement of full participation are the most important values.

Solos, duets, trios, and quartets Children have no trouble understanding that solo means one, duet means two, trio means three, and quartet means four. Give the children many opportunities to be featured as soloists or in groups of twos, threes, and fours as they play rhythm instruments or sing songs. Keep the arrangements low-key, with the emphasis on experimenting, sharing, and celebrating rather than performing.

When children are familiar with the sounds of solos, duets, trios, and quartets, play records that feature these arrangements as background music in the classroom.

Add and subtract voices and instruments. Give the children number cards. When their number is indicated, they contribute the sound of their instrument or their voice.

A group of first graders sang and played "Twinkle, Twinkle, Little Star." They began in silence. Then, one by one, the children contributed the sweet sounds of rhythm instruments and singing voices until everyone in the room was participating.

Reverse the above suggestion. After all the instruments and voices blend, stop each sound one at a time until there is silence.

Use the words "add," "subtract," "none," "everybody," and "nobody" as you explain the activity. Children need different ways to experience the concepts of addition, subtraction, and zero.

Sets and sounds One of the most important mathematical concepts for young children to learn is the relationship of like objects, or a set. Organizing your rhythm band according to like instruments is an imaginative way to convey the idea of sets. "How many drums in our drums group? How many sets of bells in our bells group? How many pairs of rhythm sticks in our rhythm sticks group?" Each group can be defined by number, shape, color, and code.

Experiment with combinations of sounds as you begin with the smallest set of instruments and sets, one by one. Sets can play the same rhythm or individual rhythms. Children enjoy varying the experience.

Musical minutes How many seconds in a minute? Sixty tick-tocks. How many seconds in a half minute? Thirty tick-tocks. Count and clap, tap, stamp, snap, or sing thirty steady beats. Count and clap, tap, stamp, snap, or sing sixty steady beats. Count thirty seconds of silence, thirty seconds of sounds. Try ten silent counts, ten claps, ten silent counts, ten snaps, ten silent counts, ten foot stamps. What an interesting minute of sound and silence.

How far can we walk in a minute, keeping the rhythm of our time? "Our room is a minute away from the office," one kindergartner exclaimed after such a measuring experience. "It's sixty claps away," a friend chimed in.

What if our musical conductors keep a minute of time while the class sings or plays instruments? At the end of sixty counts, the music stops. We have just heard one minute of music. Now, let's hear half of that, thirty seconds of music. Let's count thirty seconds of silence. Then begin the music again. This is another concrete way children discover concepts of whole and half.

Whole, half, and quarter notes Teachers who play musical instruments have a ready resource, but you do not have to be a musician to introduce whole, half, and quarter notes to your young students. A whole note is held for four counts; a half note for two counts, and a quarter note for one count. Four bouncy quarter notes equal a whole note.

After the children have experimented with these notes in their own voices, they appreciate hearing well-known arias. Play excerpts and watch your students' amazement at the range and strength of the human voice. After one such experience, a class of second graders applauded Leontyne Price. "Gosh. She ran out of whole notes to hold," one of the children observed.

Correlate this activity with movement and art. A whole note is a long note; a quarter note is a short note. Show the duration of a whole note with bodies. Take a breath and expand arms, legs, chest, fingers, and head as far as a whole note carries you. How do short, choppy quarter notes make your body move? What if you combined whole notes, quarter notes, and half notes in body patterns?

How can you show the feeling of a whole note, half note, and quarter note on paper, in clay, and with paints? Six-year-old Andy was pleased with his colorful interpretation of the whole notes he listened to as he drew. "It's the feeling of a street that just goes on," he explained as he worked.

Symphony of sounds and numbers Children develop an appreciation of music as they become more aware of sounds and rhythms. Here is an example of a story created by a class of kindergartners demonstrating their knowledge of numbers combined with a feeling for the drama of sounds. All of the sounds described in the story were made with voices and instruments.

> Once upon a time it was a very quiet morning. Not a sound could be heard. Suddenly, one rooster crowed (a child crowed cock-a-doodle-doo). The rooster woke up three ducks who quacked (three children quacked). The ducks woke up four baby chicks who peeped (four children peeped). The chicks woke up two cows who mooed (two children mooed). Oh no! Ten birds in the tree started to sing (ten children "flapped their wings" and began to sing). Just then the cuckoo clock chimed seven times (everything fell silent as the cuckoo-children chimed). What a noisy morning (everyone at once)!

Experiment with variations of this activity.

Top ten favorites Write the titles of the children's ten favorite songs, from one to ten, on a colorful chart. Throughout the week, select songs from the list, calling them by number and title. "Angela, you're our song leader today. Which song shall we sing? Oh, good. Our number four song, 'Comin' Round the Mountain.'"

Reinforce understanding of ordinal numbers by suggesting such ideas as: "Boys and girls, we have time for only two songs today. Which song from our Top Ten list shall we sing *first?* Which shall we sing *second?*" A real accomplishment is to sing all ten songs, but not in order. "OK, you folks want to sing our number five song, 'Down in the Valley,' first. Here we go. . . . What's next?"

Vary the experience by having the children pull a number card out of a grab bag and find the corresponding song on the Top Ten list. Make a number wheel and spin the spinner to decide what songs to sing and in what order. Vote. As you continue to learn and enjoy new songs, your knowledge of songs increases. The children have many more to choose from and to vote on. You'll notice your Top Ten list of favorite songs changes often.

Birthday songs What else (two wonderful words for creativity) can we do about birthdays besides singing "Happy Birthday to You'?" Enjoy some delightful extras! (Isn't "extra" a mathematical concept?) If a child is five, the class sings a song with the number five in it (handed-down or improvised). The age of the birthday children is matched to a song in the class' collection with the same number. Today is Manuel's birthday. He's six. Find the Number Six song in our songbook. Let's sing it in honor of Manuel.

Rhythm leaders Sitting in a circle with an instrument for every child, each person has a turn to set a specific rhythm and have the other musicians pick up the rhythm and join in. The children must listen for clarity, tempo, accent, tone, and beat. The children's attentiveness and response to these musical challenges will delight you. They are happy to see how successful they are in being alert to rhythms (I call them rhythm catchers!) when they use their powers of concentration.

Songs that leave out words Children enjoy the playfulness of singing a favorite song and leaving out words as the song is repeated again and again. "There's a hole in the bottom of the ———"; "Row Row Row your ———," and "Row row ——— — —"; and "My hat it has three ———."

Songs that add and accumulate ideas Good old "Old MacDonald" is an example of a building song. As each stanza is added, the summary is repeated and added to. By the time the song is over, your children can be singing and moving to ducks quacking, lambs bleating, cows mooing, horses neighing, pigs oinking, chicks peeping, roosters cockle-doodle-dooing. . . .

One song—many variations Play with a familiar song! Challenge the children with such action-yielding questions as "How many different ways can we play and sing 'Take Me Out to the Ballgame'?" Brainstorm and experiment. The children will suggest speeding it up, slowing it down, making it louder, singing it softly, singing it bouncy, singing it boring, singing it with high notes, singing it with low notes, singing it holding every note, and singing it staccato. As the tempo, rhythms, and tone change the nature of the song, the children learn about speed and timing, about counts and pauses. Time the song when it's sung fast. Contrast that time with the song sung slowly. Play the song with many instruments. Play the song with one instrument. Play! Be open to discovery.

One world—many rhythms The patterns and rhythms of music from different cultures of the world are often very recognizable. Children learn and enjoy the steady, heartbeat rhythms of many Native American chants and songs; the samba rhythms originally from Africa and played throughout South America but mainly in Brazil; the Calypso rhythms of the Caribbean; the waltz rhythms from many cultures; the steady beat of disco; the improvised, often unpredictable free-spirited rhythms of jazz; the intricate, lightning-fast rhythms of East European folk music; and the steady strum of cowhand lullabies. Around the world we journey in the diverse and marvelous music of the human family. If you think math has no place in this spread of rhythms, enjoy reading this excerpt of a note explaining the music of Ravi Shankar.[30]

> Ravi Shankar presents this afternoon Raga in the slow khyal Gayaki-Ang (style of singing). The ascending structure is Pentatonic, omitting the second and sixth notes, with a komal (flat) third and a tivra (sharp) fourth. . . . The rhythmic cycle is Ada-Chautal (14 beats divided 2–4–4–4) which is usually slow and not commonly found in Drut Laya. . . .

Numbers and number patterns are found in the music of the world!

As you flip through the pages of this book, you will find many activities that involve counting and numbers. When children clap out the rhythms of their names and cities, they are counting beats and listening to the pulse of language. When children sing about one rabbit, one turtle, or one bird, they are imagining the idea of one. When you follow "Happy Birthday to You" with the lines "How old are you? How old are you? How old is Danny? How old are you?" you and your children are celebrating the most important numbers of all. And when you teach with an openness and willingness to play with familiar materials in new ways, you will discover musical activities too numerous to number.

MOVEMENT AND PLAY TIMES

Children are always playing numbers! In commercial board games, traditional favorite games, and improvised imaginative games, the language of math is constantly in use: "My turn!" "You had a chance!" "How much?" "It isn't fair!" "I only have three left!" "We're winning! We've got five and you've got two!" "I'll trade you." "What's the score?" "Who's on first?" "Strike three—you're out!" "I'm on foursies!" So much information is gained, so many concepts learned through the natural, playful work of children. They sort, collect, categorize, compare, measure,

add, subtract, recognize patterns, make predictions, solve problems, and build on what they know.

Listen to yourself talking. How much of our own conversations have to do with math? "What time are we going? Will we have enough time to . . . ?" "Make reservations for five for sure, six maybe." "What's your phone number? Zip code? Area code? Social Security number? Address?" "I'd like a half portion. I'm on a diet." "Let's split a pizza. You take the bigger piece." "I was only going ten miles above the speed limit!" "Imagine, a speeding ticket for $50!" "I got this book at the half-price sale. It was originally $25, and I bought it for $12.50!"

What does math have to do with movement? Let's carry our imaginary tape recorder into the gym where Marlene Robbins[31] is working out with the children. Here are some things you may hear her say as they talk together in the creation of dances, in the exploration of movement ideas. Listen for the math.

"Let's divide into two groups." "Half of you work on a movement pattern that features full turns. The other half come up with a movement pattern that features half turns. We'll take about ten minutes." "Let's speed up this movement. Do it double time." "Can we connect part one and part two of your dances with a smoother transitional movement?" "Let's cross the floor in diagonal lines, one at a time." "Partners! You only have five counts to be back in your space." "Well, let's see how we want these wonderful movement sequences to go. How many parts do we want in this dance? Which shall we do first? Is there a refrain or a chorus to repeat for extra emphasis?" "Let's all get into First Position." "Notice the way Group Three came up with an interesting four count right-left pattern. Let's all try it."

Stay with Marlene and the children for a while and you'll see one of their favorite movement games in action. The children sit in a large circle. One child dances in the center then chooses another child to join the dance. Then they both move out to choose two other children. Now the four dancers choose four more children to join in. It continues from eight to sixteen dancers. The next round completes the inclusion of all the children dancing together in the circle. Hands held, they circle clockwise and counterclockwise. Twenty-seven kids, one adult. Twenty-eight pairs of hands and feet. Fifty-six tapping feet. Fifty-six clapping hands.

As you enjoy the following suggestions, number the ways children demonstrate comprehension, language development, listening skills, problem-solving skills, risk-taking, responsiveness, and ownership.

Note: Young children observe and investigate their world through play and movement. That is what they *do.* When adults tell them to stop doing that because it doesn't fit into the learning categories adults carve, children repress these natural ways of encountering their worlds. Unless they have learned to fear making mistakes, to obey structured adult directions, young children will play and move on their own. Tune into the children. Nurture their sense of adventure, of joy, of openness, of curiosity, of playfulness. They are already whole!

Inventory games Imaginative teachers and their children count everything in their rooms: smiles, crayons, loose teeth, windows, buttons, circle shapes, eyebrows, desks, puppets, and shoes. As children gather such information, be playful. Turn yourselves into detectives, scientists, or newspaper reporters. Share your findings in radio and TV newscasts, newspaper articles, graphs, reports, songs, and mime.

Guessing games Children are eager to make predictions. They never refuse challenges such as the following:

Guess how many shells are in this jar.
Guess how many pebbles are in this box.
Guess how many leaves are on our tree.
Guess how many pages are in this book.

Their guesses indicate their knowledge of and familiarity with numbers.

Nancy Roberts has a winter guessing game full of delicious treats. She fills a round jar with marshmallows and, with her children's help, tapes a strip of black construction paper around the jar for a scarf, pastes on eyes, nose, and mouth, and thus transforms the marshmallow-filled jar into a snowman. Then Nancy asks the children to guess how many marshmallows are in the jar. The children write their guesses on a piece of paper with their names. After all the guesses are in, the marshmallows are counted.

The last time Nancy played this game, the children counted sixty-two marshmallows. The closest guess was fifty-eight. "Well, we counted the marshmallows and we counted the kids," Nancy explains. "We had 62 marshmallows and twenty-nine kids, plus one teacher. We talked about this and figured out that everyone could have two marshmallows. How many did we have left over? Two, of course, which we gave to two neighboring teachers." What a delicious division and subtraction problem.

Be alert to the many opportunities to invite children into the guessing games. When reading or telling a story to your class, pause, ask the kids, "I wonder how many wishes the Princess will get. Any ideas?" or "What do you think is going to happen next?" Unless children have learned to be afraid to express themselves because the environment is harsh and authoritarian, they will be very excited to be welcomed into this open-ended process.

Children set place value Ina Mayer's first graders enjoy discovering how place value works by making sets of sticks, tongue depressors, toothpicks, blocks, and straws. But one of their favorite ways is to use themselves. Each child stands for one unit of ten. When ten children are grouped together, Ina ties a loose string around them.

How many groups of ten children are in your class? If there are twenty-four children, you have two groups of ten children and four individuals with no strings attached.

Addition and subtraction in action Children need experiences that are more involving than workbooks and ditto sheets. Remember the word "action" in "subtraction."

Many children's games involve subtraction ("you're out") and can be unhappy experiences for the children who always seem to be eliminated first. Take the tension out of such games by improvising some with built-in safety belts.

If you start from nothing (zero) and add one idea at a time, every child is included without anyone choosing favorites. After all of the children have been included, the subtraction process begins with a tiny tap on the head as each child pulls back from the whole until no one is left.

Correlate this idea with animals, robots, airplanes, cars, clowns, rollerskates, and fire fighters. Whatever your class is studying, whatever your children's interests, turn them into a game of addition and subtraction.

Body machines of moving parts When you control all of your muscles and hold your bodies still, you are on zero. Now one part moves. Tap out a rhythm on a drum, tabletop, or tambourine. The children decide which part they want to move. Then two parts move. Each child has a different pattern. Then three parts move. Some children move two feet and one hand; Tarik moves two shoulders and one wiggly nose. Try to match the rhythm with the number of parts moving. Continue to five or six parts. Then turn on the body machines and move all the parts you can.

One at a time, each machine stops (gently touch each head) until no machine is moving.

Our magic-trick fingers Children are enthusiastic magicians. The best tricks need no props. Hide all fingers in fists. "Where are our fingers? Where did they go? They disappeared? How many fingers shall we make appear? Two!"

"Do you think you can do this incredible trick, magicians? What are the magic words? Abracadabra, peanut butter and jelly. Watch two fingers appear or I'll tickle you in the belly! (This is our students' favorite incantation.) Ta Da! Pow! Two fingers? What a trick!" Then three fingers appear, then four. Oh no! Ten fingers pop up!

Remember, magicians and teachers perform the best trick of all—changing something ordinary into the extraordinary. What is more ordinary than showing the fingers on our hands? Change the experience into magic fingers.

Number questions Louise Johnson's first graders[32] were kept on their ten toes because Louise constantly challenged them with such questions as: "Look at this picture. *How many* things can you see in it? I'll write all your ideas on the board" or "It's time for a round-robin story. When it's your turn, be ready to *add one idea* to the story. Here we go" or "What's your favorite number? Don't tell us, show us by doing something a certain number of times. We'll try to guess."

Ina Mayer also reminds her first graders about numbers in almost everything they do. "When we turn to page 41 in our book, I'll nudge: 'Hmmmm. How many tens in 41? How many ones?' We don't relegate math to a specific period of the day. We are always reminded of the ways math is part of our lives.

It's easy to get children moving and thinking with questions: "Can you demonstrate ten jumps? Nine jumps? Eight jumps? Seven jumps?" or "Let's act out the first part of this story. What came first?"

Number your exercises and dances Throughout the guides, improvised exercises and dances have been encouraged. As children design group and individual patterns, challenge them to decide such questions as: How many jumping jacks? How many sit-ups? What shall we do first? How can we combine the two ideas? How many times shall we repeat this pattern? What if half the class does exercise A and the other half does exercise B?

When children are constantly working with number patterns as part of their activities, their comprehension is enriched and their feelings of success are multiplied. Illustrate their ideas with words and pictures.

Weird recipes Numbers and recipes are inseparable. Nancy Roberts's first graders are familiar with recipes from easy cooking sessions to mixing science and crafts materials. She and her lively students enjoy playing with the idea of recipes.

How to Make a First Grader

1 cup giggles	1 cup fingernail polish
1/2 cup snakes	5 cups shoelaces
1/2 cup sugar	6 papers
1/2 cup worms	2 cups American flags
1/2 cup teeth	800 lunch boxes
1/2 cup butterflies	10 cups games
1 cup whales	5 cups chalk
3 cups songs	800 workbooks
1/2 cup hair	8,000 cups mud
2 books	800 pencils
1/2 cup shoe polish	

Mix well and enjoy!

"What the children really enjoyed in creating this recipe," Nancy explained, "was the chance to use big numbers like 8,000 and 800. Young children don't have many opportunities even to talk about those numbers."

Try working out recipes with your children for a goldfish tank, a toy box, a babysitter, a puppy, a zoo, a pet store, a birthday party, and a playground.

Birthday exercises How old is the birthday child? Seven! Seven-year-olds need movement presents in sevens. What special things can we do seven times each for our birthday child? Here are some of the suggestions made by thousands of children over the years.

7 claps	7 turnarounds
7 stamps	7 jumping jacks
7 kisses (throw kisses)	7 hops
7 spanks (spank the floor)	7 finger dances
7 cheers	7 jumps
7 smiles	7 blinks
7 waves in the air	7 kicks (kick legs out)

Another of the many variations of birthday celebrations and numbers is to ask the birthday child to choose the birthday number of exercises to be featured that day. Last Friday, Molly was five. These are the exercises she chose for her class to perform:

1. Run
2. Touch-toes
3. Tiptoes and stretch arms
4. Twists
5. Turns

We practiced the five exercises in order. Soon the children remembered them by number, so when we played lively music we simply called out: "Number one" and the children ran, "Number two" and the children touched their toes. Be playful. Rearrange the number patterns!

Add movement ideas to the birthday chart or card.

For Kelli's Fifth (5th) Birthday We Gave Her:

5 hugs
5 cheers
5 claps
5 laughs
5 funny faces

These Were Antonio's Birthday Exercises:

1. Run
2. Touch-toes
3. Tiptoes and stretch arms
4. Twists
5. Turns

Parades of numbers Children are always ready for a parade. Mix parades with numbers. Organize a parade of ones. Each child marches separately, one behind the other. The children can play instruments (real or imaginary), carry flags, twirl (imaginary batons), or just swing their arms.

After the fun of ones, you are ready for twos. Organize the parade with the children marching, prancing, and dancing two by two. As they enjoy the rhythm and life of the parade, they realize that twos are different from ones. Continue with parades of threes, fours, and so on.

Mix numbers with animals, TV characters, and story characters.

A parade of animals (everyone turns into a favorite animal as ones are featured)
A parade of Noah's Ark animals (animals in twos)
A parade of robot trios
A parade of four superheroes or superheroines
A parade of number groups of colors
A parade of number groups of shapes

Dances of numbers Encourage the children to dance by themselves, a company of soloists, each dancer experimenting with individual movement patterns in response to the music. Then quickly organize the children into partners. "Ladies and Gentlemen, here is the world-famous company of dancers dancing by twos!"

Three is a fine number for small circle formations. "Ladies and Gentlemen, before your eyes you will see a dance of threes. Three people in a dancing circle!" Start the music and watch the variety of movements your children improvise.

Your only limits in choreography are safety precautions. As long as the children are paying attention, following directions, and moving in response to music and idea, their dances are excellent. Plan for success. Keep challenging the children with new combinations, play a variety of music and rhythms.

Folk dances So many children miss out on the fun of enjoying basic folk dancing because their teachers feel unqualified to teach such movement styles. Young children naturally respond to any rhythmic music from anywhere. With encouragement and reassurance, they will (and please join them) keep the beat of any culture's music by clapping, tapping, bouncing, and jumping. We recently attended a concert by Pakistani traditional singer Nusrat Fateh Ali Kahn and his group. For most of the audience, the music was completely unfamiliar, but everyone clapped and bounced and many danced in the aisles.

When sharing easy-to-move-to music from cultures around the world, remember the simplicity of forms: the children can move as a whole circle or line. Move in one direction, then the other. The children can face the center of the circle and together move toward the center, then still holding hands, move backwards to create a wider circle. Children can take turns, one at a time, or two at a time, dancing in the middle of the circle while the others follow. Children can form two lines facing each other while two by two they take turns sliding or strutting down the center of the row. Children can dance by themselves in a group with others and then form small circles of threes or fours as a chorus. Lines, circles, partners, rows, and groups of soloists—play with the forms easiest for you and your children. Don't get so technical that the joy of the dance is squeezed out.

You'll hear yourself use numbers throughout—"Let's all slide around together," "Half of us will hop this way—half the opposite way." The children will have many wonderful ideas for choreography as they respond to the rhythms. Usually the music tells you what it wants you to do! One prekindergartner shouted the news, "We have to jump in the jumpy part!" Hang loose. Be open. Be ready to share and enjoy!

Moving moments How many seconds in a minute? Sixty. If I tap you sixty beats can you keep wiggling for one minute? Don't stop! Can you keep hopping for sixty beats? How many hops did you get in that minute? Can we keep walking for one minute? How far did we get? Let's try *half* a minute. How many beats? Right! thirty! Measure your time in jumps, jiggles, taps, and wiggles. What about . . . no one moves for sixty seconds! What a challenge![33]

Giant steps, baby steps "How many giant steps does it take to get you from your chair to the front of the room? How many giant steps do you need to cross the hall? How many giant steps from here to the office? How many giant steps take you around our room?"

How many baby steps do you need to get from your chair to the front of the room? How many baby steps do you need to cross the hall?" Experiment with half-giant steps. Correlate giant steps with whole notes and baby steps with quarter notes. This activity is a good way to help children discover interesting facts about numbers and fractions.

Fairy tales and folk tales are full of numbers How many wishes? How many billy goats? What are their sizes? How many little pigs? How many challenges for our hero/heroine? How many dwarfs? How many guesses? What are the three magic words? How many brothers? How many sisters? How many days in the journey? Our folk literature is packed with the importance of numbers. As you read to the children, note the significance of numbers. As you create your own original stories to show and tell to illustrate and write, be sure numbers are clearly highlighted.

Play dough In many children's improvised games and stories, money is featured. Jack is to sell the cow for coins. The miller's daughter is to spin the chaff into gold coins. When children play store, house, service station, garage, and fairy tales, money changes hands. Eavesdrop on their dialogue and you'll hear the language of making change, of addition and subtraction, of denominations (quarters, dollars, and pennies). Encourage expanded thinking. Without being heavy-handed you might suggest, "Oh, how much do these vegetables cost? Maybe this store needs some signs with that information." When play becomes real, such as play restaurants evolving into real restaurants (as described in previous chapters), you'll need real menus and real money. You'll need to make real change! And what will your class use the money for? Let's try to gather at least ten ideas! One more! Another one?

Countdown, blast off! Our space-age children know all about counting backwards from 10. Turn yourselves into rockets. Scrunch way down, close to the floor.

Slowly, gradually, stretch up. 10–9–8–7–6–5–4–3–2–1. Now you are on tip-top toes, arms to the sky. Blast off! Jump as high as you can.

Elevator going up, going down Counting up and counting down are part of playing elevator. Start at the bottom, as low as your body will go. Move slowly upward, stopping on each floor. When you reach the top, bodies are stretched to their tallest.

Uh-oh, the elevator is going down—tenth floor, ninth, eighth . . . first floor, when bodies are once again as low as possible.

Sequence stories A fine way to reinforce comprehension of ordinal numbers is to improvise stories and situations that feature a special order of events and characters. Talk times are the best inspiration for such experiences. If the children are interested in and excited about a topic, character, situation, or event, their ideas are charged with vitality.

Here are two examples of sequence stories that came from lively group discussions. Each activity was expressed in movement and mime. The children practiced ways to demonstrate each idea.

Some first graders talked about winter ideas. They decided to show a winter day in five movement improvisations.

1. Brrrrrrr. (The children hug themselves and shiver.)
2. Penguins are birds that live in snowy places. (The children move like penguins.)
3. Rub hands together to make them warmer.
4. Make snowballs and throw them.
5. Lie down and make snow angels.

The prekindergartners at one school had a big project. They went to the pet store to buy a pet with money they had earned from their *real* restaurant. There were so many different pets in the pet store that they had a hard time deciding which pet to buy, but when they saw the little black rabbit, their hearts melted. They named her Bruce, and she is their pride and joy.

The children made a movement story of their experience. All the children moved to all of the ideas.

1. The first animals we saw were the fish.
2. The second animals we saw were the puppies.
3. The third animals we saw were the snakes.
4. The fourth animals we saw were the turtles.
5. The fifth animals we saw were the birds.
6. The sixth animals we saw were the gerbils.
7. The seventh animals we saw were the rabbits.

The children enjoyed turning into each of the seven different animals and exploring their distinct movement patterns. These stories are easily expressed in pictures, poetry, posters, movement, and song.

Many counting books feature sequence stories that are easy to move to, play to, and interpret in drama and dance. For example, in *Snoopy's 1, 2, 3,*[34] Snoopy and a friend start out on a hike. Soon, they're joined by others, two at a time, three at a time, and so on. They have a wonderful day and then, two by two, three by three, they leave. At the end, it's just Snoopy. This is a fun "game" with which to bring everyone in. Watch what happens when everyone leaves.

In *The Sheep Follow,*[35] five cheery sheep are the constants in adventures that change on every page. No matter what else happens—geese waddling, butterflies flying, or cats walking along the fence—the sheep follow. Children can take turns playing the sheep, and the rest of the class can move like butterflies, ducks, cats, and so on. Add ideas. The children will want to create their own stories and pictures when they're inspired by such movement and drama experiences.

The old counting rhyme, "Over in the Meadow," is a wonderful example of sequences, numbers, progressions, accumulation mixed with movement, play, and drama. If you don't know it by heart, read (chant) it while the kids do it (show it!) The rhyme is featured in a book, *Over in the Meadow.*[36] Remember? "Over in the meadow in the sand in the sun/lived an old mother turtle and her little turtle one." Be sure every child is included in the poem. I rarely choose parts. We all take turns or together express the ideas. Keep it simple!

Count on nursery rhymes, cheers, raps, and chants Rhymes for young children are filled with numbers, for example:

One, two, buckle my shoe.
Three, four, shut the door.

A diller, a dollar,
A ten o'clock scholar,
What makes you come so soon?
You used to come at ten o'clock
And now you come at noon.

Baaa, Baaa, Black Sheep,
Have you any wool?
Yes, sir, yes, sir,
Three bags full.

(Change colors and numbers: "Baa, Baa Green Sheep . . . 5 bags full.")

Children know many cheers with their rhythmic counts and bouncy beats. Make up your own, be playful with numbers. "3 2 1—We're number one!" "From 10 to 1, we have fun!" "Gimme a 1—One! Gimme a 2—Two!" Accompany every count with claps or jumps.

Many of the raps making their rounds (of course, be selective) feature numbers in their text. Children enjoy creating their own number raps. Try some with times of day, with lists, with ordinal numbers. Here's an original kindergartner chant:

When I woke up at six o'clock
I first jumped out of bed.

Combed my hair, one-two-three.
Brushed my teeth, one-two-three.
Down the stairs, one-two-three
This is me! One-two-three.

Jump rope chants, bouncy ball games, and action games all feature numbers. Adapt any refrains for choreography, extended musical choruses, and drama. Add illustrations and original words. Always think *more!* Only time limits us.

"Eighteen Flavors," Shel Silverstein's delicious poem about ice-cream flavors, is another example of how much fun it is to count as you pretend to lick.

Eighteen Flavors

Eighteen luscious, scrumptious flavors—
Chocolate, lime and cherry,
Coffee, pumpkin, fudge-banana,
Caramel cream and boysenberry,
Rocky road and toasted almond,
Butterscotch, vanilla dip,
Butter-brickle, apple ripple,
Coconut and mocha chip,
Brandy peach and lemon custard,
Each scoop lovely, smooth, and round,
Tallest ice-cream cone in town,
Lying there (sniff) on the ground.[37]

Ask the children to name their favorite flavors. "Shall we make up our own eighteen flavors? How about twenty? Let's pretend to taste each one."

The bear facts Here is an example of how numbers can be included in celebrations and special events. Lynn Salem's first graders are bear-crazy. They fell in love with Winnie the Pooh and soon were in love with all bears. The children decided to have a weeklong celebration of bears. They collected poems, stories, and pictures about bears and learned all about different kinds of bears, including polar bears, koala bears, brown bears, and Pooh bears. They designed bear wallpaper, note cards, and story illustrations.

At the end of the week, the children had a bear party. To help them celebrate, they brought in toy bears from home. They counted all the bears in the room and all their books about bears. They made up songs about bears that included numbers.

One of the children, Katie, insisted on bringing *all* her bears to school that day. Her mom tried to discourage her: "Katie, you need just *one* bear, not all of your bears." But Katie paid no attention. She was busy covering her five bears in a straw basket. Katie's mother tried again: "Katie, I don't think you need to take five bears to the party. One will do, dear." Katie looked up at her mother with narrow eyes, her hand firm on her hip. She hissed, "I am so glad these five bears are sleeping and didn't hear you ruin the surprise of the party for them!"

A few more books we can count on to get you moving and playing Every theme is mathematical. Think numbers. Many books are at your fingertips to move you along. For example, Peter Sis's silly book, *Waving—A Counting Book,*[38] will have everyone counting, waving, and laughing as the story is enacted: "9 Girl Scouts waved at the school children. 10 joggers waved back at them." Joggers, tourists, Little Leaguers, police officers, and more characters join the wave of numbers and friendliness.

Circus Numbers—A Counting Book[39] will add excitement to any circus theme, with such brightly illustrated suggestions as "four jugglers" and "seven acrobats." Remember, circuses have *three* rings! How many exciting events are happening in each ring? In what sequence? Involving how many animals and characters?

Donald Crews's *Bicycle Race*[40] plays with colors, numbers, and racers, with the order changed on every page as different bikers move to the front, then fall behind. In the story, there are twelve bikers, designated by number and color. You could have two groups play the story at the same time. They could hold up their colored number cards as different sequences are called: "three, ten, two, twelve, seven, five, eight, one, eleven, four." Improvise your own numbers and order after the story is interpreted. The children will enjoy designing their own bikers, colors, and numbers.

A dialogue-rich book, *Nine Ducks Nine,*[41] is a silly subtraction story involving nine ducks and a threatening fox. Each page is sparked with dialogue bubbles with remarks such as, "We'll get that fox" or "We've got a plan." This is a delightful story for the children to play along to as you read. Let them interpret and add to the action and the natural, likable dialogue.

One Good Horse—A Cowpuncher's Counting Book[42] is an example of enriching a theme with words, images, and numbers. From one good horse through the expanding scenes to a hundred head of cattle, the progressions are clear and exciting. Play western music—banjos and guitars—to accompany the action.

How many good books are there for you and your children? Too many to count! Enjoy the gathering.

We have so many pages (count them) and so much time (measure it) and too many ideas (countless) that only a few are possible to share. As I travel the country, I see so many enriching works in progress as the children learn in the *best* ways. For example:

Counting their days From day one in school, they mark walls, charts, and calendars. Some schools celebrate on the twenty-fifth school day, others the fiftieth and many, the one hundredth.

Collecting things in hundreds This is popular and effective. Children bring in their collections of 100 things. They label their collections, talk about them, illustrate them, and display them. The exhibits are astonishing in their variety and originality. Imagine how many things that could be collected in hundreds!

Measuring journeys I have seen models of the Mayflower crossing a graphed ocean, marking the days as it floats along on mural waves until it comes to America. Count on history and story books to provide you with information on how long journeys took. Such excitement when the ship landed!

There are so many more activities that include numbers, only a few of which can be mentioned here. These are: playing restaurant, store, post office, and house; playing games with dice and wheels of numbers; playing measuring games, guessing games, comparing games, and adding games; playing card games, bingo, hide and seek, and scavenger hunts (with number clues); and playing sort the pumpkin seeds, apple seeds, and orange seeds.

When we introduce our young children to the world of numbers, let us do it with a sense of wonder.

As we teach our children the important rules of measuring with yardsticks and rulers and counting with calculators and computers, let's be sure they have the fun of using french fries, inchworms, and, yes, nostrils, too!

CLASSROOM VISITORS AND FIELD TRIPS

Just as every classroom visitor is a language experience, so every visitor is a math experience as well. What time, what day will the visitor arrive? How long is the session? How many questions should we have ready for our guest? Which welcome song shall we choose to greet our guest? What do you think will happen first? Let's see, we have twenty-one children in our class, so that's twenty-one different thank

yous for our guest. Oh, right. We have one person absent. So how many thank-you papers shall we give out?

Classroom Visitors

In case you are running out of ideas, here are a few:

Folk dancers Most communities have resource people who share folk dances from different cultures. Be sure to ask such guests *not* to stress perfect form and style with the children. This should be a relaxing, enjoyable time with clearly conveyed and illustrated directions that yield immediate success and fun. Numbers play an important part in such instructions. "Ten little runs to the right, ten little runs to the left."

Cheerleaders Middle schools, high schools, and colleges will send along their pep leaders or cheerleaders to visit schools and share a few simple cheers with the children. Ask them to emphasize how important it is for them to be attentive listeners and good counters. "Are you ready? Three–two–one—GO!" They are precise and to the count! Your children will want to create their own cheers.

Computer facilitators Our high-tech kids need no introductions to the world of computers and calculators. They are fascinated by new programs, exciting combinations of ideas, and the newest technology. Remind the children that computers are the invention of the human mind.

Family and community members Whatever their skill or interest, people can add the component of numbers-awareness with validity. Shopping, car pooling, public transportation, schedules, allowances, budgets, trips, savings, scores, categorizing, sorting, and selecting: children see that in daily life numbers play a significant role.

Folk singer These visitors use numbers to introduce songs: "For my first song . . ." "Today, I'd like to sing ten songs with you." Suggest that your guest include songs that feature numbers.

Storytellers Without being told, storytellers usually know that children are more attentive when they hear numbers as part of the tales. Ears perk up to hear about "the three promises," "the four challenges," and "the six brothers." Most stories have words or phrases that have magical powers when they are spoken or sung a number of times. Be sure the children join in the repeating of such chants.

Stamp collectors or coin collectors Collectors usually organize their materials nicely. Children can easily see which countries are most often represented. They can count the stamps or coins and note the numbers on their faces.

Magicians Be sure to ask your local magician to perform tricks featuring numbers, especially card tricks. The sharpness of your students' observations and guesses will surprise you.

Artisans and craftspeople When painters, potters, weavers, designers, sculptors, and woodcarvers visit your room, concepts of sequence are usually part of their discussion of methods and techniques. It is to be hoped that visitors give your students and you a chance to participate in the creative process. If a guest is unaware of communicating a sequence clearly, politely ask such questions as "What shall we do first?" and "After we place our colors on the table, what comes next?"

Plumbers, mechanics, accountants, bus drivers, doctors, nurses, social workers, bank tellers, cashiers, and clerks all work with numbers and, as visitors, can help improve children's knowledge about and interest in numbers. Do not hesitate to stop the letter carrier, cook, secretary, messenger, and custodian in the school and invite them into your room to share some of their practical experiences.

Field Trips

Trips to such places as restaurants, supermarkets, clothing stores, airports, train stations, post offices, design studios, toy stores, libraries, and greeting card shops provide opportunities for children to learn number concepts through prices, cash registers, menus, zip codes, scales and measurements, credit card numbers, transportation schedules, dates, times, aisle and shelf numbers, addresses, and the exchange of money.

Numbers and counting walk Take a walk and count cars, houses, trees, colors, people, buses, bicycles, and dogs. What a sensational chart or graph you will have when you compile your counts! Take notes and write down numbers you see on your walk: numbers of houses, speed limit signs, license plates, posters, mailboxes, calendars, and so on.

Pet stores In addition to all the other pleasures of this experience, count the different kinds of pets you see. "Aren't the puppies cute? Let's count them. I wonder how many there are in that cage. What do you guess? Let's see, are there more hamsters than guinea pigs? Let's count them and find out."

The zoo As you admire the variety of animals with your children, take notes on how many of each kind you see, for example, the number of brown bears, white bears, and black bears. What did we see the most of?

Pizza place Fractions at work!

Office building Most office buildings have directories in the lobby that are filled with floor, room, and telephone numbers. The children ride the elevator and watch the numbers change. Mail and messages are delivered daily. The switchboard operator fascinates young children with an array of flashing buttons.

Athletic teams or cheerleaders in practice Your local high school or college will be honored to have you and your students as guest observers while their teams practice. Football fields have yard lines, uniforms carry numbers, and scores are numbers.

Science laboratory If there is no government or commercial science research lab in your area, the local high school or college offers this resource. Children are fascinated by the skill and concentration of labworkers because of the need for accurate observations and careful measuring and recording.

Dance group in rehearsal Check the Yellow Pages for dance teachers and studios, or find out if a community dance group is rehearsing for a program. As the children watch the dancers mark time, movement, and place, they realize how important numbers are to the total effort. Ask the group to share a dance with the children.

A bank What better place to see numbers in action than at a bank? Checks are deposited, bills counted, and adding machines punched. When they return to the classroom, children will want to make paper money and play bank.

Computer center As we know, our children live in a computerized society. Numbers, letters, and words flash instantly when buttons are pressed. Children are fascinated by the speed, complexity, and excitement of computers. They need to be reminded that computers are the creation of the inventive human mind, the most dazzling computer.

Wherever you go, encourage children to make careful, meaningful observations. Ask such questions as How many? How much? How big? What kind? Which is the smallest? and Who has the most?

IT ALL COMES TOGETHER

As I write this, I am looking at my bulletin board, which holds a quotation from John Muir on a postcard: "When we try to pick out something by itself, we find it hitched to everything else in the universe."

This is a fitting reminder as Chapter 13 (my mother's lucky number) comes to an end.

I have two examples of such synthesis to share. They come from the same school. One involves a kindergarten class, and the other involves everyone in the school. Let's start with the kindergarten class.

Marilyn Cohen and her kindergartners at Bet Shraga Hebrew Academy[43] talked about the importance of and the taste of fruit as part of their nutrition study. The discussion led to the question: "Which is your favorite fruit?" After the children named all the kinds of fruit, Marilyn suggested that the next day, they bring in a piece of their favorite fruit. Assorted fruit would be available in case the children forgot or were unable to bring in their own. The next day Marilyn spread out her handmade floor graph labeled with pictures and words describing many of the fruits the children described. Delighted, the children had no problems finding the column that described their fruit and placing their fruits in the clearly marked spaces.

In a little while, the floor graph was filled with the children's favorite fruits. As they admired the graph, they talked about which fruit was chosen the most often and how many more children chose apples than bananas, and so on.

"We can't leave the graph on the floor," Marilyn said. "How can we hold onto this important information?" The children decided that they could each draw a picture of their fruit on a separate paper; the numbers of papers would match the numbers of actual fruit. Of course, this evolved into a wall graph, to which the children added pictures and their own names to the fruit columns.

The children sang improvised songs like "Is your favorite fruit an apple? Mine is too. . . . Is your favorite fruit a banana? Mine is too. . . ."

They made a fruit salad, counting, cutting, discovering fractions, making patterns, and sharing the fruits of their labor. They remembered how fruits give energy and are full of vitamins. They demonstrated how energetically they could do their exercises and dance. That day, they created fruit salad poems and pictures.

The second event (series of events) I want to share has to do with kids caring. Around the country, in every state, city, and town, we have great evidence that children are compassionate and altruistic. We need to give them numerous opportunities to practice empathy and concern for others. The K–8 children in Bet Shraga were reminded daily of hunger in America. This one Thanksgiving season, teachers and children decided to pool their ideas and efforts to really reach out to others. Every child was given a paper turkey and asked to do meaningful chores at home to earn money to cover the turkey with coins.

Even the youngest children worked to earn money (many pennies), which was taped to their turkeys. Counting and sorting all the coins was a monumental job for the children. Each class did its own tallying. Their turkeys were tallied with the others. The children excitedly announced the grand total: $380 to be contributed to a local food pantry.

Talking with the social agencies who were in touch with people living through hard times, the children learned that there were many families that were going into the holiday season with meager supplies. The children and teachers decided on sixteen specific categories of need, such as soup, vegetable, macaroni, and personal toiletries. Every child drew a number that corresponded with one of the sixteen items. As the items were brought into school, the children sorted them and counted them. Each class decorated a large cardboard box with designs and colors. Greeting cards were written and illustrated but signed only "From a friend" and included in the boxes. The children of the school filled more than twenty boxes with sixteen different items in each one. They were given to twenty families in time for the holidays.

Our wonderful children are caregivers and caretakers! They are always ready to share. They make their learning count as they count their blessings, multiply blessings, adding to the lives of others, who are connected to us, one to the other.

NOTES ❤

1. Carl Sandburg, "Arithmetic," *The Complete Poems of Carl Sandburg*. New York: Harcourt Brace Jovanovich, 1960, p. 39.
2. Theodora Kroeber, *Ishi in Two Worlds*. Berkeley, CA: University of California Press, 1961, pp. 144–146.
3. Caryn Miko Falvey teaches at Poquonock Elementary School in Windsor, Connecticut. Caryn was one of a hundred teachers in the country to receive the Sallie Mae First Year Teachers Award for Excellence 1990–91.
4. National Council of Teachers of Mathematics, *Commission On Standards for School Mathematics: Curriculum and Evaluation Standards for School Mathematics*. NCTM, 1906 Association Drive, Reston, VA 22091.

5. Patte Barth's comments were reprinted in "How Kids Learn" by Barbara Kantrowitz and Pat Wingert, *Newsweek*, April 17, 1989, p. 51.

6. Jane C. Pelmutter, Lisa Bloom, and Louise Burrell, "Whole Math Through Investigations," *Childhood Education* (Association for Childhood Education International). Fall 1993, pp. 20–24.

7. Howard Gardner, *Frames of Mind*. Tenth anniversary edition, 1993. New York: Basic Books.

8. Ron Brandt, "On Teaching For Understanding: A Conversation with Howard Gardner." *Educational Leadership* (Association for Supervision and Curriculum Development), April 1993, pp. 4–7.

9. Louise Bogart is Associate Professor of Education and the American Montessori Society director of Early Childhood Programs at Chaminade University in Honolulu. The project described happened at Kalaheo School, Kauai.

10. Fred M. Newman and Gary G. Wehlage, "Five Standards of Authentic Instruction," *Educational Leadership*. Association for Supervision and Curriculum Development, April 1993, pp. 8–12. The theme of the April issue was authentic learning.

11. Ibid. P. 8.

12. Ken Goodman, *What's Whole in Whole Language?* Portsmouth, NH: Heinemann, 1986.

13. Carol Price shared ideas with children as a teacher and principal in the Worthington, Ohio, public schools. She is now principal of Colonial Hills School. See Mimi Brodsky Chenfeld, "Flamingos in the Bathroom, Love in the Classroom," *Phi Delta Kappan*, January 1993, pp. 413–414 for more about Carol, teachers, children, and flamingos.

14. Lynn Salem measured children at Immaculate Conception School in Columbus, Ohio. She now teaches at Thomas Elementary School in Dublin, Ohio. Lynn and Josie Steward create little books for beginning readers available from Seedlings Publications, 4079 Overlook Drive East, Columbus, OH 43214.

15. Fran Avni travels the country singing with and to children. Write to Lemonstone Records, P.O. Box 607, Cote St. Luc, Quebec, Canada H4V 2Z2.

16. Maurice Sendak, *One Was Johnny*. New York: Harper & Row, 1962.

17. Anne Rockwell, *Willy Can Count*. Boston: Little, Brown, 1989.

18. Misumasa Anno, *Anno's Counting Book*. New York: Crowell, 1977.

19. Ina Mayer played "dumb" with children at Olde Sawmill Elementary School in Dublin, Ohio. She now teaches at Daniel Wright Elementary in Dublin.

20. Nancy Roberts and her children conducted these surveys at Immaculate Conception School in Columbus. Nancy now teaches at Thomas Elementary School in Dublin.

21. Ken Gillies teaches at McGirr Elementary School in Nanaimo, British Columbia.

22. David Schwartz, illustrated by Steven Kellogg, *How Much Is a Million?* New York: Lothrop, Lee and Shepard, 1985.

23. Meredith Hooper, illustrated by Terry McKenna, *Seven Eggs*. New York: HarperCollins, 1985.

24. Nikki Giovanni, "Two Friends," *Spin a Soft Black Song*. Illustrated by George Martins. New York: Farrar, Straus and Giroux, 1985, Sunburst edition, p. 25.

25. Elizabeth Lee O'Donnell, illustrated by Karen Lele Schmidt, *The Twelve Days of Summer*. New York: Morrow, 1991.

26. Brian Wildsmith, *Brian Wildsmith's 1, 2, 3's*. New York: Franklin Watts, 1964.

27. Lois Ehlert, *Fish Eyes—A Book You Can Count On*. San Diego: Harcourt Brace Jovanovich, 1992.

28. Tasha Tudor, *1 is One*. Chicago: Rand McNally, 1956.
29. Jim Aylesworth, illustrated by Ruth Young, *One Crow—A Counting Rhyme*. New York: Lippincott, 1988.
30. This excerpt is from the notes on the album, *Portrait of a Genius—Ravi Shankar*. World Pacific Records, Hollywood, CA.
31. Marlene Robbins is a movement specialist on the Arts Impact Team at Indianola Alternative Elementary School and Reeb Elementary School in Columbus, Ohio. Jay Brand, Sharon Sazdanoff, and Jim McMahon are the three other members of the team.
32. Louise Johnson taught many lucky children in Hilliard, Ohio, for many years.
33. See Mimi Brodsky Chenfeld, "Moving Moments for Wiggly Kids" reprinted in *Teaching in the Key of Life*. Washington, DC: National Association for the Education of Young Children, 1993, pp. 21–26.
34. Nancy Hull, illustrated by Charles Schulz and Art and Kim Ellis, *Snoopy's 1, 2, 3*. Racine, WI: Western, 1987.
35. Monica Wellington, *The Sheep Follow*. New York: Dutton, 1992.
36. David Carter, *Over in the Meadow—An Old Counting Rhyme*. New York: Scholastic, 1992.
37. Shel Silverstein, "Eighteen Flavors," *Where the Sidewalk Ends*. New York: Harper & Row, 1974, p. 116.
38. Peter Sis, *Waving—A Counting Book*. New York: Greenwillow, 1988.
39. Rodney Peppe, *Circus Numbers—A Counting Book*. New York: Delacorte, 1969.
40. Donald Crews, *Bicycle Race*. New York: Greenwillow, 1985.
41. Sarah Hayes, *Nine Ducks Nine*. New York: Lothrop, Lee and Shepard, 1990.
42. Ann Herbert Scott, illustrated by Lynn Stewart, *One Good Horse—A Cowpuncher's Counting Book*. New York: Greenwillow, 1990.
43. Marilyn Cohen teaches at the Bet Shraga Hebrew Academy of the Capital District in Albany, New York. The children at Bet Shraga join with children the country over to reach out to others. They need many opportunities to say, "Count me in!"

BOOKS FROM MY KNAPSACK FOR CHILDREN ♥ ♥

Bang, Molly. *Ten, Nine, Eight*. New York: Morrow, 1983.
Blumenthal, Nancy. *Count-a-Saurus*. Illustrated by Robert Jay Kaufman. New York: Macmillan, 1989.
Bourgeois, Paulette. *Too Many Chickens!* Illustrated by Bill Slavin. Boston: Little, Brown, 1990.
Charlip, Remy, and Miller, Mary Beth. *Handtalk Birthday: A Number and Story Book and Sign Language*. New York: Four Winds, 1987.
Christelow, Eileen. *Don't Wake Up Mama!* New York: Clarion, 1992.
Clements, Andrew. *Mother Earth's Counting Book*. Illustrated by Lonnie Sue Johnson. Saxonville, MA: Picture Book Studio, 1992.
Fleming, Denise. *Count*. New York: Henry Holt, 1992.
Garne, S. T. *One White Sail—A Caribbean Counting Book*. Illustrated by Lisa Etre. New York: Simon and Schuster, 1993.
Giganti, Paul Jr. *Each Orange Has Eight Slices*. Illustrated by Paul Giganti, Jr. New York: Greenwillow, 1992.
Halpern, Shari. *Moving from One to Ten*. Illustrated by Shari Halpern. New York: Macmillan, 1993.
Hartman, Gail. *As the Crow Flies: A First Book of Maps*. Illustrated by Harvey Stevenson. New York: Bradbury, 1991.
Haskins, Jim. *Count Your Way Through Russia*. Illustrated by Vera Mednikov. Minneapolis: Carolrhoda Books, 1989.

Hopkins, Lee Bennett. *It's About Time.* Illustrated by Matt Novak. New York: Simon and Schuster, 1993.

Kitchen, Bert. *Animal Numbers.* Illustrated by Bert Kitchen. New York: Dial, 1987.

Lindbergh, Reeve. *There's a Cow in the Road.* Illustrated by Tracey Campbell Pearson. New York: Dial, 1993.

Linden, Ann Marie. *One Smiling Grandma.* Illustrated by Lynne Russell. New York: Penguin, 1992.

Lobel, Arnold. *Uncle Elephant.* New York: HarperCollins, 1981.

McMillan, Bruce. *Eating Fractions.* Photographs by Bruce McMillan. New York: Scholastic, 1991.

Medearis, Angela. *Picking Peas for a Penny.* Illustrated by Angela Medearis. New York: Scholastic, 1990.

Peek, Merle. *Roll Over! A Counting Song.* Boston: Houghton Mifflin, 1981.

Pinczes, Elinor. *One Hundred Hungry Ants.* Illustrated by Bonnie MacKain. Boston: Houghton Mifflin, 1993.

Rochlin, Joanna. *Musical Chairs and Dancing Bears.* Illustrated by Laure de Macharel. New York: Henry Holt, 1993.

Sheppard, Jeff. *The Right Number of Elephants.* Illustrated by Felicia Bond. New York: Harper & Row, 1990.

Sloat, Terri. *From One to One Hundred.* New York: Dutton, 1991.

Tryon, Leslie. *1 Gaping Wide-Mouthed Hopping Frog.* Illustrated by Leslie Tryon. New York: Macmillan, 1993.

Wallwork, Amanda. *No Dodos—A Counting Book of Endangered Animals.* Illustrated by Amanda Wallwork. New York: Scholastic, 1993.

Voake, Charlotte. *First Things First.* Boston: Little, Brown, 1988.

Wellington, Monica. *All My Little Ducklings.* New York: Dutton, 1989.

Weston, Martha. *Bea's 4 Bears.* New York: Clarion, 1992.

Yolen, Jane. *An Invitation to the Butterfly Ball—A Counting Rhyme.* Illustrated by Jane Buskin Zalben. Homedale, PA: Boyd Mills, 1979.

BOOKS FROM MY KNAPSACK FOR TEACHERS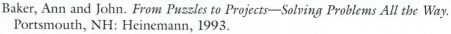

Baker, Ann and John. *From Puzzles to Projects—Solving Problems All the Way.* Portsmouth, NH: Heinemann, 1993.

———. *Raps & Rhymes in Math.* Portsmouth, NH: Heinemann, 1991.

Baratta Lorton, M. *Mathematics Their Way.* Menlo Park, CA: Addison Wesley, 1976.

Bodenhausen, J. N., Denhart, A., Gill, M., et al. *Thinking Mathematics: Volume 1, Foundations.* Washington: American Federation of Teachers, 1993.

Burns, Marilyn. *About Teaching Mathematics: A K–8 Resource.* New Rochelle, NY: Cuisenaire Company of America, 1991.

Gill, A., and Grover, B. W., eds. *Thinking Mathematics: Volume 2, Extensions.* Washington: American Federation of Teachers, 1993.

Stoessiger, R., and Edwards, J. *Natural Learning and Math.* Portsmouth, NH: Heinemann, 1992.

Weiss, Harvey. *Maps: Getting from Here to There.* Boston: Houghton Mifflin, 1991.

Whitin, David J., and Wilde, Sandra. *Read Any Good Math Lately? Children's Books for Mathematical Learning.* Portsmouth, NH: Heinemann, 1992.

Postscript

Aminah Robinson, a gifted artist you met earlier in the book who is such an inspiration to all who know her, describes herself as "a person walking." This book is like a journey, and we are walking and talking together along the way. For those who may miss the walk, I am mailing you the notes from the journey.

Even as I walk to the mailbox to drop in these notes, I am thinking of important things to add, last minute reminders, advice, and nudges! That's why we have postscripts.

One thing I forgot to include: Jane Johnson and Jean Griffith's letter to families explaining philosophy, sharing information, and requesting specific cooperation in enriching the education of their children. These kinds of letters and conversations, from school to home and back again, strengthen the "ties that bind." It is not enough for us to develop meaningful, challenging, life affirming, learning experiences for the children. It is not enough for us to talk only among ourselves. We have important stories to tell the families and the community. They are our partners in this most sacred and noble endeavor.

Most families want what is truly best for the children. They need to be informed and persuaded. They need to see the wholeness of whole language, to be convinced of the value of a truly integrated, multicultural curriculum where themes and people connect. They need to understand how skills are best learned within contexts of relevancy, not in isolation or related to nothing except a schedule. Don't keep the good news to yourself. Communicate! When families and community members understand *what* you are doing and *why* you are doing it, your support system will widen.

An excerpt from Jane and Jean's letter to the families of Deer Run Elementary School, Dublin, Ohio, will give you an idea of the valuable information we must share:

> . . . Never let the child's reading time lead to frustration. Do small positive sessions each day with some "reading to" and "reading with" time, and together we will find success. Give an abundance of praise. If there are occasions to write letters, make grocery lists or write "love" notes to family members, this reading–writing activity is great, too . . . .
>
> We're looking forward to our working TOGETHER to make all of the whole language experience positive for young [children]. The Bear's Den is a very happy place and we are glad to be working with your child . . . Thank you for your help at home . . . .

On my way to the mailbox, Rose Stough called to share a poignant telephone call. One of her former third graders, now nineteen years old, phoned her. He told her that when he watches television and sees parents and grandparents reading stories to kids, he feels very sad.

"No one ever read to me when I was a kid," he told Rose.

As he watched the program feeling more and more deprived, he remembered how in third grade Rose read to the children every day. He told her, "My happy childhood memories are when you read to us."

His phone call was a way to thank her.

Our days as teachers are packed with little things that may not appear on the pages of our planning books. Sometimes those little things are the most meaningful, deeply appreciated, and remembered of all our big activities, projects, and programs.

Rose said, "We touch children's lives in ways we will never know."

Communicating the idea of creative education is *not* easy. In the name of creative education, I have seen creativity dittos, whole language exams, and programs labeled "peak experiences" (so much for spontaneity and serendipity). I have seen agendas written on chalkboards: 1:30 PM—Surprise Story—*The Little Red Hen*. So much for surprises! We may title it, label it, proclaim it, broadcast it, and schedule it but that doesn't necessarily mean we *do* it!

And what is *it*? Although over a decade has passed since the publication of the first edition of this book, I have never heard a more beautiful explanation of creative education than that of Dr. Herb Sandberg, beloved professor, storyteller, story lover, kid lover, from the University of Toledo. He, too, was searching for ways to explain creative education and growing more frustrated by the hour.

Finally, like receiving a gift, he remembered the story of "The Nightingale," by Hans Christian Andersen. In that story, you may remember, the nightingale with the sweet voice is replaced in the emperor's palace and heart by a shiny, bejeweled, artificial nightingale. The mechanical bird is of the brightest colors; its voice is almost as lovely as that of the banished nightingale. Whenever the emperor wants to hear its music, it automatically performs for him. Everything is fine until the emperor gets sick. Nothing and no one can cure him. He calls for his mechanical nightingale, but it is broken. Death sits on the bed of the emperor. Suddenly, the most beautiful, sweet, pure sound is heard—the song of the real nightingale so powerful that even Death is moved and leaves the emperor. The emperor is cured.

Herb shares this metaphor: "Too many of our children have never heard the song of the real nightingale!"

Creative teaching means helping our children and ourselves listen with hearts and minds to the songs of the real nightingale, who sings of the beauty of poetry, literature, music, visual arts, dance, and drama. That nightingale sings of the excitement of learning and discovery; its song is the song of wonder.

If we listen to the song of the real nightingale, we will help our children develop lifelong love affairs with learning, gathering treasures to last for years to come that they will cherish and remember. If we listen only to the mechanical bird, we will become disoriented, enticed by the glitter of mechanical marvels and seduced by methodology and strategies.

All of our children are waiting to learn in loving communities where the song of the real nightingale is the music in the air they breathe. Soon, Callie Rose, Len the Muffin Man and Kimani will walk into your room along with thousands of their classmates. Will your room be Room 2, or will it be *hallowed ground*? As the children step in, will they be affirmed, challenged, and welcomed into a world of active, exciting days that are never long enough? Will the poem circulated by the Children's Defense Fund be at your fingertips, at the core of your heart, reminding you of how much you mean to all of the children?

> We pray for children
> who put chocolate fingers everywhere,
> who like to be tickled,
> who stomp in puddles and ruin their new pants,
> who sneak Popsicles before supper,
> who erase holes in math workbooks,
> who can never find their shoes.

And we pray for children
　　who stare at photographers from behind barbed wire,
　　who can't bound down the street in a new pair of sneakers,
　　who never "counted potatoes,"
　　who are born in places we wouldn't be caught dead,
　　who never go to the circus,
　　who live in an x-rated world.
We pray for children
　　who bring us sticky kisses and fistfuls of dandelions,
　　who sleep with the dog and bury goldfish,
　　who hug us in a hurry and forget their lunch money,
　　who cover themselves with Band-aids and sing off key,
　　who squeeze toothpaste all over the sink,
　　who slurp their soup.
And we pray for those
　　who never get dessert,
　　who have no safe blanket to drag around behind,
　　who watch their parents watch them die,
　　who can't find any bread to steal,
　　who don't have rooms to clean up,
　　whose pictures aren't on anybody's dresser,
　　whose monsters are real.
We pray for children
　　who spend all their allowance before Tuesday,
　　who throw tantrums in the grocery store and pick at their food,
　　who like ghost stories,
　　who shove dirty clothes under the bed and never rinse out the tub,
　　who get visits from the tooth fairy,
　　who don't like to be kissed in front of the carpool,
　　who squirm in church and scream in the phone,
　　whose tears we sometimes laugh at and whose smiles can make
　　　　us cry.
And we pray for those
　　whose nightmares come in the daytime,
　　who will eat anything,
　　who have never seen a dentist,

who aren't spoiled by anybody,
who go to bed hungry and cry themselves to sleep,
who live and move but have no being.
We pray for children who want to be carried and for those who must,
For those we never give up on and for those
who don't get a second chance.
For those we smother . . . and for those who will grab the hand of
anybody kind enough to offer it.

Ina Hughs

I stand at the mailbox remembering what we circular thinkers know—sometimes the end is only the beginning and often the last day of school should really be the first day! We keep going around, gathering and combining, saving and shedding, remembering and forgetting, and then remembering again.

As we walk along together, let us always vote "life." With our children, may we always hear the songs of the real nightingale.

Copyrights and Acknowledgments

Letters of Introduction
11   "Four Easy Nudges" reprinted with the permission of Mimi Brodsky Chenfeld.

Chapter 1
26   "Thumbprint" from A SKY FULL OF POEMS by Eve Merriam. Copyright © 1964, 1970, 1973 by Eve Merriam. Reprinted by permission of Marian Reiner.

Chapter 2
55–56   "Mean Song" from THE SINGING GREEN by Eve Merriam. Copyright © 1962, 1964, 1966, 1973, 1992 by Eve Merriam. Used by permission of Marian Reiner.
70   "Hope" from SELECTED POEMS by Langston Hughes. Copyright 1942 by Alfred A. Knopf, Inc. and renewed 1970 by Arna Bontemps and George Houston Bass. Reprinted by permission of the publisher.

Chapter 3
74   "See Me Beautiful" by Red and Kathryn Grammer © 1986. Smilin' Atcha Music from "Teaching Peace," Children's Group Records.
74   "I am a nice nice boy" by Martin O'Connor is from MIRACLES: POEMS BY CHILDREN OF THE ENGLISH-SPEAKING WORLD. Edited by Richard Lewis. Used by permission from Richard Lewis. © Richard Lewis, 1966. Distributed by The Touchstone Center for Children, Inc., New York City.
77   "Letter to a Fledgling Teacher" reprinted with permission of the publisher, Allen Raymond, Inc. From the Sept. 1975 issue of *Early Years*.
79   Excerpts from "Tuning Into Childhood" reprinted by permission of Elizabeth Hunter and the Association for Childhood Education International, 11501 Georgia Avenue, Suite 315, Wheaton, MD. Copyright © 1975 by the Association.

401 Nootka and Quileute music by Frances Densmore, 1939. Bureau of American Ethnology, 124. Smithsonian Institution, Washington, DC. Courtesy Smithsonian Institution Press.

401 Six lines from AMERICAN INDIAN POETRY by George Cronyn, ed. Copyright 1918, 1934 and renewed 1962 by George Cronyn. Reprinted by permission of Ballantine Books, a Division of Random House Inc.

Chapter 12

410 "In Praise of ABC" by Nancy Willard, from CARPENTER OF THE SUN, is reprinted with the permission of Liveright Publishing Corporation, first appeared in *Hudson River Anthology,* Winter 1973. Copyright © 1973, 1974 by Nancy Willard.

422–423 From ONE DAY AT A TIME by David McCord. Copyright © 1961, 1962 by David McCord. By permission of Little, Brown and Company.

427 "All Mixed Up" by Pete Seeger. Copyright © 1964 (renewed) by Stormking Music Inc. All rights reserved. Used by permission.

437 Line from THE WORLD IS BIG, THE WORLD IS SMALL reprinted by permission of Ella Jenkins.

Chapter 13

454 Excerpt from "Arithmetic" in COMPLETE POEMS, copyright 1950 by Carl Sandburg and renewed 1978 by Margaret Sandburg, Helga Sandburg Crile and Janet Sandburg, reprinted by permission of Harcourt Brace & Company.

463 Words and music © Fran Avni and Jacki Cytrynbaum. Their tapes are available from Lemonstone Records, P.O. Box 607, Cote St. Luc, Quebec H4V 2Z2, Canada, and in assorted children's bookstores, libraries and education resource/teacher centers across the U.S.

488 "Eighteen Flavors" from WHERE THE SIDEWALK ENDS by Shel Silverstein. Copyright © 1974 by Evil Eye Music, Inc. Selection reprinted by permission of HarperCollins Publishers.

Postcript

498–500 From A SENSE OF HUMAN by Ina J. Hughs, columnist for the Knoxville News-Sentinel, Knoxville TN. Used with permission.

Photo Credits

Letters of Introduction
5 © Larry Hamill
6 © Larry Hamill

Chapter 1
16, 36 © Larry Hamill
18 Mimi Brodsky Chenfeld
32 Allen and Leslie Zak
40 Alan J. Rubin

Chapter 2
44, 65 © Larry Hamill
46 Allen and Leslie Zak

53   Stuart Appelbaum
63   © Larry Hamill

Chapter 3
74, 85   Allen and Leslie Zak
77   Stuart Appelbaum
80   Kimberlee L. Whaley & Rebecca Kantor
95   Allen and Leslie Zak
98   © Larry Hamill

Chapter 4
108, 117   Allen and Leslie Zak
111   Allen and Leslie Zak
113   Allen and Leslie Zak
122   © Larry Hamill
129   © Larry Hamill
134   Stuart Appelbaum

Chapter 5
142, 161   Enos Austin
150   Kimberlee L. Whaley & Rebecca Kantor
156   Liz Core-Orts © 1993
157   Liz Core-Orts © 1993
160   Laura Walcher
166   Laura Walcher
167   Kimberlee L. Whaley & Rebecca Kantor

Chapter 6
176, 206   Eva Gaber Rase
178   Allen and Leslie Zak
180   © Larry Hamill
184   Scott Orts © 1993
186   © Larry Hamill
189   Eva Gaber Rase
190   Eva Gaber Rase
193   Debbie Charna
208   Liz Core-Orts © 1993
209   Kaye Boiarski

Chapter 7
218, 222   Kimberlee L. Whaley & Rebecca Kantor
220   © Larry Hamill
228   Kimberlee L. Whaley & Rebecca Kantor
241   Kimberlee L. Whaley & Rebecca Kantor
248   Kimberlee L. Whaley & Rebecca Kantor

Chapter 8
256, 274   Liz Core-Orts © 1993
258   Rhoda Linder
259   © Larry Hamill
262   Kimberlee L. Whaley & Rebecca Kantor
272   Barbara Vogel, photographer
273   Mary Bornstein